Sacred Games, Death, and Renewal in the Ancient Eastern Woodlands

Sacred Games, Death, and Renewal in the Ancient Eastern Woodlands

The Ohio Hopewell System of Cult Sodality Heterarchies

A. MARTIN BYERS

ALTAMIRA
PRESS
A Division of
ROWMAN & LITTLEFIELD PUBLISHERS, INC.
Lanham • New York • Toronto • Plymouth, UK

Published by AltaMira Press
A division of Rowman & Littlefield Publishers, Inc.
A wholly owned subsidiary of The Rowman & Littlefield Publishing Group, Inc.
4501 Forbes Boulevard, Suite 200, Lanham, Maryland 20706
http:// www.altamirapress.com

Estover Road, Plymouth PL6 7PY, United Kingdom

British Library Cataloguing in Publication Information Available

Library of Congress Cataloging-in-Publication Data

Byers, A. Martin, 1937–
Sacred games, death, and renewal in the ancient Eastern Woodlands : the Ohio Hopewell system of cult sodality heterarchies / A. Martin Byers.
p. cm.
Includes bibliographical references and index.
ISBN 978-0-7591-2032-7 (cloth : alk. paper) — ISBN 978-0-7591-2034-1 (electronic)
1. Hopewell culture—Ohio River Valley. 2. Ohio River Valley—Antiquities. 3. Earthworks (Archaeology)—Ohio River Valley. 4. Indians of North America—Ohio River Valley—Rites and ceremonies. 5. Indians of North America—Ohio River Valley—Social life and customs. 6. Indians of North America—Games—Ohio River Valley. 7. Indians of North America—Material culture—Ohio River Valley. 8. Cults—Ohio River Valley—History—To 1500. 9. Confraternities—Ohio River Valley—History—To 1500. 10. Social archaeology—Ohio River Valley. I. Title.
E99.H69B95 2011
977.1'01—dc22

2010037667

∞™ The paper used in this publication meets the minimum requirements of American National Standard for Information Sciences—Permanence of Paper for Printed Library Materials, ANSI/NISO Z39.48-1992.

Printed in the United States of America

This volume is dedicated to my immediate family, who have strongly supported me in my endeavors over the years. In particular, I dedicate this book to my loving wife, Joy, and my dear daughter, Jennifer, and to my two wonderful sisters, Mary Brule and Dorothy Byers. I also want to include my brother, Robert Byers, who unfortunately did not live to see this particular volume, although he did see and appreciate my earlier two volumes. I have greatly appreciated my family's encouragement over the years.

Contents

Figures and Tables

FIGURES

TABLES

I

THE OHIO HOPEWELL AS A SYSTEM OF CULT SODALITY HETERARCHIES

1

Introduction

One of the most interesting and complex eras of the prehistory of the Eastern Woodlands of North America is referred to by most archaeologists as the Middle Woodland period. It dates approximately between 100 B.C. and A.D. 400–500. Its interesting complexity arises from a complex historical process of ceremonialism that was played out within and among many regions of the Eastern Woodlands; and it is the material cultural assemblage mediating the events constituting these regional Hopewell episodes that constitutes what many recognize as among the most interesting and, indeed, most spectacular expressions of ceremonialism in the Native North American archaeological record. While these Hopewell episodes of ceremonialism occurred more or less contemporaneously across many regions, there is little debate that the material culture assemblage that mediated the Ohio Hopewell episode manifested the most complex, varied, and richest set of attributes of all the regions of the Middle Woodland period and it particularly played itself out in the southwestern, central, south-central, and southeastern subregions of Ohio (Byers 2004).

The range of features, facilities, and artifactual contents that mediated this episode of intense ceremonialism makes the Central Ohio Valley archaeological record unique and, indeed, this particular assemblage in all its richness is often referred to as the "classic Hopewellian" expression. Probably the most visibly outstanding and certainly quantitatively most impressive material category of this Ohio Hopewell assemblage consists of the monumental embankment earthworks and the often-associated mortuary mounds. These earthworks are located on both the wide floodplains and valley floors and on higher plateau-type ridges. The embankment earthworks on the higher ridges and terraces have often been referred to as "fortifications" both because of their isolated locations and because the embankments, often 2 or more meters high and 1 to 5 km long, tend to follow the edge of the plateau-like ridges on which they were built (figure 1.1). Embankment earthworks found on the floodplain typically display geometrical forms, some as large stand-alone circular or rectilinear embankments, but also a good number being complexes of conjoined circles and rectilinears. These "geometrical" forms often incorporate mounds, both mortuary and nonmortuary, within the extensive plaza-like areas that the embankments incorporate (figure 1.2). Some of these mounds are among the largest in the Eastern Woodlands, between 100 m and 250 m long, and 30 m to 100 m wide, and 3 to 5 m or higher. Excavations have demonstrated that most of them, particularly the largest, covered the remains of timber structures associated with human mortuary residue and accompanying artifacts. The mortuary structures were typically built on prepared floor "foundations" consisting of a series of gravel, sand, clay, and earth strata. These structures are now widely regarded as serving the needs of mortuary and related ceremonialism. The importance of the mortuary aspect of this ceremonialism is clearly manifested since the prepared floors usually included multiple closely dispersed mortuary-related features. Typically, these would be timber cribs plastered in clay and containing mortuary residue, both human remains and associated artifacts. Also, there were carefully prepared clay crematory platforms or basins that while displaying signs of intense burning were usually carefully emptied and cleaned of any crematoria remains. Also there was usually a range of hearths or areas displaying residue of intense burning. These are all signs that most of these features were used to mediate complex human mortuary practices, although some may have also been used to mediate other forms of ritual.

Found in association with many but not all of the burials and also found in large mass deposits not directly associated with any human mortuary remains were the items that make up collectively one of the most elaborate artifact assemblages known in prehistoric Native North America. These ranged from native copper earspools, fresh water pearl beads, both fresh water and marine shell beads and necklaces, multiple decorative items made of animal teeth and jaws (both actual teeth and jaws or ones made as effigies from various materials), elaborately carved (actual) human bones, and exotic resources such as native copper and silver nuggets, fine blades made of imported cherts, obsidian, and rock crystal, and so on. Many deposits of the most elaborate artifacts, usually copper plates, copper headdresses, copper celts, human skulls, mica cutout effigies and other symbolic icons, and so on, were carefully treated and placed in the mounds associated with deceased.

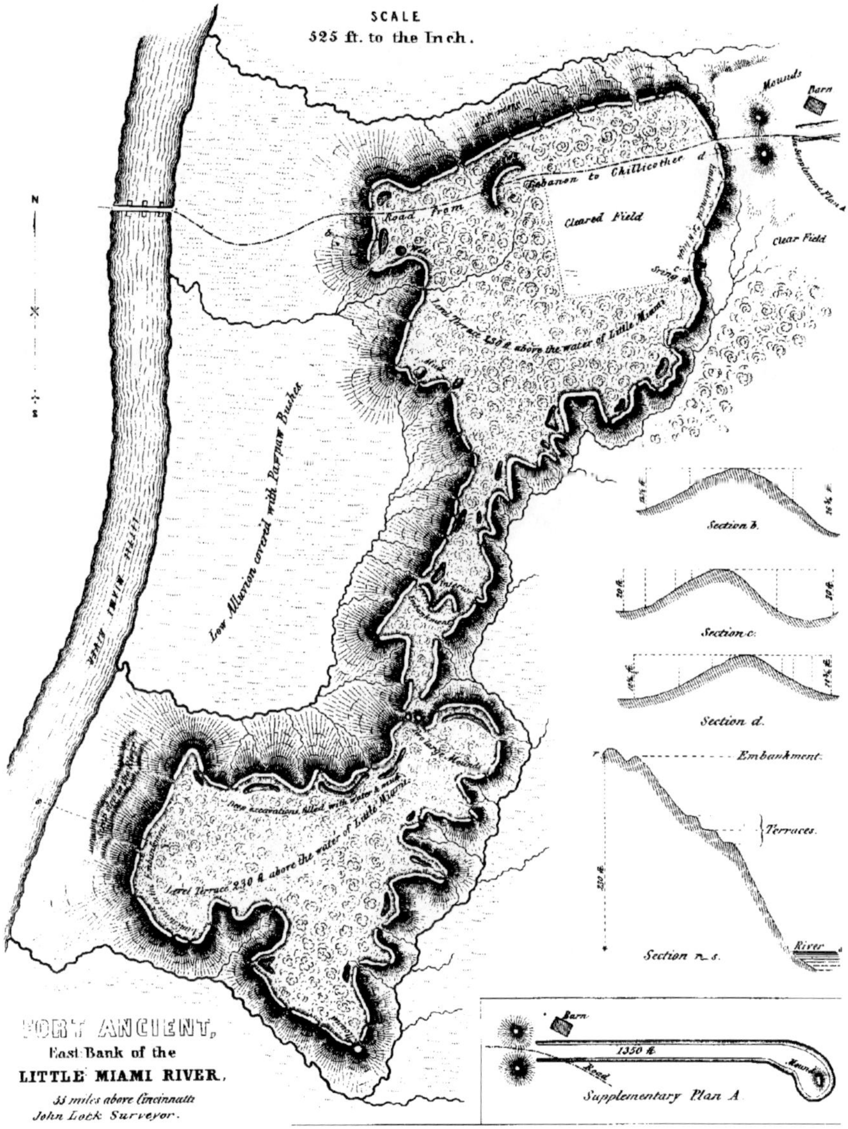

FIGURE 1.1
Fort Ancient
Source: Squier and Davis 1848, plate VII.

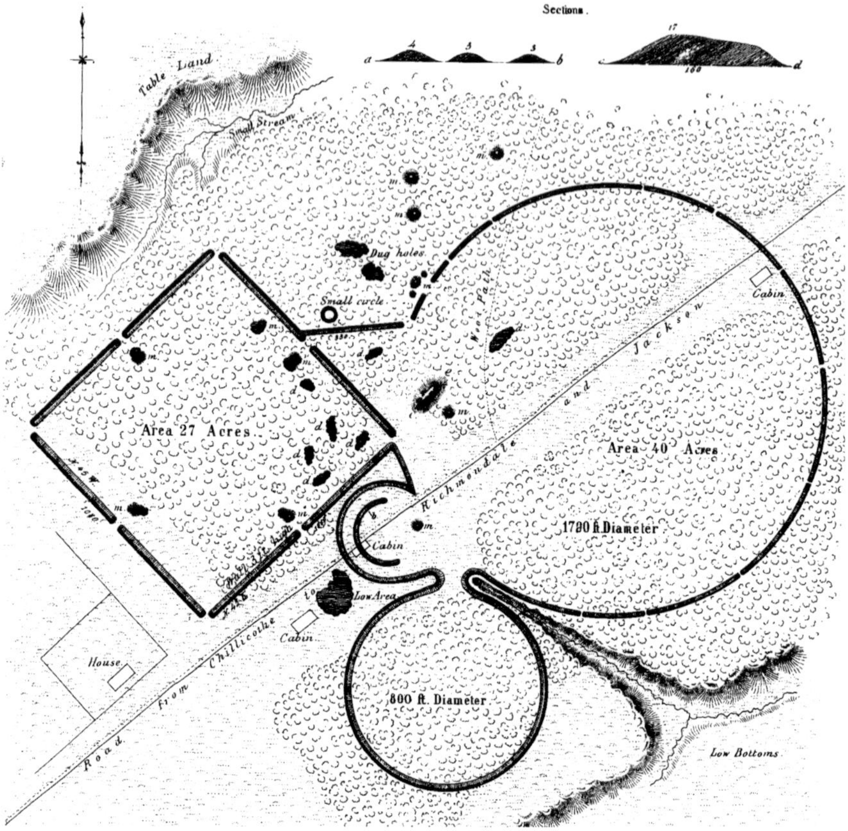

FIGURE 1.2
Liberty Works
Source: Squier and Davis 1848, plate XX.

Clearly, while the monumental Ohio Hopewellian earthworks, both embankments and mounds, are the most visibly outstanding material cultural features of the Ohio Hopewell episode, there is no doubt that the artifactual assemblage content is equally unique—both in terms of its elaborate iconographic forms and the range of materials used. In archaeology the term *exotic* is used when speaking of artifacts not only to indicate special qualitative attributes they have in terms of form, care of production, color and uniqueness of style, and so on, but particularly to emphasize that the material used was usually imported from sources that were at a considerable distance from the site where they were found. These distances could be several hundred kilometers and, therefore, would entail significant modes of long distance interaction. My reference to "exotic lithic" materials means a procurement process requiring at least 100 or up to 300 kilometers of travel and the presence of obsidian required much greater distances since the closest natural source to Ohio was from Yellowstone Park. Fine and colorful chalcedony and flints from both within and outside Ohio, crystal quartz, and other types of stones were regularly procured to make ceremonial-like blades that in many cases were deposited with these human remains. Even the prolific use of mica and copper required procuring this material several hundreds of kilometers from southern Ohio. Many of the more exotic and fine flints were also used to produce a very simple, elongated unifacial flake that is termed a bladelet. These bladelets are ubiquitous on these ceremonial Ohio Hopewell sites. However, they are also found in significant quantities on Middle Woodland period sites apparently displaying no significant Hopewellian ceremonialism. These non-earthwork-based sites are now widely interpreted by most Hopewellian archaeologists of the Ohio Middle Woodland period as domestic hamlets, an interpretation that I have attempted to significantly qualify in the course of writing this book.

In sum, the unusual components of this assemblage of the Ohio Hopewell episode were ceremonial artifacts made from mica (often in the form of effigy animals and human body parts) and procured from the Carolinas and Georgia, as well as Native minerals (such as copper and silver derived from the Great Lakes region and central Ontario) and iron-rich meteorites, and other colorful minerals (including red hematite and yellow ochers). The native copper was used to produce the above noted elaborate plates, earspools, gorgets, and flute covers, as well as ceremonial axes and adzes. The native silver was also used to produce earspools, often as a foil covering wooden, stone, or clay forms. The minerals, it is assumed, were used to produce colored powders and paints that were, in turn, used in various rituals performed at these ceremonial sites. Ceramics produced with specific figural motifs, particularly water birds and raptors, as well as other figures, were outstanding and various pipestones were procured to produce elaborate pipes, both plain and effigy in form. Marine shells procured from the Gulf coast were used as ritual containers and also as a source of shell beads and, in fact, the list of artifact categories and raw materials, often procured through long distance connections, could be continued.

While similarly formed and varied artifacts were components of other regional Hopewell episodes, only a few of these regions approached the variety and quantity that is identified with the "classic" Ohio Hopewell episode. Importantly, however, it is widely interpreted that formal similarities across these regions marked significant sharing and interaction. Seen in interregional terms, therefore, this widely dispersed material cultural assemblage articulates what is often referred to as the Hopewell Interaction Sphere. As interesting as it would be to use this book to characterize the nature of the interregional process, the Hopewell Interaction Sphere, this will be postponed in order that this book can achieve a more modest goal, this being to build on my earlier discussion of the Ohio Hopewell episode by developing a better understanding of its nature and the likely history of its development. That is, I believe that the basic cultural premises that I can develop in this book by addressing the nature of the Ohio Hopewell episode and models of the social mechanisms that generated and sustained it are necessary in order to use these to illuminate and account for the larger Hopewell Interaction Sphere. This raises an important ontological issue, this being that, in my view, the global Hopewell Interaction Sphere episode cannot be treated as simply the aggregate sum of the multiple regional Hopewell episodes; nor can a regional Hopewell episode be properly understood divorced from the wider pan-regional context that made it possible. The two levels, regional and interregional, therefore, are treated by me as mutually emergent and interdependent.

This presents an interesting dilemma, of course, in that it suggests that understanding the larger phenomenon is required to fully understand the parts but, at the same time, we can only come to understand the larger if we have an adequate understanding of the parts. However, this is not an overwhelming problem—as long as achieving understanding is understood to be a recursive interpretive-explanatory process by which our current understanding of the regional level becomes the basis for building further understanding of the larger process and in achieving the latter, recursively correcting the inadequacies in the earlier understanding of the regional. Hence, research and learning is an expanding circle. In fact, rather than imagining this process of knowledge building as an expanding circle of knowledge I prefer to imagine it as an expanding spiral. This image expresses the notion that knowledge grows by depth and width, each cyclic repetition adding new insights and understandings of the nature of the phenomena under study.

In any case, because I consider the construction and use of the Hopewell assemblage to be an intensely local process that played itself out at the *regional* level through *intraregional interaction*, I consider our understanding of the Hopewell episode is most effectively initiated by focusing at this regional level; and to say this means focusing on the interaction among major subregions of the Central Ohio Valley, those in which the Ohio Hopewell episode was successfully realized and those where it failed to be realized. The former case would primarily embrace the drainages of the Greater and Little Miamis, the central and lower Scioto drainage, and the Licking-Muskingum drainage. The latter case includes much of the Kentucky region as well as parts of the Ohio region, in particular the Hocking River Valley. Why I think it is important to clarify the nature of the Hopewell assemblage and its variation at this interdrainage level is because, as I develop the story in this book, the activity that was carried out at major sites displaying significant Hopewellian materials was a result of transdrainage interaction among several different and mutually autonomous local groups. Despite their mutual autonomy and individual commitment to their particular drainage zone, they nevertheless shared a common commitment that promoted their interaction between and among each other in the major drainages. It is this commitment to a common interest that motivated these different and spatially separated local groups to work together. In this book, I will argue that, as autonomous groups, they consensually agreed to cooperate in performing rituals of a world renewal nature. In short, I am claiming that not only were they all committed to performing the same range of valued activities in their respective drainages, they also recognized that effectiveness of the rituals they performed in their local drainages to some degree hinged on the effectiveness of similar rituals in neighboring and more distant drainage and that, indeed, in some cases, the full suite of rituals entailed interdrainage performances. Therefore, coordinating and mutually cooperating to enhance the rituals performed in neighboring drainages recursively enhanced the performance of rituals in their local regions. From this it follows that not only could the autonomous groups that constituted the complex in any one of these drainages be from several different communities dispersed in the local region that they collectively occupied but also, in some cases, they could be from communities in neighboring drainage regions. Furthermore, with respect to each other, these different and dispersed autonomous groupings were also mutually autonomous.

This principle promoting *intraregional* cooperation presupposes a logic that could equally promote *interregional* cooperation. Of course, interregional cooperation might need to be instigated by groups already committed in their own region by some of them undertaking "missions" to neighboring regions to promote the value of these ritual performances and showing their hosts that similar conditions in their region would call for and respond positively to similar rituals. Hence, they would undertake to transfer to their hosts important ritual prerogatives, and so on. Out of this process would emerge the Hopewellianization of this neighboring region. As groups within this region entrenched their commitment to this world renewal ritual and, no doubt also incorporated further rituals, they would also take on "missions" by visiting neighboring regions that were even more distant from the initial source of the ritual prerogatives, thereby transferring these same rituals. That is, the operation of the principle that specifies that performances of these renewal rituals at the local drainage level are enhanced by local groups cooperating in performances of the same rituals performed by equivalent groups in neighboring drainages would generate a dynamic that would account for the Hopewell Interaction Sphere. This also means that, despite the widespread distribution of the Hopewellian assemblage displaying common motifs and forms, there would be no centralized control hierarchy that governed the interaction processes. Instead, it was the outcome of many locally based groups, individually and in alliance, performing a set of coherently linked rituals and ceremonies, including constructing all the facilities that these rituals required, in order to discharge mutually recognized and self-identified commitments to achieving a set of shared and valued goals. As noted above, I have characterized these goals as embracing and enhancing the sacred powers of the world as they understood it to be and I have termed these goals as the ongoing pursuit of world renewal. The unique nature of committing to ritual activities that are perceived as renewing the world is that it entails having a vision of conditions of satisfaction that transcend the immediacy of the here and now, of this drainage, while, at the same time, embodying this valley and this region. Hence, in discharging world renewal duties, local autonomous groups would experience their own activities as enhancing not only the immediate region but also, of course, as participating in enhancing the wider region of which theirs was only a part. In an important way, then, the local groups necessarily would be aware of and attuned to the activities of groups of other localities in neighboring drainages committed to the same type of activities, realizing that the full felicity of locally performed rituals is partly dependent on the felicity of similar rituals being performed in both neighboring and more distant regions since, despite living in different areas, they shared a single intrinsically structured world or cosmos and the state of sacredness of one part was effected by and in turn effected the whole.

The upshot of this locally held vision that transcended the immediacy of the "here and now" is that in general local planning for ritual performances would be attuned to how similar performances may or may not have been and how they were being performed elsewhere. Sharing by any local group of their material cultural goods, social organizational capacities, and ideological know-how and ritual resources with other autonomous groups—both intraregional and interregional—would come to be part of an active world renewal global program. At the same time the principle of local autonomy would prevail so that such sharing could not transform into a form of centralized, dominance-based hierarchical control.

Now none of this should seem baffling to archaeological readers since the current view of the Middle Woodland communities in the Central Ohio Valley regions caught up in the Hopewell episode were mutually autonomous kinship-based groupings, and each constructed its own earthwork, and/or several such communities dispersed over a zone in a local valley may have allied to build and use one of the larger Ohio Hopewell embankment earthwork sites. Hence, it seems pretty straightforward to simply note that what I am referring to as autonomous groups responsible for a given Ohio Hopewell site complex were, in fact, *autonomous Ohio Hopewell communities.* Indeed, this is pretty well the current view, which firmly identifies a local Ohio Hopewell embankment earthwork and/or mound site with a local community or alliance of communities sharing the valley or nearby valleys with their multiple domestic family-based hamlets dispersed across the ambient landscape. This means that, for the most part, the large earthwork sites such as Fort Ancient (figure 1.1) and Liberty Works (figure 1.2), the type I illustrated above, are interpreted as manifesting an alliance of such dispersed-hamlet Hopewellian communities.

But this is what I am not saying. In fact, I am precisely *not* identifying the Ohio Hopewell embankment earthwork or mound site with this type of dispersed-hamlet community. To say this is not to deny that the Ohio Middle Woodland period had communities that consisted of kinship-based domestic residence groups, that is, nuclear family or small extended family, that were widely dispersed across the landscape. Nor does it deny that these family-type hamlets were likely the basic units of the more complex kinship structures of these Middle Woodland period communities, for example, the clans and moieties. What it does mean, however, is that describing these communities in terms of kinship structures alone does not complete their social characterization. These communities also had a set of non-kinship-based groups and I claim that these groups were common to all the Ohio Middle Woodland communities, but they were also relatively autonomous groups of these communities and, therefore, under certain conditions the relatively autonomous groups from different communities could and regularly did ally. It is these alliances that I claim were responsible for the Ohio Hopewell system of embankment earthworks and mounds. Another way of putting this is to say that it is a serious mischaracterization to speak of Ohio Hopewell communities. Rather, there were Ohio Middle Woodland period communities that embodied autonomous groups that allied with each other and these produced and used the Ohio Hopewell earthwork system.

A PERSPICUOUS CONTRAST

Now it is usually assumed that traditional preindustrial type communities are structured by kinship-based relations and any two or more persons who cannot trace common kinship connections must be "strangers." While this may be the case for many such communities, I do not accept that it is for many traditional Native North American communities. Anthropologists have long recognized that persons who share formal characteristics unrelated to kinship find many common grounds on which to interact and the stabilization of these interactions very commonly underwrite the emergence of recognized groupings that are reproduced with every new generation. Anthropologists have long recognized these and refer to them as sodalities. The most common sodalities are based on the formal attributes of same-sex/same-age and the substantive core value that structures these formal kinds of relations is companionship or friendship. Possibly because a person is born into a set of kin relations while the same person must create a set of friendships, it is assumed that only the former can be treated as truly social while the latter is personal and individual. However, under a certain constellation of conditions kinship can be dependent on its complementary opposite, friendship, and I propose that these conditions were fundamental to most traditional Native North American communities. Hence, these communities were characterized by dual kinship-companionship social structural axes and it was this structure that made the emergence of the Hopewell episode possible since it was the companionship axis that served as the armature to constitute complex alliances of companionship groups, what I will term generically sodalities, and it was these sodalities, not the communities to which they belonged, that allied and constructed and used the Ohio Hopewell earthworks.

Are the Ohio Hopewell earthworks the products of autonomous kinship-based communities, as the orthodox view would claim, or are they the products of autonomous sodalities that were themselves components of the Ohio Middle Woodland communities? This question may seem to be trivial and largely simply a matter of semantics. I would strongly disagree. If the latter case were correct, and in fact the Ohio Hopewell embankment earthwork sites were the outcome of sodality alliances, then it would be quite wrong and misleading to speak of these social groups as Ohio Hopewell communities—except possibly in a figurative sense. But even the figurative sense could be misleading since the term *community* as normally used in archaeology treats this type of group as constituted by kinship structures. However, if it is desired by the archaeologist to use the term in a figurative sense, then he or she would have to clearly modify it by adding a term that expresses the particular structural nature, such as speaking of it as a "sodality community." Why is this necessary? Simply because the core social components of the Hopewell embankment earthwork groups would be sodalities of various sorts and the members of these sodalities would occupy positions of companionship, not kinship—even if the members of any given sodality could also recognize each other in kinship terms. Because of the principle of the autonomy of kinship and companionship groups, however, even though the members would be perfectly aware of the kin standings that existed among them, in the *context* of the embankment earthworks and related locales they would understand that the relevant standing, the one that counts, was their relations as companions. Therefore, there would be an ingrained understanding that kinship obligations and duties were not operable in this context. Therefore, even though it is easy to imagine particular sodality contexts in which the sets of same-age males were accompanied by their families, the grouping of these families in that locale would not warrant referring to it as a transient residential settlement of nuclear families forming an extended family of the community. Rather, to characterize its social nature it would have to be spoken of as a transient residential settlement of a sodality consisting of the members and their immediate families.

What is implicated in the above is a realist ontological or theoretical posture and it strongly argues that the way we characterize an empirical patterning that is generated by a social group is the way we characterize the social nature of that group. It also perfectly recognizes that it is possible that two discrete socially generated empirical patternings can look much alike, and therefore, we are inclined to say that they are the outcome of two instances of the same type of social group. However, great care must be taken. Since different types of social groups are constituted by humans and the fundamental needs of the participants in both groups will be the same, there can be a great deal of overlap of the empirical patterning that each generates; for example, whether the men with their families are in their hamlet or earthwork settings, the families still need to carry out domestic activities. However, a careful assessment of both the overall material context and content of the two patternings will likely reveal systematic variation that can be empirical grounds for demonstrating that, despite sharing of many formal attributes, these two data sets can be recognized as generated by human groups that were constituted as socially distinct in nature.

To establish this it is necessary to theorize different social possibilities and the likely empirical differences these could generate. And this means first starting with abstract notions that articulate social properties that we have reasons to believe, given our background anthropological and/or sociological theoretical knowledge, are relevant to the case in hand. I have already presented two major alternatives with regard to speaking of the Ohio Hopewell embankment earthworks: are they the product of autonomous dispersed residential communities based on kinship structures that carried out different degrees of intercommunal alliances; or are they the product of the autonomous sodalities of autonomous dispersed residential communities based on dual kinship and companionship structural axes? If the former is correct, then the Ohio Middle Woodland community system is pretty well identified with the Ohio Hopewell system of earthworks and the Ohio Hopewell episode is simply the working out and unfolding of the interaction of these communities in the region where these earthworks are prominent over approximately five centuries, from ca 100 B.C. to ca 500 A.D. If the latter is correct, then clearly we must carefully distinguish between Ohio Middle Woodland period communities and Ohio Hopewell social structures.

Accordingly, the realist approach I am taking, because the nature of the social structuring implicated by the nonidentification perspective, namely, that Ohio Hopewell groups and Ohio Middle Woodland period communities are not identical, requires some fairly heavy theorizing. This is not because anthropological theories of Native North American societies do not exist, since clearly they do. There is a fulsome theorizing of settlement, subsistence, and social structure, particularly kinship and sodalities, and a fulsome theorizing of the related cultural traditions—cosmology, ethos, world view, and ideology. However, the use of this well-grounded theoretical knowledge in archaeology has been overly selective, focusing particularly on kinship structures to the detriment of sodalities and how the two relate, and most importantly, it has largely ignored the well-established theoretical knowledge of cultural traditions, not only treating the latter as largely ineffable and nonreconstructable since archaeologists do not directly interact with the communities of the past, but also because—in my view—there is a strong materialist bias in archaeology favoring explanations of patterns that can be tied to the produce of humans resolving concrete, everyday practices. I think that both tendencies, overselectivity of social structures and ignoring of cultural traditions, are a problem and require critical reflection and correction. The method I follow in this book is critical comparison. In this case, a terminology of perspicuous contrast is needed since only in this way can the strong critical comparison be effectively used to test against the empirical patternings. I use this terminology to articulate two equally plausible alternative and contrasting social systems models characterizing the nature of the Ohio Hopewell episode and its associated material cultural assemblage using the above range of anthropological theoretical knowledge—ecological, social, and cultural. Each model will be elucidated as a set of basic premises that perspicuously contrast. These social system models then become the major focus of a comparative method by testing them against the same body of empirical data. The goal is to establish which of these models most coherently interprets and explains the above archaeological assemblage that has come to be termed generally the Ohio Hopewell. The critical comparative method maintains that it is rational to accept the model that gives the best explanation of this complex assemblage while realizing, of course, that it is not the last word or "God's truth." Rather, I claim that the accepted model is still only approximately true of its real object, although certainly the best approximation so far in that it explains the data best. This leaves open the likelihood that critical assessment of this model will lead to presenting and demonstrating a new approximation of the nature of social system that actually explains the same data even more coherently, and so on. I have used the term *hermeneutic spiral method* to refer to this process of testing perspicuously contrasting models against the same data and it is the primary method of this book (Bhaskar 1978, chapter 3, 143–227; 1979, 11–28, 164–69; Byers 2004, 106–7).

Immediately, the skeptic might certainly acquiesce that it is rational, given the comparative method, to opt for the more coherent of the two accounts. However, she or he might go on and claim that the method begs the question in that, even though it is rational to opt for the model that gives the most coherent account, logic does not always follow reality. Therefore, even though it gives a good account, it does not demonstrate that the social system it articulates really existed. My immediate response to the skeptic is that she or he is quite correct. All we can be very sure about is that, given our archaeological knowledge about how humans mess up the world, some sort of human social system generated this particular "mess." Indeed, both models share that same basic assumption. Hence, this method does not guarantee that the social system that is responsible for this mess is well characterized by the model we rationally choose. All it can say is that it is more likely to be true than the one that we have rejected on the same rational grounds. This simply characterizes the critical comparative method I am using. It insists that we cannot start the process by assuming that one of the models is privileged, for example, because it draws on theoretical knowledge with which the model builder is most familiar. Even though it may be the case that one model articulates a very familiar set of premises, this familiarity does not alone privilege the model such that we have confidence that the social system it articulates really did exist. That is, the skeptic's begs-the-question claim, particularly when she or he acquiesces to the rationality of choosing this model over the alternative, reveals that she or he has already assumed a privileged stance toward the model that was rejected. This puts the cart before the horse, putting an onus of demonstrability on one of the alternative models that is not demanded of the other. It also misses the point that the "proof" is in the comparative explanation itself and not in some other method, such as hypothetic-deduction.

I will immediately point out that I consider that most archaeologists of the Ohio Middle Woodland period privilege the orthodox model. Of course, this privileging does not eliminate debate and disagreement. However, the existing contentiousness among the proponents of the orthodox model addresses less abstract concerns than the overall nature of the social system; for example, are these communities seasonally mobile or sedentary or do they vary along a continuum according to specific regions with the settlement of some regions being more sedentary and of others being more mobile? These are all relevant questions. However, their relevance is partly determined by the more abstract concern addressing the real nature of the social systems that were responsible. In an important sense, therefore, I consider the orthodox model to be privileged and for this reason readers will quickly note that I take particular care to articulate strong perspicuous contrasts between it and the alternative—to some degree to "level the playing field." That is, I insist that the orthodox and the alternative models have to be equally articulated and demonstrated. This does not mean "starting" from the beginning since I can readily agree to accepting the "raw data" on which the orthodox model has been built and also many of the interpretations that have been made under it. However, there are many interpretations that I must critique since they arise directly from opposing premises that inform and underwrite the alternative. When it comes to these perspicuously contrasting premises, to some degree it is necessary to go to the basics. This necessarily entails full-bodied critical comparison of the two perspectives along that particular dimension.

In short, the critical comparative methodology entails my pointing out where I think that the orthodox model fails. This does not mean that the alternative is not also critiqued. In fact, I do that thoroughly; but only some of this critique is actually expressed in this book since to do so would make the book horrendously long. Instead, what I have presented here is the current outcome of critical comparison. Importantly, the stages are critiques of a selected data set determined by the premises of each model. The critique gives reasons for rejecting that particular aspect of the model and then I present the explanation of the same data under the premises of the alternative model. This explanation is then used to show how it dissolves inadequacies, anomalies, and puzzles that my critique of the orthodox model pointed out. The alternative model also often extends and enhances our understanding of empirical patterning of the data that under the model it replaces were not even seen by its proponents as being relevant to the matter at hand.

I articulated these two contrasting models in my earlier book on the Ohio Hopewell episode (Byers 2004). However, that book addressed the social nature of the groups responsible for the individual earthworks without addressing how these groups related. This book is taking on the extra task of showing how these individual groups were organized into more complex networks that linked the Ohio Hopewell earthworks together. Therefore, much new theoretical discussion is added below. However, these additions cannot be made without clearly specifying what they are additions to. This dilemma means that the most efficient method is to present the two perspicuously contrasting models and work from there. I will do this as briefly and cogently as this very abstract topic allows. I will first briefly present the core premises of the orthodox model, a model that comes in variant versions that, nevertheless, share these core premises; and then in more detail and depth I present the premises of the alternative counter or heterodox model. This differential emphasis on the countermodel seems reasonable since the orthodox is familiar to most readers, even though the terminology I use in presenting it may not be, while the latter is not familiar and will require a little more elucidation.

THE MONISTIC MODULAR POLITY COMMUNITY MODEL

There are several community-based models of Ohio Hopewell that have been presented in the literature. Although each highlights one or the other social dimension, I think all of them share the basic premises I outline here. The best known and most widely accepted is termed the Vacant Center/Dispersed Hamlet model. This has come in varying versions, such as the Vacant Center model, the Hamlet Hypothesis model, the Dispersed Sedentary Community model (Dancey and Pacheco 1997, 8), and even the Civic-Ceremonial Center model. The primary disagreement among the above versions addresses the degree of mobility the typical dispersed community had. Many supporters of this model propose sedentary communities; others propose seasonally mobile communities. Except for these differences, however, I suggest that they presuppose the same set of basic social premises. Each premise articulates one or more dimensions of the social and/or cultural structures that constituted the communities.

Treating these different versions as slight variations on the same basic model, I will generalize and term it the *Monistic Modular Polity Community* model. The terms I have used in the name of the model may be unfamiliar but none makes reference to a mysterious property or attribute, while each highlights a critical aspect that is usually taken for granted by the proponents of the orthodox model in its different versions. *Monistic* is a term I have used to refer to a community that has a single, basic, albeit possibly complex, social structural axis that acts as its primary integrative formal armature. When speaking of prehistoric communities based on foraging or simple gardening, this core structural axis is generally referred to as the kinship structure. Therefore, for this book, by monistic I mean that the dominant social structural axis is kinship. Of course, kinship is extremely variable across cultures. However, within any given culture, it is usual that there is a complex but finite system of kinship rules and their permutations that generate a complex but finite set of kinship relations and kinship groups. *Modular* is a term derived from the notion of a module and it highlights the nature of the territorialism that is usually argued to be central to monistic communities. That is, a monistic community is recognized as having a module of territory that it regularly exploits, the assumption quite correctly being that without regular access to resources, the community cannot survive. As I noted, this is a very reasonable position; but this survival thesis goes beyond the practical, biologically entailed necessity to characterize a very special cultural dimension to this territorial module. In effect, it assumes that at this basic survival level cultural rules are determined by objective necessity. As Charles and Buikstra (1983) argue, in conditions of rising scarcity of resources, neighboring kinship-based communities will compete for land or for the limited resources on this land. Hence, rising resource scarcity "naturally" promotes competition, which in turn promotes the regular exploiters to identify the territory as their exclusive property, that is, as "belonging" to them, or, if not the territory, the natural resources in the territory that they regularly use. In my estimate, this view of the relation a people have with their territory reduces what is essentially a cultural, intersubjective property to a naturalized phenomenon, a "territorial imperative." This territorial imperative, whether expressed in terms of special relations with the land or with the resources on the land—or both—then determines the core concern of a community (maintaining control) and, therefore, it necessarily generates boundary-producing-and-securing behaviors, from communicative threats against the "outsiders" who might be suspected of planning to transgress to physically aggressive behaviors against them when they do. Therefore, a kinship-based community in material conditions that "naturally" promote competition translates this natural tendency into the cultural principle of exclusive territorialism, or what we call proprietorship, or ownership. The dominance of the kinship structural axis then fuses with the notion of ownership or exclusive territorialism to generate corporate kinship proprietorship. From this it logically follows that the community takes on the character of a polity since, by claiming exclusive control to a spatially delineated module of territory and its contained resources, its members must collectively sustain a defensive attitude to "outsiders" and, of course, an autonomous one at that since the boundaries entail maintaining such a status vis-à-vis neighbors.

The Monistic Modular Polity Community model, therefore, articulates the cultural principles—kinship, exclusive territorialism, and political autonomy—that I contend are presupposed by the orthodox Ohio Hopewell community views and, of course, as these are corporate communities, the only way the Hopewell embankment earthworks could be built is by such a community building them. Finally, since each community is effectively a unitary group with respect to all its neighbors, then in order to build large embankment earthworks it is necessary for several local monistic modular polity communities to ally—despite the fact that such an alliance might contradict the exclusive territorial principle. Hence, this model entails treating the Ohio Hopewell earthworks as civic-ceremonial centers of either individual polities (small-scale earthworks) or allied regional polities (large-scale earthworks).

This also means that it is quite unproblematic to identify the Ohio Hopewell embankment earthworks with Middle Woodland period communities, at least in those areas of the Central Ohio Valley where this regional Hopewell episode unfolded. Hence, in this view, the Ohio Middle Woodland period communities where the Ohio Hopewell episode unfolded *and* the Ohio Hopewell communities *are treated* under this model as being one and the same social phenomenon.

To further elaborate this model as it particularly applies to the Ohio Middle Woodland period settlement pattern, it is widely recognized that the latter is characterized as consisting of modular community polities having family-based groups dispersed across the landscape of its proprietorial domain while the ceremonial and decision-making locus of the community was focused in the embankment earthwork locales. Indeed, the earthworks are often explained as necessary for the perpetuation of the community by serving to integrate and sustain their internal unity despite the fact that the individual kin-based family hamlets are widely dispersed in the territory immediately surrounding the civic-ceremonial earthwork center. This "splitting" of the community settlement pattern into ceremonial centers and dispersed family hamlets is widely recognized among Ohio Hopewell archaeologists and it grounds what often is termed the domestic/ceremonial dichotomy. Hence, the domestic sphere is largely identified with the family-based hamlets, whether these are argued to be sedentary or mobile in nature, and the ceremonial sphere is largely identified with the earthworks. In short, the embankment earthworks are treated as serving as the epicenter of the corporate kinship-based community polity (or allied polities) and the surrounding lands constitute its exclusive domain, albeit the precise boundaries in the uplands may be somewhat vaguely defined.

However, this domestic/ceremonial dichotomy is recognized as particular to the Ohio Middle Woodland period monistic modular polity communities. Structurally speaking the same type of community can exist in a nucleated form, this being simply the result of the dispersed hamlets/households/farmsteads being spatially concentrated into one central nuclear locale. However, when nucleation of the dispersed community happens, it is argued, the need for the earthwork disappears as the community forms a village in which everyday and not-so-everyday life proceeds. This shift does not change the deep structures since kinship remains dominant and the surrounding land remains an exclusive territory. Even the gardens tend to be made in the land closer to the village while the men and women go out to forage for wild food in the forest and upland zones of the community's territory. Hence, under this model only the settlement patterning and not the structural nature of the community changes and, in fact, the only reason this change occurs is either because some sort of subsistence innovation must have occurred that enabled the community to nucleate into a single center, or, alternatively, possibly intensifying interpolity aggression promoted this nucleation as a defensive strategy.

Critical Discussion

There are two other major cultural dimensions related to the Monistic Modular Polity Community model. One is entailed by the logic of the model and the other is contingent. The entailed perspective is generally not recognized by its proponents and this relates to cosmology and ethos; the contingent perspective relates to the mortuary sphere. Speaking of cosmology and ethos may make some uncomfortable since, of course, these appear to link archaeology with the abstract and the unknowable. These concepts are certainly abstract and they refer to equally abstract phenomena. But as I define the cosmology and ethos of a prehistoric community, I maintain it is not unknowable to the archaeologist and much of this book will develop this claim and ground it in the empirical data. In fact, the hermeneutic spiral method promotes theorizing abstract or intangible phenomena by asking what conditions must have existed for certain types of empirical, that is, tangible data to exist. The latter are observable and if their existence can only be explained as being expressions of intangible phenomena, such as beliefs and values, then it follows that such claims can be tested by means of postulating alternative models. Again, the model that most coherently explains the empirical data is the one that is contingently accepted and using this theoretical model as an empirically grounded claim, further models can be articulated to address other data of the same order but differently patterned. Hence, this approach denies that the intangible phenomena (beliefs and values) or the tangible phenomena (subsistence tools and practices) that make up the social world are beyond our capacity to characterize and empirically demonstrate. Therefore, "unknowability" is not a relevant reason to ignore such notions as cosmology and ethos since, in fact, they simply articulate two aspects of a people's cultural traditions, those dealing with the nature of the world as they perceptually and behaviorally experience it in virtue of their cosmological beliefs and those dealing with the way they should properly conduct themselves in virtue of the way their cosmology informs their ongoing perceptual and behavioral experiencing of the world. Hence, this view entails recognizing that a people's cosmology and ethos are very important factors in terms of shaping behavior and this would mean recognizing that, as important as material needs are for food, defense, protection from inclement weather and climate, and so on, in shaping behavior, a people's beliefs and values of an abstract sort are also and possibly even more important and, therefore, specifying their nature and content must be part of explaining the particular behavioral patterns that are routinely carried out by a community.

A very important sphere of behavior is the way that a human population relates to the land. This can be termed "tenure." Usually tenure is treated under the orthodox model as simply another term for corporate ownership. However, ownership or exclusive tenure is firmly grounded on the ethos of a people. An ethos is constituted of fundamental values, attitudes, and principles or standards, and these are ground rules of conduct. Such rules constitute the *deontic sphere* of a community's cultural traditions, this being the sphere of rights, duties, and obligations, as well as the rules that stipulate what particular behavioral forms will count as appropriate actions that thereby discharge obligations, fulfill rights, and generally constitute a good life, and so on. However, an ethos does not exist in a cultural vacuum since its principles and standards presuppose beliefs about the nature of the world, that is, a cosmology of the natural world and a sociology of the human world or sociality. For example, we recognize that the nature of human beings as responsible agents makes it wrong to own another person. Ownership is strongly weighted with deontic rules and moral standards; and these presuppose cultural knowledge about the nature of the world and the things in it and states of affairs that make it up, such as the nature of being human beings and the obligations that the knowledge we have entails concerning how we conduct our interactions and relations.

As I noted above, the Monistic Modular Polity Community model is strongly committed to the view that Ohio Middle Woodland communities were based on the principle of exclusive territories. Such territories are defined and constituted as corporately owned by kinship-based communities. Hence, it is morally proper to preserve the community by excluding neighbors and not to do so is to morally fail. Besides, the exclusive territorial imperative is usually enshrined by its defining and recognizing the ancestors as the owners and they "give it" to their children. The tenure characteristic of monistic modular polity communities then consists of the set of principles and rules that define what is termed ownership, exclusive control of land and its resources. I will call this the proprietorial ethos and it presupposes what I have termed a transcendental cosmology. Such a cosmology enables, but certainly does not entail, treating the land as divisible and thereby ownable, as simply an object separate from the transcendent powers that created it. Of course, it is an important object, but it has no rights. Rather it is the object of rights and in a modular monistic (i.e., kinship-based) community, it is the object of kinship corporate rights. Of course, some land may be sacred and, therefore, have a type of life that makes it immune to or certainly strongly limits how humans intervene in its order. Hence, defined lands or particular pieces of land will be treated by the community as inviolate, possibly because the gods dwelled there when they came down to earth once in a while or because the ancestors dwell there. However, the rest of the land is divided among the communities as exclusive modules of land.[1]

I have already implied the second but contingent presupposition of the Monistic Modular Polity Community model, this being the mortuary sphere and the way it is handled. This happens to be a very important sphere since, of course, one of the most outstanding aspects of the Ohio Hopewell is the complex manner of treating the dead. In any case, this sphere is typically treated under this model in the same way Euro-American culture constitutes the proper treatment of its dead; that is, the mortuary sphere is treated as a complex set of funerary behaviors. This pretty well limits mortuary ceremonialism to funerary practices. The collective burial locale is referred to as a cemetery, the individual burial deposits are termed graves, crypts, tombs, depending on the magnitude of construction and time investment, and so on. Typically, a direct connection is made between the varied treatment of the deceased and the complexity of the community. I have used the term *funerary paradigm* to characterize this near identification of the mortuary ceremonialism and burial sphere with the funerals (Byers 2004, 172–76). I also think it is a serious mistake (Charles and Buikstra 1983, 120–21; Buikstra and Charles 1999, 207–8). However, I will discuss this in more detail later.

A final variant of the model can be recognized by cutting across the Monistic Modular Polity Community model with contrasting dimensions that distinguish between communities that are egalitarian, that is, tribes or tribal-like or band-like, and nonegalitarian, such as chiefdoms. Hence, the model can come in two versions, the Egalitarian (tribes and bands) and the Nonegalitarian (chiefdom or ranked) Monistic Modular Polity Community models.

THE HETERARCHICAL POLYISTIC LOCALE-CENTRIC COMMUNITY MODEL

As noted earlier, my heterodox view of the Ohio Hopewell is to treat it as the material manifestation of autonomous companionship-based groups or, as I refer to them generically, sodalities. Of course, as autonomous groups, these sodalities usually each individually identified with a particular community, which would also be autonomous. However, the individual communities from which the sodalities constituting a given Ohio Hopewell alliance came were not themselves part of the organization of this alliance. In sum, then, it was the alliances of these many autonomous companionship-based sodality groups from the many different autonomous communities of the Ohio Middle Woodland period that were responsible for what we have termed the Ohio Hopewell. Of course, the skeptic might well ask how the individual sodalities that identified with their respective Ohio Middle Woodland communities could ally and be responsible for these great earthworks and their contents while the individual communities to which the sodalities belonged were not. To answer this question, it is necessary to model the core structure that is postulated to have constituted these Ohio Middle Woodland communities following the same format as I did for the Monistic Modular Polity Community model. I call this the Heterarchical Polyistic Locale-Centric Community model. Of course, as suggested by the two different terminologies, these two models stand to each other in perspicuous contrast. It is important to note that these two postulated core structures address the *same* empirical data, and therefore I demonstrate which model gives the more coherent explanation of these data through critical comparison, both by arguing the validity of the theoretical premises of each and by showing how well or poorly each explains the same data. This is the hermeneutic spiral method and, following the elucidation of this alternative model of the community system, the rest of the book is devoted to demonstrating which model is the preferred one.

In terms of the Heterarchical Polyistic Locale-Centric Community model, the core structure of the Ohio Middle Woodland community was based on complementary structural axes, kinship and companionship. I use the term *polyistic* to speak of community structures based on two or more social axes. This contrasts with the above notion of the monistic community, which forefronts kinship, and if there is companionship, this is subsumed to kinship obligations and rights. I use the term *sodality* generically to refer to groups based on companionship and, similarly, groups based on kinship I refer to generically as *clans.* Clans are based on the rules of kinship filiation that characterize the community; and sodalities are based on the rules of shared age, gender, and expertise/experience. Ritual expertise may operate to constitute sodalities we can call shamanic colleges, artisan societies, and so on. Same-age/same-gender organizes young boys of the same age and young girls of the same age to constitute complementary and mutually autonomous male and female age-sets. The members of these same-sex/same-age groups of companions build up shared experiences that entrench mutual trust and sustain the group into adulthood and often to death, in parallel with but separate from the complementary trust and cooperation they experience in their clans. Indeed, the complementary nature of these two settings, sodalities and clans, is based on the complementary social meaning of kinship and companionship. These two social positions are internally related in that the social properties characterizing kinship are defined in complementary contrast with social properties characterizing companionship and, therefore, in a sense, kinship relations are what companionship relations are not, and vice versa. This means that typically careful and largely implicit, sometimes explicit, sets of rules develop by which to avoid or minimize conflict that might arise when the same people have to be both kin and companions. Hence, kin and sodality groups assiduously avoid intervening in each other's affairs. Since both groups constitute collectively the same community, the unquestioned operating assumption is that both clans and sodalities will behave in their respective spheres so as to enhance and not diminish the common interest they both have in benefiting their community. I have used the term *relative autonomy* to characterize the standing that clans and sodalities have toward each other. It presumes that each is autonomous in the sense that each is solely responsible for its own actions and one group does not interfere in the activities of the other.[2] The polyistic community, then, is a community based on at least two, complementary structural axes (more than two is possible, that is why I use the term *polyistic*), and I claim that the clan/sodality structural duality was basic to most of the traditional historic Native North American communities.

The term *heterarchical* expresses a new dimension that I have added to my original characterization of the polyistic community and it relates to my above comment that clans and sodalities stood to each other as relatively autonomous. As I understand the traditional Native North American culture, the central core or ethos value was *agentive autonomy.* As I noted above, I define autonomy as the right of an agent (an individual or a collective group) to be responsible for those activities recognized as appropriate to her, his, or their social sphere and, of course, this right included the entitlement that other autonomous agents recognize this responsibility. This definition does not at all mean that an autonomous agent or group is independent of other agents or groups, in the sense of not being responsible for and indifferent to or socially separate from other agents or groups. Of course, this state of affairs is quite possible. However, being independent does not define agentive autonomy. Agentive autonomy defined in the manner that I prefer, namely, as a social property of recognizing and being recognized as responsible for one's appropriate sphere of social actions/activities, does not contradict the notion of equality nor, for that matter, does it contradict the notion of inequality. Two autonomous agents (individuals or groups) can be unequal in terms of their respective action spheres; for example, elders can do X while juniors cannot, but juniors can do Y while elders cannot. What being autonomous means is that this difference and inequality cannot translate into dominance of one agent or group over another. For example, while seniors can do X, and X being done is important for the juniors, and while this social action power gives seniors the power to act in ways that their autonomous juniors cannot, the principle of autonomy entails that seniors cannot dominate the juniors. Rather they are constrained by their rights to autonomy to ensure that they do X so that the autonomy of juniors' rights to do Y are not diminished. This can be reversed also, of course. Only juniors have the rights to do Y and the seniors need such actions to be performed to maintain their capacity to do X. In a social world based on agentive autonomy, those who have special social powers are obliged by the very principle of autonomy that defines them to exercise these social powers in conditions that are important to the integrity of those who do not have such powers.

With this definition of agentive autonomy understood, it becomes rather easy to define heterarchy. A heterarchy is a structured group of autonomous agents or of autonomous groups. A heterarchy can embody rank and differentiation, thereby constituting what I call an enabling hierarchy. An enabling hierarchy is constituted as a built-in recognition of difference and this differentiation enables the group to carry out responsible activities without, however, generating dominance of the higher ranking over the lower ranking participants. In contrast, a dominance hierarchy, also based on difference, is such that these differences ensure those who are high in the hierarchy have control or dominance over the actions of those who are lower. For my purposes, since I consider agentive autonomy as the core ethos principle of the Ohio Middle Woodland period social system, then organized groups of agents having differential access to material resources and prestige would be constituted as enabling hierarchies. Hence, if age-sets differentiated by seniority join together, namely, ally, they constitute a ranked sodality based on an enabling hierarchy determined by seniority and the activities of the sodality will be allocated according to the traditional types of actions that the seniority of each age-set enables it to perform. Since this ranked sodality consists of autonomous age-set components, it is a heterarchy (Byers 2010a, 281–82; 2010b, 230–31).

However, the notion of communities as based on complementary kinship and companionship structures makes it important to speak of two different types of heterarchies according to whether the groups that constitute them are of the same or contrasting social natures. If the autonomous groups that are integrated are of the same social nature, such as groups of age-set companions, namely, sodalities, then they constitute a mutualistic heterarchy. Therefore, the above ranked cult sodality would be a *mutualistic heterarchy* or *heterarchical organization*. If the autonomous groups constituting the heterarchy are of different, particularly contrasting natures, for example, kinship-based and companionship-based, then what they constitute is what I term a complementary heterarchy. Since I have characterized a heterarchical polyistic locale-centric community as based on the dual complementary clan/sodality structure, it follows that this type of community is a *complementary heterarchical community*.

I consider these latter concepts, the mutualistic and complementary heterarchies, to be central to understanding the Ohio Middle Woodland period and the settlement domestic/ceremonial dichotomy. Therefore, there is more than formal distinction between these two types of heterarchies. They also define two different types of organization based on contrasting forms of autonomous relations: mutualistic and relative. With respect to the complementary heterarchical community, the clans and sodalities are complementary in their social nature and, as I noted above, this means that they are *relatively autonomous* with respect to each other. As I also noted earlier, there are two senses to this notion of "relative autonomy." The first emphasizes that the clans and sodalities are internally related in the sense that kinship is defined relative to companionship, and vice versa. Another sense, however, is that every member of a sodality in a given community is also a member of one of the clan groupings of that community and, therefore, even though the clans and sodalities are autonomous with respect to each other, they are only *relatively autonomous*. Therefore, while the clans do not intervene into the activities of the sodalities or vice versa, it is normally the case that the decisions of a sodality and the follow-up actions they perform are always in relation to the interests of the total community, and this also applies to the clans. This means that even when a sodality allies with sodalities from other complementary heterarchical communities, it remains loyal to and identified with its own community since its autonomy is only relative to the clans themselves. Hence, the welfare of the complementary heterarchical community remains as the primary interest of the sodality.

A mutualistic heterarchy as an alliance or affiliation of autonomous sodalities, of course, also respects the autonomy of its constituent components. These sodalities ally in order to carry out collective activities that they otherwise would find difficult or impossible to perform individually. Hence, according to this model, it is this type of *mutualistic heterarchy* that underwrites the Ohio Hopewell system. Importantly, a mutualistic heterarchy has special demands and this would be to ensure that its constituent components can effectively carry out the activities for which they are responsible. If a sodality finds its activities or concerns are ignored by the others in the heterarchy, it would be grounds to disaffiliate. This need for public and fairly constant recognition of the component groups' respective autonomy translates into governance by *consensus*. Hence, councils and consultations entailing a great deal of back-and-forth mobility would be characteristic of this type of organization, even more so than of the complementary heterarchical community. Indeed, in the latter case, there would be a tendency for the clans and sodalities to avoid schedule conflicts so they would convene separately, just to ensure that one is not seen as intervening in the affairs of the other. The consensual governance demands of the sodality heterarchical organization, moreover, would promote the construction of meeting places that could be used to publicly sustain the ongoing consensual governance and, of course, the ongoing performance of activities that reaffirmed the autonomy of each of the components.

Critical Discussion

Presupposing the Heterarchical Polyistic Locale-Centric Community model is the existence of cultural traditions that contrast with those presupposed by the monistic modular view. In this case, they constitute a complementary immanentist cosmology/custodial ethos cultural tradition.[3] An immanentist cosmology can nicely conform with what we know of traditional Native North American world beliefs. For them, typically the world is experienced as being intrinsically or immanently sacred. The natural order and the sacred order do not stand apart in some sort of infra/transcendent state. Rather, the natural order "contains" the sacred order and modifying the natural order entails modifying the sacred order. This belief in the immanent sacredness of the land has profound consequences in the way the community relates to the land. First, land cannot be treated as ownable, divisible, and subject to being modularized by human fiat. This also means that boundaries cannot be socially or arbitrarily created by which to exclude others. I have called this notion of tenure inclusive territorialism. It presupposes the obligation of the autonomous community to care for the land that it habitually exploits and to ensure that neighbors share both in using and in caring for it. Caring for the land is enshrined in the ethos as *custodianship*. A community becomes the custodian of the land it habitually uses and as a custodian it cannot refuse others access to the resources without just cause; for example, just cause may be having reasons to suspect/know that these people will not use the land properly since they are known to kill animals in ways that are unwarranted. As with all material practices, hunting is an activity that directly intervenes into the natural order and, therefore, into the sacredness that is immanent in this order. This dual form of intervention entails treating it as both a ritual as well as a practical ecological activity and, as such, it has to be warranted and performed according to traditional rules. Since usage and not ownership of the land defines the land-community relation, I have called this tenure a form of custodial usufruct. Under custodial usufruct tenure, manmade boundaries become largely irrelevant to social definition of responsible tenure and, instead, places and the paths that connect them become the focus of the custodial domain while land becomes the focus of custodial usufruct. The rights of usage of places and the paths that connect them are exclusive to the custodians. The places and the paths that connect them are theirs and noncustodians must gain permission to use them. Of course, it is only through permitted usage that they have access to the resources of land.

In practical terms, therefore, a custodial community will control and regulate but normally not exclude others (unless having sound reasons) from the use of their paths and places and, thereby, control the usage of the land and its resources. It is from this conceptualization of a custodial domain as a set of places and the network of paths that radiate from them and link them to the paths and the places of other communities that I derived the notion of the *locale-centric community.*

This immanentist cosmology/custodial-squatter ethos complex grounds the notion that land usage necessarily entails intervening into the sacred order of the natural world and this means that the mortuary sphere is itself treated in a strongly contrasting manner under the Heterarchical Polyistic Locale-Centric Community model compared to the way it is treated under the Monistic Modular Polity Community model. In the former case, the land is immanently sacred and, therefore, ecological practices necessarily disorder the sacred order. However, this systematic disordering has an important consequence in that it serves to transfer the sacred powers of the land to humans as energy immanent in the comestibles derived from the plants and animals that are sacrificed to this good. To partly rectify this sacrificial gift from the land and the disturbing of its natural sacred order, when humans die, they have much of their sacred powers returned back to their source, the land itself, and under this immanentist cosmology/custodial ethos view, an important part of the ceremonialism of the mortuary sphere is designed precisely for this purpose. Even though one of the rituals making up the mortuary sphere will involve releasing the personal soul to travel to the land of the Dead, constituting this and associated mortuary rites as equivalent to the Euro-American funeral, the rest of the activities constituting the mortuary ceremonial sphere will be devoted to releasing the spiritual powers immanent in the body that were originally derived from the land during the lifetime of the deceased. Hence, releasing these powers is a matter of returning them back to the land, thereby revitalizing the sacred powers of the cosmos. Much more will be discussed later concerning this conception of the mortuary sphere in order to tie it to the Ohio Hopewell episode.

CONCLUSION

The elucidation of the Heterarchical Polyistic Locale-Centric Community model has enabled me to present a theoretical frame characterizing the nature of the Middle Woodland period social system of the Central Ohio Valley that perspicuously contrasts with the theoretical framework of the orthodox model(s). I think that it can be broadly generalized across the Hopewell Interaction Sphere, although doing this is not my current purpose. This model can now be used to articulate the primary approach to the Ohio Hopewell episode that I will develop in this book. First, it is important to note that elucidating this alternative model has enabled me to generate two new social structural concepts to highlight important postulated aspects of the social system of the Ohio Middle Woodland period: the *complementary heterarchical community* and the *mutualistic cult sodality heterarchy*. I consider these concepts as critically important to interpreting and explaining the Ohio Middle Woodland period settlement patterning. Since I have now defined the complementary heterarchical community as the type of community postulated under the polyistic locale-centric view, I will now use this term when speaking of the Ohio Middle Woodland period community under this model. To maintain symmetry, I will refer to the community as defined under the Monistic Modular Polity Community model as the monistic community.

In the former terms, the Ohio Middle Woodland period community has a complementary heterarchical organization because it consists of two contrasting and complementary groups, generically referred to as clans and sodalities. As such these are relatively autonomous toward each other. This is a critically important theoretic claim for it grounds the possibility that under special conditions, specifically related to intensifying ecological practices, the autonomous sodalities of different communities would be relatively free to interact with each other and, thereby, to ally to form what I called above *mutualistic cult sodality heterarchies*. That is, instead of using the adjectival form "heterarchical," as in the notion of the complementary heterarchical community, I will use the nominal form, "heterarchy," to speak of such an affiliation of autonomous cult sodalities. A mutualistic cult sodality heterarchy is itself autonomous and, therefore, in principle more autonomous cult sodalities could join; and, as a unit, it could affiliate with another equivalent heterarchy. This iteration of cult sodalities requires further modeling, which I carry out in some detail later in the book, treating levels of alliances as first-order, second-order, and third-order cult sodality heterarchies. This model is the basis for postulating that allying and affiliating of autonomous cult sodalities occurred in the Central Ohio Valley and that the Ohio Hopewell episode was the unfolding of this process. In fact, I will argue that two major third-order cult sodality heterarchies, as well as probably one or two others, embodied and generated the Ohio Hopewell archaeological assemblage. Since the third-order cult sodality heterarchy was not localized in a given site, I will also define this as a *dispersed* third-order heterarchy.[4] Conceptualizing Ohio Hopewell as an autonomous system of heterarchies that stood at arm's-length to the system of autonomous complementary heterarchical communities constitutes what I will call the *Ohio Hopewell Cult Sodality Heterarchy System model*, and this book is devoted to developing the content of and empirically grounding this model in order to account for the archaeological record of the Ohio Hopewell episode.

2

The Domestic/Ceremonial Dichotomy

A key attribute of the Ohio Middle Woodland period settlement pattern is what is widely recognized and referred to as the domestic/ceremonial dichotomy. Now that I have outlined the two community views, the monistic community and the complementary heterarchical community, it may be very useful to apply these alternative theoretical models to show how each interprets this dichotomy. I will then elaborate on this treatment by showing how a recent and promising reformulation of the monistic community perspective has treated it. This was referred to by its authors as the Multiple Community model. As I noted, it contains important theoretical premises that pointed in the direction I have already presented under the complementary heterarchical view. However, the application of the model to Ohio Hopewell failed to live up to the promise, as I argue in some detail.

First I want to address more generally the alternative ways that the domestic/ceremonial dichotomy has been described and characterized. In this regard, it is important to note that this domestic/ceremonial dichotomy is characterized in very different ways according to whether treated under the monistic community view or under the complementary heterarchical community view. Under the former, the community is responsible for both the embankment earthwork and its associated features, such as mortuary structures, mounds, the mortuary remains, including the exotic and ordinary mortuary artifacts, and so on, as well as the multiple small domestic sites dispersed across the land surrounding each earthwork. This dispersal is enabled by the exclusive control of this land by the community; the earthwork and its contents, therefore, are simply the symbolic expression of the standing commitment of the community to defend and maintain their exclusive control of this land. This unitary characterization of the dichotomy raises multiple issues, probably the most important relating to the larger earthworks. It is generally recognized now that these were the outcome of alliances of communities that, while allied, nevertheless maintained their individual autonomy and, therefore, control of their individual territories. However, this type of alliance contradicts the basic premises of the monistic community itself in that somehow the fundamental principle of kinship-based exclusive territorialism is able to be overridden or suppressed without diminishing the political autonomy of the kinship-based community. In my view, alliances of this nature are extremely limited in their capacity to develop. Each member of the alliance would jealously guard the integrity of its own territory and this would effectively make it impossible to build large earthworks in prime gardening land. This also means that there would be little need for a major alliance since the demand for labor that large earthworks require would not exist. However, if somehow alliances of monistic communities were able to build earthworks of the magnitude characteristic of the Ohio Hopewell—and clearly these were built—then this could only be possible if the principle of autonomy was breeched as one or more kinship-based communities came to successfully dominate the others. But this immediately transforms the "alliance" of autonomous community into a dominance-based hierarchical structure of monistic communities ranked in order of relative power and prestige. That is, this takes on the characteristic of a chiefdom. Few archaeologists focusing on the Middle Woodland period identify the earthworks, whether burial mounds alone or embankments with associated mounds, as representing chiefdoms (Brown 2006, 198–99). Another problem with this monistic community view construal of the dichotomy, a problem that I will be particularly addressing later, is that it promotes a high degree of lumping of sites. In this scheme pretty well all non-earthwork-related locales are identified as the contexts of domestic, family-based activities; that is, they are sedentary or seasonal hamlets of the autonomous monistic communities, and all earthwork-related locales are the ceremonial contexts of the same communities or of alliances of these communities. This results in collapsing almost all sites that are spatially separate from earthwork-related sites into the "domestic hamlet" category, even if they should have attributes that suggest the behaviors carried out there are just as or even more closely related to ceremonialism than to domesticity; and even sites having a rich expression of ceremonialism and that are spatially close to earthworks, we might say "within a stone's throw," tend to be characterized as domestic hamlets if they display attributes that are identified as necessary to conduct everyday domestic tasks.

In contrast, under the alternative view, it is the cult sodalities—not the total set of communities to which they belong—that form alliances responsible for the earthworks and since custodial tenure and inclusive territorialism are the governing principles of land usufruct, access by the cult sodalities of these alliances to a central locale within the lands habitually occupied by a given complementary heterarchical community is unproblematic. The earthwork locales are not under the custodianship of the local custodial complementary heterarchical community but of the alliance of cult sodalities from the communities of the region; and the paths that the members of this alliance must use to cross the land to access these locales can be jointly used for foraging and for traveling to the ceremonial center without contradicting the basic custodial usufruct rules. Of course, this also opens up the range of possible site types that can be postulated since both communities and sodalities will have spatially separate and functionally complementary sites. Clans will have everyday family-based domestic sites but also clan-based ceremonial sites and cult sodalities will have a range of site types according to their needs, from the level of the individual cult sodality that builds a local place to aggregate in seclusion to ceremonial nodal sites of a set of sodality allies to large earthwork sites incorporating a large complex alliance of multiple cult sodalities. These latter may in turn have auxiliary sites that participating sodalities and their members may need and these may require only transient use, thereby constituting what we might call sodality "way houses" and "hostels," and so on.

Hence, under the complementary heterarchical community view, the tangible domestic/ceremonial dichotomy becomes the expression of the dual clan/sodality social structure. In this case, the *primary* component of the ceremonial aspect of the settlement dichotomy and its supporting locales embodies the sodality component of the community system and constitutes the system of first-order, second-order, and third-order cult sodality heterarchies that I alluded to in the introductory chapter. However, there is also a *secondary* component of ceremonialism, this being embedded in the clan component. In a complementary nature, the *primary* component of the domestic aspect is embodied in the small, dispersed "hamlet" sites occupied by family-based residential groups of the clan component of the complementary heterarchical communities, while the *secondary* component of the domestic aspect would be embedded in the sodality component manifesting the everyday domestic-like behavior that sodalities would need to carry out in the discharging of their ritual duties. What all this should clarify is why, as I noted in my introduction, it is very important *not* to identify the Ohio Middle Woodland period communities with the Ohio Hopewell earthworks. Ohio Middle Woodland period communities certainly existed, but as complementary heterarchical community types. In these terms, therefore, I propose that these earthworks manifest only the cult sodality component of this community system. Hence there were no Ohio *Hopewell* communities, that is, as the term *community* is usually defined in the standard anthropological sense of residential kinship-based units. Rather there were Ohio Middle Woodland period complementary heterarchical communities, on the one hand, and Ohio Hopewell cult sodalities and cult sodality heterarchies, on the other. This arrangement is possible largely because of the relative autonomy that the dual clan/sodality structure constituted enabling the clans and sodalities to operate largely autonomously of each other.

THE INTEGRATED-BIFURCATED SETTLEMENT ARTICULATION MODAL CONTINUUM

The dual clan/sodality structure and the associated core cultural principle of agentive autonomy endow the complementary heterarchical community with quite extraordinary flexibility while sustaining the community's basic integrity. To understand this it is necessary to think in terms of levels: the tangible settlement patterning and intangible but social structures that generated it. Above, I noted that the domestic/ceremonial dichotomy manifested a complex of settlement types that can be articulated in two parallel clan-based and sodality-based terms. The resultant settlement pattern represents what I call the bifurcated settlement articulation modal posture of a regional set of complementary heterarchical communities. Hence, to put it in its simplest terms, the earthworks embody the sodality component and the dispersed residential locales embody the clan- or kin-based component of the communities. However, the regional set of complementary heterarchical communities can manifest a contrasting settlement pattern, one in which the clan and sodality components "reassemble" in a single locale to form what I call an integrated community or village. This would appear much like a nucleated settlement with a set of structures for the clans and subclans, some possible structures serving as "club houses" for the sodalities, a central plaza, and so on. Importantly, the fundamental social structure of dual clan/sodality remains constant, as does the core cultural principle of autonomy. I have called this empirical pattern the result of the regional set of complementary heterarchical communities occupying the integrated settlement articulation modal posture. These two postures can be extreme poles of a settlement continuum and I call this the integrated-bifurcated settlement articulation modal continuum. Seen in these terms, I would characterize the settlement pattern of the complementary heterarchical communities of the Ohio Middle Woodland period as being in a rather extreme bifurcated settlement articulation modal posture. This occurs when the kinship components distribute themselves as a network of small kin-based groups across the landscape, for example, as nuclear or small extended or small joint families, while, simultaneously, the sodality components organize themselves as small spatially distinct groups of autonomous cult sodalities. The reason for this posture emerging, in fact, is probably because the communities see the posture as a strategic accommodation to the perceived objective conditions in terms of population and subsistence. Hence, it is not that the sodalities are freed up by this posture to pursue intersodality alliances so much as the communities actively shift into this posture so as to more effectively adapt to objective conditions that they find troubling in that the exploitation of the land is intensifying, and this bifurcated posture serves to redistribute the exploitation load more evenly across the region while enabling the sodalities of the responsible communities to enhance the level of world renewal intensification.

Therefore, the communities and their clan and sodality components are not in some sort of negative competition. Rather, moving into this bifurcated posture is the result of region-wide consensual decisions. As such, since it is the core principle of agentive autonomy and core social structure of dual clan/sodality that enable this strategic shift, these deep structures are reproduced and not weakened. What does change, of course, are the settlement rules that specify how the communities should deploy themselves and, along with this, the ritual rules that govern the construction of sacred ritual locales and how these rituals are most felicitously performed. However, these are not deep structural rules. They are changes to the ideological structures, the rules by which behaviors are governed so as to count as felicitous types of social activities intended. These ideological rules of settlement and ritual, therefore, can change quite rapidly and consensually while reproducing the cosmological beliefs and ethos principles that were the deep cultural traditional sources that guided the people in making these ideological rule changes. Hence, deep structures of cultural tradition remain stable while surface structures of ideology can change quite rapidly. It is this surface/deep structural stratification that I propose underwrites the integrated-bifurcate settlement articulation modal continuum and, therefore, the Middle Woodland period is the manifestation of the bifurcate extreme.

CRITICAL DISCUSSION

No models are to be privileged and, therefore, all models are subject to critique. Hence, before moving on to the next step, which is a critical discussion of the Multiple Community model, I want to critique the above Complementary Heterarchical Community model of the Ohio Hopewell episode by presenting and critically addressing the Mapuche as an analogical model for understanding the above dichotomy. This has recently been presented by Paul Pacheco (1996, 22–24). He made this comparison between the Mapuche and the postulated Ohio Middle Woodland period social system in order to give substantive theoretical support to his particular Monistic Modular

Polity Community model version of the Ohio Hopewell. He has termed the latter variously as the Vacant Center model (1996, 18, 21; 1993, 20–24), the Hamlet Hypothesis (1993, 84–89; 1997, 43–44), and its most recent version presented jointly by William Dancey and Paul Pacheco (1997, 8–10), the Dispersed Sedentary Community model. Certainly, drawing on the ethnology of the historic Mapuche community, a known South American Andean cultural community, to support the validity of the Vacant Center model in its different versions is an astute choice on his part since the Mapuche manifest several central attributes that correspond to the core premises of the Monistic Modular Polity Community model, particularly the attribute of Mapuche land tenure, which is a form of exclusive control of land use by descent-based communities (Pacheco 1996, 22–24). However, to make it even more critically interesting, the Mapuche also manifest core premises of the Complementary Heterarchical Community model, in particular, the practice of an immanentist cosmology and a qualified custodial ethos. I say qualified because, in practice, the Mapuche are not "squatters" nor do they treat the occupation of their lands as temporary. For this reason, assessing the Mapuche social system as the analogical source for characterizing the Middle Woodland period settlement system would appear to be a good test to assert which of these alternative models is the more adequate characterization of the domestic/ceremonial dichotomy, the Monistic Modular Polity Community model or the Complementary Heterarchical Community model. I think it is also quite germane to note that Olaf Prufer, the earliest and strongest proponent of the Vacant Center thesis, as he termed it, has fully approved Pacheco's use of the Mapuche analogy. "I also agree with Pacheco's Mapuche analogy. These people seem to embody, and verifiably so, much of what I had in mind when I developed my 'model'" (1996, 410).

Besides the above abstract sociocultural attributes that are at the core of Mapuche communities, there are good and reasonable formal grounds in the tangible patterning of the settlement system for Pacheco's choosing the Mapuche as the substantive basis for modeling the Ohio Hopewell archaeological record. Given the descriptions of two major ethnologists of these people, Tom Dillehay (1992) and Louis Faron (1964, 1968), the Mapuche display a settlement dichotomy that can be equated in formal terms with the Ohio Middle Woodland period domestic/ceremonial settlement dichotomy. These indigenous communities live in the valleys in the interior of south-central Chile. They are mixed horticulturalists, herders, and foragers organized into exogamous patrilineages termed *trokinches*. The individual families are distributed in a pattern of dispersed farmsteads, each usually located spatially separate from related families, albeit not overly so. Particularly important for Pacheco's purposes, the families constituting the *trokinche* cooperated to build and sustain a collective ceremonial ground consisting of a large plaza with the patrilineally related families building their individual shelters around the perimeter in a U-formation (Dillehay 1992, 382–84). These shelters, apparently quite substantially built, were occupied by the families of the patrilineage during community-wide ceremonials. The arrangement of the shelters effectively delineated the central field as a U-Form and, very interestingly, it was referred to as a "puma" and figuratively represented the cosmos. The open side of the U-Form normally faced east, the rising sun, and when possible it was terminated at a body of water.[1] Two major sets of ceremonies were performed, funerary and world renewal. The Mapuche even constructed one or two burial mounds for former "chiefs" and, in some cases, a low rectangular platform was constructed where major renewal rituals mediated by animal sacrifice were performed (Dillehay 1992, 405–7).

Although this cultural attribute is not specifically mentioned by Pacheco, according to the description of the culture that both Dillehay and Faron have given, there is little doubt that traditionally the Mapuche took the world to be immanently sacred and they treated the territories that they used as nonownable, and, for this reason, they recognized that occupiers could only use the land and that this usage established and manifested usufruct rights and obligations on the part of a *trokinche* community. Hence, it is clear that land ownership was not a concept that the Mapuche had and, therefore, their tenure would be more appropriately termed *custodial usufruct.* However, as I argued in the introductory chapter, since they took the world to be immanently sacred and territorialism was based on custodial usufruct, agentive autonomy should be the core of personal and group interaction and this interaction should generate and sustain a dual kinship and companionship structure. However, agentive autonomy as I have defined it was not the case for the Mapuche. Instead, notwithstanding their custodial usufruct notion, they had differential and largely exclusive access to land and this exclusive access sustained dominance structures mediated along kinship lines, particularly emphasizing the subordination of the junior generation of the *trokinche* lineage to the senior generation. Now this makes the Mapuche particularly important as a test of the premises underlying the postulated Complementary Heterarchical Community model and the nature of Ohio Hopewell as a complex structure of cult sodality heterarchies. That is, even though the Mapuche recognized custodial usufruct of land, the kinship groups were based on descent in virtue of the fact that a type of *exclusive* custodial usufruct of land was practiced and this was entrenched by *inheritance* traced through the male line and ranked by seniority. Along with this was the absence of sodalities. Hence, a set of patrilineally, not patrilaterally, related families constituted an internally ranked patrilineage identified with an area of farmland that they habitually gardened and the *use of the land for gardens* that made up this farmland was inherited by the junior male generation from the senior male generation, that is, father to son, sometimes also from mother to son. How would this be possible given that land *usufruct* and not land *ownership* was recognized?

In fact, Dillehay (1992, 384) specifically recognized the difference between ownership and usufruct tenure and explicitly notes that what was inherited by Mapuche was *land usufruct*, not land ownership. That is, a form of exclusive usufruct of land was established as an important kinship-based right that was normally sustained from generation to generation through descent-line inheritance. Of course, if a kinship descent group abandoned its usufruct-based domain, then the land would be available on a first come basis to others. However, Dillehay notes that, at least within the primary territory that the Mapuche occupied, there was no abandoned land and if a young man was denied access to land by his patrilineage leaders, for example, for not recognizing the authority of his senior relatives, his "fathers," then he would have to leave the territory and go into an unoccupied region, effectively isolating himself from his patrilineage. The benefit of moving was that he could open the unoccupied land for his own use to support his family. Hence, if successful as a farmer he could become a founding apical ancestor of his own patrilineage.

Now none of this detail is discussed by Pacheco, even though, at this point in my elucidation, it would certainly appear to reinforce the validity of his using the Mapuche as his analogical example for modeling the Ohio Middle Woodland period dispersed community system. However, things get a bit more complicated. The success of a young man striking out on his own in this manner obviously depended on his having a wife or having access to a wife since gardening was the duty of the in-married women. However, according to Mapuche marriage practice, one of the requisites for gaining a wife was having access to gardening land usufruct, and the usufruct, not the land to which it gave access, was given to his wife as a marriage payment. Unsurprisingly, the Mapuche had exogamous patrilineages that controlled usufruct to the land that it had historically exploited. Being exogamous, patrilineages were caught up in a network of marriage exchange relations in which women and material goods figured. Therefore, each lineage stood in one of two relations with other lineages, being wife-givers to some and wife-receivers from others. The wife-receivers had to give bride wealth to the wife-givers in the form of special textiles and silver objects, as well as transfer to the in-marrying woman custodial usufruct rights to gardening land that the wife-receiving patrilineage controlled. Typically, patrilineages related as wife-giver/wife-receiver were ranked with the latter being subordinate in honor to the former. Now mobilizing bride wealth and allocating land usufruct was not in the control of the young man who needed a wife. Rather, these powers were in the control of the senior males of a *trokinche.* Indeed, historically it was common that senior male leaders of a *trokinche* reserved more women as their own wives than they allowed the junior males of the patrilineage to receive. Although senior males probably no longer monopolize the women as wives for themselves, the fact is they still control the distribution of the in-marrying females and can favor some males over others. The result is a form of polygyny dominated by the senior males and through this control of marriageable women and land, the senior male generation also dominated the younger males. Hence, control of land usufruct and control of women distribution came to be and still are monopolized in the hands of the senior males of the patrilineage with the ranking senior male occupying the leadership position, namely, the "chief." Dillehay cites one historically remembered dominant "chief" who had about 24 wives and almost 100 offspring (1992, 407).

One upshot of this dominance structure was, of course, differential inheritance of land usufruct and allocation of women combined with a complex system of interpatrilineage relations of dominance and subordination mediated through the history of women exchange. This state of affairs is explicitly noted by Dillehay (1992, 413). Another upshot was the suppression of any tendency toward same-age/same-gender companionship. Neither Faron nor Dillehay mention companionship groups specifically, which is itself very indicative since companionship sets have been consistently recognized by the ethnologists of traditional Native North American communities, as I discuss in considerable detail in subsequent chapters. Dillehay notes that the major labor mobilization that was necessary for building, maintaining, and using the ceremonial plaza for the patrilineage's rituals was carried out by the lineage "chief" and, of course, this means that the junior generation of males of the patrilineage, his "sons," would be the major source of labor. Faron discusses labor mobilization and relations and in all cases this is carried out through dominance relations. Customary labor mobilization, *mingaco,* was carried out by the chief inviting "the household heads of his reservation to assemblage at his house on a certain day to begin plowing his fields. . . . After the chief's land had been prepared there was a round of similar activities in which each household head acted as host, fêted the participants, organized the work, and so on" (1968, 19). Faron goes on to define *mingaco* as "a word used by the Mapuche to describe cooperative labor . . . [that was] organized around a core of males of a dominant patrilineage . . . and headed by a lineage elder who is chief" (1968, 20). Pervading the Mapuche social structure, therefore, is a dominance hierarchical order and by default, no autonomous age-set sodalities existed. And, of course, the fact that junior males would compete with each other in order to gain wives through the good will of their senior male leaders would ensure that autonomous companionship groups would likely not emerge, at least of the type I have claimed characterized traditional Native North American communities of the Eastern Woodlands peoples.[2] In short, agentive autonomy appears to be a nonexisting concept in the Mapuche culture. Along with this absence would be an absence of inclusive custodial usufruct as such, and instead, exclusive custodial usufruct prevailed.

What then does the Mapuche example illustrate that is of value for understanding the Ohio Hopewell? Importantly, it illustrates that while an immanentist cosmology and a custodial ethos can indeed prevail, nevertheless the expected principles of agentive autonomy, both individual and group, and the development of dual kinship and companionship structures may not. The Mapuche teach us, therefore, that even when an immanentist cosmology and custodial ethos are in place, agentive autonomy and the generation of dual kinship/companionship structures will not be manifested and this presupposes that some intervening factor emerges that is capable of transforming the principle of custodial usufruct into a type of pseudoproprietorship. This is what I claim occurred among the Mapuche and I will use the term *exclusive custodial land usufruct* to refer to their tenure practices. In the Mapuche case, the intervening factor that transformed inclusive custodial usufruct into exclusive custodial land usufruct, thereby mimicking the conditions of proprietorship of the land and, as a result, promoting dominance of the senior kinship generation over the junior generation, was the monopolization of access to marriageable females through the senior males controlling exogamic patrilineal polygyny. This monopolization may have deep historical roots since the Mapuche have had a history of ongoing warfare against the Spanish invaders, and this history of violent and losing struggles may have promoted such intergenerational dominance. However, it may be that it preexisted the arrival of the Spaniards. The point is that commitment to using the Mapuche as a model of the "Ohio Hopewell community" also entails commitment to some type of social practice that would have had the same effect as I claim was generated by the Mapuche practice of the senior males of a patrilineage controlling the distribution of marriageable females. Since Pacheco specifically constructs his model on descent-based kin groups, it would appear that the same type of senior generation monopolization of polygyny would be the most logical candidate. And of course, if this assumption is applied to the Ohio Middle Woodland period communities, this would also entail commitment to the view that autonomous sodalities did not exist among these communities of the Central Ohio Valley.

While I accept that the Mapuche had senior male dominant polygyny, I do not recognize that this type of polygyny ever emerged in traditional or prehistoric Native North American communities, at least not those that occupied the region east of the Rockies (Kirchhoff 1959; Knight 1990). Indeed, the historic Native North American communities were also under great military pressure against the Spaniards, French, and English. Yet they retained their principles and practices of autonomy, inclusive custodial usufruct of land, and the norm of monogamy rather than polygyny. Of course, in normative terms, polygyny was practiced in many historic Native North American communities. However, this practice came under the constitutive principle of the agentive autonomy. Therefore, it was often the duty of a man to marry the widow of his brother in order to assure the autonomy of the widow and her children. Hence, sororate and levirate were normative practices, but they were not the statistical norm for marriage. Among the Mapuche, apparently polygyny controlled by the senior males was both normative and the norm with senior males typically having more than one spouse, thereby ensuring that younger males would find it difficult to marry unless they retained a near servile relation toward senior generation males.

It turns out, therefore, that the Mapuche can serve as an important disanalogy for modeling the Ohio Middle Woodland period community structure. The Mapuche may be best viewed as an example of a community based on immanentist cosmology with a custodial ethos supporting a form of exclusive land usufruct tenure that thereby generated a pseudoproprietorship of land; and the latter effectively constituted the same structural constraints that an actual regime of proprietorial land ownership would constitute.[3] Therefore, instead of encouraging companionship and autonomy it suppressed both and this generated conditions that largely precluded the formation of companionship-based groupings, while enabling and almost entailing dominance and subordination, descent inheritance, and differential control. Therefore, even though the Mapuche manifested a type of settlement dichotomy that could be formally similar to the patterning I have termed the bifurcated settlement articulation modal posture, it really would in fact be simply a vacant center/dispersed hamlet pattern, that is, a patterning manifesting a lineage-based modular polity, with dominance prevailing between men and women and the senior and junior generations. If such is the case, then it would raise a major problem for understanding the Ohio Hopewell pattern since it is also notable that, while the patterning of the Mapuche centers could certainly be interpreted as manifesting the immanent sacred powers of the cosmos, they are also somewhat puny and plain in comparison to the Ohio Hopewell embankment earthwork locales. The latter involved scales of labor organization that, apparently, the Mapuche could not match, even though their population numbers were easily equivalent if not greater (2,000 to 10,000 per center). I suggested above that not only were the patrilineages dependent primarily on their own labor sources to construct these, not being able to call on other patrilineages except those to which they stood as superior through being wife-givers, the dominance-based mobilization of the junior generation as the major source of labor was largely self-limiting and narrow. If sons felt that their fathers were demanding too much and giving too little, even though land was based on the exclusive custodial usufruct system, it also ensured that, when overly stressed, they could abandon the local region and find the land that they needed. Therefore, if labor demands became too onerous and rewards too skimpy all they needed to do was to leave the patrilineage's exclusive usufruct land area by going to a more distant valley that was unoccupied and start a farm there. That is, they could exercise primary inclusive territorial rights. This may explain why, for all their formal similarity to the Ohio Hopewell, the Mapuche ceremonial centers were somewhat limited in earthwork size and content. The somewhat limited size and labor investment in the Mapuche ceremonial locales compared to the monumental earthwork locales of Ohio Hopewell also reinforces the point I made earlier that communities based on some form of exclusive territorialism, and for the Mapuche this would be exclusive custodial land usufruct, alliances contradict the latter principle in that it gives access to the land by "foreign" communities.

THE MULTIPLE COMMUNITY MODEL

Bret Ruby, Christopher Carr, and Douglas Charles (2005, 123–25) have elucidated in considerable detail a general model to be applied to the settlement patterning of those regions that manifested a Hopewell episode. They term it the Multiple Community model. Interestingly, Paul Pacheco (2010a) has recently endorsed it as very close to his own Dispersed Sedentary Community model. In any case, the authors claim that the orthodox model, exemplified by the Vacant Center/Dispersed Hamlet model and its various versions, treats the community in unitary terms, or as I have called it, monistic terms. In contrast, the Multiple Community model recognizes multiple formations of different types of community. In particular, it treats each of these regional social systems as a tripartite level of community formations—residential, symbolic, and sustainable communities: (1) The residential community consists of social formations based on common kinship-based residency; (2) the symbolic community consists of formations based on cooperative interaction across many regions mediated by symbolic features, such as the Ohio Hopewell embankment earthworks, mortuary, and other ceremonial mounds; and (3) the sustainable community emerges from the interaction of the latter formations as the medium by which the biological needs to reproduce the residential level are fulfilled and the social needs to reproduce the symbolic level are fulfilled.

In this theoretical scheme the residential community is the lowest level or stratum of this multiple system of community formations. It consists of the residential groups of a local sector of a valley, the members of which are related by everyday face-to-face residency. In effect, they are kinship-based groups—families. And these resident groups can be either nucleated or dispersed without, apparently, having any differential social significance. The second level, which they specifically characterize as the Hopewellian formation, consists of the symbolic community level. "Of particular interest in the case of Hopewellian studies is the notion that monumental architecture may constitute a symbolic means of community formation: mounds, earthworks, and other manmade elements of the landscape may have been used as symbols to define community membership and boundaries" (Ruby et al., 2005, 122). In their terms, the "symbolic community" emerges when "individuals and households actively construct and negotiate group identities and affiliations that may cross-cut residential units and be quite fluid in membership . . . [and that] symbols (e.g., ornamentation, dress, public architecture, etc.) may be used to define, communicate, and negotiate membership in a social group that transcends or crosscuts local residence groups . . . for common political, economic, social, and/or religious purposes" (2005, 123). Clearly their characterization of this level entails a sense of fundamental social distinction along the lines that I have already argued. Reinforcing this distinction is the illustrative list they make of a number of anthropological examples of group formations that they consider to be symbolic communities: age-grade-based groups, gender-based groups, cults and other specialized sodalities, and even networks of families linked through exchange systems. In particular, again paralleling my notion of inclusive territorialism, they note that such groups are usually not tied down to territories and, indeed, transcend them, as when they say that "symbolic communities . . . are not defined by the physical imperatives of residential or sustainable communities" (2005, 124).

The third and most abstract level is the sustainable community. This formation functioned as the marriage alliance sphere and as a "community" formation it was emergent from the symbolic community level. I assume that this emergent relation was not strategic in the manner that the symbolic community level was since they imply that the reason the symbolic communities transcended and crosscut the residential communities was to achieve special interest goals. Those involved strategically in the symbolic community level necessarily came from different residential communities and by interacting at the symbolic community level they developed relations with each other that would become an excellent medium for marriage exchange. Hence, they seem to treat the sustainable community as an unintentional but, nevertheless, critically important structural level that ensured the reproductive needs of the residential communities and of the symbolic communities within a wider region. However, they equivocate on this when they also specifically recognize that some symbolic communities generated very large and elaborate earthworks such that the membership of these "symbolic communities" was largely congruent with the "sustainable community." They refer to these large Hopewellian locales as "regional symbolic communities," in contrast to "local symbolic communities," and suggest that they were this size in part because they ensured that the residential communities of the membership could sustain and fulfill their organic reproductive needs in terms of both marriage and subsistence.

Several points they raised led me to find this Multiple Community model intriguing, in particular, their promoting the notion that symbolic communities transcended territories and that non-kin social parameters (e.g., sodalities, artisan specialists, and so on) could serve as the organizing framework of the symbolic communities. Certainly, these suggested that their approach seemed to be breaking with the tradition of thinking of the past in monistic kinship-based community terms. Their definition of symbolic community also reads as if these would be able to constitute their own common goals independently of residential kinship-based communities, and, therefore, that they would be excellent vehicles for constructing and using monumental architecture for purposes that were unfettered by the needs of residential kinship-based communities who, by their nature, would tend to be focused on everyday domestic concerns. I certainly think that these points are on the right track such that, in principle, their notion of multiple communities would be very compatible with the premises underwriting my own view of Ohio Hopewell.

However, their exposition of this model through applying it to the Middle Woodland period settlement patterning of three regions, the lower Illinois Valley, the region at the confluence of the Wabash and Lower Ohio Rivers, and the central Scioto Valley of Ohio, did not conform to its own premises. While they recognize the necessity for what they term the "symbolic community" formation in order to account for the Hopewell ceremonial-related earthwork sites, they sustain the privileged nature of both the residential kinship-based community and exclusive territorialism, namely, territorial modules, by treating the residential community level as the "natural" community. This leads to their treating the symbolic community level as simply permutations of alliances of the residential communities of a local region. As I noted above, they even distinguish two levels of symbolic communities: local and regional. Hence, local symbolic communities are not groupings that are structurally distinct from the dispersed residential communities. Rather, they are reduced to being simply alliances of these residential communities and since the latter are kinship-based, the local symbolic community is also a permutation of kinship structures, for example, multiple clans constituting what many anthropologists term a tribal community. These local symbolic communities are marked by displaying a Hopewellian assemblage that is rather modest in size, complexity, and content. The regional symbolic community then comes to be simply a second-level alliance of the local symbolic communities in the region, that is, a tribal alliance, and it is demarcated by the greater magnitude, complexity, and wealth of its material forms and contents.

This rendering of the multiple community levels reduces their uniqueness since there is no distinction in *social structural nature* between the residential community, the local symbolic community, and the regional symbolic community. These latter two levels, local and regional, are simply iterations of the same social structures that constitute the residential community. Since the residential communities reproduce themselves through marriage alliances mediated by the symbolic community level, it follows that—despite their explicitly recognizing the possibility that sodalities or even unrelated individuals could independently ally to form these symbolic communities—the core social structures at all levels are kinship structures, and each level is simply the assimilation of kinship groups of the same order into composite groups of the same order, such as kin-based residential groups into clan-based "symbolic" groups.

Furthermore, in each illustrative case, the core kinship nature of the residential community level is affirmed and, moreover, the notion of exclusive territorialism is also affirmed. In the lower Illinois Valley, the kinship-based residential communities of a given sector of the valley are identified as constituting the local symbolic community, each such community delineated by its own bluff-top burial locale(s) and claiming as its corporate property that linear segment of territory—about 5 or 6 km wide and bracketing the bluff-top mortuary mound locale—that passes from the uplands, through the mound locale, and down to the valley bottom to extend and incorporate as its exclusive territory the associated floodplain and fluvial sector. Hence, the local symbolic community is not emergent from nor does it transcend the multiple dispersed kinship groups constituting the local region's residential communities. Rather it is simply the aggregation of the kinship structures, thereby being constituted as a set of clans/lineages forming a complex kinship-based proprietorial corporation, that is, the monistic modular tribal polity that is so close to the heart and imagination of anthropologists and archaeologists. It is only the second-level symbolic community, what they term the regional symbolic community, that takes on some semblance of social structural autonomy. However, this is a weak autonomy since this second level is itself simply the alliance of the local symbolic communities of the region. Since the latter are themselves kinship-based (i.e., monistic) communities consisting either of multiple lineages or of clans, this seems to give no opportunity for non-kin groups, such as age-sets, specialized religious cults, or other sodalities, to establish themselves as autonomous social groups that can transcend the interests of the communities to which their members belong.

However, this may not be a fair assessment of their model since they specifically claim that a whole range of "Hopewellian" ceremonial sites could exist that were functionally different and specific and could have been used by non-kinship groups. They assert this functional variation thesis quite strongly. "Specifically, in each region are found ceremonial centers of diversified functions rather than centers of one kind. Some centers served primarily for holding mortuary ceremonies; others as the locations of predominantly or exclusively of other kinds of ceremonies. Some mounds and mound groups were built and used by relatively small, local groups drawn from farther afield, forging symbolic and sustainable communities. Local symbolic communities used multiple kinds of centers within their own territories, and some centers were used by multiple local symbolic communities. Ceremonial precincts used by singular local symbolic communities were sometimes segregated from and sometimes combined with ceremonial precincts used by multiple local symbolic communities that constituted a broad, sustainable community. Individuals in each region likely visited a range of these ceremonial centers for different purposes, each event a potential context for the construction of group identities and affiliations of varied membership, duration, and spatial extent" (2005, 12). Now this mix of functional types certainly echoes my own claim that if the Ohio Middle Woodland period complementary heterarchical communities of a region were in the bifurcated settlement articulation modal posture that we could expect a range of different types of sites by function, one constituting the clan component of the region and the other the sodality component. Therefore, I can endorse this claim. Furthermore, the multifunctionality of this variety would certainly enable adequate flexibility for age-sets and shamanic colleges, specialized artisan groups, and so on, to aggregate fairly regularly and carry out the different activities and tasks that would be particular to their interests, capacities, and needs. In fact, as I develop the characterization of the Ohio embankment earthworks, I directly address some of the functional variation they note here. However, I do this within the theoretical framework of alliances of cult sodalities as social groups that were relatively autonomous of the communities from which they came. I recognize the specialized needs of these groups and they would necessarily incorporate and be able to comfortably incorporate this range of experts, many of them being drawn from their own membership. That is, functional variation alone does not characterize the social nature of the groups that performed these functions. These groups, which they claim would constitute symbolic communities, local and regional, must be structurally distinct from the residential groups. They seem to realize this but their illustrative examples do not demonstrate it. I will particularly critique the auxiliary model of the Hopewellian assemblage and distribution as it unfolded in Ohio to show that, in fact, the local and regional "symbolic communities" are treated under this model as complex iterations of monistic modular polity communities. I focus on the Ohio example since, of course, this book addresses the Ohio Hopewell. However, my reading of their modeling of the other two regions they discuss, the lower Illinois Valley and the Wabash-Lower Ohio confluence lowlands, convinces me that these also treat the symbolic community notion as complex iterations of kinship-based residential communities.

Of course, I want to stress that their affirming that the Middle Woodland period domestic/ceremonial settlement pattern dichotomy can be treated in "multiple community" terms is the most important point that their approach and mine share, except, of course, I have specifically avoided using the term *community* to refer to the groups responsible for the Ohio Hopewell component, preferring to speak of these as mutualistic heterarchies and, of course, my reason for doing this is precisely to emphasize the structural distinction of the Ohio Middle Woodland *community* as a dual clan/sodality social organization from the Ohio Hopewell as a complex structure of a singular type of social organization, that type based on companionship-based sodalities only. As I also noted earlier, sodalities are not constrained to same-age/same-sex. Rather, they are characterized by companionship, sharing a property that exists in complementary opposition to kinship and, therefore, as I noted above, under special conditions there is no difficulty modeling a complex sodality constituted by sectors based on a range of specialized expertise along with nonspecialized age-set and gender-specific groups. It is this type of group, I maintain, that would make the combination of "symbolic" earthworks and functional variation possible.

CONCLUSION

As noted above, the main problem I have with the Multiple Community model is its not adequately characterizing how the variable functionality that they recognized in the Hopewell site system could emerge and be sustained without some form of social structural means of generating autonomous groups. To demonstrate that this is the critical problem with the model, the next chapter is used to initiate a summary and critique of the Tripartite Ceremonial Alliance model. This model was explicitly constructed by Christopher Carr as the application of the more general Multiple Community model to the south-central Ohio region of the Middle Woodland period; and this will be followed by a detailed critique of the model. This detailed critique is necessary because, despite the affirmations of the proponents of the Multiple Community model that the latter treats the domestic/ceremonial settlement dichotomy in a radically different manner from the orthodox view, what I referred to earlier as the Monistic Modular Polity Community model, it quickly becomes clear that, rather than being different, the Tripartite Ceremonial Alliance model is a very good and quite sophisticated expression of this model as applied to the Middle Woodland period of the Ohio region. Therefore, my critique of the model serves to critique this whole monistic modular tradition. This critique then clears the way for me to present and develop the alternative account of the same archaeological record by means of elucidating and empirically grounding both the Complementary Heterarchical Community model and its auxiliary, what I will call the Cult Sodality Heterarchy Systems model.

3

The Tripartite Ceremonial Alliance Model

A Critique

The Tripartite Ceremonial Alliance model of the central Scioto Valley region was explicitly presented by Christopher Carr (2005b) as a version of the Multiple Community model directly addressing and accounting for the Ohio Hopewell, or at least the Middle Woodland period settlement pattern in that region of Ohio displaying what archaeologists recognize as the most intriguing set of major Ohio Hopewell geometrical embankment earthwork sites. These display the well-known tripartite patterning of interconnected geometrical embankments (small circle–large central circle–square) as illustrated by Liberty Works (figure 1.2). The largest set of these embankment earthworks is concentrated in the central Scioto–Paint Creek region (figure 3.1). The monumental earthwork sites of Frankfort, Seip, Baum, and Works East (figures 3.3, 3.5, 3.6, and 3.8, respectively), along with their major features, ceremonial and mortuary facilities, and their associated artifact assemblage constitute the primary empirical data set of Carr's Tripartite Ceremonial Alliance model. However, similar types of tripartite and even dual circle-rectilinear monumental geometrical embankment earthworks are found in the Scioto River region downriver at Portsmouth, up the Ohio River at Marietta, a small city at the mouth of the Muskingum River in eastern Ohio, and at Newark, arguably the most geometrically elaborate embankment earthwork complex (figure 3.2). This major site is located at the head of the Licking valley of the upper Muskingum drainage and its remains are today surrounded by Newark, a medium size city only about 60 km east of Columbus, Ohio. There are also variant expressions of these geometrical types found in the Little and Great Miami Valleys in the southeast corner of Ohio. However, as noted above, the focus of Carr's model is the set of five tripartite

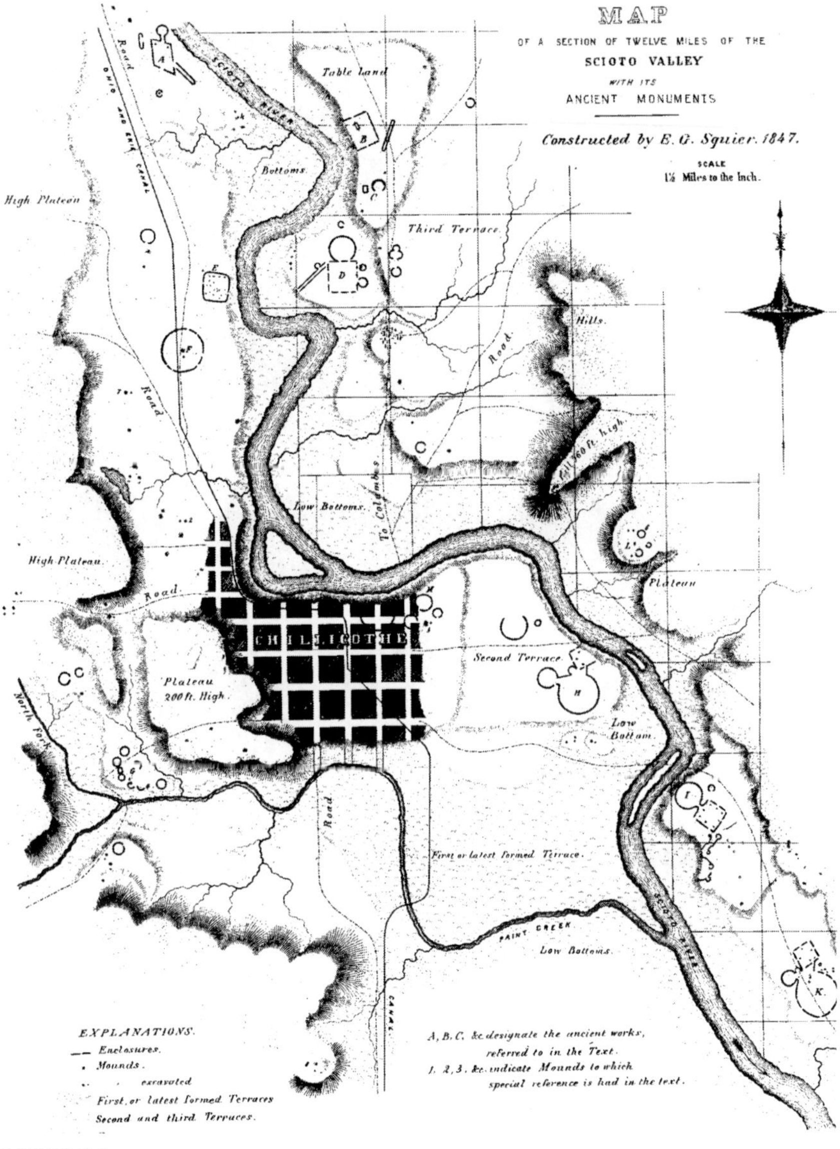

FIGURE 3.1

Map Overview of Embankment Earthworks of the Central Scioto River Valley

Source: Squier and Davis 1848, plate II.

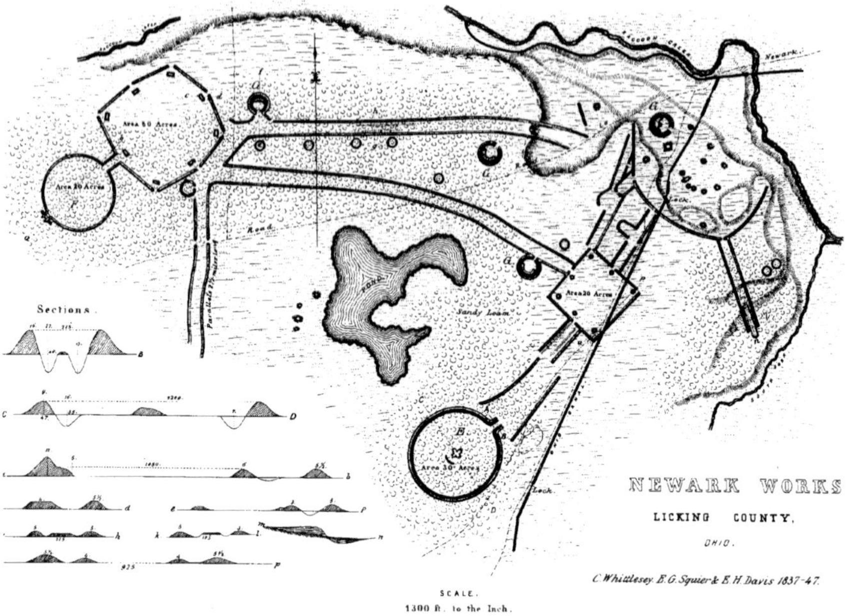

FIGURE 3.2
Newark Earthworks
Source: Squier and Davis 1848, plate XXV.

embankment earthworks plus the eponymous Hopewell site and these are located in the central Scioto–Paint Creek region in and around Chillicothe, a small city in Ross County of southern Ohio (figure 3.1). In fact, Ross County is considered by many archaeologists to be the epicenter of Ohio Hopewell, and, according to N'omi Greber (1991), it is likely in this region that critical components of the Hopewell style assemblage emerged out of the preexisting Adena background.

I have carried out an in-depth interpretation of the tripartite (circle-circle-rectilinear) embankment earthwork type (Byers 2004, 1987). When speaking in formal terms, I have called it the Paint Creek C-R configuration, the "C-R" representing the core circle-rectilinear coupling. When interpreting it in culturally meaningful terms, I have called it the Paint Creek C-R motif. It is well represented in this case by the Frankfort site (figure 3.3). To be quite clear here, when I speak of the "C-R" coupling as the core of the pattern, I am *not* referring to the large central circle. Rather, I am referring to the large square and the small circle on the perimeter of the large central circle. That is, the C-R coupling is mediated by this large central circle, which I have called the infix component. I have chosen this term because I envision the large central

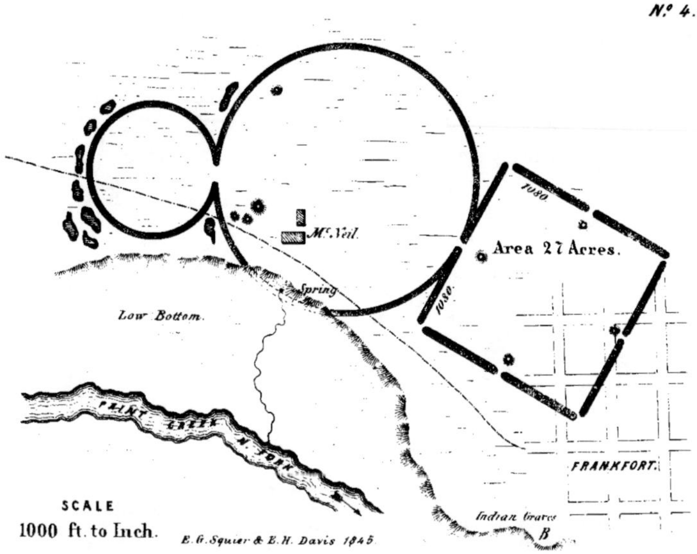

FIGURE 3.3
The Frankfort (Old Town) Site
Source: Squier and Davis 1848, plate XXI, no. 4.

circle as deliberately fixed in to separate and also conjoin the large square and the small circle. In an important sense, then, the large circle—despite being the largest component of the total motif configuration—is an auxiliary component. In terms of the overall configuration, it served as an "auxiliary" or connecting component. To claim this, however, is certainly not to claim that it was unimportant. To the contrary it had an important action meaning to play out, as I discuss later.

Hence, even though the tangible patterning of the Paint Creek C-R motif displays a tripartite configuration, I have argued that the C-R coupling manifests its core structural nature. In my view it is actually one variant configuration of a primary motif that I call the C-R motif. The second variant is manifested in the embankment earthwork patterning of what is referred to in the literature as the High Bank earthwork site (figure 3.4). Here the C-R motif is manifested in a straightforward circle-rectilinear coupling. I call this variant of the C-R motif the High Bank C-R motif. I treat these two formal configurations as complementary and, therefore, in cultural motif terms, as meaningfully interactive. The meaning of the High Bank C-R motif is the complement of the meaning of the Paint Creek C-R motif. This claim commits me to the view that although a given Paint Creek C-R motif site and a given High Bank

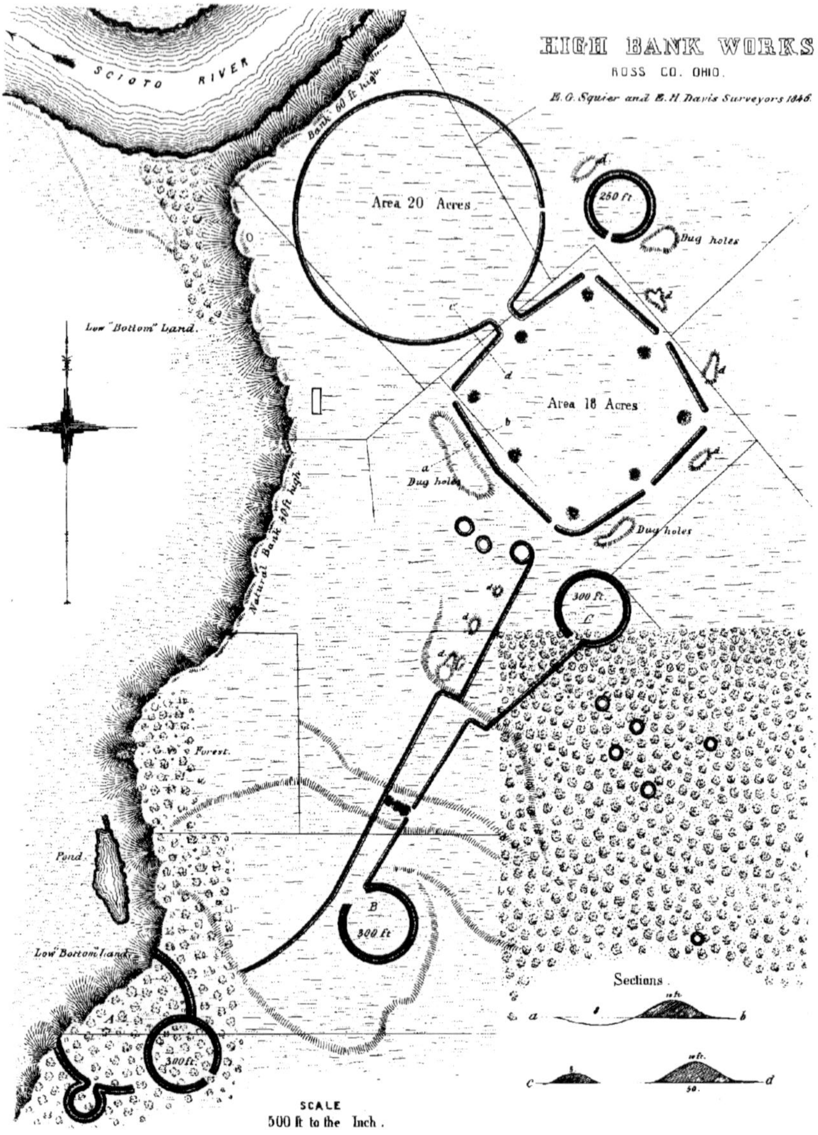

FIGURE 3.4

The High Bank Site

Source: Squier and Davis 1848, plate XVI.

C-R motif site—or their equivalents manifested in some other variant formal patterning as I discuss later—may be spatially separate, their builders and users perceived them as constituting a single complex monumental icon representing and participating in the complementary properties of the cosmos (Byers 2004). In effect, the group responsible for a particular Paint Creek C-R motif site, such as the Liberty earthworks, would also be responsible for its complementary opposite, a High Bank C-R motif site (which is actually only a few kilometers immediately north of Liberty Works), or if not solely responsible, it would share responsibility with a like group. In speaking of it as the material expression of a complementary duality, I refer to it as the Sacred Dual C-R motif. In this regard, I have argued that the Sacred Dual C-R motif was understood by those responsible for building and using it as necessary for the performance of the total suite of rituals characteristic of Ohio Hopewell (Byers 1987, 2004).

Not only does this claim entail treating the C-R motif in symbolic terms, but it also implicates what I have spoken of as the symbolic pragmatic view of material culture. This view claims that a human community uses the symbolic aspect of its material cultural assemblage to constitute their social activities as the type they are recognized to be. In short, through the symbolic mediation of their material culture they perform social actions, thereby discharging their duties and realizing the values that motivate and organize them—whatever these may be. In effect, I claim that without the range of appropriately formed material cultural symbols, a group cannot perform the set of activities that constitutes its raison d'être. I consider this claim, which I call the intelligibility principle, to be fundamental to explaining the construction and use of such monumental constructions as the Ohio Hopewell earthworks. I will elucidate this view of the meaning and role of material culture later, referring to it as the symbolic pragmatic perspective, since it clearly plays a critical role in the development of my interpretation of the Ohio Hopewell episode.

The High Bank C-R motif configuration as represented by the High Bank site (figure 3.4) played a minor role in the Tripartite Ceremonial Alliance model, even though the site is just east of Chillicothe and about 4 km north of Liberty Works, and the latter is among the five Paint Creek C-R motif earthworks that are the empirical focus of this model. While Carr acknowledges that there were embankment earthworks of this configuration, he does not address the relation between the "tripartite" embankment earthwork form I term the Paint Creek C-R configuration and any other embankment earthwork form, with the exception of the embankment of the Hopewell site itself. The distribution of these five Paint Creek C-R motif sites plays an important role in his analysis since this distribution defines for him what he terms three local symbolic communities. Two of these sites are located in the Paint Creek,

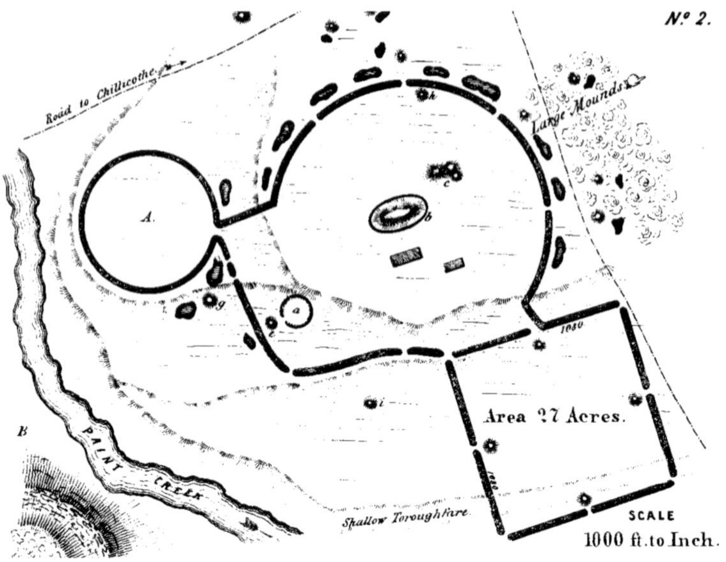

FIGURE 3.5
The Seip Site
Source: Squier and Davis 1848, plate XXVI, no. 2.

Seip (figure 3.5), and Baum (figure 3.6). They are several kilometers west of its confluence with the Scioto and are located on opposite sides of the creek. Seip is on the north bank and is the farthest west and Baum is on the south bank about 5 km downstream from the former. Frankfort (or Old Town) is another of the Paint Creek C-R motif sites (figure 3.3) and it is on the North Fork of the Paint Creek about 5 km upstream from the Hopewell site. Most importantly, Carr includes the Hopewell site (figure 3.7), which is downstream from Frankfort.[1] Although the primary embankment earthwork of the Hopewell site is what I term a C-Form, he implies that the overall site is a variant expression of the tripartite configuration. I believe he is right in this regard since I have argued that some time following the construction of the original C-Form embankment, two more embankment forms were added, in particular, a circle and a square, and in my view these effectively transformed the total site into a variant of the Paint Creek C-R motif.

The Liberty Works site (figure 1.2) and the Works East site (figure 3.8) are situated, the former, on the east bank, just south of the Paint Creek–Scioto confluence, and the latter, Works East, on the west bank, just north of this confluence. Therefore, these two almost mirror image sites are within a few kilometers of each other and on opposite sides of both the Scioto River and the Paint Creek–Scioto confluence, a patterning that echoes the relative

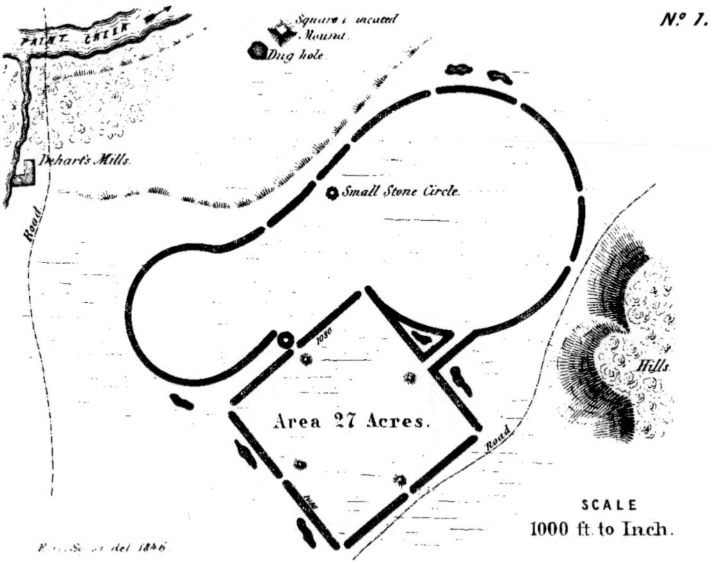

FIGURE 3.6
The Baum Site
Source: Squier and Davis 1848, plate XXI, no. 1.

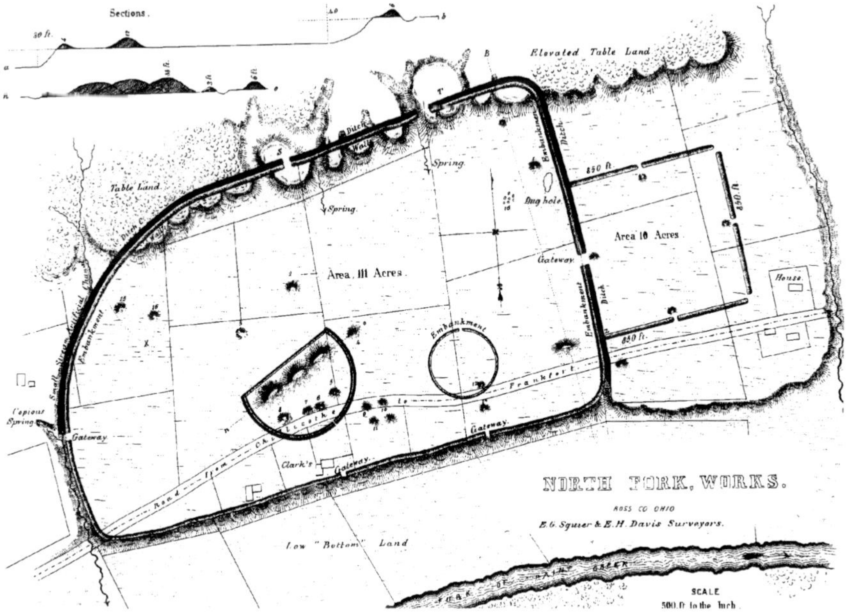

FIGURE 3.7
The Hopewell Site
Source: Squier and Davis 1848, plate X.

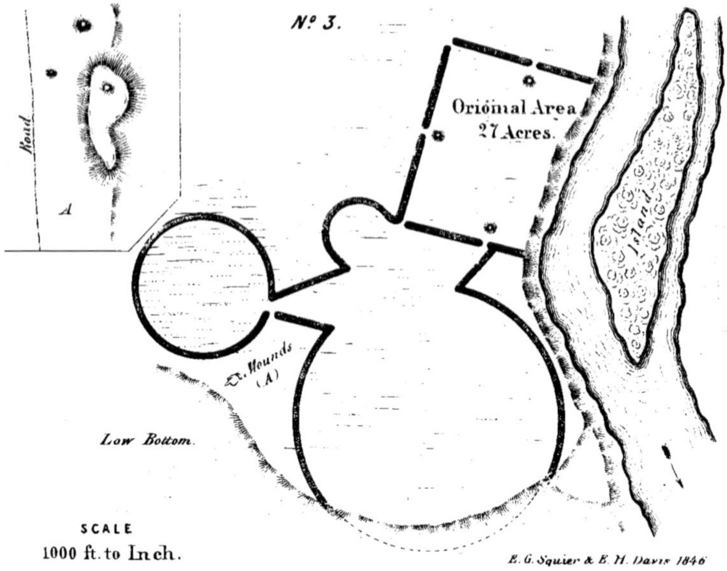

FIGURE 3.8
The Works East Site
Source: Squier and Davis 1848, plate XXI, no. 3.

positioning of Seip and Baum on the Paint Creek proper. Furthermore, I think that it is notable that the High Bank site—its large circle and octagon embankment earthworks representing the High Bank C-R motif—is not only found in the same region, it is also on the west bank of the central Scioto River effectively opposite the juncture of the Paint Creek with the Scioto and, as noted above, only approximately 4 km north of the Liberty Works site. I consider this spatial propinquity of two of the major embankment earthworks representing the complementary variants of the C-R motif to be very significant in that, viewed together, they manifest what I termed above the Sacred Dual C-R motif. However, despite the spatial association and formal similarities of the Liberty Works and High Bank sites, the Tripartite Ceremonial Alliance model pretty well ignores the latter. This suggests a serious limitation of that model, as I discuss more fully later.

In sum, the Tripartite Ceremonial Alliance model divides the central Scioto drainage into three interrelated subregions: the middle-lower sector of the Paint Creek proper, the North Fork of this drainage, and the central Scioto–Paint Creek confluence zone. Each subregion accommodates at least one pair of "matching" Paint Creek C-R motif embankment earthworks: Seip and Baum, Hopewell and Frankfort, and Liberty Works and Works East, respectively.[2] As an auxiliary model designed specifically to interpret and explain the earthworks of this region in terms of the premises of the Multiple Community model, the Tripartite model characterizes these three paired clusters of sites as constituting three autonomous *local* symbolic communities that allied to form what it postulates to be a single *regional* symbolic community with its seat being the Hopewell site. Its claim is based on several grounds. First, assuming the estimated demographics of any one of these three subregions is correct, Carr has noted that the magnitude of physical labor that each local symbolic community could mobilize could not have been adequate to move the earth fill required to build the embankments and mounds found in each community's territory. Therefore, the labor required for any one of the three earthwork sites must have been combined from the labor available in all three communities. In his view, partly confirming this labor thesis is the formal patterning of the earthworks. Not only did all the embankment earthworks share the same basic tripartite formal configuration, one tripartite earthwork in each territory contained at least one major mound that covered the remains of a large "charnel house or houses," to use the term favored in this model. The four earthwork sites were the Hopewell site (Mound 25, figure 3.7), Frankfort (figure 3.3), Seip (figure 3.5, Seip-Pricer and Seip-Conjoined, covering one structure each), and Liberty Works (figure 1.2, the Edwin Harness mound). The remains of at least three of these charnel houses, those at Seip and Liberty Works, were formal look-alikes with each charnel house built as a tripartite pattern of rooms arranged along a single axis—two rectangular rooms being immediately linked to each other by a short central rectangular room (figure 3.9). Each of these three charnel houses had three discrete burial

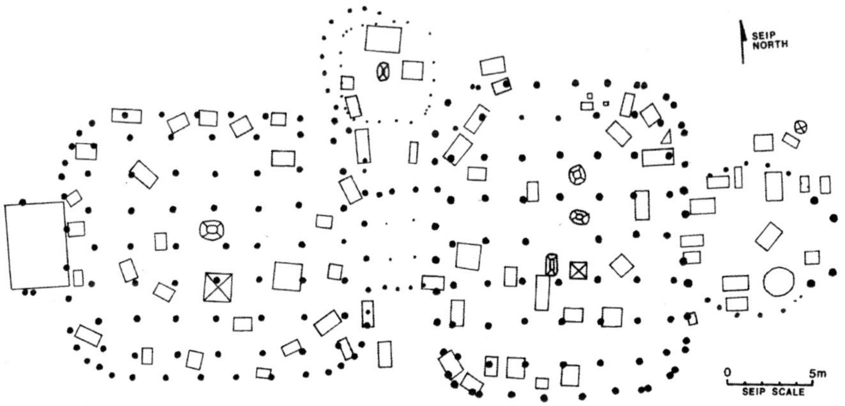

FIGURE 3.9
The Seip-Pricer "Big House or Great House" Estimated Floor Plan
Source: Greber 1983, 88, figure 10.1. By permission of *Midcontinental Journal of Archaeology.*

clusters delineated on the prepared ground that was exposed when the covering mounds were removed by excavating and most burials in each cluster were cremations, many of which displayed the residue of elaborate mortuary practices in the form of artifacts and burial features.[3] The model claims that the mortuary sphere was recruited by the three local symbolic communities (in my terms "monistic modular polities") and subsumed to their political needs by ensuring that each community had selected deceased buried in the charnel structures of each of the other communities. Its basic premise, in this regard, is that the physical forms and their internal divisions of each of these charnel structures were such as to ensure that each polity had a dedicated charnel room (above) and floor space (below) and that the distribution of the artifacts among the deceased in each room was determined by their social standing in their respective communities at the time of their deaths. By each community having some of their deceased buried in the space dedicated to it in each of the two other charnel structures of the allied communities, all three communities would be motivated to sustain their political alliance.

> [I]n the case of Scioto Hopewell mortuary remains, *the foundation determinant of their content and organization was intercommunity alliance organization and its associated ideology not internal social organization.* This foundation determinant is concluded here to have been responsible for the triads of burial clusters and/or charnel house chambers under each of Seip-Pricer, Seip-Conjoined, Edwin Harness, and Hopewell Mound 25. . . . Upon this basic mortuary theme of alliance, the effects of other determinants of mortuary practices and mortuary remains, such as the marking of leaders, sodalities, and clans, were then overlaid at the large mounds studied here. (Carr 2005b, 323)

CRITICAL DISCUSSION

First, the overall discussion that Carr gives of the structure of these "local symbolic communities" neatly conforms with the premises of the Monistic Modular Polity model. Each community was ensconced in its particular valley sector and it was constituted of dispersed kinship-based residential communities, or, domestic habitation units. Although the possibility that sodalities existed is recognized, these are subsumed to the total local symbolic community as one among several different group types, including clans, and so on, as I discuss shortly. Certainly these do not carry any special social structural significance. The only property these basically monistic polity communities have that deviates from the orthodox view is that they assiduously divided up their deceased and allocated them to the different dedicated burial spaces of the three charnel structures; however, these charnel structures were themselves the property of the specific communities that had exclusive control of both the specific embankment earthworks in which each was built and the ambient territory of that sector of the valley. Furthermore, the claim of the Tripartite Ceremonial Alliance model that the formal earthworks represent the alliance of several autonomous monistic modular polities is not unique. It is consistent with the notion that the earthworks were the civic-ceremonial centers of such communities. However, when the magnitude of the labor needed to build one of these earthworks appears to surpass the manpower resources of a single community, then alliances are invoked, as I noted earlier, despite the basic contradiction between the notion of exclusive control of territory and the sharing of the requisite construction labor to build each other's earthworks. For example, William Dancey and Paul Pacheco (1997, 9–10) have postulated a type of peer polity alliance system to account for the larger earthwork sites, such as the Hopewell site and the Newark site. N'omi Greber (1997, 219–20; 2006, 100–102) has also argued that these earthworks manifest civic-ceremonial center polity communities that were in a type of alliance association, although her analysis did not consider the Hopewell site to be a Paint Creek C-R motif variant. Where she differs from Carr is that she differentiates between those sites generated by alliances from those generated by individual polities. For example, in her modeling of Seip and Liberty Works, the mortuary deposits on the floors of each mound consisted of the deceased only of the community responsible for that mound (Greber 1979, 36–38; 1997, 214–20). Her model also postulated these communities were based on kinship descent structures, probably constituting ranked clans as manifested in the differential distribution of mortuary data marking degrees of privilege, power, esteem, and wealth (Greber 1976, 89–98; 1979, 32–36). Recently, she has developed her ideas in this regard by arguing that rather than three, there were at least four separate but more or less contemporary polities in the central Scioto drainage area: the Paint Creek polity, the North Fork polity, the Chillicothe North polity, and the Chillicothe South polity (Greber 2006, 100–102). She has not elaborated on the relations among these, but she has made it clear that for her they were mutually autonomous and each was responsible for the embankment earthworks with the associated mortuary structures in their respective and rather constrained territories.

Carr, however, considers his Tripartite Ceremonial Alliance model to be radically distinct from the various versions of the Civic-Ceremonial Center model that I have discussed, the paradigm being Prufer's dispersed hamlet/vacant center view. However, since all these models presuppose the basic premises that I articulated under the Monistic Modular Polity Community model, I disagree with him. Apparently the basis of his claim hinges on the way the "tripartite alliance" sustained its formation. While he critiques

Greber's treatment of identifying the mortuary record of each site with the particular (modular polity) community that built and used it as its civic-ceremonial center, he claims that these same mortuary records of each separate site incorporated deceased members of all three communities. This is an intriguing claim and I summarize and critique his argumentation and the interpretation of the mortuary data that he presents shortly. However, even if his claim were supportable, and I believe it is not, I do not consider his model to be anything else but a more complicated version of the orthodox view.

What it nicely illustrates is just how convoluted the argument can become when trying to account for the construction of large earthworks carried out by monistic modular polities. For example, as I noted above, the model presupposes that each valley region was the exclusive territory of the "local symbolic community" that "owned" the particular earthworks in that territory. In fact, he claims in his model that the Seip community "owned" both Seip and Baum, and the Liberty community also "owned" Works East, immediately northwest and across the Scioto River from it. Drawing on Greber's research in this regard, he argues through the model that the large timber structures on the prepared floors covered by the major mounds were internally divided into three spatially discrete mortuary spaces, each one dedicated to the deceased of one of the three allied local symbolic communities. Hence, some of the deceased of each of the three allied communities were distributed in each of the three separate charnel houses or complexes across the three regions. This ensured, he claims, that while each community had its main charnel house in its own territory, each also had a dedicated space for its exclusive mortuary use in each of the "allied" charnel complexes. Despite the complexity of the social interaction that would have to have occurred to generate this postulated mortuary patterning, it is still clear that he is committed to the premises of the monistic modular polity community view, particularly exclusive territories, and dominance of kinship structures. He does, however, recognize the likely existence of sodalities, and he accepts the view that the population of each community was dispersed as clusters of families across the landscape, both of these attributes being sustained by the generic Multiple Community model. He also has a fairly strong commitment to the mobile version of the Monistic Modular Polity Community model in that he argues that the families probably occupied seasonal base camps and moved to the uplands during the cold season and reoccupied the lowlands near their local symbolic community embankment earthworks during the warm season. Hence, I consider this model to be simply a complex variation of the orthodox view.

To demonstrate the model empirically, Carr combines analogically based a priori argumentation with "middle range" theories of mortuary practices and the symbolic meaning of material culture, using these latter to interpret the mortuary-related empirical data in functionalist terms. His analogical argument is critical since it warrants projecting onto the prehistoric archaeological record the current and rather orthodox anthropological knowledge of the historic Eastern Woodland. In this case, he targets the Feast of the Dead of the historic Huron and Algonkian speaking peoples. Until driven out by hostilities with the Iroquois Confederacy, the Hurons were maize gardening peoples who occupied the small region between Lake Simcoe and Georgian Bay of the upper sector of Lake Huron, Ontario, Canada (Heidenreich 1978, 368). The Huron were also in contact with the Algonkian peoples of the boreal region just north of the Great Lakes, who for a brief time also practiced a formally similar Feast of the Dead (Hall 1997, 37–40). In the case of the Huron, a central element of the Feast of the Dead was for a village to gather their curated deceased for collective bone burial. They also invited neighboring villages to participate by bringing the cleaned and bundled bones of some of their own deceased. The bundled bones of all the deceased were then deposited helter-skelter in a large ossuary pit (Heidenreich 1978, 380; Trigger 1976, 87). Carr argues that this collective or mass ossuary burial was strategically performed so as to serve to unite the local regional villages, the premise being that by burying the deceased of different nucleated residential communities in one shared facility, the allied villages recommitted themselves to mutual support. That is, nucleated residential communities constitute and reconstitute their alliance as "symbolic communities" through sharing the funereal burial of the bones of their ancestors. "The purpose of this joint burying of the dead was to express cooperation among the three communities and to solidify a three-way ritual alliance among them" (Carr 2005b, 296). He adds to this claim the spiritual and ideological dimensions, implicating a form of ancestor worship, again citing anthropological claims about the historically known Eastern Woodland Feasts of the Dead and specifying that this logic underwrote the cultural mortuary practices of the Ohio Hopewell symbolic communities. "This was the logic of the historic Woodland and Algonkian Feasts of the Dead. . . . This act [of collective burial], by its mortuary and spiritual nature, would have been a very substantial, structurally and ideologically potent, and long-lasting means of fostering cooperation. In particular, burial of the bodies of the dead from multiple communities together within one charnel house could have symbolized the eternal cooperation of the ancestors from those communities with each other—a sacred contract" (2005b, 296).

By this analogically grounded argument, Carr not only accepts as unproblematic the adequacy of the interpretation of the Feast of the Dead as a mortuary-mediated means of alliance among the traditional Native North American communities, but he presupposes the Monistic Modular Polity Community model as also adequately characterizing these Eastern Woodland historic social systems. It is also clear that he is committed to a particular mortuary perspective, what I have referred to in the introductory chapter as the *funerary paradigm*. This treats burials, whether single or collective, extended or secondary, bundles or cremated, as the conditions of satisfaction of the same type of mortuary intentions and these intentions are adequately referred to as funerary in nature, with the latter word largely defined in Euro-American cultural terms. As I noted earlier, the funerary paradigm fits "naturally" with the premises of the Monistic Modular Polity Community model since it argues that these kinship-based polities recruited mortuary practices to legitimize their exclusive claims to modular territories. It is argued that by collectively burying their dead in centralized locales, these communities symbolically presenced the ancestors, thereby legitimizing the claims by the living descendants to exclude non-kin from access to "their" territories (Charles and Buikstra 1983, 120–21; Buikstra and Charles 1999, 207–8).[4] Of course, if territorialism is inclusive, as I argued earlier, then the logic of invoking the spiritual authority of the dead, either to warrant the living descendants to exclude others or else to seal alliances with others, becomes largely otiose and irrelevant, even contradictory. However, far from eliminating the importance of mortuary practices, I have argued that under systems of custodial tenure they can constitute a sphere of activity that becomes a complex arena for both honoring the dead and recycling their spiritual powers, and this recycling process was perceived by those involved as having reproductive and transformative consequences that revitalized and renewed the immanently sacred procreative powers of the cosmos (Byers 2004, 177–85, 261–63).

In short, as I noted briefly in the previous chapter, it would be more rational to treat the mortuary sphere of the Middle Woodland period under the Complementary Heterarchical Community model as a multistaged process of rites from initial funerary rites (using this term in the Euro-American sense) through a series of postfunerary mourning → memorial → spirit-release → personal-social-world renewal rites performed incrementally, each marking the release of a range of different spiritual essences of the deceased, constituting social and ultimately world renewal rites (Byers 2004, chapters 8 and 10; 2006a, chapters 3, 12, 13; Hall 1979, 260–64; 1997, 156–62). In fact I detail this approach in the next chapter and show that, rather than the Huron Feast of the Dead conforming to the funerary paradigm or its performance being carried out to serve as a mechanism of intervillage alliance, it is more coherently understood in the above world renewal terms, and these are the terms that I will apply to the Ohio Hopewell mortuary sphere. I have called this mortuary perspective the Mourning/World Renewal Mortuary model and I consider it to be an important ancillary model of the Complementary Heterarchical Community model.

In any case, characteristic of most proponents of the Monistic Modular Polity Community model, in whatever versions, Carr is explicitly committed to the funerary paradigm view and the claim that separate exclusive territorial polity communities strategically recruited and subsumed their mortuary spheres to the making of political and economic alliances by burying their "ancestors" together, despite the contradictions implicated in sharing deceased among mutually exclusive territorial polities. In order for him to explain the distribution of the mortuary data in these terms, therefore, as noted above, it required his arguing that the charnel house form was determined by the alliance needs while the distribution of the artifacts and mortuary treatments manifest primarily the social standing of the deceased in his or her specific community at the time of death.

Using this dual theoretical and methodological framework, Carr proceeds to address the empirical data. Of course, the most important assumption he starts with is that these data are the expression of monistic modular polity communities, albeit he calls them "local symbolic communities." Therefore, he immediately starts by postulating a priori what he considers to be the total logically plausible range of mortuary-distribution possibilities that such communities would follow that could explain the patterning of the mortuary data: group rank, leaders versus followers, age-sets, gender divisions, sodalities, different totemic groups, circumstances of death, religious beliefs, and members of different local symbolic communities based on residential communities constituted of dispersed hamlets (Carr 2005b, 286–94). The last possibility on the list implicates, particularly, the Tripartite Ceremonial Alliance model, of course, since the latter claims that the tripartite burial spaces associated with each charnel structure and the particular distribution of burial artifacts across these three spaces together manifest a pattern that could only be produced by an alliance of the type of local symbolic communities postulated by the Tripartite Ceremonial Alliance model. By eliminating the other possibilities, he then shows that the distribution "fits" what could be expected if, in fact, an alliance of the local symbolic communities existed. As he expresses it, the burial clusters consisted of "members of different dispersed hamlet communities who were buried together to solidify an alliance among the communities," and he concludes that "[t]he last interpretation is the only one found acceptable" (2005b, 286).

It is only fair to note that his method to demonstrate his model parallels the method I prefer, that is, the hermeneutic spiral method, but in a truncated form. His list consists of a priori necessary conditions, given all that is generally known in anthropology and archaeology about the phenomenon being studied, namely, prehistoric Native North American communities and their mortuary practices. He sets up contrasting models, his own versus, for example, the Civic-Ceremonial Center model. The contrast he focuses on, however, is quite trivial rather than fundamental, namely, the congruency/noncongruency of cemetery/community patterning with the "standard" view being congruent, that is one community–one cemetery, and the former, his own, postulating crosscutting community/cemetery structures. He eliminates all the factors in the list except one while arguing that the latter fits the crosscutting view. He concludes, therefore, that his model is the only acceptable one. However, what he does not do is critique the basic model itself, namely, that these were monistic modular polity communities; this is why I noted above that his is a truncated version of the hermeneutic spiral. He takes the monistic modular polity perspective as a given.

Now, because of the apparently exhaustive listing of possible causes, at least under both the funerary paradigm and the (unstated) background assumption that he is dealing with monistic modular polities, and because he empirically claims to have eliminated all but the final possibility, it is clear that if this possibility can also be shown to be inadequate in the same terms by which he eliminated the other possibilities, then this pretty well eliminates the plausibility of the Tripartite Ceremonial Alliance model and clears the way for me to present my alternative model. By showing empirically that the alternative Complementary Heterarchical Community and Cult Sodality Heterarchy System models can resolve all the inadequacies that the Tripartite Ceremonial Alliance model was unable to do, and by extension this would apply to the alternative Monistic Modular Polity Community model, it reasonably follows that the heterarchical accounts are preferable, at least for now. Adding "for now" qualifies my own conclusions and I do this to emphasize that I do not consider my account to be the "God's truth." Rather, I treat it as the currently preferred account since it gives a more coherent interpretation and better explanation of the empirical data than is available under both the tripartite and related monistic modular polity views. If it is the best current approximation of the social system that must have existed for the empirical data to exist in the form that has been demonstrated, the most reasonable course of action is to accept it for now, contingently, and set the others aside. However, since this is only a contingent truth, it is also open to critique and replacement by another model using the same methodology. That is, my model should also be critiqued to show where it fails and then be replaced with an alternative model on the grounds that the latter is able to give an even more coherent interpretation and better explanation. This is a process of knowledge construction that in the previous chapters I termed the hermeneutic spiral method (Bhaskar 1978, chapter 3, 143–227; 1979, 11–28, 164–69; Byers 2004, 106–7).

EMPIRICAL GROUNDS OF THE TRIPARTITE CEREMONIAL ALLIANCE MODEL

It is very useful to summarize the reasons Carr gives for rejecting all but one of the above possibilities since some of these reasons firmly commit him to theoretical claims and empirical facts that he uses to reject these alternatives and which I then use below to criticize his own account, showing that it turns out to be inadequate. First, it is notable that he treats these different causes as operating independently of each other. That is, the mortuary patterning, he assumes, cannot be the result of a conjunction of causes. Intracommunity group ranking as the cause of the differential patterning of the three clusters is rejected by him because there is no segregation of what he sees as rank-defining artifacts within only one of the three discrete clusters. "No class or trait simultaneously is common within a single cluster, distinguishes among clusters, represents a significant investment of energy, and occurs with multiple age groups and both sexes within a cluster" (Carr 2005b, 287). Carrying this further, he particularly argues that if the clusters were based on rank-order differences among groups, a pyramidal order of artifact and mortuary differentiation should occur so that not only would there be an exclusive segregation in one burial cluster of rank-constitutive material features and artifacts but also, while the highest ranking of the three burial clusters should have the richest burials, they should have the lowest number of burials since they constitute an elite. Instead, not only do all three clusters share (almost) the same range of contents while having the same set of burial features (at least, for all those placed on the burial floors), there is, in his terms, an "inverse pyramidal order of prestige distribution" (2005b, 295). By this he means that the largest burial space has the most commodious space per burial, the proportionately greatest concentration of prestige-endowing artifacts, and the largest rather than the smallest number of burials of the three clusters. Then the middle size space has the second largest number of burials and the second most commodious space per burial, and proportionately the second largest concentration of prestige-endowing artifacts. Finally, the smallest burial space scores the lowest in all three categories.

He then addresses the second possibility, that "each cluster might have distinguished leaders of different roles from each other and from a portion of followers," rejecting it on the grounds that, again, no artifact class "that conceivably might have been badges of leadership roles is found in only one cluster of burials and found with most burials in that cluster" (2005b, 292). Instead, these possible leadership "badges" are found with select individuals across all clusters. Age-sets and gender-sets receive similar short shrift. Not only do artifact categories crosscut age and gender, the limited age and gender differentiations that can be reconstructed empirically from the human residue, essentially cremations, indicate that both male and female adults are found in all clusters. However, the possibility that the three separate clusters might represent ceremonial-based sodalities does give him pause. For this reason he hypothesizes the possibility that there were three individual sodalities, one each occupying one of the three separate spaces. Since he also recognizes copper breastplates and copper earspools as markers of prestige of two different sodalities, and items of these two categories are found in both rectangular spaces under Seip-Pricer, he suggests that it is "possible that the spatial clustering of burials under the three mounds represented ceremonial sodalities other than those marked by breastplates and earspools" (2005b, 292). His reliance on anthropological analogy licences him to go along with this possibility since, given the ethnological literature, "it is not uncommon for persons to be allowed to join multiple sodalities" (2005b, 292).

While he concludes that each burial space might represent a separate sodality, over and above the two he recognizes as marked by breastplates and earspools, he qualifies this conclusion as being only a weak possibility since, "other than spatial segregation, there is no material marking or badge of those posited sodalities to be found in the tomb forms or artifact classes associated with corpses in the three clusters" (2005b, 292). This comment seems to contradict his later generalization about spatial segregation. In his terms, "of the many and diverse determinants of mortuary patterns examined, the horizontal social positions of the deceased was the one factor most frequently associated with the location of the deceased's grave within a cemetery" (2005b, 294). As he defines them, "horizontal social positions" are those making up kinship, residential, and sodality groups. Therefore, his recognizing that spatial segregation usually marks "horizontal social positions" would seem to be as strong a generalization for interpreting the three clusters as sodalities, independently of the distribution of prestigious artifacts, as his opting for delineating them as representing three different sets of residential communities constituted as "local symbolic communities" sharing three separate charnel houses as he and his colleagues argue (Ruby et al. 2005, 163–65).

In any case, he then examines whether these three burial clusters could be based on constituent kinship-based groupings, in this case, clans or phratries. Here his notion that artifacts can be literally interpreted in terms of their sources, for example, teeth, jaws, and claws of animals are literally "totem badges" and mark off clans (and/or, presumably, material facsimiles of these natural "power parts," such as copper or bone "bear teeth" effigies). He notes that there are two major categories of such "power part" artifacts—bear and feline. However, he again dismisses this clan-associated possibility largely because these categories do not segregate either by cluster or by persons within clusters. The final possibility that he dismisses is the circumstances of death factor. He recognizes that this is a very difficult possibility to ground empirically but argues that there is a relationship between age, sex, and social role and the types of experiences of persons that could correlate with circumstances of death. War-related deaths would tend to occur more often among junior age-grade males than among senior age-grade males and, therefore, if these clusters are generated by circumstances of death, there ought to be a segregation occurring in these common risk terms. He argues however that "the occurrence of persons of a variety of ages, both sexes, and many social roles with single clusters of burials at Seip-Pricer . . . gives little indication that persons who died different deaths were segregated at burial" (Carr 2005b, 293). I am particularly interested in this comment because, in fact, I will argue shortly that circumstances of death did likely play a significant role in structuring these burial clusters. However, these clusters were related only incidentally to particular roles and this is because the primary factor was the relative age of the person at death. That is, senior and junior age-grade members (or the deceased dependents of these members) were systematically segregated in death and, therefore, differential age-at-death rates were an important factor in structuring the mortuary data, particularly the artifactual materials.

Having examined all (except the latter) of these possibilities and rejecting them on distributional grounds, this left only one from his a priori list—his own, that is, shared burials among three separate but allied local symbolic communities, or monistic modular polity communities, in my terminology. "In the case of Seip-Pricer, Seip-Conjoined, and Edwin Harness, no support was found for the notion that the burial clusters were kinship groups (clans and phratries) or ceremonial or other sodalities. This leaves residence to be investigated" (2005b, 294). He then asks the rhetorical question: "Could the burial clusters under each mound represent members of different dispersed communities, with three communities at Seip-Pricer, three at Edwin Harness, and two at Seip-Conjoined?" His answer is positive, of course, and it directly ties to the Tripartite Ceremonial Alliance model. His general reason is that this model endows the empirical evidence with order and coherence that the other possibilities fail to do. As a reason to accept this model, he particularly reiterates that this "interpretation is simply the patterning found cross-culturally in grave location as a strong material correlate of horizontal social distinction . . . as applied to the three mounds" (2005b, 294). That is, he targets the tripartite spaces as demarcating three groupings having the same social nature. Of course, this could return us to Greber's model, which precisely stipulates that these are groups of the same social nature and that they were differentially ranked. However, her model also claims that each "Great House" represents a single community and that the three burial spaces represent three constituent components of the community with the differential patterning of the mortuary facilities and artifacts marking the rank-order of the three constituents. Carr stresses that he has already discounted this possibility on empirical grounds, as summarized above. Instead, he argues that the mortuary contents of *each* burial space reflect "the characteristics of a community" (2005b, 294), and that the qualitative and quantitative differences do not reflect differential social natures but simply differences in terms of wealth and prestige among the communities, and these differences, he concludes, are themselves the consequence of differences in the absolute size of each community.

As I noted above, the reason he considers this as confirming the model is that a community based on rank-order should not have an inverse pyramidal prestige distribution. Instead, it should have fewer but wealthier burials in the larger mortuary space (or cemetery, in his terms), and more but poorer burials in the smaller burial space(s). Instead, the patterning is the reverse of this, at least in that the most prestigious burial space had the largest number of burials. This is what he calls the "inverse pyramidal order of prestige distribution" (2005b, 295). For him the only possible reason for this inversion would be if each of the three burial clusters represented the same type of social group differentiated solely by overall size and wealth. The only type of social organization this could be, in his terms, is an autonomous community and since each charnel structure had three such mortuary spaces, then they represent an alliance of three autonomous local symbolic communities that differed only in terms of overall population size and gross wealth. Therefore, he concludes that the burials in each of these charnel structures must have been some of the rather prestigious deceased from each of three separate local symbolic communities, one space dedicated to each of these, and their sharing the same charnel houses means that they formed an alliance, that is, "a regional symbolic community" (Ruby et al. 2005, 165–66).

Theoretical Critique

I will initiate this critique by presenting anomalies that arise from within the same theoretical framework as Carr is using. In this regard, as I noted above, at the theoretical level, his approach largely identifies the mortuary sphere with funerary ritual, an identification I have termed the funerary paradigm. As I argued earlier, the funerary paradigm is for the most part a projection of Western mortuary practices onto the archaeological data and it is tied to the Monistic Modular Polity Community model by claiming the mortuary sphere serves to legitimize exclusive territories. In respect to the Tripartite Ceremonial Alliance model, this presents a problem. Since Carr recognizes exclusive territories as part of the makeup of the symbolic community, it seems *unlikely* under this theory that a local community would actively encourage sharing its ancestral cemetery among neighboring communities, thereby weakening the legitimacy of its exclusive ownership of territory. However, this intercommunal sharing of "cemeteries" is precisely what Carr asserts is at the heart of his Tripartite Ceremonial Alliance model, suggesting that by the three communities burying their dead together, the living will interact amicably. Now I interpret this to mean that the living would willingly share their territories and their resources. "Burial of one's deceased ancestors with those of another group tops out this sequence [of trust among people] by employing the eternal cooperation of one's ancestors in the afterlife, and requiring analogous behavior on the part of the living" (Carr 2005b, 327).

Furthermore, to take an intracommunity perspective, the funerary paradigm also makes burying its dead play a critical role in unifying as well as legitimizing a local symbolic community. However, what happens to this unity and sense of legitimacy if a community's deceased are systematically dispersed, in particular by only some being buried in their own domain cemetery while the rest are deposited in the cemeteries of other domains? While this may enhance intercommunity alliance, as Carr's model maintains, the logic of the funerary paradigm would strongly suggest that dispersing the dead of the local community among the dead of other communities in this manner would significantly diminish its unity and, in fact, the practice would come to be a source of serious intercommunity and intracommunity dispute. Under this funerary paradigm view, this perverse consequence seems unavoidable, particularly when Carr's model argues that the differential richness of the artifactual association among the three sections of the charnel structures marks the three constituent communities as having different amounts of esteem and wealth relative to each other, suggesting some serious issues of competition for wealth and esteem among these communities and within each community. Indeed, his model specifically argues that the exceptional wealth of the mortuary-related data of the Hopewell site was the result of more of the highest esteemed members of all three communities being buried at this site than at either their own or at the site of another less esteemed alliance member community (Carr 2005b, 322–24).

In the theoretical terms that he uses in his model, this may plausibly enhance the bonds of the alliance but—in the same theoretical terms—at serious cost to the internal unity of each constituent community. If the Hopewell site, in particular the charnel complex under Mound 25, was the most prestigious of mortuary locales, then it can easily be imagined under the premises of his own model that the ranking families or lineages of each community would dispute among themselves precisely where their own deceased should, indeed, must be buried. That is, the Tripartite Ceremonial Alliance model as presented would seem to postulate a form of mortuary-related competitive interaction that would lead to *diminishing the integrity* of both the local symbolic communities and the very alliance it postulates.

In fact, with regard to the latter likelihood, Carr and his colleagues seem to note this contradiction for they raise the possibility that, specifically with regard to Ohio Hopewell, the membership in the local symbolic communities may have been extremely "fluid" (Ruby et al. 2005, 171). This "fluidity" would be the result of the dispersed residential communities in each subdrainage more often leaving than remaining in their occupational zones. They proffer this as an explanation of why the domestic hamlets of the Ohio Hopewell seem to have left such minor traces in the region compared to the more substantially marked hamlets of the lower Wabash-Ohio confluence region and the lower Illinois Valley region (Ruby et al. 2005, 166–68). However, this is problematic as an explanation since if in fact this were the case, then it is hard to accept as credible the claim that these local symbolic communities: (1) controlled their territories (why abandon them?), or (2) were sufficiently stable to bring about the monumental construction and mortuary patterning that the Tripartite Ceremonial Alliance model attributes to them. The latter requires long-term commitment, one that would seem to be precluded by the friction that internal competition would systematically generate in the community by the mortuary practices postulated under this model.

In contrast, in terms of monistic modular polity community integration, Greber's model of intersite relations seems the preferred one. That is, the dead buried in each structure belonged to the community responsible for it, albeit in her model these would be the dead of ranked constituent units, for example, clans, while they sustained intercommunity relations through nonmortuary means. Hence, if I were to choose between the two, I would opt for Greber's on the grounds of greater internal coherence. However, Carr's empirical critique of Greber's claims cannot be ignored, namely, that the differential treatment of the deceased across these three burial locales cannot register component groups of the same community, for example, clans differentiated merely by rank. Therefore, my critical conclusion is that both must be rejected. This is not surprising since, as I have already argued, both are different versions of the monistic modular polity view and the latter is not acceptable to me on both theoretical and empirical grounds.

Formal Spatial Critique

Moving away from the mortuary perspective, I now want to critique both Carr's and Greber's views in terms of their own recognition of the meaning of spatial patterns. They both recognize that for users there is typically a meaningful identification between the formal properties of constructed space and the social nature of the group that habitually uses it. As I note below, formal space is among the symbolic (pragmatic) components of group constitution. Carr clearly recognizes this since he notes, as does Greber, that spatial size correlated positively with artifact variation and quantity—the larger the burial locale, the greater and more concentrated the artifact wealth, the greater the number of burials, and the greater the burial space per "grave." The implication of Carr's claim, therefore, is that he accepts formal properties of space as having relevant social symbolic meaning. Hence, I find it puzzling that, while he notes two outstanding formal spatial attributes of Seip-Pricer, Seip-Conjoined, and Edwin Harness, he did not address them in any serious way in his model. The first is that these were apparently dual-level structures. Seip-Pricer and Edwin Harness each had raised upper platform floors supported on a series of regularly spaced and substantial timber post supports, 48 for each of the rectangular rooms (Greber 1983, 26–29; this was likely the case for Seip-Conjoined also). The ground level prepared floor was where the majority of final mortuary deposits was placed (a few others being found above the floor, usually on the surface of one of the mound mantles). Carr certainly notes this dual-level pattern but considers its significance simply as adding more ceremonial space.

Notably, however, it would appear that the equivalent mortuary complexes of the Hopewell site, those under Mound 25, Mound 23, and the lesser mounds, were all single-level structures and, indeed, the main ones may have been without roofs. Therefore, the question is immediately raised about the nature of this postulated alliance in that two of the constituent communities, Seip and Liberty Works, had mortuary structures that largely replicated each other while both deviated considerably and equally from the third, the Hopewell site. Given the social symbolic meaning of constructed space, whatever that meaning may have been, this deviation might be sufficient to suggest that Seip and Liberty Works were more closely related to each other than either was to the Hopewell site or, to put it more pointedly, that those responsible for the Hopewell site sustained arm's-length rather than close alliance relations with the other two.

The second outstanding formal spatial property that the mortuary complexes of Seip-Pricer, Seip-Conjoined, and Edwin Harness shared, while deviating from the equivalent Hopewell mortuary complexes, was their division into three major rooms organized along a single axis, two rectangular rooms linked by a connecting corridor and a single circular room attached at the far end. I have termed this the R-R-C pattern (Byers 2004, 297–98). Carr also notes this formal R-R-C contrast but, again, it does not figure in his critical interpretation of the mortuary data. Instead, he focuses on the linear and tripartite nature of the layout of rooms, possibly in order to draw parallels with the mortuary complex under Mound 25, which he also noted had a tripartite patterning. However, the layout of the complex on the floor of Mound 25 also differed significantly from the former. The complex of spaces did not display either the R-R-C contrast of the Seip and Liberty Works structures or the interroom juncture by means of a short corridor. Rather, the tripartite pattern on the floor of Mound 25 was made up of a single elongated oval structure roughly divided into halves by an internal divider, and a separate, unconnected, albeit nearby, circular structure. Thus, not only did the Hopewell site Mound 25 mortuary complex differ from the Seip and Liberty Works mortuary complexes by its complex being single level in contrast to their dual-level construction, it also differed by displaying its own unique R-R-C pattern. This is another reason to question the closeness of relations between Hopewell and the other two sites, a closeness that Carr's Tripartite Ceremonial Alliance model considers basic.

Social Symbolic Critique

I now want to focus on the symbolic relevance of the R-R-C pattern and the dual-level nature of the Seip and Liberty Works structures. When these structures were in use, the upper levels would be outstanding and they would constitute three distinctive and noticeable spaces, particularly to the users. It would seem that the complementary oppositional nature of this R-R-C pattern of these three spaces suggests a deliberate design anchored on the need to generate the appropriately meaningful spaces so that they counted as the types of contexts that the using groups required. In this case, whatever the social nature of the groups, because the former two occupied the same type of formally rectangular constructed spaces that differed slightly only in size, they would appear to be more like each other in social nature than either would be like the group that occupied the circular room. The further fact that the mortuary deposits under the raised floors were effectively maintained within the confines of the boundaries as delineated by these three upper spaces suggests that those who were buried in each of the three discrete floor spaces were active participants during their lifetimes or in some way relevantly linked to the groups that used the three discrete upper-level spaces.

Now it is also relevant that Carr has ignored this formal R-R-C distinction. In effect, each room was dedicated to the same type of group, namely, a symbolic community, despite the fact that these manifest a strong formal distinction that can comfortably be interpreted in complementary contrasts, suggesting that at least two types of social groups are involved that recognize each other as being of different social natures. That is if the R-R iteration of the R-R-C pattern is analytically collapsed, this reduces the complex R-R-C pattern to the R'-C pattern (R-prime). Correlated with this R'-C pattern was a significant difference in the artifact distribution. As I described above, while Carr notes there was a quantitative as well as a qualitative variation of mortuary deposits across the three burial spaces, he does not question that the formal variation of the space may relate to and express qualitative differences in social nature. He simply assumes that the three spaces relate to three, qualitatively similar "symbolic communities." Therefore, he also does not raise the possibility that the qualitative and quantitative variation of the artifact distribution might relate to the R'-C pattern. Using the Seip-Pricer data, Greber (1976, 91–94, 217, figure 27) has noted that the rank-order profiles of the three spaces—a rank-order profile being the ranking of all the burials in a given burial section as computed by her rank-sum method—corresponded qualitatively with the R'-C pattern. Whereas the rank-order profile of each of the rectangular spaces (R-R) was continuous or graduated with no major gaps within the total profile, the rank-order profile of the circular room was sharply discontinuous with only a few individual deceased scoring high in rank, and the majority scoring low.

As I have argued elsewhere (Byers 2004, 297–98), this correlation of graduated rank profile with rectangular burial spaces and discontinuous rank profile with the circular burial space is not what could be expected if the deceased were from three groupings of the same social nature or order, whether these are ranked clan-like components, as postulated under Greber's model, or the burial spaces of three separate local symbolic communities, as postulated by Carr's Tripartite Ceremonial Alliance model. This is interesting since, as I noted above, he emphasizes that the most common marker of "horizontal distinction" is spatial segregation. "[O]f the many and diverse determinants of mortuary patterns examined, the horizontal social position of the deceased was the one factor most frequently associated with the location of the deceased's grave within a cemetery" (2005b, 294). Hence, here we have two spatially related forms of segregation—the material form of the spaces and their relative position. Under his model not only should the deceased of the different allied communities be kept in separate dedicated spaces in each charnel house, as he argues, each community should have the *same type of formal space*, which he does not argue. However, not to respect this formal factor is immediately to raise doubts that the three groups associated with these horizontally organized mortuary spaces and upper rooms are all of the same social nature and, when the qualitative differences of the three rank-profiles are noted to neatly correlate with the formal complementary R'-C pattern, it suggests that the hyphen is demarcating groupings that contrast in social natures. This means that the two groups associated with the rectangular spaces have very similar if not identical social natures, differing only quantitatively in some shared social properties, while they equally contrast in social nature with the group associated with the circular space. Therefore, *contra* the Tripartite Ceremonial Alliance model, these three groups would likely not represent three discrete local symbolic communities of the same type.[5]

Proportionality Critique

As I noted above, Carr makes a very strong assertion in support of the Tripartite Ceremonial Alliance model by claiming that it is the only model that "makes sense of their inverse pyramidal distribution of prestige; that is, for each mound, clusters with more burials also had *higher proportions of individuals* with prestigious goods. In real-life terms, larger communities were wealthier and had higher proportions of individuals with prestige. This situation is reasonable: larger communities would have had bigger labor pools for organizing public efforts and for acquiring material resources" (Carr 2005b, 295, emphasis added). To confirm how size can make a difference he suggests that it correlates with leadership diversity. As he puts it, "One particular manifestation of this demographically based phenomenon may be greater diversity of leadership and other elite social roles represented in the larger burial cluster under Seip-Conjoined and the greater proportion of persons to these roles. The record would suggest that the largest community at Seip-Pricer, indicated by the western burial cluster, had society-wide leaders or sodality leaders of primary and secondary prestige, marked by headplates and celts, respectively, as well as somewhat less prestigious persons of achievement within sodalities, symbolized by breastplates and earspools. In the smaller, middle burial cluster, persons of primary prestige with headplates are missing, and the other three social roles are represented, but at lower percentages than in the western cluster. In the smallest, eastern lobe, no individuals accompanied by these prestigious role markers were found, although persons with a conch shell or a mica plate were present" (2005b, 295).

Is this assertion of proportionally greater prestige goods as a function of greater size and greater wealth of a community a coherent claim? I do not think so or, to put it slightly differently, the claim contradicts other claims of the model. I have no problem with part of his assessment; namely, the larger the community the greater would be its material wealth—or as he says, "larger communities would have had bigger labor pools for organizing public efforts and for acquiring material resources." Therefore, it is reasonable to claim that the burial spaces of the larger postulated communities would have both a larger number of burials overall than would those of the smaller communities as well as a larger number of prestigious burials than would the smaller communities. That is, communities of the same sort being different only in terms of population sizes may reasonably be expected to produce greater or lesser amounts of gross wealth relative to their sizes; and this would also mean that there would be a greater number of individuals with prestige in the larger communities than in the smaller communities. But these size differences should not translate into "clusters with more burials also had *higher proportions of individuals* with prestigious goods." Why should this be the case? Why should the proportion of prestigious to nonprestigious burials in the clusters with fewer burials, these marking communities of the same sort but having smaller populations, have a lower proportion of "individuals with prestigious goods" than in the clusters with more burials? That is, while the gross wealth of each community will vary in proportion to their relative size, twice the size, twice the wealth, the proportional number of wealthy and/or prestigious to less wealthy and/or less prestigious persons in the largest community should be the same in the other two smaller communities. For example, if community A has twice the population of community B, A might generate twice the number of prestigious persons compared to B (2:1); but each community should sustain the same proportion of prestigious to nonprestigious persons, for example, one prestigious to every ten nonprestigious burials. This similarity of proportionality of prestigious to nonprestigious persons across all three communities follows from the basic premises of Carr's model, in which he particularly stresses that these were mutually autonomous, and each community had one of these separate burial cluster areas in each charnel house.

I am sure that Carr has anticipated this argument since he postulates in the above quotation that the larger community would generate a greater variety of leadership positions. There would "be greater diversity of leadership and other elite social roles represented in the larger burial cluster under Seip-Conjoined and the greater proportion of persons to these roles" (2005b, 295). By "diversity" I assume he means different types of leadership positions across communities and not simply greater numbers of the same types according to size and wealth. And, of course, it is an empirical fact that, indeed, the three rooms display an "inverse pyramidal distribution of prestige" with the larger burial locale in each case having the larger number of prestigious to nonprestigious deceased than in the smaller locales. However, as long as the communities are mutually autonomous, while there would be more leadership positions in virtue of the greater size and more groups, there is no reason in my view for greater variety or diversity of positions—unless, of course, we are speaking of differential power relations. That is, if in fact these deceased manifest three communities with differential diversity of positions, as Carr asserts, then these could *not* be autonomous communities since differential proportions of prestigious to nonprestigious burials in each room could only be the result of the wealthier community, as measured by the greater proportionality of prestigious to nonprestigious having *a greater than proportional concentration of community leaders.* Such a state of affairs would entail that the wealthier community was dominant over and able to exploit the smaller and less wealthy, and the mechanism to enable this is to have a "greater diversity of leadership and other elite social roles," and since the greater wealth would be a consequence of exploitation, then these positions would be ranked. Dominance and not demographic size, as such, would explain the disproportionality that he asserts is manifested in this "inverse pyramidal distribution of prestige." Therefore, the primary reason for the communities with smaller burial locales having lower proportions of prestigious to nonprestigious burials is not that they are demographically smaller (although that may be the case as well) but because the wealth they produced was being systematically transferred to the benefit of the dominant community and the dominance hierarchy of administrative leaders of that community. Another term for such ranked leaders, of course, would be "chiefs" and these positions constitute the dominance hierarchy of chiefdoms. This dominance relation immediately contradicts the basic premise of the Tripartite Ceremonial Alliance model, which is that the three communities were mutually autonomous allies and differed only in relative size and wealth, not social power. Of course, such an exploitative relation also immediately dissolves the relevance of the claim that the communities involved shared their deceased *in order to cement friendly relations.*

In contrast, if the Ohio Hopewell mortuary sphere manifests a system of mutualistic heterarchies having a set of cult sodalities as its constituent components, then the three separate spaces could manifest three components of the typical cult sodality. In fact, I have carefully theorized the structure that such a sodality should have, calling it an ecclesiastic-communal cult sodality (Byers 2004, 269–78). I consider the latter group to be the basic sodality of the typical Ohio Middle Woodland period complementary heterarchical community in the bifurcated settlement articulation modal posture. I will give a fuller elucidation of this social organization in the next chapter. For current purposes, I will note that it is a complex cult sodality congregation based on a laity-clergy structure. This means that the congregation consists of two complementary sectors, laity and clergy, that is, the laity-clergy structure, and this means two arm's-length groups, lay persons and shamanic-like priests. I claim that the laity is further structured by seniority into senior and junior age-grades. Very quickly it can be seen that the R-R-C neatly manifests a structure of this order. The R-R pattern is an iteration of the same type of social space and if the latter is constitutive of the social group, then the rectilinear rooms manifest the two laity sectors, and their senior-junior standing is expressed by the difference in size. The C or circular space, therefore, is associated with the clergy, namely, a shamanic priestly order that is an intrinsic complementary component of the cult sodality. In these terms, then, all the deceased would be members of the cult sodalities that constitute the mutualistic cult sodality heterarchy responsible for the monumental embankment earthwork and its major mound and building features. The very few infants and children also found would probably be deceased dependents of the living members of the same cult sodalities. As I more fully discuss it in the next chapter, this structure can very comfortably and coherently explain the "inverse pyramidal distribution of prestige" of the mortuary artifactual pattern that the Tripartite Ceremonial Alliance model failed to explain, even though Carr explicitly claimed otherwise and, in fact, claimed that only this model could explain.

CONCLUSION

I argued earlier that the Tripartite Ceremonial Alliance model is simply a version of the Vacant Center/Dispersed Hamlet model, and both are versions of the Monistic Modular Polity Community model. However, I think it is only fair to say that the former is a special version of this monistic modular perspective in that it is an alliance version. Of course, I have already noted that the version of the Vacant Center/Dispersed Hamlet model that Dancey and Pacheco have promoted, the Dispersed Sedentary Community model, recognizes that several of these local symbolic communities would ally to form an association of peer polities that would undertake building and using major embankment earthwork sites, such as the Hopewell site and the Newark site. However, they do not model how this alliance would be structured. Carr has, in fact, attempted this, in this case by claiming that it would be a two-leveled symbolic community structure. That is, for him the alliance of three local symbolic communities constituted a regional symbolic community with the Hopewell site on the North Fork, and downstream from Frankfort and Ater, as its "seat." It is because the Hopewell site is the "seat" of the regional alliance that its mortuary record manifests such wealth and uniqueness. This would be the place of choice for the most prestigious families making up the three local symbolic communities to share their deceased. "The distinction of Hopewell from Seip, Liberty, and Ater in its material richness, and apparently its almost completely adult burial population with a predisposition for males, suggests that it was a burial place for persons of import: those who had lived to be old enough to accumulate prestige or to demonstrate the prestige they might have inherited. In contrast, those buried under the Seip-Pricer mound, Edwin Harness mound, and Ater appear to represent a much broader spectrum of social actors in terms of age, balance of the sexes, and prestige. . . . In each of these sites the percentage of persons buried with elite items is more than would be expected for a single farming community, implying that some persons of lesser prestige were buried elsewhere" (Carr 2005b, 278). He follows this up with an even firmer statement that "the actual social prestige of the deceased does seem to be generally higher at Hopewell than at the other three sites, in line with the demographic evidence. Hopewell does seem to have been a place for the burial of special persons, by and large" (Carr 2005b, 279).

He places a lot of explanatory significance on this claim of the Hopewell site being a "place for the burial of special persons" since he uses this to explain not only the greater wealth displayed in the Hopewell site mortuary deposits but also the contrasts between the makeup and treatments of the mortuary populations of the Hopewell site compared to the other sites. In the Hopewell site, the deceased were primarily extended burials with a prevalence of senior males, while at Seip and Liberty they were more "mixed" in age and gender and, of course, almost exclusively cremated. "The strong contrast of Hopewell from Seip, Liberty, and Ater in the predominance of extended inhumation versus cremation within it again suggests the greater prestige of the individuals buried at Hopewell than the other sites, because body treatment appears to have reflected prestige in this region. The latter is shown by the association of certain regionally infrequent symbols of prestige more commonly with persons who were inhumed than those cremated. In Hopewell Mound 25, 40.3 percent of those inhumed (31 of 77) had a copper headplate, breastplate, celt, and/or earspools, while only 28 percent of those cremated (7 of 25) had one or more of these items. In the small mounds at Hopewell, 39.0 percent of those inhumed without charring (16 of 41) had one or more of the items, while only 25 percent of those cremated (4 of 16) had one or more of them" (2005b, 279).

In this way the Tripartite Ceremonial Alliance model attempts to clarify what the Dispersed Sedentary Community model left unexplored, namely, how monistic modular polities could constitute alliances by which to counter the contradictions that exclusive territorialism raises with regard to the need for extensive foraging and gardening communities to gain and sustain effective access to seasonal resources differentially distributed across lowlands and uplands. Based on the above critique, I would suggest that it does not succeed. However, to support this negative assessment, as I noted above, I must present the alternative model, not the Complementary Heterarchical Community model, as such, but the related model that characterizes the sodality component of these communities when they are in the bifurcated settlement articulation model posture, that is, the Ohio Hopewell Cult Sodality Heterarchy System model and its very importantly related Ecclesiastic-Communal Cult Sodality model. I cannot do this directly since there are two other theoretical formulations to present first that are critical to my overall account of the Ohio Hopewell system of cult sodality heterarchies. The first addresses the most effective way to characterize mortuary practices, particularly those performed by Middle Woodland period communities, and the second addresses a realistic characterization of the symbolic meaning and use of material culture, one that is particularly relevant for understanding the construction and use of monumental earthworks and other forms of constructions. Since mortuary and earthwork practices play such a prominent role in the unfolding of the Ohio Hopewell episode, elucidating both of these theoretical perspectives is particularly relevant and important. When I have completed them in the next two chapters, I then turn to the elucidation of the Ecclesiastic-Communal Cult Sodality model, and, especially important, the analogical and theoretical grounding that supports this model. With all this completed, the rest of the book is dedicated to elucidating and demonstrating the Ohio Hopewell Cult Sodality Heterarchy System model. This itself will require a further and ongoing application of the hermeneutic spiral method of critically counterposing relevant aspects of the orthodox and heterodox models from the complexity of the countryside settlement pattern separate from the earthworks to the nature of the interaction that related these earthworks into what I have called the system of Ohio Hopewell cult sodality heterarchies.

4

The Nature of Ohio Hopewell Mortuary Ceremonialism

As I noted in the previous chapter, models developed in terms of the monistic modular polity premises rely heavily on the funerary paradigm. The Tripartite Ceremonial Alliance model clearly illustrates this since it specifically assumes that, whatever the particular processes involved, the mortuary sphere can be characterized as basically funerary in nature. The funerary perspective is also tied to exclusive territorialism and, most importantly, to the assumption that variation in mortuary treatment is a function of the complexity of the social structure. The "universal generalization" or "law" used to validate the funerary paradigm was specified among others by Christopher Peebles, one of its major proponents, when he described and interpreted the mortuary sphere of the well-known Mississippian period site of Moundville, Alabama, as mapping the emergence and development of a centrally organized hierarchical and dominant "paramount chiefdom." "The crucial assumption which links burials with social organization is that individuals who are treated differentially in life will also be treated differentially in death. That is, the reciprocal rights and duties gathered by the individual during his lifetime will not abruptly terminate: they will carry on into his burial and, in most societies, beyond. Therefore, the patterned variation in mortuary ceremonials accorded individuals in a society ought to reflect their positions within the society during their lifetimes" (1974, 38).

Now I would be more willing to accept the validity of this assertion as a "universal generalization" if instead of saying that the "reciprocal rights and duties . . . will carry on into his burial . . . and beyond" he had said that these "will carry on" to some degree to influence some of the mortuary rites, particularly the initial ones. This leaves open precisely how extensive the causal weight of the status-of-the-deceased-in-life is on governing the postmortem treatment and, therefore, this would be an empirical matter rather than an a priori assertion that applied equally to all "normal" human communities.[1] In the Euro-American mortuary sphere, the "living status" influence is very extensive, so much so that minimal postmortem manipulation is typical and a rather quick burial terminates it. This is what Euro-American peoples call the funeral. And, of course, it is terminated by continuing "into the burial," which occurs usually a few days after the death. That is, the burial also typically terminates the mortuary treatment. However, this is not the case for most traditional historic Native North American communities. The equivalent of a Euro-American funeral may occur as a four-day mourning period with the body placed on a scaffold. Burial may then occur, giving the impression that this is "just like" a Euro-American funeral. However, in many cases, as I will note shortly, the burial is only temporary. Sometime later the body may be recovered, any remaining flesh removed and cremated, and the bones may be reserved for further treatment, ultimately to be buried a second (or third) time. Rather than treating these subsequent rites as having their own mortuary ceremonial nature, quite different from the scaffolding/burial rite, these are subsumed to the "funeral." Extending the notion of the funeral in this manner appears to be warranted since, as Peebles specifies, the "reciprocal rights and duties . . . will carry on into his burial . . . and beyond." However, the generalization "into his burial" does not specify which burial! The "universal generalization," this being the "crucial assumption which links burials with social organization is that individuals who are treated differentially in life will also be treated differentially in death," comes to embrace all the ritual steps that make up the mortuary sphere, hence reducing these to being simply variant and usually complex "funerals" (Peebles 1974; Peebles and Kus 1977, 431–32; Goldstein 1980, 5–9; Tainter 1977, 331–32).

This tendency constitutes the funerary paradigm, as I have named it, and when it is applied to such complex mortuary spheres as that displayed in the Ohio Middle Woodland period archaeological record, it might be more correctly termed the *funerary fallacy*. However, I am pleased to note that the inadequacy of the funerary paradigm as a "universal" mortuary theory is now coming to be recognized among North American archaeologists. For example, recently Lynne Goldstein (2000, 198–99) has directly questioned the limitations of the funerary paradigm by raising the issue of how to interpret the secondary burials that make up much of the archeological record. She particularly focuses on the Mississippian period by addressing the well-known mortuary contents of the 260-plus individual mortuary deposits contained in Cahokia Mound 72. She notes that secondary, possibly even tertiary, mortuary deposits make up about half the contents of this mound. She emphasizes that secondary burials are not the outcome of mortuary practices similar to extended in-flesh burials in that the latter were motivated by the immediacy of death, that is, for her these are the residue of funerals, while the former were instigated by some cause that was not itself funerary in nature.[2]

This is a very important observation, its importance being that if generalized to the prehistoric Native North American mortuary record, it implies that most of its patterning cannot be considered as directly manifesting funerary activity, as such; and, therefore, whatever the causal factors that were responsible for this complex patterning, they cannot reference the "universal generalization" that the funerary treatments of human communities tend to correspond to and vary according to community sociostatus structure. Having made this observation, however, she is only partly able to expand her conceptualization of the mortuary sphere as a field of social practice that often includes but is not identical with funerary practices. This is largely because she continues to privilege the funeral as the only "real" mortuary practice. Hence, this means that the secondary mortuary deposit is not a full-fledged mortuary activity in its own right. In her view, it only commemorates the social group to which the collective deceased belonged. "Most significantly, secondary disposal of the dead represents a ritual that can only in part be understood as a mortuary practice, because the secondary disposal of the dead is *not really a mortuary treatment* in the same way as primary burial because the secondary treatment is triggered by something independent of the death of the individual" (2000, 201, emphases added).

She is right to say that the secondary burial (or disposal) is "not really a mortuary treatment in the same way as primary burial." This is clear since a primary and secondary burial are formally different and, therefore, probably qualitatively different mortuary practices. However, in saying that the secondary burial "can only in part be understood as a mortuary practice" she is right only if, in fact, she is committed to thinking of the mortuary sphere in funerary terms. If she does so, then this would exclude the majority of the material expressions of prehistoric Native North American mortuary practices from mortuary analysis since, as I noted in chapter 1 and intend to elaborate now, it is not only secondary burials that are not funerary in nature; only a small but certainly important sector of the total mortuary process of the traditional Native North American communities can be treated as having a ritual equivalent to what Euro-Americans refer to as the funeral. Typically this ritual would occur near the beginning of the process instigated by the normal death of a person. It might also be reinstituted at the very end of the process for many but not all deceased. Subsequent or in-between ritual steps would emerge out of the initial funerary stage in a complex step-by-step process. For this reason, it is likely that the prehistoric funerary ritual performance, as such, would be materially manifested in only an indirect way in the mortuary record. As I treat formal mortuary variation, semi-flexed, fully flexed, complex secondary burial deposits such as bundle burials, body part deposits, crematory deposits, and so on, are often the unfolding outcome of a sequence of spirit-release and renewal practices that are fully mortuary in their own right. The deceased or some component of the deceased serves as a critical component by which the behaviors she, he, it, they, in full or in part, mediate, thereby constituting these acts as having their particular ritual character independently of the (usually initial) "funerary" rites.

While Goldstein's insights have this implication, it appears she may still be caught up within and therefore is privileging the funerary paradigm, as such. Indeed, her commitment to the funerary paradigm and the notion of a cemetery as the expression of a (proprietorial) corporate group based on some principle of kinship descent seems to prevent her from recognizing that the human deceased could be serving a critical function as media of collective mortuary intentions that did not include any group commemoration intentions at all (Goldstein 1980, 5–9). Even the standard archaeological term that she uses—the "secondary disposal"—seems to be a function of the constraining nature of the funerary paradigm. Presupposing the label "secondary disposal" is the notion of "primary disposal." The latter is "first," and is privileged while the former, being second, is also lesser, that is, a lesser type of funeral. Even the persons subjected to secondary disposals, then, become treated as inferior or lesser members of the community. Indeed, this systematic privileging and underprivileging of burials by formal treatment is well illustrated when I noted at the end of the previous chapter that Carr evaluated the burial deposits at the Hopewell site as generally of the more privileged members of the alliance. He based this assessment on the fact that extended, namely, "primary," burials prevailed there while cremated, or "secondary," burials prevailed at Seip and Liberty. While he also goes on to argue that this difference seems to be correlated with significantly greater burial wealth at the former, that difference is used simply to confirm that primary burials marked the "funerals" of privileged deceased and secondary burials marked the "funerals" of lesser privileged deceased.

As I noted in chapter 1, I will treat the mortuary sphere associated with communities based on immanentist cosmologies in a more expansive manner. Certainly initial mortuary events would probably include ritual akin to the Euro-American funeral. Here the deceased would be subjected to treatment that could be interpreted as according to her or his position of being the spiritual "host" or the main "guest of honor." However, subsequent mortuary treatment would move away from recognizing the deceased in these "living" terms to treating the deceased more and more as a medium of different rites.

These are mortuary rites also since the deceased or parts of the deceased would figure as symbolic media by which the behaviors of the living were constituted as the types of ritual they intended these to be. As I define a mortuary act, it is any practice in which deceased humans, portions of deceased humans, or even symbolic representations of deceased humans play an important mediation role in constituting the nature of the social activity being performed. The total ensemble of such forms of behavior constitutes the mortuary sphere of the community. In these terms I argue that we should understand this mortuary sphere as a complex and incrementally staged ritual process: funerary → mourning → spirit-release → individual ↔ social ↔ world renewal. This process incrementally reduces the deceased materially as their bodily parts were the medium by which their spiritual powers were released so that they figured as postmortem sacrificial offerings—to the community, the local region, and the cosmos in general.

I have called this the Mourning/World Renewal Mortuary model (Byers 2004, 177–98; 2006a, 112–20; 2006c, 127–30), and it is an elaboration of the notions of the nature of Native North American human spirituality that Robert Hall outlined in his series of discussions of the mortuary rites of these historically known communities. He has noted that the latter rites always have a renewal component built into them (Hall 1997, 35, 39–40, 57, 123, 129, and passim). I have picked up on his insights and argued that these historically known mortuary rites constitute a process in which the postmortem incrementally staged treatment of the deceased unfolds to realize several different purposes that can be achieved only by the use of different components or states of the deceased. Examples of these different mortuary rites can be described as the rite of separation of the personal spirit from the body so that it can travel to the land of the Dead; the reincarnating of the name spirit or spirits of the dead so that these are not left to wander and cause trials and tribulations in the community; the recalling of the personal spirit of the dead so as to associate it with spirits of its companions to travel together to the land of the Dead; the releasing of the living souls of the bones so these can rejoin the sacred natural order and revitalize its energies; the releasing of the sacred powers of potent artifacts by transferring its name spirit from its deceased custodian to his or her living replacement, thereby enabling the artifact's potent powers to return to the cosmos; and so on. Hence, while certainly funerary practices were performed, usually as the initial separation rite by which the dead person is constituted as a deceased person, that is, as a rite of passage by which the social nature of the individual is transformed, subsequent rites (which, given the very limited Euro-American mortuary vocabulary, we might only partly or possibly quite inadequately label as memorial and mourning rites) were performed and these often were intentionally performed and constituted as social and cosmological renewal rites.

Most importantly, each mortuary ritual step generated the basic material condition necessary for the performance of the subsequent ritual step—this necessary material condition being some material aspect of the human deceased, for example, specific body part (skull), certain bones, or even cremated ashes, the latter being generated by the prior mortuary ritual. The funeral constituted the dead as a deceased person, as such; then the mourning rites may have served to release the personal name spirit. This rite may have been initiated with platform or scaffolding exposure, with the personal spirit released when the body was removed and buried. Or it may have been terminated by a simple ritual of separation assigning the name spirit to the deceased's companion while sending the personal soul to the land of the Dead. The body may have been left in place on the scaffold to be subjected to extended exposure. The decaying of the flesh would count as releasing the living spirits of the flesh, constituting this exposure as a sacrificial period of "feeding the gods." After a considerable period, the exposing of the bones may have signaled the memorial rite in which the bones may have been temporarily buried to complete the flesh removal. Later, they may have been disinterred and cremated. Each of these steps would have counted as a world renewal rite by releasing the living souls immanent in the flesh and bones so as to distribute them between the Beneath World gods and the Above World gods, thereby completing the mortuary process.

Now I am not claiming that the above can actually be associated with any known community, or for that matter, that all Ohio Hopewell world renewal rituals were mediated by postmortem human sacrificial rites or that all mortuary rites were world renewal in nature.[3] Rather it is illustrative of the *type* of multiple roles that the deceased played in mediating the mortuary activity of the community, an activity that I believe it is fair to say is completely foreign to Euro-American funerary practices. However, it is a process of this nature that is the core of the Mourning/World Renewal Mortuary model. Each step in the process of postmortem modification of the body constituted a type of sacrificial offering, which I have termed postmortem human sacrifice, by which the spiritual powers embodied in human body parts—hair, flesh, blood, bones, and so on—are returned to the cosmos from where these powers were derived.[4]

There is a very important upshot of this reasoning. It effectively means that, for the responsible populations, once the personal spirit had been appropriately treated, the different material components of the human body, flesh, hair, skulls, the long bones, and so on, figured as real, practical, and highly valued *symbolic capital* by which, in their terms, human groups were able to discharge their sacred duties to the world that supported them. Seen in this light, human bones, for example, as sacred bone bundles, would take on an importance as valued practical symbolic media of critical rituals, an importance that is hard to be imagined under the funerary view. Therefore, it is quite plausible to postulate that for the communities involved, the traditional supply through natural death of this postmortem human sacrificial capital had to be supplemented by intercommunity and, in some cases, long distance ventures being undertaken by which human bones were procured and accumulated just so as to serve as world renewal sacrificial offerings. Of course, one possible mode of procurement would be warfare. However, the more likely and less costly mode would be interregional competition for the bones of those already deceased. This could be postulated as among the sort of ventures that could be initiated by alliance construction of the type that I will argue would be constitutive of Hopewellian cult sodality heterarchies.

It might be useful to think of the funerary → mourning → spirit-release → world renewal process as a causally productive chain of events, a ritual *chaîne opératoire,* by which the mortuary sphere of a community was structured into a sequence of rituals many but not all of which could be properly characterized as world renewal in nature. The *chaîne opératoire* methodology has been applied to different technologies, from lithics to ceramics. Its primary assumption is that the basic kit of technical steps of a technology is organized into different combinations of productive steps, each step producing the material media necessary to perform the next step, such that it brings about a series of different material outcomes satisfying different intentions and purposes that, however, are related to any overall strategy defining that productive sphere of activity. A lithic knapping technology may be divided into two mutually exclusive modes, for example, discoid and cylindrical core, each anchoring a different trajectory of knapping steps by which two different flaked lithic tool kits can be generated. Even though the end-state tools of the two kits can manifest very similar working edges and surfaces, their forms may vary significantly such that a glance allows the lithic specialist to see which core technology trajectory produced a particular tool. These two different sets of tools may be generated in order to mediate quite different spheres of meaningful usage, for example, one set used for domestic, everyday activities, the other to mediate special purpose activities, such as rituals of different sorts (Byers 2004, 230–39; 2006b, 66–70). A similar case can be argued for ceramics. Distinguishing everyday ceramics from fine ware is a standard procedure, the latter deemed as being used for ceremonial and honorific purposes, the former, for ordinary everyday purposes. In fact, objectively both types of ware may be equally useful for preparing, serving, and consuming food. However, to the users the two wares may be critical symbolic media by which two, largely mutually exclusive comestible spheres were generated and maintained as separate through the reproduction of both trajectories.

The basic rationale underwriting the method is "reverse engineering" and this hinges on retroductive logic, that is, given what we already know about X—for example, the material properties of stones subjected to knapping procedures—what must have been the conditions and steps that brought about these particular forms? Did certain forms emerge that were simply stages to more refined forms? What type of reuse was performed or was it typically avoided, and so on? Of course, this is also the logical basis of the hermeneutic spiral methodology as applied to reconstructing the meaningful nature of the archaeological record, namely, the cultural content and social structural framework. It is reasonable, therefore, to extend the *chaîne opératoire* methodology to interpreting the archaeological mortuary sphere—if we assume that the variations of the observable patternings that make up the sphere are the systematic outcome of a series of different mortuary activities such that each step in the chain is constituted as the completion of a different ritual or a different ritual stage; in turn, the material outcome of that stage, or some component of it, is then used as the constitutive medium of the next mortuary ritual. Indeed, the Mourning/World Renewal Mortuary model entails treating a sequentially meaningful set of mortuary behavioral events as the manifesting of a type of *chaîne opératoire process*, each event generating a material outcome that is the condition of satisfaction of the exercise of a specific prior mortuary intention in which using human remains is a critical necessity, and this outcome, or a component of it, is then recruited to serve as the practical symbolic capital to mediate a subsequent mortuary event, one that could not be performed without the human remains that the previous event generated, and so on.

The Mourning/World Renewal Mortuary model combines two basic notions, therefore. First, it treats the mortuary sphere as encompassing a ritual *chaîne opératoire*, that is, as a process generating a series of rituals through spirit-release rites that, at the same time, have strong practical human, social, and world renewal purposes. It also treats the mortuary remains as practicing symbolic media or, as I will term it, symbolic pragmatic media, that is, material media that constitute the *pragmatic or action nature* of the behaviors they enable, and this means the human deceased become valued practicing material symbols in virtue of which communities can discharge critically important duties. Such a combination immediately transforms the mortuary sphere into an interaction sphere in which the material remains serve as media of accumulation, exchange, and ritual production. If Ohio Hopewell is treated as a complex system of interacting world renewal cult sodality heterarchies, which is my intention to do, then the mortuary component of this sphere becomes a critical and dynamic force in motivating the cult sodalities, and much of their mortuary ritual will entail manifesting a process of human bodily transfers and transformations of a highly mobile nature. Seen in these terms, while the Hopewell artifactual assemblage certainly implicates long distance expeditions to procure exotic (nonhuman) raw resources and, in some cases, to exchange the finished products, the real dynamics of the Hopewell episode are manifested in the patterning of the mortuary remains themselves. Later I will elucidate what I will term the Sacred Games *Tournée* model. I will postulate that the Ohio Hopewell interaction was mediated by sacred games that were carried out among competing cult sodality heterarchies. Human remains figured as the primary rewards, and in turn, they were used ultimately to mediate critical world renewal rituals. These sacred games entailed significant expeditions of and interactions between and among cult sodality heterarchies. Later I will extend this notion of symbolic pragmatic media to characterize the great embankment earthworks, treating them as critically important media of the felicity of these games and their associated mortuary rituals.

MULTIPLE SOULS AND POSTMORTEM HUMAN SACRIFICE

What I consider to be crucially important for understanding the traditional Native North American mortuary sphere is the effectively universal cultural notion of multiple souls and the associated cultural belief that the release of these souls characterized different mortuary rites. Since these souls were immanent in the body, spirit release required the body as the medium from which the soul could be released and, very importantly, there was usually a set order in which these souls were released. In some cases, it even entailed a dual soul manipulation, recalling previously released souls in order for them to be redirected to another person, reincarnation, or to a collective body of the community to reenliven it, such as a clan or a sodality, and simultaneously, releasing the final living souls so they could reenter the natural order, thereby contributing to its sacred reenlivening or renewal. Since these rites transferred life back to the society or the world, they can be characterized in sacrificial renewal terms. As I noted above, when humans who die a "natural" death are treated in this complex manner as sacrificial media constituting the ritual nature of the behaviors these materials mediate, I have termed it postmortem human sacrifice. This is a critical component of my modeling of the Ohio Middle Woodland period and, therefore, clearly ties into the cult sodality. That is, when I elucidate the Ecclesiastic-Communal Cult Sodality model in chapter 6, I will postulate that a central purpose of such organizations was to perform an incremental series of social and world renewal rituals, many, although not all, of which were mediated by human remains constituting these behaviors as postmortem human sacrificial rituals. In my account, then, the Mourning/World Renewal Mortuary model, the Sacred Games *Tournée* model, the Ecclesiastic-Communal Cult Sodality model, and the Ohio Hopewell Cult Sodality Heterarchy System model are mutually recursive.

George Lankford (2007b, 175–76) has argued that multiple soul beliefs were widespread in Native American cultures. Each human possessed multiple souls. He has classified these souls into two basic groups: the personal or free soul(s) and the living souls. The basic criterion he uses to make this division is self-consciousness. The personal soul is the basis of the self-conscious being and it is believed that when it is released, the primary personal soul is the one that travels to the land of the Dead and carries on in the community of the deceased, this community being pretty well like the community of the living. Lankford speaks of a singular personal soul. However, I would argue that most Native American soul beliefs would include name souls and, while the personal soul would also have a name, there seem to have been name souls that were separate from the personal soul. Typically, the name soul is given to the person after birth, and when death comes, the name soul returns to its custodial group, perhaps the clan or the sodality that initially gave the name to the person (Alford 1936, 3; Callendar 1978, 626–27; Voegelin and Voegelin 1937, 617). It will subsequently be reassigned by the name-keeper of the group to another person, often a newborn or else, possibly, when the person reaches a certain age. This name soul must have self-consciousness since it is believed that using the name of a living person improperly can have unfortunate effects by invoking the soul to leave the body in response to being called. For this reason, a person's name soul is usually kept secret among a discrete group and it will be used only when that group is performing some collective activity. And there can be more than one name soul that a person incorporates so that he or she can accumulate them. For example, if a man occupies a position of chief on the community council, this occupation of the position might well be constituted by what is essentially a mortuary rite in which the name soul of the previous chief is recalled and then given to the new occupant (Tooker 1978, 424). Usually some material item embodies the name soul until it is reassigned. Hence, this item, possibly a copper plaque worn on the chest, can be treated as a symbolic device that is taken (literally) to endow the wearer with the powers of the name soul so that while wearing the item she or he can transform her or his vocal utterances into the speech acts that the wearer intends her or his behavioral utterances to be, for example, declaring that a state of hostility between the group and another is "hereby constituted."

The living souls, according to Lankford, are no less sacred than are the personal souls. However, they do not have self-consciousness. Their release is necessary so that they can return to (be reborn into) the different components of the cosmos from which they were derived by the person during her or his lifetime (Lankford 2007b, 175–76). This immanentist cosmological view supports the claim that is very commonly made among traditional Native North American peoples, this being that the land "grows" the human community that occupies it, literally by "feeding" sacred energy of the plants and animals into the bodies of the members. The sacred powers of the bones in all their variety, the flesh of the different parts of the body, the blood, and so on, are derived from the sacred earth through the medium of the animals and plants humans eat. That is, the spiritual energies immanent in plants and animals become the spiritual energies immanent in the organic bodies of humans. This is why living soul spirit-release rites noted above are so important and why they can be considered sacrificial rites. For this book, I argue that these rites are the particular specialization of the cult sodalities (Ingold 1987, 246–47).

What is implicated in conceptualizing the process postulated by the Mourning/World Renewal Mortuary model as a *chaîne opératoire* methodology is a distribution of the ritual constituting the mortuary sphere across the clan and sodality duality. Those rituals relating to the personal souls, both the soul that is reborn in the land of the Dead and at least one or more of the name souls for which the kin groups are custodians, as well as the memorial and personal mourning rites, are likely under the predominant responsibility of the kin groups; but in complementary fashion, the subsequent spirit recall and spirit-release rites of the different non-kin, namely, sodality-based name souls, and the living souls embodied in the flesh, bones, and selected body parts are under the predominant responsibility of the sodality groups. These are the souls that they release through the mediation of postmortem human sacrificial rituals.

It is very likely that not all deceased would be subjected to the same range of incremental rites. The clan mortuary rites might be limited to personal soul release and name reincarnation rites, marked by extended and/or flexed burials with little in the way of bodily exposure and postmortem manipulation occurring. This would tend to be the case when the complementary heterarchical communities of a region are in the integrated settlement articulation modal posture since, even though the age-sets would be organized as autonomous sodalities, they would be located in the jointly shared community locale, the integrated village. Therefore, they would participate in their sodality communal cult postures along with the clans in their communal cult postures in the terminating burial rites. These would primarily count as releasing the living souls to the environment and, therefore, the bones would not be given any further processing. However, when the same type of communities were organized into the bifurcated settlement articulation modal posture, as I postulate would be the case for the Ohio Middle Woodland period, since the cult sodalities would be specialized for world renewal rites, they would be the recipients of most of the bodies of the deceased *following* the clan-mediated mortuary rites and it would be their duty to conduct the subsequent living soul release rites. These rites would be integrated into the great sacred games I noted above and would probably be specialized for different components of the world and carried out according to the annual sacred game schedules, probably keyed into celestial and/or seasonal cycles. Therefore, complex partitioning of the deceased would occur and cremation, even double or repeat cremation, might mark the terminal world renewal rites mediated by the use of the body or body parts as different postmortem human sacrificial offerings. Importantly, there would probably be a large repertoire of world renewal rites, not all requiring human mortuary remains, but each specialized for a particular aspect of the sacred natural order.

I note this because a number of archaeologists claim that to treat the Hopewell as primarily mediating world renewal ritual is to be overly simplistic. Indeed, not only do these commentators consider that the role of world renewal ritual in Hopewell is somewhat limited, even the role of mortuary ceremonialism is strictly limited. The claim is usually made that both constitute only part of the ceremonialism involved in Hopewell and, for the most part, the mortuary ritual, usually treated in terms of the funerary paradigm, is emphasized as certainly not characterizing it. Indeed, I would attribute this dichotomizing of Hopewellian ceremonialism into mortuary and nonmortuary ritual subspheres as an unfortunate consequence of the funerary paradigm. In strong contrast I claim that not only would the suite of world renewal rituals be very large in number and complex in scheduling, the need for human remains to mediate these rituals would be the primary necessity that fueled the complex mortuary process and, indeed, as noted above, procuring mortuary remains would have promoted the development of the most distinctive aspect of Ohio Hopewell—the monumental earthwork embankments as the sacred context of the great sacred games. Of course, funerary-related clan rites, along with other clan-based rites, would constitute an important part of the ceremonialism of the region. However, this would be largely located outside the Ohio Hopewell sites and in the countryside at the clan locales.

This model, therefore, can be used to give a very different characterization of the Hopewell mortuary practices than that given by the funerary paradigm. For example, as summarized in the previous chapter, the Tripartite Ceremonial Alliance model takes the funerary perspective and argues that the three charnel structures and their R-R-C formal patterning are a measure of the alliance of three "symbolic communities." It then treats the differential distribution of artifacts across these burial spaces as a measure of the relative valuation of the esteem and the social standing of the deceased at death, but only related to his or her own community. Under the Mourning/World Renewal Mortuary model, these same data, both mortuary structures and artifacts, or at least a very important category of them, would have been part of what was required to perform ongoing felicitous sacrificial renewal rituals of the cosmos and these rituals would be the specialized custodial responsibility of the cult sodality heterarchies. The accumulation of the deceased in some earthworks and their paucity in others would be a product of the great sacred games *tournées* and, most importantly, as I detail later, those accumulated deceased that have been found were probably only a small fraction of the total series of deceased that were processed through these great earthworks. A more accurate measure of the numbers of deceased who were given mortuary processing would likely be the accumulation of elaborate artifacts, such as the copper plates, the copper headdresses, and so on. I have argued and will reiterate in this book that these can be best interpreted as custodial regalia that, while constituting their legitimate wearers as occupying various esteemed roles in the cult sodality, were potent agents in their own right since they participated in the essential sacred nature of the cosmic powers, namely, the gods, which they expressively represented. The role such a select category of artifacts would play in the great sacred games *tournée* and the associated mortuary practices, therefore, would be distinctly different from that conceived under the funerary paradigm and while many of the deceased who were their custodians in lifetime would be processed and ultimately removed to be given final spirit release rites elsewhere, these custodial regalia would be curated and given terminal "burial" in these earthworks.

Typically, under the funerary paradigm, such fine artifacts are treated as ancillary to or as the property of the deceased. Under the Mourning/World Renewal Mortuary model, however, the human–burial artifact relation might be more adequately characterized in reverse. This is particularly well illustrated in the Ohio Hopewell mortuary data in which, for example, while these select artifacts were materially associated with cremated human remains, they were not themselves cremated. In many cases, the artifacts, such as copper plates, or a set of different regalia types, were carefully laid out in an undamaged state, while the cremated remains of the deceased were either placed neatly on these or were scattered across these artifacts (Byers 2004, 336–42, 351–62). This contrast between the complete destruction of the bodily remains of the deceased and the careful preservation of the artifacts grounds the conclusion that, rather than the artifacts accompanying the deceased—and saying it this way implies that the deceased "owned" the artifacts, which is the standard interpretation under the funerary paradigm—it would be the reverse: the cremated residues of the deceased were accompanying the artifacts.

That is, by the time cremation of the residual remains of the deceased was performed, the personal soul aspects that constituted them as autonomous self-aware human agents in life had been released, leaving only their more impersonal living soul aspects for final release by cremation. Furthermore, this suggests that the regalia items themselves were experienced as embodying spiritual powers, what I will term their spirit names. That is, it is possible that these items of custodial regalia were named; and the latter names were actually the manifestation of the guardian spirits that they represented. These names would also likely be the names of the formal positions that the custodial caretakers occupied, thereby being empowered to invoke and presence the spirit guardians themselves. Hence, copper celts might bear the names of different aspects of the spirit power that they represented and these names would become the titles of those who were endowed with their care and use. Similarly, copper plates, a number of them having been found with the residue of textile wrappings, may have been recognized as endowing their custodians with named leadership positions, and so on. In this way the custodian would transform his or her behaviors into the type of ritual intended. When the custodian died, burial of the artifact, unharmed, but in association with the cremated remains of its custodian, his or her living souls, would return the spirit power to its spirit guardian. Of course, a new custodial regalia item would be produced as an act of reincarnating the spirit of the custodial regalia item so as to endow the next occupant of the position as the new custodian. I elaborate on this view in more detail later.

This is a theorization of the mortuary pattern and it claims, of course, that a significant burden of the mortuary rituals must be understood in postmortem human sacrificial terms. Are there any known cases of mortuary practices that could be used to ground the plausibility of this theorization? In fact, once the theory has been presented, many examples of historic Native North American mortuary practices that have been interpreted in funerary terms can be seen to make equal if not more sense when reinterpreted in mourning/world renewal mortuary terms. In the next chapter I will note the Hidatsa as performing world renewal rituals through the mediation of the deceased. For now, I will use the Huron. This is a particularly apt example since, as I noted in the previous chapter, Carr particularly relies on his funerary interpretation of this Huron practice to ground the plausibility of the Tripartite Ceremonial Alliance model that the mortuary patterning of the Big Houses manifests funerary practices used for alliance purposes. Presumably he selects this case because the Huron were historically a well-known Eastern Woodland peoples practicing mortuary rituals that manifested the sharing of many world beliefs and ethos principles with most other Eastern Woodland peoples. Indeed, this is a basic claim he has made to warrant using the mortuary behavior as the medium of political alliance claim. Therefore, a particularly appropriate grounding of the Mourning/World Renewal Mortuary model is to use the same ritual, the Huron Feast of the Dead, and showing how it can be given a world renewal interpretation that is largely unrelated to the political sphere.

THE HURON FEAST OF THE DEAD AS WORLD RENEWAL RITUAL

Many archaeologists rely on fairly standard anthropological theory and ethnographic knowledge of historically known traditional Native North American societies to interpret the prehistoric record of Native America. Carr's Tripartite Ceremonial Alliance model is an example of this method. Pacheco's use of the Mapuche is another, as I discussed in the closing of the introductory chapter. I consider this method, usually referred to as anthropological analogy, to be basic to advancing our understanding of the prehistoric archaeological record. However, the validity of this method is contingent on the adequacy of the anthropological knowledge that it is being used to transfer. In this regard, archaeologists are careful to select as their sources known cultures that seem to be appropriate and relevant to the archaeological record being interpreted. This selection, of course, means that the archaeologist already has in mind the likely type of community that was responsible for the prehistoric data, that is, he or she has established—on a priori anthropological theoretical and archaeological methodological grounds—the general nature of the social and cultural structures that these prehistoric communities must have had given their recognized archaeological record or else he or she could not make a connection of relevance for selecting one or another known culture to act as a model for the "unknown" culture. That is, there are important theoretical and methodological premises built into the use of the analogy that cannot be empirically validated. The validity of these premises is built on the general substantive anthropological theory and archaeological methodology we have. The archaeologist relies on this to establish basic premises, namely, the necessary cultural and social structures that must have existed in order for the production of that type of material cultural patterning to have occurred. These are necessary conditions, given our current state of knowledge, and are not sufficient conditions. His or her empirical study refines these necessary conditions, expressed in the form of a prehistoric community model, so as to establish them as also sufficient conditions.

Applying this model through explaining the empirical data is a very demanding a posteriori effort, and it relies on the adequacy of a priori premises to generate a satisfactory understanding, an understanding that accounts for and explains the empirical data better and more coherently than alternatives. In applying the model through explanation, anomalous empirical patternings often emerge. They are anomalous because they are not consistent with the premises of the model. This requires modifying the model until the explanations this modification enables dissolve the anomalies while not revealing any more anomalies, or at least, any more apparently serious misfits. However, achieving this state of fit between the model (in its "final" form) and the empirical data does not guarantee that the truth has been achieved since it is always possible that a critical examination of the fit will show that an alternative model can also explain the empirical data and, in fact, can reveal that what were dismissed as minor misfits, as merely "noise" resulting from severe limitations on the preservation of the record, for example, turn out to be serious anomalies under the former model. This requires postulating a new model and repeating the explanatory process of fitting the model to the data, and so on. This process of confirmation is what I have termed the hermeneutic spiral method, following Bhaskar's critical realism perspective (1978, chapter 3, 143–227; 1979, 11–28, 164–69; Byers 2004, 106–7; Sayer 1984, 214–15).

Establishing the most reasonable explanation is always dependent on the current status of theory in the discipline. This theory may open up understanding, but it can also close down many other possible avenues simply because the familiarity that anthropologists have with the most well-known theoretical view discourages exploring the observed behavior in any other way. The fact that the anthropologist's own cultural background can "blind" her or him to alternative understandings is, of course, well understood in the discipline. It is a bit surprising, therefore, to realize that many archaeologists do not fully appreciate the adequacy of the theoretical premises of the anthropological characterization of a given cultural system when choosing which historical culture to use for analogical modeling. Possibly archaeologists are intimidated methodologically by the anthropologist since the latter's knowledge of a given culture is "authorized" by the fact that often she or he personally experienced the cultures studied. Archaeologists, of course, cannot have this direct experience. Therefore, in their eyes, the direct experiences by the anthropologists give their characterizations of the communities a type of authenticity and authority that often make their adequacy unquestionable to archaeologists. Of course, some other reason may be responsible. The important point, however, is that archaeologists often only select the source culture on the basis of the relevancy it has for understanding the target culture and rarely question whether the anthropological characterization of that source culture is itself adequate in theoretical or methodological terms.

The theoretical adequacy of the accounts of historic Native North American cultures is particularly a problem since much of the earliest Euro-American knowledge of these cultures was not built on empirical observations collected by scholars trained in anthropology. These were missionaries, merchants, adventurers, soldiers, and so on. Even when they were trained scholars, they were not trained to question their own cultural background but simply somewhat naively drew on this background to understand the cultures of those they encountered—and typically this understanding was couched in terms of inferiority of the other. Hence, as missionaries or soldiers, even when educated, their recordings were heavily laden with largely unquestioned assumptions of their own cultural backgrounds, for example, that the religious beliefs and practices of the Native North Americans were essentially devil worship and that it was the missionaries' duty to save them from their own sinful life. Mortuary practices would be particularly subject to highly biased understanding. In my view, much of the interpretation of Native North American mortuary practices has been systematically misunderstood for this reason. The funerary paradigm is a particular example of this intercultural misunderstanding and the Huron Feast of the Dead is a case in point. This ceremony was described and interpreted by 17th-century French Catholic missionaries and traders. Archaeologists "modernize" and "anthropologize" these descriptions and interpretations, of course, for example, by applying the notion of rite of passage to the Huron Feast of the Dead, arguing that it was carried out as a collective terminal *funerary* event of reincorporation in order to solidify intervillage unity. Indeed, Carr repeats this claim several times (Carr 2005a, 469–70, 475–76; 2005b, 296). However, the contemporary and similarly culturally and socially structured Iroquois Confederacy under similar material constraints, including being historic enemies of the Huron Confederacy, did not seem to find it necessary to perform the equivalent mortuary practice for social integrative purposes, even though the Iroquois Confederacy stretched across a much more expansive region than did the Huron Confederacy.

Given this critical view, is it possible that, in fact, instead of the funerary aspect of Huron mortuary sphere being dominant in the Feast of the Dead, this aspect was if not absent at least rather minor? I think this was likely the case. Typically the Feast of the Dead was carried out by a village every eight to twelve years. This correlated with the community's "abandoning" its village site and, in fact, it was deliberately performed so that the community could then move. This was a result, it is claimed in anthropology, of overuse of the resources of the land, in particular the available wood (Trigger 1969, 27–28; 1976, 87–88; Heidenreich 1978, 378–80). Initiating the ritual included inviting members of neighboring villages to bring some of their own curated deceased as bone bundles so that they could be reburied with the bones of the deceased of the host village. It is important to note how this Feast of the Dead was carried out. It consisted of a series of postmortem manipulatory rites. First, the deceased of the village were removed from their bark "caskets" by their relatives and cleaned of any remaining flesh. This flesh was *cremated*, and then the defleshed and cleaned bones were wrapped in fine animal skins to form sacred mortuary bundles. Similar activity by members of neighboring villages created more sacred mortuary bundles and these were carried to the host village where the ceremony was performed. Each stage involved much ritual in the form of feasting, gifting, singing and dancing, and, I suspect, sacred games, all of which have to be understood as an intrinsic part of the total ceremony. The termination of this collective burial was suspending the sacred mortuary bundles on long poles over the scaffold that surrounded the newly dug collective ossuary pit, and then unwrapping these bundles and depositing the bones into the pit, where they were *thoroughly mixed* by chosen men using long poles.[5] Then the thoroughly mixed bones were carefully covered with the outer edge of the large shroud made of beaver skins that was used to line the pit. Logs were placed over the pit, sand over these to make a low mound, and the whole was covered by a low roofing, realizing in this way possibly the primary symbolic constitution of postmortem sacrifice.[6] Further ritual feasting and gifting occurred and then all the invited went home while the hosts abandoned the village and gathered at their new village locale a few miles away (Trigger 1976, 87–90; Heidenreich 1978, 374–76).

Before interpreting this major event in terms of world renewal, let me turn to another mortuary practice that was only performed under special conditions of death. As Trigger (1969, 104) describes it, "[t]he body of a person who had drowned or frozen to death was taken to the village cemetery and laid on a mat. A ditch was dug on one side of the body and a fire was lighted on the other. Then some young men, chosen by relatives of the deceased, cut up the body and threw the flesh and entrails into the fire, while the skeleton was placed in the ditch. This ritual was performed to appease the sky spirit or the spirit of the lake, who was believed to be angry. Failure to do so would result in dangerous changes in the weather and in accidents. Thus the men who cut up the body were rewarded for having performed a generous and public-spirited act."[7] I believe that this is a clear example of postmortem human sacrifice, using the deceased as a sacrificial offering to assuage the powerful spirits immanent in the sacred natural order. It is also notable that the defleshed skeleton was *buried* and the soft tissues were *burned*. Why this is notable is that it replicates the patterned treatment meted out to the deceased as the first step in the Feast of the Dead. Their bones were cleaned of any remaining flesh, which was then cremated, and the bones ultimately were collectively buried! Of course, in the latter case, the deceased died in a "normal" manner and had their initial "funerary" rituals terminated by their being placed as whole bodies on a form of scaffold, in this case, individual bark caskets raised on low posts. In contrast, those who drowned were subjected to immediate defleshing and skeletal burial, constituting them as postmortem human sacrificial offerings to the sacred powers of the lake or river where they drowned or of the sky if they froze to death. This suggests that one form of behavior constituting postmortem sacrifice was a two-stepped process of separating the flesh from the bones and then burning the former and burying the latter. Due to its arising from the special circumstances of death by drowning or by freezing, this particular sacrificial mortuary rite may not have been performed often. Nevertheless, it clearly indicates that *the belief, ethos, rules, and practice of postmortem human sacrifice were very much part of the mortuary sphere of the Huron.*[8] It seems very reasonable to extend this practice to the Feast of the Dead as well. Of course, the Feast of the Dead was a drawn out set of incremental rites. But the same postmortem manipulatory steps occurred as in the above explicit sacrificial process. This supports the conclusion that the Feast of the Dead was a collective postmortem human sacrifice that served to renew the spiritual powers of the cosmos, in particular, the local reproductive powers of the surrounding lands and forest.

In contrast, also citing Trigger (1976, 87–90), Carr (2005b, 296) argues that it was the spirits of these commingled bones that constituted the basis of the "sacred contract" that reconfirmed the Huron alliances. While this political spin-off might emerge from the event, I would suggest that alliance-building, as such, would not be the explicit goal that would warrant the activity. Indeed, in order to use nonpolitical practices, namely, mortuary practices, for political-ideological purpose, this motivation must be kept obscure. Furthermore, the nonpolitical practice has to have its own logic, value, and purpose independent of any political goal. That is, only if the mortuary practice was an autonomously valued collective behavior would it make sense to recruit its performance for political gain. If it did not have important collective value in its own right and if it was not performed according to the recognized constitutive rules, then it could not serve as a strategic mode for achieving political goals.

It should also be recalled that in the understanding of the Huron, the spiritual powers immanent in the collective bones were no longer relevant to relations among the living. It would appear that the personal souls and not the living souls would be the ones that would count as the media by which the living would sustain their friendly relations. However, upon their release through the Feast of the Dead, these personal souls moved to another plane of existence by traveling on the Milky Way to the land of the Dead (Trigger 1976, 87). This move conforms closely to the notion of Western Heaven, as promoted by the Catholic missionaries; but for this very reason it does not causally link the Feast of the Dead to political alliance. This confusion may be where the missionary sources might be a problem, since, in fact, most of the information on the fate of the souls derives from the missionary commentaries. In this regard, as Von Gernet (1993, 45–46) points out, while the missionaries noted the different Huron terms for "souls," they did not treat these terms as naming different types of souls but as naming different faculties or aspects of the singular soul. If this is the case, then confusing multiple souls with multiple aspects of singular souls dissolved any need for the missionaries to deal with the fate of the living souls embodied in these collective bone burials!

Now, there is no doubt that in the understanding of the Huron, these bones were still supercharged with spiritual power. It will be noted, however, that this is also the first and final time the bones were actually placed in the earth and that this collective burial marks the abandonment of the village and the usage by the village people of the surrounding custodial lands. Also, as I reiterated above, the Huron clearly believed that postmortem manipulation and final bone burial were among the primary conditions stipulated by the rules of sacrifice by which offerings of human spiritual essences could be made to the powers of the cosmos. This combination suggests that the Feast of the Dead, was both (1) a final spirit-release rite of the personal souls of the deceased, enabling them to leave this plane of existence and travel to the land of the Dead, and (2) a world renewal rite directed to initiating the revitalizing of the surrounding land through postmortem human sacrificial offering.

In short, it is quite likely that the missionary reports distorted the social reality they were reporting on. However, these distortions have become the core of the "modern" anthropological constructs and it is these that many archaeologists have accepted, largely without question, in order to model the mortuary practices of the Ohio Hopewell. In contrast, if the premises of the Mourning/World Renewal Mortuary model are used to reconstrue our understanding of the Huron social system, then the latter would be rooted on a regime of inclusive territorialism and custodial usufruct domain. Therefore, their horticultural practices would be based on inclusive custodial usufruct rights (Byers 2004, 152–55). This was clearly the case for many historic Native North American peoples. Typically, horticultural villagers recognized that a family had a right to use the same land for their gardens as long as they needed it. However, should they stop using it, then it was available to anyone who had need for it (Heidenreich 1978, 380; Hurt 1987, 67; Will and Hyde 1964, 81).

That custodial domain of an inclusive sort (in contrast to the Mapuche exclusive custodial land domain) prevailed among the Huron is clear from Heidenreich's comments in regard to their land tenure (1978, 380). "Among the Huron all unused land was common property. Farm plots seem to have been owned and operated by individuals or nuclear families, although the tasks of land clearance, as well as a large part of the produce were shared by the extended family. Every family took as much land as it could cultivate, whereupon that land became theirs. When the land was abandoned it reverted back to the community and was free to be taken up by someone else. . . . Since land could not be sold or inherited, it could not be accumulated as wealth." Of course, he uses terms that are redolent with the sense of private proprietorship and, therefore, his describing farm plots as being "owned and operated by individuals" must be reconstrued into more appropriate custodial usufruct terminology. That custodial usufruct tenure is what was basic is clearly indicated when he notes that land that was unused "reverted back" to the community. Therefore, it is quite reasonable to treat the Huron as having inclusive custodial usufruct and, as long as the land surrounding the village was regularly used by the people of that village, their custodial usufruct rights would be recognized by their neighbors.

However, both the need for wood and timber and the demands of maize horticulture required abandoning the land for a prolonged period by moving the village to new or currently unused nearby land and, indeed, the Feast of the Dead constituted this step. Possibly equally important, however, is that this ceremony would resolve a problem that the principle of custodial usufruct would raise when applied in a slash and burn horticultural system, namely, constituting the physical abandonment of a particular land area as *not counting* as the surrender of the traditional custodial usufruct of the land by the villagers who were collectively absent. As noted above, abandoned land was available to others. But this raises directly a question of what would count as "abandoned land" and how neighboring peoples would know that the land whose habitual occupants were conspicuous by their absence was not abandoned land available for use for others but was land that was simply in a state of being renewed by its current custodians for later use. I postulate that deliberately inviting neighbors to share the use of the ossuary by contributing some of the deceased would solve this problem. That is, part of what made a Feast of the Dead successful is that many neighbors would attend and participate, thereby publicly recognizing that the abandonment of the local land by the resident community was *not* to be interpreted as the freeing-up of this land usufruct for themselves to exercise. They would also welcome the opportunity to participate in this ritual because it enabled them to fulfill the duty they had to the personal souls of their own deceased who were probably assumed to be quite impatiently waiting for their release rites so they could travel to the land of the Dead.

Here is an example of how a mortuary activity can legitimately take on functions that are nonmortuary in nature. In effect, the essential core of the ceremonial practice that makes it what it is, a dual form of personal and living spirit-release ritual, could be fully felicitous without the addition of deceased from surrounding villages. However, by including a public invitation in this way, the host community was able to maintain good relations with its neighbors who, by participating, would commit themselves to continue recognizing their host's custodial usufruct rights—a recognition that everyone implicitly understood. Most importantly, this invitation benefited the guests since being invited to participate by contributing the sacred bones of their deceased relations and companions was an opportunity to discharge their duties to their deceased and the cosmos by dedicating the living souls immanent in these bones to renewing the local land. That is, their relatives' bones were media for ensuring that the Feast of the Dead was a felicitous world renewal sacrifice. Of course, all this would also serve to enhance the social integration of these communities with each other and individually.[9] Therefore, I conclude that the bones of the deceased used to mediate the Feast of the Dead can be understood as a sacrificial offering of their immanently sacred powers. This offering process constituted the collective mortuary event as a world renewal ritual by which to renew the sacred reproductive powers of the local land, thereby discharging the duties of the living to that land, while also serving as a public claim to the continuation of the village's custodial usufruct rights to the land.

I think that it should be fairly obvious that this alternative view of the Huron Feast of the Dead and the Mourning/World Renewal Mortuary model that serves as its theoretical background can be added as part of the critique of the Tripartite Ceremonial Alliance model. Under this latter model, the Ohio Hopewell mortuary pattern was interpreted as a funerary process and served to constitute intercommunity alliances. Of course, critiquing the model in these terms does not mean that intergroup alliance may not be one of the conditions that made the Ohio Hopewell mortuary patterning possible. However, as I have already argued and as I will demonstrate shortly, when treated in terms of the Mourning/World Renewal Mortuary model, a treatment that is warranted by my above interpretation of the Huron Feast of the Dead as a major medium of world renewal ritual performed jointly by communities, it will be seen that a very different form of alliance would be responsible, one that I have already referred to as cult sodality heterarchies. In the next chapter, I turn to the particular theory of symbolic meaning of material culture that informs my interpretation of the Ohio Hopewell mortuary sphere. It also stands in opposition to the theory of symbolic meaning relied upon by Carr and by many other proponents of the orthodox model.

5

The Symbolic Meaning of Material Culture

In a literate society, a warrant is an artifactual document that is issued by a court or some judicial authority. This warrant expresses and manifests the deontic power of this authority, that is, its rights and prerogatives, and through the medium of the warrant, the court authority, for example, a presiding judge, endows some of these rights on the person who is granted the duty of bearing the warrant. This constitutes the person as an officer of the court, such as the position of bailiff or sheriff. The rights and duties that the warrant endows on the bailiff's position, therefore, constitute the social powers and obligations of the occupant of this position, the bailiff, as such. Social power is a key term that I will theorize in more detail later. However, for the moment it is sufficient to note that social powers define the action capacities of social positions and these capacities attach to the legitimate occupants of the positions. Therefore, as I treat social powers, they are deontic states such as rights and duties and are not reducible to the physical powers of these persons, although the physical powers are often used to ensure that the purposes of the warrant holder's actions are met. We have physical powers, of course, and these are normally emergent from the neurophysiological structures of our bodies and are the powers by which through exercising our intentions we make controlled or willful movements. But social powers exist at a more abstract and emergent ontological level, what can be called the social level. The nature of this level can be characterized as intersubjective and is constituted as the level of ongoing human interaction. When social powers are exercised by subjects such as sheriffs and bailiffs through the medium of the "warrants" they bear, these powers transform their tangible, physical behaviors into social actions that holders of warrants of this type are recognized as having the deontic, constitutive powers to perform, for example, making arrests, seizing property, and the like.

This transformation of behaviors into social actions by means of expressing and manifesting social powers or properties of certain sorts in specific social conditions is what I mean by constituting social actions. The warrant can be used by the holder in this way because it *symbolically* expresses and manifests the social powers and properties that its user has had endowed on him or her. I have stressed "symbolically" in order to emphasize that the warrant is a conventional instrument. Its powers are dependent on the "rules of the game" that it mediates and these rules exist as the representational content of certain of the collective mental states of the "game players." Such collective mental states constitute generically what I term the cultural traditions of a people and specifically the ideological structures. I elucidate what I mean by cultural traditions in the final part of the chapter.

I speak of this constitutive transformation as an emergent moment in the sense that a different phenomenon, a social action, *emerges* from but is grounded in the tangible, physical behavioral streams of the agents involved. Also, importantly, since this expressive moment of the warrant manifests social powers, it also necessarily manifests or expresses the social and cultural source of these constitutive powers, in this case, the judicial institution we term a court. Therefore, the constitutive moment generated by the expressive meaning and by which the user's behavior becomes a definable social action occurs in the collective understanding of the parties involved—from the primary interacting parties, for example, the officer of the court bearing the warrant and the person he or she is arresting by physically seizing and handcuffing, through the usually extensive set of occupants of the network of social positions that constitutes the relevant social context of the warrant holder's behavior. And note, my saying a social action or activity "emerges from but is grounded in" means that the behavioral stream and the action stream are not two different objective movements. They are one and the same objective movement but realizing two different phenomena, the action being emergent from but rooted in the behavior. This emergent ontological status exists as real but it is only real for the human subjects involved. Indeed, their knowing that they are doing certain activities is part of constituting the action stream.

I maintain that the action is a real phenomenon and not simply an epiphenomenon, as demonstrated by the fact that the very same behavioral stream could occur and count as a very different social action simply by varying the conventional moment in which it occurs, thereby generating quite different symbolic meaning. For example, in the absence of the warrant (or an equivalent material symbol), the same behavior would be perceived and experienced as a criminal assault. And for social humans, this differential recognition is not trivial. Even though objectively the two behavioral streams would be effectively identical, except for the presence or absence of the relevant material symbols, the subsequent behaviors arising from each of the behavioral streams would be quite different. The officer of the court performing the behavior is commended by the court judge for effecting the arrest and fulfilling his or her duty; the person who assaults another is subject to legal punishment and imprisonment. These are real differences flowing from the behavioral streams having the same objective forms but quite different action natures. Therefore, these same behaviors must count as and be different social actions. The difference that counts is symbolically constituted.

Seen in these terms, one way of characterizing the meaning of the warrant is that it is action-constitutive power and it endows this power on its legitimate holder. Therefore, to ask for the meaning of the warrant you need to ask not what the warrant "points to" but what type of social (legal) action does the use of this symbol constitute. Most importantly, this meaning is symbolic and abstract in nature since, of course, it is conventional and the object it represents, "authority," exists as an abstract property, that is, its mode of existence—its ontological status—is as part of the collective understanding of the community's members. Why do I say this? Because there is no tangible object in that community that one can point to and designate "authority" in the way that you can point at an animal and recognize and call it "dog." The dog is an object in the world and the existence of dogs, in general, does not depend on their existence being recognized by the human community. However, the only "place" authority can exist is in the community's collective understanding. Certainly, one could point to a building and use the term *courthouse* to refer to it but it is the abstract meaning that this term expresses that characterizes its cultural meaning and the type of activities that occur in it. Objectively it is simply a complex of material things; but, like the warrant, it is the expressive manifestation of the collective concept of authority. That is, even the moment of recognizing the warrant *as such* or the court building *as such* or the judge *as such* is constituted by these material things (including the persons) conforming in appearance to the stipulations of social rules and norms that constitute these objects as warrants and court buildings and judges.

This distinction between the meaning of the words *dog* and *cat* as symbols and the meaning of a document such as a warrant or of a building such as a courthouse as symbols, the former having objective referents and the latter having intersubjective "referents," is critically important in my view and typically it is not appreciated in archaeology. Indeed, there is a tendency to uncritically accept that the meanings of such symbolic things as ceremonial blades and animal-like headdresses are the objects they are used to refer to and what they refer to are usually something other than the users or the mental properties of the users of the symbols. Therefore, just as the word *dog* uttered by a speaker using an appropriate grammatical context, namely, a rule-governed well-formed vocal utterance, can be understood by others as the speaker's referring to an animal of a certain sort, even and particularly when that object is not present, so it is assumed that a material symbol, such as a sheriff's star, is used to refer to something independent of it, and usually this is assumed to be the wearer. Therefore, this person is recognized as the sheriff and, of course, the badge and the person are mutually independent. This all seems reasonable, even though what the badge "refers to" does not exist independently in the way that the dog exists independently of the word *dog*.

I will use the term *referentialism* to speak of this extension of the referential meaning of object-specifying words to the meaning of material cultural symbols. It contrasts with the above construal of material symbols as having *abstract* objects and as being used not to refer to their abstract objects but to *express* them. In general, I consider referentialism to be a mistaken way to characterize the symbolic meaning of material culture, whether the item is a document such as a warrant or passport or a non-document-type artifact—such as a sheriff's star, a military uniform, or military or civilian insignia; or symbolic features, such as thrones; or monumental constructions, such as cathedrals. Instead, I treat all these as expressive symbols and, like the warrant, in expressive usage they are used to invoke, manifest, and presence the cultural abstraction, that is, the collective conceptual structure that they conventionally represent. That is, importantly what they represent is not an object that exists independently of the concept but an abstraction that only exists in the collective understanding of the community—the conceptual paradigms that make up the community's cultural traditions. Of course, a community often reifies this abstraction(s) and takes it to exist independently of their collective understanding. When a material symbol is experienced and used in this way, which is very often, I term it an iconic symbol. That is, the icon is taken to be part of and to actively participate in the properties and powers of what it represents and these properties and powers generally exist independently of the users of the icons. However, those who are privileged and burdened with the responsibility of using them are also recognized as participating in the powers of these abstract entities through the expressive mediation of the material symbols.[1] Now, as I noted above, it is also true that the word *dog* represents and expresses an abstraction that exists in the collective understanding of language community, namely, the concept "dog." However, the concept is about an object that exists independently of either the concept "dog" or the word *dog*. Dogs are among the objects of the world, whether we think of them or not and whether we speak of them or not. The authority expressed by a sheriff's badge, however, only exists as an emergent "object" and does so as a collective concept of the community's cultural traditions.

We can make and utter words such as "a sheriff's badge," symbolic terms, in order to refer to such items. After all, like dogs actual "sheriff's badges" are among the objects of the world. But this does not mean that the wearers of the actual objects use them in order to make reference to themselves as sheriffs. If they want to express their social identity (perhaps it is too dark for the badge to be seen), they simply say it. And if we want to refer to the sheriff, we also simply use the words to do so and usually the reason is because we want to talk about (term of reference) or talk to that person (term of address).[2] Words are used to refer to their objects and this usage underlines the fact that there is an ontological separation of the word *dog* and the object it refers to. If we insist on characterizing the meaning usage of the sheriff's badge as referential, then we are saying that wearing the badge is like referring to the sheriff and just as uttering the word *dog* refers to its object, an actual dog, independently of the dog itself, then the wearer of the badge must be referring to someone else because a symbol used referentially stands for and is not what it refers to. Hence, we get into a vicious regress and the wearer of the sheriff's badge is never the sheriff but only referring to someone else who is the sheriff. The point is not that the sheriff's badge does not mean "the sheriff." Rather the point is that wearing the badge is not the same as saying the word *sheriff.* Saying the word expresses the concept but refers to the person. Wearing the badge expresses the concept and *manifests* it in the person who is wearing it. In doing so, the wearer is constituted *as the sheriff.* That is, the badge mediates the expression of the concept "sheriff" and what emerges in this expression is the person as sheriff. Just as the warrant expresses the concept "authority of the court" and manifests this authority in the person of the bailiff, so wearing a sheriff's badge enables the authority to emerge, that is, manifests the authority in the wearer and, thereby, constitutes the wearer as the sheriff and her or his behavioral streams are thereby constituted as the social actions of a person occupying such a position.

In short, reference is nonemergent and stresses the separate natures of the speaker and the objects being spoken about. Expression is emergent, in nature, and presences in the user, the concept it expresses, thereby constituting her or his social identity. This identification is particularly important since, in fact, what is being expressed by the symbol can only be manifested in this or synonymous expressive symbols. It exists as an emergent phenomenon in the collective understanding of the community, and the material symbols and their distribution across a population delineate the emergent distribution of this phenomenon, that is, of the deontic reality of social powers and responsibilities.

I believe that the affinity that archaeologists have to characterizing the symbolic aspect of material things in referential terms is well motivated in that the problem they are addressing is accounting for style. If it is acceptable to speak of style as the tangible aspect of material cultural things that bears symbolic meaning such that they are the way they are in virtue of conforming to conventions and rules, then clearly archaeologists want to explain the symbolic nature of style in communicative terms. This leads them to linguistics and most discussions about language and its use emphasize reference; and, as noted above, many words are used referentially. However, there are many occasions when words are used just like material symbols in that their use is only expressive and this is because they express abstractions that exist only in the collective understanding of the language community. For example, promises and orders are expressed in words but promises and orders are abstract phenomena emerging in the behavioral moment of uttering the promises or orders and their existence is totally dependent on the collective understanding of the community. Such speech acts have at their core verbs that are termed performatives, for example, I promise . . . ; I order . . . ; I swear . . . ; and so on. In linguistics the rules and protocols for the use of performatives are termed pragmatics, and it constitutes a part of the grammar that is intrinsic to any language. These rules enable humans to perform speech actions—a very amazing skill, when one thinks about it. Searle (1983, 4–13) has spoken of several basic speech act forms: expressives, commissives, directives, declaratives, and assertives. He defines them in terms of the type of intentional state each expresses (again, I discuss intentionality later in this chapter). Let me illustrate with the commissive (generic for expressing an intention). In fact, the most common commissive is the promise. Others are agreements, bets, and other related forms of utterances by which speakers use symbols to perform an expressive action that commits them to a subsequent course of action. For example, in making a promise, the speaker commits himself or herself to doing some activity and often this commitment is to the hearer(s) of the act of promising. A commitment is a deontic phenomenon in that it ties the speaker and hearer into a moral or legal relation and, in this case, puts the obligation on the speaker-making-the-promise to perform the action to the satisfaction of the hearer-receiving-the-promise. Hence, as with warrants and sheriff's badges, the speech act generates a set of abstractions—obligations, rights, duties—that link, or (abstractly, morally, legally) relate, this speaker to the hearer(s), and this relation is itself, of course, an abstraction since it only exists in their shared understanding and its existence is only possible given that they also are part of a language community that has pragmatic rules by which such speech-mediated actions can be performed.

Of course, while the obligations exist only as abstract phenomena, they are not epiphenomenal in my view since, of course, the promise makes a difference in the social world itself. In fact, this "making-a-difference" can be labeled "a promise," and this word can be used referentially to speak about that type of speech act, just as the social power of the warrant can be labeled as "authority." Therefore, just as we have words to refer to things like dogs and cars, we also have words to refer to speech actions, such as "promises" and "orders." Promises and orders, of course, have tangible properties. When spoken we hear an order or a promise. When written they constitute "long-term" agreements: IOUs, bank drafts, and the like. However, while dogs and cats exist independently of the words we use to speak about them, promises and orders only exist when the words uttered or inscribed are heard and or read and this is because their existence is intersubjective, that is, dependent on being part of the awareness of others. It is by having appropriate grammatical form and semantic content that their utterances or inscriptions can be interpreted as expressing the abstractions we call duties and rights and social relations. The speech actions are emergent abstractions, rule-governed expressions, since it is only through expression that such abstractions can be manifested in our understanding. And the speech actions are real phenomena, despite their tangibly ephemeral nature (unless written down, of course), since they make a difference in the social world of the speakers. Thus, in the appropriate circumstances and done in the appropriate (rule-governed) manner, in uttering the words "I promise to X," I perform a real social action, namely, the speech utterance behavior transforms into a speech action. The social reality I generate consists of real social powers and obligations, both in that I can make my words count in the understanding of others as a promise and I impose on myself the obligations to act so as to fulfill the promise. The core of the performative speech act, therefore, is nonreferential and expressive and through expression it enables others to recognize in the speaker and themselves the properties of obligation, entitlement, rights, duties, and so on, depending on the particular speech act being performed. I also want to emphasize that usually among the necessary conditions of generating the speech actions intended is that the person speaking must occupy the appropriate social position. This is why the warrant or its equivalent is so important as a symbolic medium of abstract rights and duties.

I want to say that in terms of usage meaning, the symbolic meaning of material cultural items is action-constitutive in this symbolic pragmatic sense. Hence, not only are material cultural symbols, such as warrants, expressively used to transform the physical behaviors performed through their tangible mediation so that they count as arrests or legal seizures, these same symbols are often necessary to constitute the oral utterances of the users as promises and orders. The speech utterance "Attack the enemy" counts as a military order only if the person speaking is recognized as occupying the position of officer because of the uniform he or she wears and this uniform is like the warrant in mediating and manifesting the intersubjective abstraction we term "military authority." Only by recognizing this speaker as an officer are the hearers then obliged to obey. It is for this reason that I claim that treating the meaning of a uniform in referential terms, as if it is referring to the position of the wearer, is to distort the significance of material symbols. However, I can appreciate that those who do so are trying to address an important problem, this being recognizing that material culture must be seen in order for its meaning to be operative. One must see and recognize the speaker *as an* officer for the speech act to count *as an order*. And as noted above, relevant others' recognition of the wearer of a sheriff's badge is part of constituting this person's behavior as the actions that only a person in the position of sheriff or its equivalent can intend to perform and, in exercising the intention in behavior, constitute this flow as a legal action of the type that only sheriffs or their equivalents can perform.

Now, if characterizing this moment of social recognition as referencing misconstrues what is going on, as I claim it does, then I am obliged to present an alternative way of characterizing it. I have tried by analogy with the notion of a court warrant. However, this is a formal document constituting formal or official actions. I want to claim that the symbolic pragmatic moment pervades not only our formal but also our everyday lives and this moment or imperative is a strong motive for generating material cultural style. To illustrate how this pervasive nature of symbolic pragmatic meaning operates through material culture I think that the notion of the cue as used in drama is very helpful. On stage, the actors' primary medium is speech and laced through this flow of speech are verbal cues by which they not only play their parts but also cue each other's behavior so as to ensure that the interaction flows smoothly and intelligibly. Actors treat each other's utterances as cuing devices to time their own acting behaviors. However, there is much more to cuing when the drama is looked at from the perspective of the audience. From their perspective a critical part of cuing is the costume and the stage setting since the expressive meaning of the latter establishes the (pretend) social context by which the spoken behaviors of the actors are transformed into their performances. It is this use of theatrical costume and setting by the audience as cues by which the actors' behavioral streams are constituted as the actions they wish to portray that expresses the symbolic pragmatic moment of style. Therefore, the actor playing the sheriff wears the appropriate garments and the audience, who are part of the same general cultural background as the actors, can immediately cue into the nature of the activity that the actor's behavior is performing. I would argue that the actors are not wearing costumes in order to make self-reference. Rather, they are wearing costumes to manifest the roles they are playing. Indeed, the most effective dramaturgical staging is one in which the costume and material setting are effortlessly interpreted by the audience so they can "suspend their disbelief" as they immerse themselves into the ongoing behavioral flow of the actors as intelligible and believable performances of the way of life being "lived." Not referring but cuing as ongoing expressing of abstract social and personal meanings, intentions, wants, and so on, is the communicative role that material cultural symbols play and in real social life this cuing, of course, is serious, not pretend or theatrical, so that the behaviors are transformed into real sequences of intelligible social actions that simultaneously reconstitute the social context and deontic relations of rights and duties that agents occupy.

As I am using the term, the cue is any material sign, words also, intentionally used by an agent to structure (i.e., constitute) his or her behaviors so that they count as the social actions intended. Of course, the cue user may fail in satisfying his or her intentions—but that does not deny the cue function of the signs themselves. The warrant, then, is an action-constitutive cue in the sense that it both endows the user with the powers of a position and enables the user to express and thereby communicate his or her intentions in his or her behaviors so that others recognize and interpret them as the types of social actions that they are in virtue of the symbolic pragmatic meaning of the material cues.

Treating material symbols as action-cuing devices highlights the importance of the expressive nature of material cultural items and also avoids reducing understanding its usage to simply some form of referencing. Most importantly, it clarifies the communicative moment that material cultural items mediate.[3] I initiated this discussion of warranting in order to highlight the symbolic pragmatic meaning of material culture, its action-constitutive nature. To speak of a warrant as an action cue simply highlights its inter-subjective communicative moment as an expressive symbol that manifests a deontic abstraction that exists only in the collective understanding of the community. However, I can see value in using the term *action cue* as a general characterization of the symbolic nature of material cultural artifacts to supplement the more formal sense of warrants, licenses, and so on, as pragmatic devices. A warrant in our society is not only a formal action cue, it presupposes a dominance-based social hierarchy and, therefore, as I discuss in detail later, the social powers it endows are "powers-over" the actions of others. In my view, such powers were severely constrained and largely nonexistent in the Middle Woodland period social system and, instead, given the core concept of agentive autonomy, the formal action-constitutive powers of "warrants" would be enabling powers, endowing the user to constitute his or her behaviors as the social actions intended while simultaneously not endowing this person with powers over the actions of others. Therefore, I would qualify the term *warrant* and speak of these as "enabling warrants," or formal action cues that endow the user with the social powers necessary to transform her or his own behaviors into her or his own social actions. As I noted above, I discuss social powers in more detail later.

In any case, part of the benefit of using the term *action cue* or *cuing* as a supplement to the more formal terms such as warrant/warranting and license/licensing is that it enables us to reach beyond the narrow formalism that these latter terms encourage. For example, it might distort the symbolic pragmatic meaning of a shell bead necklace of the type found with many Ohio Hopewell burial deposits to speak of it as a warrant or a license of some type of action, particularly since its widespread distribution suggests that it did not define a formal social position but was part of the ensemble that was worn by many people. However, this same distribution would suggest that it certainly must have been an important symbolic medium of interaction and, therefore, it can be treated more informally as an action cue, an important but not a critical action-constitutive device. I would suggest that rather than specific social positions or specific action intentions, its action cue value was that it articulated and expressed a particular range of attitudes that wearers of these items were expected to manifest with respect to the event or events in which they would normally participate, and therefore would be worn along with many of the other portable artifacts that made up the normal costume ensemble appropriate for that or similar events. The event or events may have been the type that entailed the use enabling warrants by which some of the participants manifested their formal positions. For example, a formal rite of passage would entail that the leader of the rite wear the appropriate warrants. Supplementing these warrants would be the action cuing devices that would not be constitutive of these positions while still being important as a means of manifesting the seriousness of the event and ensure that the participants regarded it seriously. The proper action cues manifest the respect that is appropriate in constituting an event of this sort as fully felicitous in its nature, and so on. These quite outstanding artifacts, some involving procuring resources from a great distance, would serve to express the quality of attitudes and postures, the sincerity and seriousness that were constitutive of the felicity of the events. In their absence, as long as the formal warrants were being used, the interactive stream of behaviors would still count as the type of event intended, but this event would be reflexively assessed by all those involved as not as fully felicitously "pulled off" as desired. Many might raise the issue of just how seriously people took the event and many might take this absence of appropriate action cues, proper pearl or shell necklaces, copper hair clips, copper earspools, and so on, as a shortfall in the expression of proper respect and seriousness and this would be a reason to be ashamed collectively in the way the group performed the event. The importance of the term *action cue*, therefore, highlights not only the expressive mode of communication that is critically important to action constitution, expressing one's personal abstract properties, standings, attitudes, intentions, emotional involvement, and so on, but also the claim that even these "informal" items play an important symbolic constitutive role, and therefore, the total event is irreducible to the behaviors that manifest it. In sum, while formal social positions entail the use of formal symbolic media to constitute the actions of the occupant, a whole range of nonformal positioning and expressing of emotions and attitudes is also necessary for the felicity of events so that many things will display certain conventionally recognized properties in order to express the appropriate attitudes, values, and standards that persons, whether occupying formal positions or being part of the important "audience," "must" display in order to be taken as serious participants and thereby do their share in sustaining the reputation of the community involved.

As expressive symbols, items treated as action cues are not at all vague about the objects that they represent. That is, even though material symbols are not used to make reference to what they represent, they can be used to articulate and make real for their users and relevant audiences what they represent possibly better than any words. Because words can so easily be used referentially, that is, they can be used to *stand for* what they represent, they tend to objectify and displace the essential nature of the objects they represent. However, since material symbols as action cues are necessarily used expressively and, furthermore, what they express are abstractions, that is, they have no objective extensions except the action cues themselves, sometimes the material things become the media for teaching others about the abstractions they represent. Without the material symbols, the abstractions would not be able to be learned and known. That is, as material symbols, what they represent are collective intentional properties of the people who use them and in using the action cues they manifest the concept.

The significance of identifying material cultural items as symbolic pragmatic devices seems particularly obvious for archaeological interpretation since, of course, allowing for idiosyncratic "noise," the material culture that forms the basic body of empirical data in the archaeological record is the outcome and medium of systematic and regularized behaviors. In terms of the symbolic pragmatic/action cue view, these behaviors would *count as* the performances of actions and interactions—or social activities—because of the culture-specific action cue meaning of the material cultural items that mediated them. Hence, cutting deer meat with blade X under material cultural conditions A-B-C (in the domestic household) counts as domestic culinary subsistence butchering; cutting the same type of meat with blade Y (ritual bladelet) under conditions M-N-O (in a renewal lodge in the embankment earthwork) counts as ceremonial culinary butchering for a communal world renewal ritual feast. In mortuary terms, shaving the hair of the deceased with blade Y under conditions M-N-O counts as Z, an offering of the spirits of the hair to the cosmos.

This action cuing perspective, therefore, is fully applicable to the embankment earthworks. Indeed, treating these monumental earthworks in symbolic pragmatic terms, as monumental icons of the cosmos, makes their construction particularly intelligible (Byers 2006a, 34–39; 2004, 62–76; 1999, 270–72; Searle 1995, 80–86). By taking monumental earthworks as illustrative, this claim immediately requires asking what kinds of social activities and events must have been predominantly performed in these monumental symbolic pragmatic contexts. Of course, the answer is constrained by the patterning of the archaeological record so that not just any answer will do. Therefore, to establish this, two interpretive steps of the patterning must be taken. It is necessary first to establish the symbolic pragmatic or action cue meaning of the embankment earthworks, and, second, it is necessary to establish the action nature of the dominant behaviors responsible for generating the recognized patterning of these contents. The action nature of the material behaviors that generated the latter data would be determined by the symbolic pragmatic meaning of the embankment earthworks themselves. In this case, I have argued consistently and empirically grounded the view (Byers 1987, 1996, 1998, 2004) that they were the expressive (reified) symbols of the cosmos and, as such, they were treated by their builders as *monumental icons* of the cosmos. As iconic symbols the users took them to be participating in some of the basic or essential properties of what they represented, thereby manifesting or presencing the natural or "supernatural" powers of this phenomenon; and, of course, in symbolic pragmatic terms as a material symbol it was used performatively, that is, in action cuing terms, so as to transform the behaviors carried out in their context to count as critical social actions that could only be performed in these earthwork contexts. In counterfactual terms, but for the construction and use of the embankment earthworks as monumental iconic symbols of the cosmos, the builders would be unable to felicitously manifest and participate in its sacred powers and, therefore, they would be unable to perform the types of ritual actions required to discharge their duties (Byers 2004, 78–101). I have argued that these monumental icons enabled the transformation of the behavioral performances so that they counted as world renewal ceremonialism.

I think that from the empirical data it is clear what type of material behaviors played a central role in these earthworks. As I noted in the previous chapter, they were mortuary-related behaviors since, of course, the most ubiquitous residue in the two most prominent features, the two "Big Houses" (also sometimes termed "Great Houses") of Seip-Pricer and Seip-Conjoined, were human remains, in the form of cremated remains, as well as a few extended burials. Since these remains were given final treatment in these major structures, the Big Houses, it suggests that a significant part of the incremental behaviors constituting different mortuary rituals as postulated under the mourning → spirit-release → world renewal mortuary *chaîne opératoire* continuum was also played out in the context of the Seip earthworks, even though these behaviors would likely be terminated with scaffolding and/or temporary curating of the deceased in charnel structures in preparation for later cremation and, therefore, would not leave any clear evidence of human remains. The conclusion then is that the primary raison d'être of the groups who produced and used these earthworks was directed to constituting rituals of renewal of the spiritual powers of the cosmos; and, since the symbolic pragmatic media constitutive of these rituals would be human remains, the latter would figure in many of them. However, despite the size of these mortuary ceremonial structures, they actually occupy a very small area of the embankment earthworks in which they are located. I postulate in detail later the claim that the mortuary process was integrated with a complex and ongoing series of sacred games *tournées* that became the primary performative action schedule of the cult sodality heterarchies that built and used them.

In the following chapter I will elucidate the appropriate model characterizing the nature of these groups, what I earlier referred to as ecclesiastic-communal cult sodalities. Because so many—although certainly not all—of the rituals that these postulated cult sodalities regularly performed were marked by cremation, I will argue that these cremation behaviors must have been the termination of the complex incremental series of funerary → mourning →spirit-release → social renewal → world renewal rituals with the product of each ritual step being appropriated to serve as the symbolic pragmatic mortuary medium for the performance of the next ritual step (Byers 2004, 177–85).

This symbolic pragmatic/action cue approach to interpreting the action-constitutive meaning and purpose of the earthworks tightly and meaningfully ties together a set of material cultural components—embankment earthworks, renewal lodges, facilities, and artifacts; the human mortuary residues associated with them; and the earthwork mounds covering them—that under most other models, such as the Vacant Center/Dispersed Hamlet model and the Tripartite Ceremonial Alliance model, were disparate and, in terms of mortuary practices and embankment earthworks, only contingently rather than substantively related. In this case, my theoretical view and the empirical data together warrant my assertion that the social organization that was responsible would have been a companionship-based sodality rather than a kinship-based community. As such, this "symbolic community" would probably be constituted as an alliance of ecclesiastic-communal world renewal cult sodalities and, as I noted earlier, it is these alliances that would affiliate to form networks of major embankment earthwork sites, such as Hopewell, Turner, and, possibly, Fort Ancient, constituting second- or more likely third-order cult sodality heterarchies. Before turning to this argument I will first use the symbolic pragmatic view of the meaning of material culture to summarize and critique the theory of the symbolic meaning of material cultural style elucidated and used by Christopher Carr and Troy Case (2005b) to ground their claim that the leadership structure of a typical Ohio Hopewell "community" was strongly shamanic in nature.

A THEORETICAL CRITIQUE OF SYMBOLIC MEANING OF MATERIAL CULTURE

The symbolic pragmatic approach to material cultural meaning that I articulated above can now be used to critique the approach to material cultural symbolism applied by Carr and Case (2005b, 177–237). This has important theoretical consequences since their approach leads to characterizing "Ohio Hopewell communities" in ways that are diametrically opposite to the characterization given by the Complementary Heterarchical Community model. In terms I used above, their approach can be characterized as referential since they unproblematically assume that material cultural symbols are used to refer to what they represent and what they represent are formal social positions. This almost automatically eliminates thinking of symbols as having action-constitutive meaning. Also, they tightly tie the symbolic meaning of artifacts to formal social positions by speaking of them as referring to the leadership role of the users, thereby making it very difficult to think of many categories of Ohio Hopewell artifacts as having a more general social action cue role than a formal warranting role. Using this referential approach, they believe that they can use the artifacts in order to directly read off the Ohio Hopewell leadership roles from the archaeological assemblage, and their interpretation of the semantic content of the artifacts, almost all of which they interpret as "referring" to intangible powers of the type they identify with shamanism, leads to their concluding that these leadership positions were predominantly shamanic or shamanic-like in nature. While certainly recognizing that the same artifact categories can be identified with special properties immanent in the world, the symbolic pragmatic approach can show that rather than the Ohio Hopewell artifactual assemblage "referencing" a shamanic or shaman-type leadership, it is the type that could be expected to have been used to mediate the range of activities of what I have termed a cult sodality heterarchy. There was a rather limited set of "warrants" of action constituting formal positions that endowed their users with action powers necessary for them to fulfill their duties and honor their obligations and there was a much broader range of action cues that served to express and publicly articulate—and therefore presence—that range of values and standards that constituted the felicity or sincerity conditions that ensured that the users' material behaviors mediated by these items counted as worthy and reputation-enhancing activities. Confirmation of this latter conclusion will be presented in the next chapter when I elucidate the Ecclesiastic-Communal Cult Sodality model and use it to give a radically different account of the distribution of the mortuary data associated with the same sites that Carr has used as central to his Tripartite Ceremonial Alliance model.

Carr and Case make two assumptions. First, they assume that somewhat esoteric material items register their users as community leaders of one sort or another. If this assumption was made in symbolic pragmatic terms, particularly the more general action cue notion, this certainly would have merit. However, they then select items bearing figurative representations and treat these as being used to refer to what these figurative representations are about. Thus they claim a specific object category as the meaning of the artifact, as its referent. In this case, they start with a well-known series of Adena engraved tablets. They note that many of these tablets have dual depictions: human faces/raptorial birds. Based on analogy, they conclude that these depictions reference a classic shaman-into-animal (bird) transformation. They note that along with this depiction tree-like objects are depicted on the tablets and they interpret these as referring to the Cosmic Tree with the shaman transforming himself or herself into a bird spirit and ascending into the heavens. The referential view then leads them to conclude that the user of these items was a shaman. As I noted, the alternative view would be to assume that this item was used in order to transform the behavioral stream it mediated into the type of social act intended, for example, a mortuary rite. This does not entail, however, that the user was a shaman or that the action was shamanic, although this is one possibility, of course.

Setting aside the referentialism of their approach, their starting with a figurative depiction in this manner is a good step since the depiction is an excellent cue to the nature of the object that is being represented, in this case being abstract, intangible powers and properties that endow rightful users with action powers. That is, the figurative depiction must itself be abstractly interpreted to lead to the next step. Using this Adena-based figurative depiction as their conceptual base, Carr and Case then turn to several well-known

Hopewellian items: a pipe depicting a "shaman" in "trance-flight" and a bear transforming into a human. They suggest these may also be depictions of shamans. "[T]here are two pieces of representational art that illustrate the shaman in this classic sense. . . . [One is] a pipe . . . which depicts a bird-man: a man's head with the body of a bird. The bird-man appears to be in flight . . . ; [it] quite directly depicts soul flight. Significantly, the representation is made on a smoking pipe—an implement for inducing trance states in which shamanic soul-flight is experienced. The eyes of the man are closed and his mouth is drooped, as in a trance" (2005b, 192–93). And they go on to speak of the Wray figurine, which "illustrates a human largely enveloped by the image of a bear. The hand and arms of the man are fully transformed and one with the paws and forelegs of the bear and the man's feet have a clawlike appearance. . . . [T]he bear-man could be a shaman in the role of a war leader and/or a body processor and psychopomp. As a psychopomp the bear-man would be in a state of soul flight" (2005b, 193). In each case, they claim that these items are used to refer to what they depict, namely, shamans or shaman-like persons, and therefore that they refer to shaman-like persons or shamans of one sort or another. Again, this referentialism, correlating the object of meaning of the item with the formal depiction itself, for example, this looks like a "shaman" and therefore refers to a "shaman-in-trance," avoids the expressive moment, that this depiction may be manifesting an intangible property rather than a tangible "person." This again leads them to assume that those who used these objects were also shamans and the usage was to refer to themselves as shamans or as persons occupying shaman-like roles.

The next step is even more concrete in its referentialism in that, instead of using items bearing depictions, they identify most of the artifact categories that either were actual animal parts, in whole or in modified part, or else were facsimile depictions of animals or animal parts. They then treated these as being used to refer to the associated deceased as shamans or shaman-like persons that had properties of these animals as represented by their parts; or in this case, they also recognize that the users could be "lay" persons who used these items to refer to their clan affiliations. They then moved to a more abstract level by sorting nondepictive artifact categories according to natural properties they had that, through drawing on analogy, ground their claim that these had associations with shamanic behavior. These were items consisting of special stones, minerals (such as mica and obsidian), copper, shells, and so on. All these categories had specific meanings, they claimed, because they referenced shamanic powers, that is, they referred to their users' abilities to have visions, see into the future, and so on (2005b, 199–200). In this step-by-step manner, they identified the bulk of the twenty-one categories of mortuary-related artifacts that they generated as "referencing" the deceased with whom they were directly associated as shamans or as occupying shaman-like roles in their lifetimes. Since they also treated these artifacts as marking leadership, they claim that the major portion of Ohio Hopewell leaders occupied shamanic or shaman-like roles. Indeed, they specifically deny that Ohio Hopewell had any priestly roles (except possibly late in the Middle Woodland period) and that the few nonshamanic or "secular" leadership roles were limited to possibly war and governance of the community.

THE SYMBOLIC PRAGMATIC READING

If these same items are treated as having symbolic pragmatic meaning, as expressive, presencing what they represent and thereby constituting the behaviors they are used to mediate as the types of social actions intended, and if they are also treated as reified symbols, as icons, the depictions they have should be understood as *figurative* and not literal representations of their objects and these are not tangible objects but abstract objects that are not directly perceivable. That is, they are representing abstract properties, albeit, since they are reified by the users, these properties would be experienced by the user as independently existing properties that the user is able to presence through the medium of these icons. Therefore, a beaver depiction would not represent a literal beaver nor would a shaman-like depiction necessarily represent a literal shaman. Rather, these depictions would express abstract properties that are taken to make up the spiritual world. All this means that while the engraved Adena tablets and the Wray bear-human figurine depict what to our eyes look like humans transforming, these depictions represent abstract sacred entities or powers that the culturally knowledgeable participants believed were immanent in the entities making up the sacred natural order and, therefore, enabled these entities to transform their forms into other entities, such as a bear transforming into a human. Treated in symbolic pragmatic terms, therefore, these symbols would be experienced as icons, that is, as participating in the properties and powers of what they represent, thereby serving as symbolic pragmatic devices by which their users would be endowed with the abstract but real powers of the sacred entities these represented, and, as such, these powers would be presenced in the persons so endowed. In the understanding of the users, this presencing of such abstract and potent action powers enabled them to perform specific ritual activities.

Does this interpretation lead to the same result that Carr and Case made, namely, that these users were shamans? This conclusion is certainly not entailed. Indeed, the likelihood that these items would be exclusively used by shamans is very low. First, according to their argument, this would mean that shamans were leaders of the groups responsible for this complex and monumental material cultural assemblage. However, in A. F. C. Wallace's

(1966) perspective, shamanic organization is largely a crisis-oriented, reactive organization that has little or no planning depth and the participants are largely limited to those most affected by the crisis. Furthermore, as Wallace points out, shamans did not have a monopoly on this sacred power. In an immanently sacred world, everyone had or could develop the capacity, and, indeed as I have argued, this transformative power was embodied in their flesh, bones, and even the names as sacred spirits. Everyone was reliant on assistance from a range of spirit guardians with which they would establish a human–spirit guardian relation of mutual and reciprocal obligation and trust. Shamans were known as having access to these powers, as such, because they had developed particularly powerful relations of this sort with potent beings. Therefore, using images of shamans-in-transformation might be particularly apt for constituting artifacts of power, not because the shaman is being "referenced," or more correctly stated, not because shamanism is being expressed, but because these items were taken to be expressing and therefore as participating in the particular powers that the gods possessed and that shamans and others rather regularly invoked, and, therefore, these items were potent media presencing these powers in the persons that occupied the positions that the items constituted. Alternatively, the gods themselves were often imagined as supreme shamans and, therefore, depicting a shaman-like figure would be a particularly apt figurative expression of the gods. Which particular god might be represented would be specified by one or another animal attribute, feathers for a sky god, horns for an earth god, and so on.

The spirit quest was critical to the individualistic cult and was effectively a universal practice in Native North American cultures by which young men and women would deliberately undertake a dangerous quest just so as to engage a spiritual power in a lifelong relation. This relation entailed multiple rituals undertaken by the individual deliberately to build up such protective powers. Therefore, the literalness of Carr and Case's referentialism has over-specified the nature and distribution of these human–spirit guardian power relations by labeling them "shamanic," when in fact they were very widespread, indeed, immanent in the components of the world. Hence, spiritual powers were not taken to be exclusive to shamans and, indeed, anyone who emerged as a leader did so partly because they were perceived as having great spiritual power, possibly accumulated by extraordinarily successful quests, military encounters, or even powerful dreams. Therefore, as iconic symbols, even though these items depict humans performing spiritual transformations, it does not mean either that these are depictions of shamans, per se, or that the users of these items were shamans or were occupying shaman-like positions. Furthermore, while the powers that the items were used to express and presence are critical in symbolic pragmatic usage, these powers do not alone define the social position of the user. Rather, the social position is defined and constituted by the structural relations of which it is a critical part. Hence, the same powers could be invoked by different social positions and these positions need not have been formal. Indeed, many would have been positions that most if not all normal persons as agents were expected to occupy sometime during their lifetimes. As I noted above, Wallace terms the individualistic cult as constituted by the individual who goes on a spirit quest and this quest is successful when it generates a relation that binds the individual and spirit into an ongoing reciprocity of mutual assistance and aid that usually extends over the rest of the lifetime of the individual. However, structurally, this individual quester–guardian spirit relation is of the same order as the shaman–spirit guardian relation; only the latter spirits involved were considered to be exceptionally powerful. Furthermore, in principle, the same type of symbolic item could be used by both and, therefore, a particular icon of the Adena tablet type could be used to endow a "lay person" with social powers constituting the position of leadership. Indeed, the very same item could be used to mediate a priestly position. While certain artifacts, such as copper plates and copper celts, may well constitute formal positions of leadership, and I will argue later that they did, many other items that would be appropriate as part of the ensemble of the leader could also be worn by nonleaders and, as I noted above, these could be made of exotic materials that were acquired by these individuals as part of the ordeal quests.

This critique has the very important methodological consequence that we cannot use the depictions that some artifacts bear to specifically define the type of social positions of their users. The social positions are not being referenced by these items; rather, their powers are being manifested and the same powers can be mediated by different social positions ranging from formal to auxiliary, ancillary, informal, and so on. For example, shamans and priests can have the same or at least overlapping powers and this is simply because the same agent could occupy both positions, taking on the position of priest when participating in a laity-clergy relation or as a shaman when occupying a shaman-client relation. That is, it is the nature of the social relation that determines the nature of the social position the person occupies, not the other way around. Hence, to establish the possible nature and range of social positions that would require the presencing of these powers we are forced to use other evidence. First, it is necessary to postulate what kind of social actions these possible powers could constitute; and then it is necessary to ask what kind of contexts would be necessary to constitute such social actions. I raised these points earlier. The embankment earthworks are deeply involved in mortuary practices. The organizational structure entailed by the former could not be credibly provided by shamanic cults. As noted above, shamanic cults are crisis oriented, emerging when a situation calls for a shamanic séance and the séance dissolves once performed. No planning depth is required and, in general, such a cult could not organize the type of labor that the earthworks entailed. Furthermore, if the powers represented by the artifacts participate in the powers of the cosmos, then it follows that the type of religious organization that the earthworks presuppose is an ecclesiastic-communal type, as I argue in the next chapter. Such an organization is a permanent congregation having the laity-clergy structure. Therefore, there would be two types of leadership, laity and priestly, and, as I noted earlier, the mortuary activities would be sacrificial. Hence, rather than representing shamans literally transforming into animals or spirit guardians, these items could be just as reasonably treated as representing Thunderbirds; and those using the items would be priests drawing on this power to transform the mortuary ritual into the release of spiritual powers to "feed" the celestial gods. In the case of the Wray figurine, therefore, while as an iconic symbol this item depicts a bear transforming into a human (or a human transforming into a bear), what it is representing is an abstraction. Therefore, it might be more correct to say that it represents the transformative power immanent in the cosmos, particularly, given the bear motif, probably an earth deity who is taking on a human guise in order to communicate with human souls, depicted as the human head on the lap of the bear/human figurine, and so on.

In fact, while it is important to recognize the figurative and abstract level of iconic symbolic meaning in understanding the action-constitutive nature of these artifacts, it is not particularly important to pinpoint the precise conceptual meanings that those responsible would have expressed through these iconic depictions. At least it is not important to us in order to reconstruct the social system; although, of course, it was critically important to the users to know these icons and their meanings since this knowledge included know-how, the rules of proper usage, and which icons would have particular ritual purposes. That is, it is the principle of symbolic pragmatic meaning that is important here. By treating these artifacts as expressive symbols working as interpretive media figuratively representing concepts that have abstract objects, such as spirit/human or spirit/animal transformations, and by assuming that the users reify these symbolic items, they presuppose a complex of interrelated concepts, namely, a cultural tradition, that defines a structure of powers that the entities that this conceptual paradigm articulated were believed to have, *literally*. Therefore, to the users the artifacts expressively *participated* in these very same (to them) real-but-abstract and immanent powers. By these iconic symbols presencing the sacred powers, they would constitute social positions within the responsible groups. Their legitimate users, like the persons wearing sheriff badges in our social world, would therefore be recognized as the rightful occupant of these sacred positions and as having real transformative powers endowed on them by these iconic items. This symbolic pragmatic interpretation of these figurative icons immediately eliminates the claims that Carr and Case make that restrict Ohio Hopewell to shamanic type leadership. Of course, assuming for the sake of exposition that the responsible groups were cult sodalities, then there would have been shamans; but there would also have been priests (possibly positions filled by the same persons), laity sodality chiefs, age-grade peer leaders, and so on, all of whom would require iconic symbols to endow them with this complex of leadership and nonleadership positions.

Hence, in this reading, even if it were the case that the Wray figurine, for example, represents a shaman/bear spirit transformation and was an important component of the sacred bundle of the custodian of the role that the person using it was occupying, this sacred bundle bearer need not have been either a shaman or a priest. Rather, he or she could have been a lay person occupying a specialized ritual role who, in virtue of occupying this position, was among the leaders of the cult sodality and, as such, was responsible for presiding over certain ceremonies. Similarly, a copper headdress with deer antlers could mediate a social role that was performed by an agent who was not a shaman as such. In symbolic pragmatic terms, by wearing the antler copper headdress, along with the rest of the paraphernalia that constituted the total ritual gear, the wearer actively occupied a critical performative role and thereby was endowed with the authority of the spirit-powers that were expressively presenced in the total outfit. In the understanding of the wearer and of those with whom he or she was interacting, partly in virtue of this regalia, their behaviors counted as the performance of the type of ritual event they collectively agreed upon to perform as part of the religious strategy of the cult sodality.

With one outstanding exception, essentially all the Hopewellian artifacts and related materials are found almost exclusively in association with the embankment earthworks and mounds and next to none are found in association in the sites that many have interpreted as dispersed domestic hamlets.[4] The outstanding exception is the Hopewell bladelet. I have explained this as the result of the need to avoid mixing ritual tools across the locales making up this dichotomy that partly expressed and constituted the relatively autonomous arm's-length cult sodality–clan relation. Bladelets, expediently made of selected and often exotic chert, can be used as ritual tools in both contexts and they can be immediately tossed after use, thereby discouraging curation so a person performing a ritual using the bladelet in the earthwork context, for example, will not inadvertently carry this as a used ritual tool into the domestic ritual context, or vice versa, thereby averting unwittingly polluting either context (Byers 2004, 227–39; 2006b; I elaborate on this action cue nature of the bladelet later).

CULTURAL TRADITIONS AND INTENTIONALITY

"Lurking" behind and supporting this discussion of the symbolic pragmatic view of material culture and the auxiliary action cue concept is a particular way of thinking about and characterizing cultural traditions. When archaeologists and anthropologists speak of cultural beliefs and attitudes, they often use the terms *ideology* or *world view*. Less often they might speak of the *ethos* of a people or, very commonly, the *cosmology*. All these are legitimate terms. The problem I have encountered, and surely many others have also, is that the terms seem to be used in a very loose manner, almost as if they were synonymous or, at least, were being used to refer to the same phenomenon simply from different perspectives. This is a problem because I consider these notions as defining the fundamental phenomena underwriting symbolic pragmatic meaning and, for that matter, all forms of meaning, referential and expressive (Byers 2010a, 282–86). I accept Searle's pithy definition of meaning as that which emerges when there is a difference between the forms of the signs we use and deploy and the representational content of the intentionality they express. Searle puts it quite nicely: "Meaning exists only where there is a distinction between Intentional content and the form of its externalization, and to ask for the meaning is to ask for an Intentional content that goes with the form of externalization" (1983, 28). Of course, if you know the meaning of the utterance "I promise to X," then there is no reason to ask for the "Intentional content" since you know it already. Its content is its meaning and the expression of this meaning in these terms and this social context constitutes the utterance as a promise. How does this relate to cultural traditions?

Intentionality is the key concept that Searle uses. He uses the upper case *I* in writing it. I will use the lower case. For him, intentionality is central to human meaning. As I will treat them, cultural traditions are forms of collective intentionality. A culture, for example, always has a cosmology and we can identify different cultures as having different or similar cosmologies by comparing the representational contents (i.e., intentional contents) of these cosmologies. These contents can be expressed in speech as assertions, "I believe (think, guess, speculate, and so on) that X is the case." That is, an assertive is a speech act that expresses a belief. The Euro-American cosmology and the traditional Native North American cosmologies were once very similar in one sense: they both characterized the earth as flat and stable while the sun, moon, planets, and stars rotated more or less regularly from east to west, and so on. Of course, during the last few centuries the Euro-American cosmology has radically changed into the heliocentric model with the sun believed to remain constant while the earth is believed to move around it in regular cycles. What has changed is not the way the solar system operates but the representational contents of our Western beliefs about it. They still are directed at the same phenomena, the sun, moon, earth, and so on, but they characterize their movements and physical relations quite differently. I think it is quite useful to define a cosmology in these intentionalist terms, as the total and very extensive set of collective beliefs about the nature of the world, and by collective I mean both that the beliefs are shared by a people and that part of the shared beliefs includes the assumption that most (normal) persons hold these beliefs.[5] This recursive nature is intrinsic to these collective beliefs (or more correctly in Archer's terms [2007], collective ideas) in that it is part of the property of understanding that makes up the belief. This recursiveness applies to all the structural components of a cultural tradition, and even includes qualifications. For example, ideological strategies include the awareness that there are alternative ideological strategies and that these alternatives participate in the formation of the community's overall ideological strategy. While factions X and Y are more or less equally in support of strategy M, the total group's strategy, the two define themselves partly by being aware of where each disagrees and this collective awareness leads to ongoing negotiations and competition. In this sense, a cultural tradition consisting of a collective cosmology, ethos, world view, and ideology is like a language. A language is recursive in that the act of speaking includes the assumption that those to whom one is speaking share the linguistic structures being used in speaking. This recursive property of the complex collective intentionality I refer to as cultural tradition distinguishes it from states of individual intentionality.

Intentionality is a critical property of the individual human mind. As Searle puts it: "Intentionality is that property of many mental states and events by which they are directed at or about or of objects and states of affairs in the world" (1983, 1). He goes on to exemplify this property by saying that "[i]f, for example, I have a belief, it must be a belief that such and such is the case; if I have a fear, it must be a fear of something or that something will occur; if I have a desire, it must be a desire to do something or that something should happen or be the case; if I have an intention, it must be an intention to do something." That is, intentional states are always about something. He goes on to note that he follows "a long philosophical tradition in calling this feature of directedness or aboutness 'Intentionality.'" He also notes that the term has been somewhat misused and misdefined. His intention is to put it in order. He does this by first asserting that there are four basic forms of intentionality and all these can be logically analyzed as having the same structure, what can be called psychological mode or attitude and representational content. These four basic forms of intentionality consist of beliefs, desires, perceptions, and intentions. The generic abbreviation of psychological mode/representational content is simply S(r). S(r) becomes Bel(r) for beliefs, Des(r) for desires, Per(r) for perceptions, and Int(r) for intentions, and by intentions here he means the type of intentional states that requires an action as its object of satisfaction. Again, these notations cover a range of related intentional forms. Beliefs include everything from absolute belief to speculative guessing to imaginary possibilities. Also desires can be wants, hopes, striving, or, negatively, fears, despairs, and so on. Importantly, these four forms are relatively autonomous and, therefore, cannot be reducible to each other. That is, desires are not simply a weak (or strong) intention nor are perceptions simply a form of visual beliefs, although there are interrelations, of course. But each is structurally distinct and it is this distinction that is the basis of the model of cultural traditions that I present here.

Psychological attitude, namely, "S," is the property of directedness of an intentional state while representational content (r) specifies the object that the intentional state S is about—whether a Bel(r), Des(r), Per(r), or Int(r).[6] In principle, therefore, each intentional state can be distinctive in terms of directedness but linked by having the same representational content (r). Remember, the core property of intentionality is directedness, the mode by which we mentally and physically engage with the world. The four forms of intentionality differ in terms of two types of directedness, psychological attitude and psychological or intentional causality. He metaphorically characterizes these as "direction of fit" and "direction of causality," respectively. Direction of fit refers to the direction of the mind-to-world engagement. Through our beliefs, for example, we engage with the world mentally by having mind-to-world or M → W direction of fit and by this he means that the contents of our beliefs "fit" the world. If this is a good "fit," then our beliefs are "satisfied." That is, we consider them to be true about the world. If the belief is not true, that is, its contents do not fit the way the world is, then they are false and in order to get them to fit we must change their representational contents to try to improve their fit. This notion of "satisfied" is itself an intentional concept since, of course, only an intentional being can be satisfied or unsatisfied and being in a state of "satisfaction" means that the intentional state "fits" the world or the world has come to "fit" the intentional state, depending on the direction of fit that goes along with that intentional form. For example, while beliefs have M → W direction of fit, a desire, Des(r), has the opposite world-to-mind or W → M direction of fit. For the desire X to be satisfied, the world must change or be changed so that it "fits" the desire. In this case, eating the hamburger is the condition of satisfaction of my desire to assuage my hunger. Beliefs and desires, therefore, are complementary opposites in terms of direction of fit: M → W and W → M, respectively. However, this complementary direction of fit also means that desires and beliefs cannot be collapsed into one another, even should a belief and desire have the same representational contents since they differ diametrically in the direction of fit. You cannot wish the world into changing in order to fit your beliefs; you must change your beliefs. And you cannot change your beliefs about the order of the world in order to give it an order that satisfies your desires.

Notice, however, one of the reasons the above inversion does not work is that beliefs and desires do not involve any direct material engaging with the world. I can hold beliefs without the objects of these beliefs being present and I can have desires without the objects of those desires actually being present. In this sense, beliefs and desires can exist without the exercise of intentional causality, that is, the world does not cause my beliefs, although it can certainly be an important source of beliefs, nor does my desire directly cause me to act on the world, although it can be a reason for me to act on the world. In both cases, I need to exercise other intentional states in order to materially engage with the world, these being perceptions and intentions. Take the perception, Per(r), of seeing a bird flying. If I really see a flying bird it is because of the complex material process of light reflected from the bird and impinging directly on my ocular nerve, and so on, a very complicated neurophysiological process. Without that process, however, I cannot see a flying bird and if I do but there is no bird actually causing my perceptual experience, then this is a hallucinatory perception and not a real perception. The critical factor here is causality. The object of my seeing, that is, the bird itself, is a critical causal factor in the formation of my perceptual experience. Hence, real or veridical perceiving is a causal process in which the objects of world act on the mind through the mediation of both mental and physiological senses. Again this can be expressed as world-to-mind or W → M direction. However, this is a causal directionality and Searle calls it intentional causality. Based on my discussion of beliefs and desires, intentional causality entails both physiological material causality and intentional mental causality. That is, in the moment of successfully perceiving the bird, I must apply the contents of my beliefs and desires about birds to the sensory input in order to see the object *as a bird* and, of course, this immediately means that all the beliefs and desires, values, attitudes about birds constitute the emotional and cognitive content or meaning of my perception. If my cultural beliefs inform me that birds are the messengers of the gods, then I will have a different perceptual experience of the birds flying than if my culture has collective beliefs that characterize birds as the descendants of monstrous dinosaurs! That is, in order to constitute the physiological aspect of the bird-seeing as having meaning for us, we simultaneously and quite recursively draw on our collective beliefs and desires, that is, cosmology and ethos, to constitute this sensory input as the perceptual experience it is, namely, perceiving a bird—and part of this perceptual experience includes the emotional and attitudinal aspect that we have in virtue of the type of cultural beliefs about birds that we have; and this applies to all our perceptual experiences—hearing, seeing, feeling, and so on. Therefore, while perceptions like beliefs also have M → W direction of fit, unlike beliefs, perceptions also have W → M *direction of causality.* If my culture values birds as messengers of the gods, then my visual experience of the bird will have an emotional tone of approval and wonder that it would not have if, instead, my culture identified birds with monstrous lizards and dinosaurs.

As noted above, one of the problems Searle finds with the term *intentionality* is that it is often confused with or treated as synonymous with the term *intention.* Of course there is a relation of the two since intentions are among the mental states of intentionality. However, as he points out, an intention is simply one of the four basic forms of intentionality. It is like a desire in that it entails a W → M direction of fit for the intention to be satisfied. Also, just as a desire will be satisfied if the world fits or comes to fit the representational contents of the desire, so an intention will be satisfied if the world comes to fit the representational contents of the intention. Indeed, the representational contents of Int(r) and Des(r) can be the same. If all this is the case, that is, if the direction of fit and the object that satisfies can be the same for intentions and desires, what is the difference between them? A very important difference, equivalent to the difference between beliefs and perceptions. An intention can only be fully formed if the agent actually intends to behave by way of satisfying it. That is, an intention just like a desire has W → M direction of fit, but in addition, it has intentional causality, in this case, M → W direction of causality. Therefore, to be truly said to have an intention, an agent must intend to behave in such a manner as to change the world so as to fit the representational contents of his or her intention. Of course, if he or she would like to change the world in a certain way but cannot do so, then this means that the intentional state is not an intention but a desire and, of course, it is a frustrated desire, not only because the world does not fit the desire but also because the agent cannot form the intention to act so as to satisfy the desire. That is, intentions can be formed only if the holder of the intention can realistically intend to act and the intention if formed is satisfied only if, in point of fact, the agent actually behaves in such a way as to change the world so that it comes to fit the representational contents of the agent's intentions. Hence, for the agent's intention to be satisfied the agent's own behavior must change the world so that it "fits" the contents of the actor's intention. The contents of the intentions-in-action, of course, have the status of being rules, protocols, standards that specify what behaviors must be performed—and what material devices of these behaviors must be used as warrants in order for the behaviors to count as the types of social actions the agent intended.

This way of putting it makes very clear the relation between intentions and meaning treated here in symbolic pragmatic terms. A behavior counts as a social action of a certain type when it is seen to conform to the symbolic pragmatic rules. Since the agent must do this behavior by exercising his or her intentions, we can say that intentions have M → W direction of intentional causality and, since the behavior counts as the intended action only if it and the changes in the world it brings about conform to the rule contents, then intentions, like desires, have W → M direction of fit but M → W direction of causality. It becomes clear now why perceptions and intentions can be considered as complementary intentional states. They both entail complementary directions of fit and directions of intentional causality. Perceptions have M → W direction of fit and W → M direction of causality; intentions have W → M direction of fit and M → W direction of causality. In exercising our intentions we cause ourselves to behave using the requisite range of behavioral and material forms (i.e., warrants) so as to make the world fit our intentions as stipulated by the representational contents of our intentions; and the changes we make in the world in turn cause us to perceive these changes while, at the same time, our perceptions, like beliefs, have M → W direction of fit so as to determine how and under what aspect we will perceptually experience it. Table 5.1 summarizes these four basic forms in terms of direction of fit and direction of causality. It also clarifies why these constitute four autonomous but integrated intentional states. Each has a particular M → W or W → M direction of fit, while in addition, perceptions and intentions have W → M and M → W direction of causality, respectively; and the particular combination each has makes it a relatively autonomous intentional state. I say that each is relatively autonomous because, while neither can be reduced or collapsed into the other, each is related in that no perception occurs without the contents of beliefs and desires constituting the particular meaningful nature of the perceptual experience; nor can any intention be formulated without the exercise of beliefs and desires about the world and the self-awareness of the social situation of the agent. The nature of the action and whether it is such

Table 5.1. The Structure of Intentionality

	Direction of Fit	*Direction of Intentional Causality*
Beliefs	Mind → World	None
Desires	World → Mind	None
Perceptions	Mind → World	World → Mind
Intentions	World → Mind	Mind → World

as to satisfy the intentions or not is determined by the way a person perceives her or his activity as well as perceives how it is taken to be by relevant others.

Importantly, in putting it this way, I am not saying that an intention is the cause of an action. Rather, I am saying that an intention causes a stream of behavior and this behavior is transformed into an action if it conforms to the symbolic pragmatic (cultural) rules and social prerogatives. That is, the action is an emergent phenomenon that cannot be reduced to the behavior that realizes it since the individual agent cannot force or impose on others the recognition that this behavior is the type of action the agent intends it to be. This is because relevant others will be interpreting the behavior from the perspective of the social positions they occupy and these positions are independent of but no doubt related to the social position occupied by the agent performing the behavior. So both parties are behaving and interpreting in accordance to symbolic pragmatic rules and these are collective knowledge. Therefore, as I stated above, they are recursive in that all parties are aware that "normal people" generally govern their behaviors in accordance to it.

Equally important, the relationship between beliefs and desires is symmetrical, in that all desires entail beliefs that specify what things and states of affairs exist that can be objects of desires; and all beliefs presuppose some type of emotional or attitudinal posture toward them. Similarly, perceptions and intentions are symmetrically related in that to intend to act in a certain manner entails knowing the symbolic pragmatic rules and to know that one's intention is satisfied, one needs to perceive one's behaviors as conforming to these rules. Equally important, to see another's behavior as actions of a certain sort, one needs to know the symbolic pragmatic rules in order to know the intentions that the other's behaviors are expressing, thereby seeing her or him as acting in a certain manner. However, because beliefs and desires do not have intentional causality while perceptions and intentions do, the belief-desire and perception-intention levels relate asymmetrically. One can have the standard beliefs and attitudes about deer and still not intend to hunt them; however, one can only formulate intentions to hunt deer and see deer as desirable to hunt if one already has the requisite beliefs and desires about deer, and while these beliefs and desires are always held by individuals, they are simultaneously collective beliefs in that their representational contents are recursively shared. That is, having perceptual experiences of X and intending to hunt X presuppose having the appropriate beliefs and desires concerning X; but having these beliefs and desires does not alone determine one's actions. In archaeological interpretive terms, what this means is that if we have correctly identified the residue of deer butchering, it necessarily means that those who were responsible also had the requisite beliefs about deer, their behaviors, and the requisite attitudes toward deer that made it possible to formulate the deer hunting intention.

Cultural traditions, as I treat them, have the same structure as individual beliefs, desires, perceptions, and intentions (2010a, 286–90). The important difference, as I noted above, is that they are collective forms of intentionality. By collective I mean that they are the forms of intentionality the representational contents of which are recursively shared by a population and by "recursively" I mean that part of this sharing includes awareness, usually implicit and practical, that "everyone has these beliefs, etc." Collective awareness of this sort presupposes effortless reflexivity so only populations that share this neurophysiological capacity can transform their individual intentional states into collective intentional states, namely, into cultural traditions. That is, language is a collective know-how and the act of using it presupposes awareness that others know it, even though we rarely think about this sharing as part of our language use. Often we realize the collective nature of our language usage when we are in foreign contexts where we suddenly are confronted with the problem of our utterances being understood. This very fact, however, reinforces the recognition that our intentionality is both individualistic and collective; and this means that we can typically, when needed, differentiate between collective and individual intentional states so that we are never automatons of our own cultural traditions. We can be aware of them and criticize them, choosing to act in their accordance or to deliberately resist them. In any case, under normal circumstances, we effortlessly draw and act on them. Furthermore, this difference between private/individual and collective intentional states is more than simply an awareness of their simultaneous existence in that it includes the understanding that collective intentional states always have as part of their content this sense that their representational contents are shared.

Collective intentional states have a strong sense of standardization involved. Collective beliefs can be experienced as natural and proper, thereby articulating for us the nature of the world, the cosmos. This is why I call the set of collective world beliefs cosmology. To challenge the truthfulness of the cosmology can have grave consequences. Collective desires and attitudes also take on a strong emotional content, becoming what can be termed strong values. Collective values constitute standards by which ordinary or individual desires are judged. These collective standards, values, and attitudes constitute what I term the ethos of a people and it is from the ethos that the deontic force of rules and protocols is derived. Clearly, cosmology and ethos are both structured similarly to beliefs and desires and are symmetrically related in the same way that beliefs and desires are related. The cosmology articulates the nature of the world and the ethos articulates the standards and principles that humans must follow in order to realize the truth of their cosmology. Clearly part of the cosmology and ethos includes the social beliefs and standards that characterize the social structure. I call this set of collective social beliefs and values the sociality. In an immanently sacred cosmology with its complementary custodial ethos, the social structures are considered to be largely congruent with the natural order, which is itself immanently sacred so that the sociality becomes subsumed to cosmology.

I use the term *world view* to speak of collective perceptions. This is the ongoing perceptual experiencing a people have of their world, both natural and social, in virtue of their cosmology/ethos. It is only because of their cosmology/ethos that they can have the world view they have, both natural and social. In parallel, I use the term *ideology* to speak of collective intentions. Remember, just as the representational contents of individual intentions specify the form and outcome that intentional behaviors must display and the changes they must bring about to count as the type of actions intended, so the representational contents of ideology, collective intentions, specify the form and outcomes that collective intentional behaviors must display to count as, that is, to constitute these behaviors as, the kind of social actions intended. These social actions are the conditions of satisfaction of the ideology that generated them. Since ideology is collective intentions, it is clear that we have to think of intentions as being able to exist for a time in a state of nonsatisfaction while still being full-fledged intentions. Searle calls these prior intentions, arguing that in many cases the human agent must develop a plan or strategy specifying the behavioral-action steps that must be successfully undertaken prior to the performance of the action that satisfies the prior intention. Hence, collective intentions, or ideologies, are always realized as collective strategies, a plan delineating intentional steps and procedures that must be carried out in order for the collective intentions to be fully realized in collective behaviors. Hence, I speak of ideological strategies. Building earthworks, for example, manifest and are the outcome of earthwork ideological strategies. The content of this strategy specifies the schedule of behaviors that must be carried out, including by whom and when these are to be carried out, and the material media required to perform them. Therefore, the immediate content is the set of rules and protocols that I have referred to as the symbolic pragmatics of a given ideological strategy. Of course, these strategies presuppose social organizations that embody them and the strategies they develop are effectively collective promises, commitments, to perform the sequence of activities specified by the strategies. As the representational contents of the strategies, these rules and protocols presuppose a cosmology/ethos to which the group is also committed since this set of collective beliefs/values is what makes it possible for such a strategy to be formulated.

Hence, in parallel with the four basic states of intentionality, there are four basic cultural traditions that are relatively autonomous: cosmology, ethos, world view, and ideology. Each can be explicitly characterized in terms of direction of fit while world view and ideology can also be characterized in terms of complementary direction of intentional causality. Cosmology has M → W direction of fit and ethos has W → M direction of fit; and both have no intentional causality. World view has M → W and ideology has W → M direction of fit and both have complementary intentional causality with ideology having M → W direction of causality and world view having W → M direction of causality. The world view and ideology, of course, can only be formulated and experienced because the responsible agents draw on the contents of their cosmology and ethos. This asymmetry grounds my characterizing cosmology/ethos as the *deep cultural traditions,* while world view and ideology constitute what I call the *surface cultural traditions.*

This distinction of deep/surface cultural traditions is important for archaeology since it is the basis to claim that the two levels of cultural traditions have differential continuity over space and time. For any world view to be the collective perceptual experience it is and for any ideology to be the collective strategy it is, each entails a background context of a particular cosmology/ethos complex. However, the same cosmology/ethos context can be amenable to alternative and contrasting ideologies and world views. How is this possible? Ideology and world view are the way a community engages physically with the world and while in any given instance the rules that make up the content of an ideological strategy may be reified by proponents, who treat them as being "written in the heavens," they are not. The cosmology and ethos specify the way the world is (cosmology) and generally how humans should engage with that world (ethos), and, in an important sense, despite the difference between individual and collective beliefs and desires, these beliefs and standards are treated as given by the community. However, what behaviors in the world will count as fully realizing the life way according to the shared cosmology and ethos will be subject to dispute. There can be periods of time when a community's ideological strategies retain stability; but this is often at the cost of ongoing negotiations. The rules and protocols of every ideological strategy are potentially subject to disagreement, particularly if a community consists of social groupings that have contradictory interests. What will count as a proper mortuary behavior for clans may not and probably will not count as fully felicitous in the interest of a sodality, and vice versa. This ideological conflict necessarily applies to world views also. Clans may perceptually experience earthworks as less felicitous media of mortuary activities than do sodalities. At the same time, however, both sodalities and clans share largely without any disagreement the same cosmology and ethos, each interpreting the behaviors and material media associated with the other as having problematic aspects in terms of being proper ways for humans to conduct themselves in an immanently sacred social world having a custodial ethos, an immanentist custodial sociality.

The upshot of this deep/surface structuring of cosmology-ethos/world view-ideology is that since the former is the condition that makes the formation of the latter possible, an immanentist cosmology/custodial ethos complex can retain stability over wide spatial distribution and deep temporal periods while the world view/ideology complex, being subject to negotiations and changes in the light of contradictory interests, can modify quickly. Indeed, neighboring river drainages can differ in terms of ideological strategies, each perceiving the material features that prevail in the neighboring drainage as infelicitous to one degree or another. At the same time, however, this difference presupposes the same basic cosmology/ethos complex and, indeed, it is because the two regions share this complex that they can each perceive the other as somehow transgressing it in their behaviors and material way of life. Hence, even though cultural traditions seem to be very ephemeral phenomena that have little stability, in fact, their fundamental structure enables deep and broad continuity of the cosmos/ethos complex while rather rapid variability and change in terms of ideological rules and world viewing.

I have termed this approach to cultural traditions the integrated view and it stands in contrast to what I term the fused view (Byers 2006a, 60–84; 2010a, 284–92). A fused view is one that tends to treat ideology, world view, cosmology, and ethos as more or less graded differences and this is a result of undertheorizing the nature of cultural traditions. This undertheorizing is itself a result of not fully articulating the nature of intentionality and human agency. I find that Searle's view of intentionality is very useful in this way. However, he has treated intentionality in individualistic terms. I have borrowed Charles Taylor's (1985a, 1985b, 1985c, 1985d) view that humans are self-defining animals and this is in virtue of their reflexivity or, as I have called it, their effortless reflexivity, that is, our ability to be effortlessly aware of our own states of awareness. On this basis, Taylor speaks of first-order and second-order or strong desires with the latter being standards and values that we use to assess our own first-order or individual intentions and desires. I have construed ethos in these terms, as second-order or strong values by which responsible community members assess their individual values, desires, intentions and judge them as adequate and acceptable, as honorable and worthy, or as dishonest, dishonorable, and inappropriate. The synthesis of the thought of both Taylor and Searle, therefore, underwrites my above analysis and characterization of cultural traditions.

Finally, it must be fairly clear how all this ties into the symbolic pragmatic view of the meaning of material culture since, of course, symbolic pragmatics constitute the representational contents of ideological strategies. These strategies underwrite the construction of earthworks and also specify why the earthworks were important since, according to the symbolic pragmatic/action cue view, for the mortuary behaviors to count as the types of social activities intended, that is, world renewal rituals mediated by postmortem human sacrifice, they must be performed in earthworks that display the forms that count as embodying and presencing the powers of the immanently sacred cosmos. Hence, these forms presuppose an immanentist cosmology and a custodial ethos. With the completion of this discussion of cultural traditions as collective forms of intentionality, I now turn in the next chapter to articulating the core social component of Ohio Hopewell, what I have termed the ecclesiastic-communal cult sodality.

6

The Ecclesiastic-Communal Cult Sodality Model

I noted in chapter 3 that Carr topped off his argument in support of the Tripartite Ceremonial Alliance model by asserting that it was the only model that "makes sense of their inverse pyramidal distribution of prestige; that is, for each mound, clusters with more burials also had *higher proportions of individuals* with prestigious goods. In real-life terms, larger communities were wealthier and had higher proportions of individuals with prestige. This situation is reasonable: larger communities would have had bigger labor pools for organizing public efforts and for acquiring material resources" (Carr 2005b, 295, emphasis added). I argued this point, pointing out that even if the autonomous communities of the same social nature are different in size, there is no warrant to conclude that the proportion of prestigious to nonprestigious burials would differ in favor of the larger communities. Carr probably anticipated this type of critical response because he suggests that size alone would probably generate more different types of leadership positions. I can accede that this is a possibility, but size is not the condition that would spawn new types of leadership positions in the larger communities. It would be new administrative demands and this could occur only if the relations between the larger and smaller communities were quite different from that postulated under the Tripartite Ceremonial Alliance model. This treats the allies as autonomous communities of the same type, "symbolic communities"; and, therefore, as I noted above, while the number of leadership positions may be a function of size differences, the types would be the same across the communities and the numbers would remain proportionally the same. The only way greater variety of leadership positions could emerge in the larger communities would be a function of dominance with the larger community needing more administrative persons to implement the dominance relation and this means that its greater wealth, size, and *diversity* of leadership positions would be a function of exploiting the labor of the "allies." Of course, this dominance-based social structure is the antithesis of the structural relation postulated under the Tripartite Ceremonial Alliance model, and this empirical contradiction of the basic premises of the Tripartite Ceremonial Alliance model falsifies it.

I then presented an alternative account of these same burial data, arguing that, in fact, in principle there is a type of preindustrial social organization that could generate this type of "inverse pyramidal distribution of prestige" while not being exploitative. This pattern is consistent with the type of cult sodalities that I have postulated would ally with one another, thereby generating cult sodality heterarchies. I have postulated that such mutualistic heterarchies were responsible for the embankment earthworks and their associated mortuary structures, which under this view I will now term "renewal lodges," a term that is consistent with the nature of the ceremonialism I postulate they performed. As I also noted in chapter 4 the Mourning/World Renewal Mortuary model (Byers 2004, 177–190; 2006a) is a critical component of my modeling of the Ohio Middle Woodland and, therefore, it ties into the cult sodality notion since the central purpose of these sodality organizations was to perform world renewal rituals, many but not all of which would be through the medium of sacred games integrated with human mortuary practices, as I more fully elucidate in part 2.

PERSONAL NAMES AND SOCIAL STRUCTURE

I want to be quite clear here. Using the concepts I have so far developed, while the core of the Ohio Middle Woodland period complementary heterarchical community in the bifurcated settlement articulation modal posture was the dual clan/sodality structural axis, the contrasting complementary cultural principles that underwrote this structure manifests the complementary principles of kinship and companionship. These two cultural concepts are internally related. By this I mean that kinship is defined in complementary contrast to companionship. Kinship is what companionship is not, and vice versa, and when these principles are realized in social groupings, they constitute two relatively autonomous social spheres. This means that, in the typical complementary heterarchical community, most individuals during their life cycles actively participated in both spheres while keeping their activities in each more or less apart. One of the ways this would be done might be through personal names. The traditional historic Eastern Woodland Native American communities considered the naming of newborns to be a critical rite of passage. Typically, early in its life, often not too long after birth, the infant or even neonate would be named by the custodian of the names of his or her clan. These names were specific to a given clan and naming the infant endowed him or her with clan membership. However, there are known cases in which the custodian of names did not endow names of one of the parent's clans, but the names of a nonclan group and, in fact, those who share names derived from the same source, often an animal, have been termed in anthropology "name groups." The offspring of a couple would be carefully distributed among the different name groups of a community so that (1) no offspring belonged to the parents' name groups and (2) no two siblings were members of the same name group (Voegelin and Voegelin 1937, 617). Hence, while the naming was instigated by the parents, the names ensured that the offspring were connected to non-kin groups and each group was integrated by sharing names from the eponym of the group. As noted above, the eponym of the group was usually an animal or some other natural phenomenon and each name expressed some aspect of that phenomenon. That is, such name groups could be said to have been totems, but these would be non-kinship-based totems.

Hence, it is also possible that the same community could have both clans and name groups, each bearing totems. Indeed, the same animal or natural phenomenon could be used as the totems for the two different types of groups, clans and name groups. Clearly, the former would be kinship based, usually either matrilateral or patrilateral according to the filiation rules of the culture, while the latter would be companionship based. In the case of companionship-based groups, all names were related to the same eponymous phenomenon and, therefore, the members were "related" through their names articulating different properties of the same phenomenon. Hence, individuals collectively sharing names derived from the same "totem" constituted the name group. The name group was also internally structured by age and gender so that it would be sectored into male and female "moieties" and each would be sectored as age-sets and these were hierarchically organized by seniority. It is reported, in fact, that for the historic Shawnee, the name group was the context of the most agreeable and enjoyable of social activities. Thomas Wildcat Alford, a prominent Oklahoma Shawnee religious leader, reports the following. "There are six branches of Um-so-ma [name groups] . . . which is a kind of social clanship existing between members of the Shawnee tribe. When a child is named he automatically belongs to the same Um-so-ma as the person who named him. The comradeship and partisanship existing between members of the same Um-so-ma is outstanding, and the cause of much rivalry and much innocent fun. It is not to be confused however with the tribal clan divisions which constitute the government of the tribe" (1936, 3n). He further characterizes the name groups or Um-so-ma and the nature of the companionship that flourished in them while clearly distinguishing these from the clan. "The comradeship or partisanship existing between those of the same branch was outstanding, and it meant a delightful feeling of kinship or intimacy, a kind of fellowship which afforded much merriment and innocent fun among both old and young. There were many jokes, always against or at the expense of those who belonged to other branches of the Um-so-ma, though nothing sordid or vulgar ever entered into this fun" (1936, 52–53).[1] A similar practice occurred among the Pueblo, in this case the parents assigning their children to sodalities that were separate from their own sodalities (Smith 1983, 34–35).

There is some indication supporting the claim that the Shawnee name group system emerged and replaced the Shawnee clan system as a result of the great social and physical disorder that the Shawnee suffered in the 1700s and 1800s. Of course, if this claim is correct, it suggests that the traditional social structure consisted of clans while the name group only emerged with the dissipation of the clan system. However, I am not at all sure that any replacement actually occurred. It is just as likely that both systems were in operation prior to the debilitating confrontation between the Shawnees and the Euro-American communities and, as a result of the extreme disorder that this encounter created, the clan system became disarrayed and the name group system became much more noticeable. In any case, the important point I am making here is that even in those social systems known to have a strong clan structure, such as the Shawnee during their historic (and probably prehistoric) occupation of different zones in the Central Ohio Valley, there were also other strongly constituted non-kinship groups, such as the name group system, that existed and this would have been a type of sodality. Indeed, another way of speaking of the type of age-grade sodality that I postulate for the Ohio Middle Woodland period could be to characterize it as a name group sodality based on an enabling hierarchy organized by seniority of age-sets. This would mean that an individual would bear two personal names, one used in the kinship context and the other in the sodality context. The two systems might also have complementary constitutive symbols such that an individual would wear two totems, one invoking the protective powers of his or her clan's eponymous sacred guardian, for example, the wolf, and the other, the powers of his or her name group's or sodality's eponymous sacred guardian, for example, the panther.

Now, when the complementary heterarchical communities of a region were in the integrated settlement articulation modal posture, these two organizations would probably share to a significant degree the same ritual spaces and activities of the community, although there could also be a certain degree of duplicating of the locales. In any case, to the outsider the two parallel organizations might go unperceived, particularly if the outsider is from a society that had very different cultural traditions, such as the Euro-American societies. However, should the same set of regional communities move into a bifurcated posture, the name groups would become much more visible and it would be the clans that would tend to become somewhat invisible. This is because the latter would continue to be embedded in the domestic kin groups and since these would be dispersed and, in most cases, sufficient for only nuclear and possibly small extended families, the formation of clan-based ritual would tend to simply recruit these family spaces for this purpose. The clan leader's current dwelling locale might be a little larger and more complex than the dwellings of the ordinary members, but there would be no major material or formal differentiation. In contrast, the name group sodalities or the same-age/same-sex sodalities would constitute themselves into the cult sodalities noted above and through alliances would be able to construct major sacred spaces and places. These would be the type of organizations responsible for the Ohio Hopewell earthworks.

I am not claiming here that the Ohio Hopewell cult sodalities were, in fact, prehistoric versions of the historic name groups. What I am saying is that this is one possible way that this type of cult sodality organization could emerge, not as a new form of organization but as a traditional form that becomes disembedded from an integrated village structure in which clan and name groups shared ritual spaces and locales. One possible way that this disembedding could occur is if the complementary heterarchical communities of a region, initially in the integrated settlement articulation modal posture, consensually decided to shift into a bifurcated settlement articulation modal posture. Therefore, a variety of sodalities could be the basis for the emergence from preexisting sodalities, such as name group sodalities, same-age/same-sex sodalities, shared expertise sodalities, such as same artisan know-how (drum artisan sodalities), same spiritual powers sodalities (shamanic or medicine cults), and so on, into what I have termed the *ecclesiastic-communal cult sodality structure.*

The important overall point here is that the two principles of kinship and companionship would emerge in complementary organizational structures that sustained arm's-length spatial and formal structural relations. By this I mean that the companionship-based groups would likely actively distance and differentiate themselves from the kinship-based groups to which the latter also belonged by physically distancing their aggregation locales and monopolizing responsibility for a range of social activities that they performed on behalf of the total community. The spatial separation of formally different locales and the specialized tasks that the sodalities took on maximized the relative autonomy in which the two complementary groups stood to each other. These material expressions of the relative autonomy of the two can be interpreted as embodying the sodality-clan arm's-length relation. I have already postulated under the deontic ecological perspective what the conditions may have been that promoted this bifurcated posture since, in an immanently sacred world, with intensification of subsistence and of a tendency toward "settling down" emerging, the need to enhance world renewal rituals while sustaining a dispersed distribution of population to the greatest degree practicable would promote the formation of the bifurcated settlement articulation mode. In these circumstances, the preexisting autonomous age-set sodalities of a given complementary heterarchical community would tend to organize themselves hierarchically by age seniority. This emergent group would likely recruit local shamans as religious specialists. As soon as this relation becomes stabilized, a new organizational complex emerged, one that transformed the age-sets into seniority-ranked laity and transformed the shamans into clergy, namely, the laity-clergy structure. This is what I have termed the *ecclesiastic-communal cult sodality* (Byers 1996, 185–90; 2004, 269–78; 2006a, 122–32).[2] With the emergence of ecclesiastic-communal cult sodalities occurring across communities and each being relatively autonomous of the clans of their respective communities, and since all the communities were experiencing the same ecological stresses, the cult sodalities would share common concerns for innovating and expanding world renewal rituals. This would promote allying, thereby generating world renewal ecclesiastic-communal cult sodality heterarchies.

Let me clarify this. While initially the relation between the age-set and shaman was simply the classical client-shaman séance relation of a shamanic cult, with the stabilization of this relation a new, more formal and permanent social context necessarily emerges as with each component party, junior and senior laity and clergy, having distinct rights and duties vis-à-vis the other. Probably no one planned this emergence such that the shaman took on rights and duties characteristic of a priestly or clergy office, or that the age-set companions necessarily complemented this official position by becoming laity members. And, of course, many of the same religious behavioral routines associated with the shaman and client interaction would have remained largely unchanged; but sustaining this context for a while would institutionalize it. The emergent religious office could be characterized as the shamanic-priest position. Once this laity-clergy structure emerges, the total organization becomes a congregation, this being a religious group based on the laity-clergy structure. In this case, I have postulated that the laity would be structured hierarchically into senior and junior age-grades and each grade would be further structured by relative seniority into age-sets.[3] Importantly, while a new organization emerges, it reproduces the core cultural ethos principles and, in this case, it would be underscored by the principle of agentive autonomy. Therefore, even though the laity was based on age-sets and/or name-sets hierarchically organized by seniority, this would constitute an enabling hierarchy in which each level retained its autonomy, that is, responsibility for its own actions. This autonomy applies also to both the laity and clergy positions. Hence, each sector—laity structured as junior age-grade/senior age-grade, and clergy—is recognized as responsible for its own activities and these are allocated by traditional rule-governed procedures so that each sector has a range of tasks, articulated into ritual practices, particular to it and which the other sectors cannot carry out without transgressing the principle of autonomy. For this reason, the governance of the congregation is based on consensus. As I discuss later, these tasks are not simply traditional, although this is part of the mode of distribution. They are also ritualized and, therefore, have built-in usufruct rules that enable only that age-set to perform those rituals. I discuss this in more detail later.

The outline of this hierarchical structure was presented in my earlier book on the Ohio Hopewell episode, only I referred to the hierarchical order of the age-sets and age-grades as manifesting a stratified egalitarianism (Byers 2004, 297). Careful rethinking of this theoretical elucidation convinced me that the critical property was not equality but autonomy differentiated by ranking and by its nature this manifests *inequality or systematic differentiation* along the rank dimension, for example, age or seniority. However, as I noted in chapter 1, even though differentiation and inequality are embedded in the hierarchical structure, the principle of agentive autonomy (for both the person and the group) prevents this inequality and differentiation from translating into dominance of one agent, either person or group, over another. For example, while it allows for and indeed promotes unequal distribution of material wealth, this inequality must respect the principle of autonomy and this translates into generating a distribution that must remain proportional to the duties and obligations of the different positions that the membership occupies in terms of their age-set or expertise, thereby constituting the differential distribution as the expression of an *equitable* distribution of resources and labor, given the needs the recipients have to fulfill their different responsibilities. Hence, an enabling hierarchy recognizes differences while respecting material needs through equitable distribution of material resources, including the labor resources available to each age-set, given its size, age, expertise, physical capacity, and so on. This is why I have suggested that governance and decision making must be by consensus. Most importantly for understanding the Ohio Hopewell episode, in particular the monumental architecture, such an organization has structural permanence having both rules of promotion and cycling of the age-sets and a division of tasks for both laity and clergy leaders.

I suggest that this type of organization has the planning depth and capacity that is necessary for such monumental architecture to exist; and, of course, if it has a mission that embraces universal concerns, such as world renewal, then it would be very capable of producing these architectural features if its membership was convinced that the latter were iconic warrants enabling it to perform activities by which the sodality's obligations could be regularly and systematically discharged and its collective duties fulfilled.

As I noted earlier, because the postulated ecclesiastic-communal cult sodality would be based on the principle of companionship and the dispersed habitations would be based on the principle of kinship, and both would respect the principle of agentive autonomy, the two organizational types would stand to each other as relatively autonomous and this standing would be marked and constituted by the maintenance of two systems of locales: the cult sodality locales and the clan-based habitation locales, probably both dispersed, as I discuss in detail later. As I noted in chapter 2, these properties of relative and mutualistic autonomy are precisely the social properties that are *absent* from the Multiple Community model, and therefore, in my view, it is unable to characterize the "symbolic communities" as being structurally different social groupings from the "residential communities." Hence, the two "communities" are not autonomous but simply quantitatively disaggregated and aggregated, respectively, with the total set of residential communities adding up as the local symbolic community. The principle of exclusive territorialism is maintained but collectivized as a kinship-based corporate proprietorship and, as I noted earlier, the consequence is that the Multiple Community model reduces to being another type of Monistic Modular Polity Community model. My analysis of the Tripartite Ceremonial Alliance model illustrates this quite well. The latter fails to recognize that there is any autonomy between the residential and the local symbolic communities and, instead, treats the embankment earthworks as the civic centers of the kinship-based residential communities dispersed in the surrounding zones, in this case, as civic centers of the individual local symbolic communities that, nevertheless, allocate mortuary spaces in their centers that are dedicated to each other. The alliance of "local symbolic communities," that is, the "regional symbolic community," then, is simply the aggregation of these three communities. It then adds further to this mischaracterization by claiming that, despite being essentially kinship-based in nature, implicating kinship-rooted leadership, the leadership of these communities was for the most part by shamans or shamanic-like leaders.

In theorizing the ecclesiastic-communal cult sodality I have found Wallace's (1966, 84–88) theory of cults to be extremely useful. His theory characterizes the religious system of a community in terms of the combination of types of cult organizations that characterizes it. I will not summarize that larger part of his theory since it is his distinguishing among types of cults that is important for my purposes. However, as I discuss shortly, there are two problems I have with his overall theory. The first is that he frames his discussion of cults within a larger theory of the nature of societies and for him this theory is strongly underpinned by the same premises I have critically noted characterize the Monistic Modular Polity model. For him, the modular state is the evolutionary goal of simple chiefdoms and tribes. It may be for this reason that he is unable to speak in terms of, much less think about, ecclesiastic-type cults as preexisting states or, at least, complex chiefdoms. Second, he seems to equivocate between defining "cult" in behavioral terms, that is, specific types of religious behaviors, or social structural terms. I have focused on social structure as critical since, in my view, it is the social context of a person's behavior that constitutes the latter behavior as the type of social action it is (e.g., religious or cultic) and this means characterizing the particular nature of the social relations and positions, for example, as religious or economic or political or some combination.

In this regard, I constructed the term *ecclesiastic-communal* to characterize the type of cult sodality that I postulate generated the Ohio Hopewell episode by combining attributes of two different cult types that Wallace defined separately: the communal cult and the ecclesiastical cult. For him the ecclesiastical cult is characterized by the laity-clergy structure and, therefore, it was a congregation. The communal cult, however, lacked the laity-clergy structure and, therefore, it did not form as a congregation, as such. Rather it was the religious posture of a communal organization, such as a sodality or a clan. That is, a clan could undertake the duty to perform a religious ritual and to do so it would "move" into its religious posture, constituting itself as a communal cult for the duration of that event.[4] The same could be done by a sodality. In each case according to Wallace, the clan or sodality would typically contract a shaman to supply the specialized ritual powers required. When the ritual was completed, the shaman was given a gift and thanked. The clan or sodality, depending on which group was performing the ritual, would then shift back into its nonreligious posture of being a clan or a sodality.

Wallace speaks of four types of cults: individualistic, shamanic, communal, and ecclesiastical. For him the evolutionary dividing line came between communal and ecclesiastical cult since the latter had a laity-clergy structure and stood as a permanent congregation, while the first three were much more situation dependent, each emerging as a religious posture. The individual would elicit a spirit guardian and go into a self-induced séance, constituting the individualist cult posture. The shaman might do the same, in which case he or she also was in the individualistic cult posture. But he or she could also be called on by a family, for example, to cure a sick relative. The shaman and the family would go into the shamanic cult religious posture, a séance, with the shaman invoking his or her powerful guardian spirits so as to cure the sick client. As I noted above, the shaman could also be contracted by a communal group, such as a sodality, to assist it in performing specialized ritual.

Only with the ecclesiastical cult, however, does this ad hoc situation dependency not apply. Instead, the cult was permanent and autonomous and, as far as Wallace was concerned, this permanency and autonomy was only possible in complex societies, such as chiefdoms and states. This implies that for Wallace the emergence of the ecclesiastical cult type was a social evolutionary achievement. As I noted above, I think this is a mistake, however. In fact, it is clear from his own writing that he treated the Native North American community as a monistic modular polity having exclusive territories, even though he recognized sodalities. Of course, many of the historic communities he studied were in the integrated settlement articulation modal posture and this condition would likely suppress the formation of congregation-based cults. However, this would not be the case if the communities were in a bifurcated posture. I postulate that in the latter case, another type of cult organization would likely emerge, and this is what I have termed the ecclesiastic-communal cult sodality.[5] Hence, in a bifurcated posture, while the communal cult would persist as the religious posture of kinship groups, particularly clans, the ecclesiastic-communal cult would be the normal religious posture for the sodality. Hence, this would embody both the laity-clergy structure and the communal sodality structure, generating what I have termed the ecclesiastic-communal cult sodality; I postulate that it is only if this type of organizational structure existed would the planning depth and organizational scope exist to make the Ohio Hopewell monumentalism possible.

Of course, I am not claiming that shamanism was unimportant in the Middle Woodland period. No doubt individuals occupying the priestly position could also shift into the shamanic position should a crisis emerge requiring a "private" or kinship-based séance session. That is, the same agent could occupy both positions, but not at the same time. I do not accept that positions such as "shaman" or "priest" can be defined in terms of the behaviors each performs. Rather, the nature of the positions and the relations that link these positions, that is, the social structures, are constitutive of the action nature of the behaviors that the incumbents perform, not the other way around. Hence, two persons standing to each other as shaman and client and two persons standing to each other as priest and lay person could perform what amounts to objectively the very same formal behavioral stream; but the former would be counted as a shamanic ritual séance and the latter as a priestly ritual. This claim is grounded on the symbolic pragmatic view, which hinges on what I have termed the behavior/action duality. As I noted earlier, an action is emergent from intentional behaviors performed through the medium of a social position and within a recognized social context. In these terms, therefore, both priests and shamans could perform objectively the same behaviors, while the behaviors of each would constitute different types of ritual activities; and, indeed, as I noted above, the same person could occupy these different positions at different times and in different contexts. The contexts are cultic so that the relations linking the positions of shaman and her or his clients constitute the mutual behaviors as a shamanic cult ritual, a séance, and the relations linking the positions of priest and her or his laity constitute their mutual behaviors as an ecclesiastical or as an ecclesiastic-communal cult sodality rite, for example, a world renewal ritual.

Since the emergent Ohio Hopewell cult sodality organization would have been constituted by a preexisting sodality and one or more preexisting shamans taking on mutual commitments, a type of "collective promise," this collective agreement would count as transforming the two parties into a new social organization based on the emergent laity-clergy relation. This is the structure that constitutes an ecclesiastical cult, according to Wallace. However, since the internal structure of the laity retained its original communal sodality hierarchy and the two sectors, clergy and laity, retained autonomy for their respective activities, then I chose to call this organization an ecclesiastic-communal cult sodality. The laity-clergy structure could have, and most likely would have, emerged even before native terms were developed that could be used to distinguish between these two social positions. However, equivalents for these terms would necessarily emerge since using the established term designating a shaman would implicate the latter as nonmembers of the sodality organization. As such, the nonshamanic members of the sodality would need to be treated as simply traditional "clients" of a given shaman. As I noted above, the shaman-client relation is situation dependent and it is invoked, often but not always, in situations of crisis so that when the needs of the client are resolved by the shamanic séance, the shamanic cult posture is dissolved and the parties return to their everyday social standings. As long as the same terms for shaman and client were to be used by an emergent ecclesiastic-communal cult sodality, this understanding and experience would be generated every time the newly emergent priests were called upon to perform their ritual. Therefore, unless terms emerged that would express the emergent relation, it would suppress as well as oppress the interaction between participants in the two categories. This would cause an ongoing cognitive dissonance that would generate considerable tension and avoidance in the affairs of the cult sodality. Such tension would transform into mutual avoidance and this would also feed back to undermine and weaken the bonds of cooperation between the junior and senior age-grade sodality components.

As I noted when elucidating the symbolic pragmatic view, the symbols are experienced as powerful transformative devices, and this is the case even when these symbols are words. Hence the meaning of social symbols, such as the words used to express the social structural concepts of "companion" and "shaman," are partly constitutive of the social world they mediate, and, therefore, in their experience, this representational meaning is partly constitutive of the social property it is used to articulate. The relation that the user of the term will have with the subject being addressed by the term will be strongly based on that meaning. Clearly, old terms expressing properties of a shamanic nature must be modified or new ones innovated. A common way this may occur is to use the old terms in the new situation while adding a verbal marker indicating a figurative but serious (i.e., nonpretend) use. For example, the Hidatsa term for companion is *irakúu.* Two *irakúu* from different age-sets, one senior to the other, will address each other as *irakúu* "father" and *irakúu* "son," using the Hidatsa kin terms in conjunction with the traditional term for *irakúu. Irakúu* recognize each other as being of the same age-set so that, even if one is older than the other, the difference in age, possibly only one or two years, is considered inconsequential. However, the age difference between age-sets of the same age-grade generation can be five to ten years and this means that the age seniority makes a difference. Two individuals from senior and junior age-sets of the same generation cannot, therefore, relate as *irakúu* "brothers." The additions of the kin terms "father" and "son" mark and constitute the total phrase as figurative, but it constitutes the relation as having a real difference in seniority. The deliberate use of the two terms will constitute a social context for interacting in ways that combine the autonomy and mutual respect between *irakúu* and the respect a junior is obliged to have for a senior relative, for example, a senior and junior brother. This usage both articulates and reproduces an *irakúu* relation that is different from the standard *irakúu* relation but is still similar in that it is not to be counted as a kin relationship.

I would suggest that something along these lines could occur so as to facilitate the transformation of the preexisting position of shaman into an emergent position of priest. Since the context of the transformation is a sodality, itself an organization firmly grounded on the *irakúu* principle (the principle of companionship), this would logically occur by coupling the standard local term equivalent to the Hidatsa notion of *irakúu* with the standard local term for "shaman," for example, *irakúu* shaman. This "contradiction" (i.e., the shaman here is serving the needs not of a "client" but of an *irakúu* laity group) transforms the standard understanding of the religious positional term *shaman* into being a special type of religious position, an "*irakúu*-shaman," which could be interpreted in English as something akin to the notion of "priest." While persons occupying this *irakúu*-shaman position have sacred properties associated with shamans, they no longer interact with the sodality members as shamans but as *irakúu*-shamans and the rituals they perform are no longer directed to specific needs of individuals as clients but to the collective needs of the *irakúu* sodality. And, of course, this emergent *irakúu*-shaman or priest position transforms the complementary *irakúu* clients (i.e., the regular companions) into a set of *irakúu* who are different from those *irakúu* of sodalities in which there are no recognized *irakúu*-shamans. The difference might be constituted by the addition of some other marker to the traditional *irakúu* term that invokes the spiritual nature in keeping with the religious nature of this emergent congregation, for example, "*irakúu*-quester." That is, both the *irakúu* client and the shaman positions mutually transform into the *irakúu* quester–*irakúu* shaman relation, that is, the laity-clergy relation.

Of course, the transformation of the linguistic markers does not occur independently of the transformation of the material cultural symbolic markers. The traditional marker of an Early Woodland shaman might have been his or her kit of slate tablets with hematite pieces by which he or she elicited the powers of the different deities with which he or she intentionally interacted to effect the desired outcome (Dragoo 1963). It would take little modification of the latter tablets to re-form them into the type of iconic action cue, or enabling warrant, that elicits the powers of the gods that would be of particular interest to world renewal cult sodalities. Hence, an Adena ochre-producing tablet could be prepared according to traditional procedures but with the addition of symmetry so as to serve as a firm basis for engraving an iconic image. This image may be a careful rendition of what knowledgeable others would interpret as the sacred tree of the world that sustains the four quarters and three strata of the cosmos. The gods of the different strata and quarters may be depicted in bird forms having human-like faces. These instruments of action-constitutive power would be conventionally identified with the emergent ecclesiastic-communal cult sodality and exclusively kept under the custodial care of the emergent *irakúu*-shaman (clergy) group. When using or wearing this tablet, the person cues others who recognize him or her as occupying the now established position of *irakúu*-shaman and the standard *irakúu*-shaman term would likely be modified so as to include an allusion to this ocher-mediated action while bearing the powers that only the person using it has the right to exercise for the group, for example, he is called the "tablet-bearing *irakúu*-shaman." Hence, when called upon or even when talked about in his absence, the "tablet-bearing-*irakúu*-shaman" becomes one word and defines a person who occupies a position that is distinct from that of the ordinary *irakúu*-shaman, and so on.

Importantly, this does not limit elaborate symbolic pragmatic warrants to the emergent priestly group since, of course, the regular members have also taken on a special religious position since they are now "*irakúu*-questers," that is, those companions having *irakúu*-shamans as their sacred companions and, as such, they also have legitimate access to the same range of powerful properties as the *irakúu*-shamans, albeit these properties will be carefully defined and allocated as being appropriate for "laity," *irakúu*-questers, to perform. Hence the *irakúu*-questers constituting the laity and the *irakúu*-shamans, or the priests, constituting the clergy will share in the performance of rituals. This would also mean that as part of the entrenchment of the emergent ecclesiastic-communal cult sodality, a proliferation of specialization of tasks would emerge, distributed according to seniority of age-sets and between laity and clergy sectors, all requiring material symbols that differentiate and constitute the positions. A range of sequentially generated mortuary behaviors would proliferate as different types of world renewal rituals and important material components mediating these rituals would be the custodial regalia of clergy and laity leadership, as well as a range of lesser ritual artifacts.

While the ecclesiastic-communal cult sodality would be a new, emergent form of organization, the deep structures that underwrote it would be largely unmodified. Hence, the autonomous age-set of companions or *irakúu* age-set would constitute its core component. This autonomous age-set would reciprocally recognize other age-sets as being autonomous, as being responsible for their own specific tasks and activities. These activities would be entrenched in the particular rituals or parts of larger rituals that each age-set was responsible to perform. As autonomous groups, each age-set would have its own assemblage of symbolic pragmatic warrants whereby it was able to perform actions that would discharge its collective duties and obligations within the context of the sodality. Since an age-set was based on autonomous agents having equivalent properties, namely, same-age/same-gender, it necessarily recognized that seniority was a critical boundary condition of its own autonomy. Since senior and junior age-sets treated one another as autonomous, they would respect each other's sphere of activities within the sodality. Structuring the age-set by seniority, of course, would entail a hierarchy based on the differentiation of age seniority. However, this hierarchy could not be the basis of dominance by seniority since this would mean that the autonomy of a junior age-set could be transgressed by a senior age-set. If this were normatively possible, then the principle of autonomy would itself be curtailed and in its place would be dominance. Each higher level would be dominant over the lower level. Above, I termed the former an enabling hierarchy and I have termed the latter a dominance hierarchy (Byers 2006a, 129). In an enabling hierarchy, while each level is autonomous, namely, responsible for its specific sphere of activity, the levels are interdependent since the performance of the activities of each level requires that all perform their own specific activities. That is, any given age-set is able to felicitously perform its own activities only if the other sets also perform theirs. As I noted earlier, the important implication of this enabling hierarchy structure is that governance of the cult sodality is carried out under the operating principle of consensus. All participating age-sets must consent to a collective activity for the latter to be fully felicitously performed.

Also, to repeat, autonomy applies equally to the two sectors, laity and clergy. These are linked equitably. In certain endeavors, the clergy will have enabling prerogatives and in others the laity will. This difference can be properly termed a balanced equitability of task distribution, each sector having responsibility for the tasks identified with it and, therefore, being ranked in terms of prerogatives in initiating collective activities by being able to call on the other sectors that have by consensus agreed to give assistance in order to discharge those tasks. I would contrast the junior age-grade/senior age-grade laity structure and the laity-clergy structure as vertical and horizontal structures, with the former constituted as an enabling hierarchy and the latter as a sequential hierarchy, also sometimes termed a horizontal hierarchy. Since the prevailing principles underwriting the total organization are companionship and autonomy, this would constitute a *mutualistic heterarchy.* Importantly, this total organizational structure allows for differential distribution of resources across the institution. This will translate into measured or balanced differential distribution of resources, depending on the type of resources being distributed and the needs of the groups that these fulfill, namely, equitable distribution. This means, of course, that it does not allow for inequitable distribution of resources, this being the hallmark of dominance-based hierarchical organizations. The higher the level in the dominance hierarchy, the proportionately greater the concentration of resources. This, of course, is what Carr was alluding to when he concluded that the wealthier communities would have proportionately greater concentrations and a greater diversity of prestigious leadership positions and persons than the less wealthy communities in the "alliance." This entails a dominance hierarchy and translates into poverty or inequitable wealth distribution to the smaller communities, that is, lower levels, a state of distribution that not only is inequitable but often translates into crippling life chances of those occupying these levels.

By equitable, therefore, I mean the tendency for the resources to be distributed in realistic proportion to the responsibilities of the autonomous constituent components. In this case, following the same logic, since the units are autonomous, the responsibilities would be distributed according to the particular capacities of the agents making them up. Hence, the junior age-sets, being the most robust members, would be expected to provide the hard labor and they would receive the prestige as well as sacred burden associated with this labor. The ritual tasks they would perform would be built into the labor, such as constructing the earthworks. The behavioral labor of heavy construction would be evaluated as both necessary and polluting. It would be necessary since the earthworks would be perceived as monumental iconic warrants making the collective behaviors carried out in their contexts count as the range of world renewal rituals intended. However, their very construction disturbed the sacred natural order and, therefore, this material behavior would have a polluting consequence. I have argued that since the earthworks embodied the sacred properties of the cosmos, it follows that the pollution caused by their construction would not adhere to the earthworks but to those who built them. Hence, a personal sacrifice would be necessary, that is, taking on the burden of pollution that would be caused by building them. Individuals involved in building, therefore, would become personally polluted and they in turn would be reliant on the priests who would be empowered to perform the cleansing rituals by which the younger age-sets would eliminate or reduce their pollution load. Another source of rectification would be to go on vision quests, and so on. The priests, of course, would have the duty to rectify and sanctify and, therefore, their material intercessions would have the opposite outcome of the younger age-sets; they would be sanctifiers. In short, the different sectors and the hierarchically structured components would be identified with different types of labor: menial and self-polluting to esteemed and world sanctifying.

Hence, we could expect a variable distribution of warranting resources across the different sectors. In particular the laity would be divided into senior and junior age-grades and these two would be internally structured into age-sets according to relative age; and the division of labor of the laity would be distributed and marked by esteemed and mundane symbolic pragmatic enabling warrants. In keeping with the principle of agentive autonomy, each age-set would select peer leaders from among themselves. Hence, each age-set would have one or two peer leaders with their recognized enabling warrants by which the age-set would be empowered to perform its collective activities in order to discharge sacred duties. These warrants would make up the range of Ohio Hopewell artifact categories that are the hallmark of the episode. Of course, many of the categories would not be official or formal warrants but, instead, the type of material action cues that expressed the general standing of the wearers in the sodality and enabled them to manifest their respect for each other and the actions they were performing. These would be Ohio Hopewellian action cues by which the participants were able to manifest the sincerity of their intentions and their respect for the ritual events, thereby doing "their part" to ensure the reputation and honor of the sodality.

The more formal action cues, the enabling warrants, were likely constitutive of the age-set leadership and these might be accumulated by the peer leaders of each age-set as their age-set moved through the promotion process, each defining different action powers. I have termed these powerful enabling warrants the custodial regalia since those who were responsible for them were the custodians and they served as focal enabling warrants. By this I mean material things that the symbolic pragmatic rules specified were necessary for the behaviors the age-set performed to count as the type of collective activity they intended. I have treated the nonfocal or lesser action cue items of the age-set as individual personality. These are auxiliary items as contrasted to focal items. The latter empowered the age-set through its peer leaders; the former empowered individual wearers to participate with pride and mutual respect in the set of activities and rituals that were characteristic of that age-set. The custodial regalia would probably bear names and require rituals of transfer or decommissioning at the death of their custodians. I discuss this in considerably more detail later since the acquisition and transfer of custodial regalia also constituted the acquisition and transfer of the range of ritual prerogatives that these items mediated (Byers 2004, 255–67, 272–77). I postulate that it was interactions within and among organizations of this ecclesiastic-communal cult sodality type that are manifested in the mortuary deposits of the various major and lesser renewal lodges.

In these terms, then, the complementary heterarchical communities of this region would have continued to sustain the bifurcated settlement articulation modal posture established in the Early Woodland. While the ritual locales of the later Early Woodland constituted the Adena ceremonial network of autonomous senior age-grade and junior age-grade communal cult sodalities, it was the emergence of the ecclesiastic-communal cult sodality that transformed many of the preexisting Ohio Adena ritual locales into Ohio Hopewell locales so that, while this region continued in the bifurcated modal posture in conditions of intensified settlement and subsistence practices, the ceremonial locales came to be much larger than those of the Adena roots from which they emerged (I discuss this in more detail in the closing chapter). This caused a corresponding shift in the settlement distribution of the population. From a widespread distribution of population in the Early Woodland across the uplands and in the valleys, during the Ohio Middle Woodland period the population became more localized in the lower sectors of the valleys during the warm season while retaining widespread cold season occupation of the uplands.

DEMONSTRATING THE ECCLESIASTIC-COMMUNAL CULT SODALITY MODEL

While I have already demonstrated this model (Byers 2004, particularly chapters 10 and 11), for this book a condensed summary may be useful, thereby showing how the Ecclesiastic-Communal Cult Sodality model can give a more coherent interpretation of the mortuary data than can the Tripartite Ceremonial Alliance model. In this case, I first focus on the spatial forms of the major renewal lodges that Carr describes (referring to them as "charnel houses") and then I show that the burial clusters and the "inverse pyramidal distribution of prestige" (Carr 2005b, 295) that they manifest are, in fact, clearly manifesting the type of incremental prestige accumulation that we can expect between laity sectors characterized by a generational difference in age. In this case, they manifest differential material needs and developmental trajectories of persons occupying internally related junior and senior age-grade laity sectors and internally related laity-clergy sectors.

As I noted earlier, material attributes of spatial form and relations would express significant symbolic pragmatic meanings partly constitutive of the social nature of the occupant groups. If it is accepted that formal variation in space is partly constitutive of the social nature of the groups that occupy it, then these dual structural axes, laity-clergy sectors and senior/junior age-grade sectors, would entail contrasting spatial locales and since the laity-clergy relation entails a complementary opposition, then we could expect a complementary contrasting of spatial forms, for example, circle-rectangle. Of course, since the senior and junior age-grades were of the same social nature, peer-based companionship groups differentiated only by generation, then we could expect similar or parallel spatial forms possibly distinguished in size to manifest the differences in seniority. It is not surprising, therefore, that in fact the major renewal lodges of Seip and Liberty Works display this R-R-C pattern (figure 3.9). It is also salient that the rank profiles of the burials of each section of the Seip-Pricer Renewal Lodge also relate in similar contrasting terms in that the rank profiles of the burials in the two spaces under the rectangular rooms (R-R) are more qualitatively similar to each other, both showing a graduated rank distribution, than either is to the rank profile of the burials in the space under the circular room. Importantly, as Greber's work has demonstrated, the two rectangular rooms and their burial spaces are different in size and this difference correlates with a greater number of burials, as well as *greater variety and number* of esteem-endowing artifacts, in the larger of the two rectangular spaces (Greber 1983, 26–29). It was this latter distinction that Carr labeled the "inverse pyramidal distribution of prestige" (Carr 2005b, 295). As I argued above, this inverted order cannot be explained by the Tripartite Ceremonial Alliance model without generating contradiction between the premises of the model and their conclusion, thereby constituting a falsification of the claim. In contrast, under the Ecclesiastic-Communal Cult Sodality model, if we assume that the rate of death in a senior age cohort increases relative to that of the younger age cohort, we could anticipate that not only would there be a larger number of burials in the mortuary space devoted to the senior laity age-grade of companions, there would also be a proportionately larger spatial arrangement demarcating the seniority of this age-grade as well as a greater range, variety, and quantity of esteem-endowing/role-constituting artifacts, particularly custodial regalia, than there would be among the deceased of the junior age-grade laity. This is simply because of the time-dependency factor related to the development of cult sodality career trajectories as marked by the accumulating of these symbolic pragmatic devices constitutive of and necessary for successful leadership and promotion within the cult sodality. The deceased of the senior laity sector would have initiated their participation in the cult as junior laity, and therefore would, in general, have a much longer period before their deaths to accumulate responsibilities and the prestigious and esteem-endowing action-constitutive enabling warrants of positions that go along with these compared to the contemporaneous junior sector deceased who, of course, being younger at death, would have had less time and opportunity to develop their careers. Therefore, collectively, those deceased who belonged to the senior age-grade sector at death should have accumulated a *proportionately greater* number and variety of such symbolic pragmatic devices than those deceased who belonged to the contemporaneous and complementary junior age-grade sector.

This suggests that, in fact, there should also be a differential age-at-death between the deceased of the larger rectangular space, which I term Locus 1, and the deceased of the smaller rectangular space, Locus 2. This differential size would manifest the respect for seniority such that Locus 1 and Locus 2 would have been the ritual mortuary spaces of the senior age-grade sector and the junior age-grade sector deceased, respectively (or some of the deceased dependents of the living senior and junior age-grade members). And if this is the case, then those in Locus 1 should display not only a greater proportional quantity and variety of esteem-endowing artifacts, they also should display skeletal differences indicating an on-the-average greater age at death than the deceased in Locus 2.[6] This claim could normally be verified by a careful analysis of the bones for age-at-death indicators. The problem is that all floor burials were cremated. According to Lyle Konigsberg, "[a]ll adults were simply classified as 20+ years old. This classification was necessary because of the extensive damage from cremation, which obscured or destroyed the macroscopic morphological indicators traditionally used to estimate adult ages-at-death. Although recent work . . . suggests that microradiography could be used to determine ages-at-death for cremated adult remains, this technique has not yet been applied to the Seip materials" (1985, 125).

However, there is another possible source of empirical evidence to ground the claim that these two burial loci manifest the deceased of the contemporaneous senior and junior sectors of an ecclesiastic-communal cult sodality heterarchy. William Mills (1907, 113–93) first excavated and reported on the Edwin Harness mound at Liberty Works. He then excavated and reported on the Seip-Conjoined mound (1909, 269–321). He commented that while the Edwin Harness burials had only one mode of terminating mortuary rites, the Seip-Conjoined burials had two different and contrasting modes.

> As stated, the single graves in the first section [Locus 1] of the Seip [Seip-Conjoined] Mound were similar in construction to those of the [Edwin] Harness Mound, *though the final burial ceremony must have been different.* In the Harness Mound, after the incinerated remains had been placed in the grave, objects of clothing, together with straw, bark, or twigs, were placed over the remains and set on fire: while burning, clay was placed over the grave, thus preserving the cloth, the grass, and twigs in a charred state. This ceremony *was dispensed with in this section* [Locus 1] of the Seip [Seip-Conjoined] Mound, and the incinerated remains were placed in the prepared grave, and a covering of wood, usually split pieces, was placed on the top and the grave covered with earth to a depth of a few inches. (Mills 1909, 288, emphases added)[7]

He then went on to comment that, with regard to the burials of Locus 2, "[t]he final ceremony of burning straw, bark, and clothing over the remains, *similar to the burial methods at the Harness Mound,* was in evidence in 9 burials of the 19 [Locus 2 of Seip-Conjoined] found at the base of the Seip Mound" (emphasis added).

I have called these two different burial termination modes the *fire-clay rite* and the *split-log rite,* respectively (Byers 2004, 303). Thus, in the Edwin Harness mound, the fire-clay rite was used exclusively while both rites were used in Seip-Conjoined, although differentially according to locus. The split-log rite was used for all the 24 burials in Locus 1, while, as noted in the above quotation, both rites were used in Locus 2, with the fire-clay rite being used for 9 burials and the split-log rite for 10 burials.

Given his statement that the fire-clay rite "*was dispensed with in this section* [Locus 1]," this suggests that he recognized this absence of fire-clay rites implicated a chronological factor, that is, being "dispensed" in Locus 1 that it had been used earlier, that is, in Locus 2, along with the split-log rite, and then in Locus 1 only the latter rite was used. If so, then the implicated chronology of the two terminal rites appears to parallel the actual chronological order of his excavations and reports, first of Edwin Harness, where all burials were terminated by the fire-clay rite, and then of Seip-Conjoined, where both rites were performed. Since in his terms the fire-clay rite was "*dispensed with*" in Locus 1, it must be that he assumed that the earliest burials at Seip-Conjoined would have been the nine fire-clay rites in Locus 2. His reasoning may have been that since the fire-clay rite was standard at Edwin Harness, then it was probably also standard at Seip-Conjoined. Therefore, only following these nine fire-clay rites—that is, partway through the period of use of Locus 2—would the split-log rite have been introduced, possibly being innovated at Seip-Conjoined. Of course, it is possible that for a short period an overlap of usage of these two loci may have occurred with both rites being used simultaneously at Seip-Conjoined. If so, a very few of the split-log burials could have been performed in both Locus 1 and Locus 2 while the use of the fire-clay rite continued in the latter. In any case, it would be clear to him that from the initial use of Seip-Conjoined for burials, at least nine deaths would have occurred in the group occupying Room 2 while either no deaths or possibly only one or two deaths would have occurred during this same period for the group occupying Room 1, and these few would have been only when most of the nine fire-clay burial rites in Locus 2 had been performed.

If this is the case, then this suggests a differential death rate of the two groups during this same time period, nine in Locus 2 while only one or two in Locus 1; and this would be the type of gap that would be expected if there was a generational difference between them. The fact that when Seip-Conjoined was abandoned the split-log rite was in the significant majority (a total of 34 split-log rites as compared to 9 fire-clay rites) also suggests that the fire-clay rite would have been completely abandoned well before the termination of the usage of Seip-Conjoined so that most of the 24 deceased buried in Locus 1 would have died not only well after the 9 fire-clay rite burials in Locus 2 would have occurred but also after most of the 10 split-log burials in this same Locus 2 would have been performed. In short, *following Mills's apparent chronological priority in this regard,* since the fire-clay rite had temporal priority so that the split-log rite would have been introduced into the mortuary sequence of Seip-Conjoined rather late, then the numerical disparity of distribution of the split-log rite between Locus 1 and Locus 2 of Seip-Conjoined, 10 in the latter and 24 in the former, would be consistent with a differential death rate of the two groups separated by a generation, and this would be consistent with the mortuary trajectory of a social organization of the type postulated under the Ecclesiastic-Communal Cult Sodality model.

However, there is a very real problem with this conclusion. In these terms, the disparity of death rate would make Locus 2 the burial place of the senior age-grade laity sector and Locus 1 the burial place of the junior age-grade laity sector. This follows from the observation that possibly most of the nine fire-clay burials had already occurred before any split-log burials were performed in Locus 1. However, according to the "inverse pyramidal distribution" of the esteem-endowing copper artifacts, spatial size differences, number of burials, proportional distribution of esteemed goods, and so on, Locus 1 should contain the senior age-grade deceased and Locus 2 the junior age-grade deceased. This anomaly can be easily resolved, however. More than 20 years following the publication of Mills's 1909 report on his Seip-Conjoined excavation, Shetrone and Greenman (1931, 343–509) published their excavation report of the Seip-Pricer mound. They firmly established that the Seip-Conjoined Renewal Lodge was built and used *after* the Seip-Pricer Renewal Lodge was abandoned. Furthermore, all the burials on the Seip-Pricer floor were completed by the terminal split-log rite. This was the opposite for Edwin Harness, where all the floor burials were completed by the fire-clay rite. Furthermore, Greber's radiocarbon dating for the Seip-Pricer and the Edwin Harness Renewal Lodges gives a median date of A.D. 300 for both of them, suggesting that while separated in two neighboring valleys, these two structures were contemporaneous for some of their usage histories (1983, 91, figure 10.2). This means that when Seip-Pricer was abandoned and Seip-Conjoined built and used, Edwin Harness continued in tandem with the latter, and also continued to use the fire-clay terminal rite. Therefore, rather than the fire-clay rite predating the split-log rite, the two rites overlapped in time and during much of that time, the split-log rite was the norm at Seip-Pricer and the fire-clay rite was the norm at Edwin Harness.

It is reasonable to conclude, therefore, that the split-log rite was traditional to Seip and following the abandoning of the Seip-Pricer Renewal Lodge, this tradition continued in use at the newly built Seip-Conjoined Renewal Lodge. And it must have been continued in use for a considerable period before the fire-clay rite was finally introduced, probably originating from Edwin Harness. Why this must have been the case is that, as noted above, all 24 mortuary deposits on the floor of Locus 1 were terminated with the split-log rite, while only 10 of the 19 on the floor of Locus 2 were also terminated with the split-log rite. Therefore, the split-log rite was earliest and in the majority at Seip-Conjoined, occurring in 34 of the total of 43 floor burials. This means that the above chronology that Mills implicated must be reversed and Locus 1 of Seip-Conjoined accumulated possibly two burials for every one burial accumulated in Locus 2. This also means that Locus 1 would have been used for senior age-grade sector and Locus 2 for the junior age-grade sector burials.

CRITICAL DISCUSSION

With the correct relative chronology established, the differential patternings of the mortuary records of Locus 1 and Locus 2 now fit the expected senior-junior laity sectoring characteristic of an ecclesiastic-communal cult sodality. However, does it also follow that the differential distribution of these two rites between Locus 1 and Locus 2 can be more coherently accounted for by the Ecclesiastic-Communal Cult Sodality model than by the Tripartite Ceremonial Alliance model? Since the latter model postulates that each of the three burial sections contains some of the deceased of one of three separate monistic modular polity communities (i.e., in Carr's terms, three "local symbolic communities"), then they should have had comparable age-structures, with individuals of each community having similar life experiences, even when the postulated differences in prestige and wealth among the three communities are taken into account. Therefore, the death rates should have been more or less equal. Furthermore, under his model, they should have been used simultaneously. Hence, once the fire-clay rite was introduced, even if fairly late in the use history of Seip-Conjoined, it should have been distributed about equally across all loci (there were no burials in Locus 3). This is clearly not the case.

It could be argued under the Tripartite Ceremonial Alliance model, however, that, since the burials in Locus 2 were split between the two rites, while all the burials of Locus 1 of Seip-Conjoined were terminated with the split-log rite, there was some leeway between using these two ritual modes. Therefore, the community responsible for Locus 1 might simply have been very conservative. However, according to Carr, since both were the same type of local symbolic community based on dispersed residential hamlets, and presumably having the same age structures, it could be expected that the same range of attitudes toward ritual would be about equally distributed across each community, suggesting that there should be a similar mix of the two rites in both loci. Therefore, this conservative/liberal argument is not persuasive. In fact, according to the Tripartite Ceremonial Alliance model, since both the Edwin Harness and Seip "charnel structures" were used for funerary burial for some of the deceased of all three communities, it seems strange indeed that all the Edwin Harness burials were terminated with the same fire-clay rite, no matter which burial locus is examined. Under the Tripartite model, since the largest burial space marked the largest, wealthiest, and most prestigious community of the three, then the burials in the larger of the two spaces (which also had the largest number of burials) at Edwin Harness ought to have been terminated also with the split-log rites, similar to the burial-termination rites at Seip-Conjoined, since these two burial populations represented the same and wealthiest community. It was not.

In the same vein, the burials in the smaller of the two spaces at Seip-Conjoined should have all been terminated with the fire-clay rite, as they were in the equivalent locus at Edwin Harness. We have already seen that this was not the case. That is, according to the Tripartite Ceremonial Alliance model, each community had one dedicated burial space in each mortuary locale and the point of this crossover burial practice was to emphasize unity and alliance, not difference and separation. Different burial rites count and manifest the latter, not the former. Therefore, the two modes of burials should have been distributed across the equivalent burial locales in at least these two. They were not. To add further confusion to all this, it should be noted that, at the Hopewell site, which according to Carr was the wealthiest of the local symbolic communities making up the Tripartite Alliance, the majority of the deceased were interred as extended burials within large vaulted log crypts, as I discuss later. I find it quite strange that Carr does not incorporate this variation of mortuary treatment among the three postulated constituent communities of the Tripartite Ceremonial Alliance model. While he definitely notes the high incidence of extended burial at the Hopewell site, he treats this as marking these individuals as prestigious and he makes no mention of the differential terminal treatment at Seip and Liberty Works that I have termed the split-log ritual and the fire-clay ritual.

Not being able to account for this distribution in terms relevant to the Tripartite Ceremonial Alliance model reinforces the differential age-at-death claim that is consistent with the Ecclesiastic-Communal Cult Sodality model. However, were these tendencies sufficient to indicate a generational difference? In fact, at the most superficial level, it becomes fairly obvious that the answer is yes. If the fire-clay rite was introduced into Seip-Conjoined, then it suggests that all or the great majority of the split-log burials occurred prior to this introduction. Since all 24 mortuary deposits of Locus 1, Seip-Conjoined, were terminated by the split-log rite and only 10 of the 19 mortuary deposits of Locus 2 were split-log rites, then this suggests a pre-fire-clay rite differential Locus1/Locus 2 death rate of 24/10; or, during the same time period, there was the average of 2.4 burials (marking deaths) in Locus 1 for every single death in Locus 2. If we assume that, everything else being equal, the burial rate marks the death rate and the death rate of a group increases with its average age, then we could easily accommodate this 2.4:1 ratio of Locus 1:Locus 2 to the former being the senior age-grade laity sector and the latter being the junior age-grade laity sector.

However, it is more complicated than this. In my full elucidation of the Ecclesiastic-Communal Cult Sodality model, I also argued that when the senior age-grade sector becomes so reduced by deaths that it cannot effectively perform its duties, the survivors retire, become respected cult sodality elders, and the junior age-grade is promoted to the senior age-grade status, takes over the responsibilities of this laity sector, and the pre-initiate group of youths becomes the new junior age-grade laity sector and, in some cases, the old renewal lodge is abandoned and a new one constructed (Byers 2004, 269–77). This means that, as part of this retirement-promotion process, following the "last" of the 24 senior age-grade members to be buried in Locus 1 a new renewal lodge should have been built and this would mean either a complete absence of the fire-clay rite or, at the most, only one or two such rites being performed prior to this abandonment. However, this did not happen. Instead, it is clear that, following this last split-log burial in Locus 1, all or most of the 9 fire-clay burial events occurred in Locus 2, the postulated junior age-grade sector. This means that the renewal lodge was not abandoned and, furthermore, apparently there was no promotion of the junior to the senior age-grade sector. This does not conform to the Ecclesiastic-Communal Cult Sodality model expectations. Therefore, while the 2.4:1 death ratio certainly satisfies the claim that a generation separated the two groups, with Locus 1 being used by the senior age-grade sector and Locus 2 by the junior age-grade sector, other claims of the model are not satisfied. Furthermore, there are no burials at all in Locus 3.

The detailed solution to this quandary was presented elsewhere (Byers 2004, 302–21) and the upshot of that analysis was to demonstrate that Seip-Conjoined was probably a dual-cycle renewal lodge. What this means is that the cult sodality used it for two generational cycles, each cycle being 25–30 years long. The first cycle was marked by the split-log ritual occurring in both burial loci while the second cycle was marked by the split-log/fire-clay ritual distinction with the newly promoted but rather traditional senior age-grade sector continuing the usage of the split-log ritual in the second cycle usage of the renewal lodge and the junior age-grade sector, being less conservative and possibly influenced by the Edwin Harness cult sodality, introducing and promoting the fire-clay ritual. This dual-cycle renewal lodge claim also accounts for the absence of burials in Locus 3. In this case, I treat the absence in a way similar to Carr's treatment, but with appropriate differences. He sees the absence of burials in Locus 3 as the reduction of the tripartite alliance to a dual alliance. In my model, however, in accordance with the R-R-C pattern marking the laity-clergy structure, Locus 3 is postulated as being dedicated to the clergy, both priests and apprentices. Therefore, both the absence of clergy burials and the differential usage of terminal burial rituals by the senior and junior age-grade laity sectors bespeak a serious disruption of the Seip cult sodality, possibly echoed in the introduction of the "foreign" fire-clay rite by the new junior sector. I have argued that these are among the major indicators of the imminent dissolution of the Ohio Hopewell ecclesiastic-communal cult sodality system.

I have gone on to argue and empirically ground the claim that the dissolution of the Seip ecclesiastic-communal cult sodality heterarchy occurred partway through the abandonment of the Seip-Conjoined Renewal Lodge, accounting for the fact that the Seip-Conjoined mound covering its abandoned renewal lodge was not completed. However, part of abandoning this renewal lodge entailed abandoning the Seip embankment earthworks by first building a replacement. Apparently, the cult sodality sustained integration long enough so as to complete the construction of its new embankment earthwork, this being Baum. However, it seems that it had not initiated or at least had not completed the construction of a renewal lodge, since there is no evidence currently available to this effect.

Carr has a different explanation. He interprets Seip and Baum as contemporaneous and argues that they were used by the same local symbolic community for two different purposes. "At least some communities built and used more than one earthwork or mound center at a time within their lands. The different earthworks or mound centers had different ceremonial functions" (2005b, 320–21). I am not at all convinced by this argument. An important standard for models to meet is not only consistency but breadth. The model that can give the most coherent explanation of the broadest range of data is preferred over a model that leaves data unexplained, particularly when these data constitute possibly the most outstanding aspect of the archaeological record being interpreted. First, since Baum has no known mortuary residue in its context, his suggestion entails a disconnection between embankment earthwork ritual and mortuary ritual such that these rituals could be done independently of each other. Once this is conceded, then there seems little reason to have any mortuary remains in association with embankment earthworks or, for that matter, any embankment earthworks in association with mortuary remains. Second, and on a more positive note, under the symbolic pragmatic view, both Seip/Baum and Liberty/Works East paired earthworks have effectively the same formal properties and, therefore, they would have the same symbolic pragmatic meaning. If so, it is more reasonable to argue that the Baum embankment earthwork, for example, was built in anticipation of abandoning Seip with the closing of Seip-Conjoined, as was the Works East earthwork built anticipating the abandonment of Liberty Works. But before these transfers to the new embankment earthwork facilities were effected, both cult sodality heterarchies dissolved or, at least, abandoned their respective earthwork systems.

A number of indicators from other major Ohio Hopewell sites suggests that the dissolution of the Seip-Baum cult sodality heterarchy was only part of a region-wide process. As I noted above, a similar absence of a renewal lodge occurred at Works East, suggesting that the Seip and Liberty Works cult sodality heterarchies both dissolved at about the same time, clearly participating in and being important events in this widespread rupture-like dissolution of the cult sodality heterarchy system (see Byers 2004, chapters 13, 23, and 24). Indeed, as I argue in a later chapter, Seip and Liberty Works were probably two major second-order cult heterarchies that were allied into a third-order heterarchy and the introduction of the fire-clay rite into Seip practices may also have seen the clergy sector of Seip preferring burial in the Edwin Harness Renewal Lodge, thereby accounting for the absence of any burials in Seip-Conjoined Locus 3 and multiple burials in the equivalent of Locus 3 at Harness.

In sum, several lines of theoretical argument and supporting empirical evidence establish good grounds for supporting the Ecclesiastic-Communal Cult Sodality model. These grounds are (1) as understood in symbolic pragmatic terms, the intrinsic connection between the nature of the social organization, in this case, an ecclesiastic-communal world renewal cult sodality heterarchy, and the forms of the embankment earthworks and the renewal lodges, and between the latter as world renewal locales and the mortuary practices; (2) the nice fit between the complementary contrasting R-R-C pattern of the renewal lodges and the differential rank profiles across this pattern; (3) showing that the distribution of the split-log/fire-clay rites is most coherently accounted for in terms of senior/junior age-grade structure as postulated by the Ecclesiastic-Communal Cult Sodality model, while being totally ignored by the Tripartite Ceremonial Alliance model; (4) a consistent explanation of the inverse pyramidal distribution as the outcome of a proportionately greater accumulation of symbolic pragmatic devices in Locus 1 compared to Locus 2 (i.e., by leaders of the senior compared to leaders of the junior age-grade laity sectors); and (5) a symbolic pragmatic interpretation of the social structural nature of the artifacts as warrants as being consistent with the mortuary distribution of a cult sodality organization, rather than "shamanic" practitioners, among other points that could be made if the space was adequate but which have been fully covered elsewhere (Byers 2004, chapter 23).

CONCLUSION

The next step to develop from this point is to present and empirically ground the Ohio Hopewell material archaeological record as the expression and development of a complex system of first-order, second-order, and third-order cult sodality heterarchies. This claim will, in fact, demonstrate that rather than the sites that Carr has interpreted as constituting a Tripartite Ceremonial Alliance, they embody an interface separating and linking the two major third-order cult sodality heterarchies that were responsible for the bulk of the great Ohio Hopewell embankment earthworks. I will be arguing that the

North Fork–Paint Creek zones marked this interface between the third-order Fort Ancient–Turner–Hopewell cult sodality heterarchy, and the third-order Chillicothe-Newark cult sodality heterarchy. The latter heterarchy may also have included the Portsmouth zone.[8] I plan to elucidate the theoretical framework that this proposal requires and then to demonstrate empirically its likelihood in part II of this book. However, prior to moving to part II, it is necessary to demonstrate through analogy the plausibility of the Ecclesiastic-Communal Cult Sodality model by describing known historic Native North American communities that displayed all the basic social and cultural components that would be necessary to constitute such a cult sodality, if the appropriate conditions had developed. This will also allow me to elaborate on the cultural background that would be critical to the process of heterarchy construction as I intend to discuss in detail in part II. For these purposes, I will return to my comments on the Hidatsa cultural communities of central North Dakota and elaborate on their social organization during the 1700s and into the middle of the 1800s, and how this organization served to relate them to their neighbors. They are particularly appropriate for my purposes since, as discussed above, a primary component of the community was a system of ranked and specialized groups of age-set companions, namely, same-age/same-gender sodalities. Therefore, I turn to the Hidatsa age-set system in the next chapter. I also use this cultural perspective to elucidate a model of what I consider to be the primary, although not the sole, dual social mechanism by which the Ohio Hopewell episode emerged and developed. I will argue that this was a process of transferring within and among age-set sodalities the prerogatives necessary to produce and use the symbolic pragmatic devices that mediated Hopewellian world renewal ceremonialism. I have called this the Ritual Usufruct Conveyancing and Franchising model. With these two theoretical perspectives and analogical illustrations completed, I then turn to the process of the emergence and development across the Central Ohio Valley of the interacting networks of ecclesiastic-communal cult sodality heterarchies and the primary mechanisms that were responsible for it, what I have termed the processes of conveyancing within and franchising among cult sodalities of world renewal ritual usufruct.

7

The Hidatsa Age-Set System and the Ritual Usufruct Conveyancing and Franchising Model

I noted earlier that Robert Hall has persuasively argued that traditional Native North American mortuary practices have a strong component of personal and social world renewal purpose built into them. He has used this fact as a premise to argue that this world renewal aspect has a deep structural continuity reaching back to at least the Middle Woodland period. I have constructed the Mourning/World Renewal Mortuary model on his premises. Hall has also addressed the role of renewal ritual in the development of interregional interaction (Hall 1991, 31; 1997, 47, 64, 80–83). Although his most recent work in this regard has focused on the Mississippian period, I will argue that the premises of the Mississippian and post-Mississippian period interaction model that he develops are equally applicable to the Middle Woodland period. The scale of interaction mediated by renewal ritual that he is particularly interested in is very large in that it focuses on interregional interaction. Therefore, I think that a similar modified approach can be equally illuminating to characterize the Hopewell Interaction Sphere and that, indeed, he has argued this very point (1997, 155–68). However, operating at this macroscale is for another book. In keeping with the main theme of this book, what I intend to do here is develop the premises in the form of models by focusing on the *intraregional* scale of interaction, limiting my examination to the way the Ohio Hopewell episode played itself out in networking the subregions of the Central Ohio Valley. It must be kept in mind, of course, that this intraregional networking cannot be fully understood independently of interregional networking and, therefore, although I leave the large-scale nature of the Hopewell Interaction Sphere of the Middle Woodland period of the Eastern Woodlands for a later book, this interregional sphere can be treated as the background to the intraregional networking of the Central Ohio Valley and, for the most part, the same social mechanisms were operable at both levels.

THE CALUMET FICTIVE KINSHIP ALLIANCE MODEL

Hall (1991, 18–21) has pointed out that when Europeans first encountered the peoples of the Upper Mississippi and Missouri Valleys, as well as peoples farther south and west of the upper Central Mississippi Valley, they were linked into a widespread system of interaction, what has been termed by ethnohistorians the Plains Interband Trading System. He argued that the primary mechanism that sustained this interaction was the practice of Calumet ceremonies by which individual leaders of different villages entered into fictive kinship-mediated alliances by formally adopting each other as "father" and "son." He then linked this system back to the Late Prehistoric Oneota Interaction Sphere and the latter he argued overlapped with the terminal period of the Cahokian Interaction Sphere of the late Mississippian period. He has suggested that this long distance system of interaction mediated by fictive kinship-based alliances among village leaders, itself based on a Calumet or at least a Calumet-like ceremonialism, sustained continuity across large sectors of the Upper Mississippian region into the historic period.

Hall particularly emphasized the important constitutive role of the religious-mortuary moment of the Calumet ceremony, pointing out that it invokes the presence of major sacred entities, the type that are represented in well-known creation myths such as those of the Winnebago, especially the narrative of these people's sacred culture hero Red Horn and his sons and their engaging with the Giants. Red Horn engaged the Giants in a sequence of battles, which he won. However, they finally succeeded to kill him, and his sons revenged the death of their father and his companions by in turn killing the Giants. The sons then retrieved the bones of their father and his companions, as well as the villagers who were also killed by the Giants, and reincarnated them (Hall 1997, 150). The role of the sons of Red Horn was particularly important for Hall's argument in order to ground the claim that the Calumet ceremony counted as the medium by which alliance relations between unrelated persons could be constituted. He then linked this notion of Calumet ceremonialism back to the Cahokian Interaction Sphere arguing that the appearance and distribution in the archaeological record of a small artifact termed the Long Nosed God maskette maps an equivalent Cahokian-like ceremonialism based particularly on Cahokia. He presented further important data to argue convincingly that this maskette depicts Red Horn. First, he noted that in the Winnebago creation myth, Red Horn is also referred to as He-Who-Wears-Human-Heads-As-Earrings (1997, 151). He then pointed out that there are several early Cahokian era depictions of the Long Nosed God showing him wearing earrings in the form of human heads. Hall also noted that rock shelter and cave art depictions in Wisconsin and different locales in the Central Mississippi Valley have been identified in which the persona are depicted as wearing human heads as nipple inserts. This is an important variant since one of the sons of Red Horn is also named He-Who-Wears-Human-Heads-In-His-Nipples (1991, 31; 1997, 150). Hence, Hall concluded that the historically known Calumet ceremony—along with its material symbols and practices—was the continuity in different symbolic form of the Cahokian-like ceremonialism marked by the Long Nosed God maskettes and their derivatives.[1] He continued his reconstruction by arguing that the Long Nosed God maskettes probably were introduced by the Cahokian chiefly system as a mark of the superior status of the latter over the tribal chiefs with whom the paramount chief allied. "The difference I see is that the Calumet ceremony served to create bonds of kinship between persons of roughly equal status, while the maskettes could have functioned within a ritual to create fictions of kinship between the powerful leaders of a large polity and his political clients in outlying areas" (Hall 1997, 151). In sum, Hall postulates that the interaction between Cahokia and its extraregional neighbors was mediated through the construction of alliances by the Cahokian paramount chief with leaders in distant communities through the formation of adoptive kinship relations and the ceremonial events that constituted and sanctified these alliance relations invoked and presenced the deities as they were depicted in these widely shared types of world creation stories.

This is a powerful model. Of course, I think most Middle Woodland period archaeologists would not transfer it "as is" to the Hopewell Interaction Sphere since most generally recognize that the communities involved were not of the same order. Rather, the Hopewellian were "tribal-like" while the Mississippian were "chiefdom-like." Therefore, the question of dominance relations would not apply.[2] Of course, individual leaders from different communities could stand to each other in seniority terms, as figuratively expressed through "father-son" terminology. However, as I argued in the previous chapter, if autonomy was a core principle of the social systems of the Middle Woodland period, then this ranking by seniority would not translate into dominance-subordination. However, while I consider Calumet-like fictive kinship adoption to be an important social mechanism mediating long distance interaction, with respect to the Middle Woodland period, I consider this type of alliance formation would be a secondary mechanism—both in terms of intra-regional and interregional interaction. Seen in terms of the Complementary Heterarchical Community model, the fictive kinship adoption process might operate only among the clan components of the interacting communities.

The reach of these alliances would be somewhat limited since the interests being served would be governed by the type of concerns that clans and kin groups would have. These would entail primarily what Ruby et al. (2005) refer to as the concerns addressed by the "sustainable community," the community formation based on marriage alliances. Therefore, these alliances would tend to be limited to the intraregional scale and they would largely exclude the practices I have identified as generating the Ohio Hopewell episode since these practices would be the responsibility of the cult sodalities.

Of course, the cult sodalities would clearly have an interest in allying with each other both intraregionally and extraregionally. However, this also means that the religious component that would ground the alliance would not likely invoke the sanctity of mythical heroes related by kinship as exemplified by such cultural heroes as Red Horn and his sons. Instead, they would invoke the sanctity of the same-age/same-sex companionship relation between, for example, Red Horn and his *boon companions*, such as the Thunderbird Storms-As-He-Walks, Turtle, and others. Now, this raises an important limitation of Hall's model. In relating the Calumet or Calumet-like ceremonialism with interpersonal alliance construction through fictive kinship adoption processes, he actually has obscured an equally important historically performed Calumet-like ceremonialism that enabled the formation of alliances between sodalities of different communities. However, it is rather easy to resolve this since, in fact, I believe that the same myths that Hall used to ground his fictive kinship model of alliance construction can be used to warrant the construction of cult sodality alliances. If I am right, then the event of Red Horn's reincarnation by his sons would hardly be the whole story. And, in fact, this is the case since the same suite of Winnebago Red Horn creation myths, and by extension, those of most Eastern Woodland peoples, can be used to demonstrate the equal importance and sacred nature of *companionship*. All that is needed is to shift the focus of the social relations manifested in this mythology from Red Horn and his sons, the father-son relation, to Red Horn and his *boon companions*, the non-kinship relation that bonded Storms-As-He-Walks and Turtle, along with all their other god *companions*. These constituted a *male-based warrior sodality*, engaging with and succeeding several times in overwhelming the Giants in a lethally serious game of combat. Indeed, this suite of myths is presented prior to the birth of Red Horn's sons and, therefore, would appear to be about creative events that were more fundamental than those performed by his sons.

During this prior-to-his-sons suite of myths, even though Red Horn is represented as having brothers, these male kin, at least in their capacity as kin to Red Horn, do not figure in these battles and, of course, Red Horn had no sons at that time. It was through the series of victories over the Giants that

Red Horn came to have two wives. One of these wives was the daughter of the Giant's leader. His other wife, whom he married prior to marrying the daughter of the leader of the Giants, was a mysterious woman who, apparently, was unrelated to any living god-hero and, therefore, could also be treated as having no prior kinship relation with Red Horn. Therefore, she was probably a god in her own right, a female companion. In fact, prior to his becoming the adult hero that he became, when he was still an adolescent and the youngest of his brothers, he contested a race against his brothers and other kin in the community with the prize being to marry the daughter of the village chief. Even though he was refused permission by the chief to compete, he did so anyway, and using his powers to transform into a sacred arrow, he defeated all competitors, and won the chief's daughter. But rather than marrying her, as the youngest brother, he offered "his would-be bride to his next older brother, who similarly declines and offers her to the next older until finally the oldest of the ten accepts her and marries her" (Hall 1997, 149). The lesson I see in this story is that, in kinship terms, his autonomy was seriously constrained by the rules and protocols of kinship. His true nature as an autonomous agent, a Thunderbird, indeed, the peer leader of the Thunderbirds, only emerged fully when he was in the presence of his fellow companions, the other Thunderbirds; and it was in their shared persona as companions that these gods were able to save humankind against the hostile underworld gods, the Giants. In any case, from these two wives he had one son each and these were themselves companions as well as brothers since they had separate mothers. It was these companion-brothers who revenged their father's death at the hands of the Giants, as well as revenging the deaths of Red Horn's boon companions. They used the bones of their father and his companions to reincarnate them and all the humans of the original village.

Thus, the Calumet ceremonialism that Hall focuses on to warrant the fictive kinship adoption view was based on a suite of myths that derived much of their relevance from the preceding mythical events relating to the companionship-based battles. Red Horn and his companions, on the one hand, and the leader of the Giants and his companions, on the other, probably represent the primary cosmic powers of the Above World (the celestial heavens) and the Beneath World (the watery underworld), respectively—that is, the Thunderbirds and the Great Serpent in various guises (Lankford 2007a, 124). Also, it is important to recognize that the events told in these myths can be easily interpreted as world creation and world renewal events and their ritual performances under the right conditions and by the right ritual agents, those who are recognized as "pretenders" occupying allied and opposed companion-god persona sets, would constitute world renewal rites. Notably, therefore, the story of Red Horn's sons reincarnating their father constitutes the second or follow-up cycle of the myth, suggesting that in terms of *priority*, the sanctity of companionship may well sometimes trump the sanctity of kinship. Also, as I noted above, the two sons of Red Horn are half-brothers, that is, half-companions. They formed a type of dual kinship-companionship bond, one being related through his mother to the Giants, the gods of the Beneath World (the underworld realm), and the other being the son of a female god, probably associated with the heavenly Above World realm.

The Winnebago myth of the creator gods as companions, in fact, is not unique. Many of the neighbors of the Winnebago had equivalent culture heroes and myths involving companions and/or "half-brothers/half-companions" as the creator gods. For example, the Iowa, Oto, Missouri, Osage, Miami, and Illinois have stories in which the equivalents of Red Horn and his companions figured importantly (Hall 1991, 18–21). Since Hall is correct in that it is known historically that the Calumet or Calumet-like kinship adoption rites served to link communities across regions, it is equally reasonable to assume that similar and possibly even more intense long distance relations were constituted by rituals related to the formation of "fictive" companionship; although, in this case there would be no sense to add the concept "fictive" since these would become companions and, by definition, companions are non-kin. Only in a face-to-face community would companionship-based groupings require a sort of "fictiveness" to their composition since, in many cases, those relating as companions could also easily trace kinship filiations with each other. Hence, as I noted earlier, one reason sodalities may be pressed to isolate their facilities spatially from the clan facilities is to create symbolic contexts, for example, age-set lodges, which act as the constitutive media of companionship. Those "retreating" to such a sodality lodge facility do so in virtue of their being companions, even if they are also able to trace kin connections. In that sense, the members of every sodality have to subsume their kinship obligations and responsibilities that many of the members could easily invoke in relation to each other, and stress their companionship obligations and loyalties. However, long distant relations based on same-age/same-gender companionship clearly can be treated in a "pure" sense. The more spatially distant the two groups are, the less likely they need to suppress the kinship expectations. Indeed, as I suggested above, such distantly related companions probably could establish affinal alliances through sister-exchange practices.

It is possible that the tendency for archaeologists to ignore or be oblivious to the sanctity and central role that companionship plays in many creation myths might be related to our reliance on the emphases that North American ethnologists have placed on kinship. I think that this kinship-centricity is well represented by Alfred Bowers's (1965, 2004) classic studies of the historic

North Dakota Hidatsa and Mandan communities of the Upper Missouri Valley. In the following, although he does not use the term *calumet*, he clearly describes the same type of ritual kinship adoption practices that Hall speaks of as Calumet ceremonialism.

> A Hidatsa would select as a "son" a prominent member of a visiting band, usually the leader of the band, and announce he would come to visit sometime during the summer. In the interim both "father" and "son" would prepare the goods and paraphernalia necessary for the adoption ceremonies. The father would first prepare, or have prepared by some members of the Adoption Pipe *fraternity*, the principal ceremonial object; a wooden pipestem decorated with redheaded woodpecker scalps, eagle feather, and horsetail hanging as a scalp. He would also secure a good buffalo horse, complete sets of clothing for the son and family, and other fine presents such as robes, guns, and bows and arrows. In the accumulation of the necessary things, he received assistance from his own and related households, and from the members of his own clan and *age-grade* groups. (Bowers 1965, 84; emphasis added)

Except that he adds "age-grade," the content repeats much of the content that Hall gives, even to noting that the central icon of the ritual was a "pipestem" (the actual calumet item) decorated with various items, but in particular, bird parts. As Hall notes,

> The popular conception of a Hako-type round stemmed calumet pipe as simply a sacred smoking pipe obscures its ritual function in mediating a symbolic conception, either as a tube through which breath passes or as a symbolic arrow. Its associated ritual derives from the kind of background one would expect of a ritual based in varying degrees upon spirit adoption in mourning, the storey of He-who-wears-human-heads-as-earrings [Red Horn], the Morning Star sacrifice, and World Renewal ritual. Calumet ceremonialism fits the bill as the mechanism of the Oneota Interaction, while Long-Nosed God [Red Horn] earrings and tattoos are implicated, at least, in the mechanism of the Cahokia Interaction. (Hall 1997, 152–53)

Therefore, both Hall and Bowers emphasize that this Calumet ceremonialism was essentially a fictive *kinship* adoption ceremony that included a strong mortuary component of death and rebirth.

However, importantly, Bowers also points out in his discussion that Calumet or Calumet-like ceremonialism came in two forms, each constituting different relations. In one form it was used to constitute a fictive "father-son" kinship relation as described above; *and* in another form it was used to constitute a companionship relation between two men or two groups of men (or of women) from unrelated communities. In fact, both forms of ritually constructed relations played a critical role in the Hidatsa individual's constituting his reputation. This is clear when Bowers points out that "all council leaders had established, by means of adoption ceremony, 'father-son' or '*friend-friend*' relationships with a number of distinguished men of other tribes. Even the children established '*friend-friend*' relationships with individuals of the same age and sex by the formal exchange of clothing and presents" (1965, 91, emphases added). It is notable here that, in an almost off-handed manner, Bowers included the "friend-friend" relation within this type of fictive kinship ceremonialism, clearly showing how companionship is typically subsumed to kinship in the thinking of many anthropologists. Still Bowers went on to discuss the friend-friend or as he also termed it the "pal-pal" relationship in more detail, showing that it ramified well beyond boys of the same age being friends. It clearly was the key constitutive value of the age-grade system. In fact, he presented a rather balanced description of the Hidatsa kinship and age-grade systems and even stressed the importance of the age-grade system in the life of the community. But it was the intricacies of the kinship system and its clan structure to which he gave greatest attention and detail, effectively subsuming the companionship system to the kinship system by treating the former as largely a socialization agency of the latter.

This subsuming is neatly illustrated in his listing of Hidatsa *kinship terms* of address. This list includes 26 separate terms in English with their equivalents in Hidatsa, where such equivalents existed. Many of the English terms were compounded so as to delineate their Hidatsa equivalents. This required using English modifiers as in, for example, "elder brother," "younger brother," and so on. He also had to make two columns for gender-distinctive terms, that is, different terms having the same referent but used by males only or females only. Also, the spaces next to the English "husband" and "wife" were left blank, suggesting that there were no Hidatsa terms for "husband" and "wife." This actually reduced the Hidatsa terminology that he listed to 24 terms. Also a male speaker used the same term for sister without distinguishing between elder and younger sister. Interestingly, female and male speakers had separate terms to refer to elder or younger brothers. This latter point may highlight the importance that both male gender and seniority played in governing interpersonal relations, and certainly, this was the case among the male age-sets (Bowers 1965, 80, table 3). In typical anthropological manner, Bowers went on to carefully chart the distribution of these terms from the perspective of "ego," and listed and described the mutually binding rights and duties (i.e., the deontics) of paired relations, "father-son," "father-daughter," "elder brother-junior brother," and so on. However, to make this set of relations he did not need to use one of these 24 listed terms. This was the term *irakúu.* Although Bowers listed it *as a kinship term*, there is a good reason for his not using it because it clearly was *not* a kinship term. Bowers specifically translated it as "pal" (Bowers 1965, 80–90, 93–94). A synonymous term *kotomanaku*, also meaning "companion" or "pal," is found among the Mandan (Bowers 1965, 183).

Now, it might be argued that possibly this term *irakúu*—"friend," "pal," or, generically, "companion"—is simply used as a diminutive between certain kin. However, there is independent evidence showing that the Mandan, Hidatsa, and related peoples, such as the Arikara, sharply distinguished between the concepts of kinship and companionship. Virginia Peters (1995, 26) relates the creation myths of the Mandan and Hidatsa creator gods. These were two companions, First Worker (or First Creator) and Lone Man. They encountered each other and traveled together prior to turning to reforming the world into its current arrangement, that is, world creating. In their wandering together, they met up with a female mouse and addressed her as "friend." According to Peters, the busy mouse immediately responded and said "'Not so!' . . . '[Y]ou are wrong, you are not my friends; you are my grandsons!' 'You must be our grandmother,' they said. 'Yes,' she answered. Then they found other tracks which led them to a large female toad, who said the ground was her body. She said they were her grandsons too" (Peters 1995, 26). These incidents in the creation story imply to me that the meanings presupposed in the English generic terms *kinship* and *companionship* were internally related by *complementary opposition.* A friend, pal, companion, and so on, was defined as a person who was not a kin person and vice versa.[3] Finally, to reinforce the claim that kinship and companionship constitute complementary social spheres, it is notable that the Hidatsa have a number of different terms of address that have the same referent, "elder brother," "elder sister," and so on, and these are distinguished by one set being used only by male relatives and the other only by female relatives. At the same time, however, and in stark contrast, both males and females use the same term *irakúu* to address and/or refer to a person as a "pal" or "friend," whether the person is the same or opposite sex of the speaker.

Therefore, despite Bowers's listing these terms, *irakúu* and *kotomanaku,* as being among the Hidatsa and Mandan kinship term sets, respectively, their usage actually expressively demarcates and is constitutive of a non-kinship sphere, the companionship or friend-friend sphere of relations. As quoted above, two young boys, for example, can become *irakúu* by exchanging gifts. The same term is used to refer to the relation that binds a group of males who constitute an age-set. Indeed, Bowers points out that the *irakúu* relation can pair complementary male and female age-grade sodalities so that they constitute an "*irakúu* brother"–"*irakúu* sister" alliance. It can also be used to pair age-equivalent male sets from different communities. In short, the meaning is constitutive of companionship and its reciprocal and serious use between two parties delineates and simultaneously constitutes the *irakúu* relation. The fact that the persons making up the *irakúu* age-sets of a community are also the same persons that make up the unilateral kin groups of this community (the Hidatsa and Mandan are matrilateral) is what I mean by characterizing the age-set sodalities and clans as relatively autonomous and, therefore, why the total community is organized as a complementary heterarchy consisting of the clans structured into complementary moieties and age-set sodalities, substructured into male and female, and each gender sector organized into enabling hierarchies by relative seniority.

All this means that Bowers's description of the Hidatsa community strongly indicates two structural spheres, each anchoring ritually constituted intercommunity alliance relations—one mediated through the father-son adoptive relation that Hall also primarily addresses, and the other mediated by the friend-friend or *irakúu* relation. In fact, the principles of both of these relations may underwrite the age-set system.[4] Therefore, despite Bowers's listing *irakúu* as a kinship term, he actually has delineated the friend-friend relation as being critical to the constitution of age-set sodality groups who, as lifelong friends, together move up the age-set enabling hierarchy. Also, he explicitly recognizes that companionship is at the heart of intracommunity and intercommunity sodality relations. In particular, he notes that the formation of companionship bonds between equivalent age-set sodalities from different communities was very formal.

A Hidatsa age-set is a mutually self-selected group of *irakúu* and as such it can relate to other equivalent *irakúu* age-set groups in the same terms, whether male or female. In fact, as I noted in the previous chapter, male-based age-sets that are not age equivalent relate in terms of seniority by using the kinship terms that denote senior-junior generations, that is, the male age-set that is immediately senior to another will refer to the proximal junior age-set as "*irakúu* sons" and the latter reciprocally refer to the seniors as "*irakúu* fathers," even though both age-sets are in the same age-grade (i.e., same generation) and many of the males in the senior age-set would have younger brothers in the junior age-set. Female-based age-sets use the appropriate "mother-daughter" terms; separate male- and female-based age-sets relate to each other by using the "*irakúu* brother–*irakúu* sister" terms. However, this kinship terminology is being used figuratively in order to delineate not kinship but companionship, either equivalent or in terms of relative seniority. This is clearly the case since part of the process of transferring sodality duties from the senior to the junior male age-set is for the latter to offer their wives (with their consent) as sexual partners to their *irakúu* fathers. Furthermore, a member of the senior age-set will "adopt" members of the junior age-set who are of his father's (matrilateral) clan, and they refer reciprocally to each other as "father" and "son," even though they are of the same generation.[5] However, when these same males are in a shared kinship context, as same generation males related by sharing fathers of the same matrilateral clan, these males would address each other as elder and younger brother (Bowers 1965, 82). These behaviors, which actually contradict the kinship relations that are constituted by these terms, reinforce the conclusion that the kinship terms—*father* and *son*—are being used figuratively in the intrageneration context in order to recognize the difference in seniority between two *irakúu* age-set groups. As I discuss below, these relations of seniority play a major role in understanding the ritual of transferring the age-set sodality responsibilities from the senior to the junior age-set.

In short, a closer examination of the Hidatsa and Mandan, typical practitioners of Calumet ceremonialism, would suggest that Hall's description of this ceremonial alliance construction is incomplete in that while he is correct to note that the cosmology and the ethos traditions underwriting it serve as the basis of fictive kinship alliances, he has largely left out that they also serve to warrant a second, parallel, and equally if not more important form of alliance construction by which intercommunity relations, both not-so-distant and long distant relations, were constituted and sustained. I will call it *irakúu*-Calumet ceremonialism. If we follow Bowers in this regard, there are two critical expressions of this *irakúu*-Calumet ceremonialism, one ritual event that transfers the ritual usufruct rights and obligations of a senior age-set sodality to the immediate junior age-set sodality, thereby promoting the latter to the senior level while the former retires from that level and then does the same to the age-set senior to it; and the other dealing with transferring ritual usufruct rights and obligations between equivalently senior age-sets of separate complementary heterarchical communities, thereby constituting another set of intercommunity relations complementary to the fictive kinship relations.

However, as noted above, Hall has established another significant quality about the Calumet ceremonialism, this being that it was tied into mortuary ritual, from releasing the personal or free soul of the deceased in order to travel to the land of the Dead, to releasing name souls so that they can be "reborn" in the newly born, as well as releasing living souls to enable rebirth. But he locates this mortuary ritual pretty well exclusively in the kinship sphere. If we recognize the existence and widespread practice of *irakúu*-Calumet ceremonialism, however, it becomes clear that companionship-based groups, such as age-set sodalities, would also be identified with the mortuary sphere. Bowers has unwittingly presented empirical evidence to this effect.

Before presenting this evidence, it is important to remember that I characterized the Hidatsa, Mandan, Pawnee, and so on, as matri*lateral* not matri*lineal* communities. Often the terms *matrilineal* and *matrilateral*, or the generic terms, *unilineal* and *unilateral*, are used interchangeably. However, this is a serious error. As Vernon Knight (1990, 4–6) cogently argues, it is a mischaracterization to speak of the historic and probably prehistoric communities east of the Rocky Mountains as unilineal systems. Rather, they were unilateral systems and, therefore, would not have lineages, as these are usually characterized in the anthropological literature. He defines the distinction in terms of filiation and descent. Descent-based kinship groups, that is, lineal groups or lineages, involve recording genealogies and noting quite precisely the degree of relation an individual has to an apical ancestor; filiation-based kinship groups classify relatives as clan or clan-segment members and a person differentially relates to the clans of his or her parents, with the father's clan as the cognates in a patrilateral system and the mother's clan as cognates in a matrilateral system. In these terms, the Mandan and Hidatsa were matrilateral and I will follow Knight in this regard by treating these communities as matrilateral. This position is not a trivial matter since, as I argued in chapter 2, I consider unilateral filiation and unilineal descent are characteristic of the two different community types: the complementary heterarchical community and the monistic modular polity community, respectively. I have already noted that the Mapuche are patrilineal and, based on exclusive custodial land usufruct, they apparently have no age-set sodality system. Primary inheritance of exclusive custodial land usufruct is traced through the patriline and, as I argued earlier, this promotes competition among siblings and lineages. Such competition would make little or no sense in a community having unilateral filiation as its primary kinship structure. If Knight is correct that, in fact, Eastern Woodland communities were unilateral, then, assuming this would be a deep social structural rule, this would support the view that the Middle Woodland period communities of the region were also.

With this clarification made, I can now address the empirical data that Bowers uses to relate the roles that companionship and kinship groups play in the mortuary sphere. It is notable that Bowers asserts that it is not the deceased's cognates, the matrilateral or mother's clan, but his or her agnates, the father's matrilateral clan, that make up the set of persons responsible for organizing and conducting the mortuary rites. The members of the deceased's own matriclan are responsible to provide much of the requisite material goods for the organizers to conduct the mortuary rites (Bowers 1965, 75). Since both the deceased's father's and mother's matriclans operate in this complementary manner, it would appear that the mortuary practices are under the exclusive control of the clans and the companions or *irakúu* of the deceased are excluded. However, it is not so simple. Bowers particularly stresses the fact that the crosscutting networks of clans and age-sets normally allow any two individuals in the community to invoke one of several different relations in which they stand to each other by selecting the relation appropriate to the social context in which they are jointly involved. "[M]any factors of social participation affected the relationship between individuals and extended the system to include nonrelatives, age-grade associates, ceremonial participation, adoption of children and ceremonial adoptions by both men and women, and equatings of Hidatsa with Mandan clans. All these produced systems of interaction between individuals in which two people often stood in several relationships to each other. This was not mentioned specifically by informants and came out in the study of various customs" (1965, 7). As a community based on matrilateral filiation, the Hidatsa recognize that only those linked through the mother are cognatic kin, that is, treated as affiliated to the same matriclan. Father-son and father-daughter are agnatic kin, or kin affiliated with the father's matriclan. Therefore, agnatic and cognatic kin relations are differentiated by the sex of the linking parent, and this is clearly recognized by the division of mortuary responsibility between the deceased's father's (agnatic) and mother's (cognatic) matriclans. Now, while cognatic brothers could not relate as *irakúu,* namely, as companions (at best age-sets of senior and junior cognatic brothers could stand as "*irakúu* fathers"–"*irakúu* sons"), agnatic brothers could. In fact, they could become special *irakúu* combining both agnatic relations, having fathers of the same matriclan, and being "ordinary" *irakúu.* Of course, this does not mean that only agnates can form *irakúu* relations; it simply means that agnatic clan brothers who also stand to each other as *irakúu,* or members of the same age-set, would not contradict the duties and responsibilities they had to each other as agnatic kin.

Indeed, as I noted above, the *irakúu* companions making up a specific age-set sodality were usually structured into subgroups of such agnatic-brother pairings, that is, having fathers of the same matriclans. How this would come about was built into the age-set sodality system. A Hidatsa or Mandan age-set sodality that was prepared to move to the next level in seniority would approach the members of the immediately senior age-set sodality and would propose that this senior group transfer all the rituals and responsibilities that they performed as an *irakúu* sodality to them, the junior age-set, thereby promoting the latter up the age-set enabling hierarchy. This senior age-set, of course, would subsequently approach the age-set senior to them to arrange the same type of transfer, and so on. Now, as noted above, although these two age-sets stood in direct junior/senior position to each other, they would belong to the same generation. Median age difference between the two groups would likely be about five to six years. However, and despite their being of the same generation, seniority prevailed and, when agreement was arrived at for the transfer, each member of the senior age-set selected from among the junior age-set members those who were his agnates through having fathers of the same matriclan. The senior agnate then addressed his junior agnates as "*irakúu* sons" and they addressed him as "*irakúu* father." It was his responsibility (or their responsibility if more than one was involved) to teach his *irakúu* sons all the rituals of the senior age-set sodality that the junior age-set sodality was being prepared to "adopt." Each promotional step occurred the same way so that each *irakúu* subset linked by common agnatic relation (but belonging to different cognatic matriclans) would probably have remained especially close as a group within the overall age-set of companions and, in all likelihood, would have developed into sets of boon companions.

I have to speculate how this would relate to the mortuary practices. However, this suggestion is logically very plausible. Bowers points out that the Hidatsa practice was for an individual to select from among his or her companions those who would receive special gifts on his or her death and these would also participate in special ways during the mortuary rites. Now, a point that Bowers noted with regard to the deceased's agnatic matriclan is that "the members of the father's clan who officiated were selected in advance, sometimes years beforehand. It was the duty of the clan to provide goods, horses, and food for the funeral rites as payment for the official mourners who comprised the adults of the [deceased's] father's clan" (Bowers 1965, 75). However, the actual selection was usually made by this person in anticipating her or his own future mortuary rites and, therefore, for males this would amount to choosing their boon companions as an important part of these rites, these latter being his agnates in virtue of sharing his father's matriclan, and, indeed, they probably would take on special responsibilities in their dual capacity as agnates and companions who had shared experiences from self-torture in pursuit of sacred powers, to battle, to long distance travels. Therefore, while Bowers stipulates that the deceased's father's matriclan was responsible for organizing the mortuary rites, his own analysis of the age-set system supports the conclusion that several of these agnates would also be age-set companions of the deceased and, indeed, probably boon companions who would take special responsibility in these rites, including the honor of pursuing vengeance if their companion had died in battle.

This relates the age-set sodalities directly to mortuary practices and, furthermore, the latter can easily be seen as having world renewal rituals built into them. In this case, what Bowers has to say about the mortuary rituals, or as he calls them, funeral rites, is very germane; but also it is very puzzling since he describes a bifurcation in the total mortuary process and does not explain it. Following the first night of separation rites in the deceased's lodge, this deceased person was wrapped and taken by members of his agnatic matriclan, among whom would probably be his boon companions, and placed on the village scaffold, which was typically outside the village and associated with a skull circle or skull shrine, this circle being made up of the skulls of the dead of the village and of selected bison skulls (Bowers 1965, 170–71). These skull circles and mortuary scaffolds were particularly important as sacred places for young men who wanted to invoke spiritual aid through self-torture and fasting in their pursuit of sacred power. The actual length of the scaffolding period varied, however. It might be terminated after four days, at which time the rites of mourning were performed, thereby releasing the free soul to travel to the land of the Dead, and the body was removed and buried either under the floor of the lodge that the deceased had occupied or immediately outside this lodge. Alternatively, while the rites of mourning would be performed on the fourth day, again, releasing the free soul, instead of removing the body, it would be left on the scaffold until the flesh had completely decayed. At that point it was removed, the skull was set aside to be deposited in the skull circle later, and the bones bundled and usually buried in the stream bank, although Bowers also comments that sometimes the bones were deposited "within the refuse accumulation of the village itself, apparently without ceremony" (Bowers 1965, 331).

Bowers does not explain this variation between extended burial immediately after a four-day period of scaffold exposure, on the one hand, and long-term scaffold exposure followed by bone-bundle burial, on the other, except to say that it was the custom for some Hidatsa and Mandan lodges to do it one way, some to do it the other way, and some to do it both ways by alternating between mortuary rites for deceased. "During the summer months, while occupying the permanent villages, scaffolds were erected on a four-post frame at the edge of the village. The area might contain both burials and scaffolds. In some instances all the members of some households would be placed on scaffolds, while all the members of other households would be buried in the ground. In other instances a household might practice both scaffold disposal and interment" (Bowers 1965, 170).

Typically, the rules and protocols governing mortuary practices tend to leave very little in the way of discretionary choice to the mourners. Thus, this bifurcation of the mortuary process probably represents and is the outcome of rules that had varied application according to circumstances. That is, this bifurcation represents alternative mortuary *chaîne opératoire* trajectories. The choice that is implicated between extended burial and long-term scaffold exposure terminated by bone-bundle burial was probably the result of the influence of social groups and the exercise of mortuary-related rules that are left unexamined by Bowers; and yet these governed the proper way for disposing of the body according to a complex of conditions. Clearly, there would have been three major groups involved, each having common but also crosscutting interests: the deceased's own matriclan or, more precisely, matrilateral lodge; the deceased's father's matriclan; and, as I postulated above, the deceased's age-set sodality. Assuming that the deceased was male, then, in the latter case, while the whole sodality was called upon by the deceased's matriclan to contribute to the costs of the mortuary process, particularly to supplying the requisite gifts to be distributed on his behalf so as to be a proper measure of his reputation and standing, a core group within his sodality, whom I suggested above may be appropriately termed his "boon *irakúu*," most of whom would probably have been related to him as *agnatic* kin, might have considerable say in how the deceased was to be treated. It is likely, in fact, that it would be these men, or some of them, who had been selected by the deceased before his death to be the main organizers of his mortuary rites and he would have gifted to these same men some of his most valued possessions at death, such as his favorite horse, his most potent weapons, his personal sacred bundle, and so on. Therefore, the above decision of continuing the exposure of the body on the scaffold after the requisite four-day mourning period may have been strongly influenced by them. If all the parties consented, this would mean that instead of the mortuary rites being terminated after the four-day mourning period and the deceased being given an extended burial in or near the matrilateral lodge, these rites would be continued, ensuring the body fully decayed, followed by collecting the bones, bundling them, and then burying them in the river bank or near the scaffold, and setting the deceased's skull in the skull shrine.

Hence, the fact that the same matrilateral residential lodge might have its deceased members treated one or the other way strongly argues that discretion was not left to the deceased's matriclan alone. Among other conditional factors could be the relative age of the deceased. Younger men, for example, may have had a more intense commitment to their age-set sodality than to their matriclans and, given that it was the deceased who, prior to death, selected how he was to be treated at death, as a younger person he would have been particularly caught up with his companions. Older men, however, caught up with matriclan concerns, may have tended to ask old companions to ensure that he was quickly buried so some of his spiritual essences, his living souls, remained close to his matrilateral lodge in order to protect the occupants against invading spirits, and so on. Finally, it is particularly germane to note that, for the Hidatsa, extended scaffolding was interpreted as a mode of *postmortem human sacrifice* to the Above World gods. They interpreted the deterioration of the flesh as "feeding the gods." In terms of the Mourning/World Renewal Mortuary model, the gathering of the bones and burying them by the riverside would probably count as a transfer of the spiritual powers immanent in the bones to the Great Serpent, the god of the Underworld—often associated with bodies of water (the Hidatsa referred to the Missouri River as a Great Serpent). Hence, according to the above postulated process, the age-set sodalities of the Hidatsa were directly implicated in world renewal rituals and supervised certain of the mortuary rites of their companions for this purpose.

Of course, my claim that the boon companions would have promoted postmortem human sacrifice cannot be experimentally demonstrated. Rather, all this discussion does is bring together separate and apparently discrete conditions, different mortuary practices, obligations, relations, and articulate them into an explanation of a puzzle: why were there two types of mortuary practices performed? Bowers could only describe the practices. He made no attempt to explain them. This is an explanation. In terms of retroductive logic, it makes sense. It probably is corrigible. However, to reject the explanation on the grounds that it is not deductively demonstrated would mean preferring no explanation. This seems to be an irrational choice. I recommend accepting this explanation as the best approximation for now and use it as a means for accounting for further Hidatsa practices and, if the latter show inconsistencies that can be corrected by modifying the boon companion explanation, then it would be rational to do so. Hence, the hermeneutic spiral method enables the reasoned and rational growth of knowledge.

CONVEYANCING AND FRANCHISING OF SODALITY RITUAL USUFRUCT

As I noted above, Bowers makes it clear that there were two types of Calumet-like ceremonials, one constituting fictive kinship alliance and the other intersodality alliance. However, he also gives clear grounds that, in fact, there were two types of sodality ceremonials, one dedicated to transferring ritual prerogatives between senior and junior age-sets of the same community, as discussed briefly above, and one dedicated to transferring ritual prerogatives between equivalent age-sets from different communities. The former ensured the continuity of the age-set system in the community; the latter was fundamental to constituting sodality alliances between and among age-sets of separate and sometimes quite spatially distant communities. Both of these are important in order to give some analogical content to the development of the Ohio Hopewell episode.

Conveyancing of Ritual Usufruct

As noted above, when a junior age-set sodality considered itself sufficiently mature to take over the responsibilities of the age-set sodality immediately its senior, it made overtures to this senior age-set in order to negotiate the transfer. Of course, a major cost was involved in that the junior age-set must mobilize considerable material wealth as gifts for receiving the rights from the senior age-set to perform the rituals. I also outlined above the actual way this relation was expressed, with the senior and junior age-set sodalities referring to each other figuratively as "fathers" and "sons." Probably the most important and detailed part of the transfer was the instruction of the ritual by the "fathers" to their "sons." This instruction involved all the stories, songs, performances, as well as the proper way to make, repair, treat, curate, and use the sacred material media of the sodality. All this consists of two forms of cognition: existential knowledge and know-how rules and practicality. The knowledge consists of the stories and related songs they had to learn, as well as the way these fitted into the cosmology; the know-how consists of the rights, duties, and values as embedded in these stories, as well as both the conditions under which the ritual had to be performed and the complex set of rules and protocols that governed the group's individual and collective behaviors so as to ensure that these counted as fully felicitous ritual performances.

In our own society, we would class all this symbolic expressive knowledge and especially the know-how as "intellectual property" and, as a proprietorial society, the law governing the ownership of this property is termed proprietorial copyright. However, in my discussion of the deontic ecological perspective, I argued that prehistoric Native North American communities were based on inclusive territorialism and that this constituted the community that habitually used and occupied a territory as its custodians, not its owners. Custodianship of territory is based on the notion that those who habitually occupy and exploit it must both care for and share the resources. The social powers of the occupants that endow them as the custodians arise from their taking on these responsibilities and obligations as autonomous communities. In the world experienced by the prehistoric Native North Americans, then, while the notion of copyright would be perfectly logical and intelligible, the supporting notions of "proprietorial copyright" and "intellectual property" would not. Rather, the equivalent English terms would possibly be expressed as *custodial copyright* and *intellectual usufruct.* This means that having custodial copyright of *intellectual usufruct* means having the copyright, that is, the exclusive right and responsibility in that community to perform that activity as stipulated and defined in the representational content of the intellectual usufruct (know-how). When it comes to the custodial copyright of intellectual usufruct of ritual, or what I will term *ritual usufruct,* I would suggest this means that while custodians have exclusive rights in the community to perform this ritual, they also are obligated to exercise the ritual usufruct on behalf of the community and, when no longer able or willing to exercise it, they are obliged to pass on the custodial copyright to another party who becomes the new custodian of this ritual usufruct. Therefore, custodial copyright to ritual usufruct would be defined as the right and duty to perform and, under the appropriate circumstances, to pass on the custodial copyright of this distinct body of sacred knowledge and ritual know-how, namely ritual usufruct. This custodial copyright includes the obligation of the custodians to ensure that this body of ritual usufruct is used properly and also that they pass it on in good order to those whom they recognize as having qualified and demonstrated that they would continue respecting the imperatives of this important body of ritual practice. These obligations of usage and transfer distinguish custodial copyright from proprietorial copyright since, in the latter case, as represented in Euro-American culture, the copyright holder is an *owner* of intellectual property and has the exclusive right *and* discretion to use or not to use the knowledge and know-how. The holders of custodial copyright, however, are the custodians of ritual usufruct and while such rituals can only be performed by them, they do not have the discretionary right to withhold exercising the usufruct when requested. They are custodians and have the overriding obligation to preserve and exercise the ritual usufruct on behalf of the community and its members.

Traditionally, Native North American peoples have a great respect for the custodial copyright of ritual usufruct. It is firmly believed if this ritual usufruct or any of its material icons, such as sacred bundles, are used by noncustodians, the consequences for the unwarranted users can be devastating and even the custodians can be materially and/or spiritually harmed, particularly if they were party to this improper usage. Of course, at the same time, the custodians are responsible to transfer the ritual usufruct at the proper time and, just as proprietorial copyright to intellectual property can be transferred in several different ways in proprietorial regimes (e.g., buying, inheriting, licensing), so custodial copyright to ritual usufruct can also be transferred in different ways. These transfers are typically effected by means of the custodians teaching the body of ritual usufruct to the proposed recipients with the latter then being required to perform the specific rituals under the master custodian's guidance.

I have already outlined the way the transfer can be made from a senior to a junior age-set. This is an absolute form of transfer that I will call *conveyancing* of ritual usufruct. It is absolute in the sense that when the current custodians perform the transfer, they *extinguish* their custodial rights. That is, even though they clearly have the knowledge and know-how of the ritual usufruct, their rights and prerogatives to perform the ritual are extinguished by their consensually conveying them to the recipient party. As in the Hidatsa case, when the ritual usufruct is the custodial copyright of an age-set sodality, the latter can convey its copyright to the junior age-set, and thereby surrender all rights.[6] The recipient age-set members become the new custodians and they also take on all the obligations this involves. Clearly, usufruct conveyancing of ritual from senior to junior sodality is typically done only within a community and between age-sets that stand as senior-junior to each other or, in an *irakúu* father–*irakúu* son relation. Being of the same community is important; otherwise, as an absolute form of transfer, the community would lose the ritual usufruct if the latter was conveyed to parties who did not belong to the community.

Franchising of Ritual Usufruct

Conveyancing is not the total story. As I noted above, equivalent age-set sodalities of different autonomous communities also were able to transfer a ritual usufruct but in a manner that did not extinguish the rights of the donors. Bowers gives an example of this type of transfer. In 1870, an age-set of Crow warriors approached their age-set equivalent, the Crazy Dog sodality of a Hidatsa village, and asked the Crazy Dogs if they, the Crow age-set, could receive the rights from the Crazy Dogs to perform the Hidatsa Grass Dance ritual. Considerable preliminary negotiations occurred and the upshot of these was that the Hidatsa Crazy Dog sodality group agreed. How this transfer of ritual rights and prerogatives occurred was through a complex Calumet-like ceremony (Bowers 1965, 91–92). Interestingly, what concerned the Crazy Dogs was that the Crow age-set not insist on an outright, or what I termed above, a conveyancing transfer. They were quite adamant in this regard because, as I noted above, conveyancing would mean that the sodality would no longer have the right to perform the ritual and this would not be in the interests of the community. Bowers put it this way: "The Hidatsa were unwilling to sell in the sense of extinguishing their rights, which would have happened had a 'father-son' relationship been established. The Crows, therefore, agreed to a 'friend-friend' relationship so that the Hidatsa could transmit the rite and the information while still holding their own rights. Then each member of the society selected a friend to whom he supplied a duplicate set of society equipment" (1965, 92).[7] In effect, the two equivalent age-sets from these culturally related but mutually autonomous communities, the Crow and the Hidatsa, were replicating a relationship that would be akin to those that bonded the three Winnebago boon companion gods—Red Horn, Storms-As-He-Walks, and Turtle. The contrast to this would be to act in terms of the relation between Red Horn and his sons, namely, a kinship relation.

Bowers also notes that the friend-friend or, in the equivalent terms I am using here, the *irakúu* brother–*irakúu* brother transfers constituted alliances between the two equivalent age-sets. Traditionally, they could offer and call on one another for assistance unrelated, as such, to the ritual usufruct that linked them. For example, he reports that it was not unusual for this alliance to enable one age-set—or volunteers from it—to participate in acts of vengeance against the enemies that killed one of the members of an allied age-set sodality. Therefore, this was a very important type of intercommunity alliance construction.

As I noted above, Bowers specifies that the Hidatsa Crazy Dogs insisted on transferring the custodial copyright of the ritual usufruct while "still holding their own rights" to it. Hence, this intersodality transfer was distinctly *not* a form of conveyancing of ritual usufruct. Unfortunately, Bowers does not use a term to clearly distinguish it from the conveyancing type, as discussed above. However, the transfer is significantly different since, as illustrated in the case of the Hidatsa-Crow transfer, not only did the Hidatsa custodians of the ritual usufruct retain custodial copyright of the ritual usufruct, thereby maintaining the right to continue performing the rituals for its community, but also the recipient Crow age-set, in gaining the full right to the ritual usufruct, could proceed to transfer the same ritual usufruct to another equivalent age-set of a community unrelated to either themselves or the Hidatsa, while retaining rights to its own ritual usufruct, and so on.

The above "and so on" is very important for it implicates a process of linking together more and more-distant age-set sodalities, a type of "chain reaction" of ritual usufruct transfers. I think that the sense expressed by the English term *franchising* usefully articulates the type of transfer process this is and I will use the term *ritual usufruct franchising* to refer to this intercommunity *irakúu* age-set transferring of the custodial copyright of ritual usufruct. If this transfer of ritual usufruct is treated as a type of franchising, then the vocabulary of franchising is appropriate. In principle, because the initial *franchiser* retains the copyright, and the *franchisee* also has the right to subsequent franchising of the same usufruct, then only practicality and the perceived intrinsic value of the usufruct limits the number of times this same ritual usufruct can be transferred to other equivalent sodalities while all the franchisers retain their custodial copyright to it. Importantly, in fact, it almost becomes a moral obligation to franchise the usufruct to another sodality since, as a custodial rather than a proprietorial phenomenon, part of the custodial copyright includes the moral responsibility and obligation to "pass on" the ritual usufruct to equivalent parties in other communities. Therefore, in an important sense, not only does this type of ritual usufruct franchising transfer make it possible to distribute the ritual while the franchisers retain the original ritual usufruct, there is a built-in obligation on their part to do so. Equally importantly, each recipient age-set sodality, the ritual usufruct franchisee, also receives the right and obligation to become a franchiser of the same usufruct ritual by transferring it to an equivalent age-set sodality of another community. Typically, this second-degree recipient age-set could be even farther away from the original franchiser sodality so that, in effect, a "down-the-line" chain-like serial reaction of franchising events could occur, probably in multiple directions. Archaeologically, of course, the signature of these chains would be typical "down-the-line" exchange patterning. The material content of these exchanges would tend to be of exotic rather than everyday artifacts and features since part of the franchising of important ritual usufruct would include producing and using the symbolic pragmatic warrants necessary for the felicitous performances of the rituals.

Therefore, ritual usufruct transferring entails two complementary forms of transfer, conveyancing transfers and franchising transfers. I will call this dual process the *Ritual Usufruct Conveyancing and Franchising model.* It postulates two processes by which particular material cultural patterns related to ritual can be distributed *within* a given group across time and both within a region and across regions, both near and distant. These two mechanisms are continually at work. Within a given region, conveyancing occurs within the ritual units, that is, within a given cult sodality, and this is how junior age-sets replace senior age-sets and, at the same time, become promoted to the senior level. However, also within a given region, franchising between cult sodalities will occur. This ensures the dispersing of a new ritual usufruct or an innovation to an established ritual usufruct among the regional cult sodalities. Franchising, of course, is also the main mechanism by which extraregionally derived usufruct rituals and their constitutive warrants are procured. The responsible cult sodality will likely quite quickly promote intraregional franchising, thereby fulfilling its obligation as a custodian of the new ritual usufruct to pass it on to its allied cult sodalities.

Of course, I have relied on using the notions of proprietorial copyright and intellectual property analogically to model custodial copyright to ritual usufruct. However, while these have important similarities, it is also important to note where they significantly differ, that is, where they perspicuously contrast. Otherwise I risk simply projecting the Euro-American cultural practices onto the Middle Woodland period communities. This particularly applies to modes of transfer. A common form of franchising intellectual *property* entails maintaining exclusive control by the franchiser, and this is done by a contractual license to constrain the use of the intellectual property by a franchisee under quite specific conditions. The recipient party *leases* or derives strictly monitored usufruct rights by paying first a franchising "down payment" and then a scheduled franchising fee. This fee is set by "free market" negotiation and typically it is also scheduled so that every month or so, the franchisee must pay a licensing fee to the franchiser plus a proportion of the profits. This generates a franchiser–franchisee relation that has strong deontic similarities to the landlord–tenant relation. Furthermore, the copyright owner or proprietor, the franchiser, usually retains the right to franchise to as many parties as the owner can contract. Sometimes a franchisee can also contract the right to subfranchise within a defined territorial module and these subfranchisees also must pay constant renewal fees and the first-degree franchisee typically is required under her or his original franchise contract to pass on a specified proportion of these second-degree franchising fees to the primary or first-degree franchiser. Hence, a hierarchical structure emerges that is characterized as permanent and dominance-based in nature.

However, I postulate that this is *not* the case for the ritual usufruct franchising of custodial copyright. As noted above, one of the reasons the franchiser transfers the ritual usufruct is to fulfill the custodial responsibility to ensure sharing, continuity, and effective practice of the sacred knowledge and know-how. Therefore, actively pursuing franchising so as to expand the distribution of the ritual and ensure the continuity of the know-how is part of each franchiser's custodial duty. Importantly, the franchising event is a form of reciprocal gifting since it entails significant material exchange by the recipient of the ritual usufruct (i.e., the franchisee) to the donor of the ritual usufruct (i.e., the franchiser), and vice versa. In fact, the most important material gifts are probably the material items that constitute the primary symbolic pragmatic media of the ritual usufruct being transferred. This is typically the responsibility of the franchisers, since they possess the know-how and have access to the requisite exotic materials, and these are gifts to the new franchisees, who use them for their first performance of that ritual. Alternatively, the gift can be in the form of the ritual know-how guided by the franchisers; in which case the requisite material media will be locally produced by the recipients acting as ritual apprentices under the guidance of the franchisers. The initial performance, guided by the franchisers, counts as the completion of the franchise transfer of the ritual usufruct. However, if the Hidatsa system can be used as the model, the recipient party as host is obligated to house and feed the donor party as guests for the duration of the franchising event. Since the duration involves a period of intensive apprenticeship, learning all the oral mythical knowledge and ritual know-how, including how to produce and treat the material media, this franchising event can last for several months. Furthermore, the hosts must also ensure that their guests are given a good send off by loading them with gifts made from local and even more distant regional materials. Because the gifting discharges the obligations of the recipient franchisee to the donor franchiser, and in fact sets up expectations of reciprocity from the franchiser, no controlling hierarchy of franchiser–franchisee emerges as in the case of proprietorial franchising. Rather a network of autonomous franchisers–franchisees emerges. These constitute a network of mutualistic alliances stretching over space and time. In short, since the custodial copyright includes rules and protocols that spell out the exotic forms of artifacts and features that must be used to constitute proper ritual performances, mapping the expansion of the latter in space and time is also mapping the distribution of the ritual and the alliances that it constitutes.

Finally, under a custodial regime, the mutualistic heterarchical alliance relations are primarily maintained not by the coercive imposing of fees, as is the case for proprietorial copyright franchising, but by the cycling of reciprocal gifting satisfying the need of the recipient sodality to replenish the symbolic material media by which the felicity and efficacy of the ritual performances are ensured. The source of this replenishing, of course, would normally be the initial franchisers relative to the recipient franchisees. Note that the makeup of these two groups also changes over time through internal transfers, conveyancing, from seniors to juniors. That is, over time the primary franchisers would be replaced as they aged and their junior age-sets were promoted to senior age-sets by the conveyancing of the ritual usufruct. Furthermore, it should be noted that the same franchiser–franchisee network would likely mediate innovations to established ritual usufruct and/or introduce new ritual usufructs arising from changing conditions within and beyond the initial network, thereby being an active medium in cultural transformations.

David Penney has very astutely postulated a form of ritual franchising as the primary mechanism by which the Middle Woodland period Hopewell interregional system of exchange came about (Penney 1989). While the same basic notion of interregional exchange as being mediated by the franchising of ritual usufruct is at the core of both our models, it is important to point out where we differ. He refers to long distance interaction mediated by ritual procurement as the pursuit of ritual prerogatives, and this is effectively what I mean by custodial copyright of ritual usufruct. "Prerogative" seems to be a very apt term. However, he treats this is a type of individualized proprietorial copyright passed from master to apprentice. He also highlights the process as the outcome of a type of individual personal power quests. These are carried out not by collectives such as sodalities but by independent individuals pursuing the enhancing of their personal reputations and prestige at the local level. Therefore, an independent agent actively undertakes travels (vision quests and the sort) to learn the ritual prerogatives from a shaman or a learned person(s) in distant regions. This person then returns to the home area with the personal and exclusive control to these ritual prerogatives—implicating a type of proprietorship—consisting of esoteric knowledge and ritual know-how and, through exercising this ritual in his local region, he or she comes to reproduce the exotic materials.

He also cites the Hidatsa and other historically known peoples, in this case emphasizing such individual pursuits of power that have been recorded among them. He notes, for example, an individual "purchasing" a sacred bundle was, in effect, acquiring the prerogatives to the use of the rituals attached to that bundle. "Ownership of a medicine pipe bundle offered spiritual powers useful in healing, warfare, and seeking buffalo. The bundles were purchased with horses and blankets during an elaborate ritual in which the purchaser learned the songs, rituals and other sacred lore associated with the pipe during an extended period of tutelage. When the training and transfer was complete, the recipient of the pipe bundle received the right to make replicas of the bundle which he could then transfer to others" (1989, 170). Clearly, he has particularly focused on the type of interaction mediated by shaman-apprentice and father-son adoptive kinship relations that Hall has argued were at the basis of the Calumet ceremonialism. Also, just as Hall did, he has focused on the person-to-person relation that this exchange established. "Among the Hidatsa, a Siouan speaking village tribe of the upper Missouri river, men gave sacred pipe stems to their adopted 'sons' or trading partners who belonged to one of the several alien bands that visited Hidatsa villages to trade for corn. Medicine pipes . . . were the focus of a series of sacred bundles that circulated among the Crow, Hidatsa, Blackfeet [and so on]" (1989, 169–70). While I certainly can endorse Penney's proposing the pursuit of religious or ritual prerogatives as the mechanism by which the Middle Woodland Hopewellian assemblage was dispersed, I find his individualistic focus on the process as well as his tendency to treat prerogatives in proprietorial rather than custodial terms to be problematic. I prefer to argue that the widespread distribution of the major and unique Hopewellian assemblage is more likely to be the result of collective endeavors in the pursuit of custodial prerogatives than personal endeavors in pursuit of private gain. Of course, caught up in my proposed ritual usufruct franchising could be "sideline" forms of interaction in which individual participants took the opportunity to pursue personal ritual power, and even possibly meet up with future spouses. However, these endeavors would be parasitic on the primary process of collective ritual usufruct franchising as articulated by the above Ritual Usufruct Conveyancing and Franchising model.

THE EMERGENCE OF THE ECCLESIASTIC-COMMUNAL CULT SODALITY

This discussion of the relations among senior and junior age-set sodalities and among equivalent age-set sodalities of different communities can be used to refine the nature of the age-grade hierarchy that this ecclesiastic-communal cult sodality type is postulated to have and that I described in the previous chapter. Given my above discussion of Hidatsa villages as constituted by clans and sodalities that stood to each other as relatively autonomous organizations, it is clear that I am treating them as complementary heterarchical communities. It is also important to note that when encountered by Euro-Americans, the historically known Hidatsa villages were in the integrated settlement articulation modal posture. As I noted earlier, Wallace treats both clans and sodalities as the bases of communal cults, kinship and non-kinship, respectively, and, in fact, the "cult" was simply the sodality or the clan in its (temporary) religious posture. I also noted earlier that communal cult formations are to be expected of communities in the integrated settlement articulation modal posture since it was more likely in the material conditions of the bifurcated settlement articulation modal posture that the emergence of the ecclesiastic-communal cult sodality type might occur. In that discussion I also noted that these two postures manifested surface social structural articulations that, seen overall, constituted the integrated-bifurcated settlement articulation modal continuum. Such surface structural fluctuations, however, presuppose the continuity of deep social structural conditions, namely, the dual clan/sodality structure that defines what I have called the complementary heterarchical community. Hence, since a historic Hidatsa or Mandan community consisted of an integrated village, the age-set sodalities in each were mutually autonomous while being relatively autonomous to the clans, as described above. This also means that the sodalities operated in the religious posture as communal cults, not ecclesiastic-communal cult sodalities (i.e., being congregations based on the laity-clergy structure). However, I have postulated that the complementary heterarchical communities of the Ohio Middle Woodland period were in the bifurcated settlement articulation modal posture and that the latter posture was a necessary (but not sufficient) condition for the emergence of an ecclesiastic-communal cult sodality system. Does the fact that the Hidatsa and Mandan sodality systems enabled the shift into communal cult postures within their integrated villages discount them as useful analogically for understanding the Ohio Middle Woodland period social system? I think not. In fact, they become particularly useful since understanding the operation of the Hidatsa sodality in their communal cult postures highlights the sort of internal structural changes to this type of sodality system, one sustaining *communal* cult sodalities, that would need to occur to make it possible for an *ecclesiastic-communal* cult sodality system to emerge.

As I noted above, within an age-grade the conveyancing of custodial ritual from a senior age-set to its immediate junior age set, that is, from *irakúu* fathers to *irakúu* sons, constituted a promotional step and this motivated the senior age-set to then turn to their own *irakúu* fathers in order to ask them to convey their custodial ritual to them, their *irakúu* sons. Since each age-set was autonomous, this could be worked out without too much disorder, although, as I discuss below, it probably was not always quite so simple. However, I have postulated that an ecclesiastic-communal cult sodality would have a major promotional conveyancing event whereby the junior age-grade would become the senior age-grade when the few remaining current seniors retired en masse, and the pre-initiated age-sets would in turn be incorporated en masse as the new junior age-grade. How could the Hidatsa-type individual age-set to age-set conveyancing practice modify to enable the total age-grade ecclesiastic-communal cult sodality conveyancing to occur, or do I have to modify the latter? I do not think so. As I just noted above, Hidatsa practice had significant quirks and problems that were also resolved and the method used could serve as the basis to evolve a new age-set conveyancing mechanism that would enable the ecclesiastic-communal cult sodality inter-age-grade conveyancing to occur en masse.

For the Hidatsa, as for any community with an age-set sodality system, the conveyancing of ritual custodial usufruct from the senior or *irakúu* fathers age-set to the junior or *irakúu* sons age-set is a time-dependent process and since normally an age-set of companions is closed to accepting new members as companions, all the age-sets of the community will be affected when any one of these autonomous groups decides it is time to "move up." In this case, "moving up" means to initiate negotiations with the immediately senior age-set, their *irakúu* fathers, to enter into the ritual conveyancing process. However, this senior age-set may not be prepared to proceed, either because they believe that their *irakúu* sons have not achieved sufficient maturity to take over the senior ritual usufruct or else because their own *irakúu* fathers in the next more senior age-set do not themselves feel it is time to move up. This type of blockage, in fact, could lead to a splitting of the integrated village since it was not unknown for a dynamic peer leader of a more mature age-set, frustrated by the senior age-set's postponing conveyancing of their usufruct ritual to his age-set, to lead his companions and their families to separate from the village and establish their own integrated village. Since the members of this more mature age-set would likely have families and they would be drawn from across the clans of the village, as well as possibly encouraging younger siblings to come with them, a viable new village could be possible that combined representatives of all the clans and most of the age-sets. The Hidatsa historical experience may be instructive in this case since it suggests what changes would have to be innovated to overcome this problem of fissioning, although even if such a buffering or avoidance process emerged, it certainly would not be guaranteed to succeed all the time.

For the Hidatsa the most important and active age-set sodality was the Black Mouths. This group occupied the "middle" position. They were the junior of the senior age-grade sodalities consisting of mature men in the prime of life. They were active in warfare and, in fact, they had important intravillage responsibilities as the community's "police." If a major ritual event involving the total community was planned, the community leaders from the clans and the senior age-set sodalities would meet in council to plan the event and, of course, the leaders of the Black Mouths were there. Usually the latter consented to act to ensure peace, and good order would prevail, and by their consenting the leaders of all the other groups recognized the responsibilities of the Black Mouth society in this regard, effectively endowing them with the necessary authority to act in terms of their traditional responsibilities at such public gatherings. This general consensus meant that the Black Mouths could physically intervene in another's behavior if they judged this person's behavior was an inappropriate form of conduct in the context of the public event. In effect, the Black Mouths had the consensual approval of the community, that is, a temporary and conditioned dominance authority to invade the autonomy of an individual agent, a member of their own community, if they judged that person's behavior threatened the well-being of the community. Often such actions required on-the-spot decisions and this meant that the Black Mouths had to be mature and physically strong men. At the same time, as an autonomous sodality, only the current Black Mouths had the right and responsibility to decide when they should surrender this responsibility to the next junior age-set, their *irakúu* sons, and they could refuse initial approaches on grounds that they did not judge their *irakúu* sons to be sufficiently mature. Usually, prior to making such a negative judgment, they would consult with their own *irakúu* fathers, the one-step-more-senior Real Dog sodality, for their advice. The leaders of this sodality, chosen as such by their own companions, were men who had advanced in prestige and respect in war and alliance construction and their advice would add serious weight to the decision of their *irakúu* sons holding the Black Mouth custodial ritual usufruct sacred bundles and the associated responsibilities.

Normally the *irakúu* sons of the Black Mouths would accept a negative response from their *irakúu* fathers in the first case, recognizing their wisdom and also the wisdom of the Black Mouths' own *irakúu* fathers. However, if a second approach was also spurned, then problems could arise. In fact, as I noted above, the refusal of those occupying the Black Mouth sodality to perform the conveyancing ritual to transfer the custodial ritual usufruct rights to their *irakúu* sons was one of the reasons a Hidatsa village split in the 1870s. The leader of the sodality that wished to move into the Black Mouth position took his age-set and all their families out of the village and established a new one. This indicates how central the age-grade system could be to the traditional Native North American complementary heterarchical community. In fact, as I noted briefly above, since membership in an age-set is independent of the clans of the community, it incorporates members from all or most of the clans and, added to the fact that equivalent but complementary male and female sodalities were often paired as *irakúu* brothers–*irakúu* sisters, it is likely the female-based sodality would leave with its *irakúu* brothers. As age-sets, the two would together have representation of all the clans. Also, their offspring would probably accompany them and they would be organized into their own junior age-set sodalities. Therefore, not only would the separating age-set group make up a significant portion of the active adult population of the home community, they would incorporate the ritual usufruct and social structures that would be sufficient to constitute a viable independent community. It is not surprising, then, that a community will have some flexibility built into the age-grade system in order to maintain as smooth a process of promotion as possible and avoid such community fracturing.

For the Hidatsa, the male-based age-set system was divided into two major categories by junior and senior age-grades or generations: males of the preadult, young adult, and the younger mature adult categories constituted the age-set sodalities of the junior male age-grade; and the active middle aged and elder male adults constituted the age-set societies of the senior male age-grade (an age-grade was a generation having about a 25-year youngest-to-oldest spread). The formal junior age-grade entry level was the Stone Hammer society, occupied by 12- to 14-year-old boys. They rather smoothly moved through the Little Dog and Crazy Dog age-set societies (i.e., "society" being generically a sodality), building up their ritual powers and honing their warrior and hunting rituals and skills. All these societies sustained their autonomy through maintaining founding myths usually rooted in the Hidatsa world creation stories where culture heroes played critical roles, some of them being the mythical founders of the sodalities. Each had the same basic organizational structure of peer-selected leaders, a public speaker who would orally announce to the village the society's upcoming ceremonies and other activities, and so on.

In general, the Stone Hammer society would advance to the next level, the Little Crazy Dogs, and from this level they would move to the Crazy Dogs. The next was the Lumpwood society. These were young men entering into adult status. Hence, they could be labeled as the bachelors of the community, prospective husbands as well as young warriors who had already received their apprenticing as Stone Hammer, Little Crazy Dogs, and then Crazy Dogs. By the time those of the Lumpwood society approached the next level, the Half-Shaved Head society, to request conveyancing rituals they may have been eight or more years as Lumpwoods and they would be "champing at the bit." The conveyancing of the Half-Shaved Head society copyright was a critical transfer because it was the most senior of the junior age-grade societies. This would place them just below the Black Mouth society, the first of the senior age-grade societies. As noted above, the responsibilities of this society required mature males who were respected for their military as well as "diplomatic" skills and who were still physically very capable. However, by this time, so were the Lumpwoods, although clearly more junior. Bowers argues that it is for this reason that the Half-Shaved Head society "served as a buffer society to protect the Black Mouths from premature purchase until the younger men had sufficiently distinguished themselves in warfare, ceremonial activities and fasting, and had shown evidence of good judgment so that the group could be entrusted to fulfill the many social obligations and responsibilities of the Black Mouth society" (Bowers 1965, 183). Therefore, typically when the Lumpwood society approached the Half-Shaved Head society to initiate the conveyancing transfer, the men they spoke to were not only holders of the latter ritual usufruct, they were also the Black Mouths.

To clarify, it is necessary to step back a bit. Typically when the Half-Shaved Head society males became Black Mouths, they *retained* custodial ritual usufruct of the Half-Shaved Head society. Hence, the Black Mouths, in their capacity as custodial copyright holders of the Half-Shaved Head society ritual usufruct, would only convey this latter copyright to the males of the Lumpwood society when they perceived this junior group was ready or almost ready to become the next Black Mouths. That is, a two-step process would occur. The Black Mouths would first convey the Half-Shaved Head rituals to the Lumpwood society males, and then typically a year later, or thereabouts, the Black Mouths would convey their Black Mouth custodial copyrights to the Half-Shaved Head society members and move on to more senior age-sets, such as the Real Dogs (Bowers 1965, 194).

The only drawback to an age-set doubling up its custodial usufruct load, such as the Black Mouths retaining the Half-Shaved Head custodial ritual usufruct, at least for the Hidatsa and Mandan, was that normally the age-set sodality responsible for both sets of rituals would not perform those of the more junior age-set for which they were custodians. However, this Hidatsa practice is not based on any entrenched or warranted necessity and, in fact, it was a form of transgression in that the age-set was not discharging its custodial duties to perform the ritual usufruct for which it had responsibility. Therefore, there would be moral pressures to contend with that, under special circumstances, could lead this "doubling up" to instigating important ritual innovations while maintaining the respect for age-set autonomy. In this case, under special conditions, "doubling up" could be an opportunity for both *irakúu* fathers and sons to develop a closer, more everyday relation. Using the Hidatsa for illustrative purpose, instead of a senior age-grade sodality like the Black Mouths suspending the rituals and duties of the Half-Shaved

Head society while devoting themselves to the rituals and duties they have as Black Mouths, they could decide to recognize their *irakúu* sons, the current Lumpwood society, as apprentice Half-Shaved Heads "in waiting," conditionally franchising, not conveyancing, the right to perform the rites and duties of this latter sodality while acting under the authority of their *irakúu* fathers, the Black Mouths, who also, of course, actually held the Half-Shaved Head exclusive ritual usufruct. This would maintain the formal age-set separation and thereby respect the principle of autonomy between the Lumpwood and Black Mouth societies, while reducing any potential friction caused by the latter retaining the Half-Shaved Head ritual usufruct. At the same time, this conditional franchising, a form of "learner's permit period," would allow for the Lumpwood society to receive a thorough training and experience in the Half-Shaved Head duties and, of course, the community would benefit by having the custodial ritual usufructs of the latter sodality being performed. Hence, the members of the Lumpwood society would continue possibly for eight to ten years in this position while devoting more and more time and effort to the Half-Shaved Head and even, as apprentices to the Black Mouths, some of the Black Mouth tasks. Since the Half-Shaved Head society was recognized as the most senior of the junior age-grade sodalities, the Lumpwood society males would be respected for doing activities traditional to this group while assisting the important first-level senior age-grade Black Mouth society, without, however, transgressing the junior/senior age-grade distinction. When they did carry out the formal conveyancing ritual, they would be fully recognized as the Half-Shaved Head society. They would willingly convey the Lumpwood ritual usufruct to the next lower society, the Crazy Dogs, their *irakúu* sons, knowing that one year later they, the Half-Shaved Heads, would have the full custodial copyright to the duties and ritual usufruct of the Black Mouth society conveyed to them. Their *irakúu* fathers would then become the new Real Dog society, recognized as among the more senior and most respected of the male age-set societies. "[T]he Dog society was an important one to which chiefs or leaders of various subgroups of the village belonged. They were the mature men who had distinguished themselves in many ways" (Bowers 1965, 185).

How would this sort of overlapping apprenticing program play out? The Black Mouth society consists of mature men who would be at the prime of their lives. The median age of a new Black Mouth age-set would be 34–35. They had initiated their age-set careers as adolescents at the age of 12–14. They progressed through the Little Dog and Crazy Dog societies, the former between 14 and 16, and the latter between 16 and 20. When they became the Lumpwood society, they would have been 20–22 and would have remained at this level until 30–32 or 33. During this period they progressively took on

Half-Shaved Head society duties until, at 32 or 33, they formally became the Half-Shaved Head society. In one year, at the median age of about 34 or 35, they officially became the Black Mouth society. The total experience of this set of males as a sodality group would be from about the median age of 12 to 35, a generation. Of course, all this means that doubling up as apprentices for the senior age-set society in addition to being the occupants of the junior age-set society would probably occur at every level. This is because the ten years from 20–22 to 30–32 that they were officially the Lumpwood society, those in the Crazy Dog society were "frozen," as were those of the Little Dog society and those in the Stone Hammer society. However, the Lumpwood society would retain custodial copyright to the ritual usufruct and duties of the Crazy Dog society while apprenticing those of the Little Dog society, and when the Lumpwoods officially became the Half-Shaved Head society, they would officially convey the Crazy Dog ritual to those holding the Little Dog society ritual usufruct and, one year later, the new Crazy Dog society would receive the Lumpwood ritual usufruct and ask their Little Dog society *irakúu* sons to apprentice in the Crazy Dog ritual, and so on.

Of course, the same doubling up would have occurred in the senior age-grade. Bowers points out that the age-set society senior to the Black Mouths would often have the Real Dog society (also known as the Old Dog society) ritual usufruct and other duties conveyed to them well before they would in turn convey the Black Mouth ritual usufruct to their "sons." This is not at all improbable since the Old Dog society would normally be made up of quite senior, that is, older, men and their numbers would probably reduce fairly quickly through natural attrition. Still, the critical factor here was the extended Black Mouth period. Clearly, this could be reduced if the junior age-set-in-waiting was patently competent and this would from time to time effectively reduce the generation span possibly by five years, in effect, extending the senior generation by five years. This flexibility would allow maintaining the junior/senior age-grade structure and the internal age-set structuring and, therefore, maintain the overall stability of the age-set system. As I noted earlier, if the system became unstable, it could lead to the fissioning of the community along the junior/senior age-grade fracture line. Therefore, it becomes even more important when speaking of an ecclesiastic-communal cult sodality since if this junior/senior age-grade division is broken the cult sodality would likely dissolve, leaving the junior age-grade to establish a new one, if possible.

I have taken some care to outline the Hidatsa age-set system in order to demonstrate that even though the age-set societies or sodalities are mutually autonomous communal cult sodalities, the system has embedded in its structural relations the potential to be transformed into an ecclesiastic-communal cult sodality organized as an enabling hierarchy based on age seniority. The critical factors are the ongoing junior–senior *irakúu* relationships, here termed the *irakúu* father–*irakúu* son relation. Age-set sodalities normally are community specific, relating across communities through the *irakúu* brother–*irakúu* brother, *irakúu* sister–*irakúu* sister, or *irakúu* brother–*irakúu* sister relations. Should the Hidatsa complementary heterarchical communities shift into the bifurcated settlement articulation modal posture, even though the age-set cult sodalities would be freed up to establish autonomous locales sustaining spatial arm's-length relations from the dispersed clan-based habitation locales, the *irakúu* father–*irakúu* son relation would promote these age-sets to cooperate in building *shared* locales in order to perform the critical world renewal ritual. The practices of "splitting" the custodial ritual usufruct of each named sodality could easily be accommodated to the need to maintain good relations among these groups and, of course, endowing a junior age-set with auxiliary legitimacy to perform rituals of the senior age-set would enable the latter to continue to draw on the labor of the younger groups while also assigning them to the important but difficult tasks of going on long distance expeditions to procure exotic resources and, in fact, carrying on franchising transfers of selected ritual usufruct to distant equivalent age-sets, creating long distance intercult sodality alliances, and so on. The sodalities of these distant regions in their communal cult posture might also be stimulated to exercise their own *irakúu* father–*irakúu* son relations to emulate the ecclesiastic-communal cult sodality structure of their Ohio Hopewell allies and emerge as new ecclesiastic-communal cult sodalities.

Of course, if the Ohio Middle Woodland period communities were already structured in *clans* and *name groups*, as I earlier described these latter for the historic Shawnee, then structurally integrating the ranked age-sets would not be necessary since the Shawnee name group system already was constituted as a strongly established enabling hierarchy of ranked age-sets and, of course, it also had a dual sectoring into male and female groups. The only structural component it lacked was a clergy. Therefore, to be transformed into an ecclesiastic-communal cult sodality, it would have to incorporate a laity-clergy structure. However, I have already described how this could be done under conditions I have postulated for the Middle Woodland period of this area, namely, intensifying subsistence and settlement promoted both the dispersal of the habitation system, the latter being the focus of the clan component, and the promotion of new world renewal ritual through alliance construction among the multiple sodalities (name groups) of the region. The increasing demand for labor to build iconic monumental earthworks would not only enhance the need to build alliances but shamans would no longer be "mobile." They would tend to sustain ongoing relations with a set of name groups and this would transform into a permanent shaman-client relation that would quickly transform into the laity-clergy relation. I will now turn in the next chapter to a full elucidating of the Ohio Hopewell Ecclesiastic-Communal Cult Sodality Heterarchical System model and this will lead into my empirical validation of the model.

8

The Ohio Hopewell Cult Sodality Heterarchy System: From the Bottom Up

As I noted in chapter 1, under the Complementary Heterarchical Community model, it is incorrect and misleading to identify the Ohio Middle Woodland period system of complementary heterarchical communities with the system of social groups responsible for the *Ohio Hopewell* embankment earthworks. Of course, these two systems of organizations were related, but in an arm's-length manner. No doubt the communities that habitually exploited the resources of a valley bottom and its nearby upland regions had a greater interest in the large embankment earthworks around which their seasonally based family or domestic habitation locales were dispersed than they had for equivalent embankment earthworks in neighboring valleys or in farther reaches of the same valley. But this was not because these earthworks served as their community "centers." It was because many of the occupants of these dispersed clan-based habitation locales, most of whom were unilaterally related and practiced some form of exogamy with unilocal postmarital residency, that is, their spouses were from similar communities in neighboring and more distant valleys, were also members of the cult sodality alliance that was responsible for the building and using of these nearby earthworks. I have called these organizational alliances cult sodality heterarchies. Since the cult sodalities and the clans that constituted the typical complementary heterarchical community stood in an arm's-length relation, only the cult sodality could identify with the local earthwork and since each earthwork was built by an alliance of the autonomous cult sodalities of the local communities, the total organization could not be identified as the "civic center" of any given complementary heterarchical community. To add to this lack of one-to-one identification of the community and the local earthworks, there is the likelihood that these earthworks were themselves only part of the network of earthworks built and used by the alliance of the cult sodalities of the communities of the local region. This would be the result of the local cult sodality heterarchy being allied to other similar local sodality heterarchies in other regions; and these two or more affiliated heterarchies cooperated to build and extend the earthworks in the areas where its participating heterarchies were located.

What I mean by speaking of the Ohio Hopewell, therefore, applies only to part of the Middle Woodland period settlement pattern, that part articulating the network of mutualistic cult sodality heterarchies; and it presupposes the ongoing existence of clusters of dispersed but regionally constrained clan-based seasonal base-camp domestic habitation locales, the latter being the habitation units of the families of the local complementary heterarchical communities dispersed across the region. For this reason, I speak of two organizational structures responsible for the habitation/earthwork dichotomy of the Ohio Middle Woodland period: the system of complementary heterarchical communities (in the bifurcated settlement articulation modal posture) and the system of Ohio Hopewell cult sodality heterarchies.

How is this network to be conceptualized from the bottom-up perspective? I postulate that in a given region, the complementary heterarchical communities in the bifurcated posture will be embodied by *two relatively autonomous and spatially disengaged site clusters*, the dispersed clusters of *seasonal kinship-based habitation sites* and the serially occupied clusters of *mutually autonomous cult sodality sites*. While the occupation of the habitation sites would probably change with each season, some of these being reoccupied from time to time, the autonomous cult sodality sites would probably be "permanent" in the sense that while only seasonally occupied, they would be regularly reoccupied each season.

As I argued in the previous chapter, the ecclesiastic-communal cult sodality was based on the clergy-laity structure and the laity component was itself structured into the senior/junior age-grade sectors. The age-grades were further structured into age-sets. In general, a given ecclesiastic-communal cult sodality would consist pretty well of all the active males and females of the community (I allow for the laity to be sectored into female and male subsectors), although all of them would not be equally active in the affairs of the cult sodality. Activity levels would be largely a matter of age and the burden of kinship-related duties. Therefore, probably generally a smaller proportion of active females would be participating at any given time compared to the active males and among the males, a smaller proportion of active senior compared to active junior males of the community. I postulate that the cluster of sites associated with the typical autonomous cult sodality would be structured into three categories by size and complexity. The largest and most complex site of the cult sodality cluster I will call the *ceremonial nodal locale.* Here both the clergy and laity components would congregate for collective activities. Therefore, it would serve as the primary sodality center, the "headquarters," where sodality-wide ritual would be carried out. It would likely be a permanent structure with associated ritual features.

The other two categories of sites of the autonomous ecclesiastic-communal cult sodality cluster would be specialized for the laity sector. I will call these the *auxiliary locale* sites of the sodality and they would likely be dispersed around or near the cult sodality ceremonial nodal locale, thereby constituting the total ecclesiastic-communal cult sodality cluster. The auxiliary sites would be subcategorized into two formal types also distinguished in terms of size and internal structuring with one set being small and somewhat "ephemeral" in content and the another set being larger and more complex in content. This is simply because these two manifest the laity structure of age-sets and age-grades, respectively. Since an age-grade consisted of four or five age-sets ranked according to seniority, these site locales would be used when the age-sets were conducting collective tasks and these would likely be devoted to specialized production of Hopewellian artifacts and preparation of ritual performances. This age-grade site, therefore, would occupy the larger and more complex of the two types of auxiliary locales. In some cases, a cult sodality might have only one age-grade locale that was jointly but serially used by both the senior and junior age-grades. When possible, however, a cult sodality would sustain two separate age-grade site locales, one for the senior and one for the junior age-grade. In this regard, I would also suggest that only the age-sets of the junior age-grade would also have age-set locales, for reasons I discuss shortly.

In contrast to the age-grade site locales, the age-set sites would be small. These also may have been serially or jointly used by more than one age-set of a given age-grade. Given four or five age-sets per age-grade, there could be four or five age-set sites for each age-grade site, thereby manifesting the basic laity structuring of the cult sodality and, by extension, of its labor distribution. The age-sets would use their individual locales to carry out activities particular to their own responsibilities, including dressing the animals that the group hunted in preparation for both cult sodality meals and for sharing among the members who would take their shares back to their kin groups. The age-set of companions, possibly only eight to ten persons, would also carry out preparation for those aspects of the sodality-wide ritual in which they participated. That is, I postulate that the age-set locale was jointly used by its companions to cooperatively discharge cult sodality and kinship-based preparatory tasks. Therefore, this locale would tend to take on the appearance of a special task force locale, such as a logistical hunting camp or gardening and gathering camp. It is notable that I have implied above that these responsibilities would often include both cult sodality and domestic-related collective duties so that at this basic labor unit level, cooperative planning could resolve demands of both sodality and clan for which the same individuals were equally responsible.

In contrast to the overlapping tasks carried out in the age-set auxiliary locale site, the auxiliary age-grade site locales would be devoted to the activities particular to the total cult sodality. Since sodality-wide ritual activities would be undertaken in the cult sodality ceremonial nodal site locale, for this reason I postulate that the primary activities of the auxiliary age-grade site locales would be centered on productive tasks necessary for the well functioning of the sodality, as well as sharing subsistence tasks that would produce comestibles required for collective feasting, although when ready these might actually be carried to the relatively nearby ceremonial nodal locale where the feasts occurred. The age-grade site locales would also focus on the preparation of ritual-related devices, from copper and other exotic artifacts to the ubiquitous bladelet cores and bifacial blanks for the production of ritual tools. In short, these auxiliary age-grade sodality locale sites would tend to be specialized Hopewellian production sites.

In sum, this structuring of clan and sodality components means that each complementary heterarchical community in the bifurcated posture will consist of two spatially separate and relatively autonomous clusters: the household component consisting of the clusters of dispersed seasonal base camps occupied by the core kinship units linked by clan, on the one hand, and on the other the companionship-based component consisting of the cult sodality ceremonial nodal locale and the dispersed auxiliary sodality locale sites: the age-set task site locales and the age-grade specialized production locale sites. This Dual Complementary Clan/Cult Sodality Clusters Community model addresses the overall patterning of the complementary heterarchical community in the bifurcated settlement articulation modal postural; but it can be further resolved into two related models, one addressing the dispersed domestic, clan-based component, which I will term the Dispersed Kinship Habitation Cluster model, and one addressing the sodality-based component, which I will term the Cult Sodality Cluster model. However, since I am characterizing the spatial organization of an ecclesiastic-communal cult sodality, this could also be called simply the spatial distributional aspect of the Ecclesiastic-Communal Cult Sodality Cluster model. It is the social organization characterized by the latter model and the complex bottom-up iterations of the ecclesiastic-communal cult sodality clusters that is properly referred to as the Ohio Hopewell complex—a complex of cult sodality heterarchies.

How does this work? Since agentive autonomy, both personal and group, was a core principle of the postulated custodial ethos, the emergent Ohio

Hopewell ecclesiastic-communal cult sodalities would respect the tradition of age-set autonomy. Therefore, even when the age-sets of a community integrated into the ecclesiastic-communal cult sodality congregation and the latter established its own ceremonial nodal locale for performing its collective rituals and related activities, the component age-sets would continue to sustain separate auxiliary age-set sodality locales where they could conduct those affairs that were their particular responsibility but did not entail the participation of the total sodality. These locales would serve as places where the age-set could plan and organize its sodality activities, prepare their ritual materials, and so on. I postulated earlier that even when the community was in the bifurcated settlement articulation modal posture, many of the tasks that sustained the domestic family groups would be carried out by age-set groups cooperatively serving to pursue game or prepare gardens and the companions would equitably divide the benefits this cooperation accrued between the needs of the sodality and their families. Therefore, the group would set aside the resources required for cult activities and distribute the rest among themselves, and the individuals would typically return with their shares to their families, thereby performing cooperative labor that discharged both sodality and kinship duties simultaneously—and probably more effectively than if these tasks had been done separately. It would also be flexible since two or more junior age-sets of the community could reciprocally share among themselves the subsistence domestic and cult sodality ritual duties so that when an age-set had to travel some distance to a chert quarry to procure special chert for ritual production, their proximal senior (or junior) age-set could double up their close-to-home cooperative labor to ensure that the subsistence needs of the families of their *irakúu* sons or *irakúu* fathers were met. Being reciprocal, this means that an age-set that had covered the subsistence needs of families whose fathers or sons had gone on a long distance logistical procurement exhibition for their cult sodality would be reciprocated by this age-set when they also had to perform cult sodality tasks that took them away from their family duties. Therefore, the age-sets would combine family and sodality duties but in their capacity as cult sodality members. These age-set locales would be very important to the companions since it is here where their autonomy as a same-age/same-gender peer group would be most fully realized.

However, when a junior age-grade was promoted into the senior age-grade, I postulate that its component age-sets would leave these auxiliary locale sites to the age-sets of the new junior age-grade sets while focusing their activities on the age-grade-based specialized production locale sites. This would not likely reduce their sense of autonomy since, as members of the senior age-grade, the structuring by seniority would be somewhat mitigated. Men of the same senior age-grade would relate to each other primarily in terms of individual reputation and skills while age seniority would tend to be largely downplayed. Here several age-sets of the senior age-grade would probably cooperatively undertake sodality tasks related to their traditional ritual responsibilities, the latter being interrelated by mutual dependence. For a senior age-set to perform ritual task A, this might require that its proximal less senior age-set perform ritual task B. In sum, I will speak of this settlement pattern consisting of the ceremonial nodal locale of the autonomous ecclesiastic-communal cult sodality along with its cluster of auxiliary age-grade and age-set sites as the *ecclesiastic-communal cult sodality cluster.*

As I noted above, in parallel with this cult sodality cluster would be the dispersed kinship habitation clusters consisting of autonomous families of the clans. Each clan would consist of a dispersed cluster of seasonally based family habitation camps. The two clusters, the ecclesiastic-communal cult sodality cluster and the dispersed kinship habitation clusters, would identify with and share the custodianship of the same general precinct of land that they collectively gardened and foraged, although the cold season uplands, in particular, would probably be large precincts under the joint custodianship of many communities from disparate lowland regions. In the lowland setting, the locales of the clan and sodality clusters constituting a given complementary heterarchical community would maintain an arm's-length spatial relation. Since a community would have only one ecclesiastic-communal cult sodality while it might consist of several clan clusters dispersed over the community's custodial domain, the latter clusters would be more numerous and more widely dispersed while the former cluster would tend to be less dispersed and, in general, located in a part of the custodial domain of the complementary heterarchical community that was convenient to all members.

However, this means that the autonomous ecclesiastic-communal cult sodality cluster of a local complementary heterarchical community—namely, its ceremonial nodal locale and its two sets of auxiliary age-set and age-grade locales—does not exhaust the range of cult sodality locales. At this point, I have not mentioned the great embankment earthworks, which I firmly categorize as the crowning locale of the cult sodalities of the Ohio Middle Woodland period. As I noted in chapter 1, the ecclesiastic-communal cult sodalities of the complementary heterarchical communities of a region would actively pursue alliances with each other. That is, two or more ecclesiastic-communal cult sodalities would ally to form what I call a first-order cult sodality heterarchy. I term it a first-order heterarchy since its constituent units are autonomous cult sodalities that have allied directly with each other. Typically the first-order heterarchy would construct a locale where they could cooperatively conduct their suite of collective rituals. This could be built near the ceremonial nodal cult locale of one of the founding members of the first-order heterarchy, particularly if this cult sodality was the primary franchisee of a major ritual usufruct that it had received from the primary franchiser, itself a first-order cult sodality heterarchy located in a neighboring region. Alternatively, the cult sodalities constituting a first-order heterarchy might choose to build an entirely new locale so that it was more or less equidistant from the ceremonial nodal locales of all its member sodalities. In any case, these locales are typically marked by *moderately sized* embankment earthworks and one or two associated mortuary features that, in time, become the burial floors of mortuary mounds. Isolated mortuary mounds, those that have no embankment earthworks in association, in fact, may be part of a local clan cluster, particularly if it is one of the lesser mounds (more on these mound types later). If it is a fairly large mound, however, it might mark either the initial stages of a first-order heterarchy or, more likely, the evolved stage of an autonomous ecclesiastic-communal cult sodality.

Importantly, since a first-order heterarchy is autonomous, its governance being based on consensus among the ecclesiastic-communal cult sodalities that constitute it, there is no structural constraint preventing it from allying with one or more other first-order cult sodality heterarchies, thereby constituting a second-order cult sodality heterarchy. In fact, I will call a second-order cult sodality heterarchy not an alliance of cult sodalities but an affiliation of first-order cult sodality heterarchies. The affiliation is also autonomous so that its first-order allied heterarchies will participate in its activities, including the governance of the second-order heterarchy, by means of cult sodality-wide consensus. Typically the second-order heterarchy will build a fairly elaborate embankment earthwork in which to perform their collective world renewal and related rites. (In fact, as I argue later, a second-order heterarchy typically builds at least two formally contrasting embankment earthworks. The theoretical and empirical basis for this claim will be elucidated later.) Hence, there will be both first-order and second-order cult sodality locales and associated constructions where collective rituals would be performed. In the second-order heterarchy, these rituals will involve the construction of special cult sodality renewal lodges, probably one or two for each of the first-order heterarchies constituting the affiliation (more on these details later). Also, the first-order heterarchy components of the second-order affiliation will usually collectively construct a central renewal lodge where the major final set of incremental renewal rites is performed. These typically require different forms of postmortem sacrifice, including the use of the custodial regalia that the deceased had accumulated during their lifetimes and for which they had been primary custodians. I propose that Liberty Works with the Edwin Harness Renewal Lodge, and Seip with its two known large renewal lodges, Seip-Pricer and Seip-Conjoined, were each second-order heterarchies that were also affiliated to each other. In fact, the affiliation of two or more second-order heterarchies constitutes a third-order level of the heterarchical system. The embankment earthwork locales of the second-order heterarchies making up a third-order heterarchy might be spatially quite distant from each other, occupying different valleys or possibly different river drainages. While the third-order heterarchy may also generate an independent embankment earthwork site, which the two or more second-order cult sodality heterarchies constructed (one example of the latter that I will postulate and examine in detail later being the Hopewell site), it is also very possible that a third-order heterarchy could exist without a centralized embankment earthwork site. Rather, the second-order cult sodality heterarchical affiliations would probably come to specialize their second-order sites, each second-order site becoming the locale where certain major world renewal rites were performed or where certain portions of the world renewal process were performed. If this were the case, then the second-order affiliations that made up the third-order level may have cooperatively cycled among their respective locales the performance of such major rites or different stages of these major rites. These probably entailed postmortem and possibly some lethal human sacrifice.

What this bottom-up perspective means is that the third-order cult sodality heterarchy does not necessarily have a singular locale where the total ritual complex is performed. Rather, either it has a specialized locale where certain major or critical ritual practices are performed or it has two or more major locales where the same terminal set of core ritual practices is performed but in a balanced or reciprocal manner so that each locale carries out its overall "fair share." In both cases, the third-order cult sodality heterarchy consists of a dispersed set of embankment earthworks and mounds, some of which could be many kilometers separated, as I discuss in more detail in part 2. It is this spatially dispersed nature of the third-order cult sodality heterarchies that particularly characterizes the Ohio Hopewell cult sodality heterarchy system, a system that transcends the major river drainage systems of southwestern, south-central, central, and southeastern Ohio.

CRITICAL COMMENTARY

The Dual Complementary Clan/Cult Sodality Clusters Community model and the Vacant Center/Dispersed Hamlet model both recognize the Ohio Middle Woodland period settlement patterning as complex and both recognize that it is bifurcated. However, the way the latter treats this bifurcation allows for speaking of the community interchangeably as either the Ohio Middle Woodland period community or as the Ohio Hopewell community. This is because under this model the ceremonial/everyday domestic habitation dichotomy correlates the dispersed domestic habitation component with the family, usually referring to it as either a sedentary hamlet or a seasonal base camp, according to whether the sedentary or seasonally mobile version is being promoted, and the ceremonial sphere is correlated with the earthworks acting as the civic-ceremonial center of the monistic community. This view also recognizes ancillary sites, of course, for example, short-term task sites in close spatial association with habitation sites and specialized base camps for production of ritual materials in spatial association with the ceremonial sites. Even mortuary mounds not in association with embankment earthworks are recognized and are treated more as part of the habitation sphere rather than the ceremonial sphere. Hence, all settlement loci come to be classified as either habitation or ceremonial and the few that do not seem to fit either are shoehorned into one or the other category largely on an ad hoc basis.

However, the complementary heterarchical community view treats this dichotomy quite differently and, as noted earlier, this treatment makes it interpretively basic *not* to identify the Ohio Hopewell settlement assemblage with the Ohio Middle Woodland period community. This is because it recognizes two relatively autonomous arm's-length clusters, one kinship/clan-based, and the other companionship/sodality-based: and the dichotomy is the expression of what I have called the bifurcated settlement articulation modal posture. Therefore, overall, the settlement pattern is characterized as consisting of a much more socially complex range of settlement locales than contemplated under the monistic view. One set constitutes the kinship/clan-based cluster and the other, the companionship/sodality-based site cluster. The former will display a major focus on domestic habitation residue while the latter will display a varied range of degrees of ceremonial and habitation attributes and, for this reason, some of these can be *mistaken* for kinship/clan-like habitation sites. This varied range includes the auxiliary age-set and age-grade sites and the cult sodality ceremonial nodal sites, the latter constituting the cult sodality cluster, as well as a complex range of earthwork sites and their associated structures and facilities manifesting first-order, second-order, and third-order organizational levels. Also, since these different levels correlate with scale of distances separating local cult sodalities from different first-, second-, and third-order heterarchy sites in which they participated, this would entail a range of auxiliary sites I have not mentioned. However, these would have been an intrinsic part of the cult sodality component of the bifurcated settlement pattern. For example, most sodality groups may have had to travel for many kilometers to attend rituals at second-order or third-order sites and these expeditions would require hostel-like accommodations. Hostel-like attributes would appear as marking both sodality "way stations" to accommodate age-sets or groups of age-sets en route to ritual events in more distant earthwork locales and at the great earthworks themselves. Of course, the hostel-like nature of these sites would entail domestic residue, cooking and storage features, and so on, not too different from what could be anticipated at family habitation locales, although likely on a larger scale. The important point, however, is that the Dual Complementary Clan/Cult Sodality Clusters Community model opens up a much broader range of possible site types and elucidating this range can and will be developed as part of the interpretive process of the settlement pattern that this book pursues. This prevents ad hoc shoehorning of sites into either the habitation or the ceremonial category and, at the same time, enables developing the more subtle characteristics of the social nature of the settlement pattern.

This difference is not trivial since, in terms of the hermeneutic spiral methodology, the adequacy of the model to explain the empirical data is assessed by the coherence with which it endows these data and this means minimizing contradictions and anomalies while expanding the range of empirical data that it can be used to perceive, classify, interpret, and explain. A conceptual scheme that is not adequate to the interpretative and explanatory task actually tends both to conflate empirical data into a single category that should be discrete and to split the empirical data into separate categories that should be treated as variants of the same category (lumping and splitting). A conceptual scheme that promotes a somewhat arbitrary process of lumping and splitting basic sites is characterized as a chaotic scheme simply because this generates many anomalies and anachronisms, thereby revealing itself as incoherent. Of course, all conceptual schemes used in modeling generate anomalies and indecisiveness in the interpretation of the empirical data, thereby revealing themselves as only approximations of the reality that they are addressing. These anomalies, often revealed by critique, call for correction through changing the model. Sometimes this requires simply a minor adjustment to the model or, in extreme cases, it requires model replacement. I am suggesting, of course, that modeling the settlement bifurcation in terms of the unitary or, as I prefer speaking of it, the monistic modular polity community view is seriously inadequate and generates many anomalies in our understanding of the empirical data. However, as I hope to demonstrate as I proceed, anomalies are fewer when the same settlement bifurcation data are interpreted in terms of the complementary heterarchical community view.

Demonstrating which of these two contrasting models is the preferred one must now proceed. I will do this first by critically addressing the Vacant Center/Dispersed Hamlet model. This model actually strongly relies on Bruce Smith's (1992, 241–43) notion of the Hopewell household unit and his empirical grounding of this notion in the Middle Woodland period settlement pattern. I have chosen to start with his view since he made an important breakthrough in settlement studies, essentially arguing that there were no

"Hopewell villages" or "nucleated" settlements, as was assumed to be the case prior to his research. Instead, he claimed that the countryside was dominated by dispersed household units or, as he termed them, Hopewell household units (HHUs). In fact, he drew on Prufer's earlier work in Ohio for his inspiration. Therefore, Smith's claim for the HHU and his listing of the major attributes that it should have, these coming to be delineated as the attributes of a *sedentary hamlet*, has played a major role in the development of settlement pattern interpretation in the Middle Woodland period of the Central Ohio Valley. Indeed, it has become the basis for classifying a site as belonging to the everyday habitation component of the habitation/ceremonial dichotomy (Smith 1992, 211–14, 220, 225, 229, 235–36, 243). This feeds directly into the next two steps I will take, summarizing the excavations of two sites that have been particularly influential in articulating the range of attributes that an Ohio Middle Woodland period habitation site should display: the Jennison Guard site (Blosser 1996; Kozarek 1987, 1997) or also referred to as the Whitacre site (Whitacre and Whitacre 1986), and the Murphy site (Dancey 1991; Dancey and Pacheco 1997; Pacheco 1996, 1993). I will then critique these interpretations, arguing that treating them as sedentary hamlets, and as exemplary of this category, is a serious mischaracterization of their real social nature. Rather, the attributes of both sites fit most reasonably what we would expect cult sodality age-grade site locales to display, the type of site that specialized in Hopewell production technology and that would be the responsibility of every Ohio Hopewell autonomous ecclesiastic-communal cult sodality.

Based on the conclusions of the excavators that these two sites represent classic HHUs, an important follow-up of the Murphy site region was carried out by Paul Pacheco (1993), who used his intensive and systematic survey of the 50 ha area in which the Murphy site was initially found as the basis for his dissertation. This was the medium for theoretically elucidating and empirically grounding what he called the Hamlet Hypothesis. This hypothesis was explicitly developed to demonstrate the Vacant Center/Dispersed Hamlet model. Drawing on Smith's conclusion that the ceremonial/habitation dichotomy manifested "corporate-ceremonial sites" and dispersed HHUs, and bolstered by the claims that dispersed sedentary hamlets had been empirically established (Jennison Guard and Murphy), Pacheco concluded that the multiple clusters he revealed through surface surveying of the Murphy Tract were, indeed, the residue of dispersed sedentary hamlets and their associated short-term special purpose locales and that this patterning confirmed Prufer's Vacant Center/Dispersed Hamlet model of the Middle Woodland period Ohio settlement system.

This series of excavations and surface surveys has strongly but not absolutely entrenched the Hamlet Hypothesis interpretation of the Ohio Hopewell and, of course, it has entrenched the view that indeed Ohio Hopewell settlement patterning manifests a ceremonial/habitation bifurcation of a social system of monistic modular polity communities. Nevertheless, there is a strand of opposition to the sedentary hamlet view. However, it also largely recognizes the monistic modular polity perspective and its associated ceremonial/habitation dichotomy. The primary way it differs is that it claims that the Middle Woodland period communities consisted of mobile and not sedentary kin groups, probably nuclear families that spent much of the year in a widely dispersed settlement mode while regularly aggregating at ceremonial locales, often different families aggregating at different ceremonial locales. Therefore, it is possible that no particular aggregation at a ceremonial locale consisted of a preexisting organized group that treated a given locale as its particular ceremonial center (Cowan 2006; Cowan et al. 2004; Lepper and Yerkes 1997; Yerkes 1994, 2003, 2006).

Finally, as I discussed earlier, there is the Multiple Community model recently elucidated by Bret Ruby, Christopher Carr, and Douglas Charles (2005) that claims the ceremonial sphere can be understood as consisting of several social levels above the residential community level, that is, the local and regional symbolic community level, and, sometimes, the sustainable community level. However, as I critically noted earlier, while this model has merit, unfortunately, it fails structurally in that these levels are not postulated as being autonomous but as being simply the outcome of either partnerships among individuals who are prominent in their different regions or, more likely, kinship "alliances" among kinship-related communities. By the way, this lack of structural distinction is the same problem that Berle Clay's model of the Adena faces (1991). He has argued that the Adena ceremonial locales constitute an organizational type, not a community. This certainly is akin to my own view, as I discuss in more detail in the final chapter. However, he then denies that the groups responsible for the Adena locales are autonomous units of the communities from which they came. Rather, they directly represent these communities in the Adena alliances. The result, therefore, is to constitute the Adena symbolic community as a federation of clan-based residential communities.

I will now use the second half of this chapter to proceed in terms of the hermeneutic spiral method to summarize and critique the claims that the Jennison Guard and Murphy sites are sedentary hamlets. I follow this up briefly by showing that, in fact, these sites nicely fit what we could expect under the Cult Sodality Cluster model, namely, sets of primary age-set and age-grade components of a cult sodality cluster. Since Pacheco's interpretation of the Murphy Tract as the dispersed hamlets of a monistic community hinges on his accepting the Murphy site as a sedentary hamlet, my critique of the Jennison Guard and Murphy sites applies to his thesis also. Therefore, it is not necessary to critique his Hamlet Hypothesis, as such. However, his research is especially valuable for grounding the Cult Sodality Cluster model in the empirical data that his work revealed. Therefore, in the next chapter I summarize Pacheco's empirical data and critique his interpretation in order to clear the way to use the same data as empirical grounds for interpreting the Murphy Tract under the Cult Sodality Cluster model, showing that indeed it displays almost the total range of sites that I have postulated would fulfill the needs of an autonomous ecclesiastic-communal cult sodality, in particular age-grade and age-set locales and, very possibly, a cult sodality ceremonial nodal site.

THE DISPERSED SEDENTARY HAMLET VIEW

In his 1992 book, Bruce Smith claimed that the emergence of domesticated plant agriculture occurred in the Eastern Woodlands by the Early Woodland period, if not earlier. He particularly argued that the intensification of indigenous cultivated and domesticated practices correlated with the emergence of the Middle Woodland period. He saw the main opposition to this position arising from those whom he interpreted as trivializing this independent emergence of what he considered to be a major evolutionary step by the claim that the achievement of some indigenous practicing of manipulating plants might, at best, be treated as a form of limited horticulture by peoples who were still at heart foragers of wild foods. For Smith (1992, 203–5), this was a denial by some archaeologists of the significance of what was essentially an independently achieved evolutionary step in domestication by prehistoric Native North Americans, and he was very insistent that rather than being superficial and basically ephemeral, the horticultural practices of the Middle Woodland period were best characterized as the entrenching of widespread farming. This is a position that I have accepted as foundational for the reason that it articulates the fundamental change in the deontic human–environment relation that constitutes the heart of my deontic ecological argument that the Hopewell episode of the Middle Woodland period was a creative response to the perceiving that the requisite degree and level of changes in the subsistence and settlement practices were unavoidably generating intensifying levels of sacred pollution. It is in response to this collective world view perception that the reorientation in the dispersed settlement practices was occurring that promoted the emergence of the ecclesiastic-communal cult sodality heterarchy system that I earlier detailed.

I want to make it clear, therefore, that my approach is committed to affirming Smith's views concerning the nature of the emerging subsistence practices. However, his modeling of the settlement pattern in social terms diverges from my own and is more in harmony with the monistic modular polity community views. In this case, as I briefly noted earlier, he argued that this farming system was based on regional systems of economically autonomous dispersed homesteads of nuclear and small extended families. He postulated the basic settlement component was a small *sedentary* farming site displaying a combination of features, including some form of permanent dwelling, typical of everyday sedentary domestic life, including earth ovens, hearths, and storage pits, and sometimes a lightly built wind break–type shelter that, in fact, may also have served as a summer dwelling residence. Therefore, the typical family, in his view, was an autonomous residential unit practicing sedentary farming, although of course it could also sustain logistically organized task groups.

Now I can understand his motive at this time for emphasizing the sedentary nature of the basic family unit since it would reinforce his claim that the Middle Woodland period subsistence and settlement system was more properly referred to as a farming than a slash-and-burn or swidden horticultural system. As will become clear later, however, I am of the view that, given the very existence of the Ohio Hopewell system of heterarchies as centers for focusing and expanding the benefits of mortuary-mediated world renewal ritual, the culture-wide concern for minimizing sacred pollution would override any serious move toward sedentary farming, not simply because of deontic standards, but also because of concern about overstressing the wild faunal resources that sedentary settlement would encourage. Again, in assessing the causes of the particular settlement and subsistence practices of a people, it is important to note that the deontic ecological view encourages taking into account the cultural traditions, that is, the emic perspective. In a world experienced by the people as immanently sacred, hunting game was assessed as both an exploitative and species-reproductive activity. It was the moral obligation of the hunters not only to avoid stressing the species they exploited but also to distribute their exploitation practices so as to ensure ongoing reproduction of the species; that is, the killing of an animal was experienced as the first sacrificial step leading to the rebirth of its spirit in a newborn. Focusing on deer hunting in the main valleys where *sedentary* hamlets would primarily locate would have a double polluting effect, the unwarranted stressing of the local herds by oversacrificing the individual animals and unwarranted stressing of the reproduction of the upland herds by undersacrificing these. In an important sense, I am suggesting that cycling of settlement from warm-season lowland domestic habitation sites where field horticulture was carried out to cold-season upland foraging habitation sites would be part of a refined proscriptive subsistence-settlement system by which the material needs of the kinship/clan-based component of the community were achieved at minimum polluting costs in parallel with a prescriptive or intensified system of world renewal rituals performed in the emergent cult sodality heterarchies.

In any case, Smith called the basic sedentary domestic site the Hopewell household unit (HHU [1992, 213]). Importantly, any given zone in which there were dispersed Hopewell household units would have one or more ceremonial sites that served as the collective corporate center of the dispersed families, the implication being that these families were related by descent of one sort or another. In short, he postulated a version of the Vacant Center/ Dispersed Hamlet model as characteristic not only of Ohio but of most regions of the Eastern Woodlands of the Middle Woodland period. Therefore, not only was he arguing for the emergence of farming practices based on this dispersed set of homesteads integrated around a central ceremonial site, he was arguing against the widespread assumption at that time that the primary settlement component of most Middle Woodland period regions of the Eastern Woodlands was a nucleated settlement, for example, a village, in association with a Hopewellian ceremonial corporate headquarters. In order to empirically support his argument, he carried out a multiple regional review of the most up-to-date surveys and excavations at that time in several separate regions, particularly focusing on local regions in central Tennessee, west Tennessee, the American Bottom, and the Illinois River Valley, but also touching on Alabama and Georgia (1992, 215–39). He noted in each case that the Middle Woodland period settlement pattern in these separate regions conformed to his above postulated model. He also included Ohio, in particular the central Scioto Valley, although he noted that despite Prufer's initial research in the 1960s there was at the time of his survey little up-to-date published research of the settlement patterning of that region. His conclusions were that "[w]hile Hopewellian farming settlements were small, dispersed, apparently independent, and redundantly egalitarian in appearance, excavation has often illuminated rich elaborately expressed, and regionally quite variable programs of social ranking . . . along with considerable evidence of community-scale social integration in the form of corporate labor efforts (corporate-ceremonial structures, mounds, geometric earthworks)" (1992, 243).

It is also important to note that much of the basic material of the overview that Smith made in his 1992 book, *Rivers of Change*, had already been published by him in articles and books published from the mid-1980s. This 1992 work was published shortly before two important volumes on the Ohio Middle Woodland settlement pattern were published, which, in most cases, converged with his claims. These were *The View from the Core*, edited by Paul Pacheco (1996) and *The Ohio Hopewell Community Organization*, edited by William Dancey and Paul Pacheco (1997). Therefore, this convergence had been developing prior to the above two major Ohio Hopewell publications.

Two publications of site reports that seemed nicely to fit the HHU view that Smith was developing will be critically examined here: the Jennison Guard site (Kozarek 1987) and the Murphy site (Dancey 1991). These are located quite distant from each other. The first is in Dearborn County in the extreme southeast corner of Indiana on a major upper terrace of the Ohio River just a short distance downstream from the mouth of the Great Miami River. About 350 km to its northeast is the Murphy site, located on a high terrace of the Raccoon Creek about 3 km west of Newark, which is at the confluence of the Raccoon Creek and the Licking River. The Licking River is a tributary of the upper Muskingum River, which joins the Ohio River at Marietta in the southeast sector of the state.

Sue Kozarek, who interpreted the Jennison Guard site, actually drew theoretical support concerning the early emergence of agriculture from the Illinois Middle Woodland literature, prior to Smith's 1992 work. At the time of her work, it was assumed that the nucleated village settlement pattern prevailed in Illinois, and Kozarek worked within this assumption. However, she did not apply it to the Jennison Guard site and, instead, relied on Prufer's Vacant Center thesis and recognized that Ohio subsistence and settlement practices were likely based on dispersed hamlets. Therefore, she was prepared to argue that the Jennison Guard site was a sedentary hamlet. She considered this site as particularly important to ground this dispersed sedentary hamlet view since it was the only known site at that time that seemed to fit Smith's HHU criteria and, furthermore, it was not near a major Hopewell ceremonial locale. Therefore, if it could be demonstrated to be a sedentary hamlet, then it would nicely reinforce Prufer's claims and converge with Smith's 1992 book. Dancey also published his report on the Murphy site without reference to Smith's view. Instead, like Kozarek, he saw the Murphy site data in the context of Prufer's thesis and, as noted above, he recognized that this site was close to several major Ohio Hopewell embankment earthworks, as I discuss later.

THE JENNISON GUARD SITE

The excavated portion of the Jennison Guard site seems to conform to Smith's HHU model quite nicely. Kozarek described the site as organized into several discrete components. In terms of cultural features, the two most important were in the most extreme southeastern portion of the site and the other in the northeast portion (1987, 5). The northeast sector was termed by her Transect A. Although no post holes were found, she noted that there was some twig-impressed mud daubing, implicating some sort of shelter. Importantly, there was an array of 18 (possibly 19) cultural features consisting of hearths, earth ovens, and piles of fire-cracked rock that formed a rough ovoid incorporating a cleared area. She asserted that these features, along with the cleared area that they delineated and the possible residue of a shelter, were all consistent with a sedentary hamlet of the type postulated by Prufer and that Smith was shortly to postulate under the HHU model. She also noted several discrete midden areas, some with a great deal of content. One was north of Transect A and was characterized by large quantities of lithics, including fire-cracked rock, and ceramics. One was east and, in fact, was associated with a male human burial. Another was west of the Transect A, and this apparently incorporated residue of organic waste, shells, ceramics, and animal bones. A female burial was also found associated with this midden. Thus, two major middens existed: one largely dedicated to lithic debitage and one dedicated to organic and ceramic debitage. And each had a burial in association. Other hearths were found farther southwest of this midden, suggesting that another activity area component existed separate from Transect A. "[T]he majority of these features were cooking facilities . . . [displaying some] sequential use phases. The spatial distribution of the cooking facilities suggests considerable organizational effort, and the contents indicate that this particular portion of the community was the locus of a series of cultural activities" (1987, 62). For her, all these features and the layout were largely contemporary.

One of the most intriguing observations, she claims, was the careful organization of this site layout and the practice of site maintenance. Not only were there the large, discrete and separated midden deposits as noted above, but the cleared area embraced by the ovoid array of cultural features was itself remarkably clean. The features contained secondary refuse, particularly a great deal of chert debitage (over 15,000 fragments). Moreover, as she noted, the excavation revealed that the floor of the cleared area contained many small fragments of ceramics and lithics. The size and positioning of these indicated that they were probably overlooked when the area was regularly cleaned (many were "ground" into the surface). She attributes this ongoing sustaining of the basic sections of the site as specialized locales—cooking and storage, midden deposition, open cleared area, and some sort of dwelling structure off to one side—combined with intensive site maintenance practices as manifesting fairly long-term, year-round sedentary occupation.

Critical Commentary

There are two outstanding contents of the site: its lithics and its nonlithic exotics. In regard to the former, there are three reasons the lithics are outstanding. Besides the fact that much of the larger debitage was concentrated in one of the two major midden deposits, the lithics displayed the total range of standard Middle Woodland lithic production from decortication of the quarry-derived chert to the final end product in the form of bladelets, bifaces, and even utilized flake tools. Second, the vast majority of the lithic debitage consisted of two varieties of chert, the largest proportion being Wyandotte chert derived from known quarries about 140 km downriver from the site, and the next largest quantity, although distinctly minor in comparison, being Flint Ridge chert derived from the Flint Ridge quarries about 350 km northeast of the site (and only 20 km southeast of the Murphy site). The third outstanding reason is the near absence of locally derived chert or of fine quality chert that was abundantly available within a radius of 20 km from the site.

Along with these two types of chert, both requiring overcoming considerable logistical problems to procure, there were also small quantities of other exotic resources, particularly mica and copper. It is interesting to note that Kozarek was not particularly puzzled by the presence of copper or multiple mica fragments; nor for that matter, as I discuss in some detail below, was she particularly puzzled by the large quantity of Wyandotte chert debitage manifesting the total range of the Middle Woodland lithic *chaîne opératoire* and the smaller quantity of Flint Ridge chert manifesting only the end-use aspect. In the case of the exotics, she comments that the presence of mica and copper simply confirms for her that such exotics must not be identified as exclusive to the ceremonial locales. "The presence of these items at the Jennison Guard site attests to the fact that the occupants were actively participating in the exchange of Hopewell Interaction Sphere items. More importantly, the context from which these items were recovered (i.e., along with typical domestic refuse) suggests that these items permeated the daily lives of Hopewell, rather than being strictly reserved for ceremonial purposes" (1987, 121). Interestingly, Jack Blosser, who also excavated at this site, makes effectively the same comment, even though he also notes that the Jennison Guard site is the only "hamlet" that he knows that seemed to actually specialize in the production of Hopewellian mica exotics. As he points out, over 600 pieces of mica, most of which displayed cut edges, indicated that it was probably modified on the site (Blosser 1996, 58). Furthermore, while many of these pieces were fragments resulting from manufacturing steps, several can be identified as effigy artifacts in the form of projectile points (Snyders point, Ross Barbed), as well as an effigy fan or bird's wing. "Nowhere in the archaeological record of the Ohio Valley has a Middle Woodland habitation site produced sufficient evidence to warrant an interpretation of craft specialization of exotic material for the modification or manufacture of specific materials for mortuary purposes. Evidence from the Jennison Guard–south excavations however does suggest the modification and manufacture of sheet mica into forms for ceremonial activities or trade" (Blosser 1996, 58).

Critique

I find the juxtaposing of a habitation site with the presence of exotic materials, Hopewellian ceremonial production, and major quantities of selected nonlocal cherts to be radically anomalous. Certainly, Smith did not specify these attributes as part of what he defined as a Hopewell household unit. However, rather than reflecting on these exotics in a habitation site as anomalous and rather than raising the possibility that this site was not a habitation site, as such, both archaeologists simply redefined or, more correctly, expanded what can be expected with regard to the attribute distribution between the ceremonial/habitation dichotomy. In short, "they moved the goal posts," and without any particular warranting argument being made. That is, while they recognized that long distance procurement of copper and mica was a prerequisite of Ohio Hopewell ceremonialism, they claimed that sometimes it was also part of everyday domestic life! Therefore, while the pursuit and exchange of exotic or selected cherts and their transformation into a whole range of blanks of the type found, for example, in huge ritual deposits at the Hopewell site seems clearly a prerequisite of Ohio Hopewell ceremonialism, sometimes (in fact often in their view) it is also a part of everyday domestic life. Is this a legitimate redefinition or is it an example of ad hoc redefining of categories? I think it is an ad hoc and unwarranted redefinition. I say this because it was not the only case of ignoring attributes that seemed to fly in the face of what we could legitimately expect everyday habitation sites to display, whether sedentary or not. In this case, rather than the presence of large quantities of select cherts derived from very distant quarries suggesting that this site was caught up in activities characteristic of the ceremonial sphere, Kozarek argued that this long distance procurement and systematic production of specialized lithics demonstrated that the site must have been not only an everyday domestic habitation locale but, in fact, one that was established as a long-term sedentary habitation locale.

To this end Kozarek presented a careful analysis of what type of settlement Jennison Guard must have been in order to explain how the patterning of the Wyandotte chert and the Flint Ridge chert came to be. Again, the primary working assumption was that this site was a domestic habitation, the locale of a family or several families. This was taken as self-evident. Therefore, the question this assumption raised was the kind of mobility these families must have practiced in order for the Wyandotte and Flint Ridge cherts to be there in the quantity, variation, and distribution that they were. Kozarek proposed four possibilities that would result in a *sedentary hamlet* having this content: (1) regional exchange, (2) residential mobility, (3) subsistence-based logistical mobility, and (4) specialized procurement-based logistical mobility (Kozarek 1987, 99). She eliminated the first or exchange possibility on the grounds that the Wyandotte chert displayed the full range of production steps, including decortication. Procurement by exchange would suggest only finished products would appear in the site. She also dismissed the possibility that procurement was by residential mobility on the grounds that (1) there would be no reason for a family unit, as such, to travel 140 km as part of its seasonal rounds since the local environment of the Jennison Guard site and the environment where the Wyandotte chert quarries were based were effectively identical; and (2), again, even if they had, they would have reduced the chert at the quarry in order to avoid being excessively burdened on the trip back home. She eliminates the third or subsistence-based logistical mobility possibility on the grounds that if a community sent out logistical subsistence task groups, these would usually be only short distance trips. The Wyandotte chert quarries were 140 km distant. It follows, therefore, that logistical task groups of the sedentary hamlet must have been specialized and sent specifically to procure this chert. Furthermore, since the domestic grouping of the Jennison Guard site would have only a small number of persons available to make this 300 km round trip, the task force would have to sacrifice by moving fast and carrying the full nondecorticated chert. "In order to limit the disruption to daily activities relatively few individuals would have been involved in so specific a task. These individuals may or may not have been the ones responsible for tool production [at the site itself]" (1987, 104). Having eliminated exchange, residential mobility, and subsistence-based logistical mobility, this left only one possibility, specialized procurement-based logistical mobility. Therefore, the Jennison Guard site was a sedentary hamlet, as was already presupposed by the argumentation. "I have demonstrated that (1) a high degree of site maintenance was practiced by the Jennison Guard site's occupants, (2) refuse disposal at the site was highly systematic, and (3) a tremendous volume of refuse had accumulated in the refuse areas. These data indicate that the Jennison Guard site was occupied for a relatively long, uninterrupted period of time and that the occupants of the site were *residentially sedentary*" (1987, 131–32). She effectively repeats this position in a chapter in a later publication (Kozarek 1997). Before completing my critique of Kozarek's and Blosser's interpretation of this site as a sedentary hamlet, I will summarize the Murphy site. I will then carry out an overall critique of both claims together.

THE MURPHY SITE

This site was excavated and reported by William Dancey (1991). It is now treated as one of five "hamlets" making up what Paul Pacheco (1993) has termed the Murphy Tract. The latter is a 50 ha land area located on an alluvial terrace of the Raccoon Creek only about 3 km upstream from Newark. Dancey revealed a patterning that was largely akin to the patterning revealed at the Jennison Guard site, including a scattering of mica debitage redeposited in several of the features. As in the latter case, the most abundant artifact content was lithic debitage. Dancey comments on the density, distribution, and content of the debitage, in particular that it manifested the total range of knapping reduction from the decortication to the production of blanks and cores, particularly bladelet cores and a superfluity of bladelets. "The flake sample from Murphy is immense. Test pitting of the plow zone produced a sample of approximately 10,000 items in 57 units (1 × 1× 0.3 m); test pits in the densest part of the distribution contained between 500 and 1,224 items. The post hole digger tests recovered >5,500 flakes, and screened examples of feature fill have produced >6,000. The bulk of this material probably derived from biface production, although some flakes undoubtedly are related to the bladelet industry" (Dancey 1991, 55). He goes on to comment that in this site alone he retrieved 84 bladelet cores, and more than 300 bladelets, the bulk being found in the plow zone. Thirty-six percent of the bladelets was recovered from feature fill. However, it is important to note that a few bladelet fragments of Wyandotte chert were also found, as well as Knife River chert from North Dakota. All this material (Flint Ridge Vanport variety) was produced from chert brought in from the Flint Ridge quarries and, in fact, stored for future production use. "Handsized, weathered, unmodified blanks were transported to the site and stockpiled" (1991, 59). He goes on to describe the distribution of the lithics as forming a "uninodal (or 'bull's-eye') pattern in which the largest quantity of artifacts exposed on the surface occurs in the site's northeast corner" (1991, 65). It is here that he test pitted and derived the 10,000-plus lithic items.

Dancey summarizes the settlement plan noting that the uninodal dump zone was on the northeast quartile of the site, where "the waste products from knapping at another location were dumped, along with other refuse" (1991, 66), with a clustering of earth ovens and basins in the northwestern zone where, he suggests, food preparation was carried out, and along with these were scattered post molds that marked possibly fences, racks, benches, and even possibly a floor of a structure, although he notes that plowing in this zone may have ruined any evidence supporting this latter claim. Most importantly, as with the Jennison Guard site, there was a large ovoid area making up the southern half of the size, which formed what he called an "open-yard zone." "The open-yard zone consists of that part of the site largely devoid of features and exhibiting a low frequency of cultural items in the surface and plow zone samples" (1991, 66). Although carefully troweled it only "yielded a small sample of chipped-stone items, a number of which exhibited use wear. . . . Potentially, this is where manufacturing, along with a host of other daily activities, took place" (1991, 66). He explains this overall patterning in similar terms that Kozarek used to explain the similar patterning at the Jennison Guard site, namely, as a result of long-run site maintenance of a sedentary hamlet site. As he claims, "The Murphy site appears to contain a prominent manifestation of continuous occupation sometime between approximately 100 B.C. and A.D. 225. The occupants were members of a household group and their residence was year-round. Their economy combined hunting and gathering with horticulture, possibly in a swidden system. They maintained institutionalized exchange relationships with other households in the community and shared a central cemetery and community area. It is the embodiment of the Hamlet Hypothesis settlement" (1991, 66).

In short, these are effectively the same conclusions that Kozarek came to with regard to the Jennison Guard site. In both cases, rather than ask if these attributes are what could be expected of small sedentary family habitations, the excavators assumed that they were family habitations and, therefore, the attributes demonstrate that they were sedentary locales that also happened to participate in the Hopewellian Interaction Sphere. Dancey was aware, however, that the superfluity of lithics and the absence of used implements raised the possibility that the Murphy site could be a specialized production site. But he chose to sustain the sedentary hamlet characterization. "Although implements are rare, the presence of food processing facilities together with ceramic and food waste suggests that Murphy represents the trace of a residential settlement rather than a special purpose site such as a bladelet and biface 'factory.' The microwear analysis lends support to this since a wide range of domestic activities was found to be represented in the edge wear on chipped-stone tools. No evidence of craft specialization was identified by the microwear analysis" (1991, 67). In this regard, however, he notes that Yerkes, who carried out the microwear analysis, disagreed and claimed that the lack of hafted tools, the absence of tool-sharpening debitage, and limited microwear usage indicates short-term and seasonal occupation by small groups (1991, 68). While noting this disagreement, Dancey concludes that "[t]he small size of this settlement . . . the coherent site plan, and archaeobotanical remains of mixed domesticated and wild plants suggest that the notion of Middle Woodland populations living in dispersed, sedentary hamlets or households based in part on a food-producing economy is correct" (1991, 67). He even accounts for the presence of exotics in the same terms as did Blosser and Kozarek for the Jennison Guard site. That is, he claims that these simply confirm that Middle Woodland families living in their sedentary hamlets were tied into the ceremonial sphere. "The presence of exotic cherts, ceramics, and mica, although rare, demonstrates the participation of this household unit in pan-regional exchange. Such objects probably also are the remains of intercommunity, pan-regional exchange networks" (1991, 67–68).

OVERALL CRITIQUE

I will suggest that if the lithic residue in both the Jennison Guard and Murphy sites was analytically separated out, the remaining content and patterning of these sites could be plausibly argued as manifesting the type of site that Smith has claimed would be generated by a sedentary nuclear or small extended family unit, namely, a Hopewell household unit. Of course, we would then have to factor back in the lithics since this type of habitation unit would necessarily generate *some* lithic debitage, broken tools, and so on. However, the shear quantity of lithics might give the analysts pause to wonder—as it did for Dancey. This might also serve to motivate a reassessment of the presence of exotic resources such as copper and mica, even in small amounts. Would these two factors by themselves be sufficient to deny these sites were kin-based sedentary habitation units? In my opinion, if only a fraction of the lithics were factored back in, then the other exotics might pass muster as not being unreasonable for a sedentary domestic family that participated in the Hopewell ceremonial system, although the level of ceramics might still be questionable for a sedentary site. However, when the actual character and quantity of the lithics that were identified in both sites are factored back in, then not only should this raise some puzzlement, but the presence of the exotics, particularly the cut mica effigies at Jennison Guard, should definitely be considered anomalous. For example, what is a sedentary nuclear family, or even several nuclear families, doing with so much select nonlocal chert, particularly when qualitatively equivalent chert was rather easily available nearby? In the case of Jennison Guard, this procurement required a specialized 300 km round trip! When these two aspects, the specially procured lithics and the exotics, are seen as anomalous given the assumed sedentary domestic habitational nature of these sites, then the rest of the attributes deserve being reassessed, such as the apparent site maintenance that was undertaken, and so on. Once looked at in alternative terms, assimilating all this to the sedentary family dwelling unit view needs to be rejected.

None of this skepticism denies that, in fact, the Ohio Middle Woodland period domestic settlement system followed the Hopewell household unit pattern that Smith has outlined. As noted above, I happen to think that it does so only partially and, overall, requires rearticulation. But this is not the issue. What I suggest is that it makes it highly difficult to assimilate these to the HHU model—given that both the Jennison Guard and the Murphy sites display a very similar content and patterning of materials that would be superfluous to the needs of a small hamlet, sedentary or not. That is, if Smith's model is right, the type of social unit it postulates is not being manifested in these two sites. However, I can agree with Kozarek's careful analysis that the likely mode by which the Wyandotte chert was procured, brought to, and used at the Jennison Guard site is essentially correct. That is, it is very reasonable to conclude that the chert was procured by direct specialized logistical procurement undertaken by task forces whose primary purpose for these expeditions was to collect the desired raw material from the Wyandotte chert quarries 140 km distant from the site and bring it back largely unmodified to be fully worked at the site. Importantly, three points that she made support this conclusion. The need for this chert was specialized, given that the distances involved required such focused methods requiring major labor and time investment. The chert was desired for reasons not related to everyday life since she pointed that, in fact, there were plentiful sources of qualitatively equal cherts much closer to hand. Finally, there was no problem with using nearby lithic sources since, in fact, nonchert lithic sources were regularly used by the group or groups occupying the site. "[E]ven though other types of available lithic resources (e.g., limestone, glacial erratics) were exploited by the site's occupants, the majority of chert recovered from the site consisted of two *nonlocal* varieties" (1987, 67). This third point, using nearby nonchert lithic resources, suggests that the community certainly exercised economy when procuring such resources, for example, selecting nearby limestone and other stones to serve as cooking stones for earth ovens, and so on. However, when the latter is added to the first and second points, it also suggests that such economizing did not apply to Wyandotte chert. This is not to say that the Wyandotte chert procurement and usage was not effected in as efficient or economizing a manner as possible. Rather, what it says is that Wyandotte chert usage manifests a set of values and imperatives that warranted the extra costs required to procure it rather than using the more locally available cherts. Such values cannot be reduced to the instrumental, everyday needs that any good grade chert can serve to fulfill since there were qualitatively adequate cherts much more closely at hand that would serve the same instrumental needs as the long distant cherts did.

Kozarek is aware of this special valuation attributed to Wyandotte chert. She deals with it by noting that it is not only Wyandotte chert that came from a great distance but also Flint Ridge chert. Hence, she recognizes that two nonlocal cherts were used to produce tools used for "everyday" tasks. Even though other types of stone resources used for everyday tasks were procured on the basis of economizing, that is, stones that were conveniently at hand, rather than this usage of exotic cherts for equally everyday purposes raising a puzzle for her, she simply asserts that it has been widely recognized by archaeologists that the pairing of exotic or at least selected nonlocal cherts, excluding perfectly adequate cherts that may be more conveniently at hand, has been observed as occurring in many separate regions where the Hopewell episode was played out and, therefore, the Jennison Guard case was simply replicating this common pattern. "The use of nonlocal chert varieties was widespread during the Middle Woodland period" (1987, 95). However, this is hardly an answer. Rather, it raises an even more serious puzzle. Why would the long distance procurement of select cherts be regularly carried out by "sedentary hamlet groups" in order to produce such everyday expedient tools as bifaces and bladelets when all these Hopewellian regions typically had qualitatively equivalent local cherts close at hand?

As I noted above, while at Jennison Guard the dominant chert was Wyandotte and the lesser chert was Flint Ridge, at the Murphy Tract, it was the reverse. Flint Ridge chert was dominant while Wyandotte was in much lower proportion. However, the dual pattern still prevailed. Now while the exotic nonlocal nature of the Wyandotte chert at the Murphy site is clear (after all, the quarry resources were over 300 km away from this site), it is hard to make the same argument for the Flint Ridge chert. The Flint Ridge quarry region is only about 20 km southeast of the site. Nevertheless, Flint Ridge chert had special value for the occupants and users at the Murphy site. Not only is the special value of this chert demonstrated by its being ubiquitous across all the ceremonial earthwork sites of Ohio and, of course, even in Indiana and, less so, in Illinois, it is important to note that the Murphy site is in an exceedingly rich chert region. There are several major chert quarries with qualitatively equal cherts in the region, some of which are even closer to the Murphy site than the Flint Ridge quarries. Indeed, in pre– and post–Middle Woodland period components of the Murphy Tract, Flint Ridge chert was largely absent and these other cherts were primarily used. Hence, it is clear that, even though the labor requirement involved in procuring Flint Ridge rather than some other locally available chert was not of the same magnitude as the labor demands imposed on the Jennison Guard site occupants to procure Wyandotte chert rather than use more locally available cherts, preferential selection was still being exercised at Murphy. Such selectivity suggests deontic values and standards being exercised that cannot be adequately explained in instrumental, practical terms. That is, seen in symbolic pragmatic and integrated cultural tradition terms, the needs that the use of these two cherts fulfilled at both sites simply could not be fulfilled by substitutes, even if the latter were qualitatively the instrumental equivalent. Another way of putting this is to say that the cherts possessed tangible attributes that served to constitute the items they were used to produce as essential symbolic pragmatic devices by which the tasks that these mediated would be constituted as the type of social activities (rituals) intended. Even though other cherts were equally efficient in objective terms, they were ineffective in symbolic pragmatic terms.

This does not deny, however, that local cherts were not used. In fact, there is a small percentage of local cherts in both these cases, indicating that some tasks that were performed in these sites could be adequately mediated by them. At this point, the symbolic pragmatic view would suggest that the select cherts were required to serve tasks of a special ritual nature and, in contrast, the ordinary cherts served nonritual needs, the type of needs that would be paramount in a domestic, family-based everyday setting. Since such local cherts were rare at both Murphy and Jennison Guard, it suggests that, despite the presence of earth ovens, hearths, and possibly storage pits, the domestic-like tasks these features served were not quite like the domestic-like tasks that would be performed in an everyday habitation setting, whether this was a sedentary hamlet or a seasonal base camp. As I noted above, Dancey chose between two possibilities when he characterized the Murphy site. He noted that its small size and domestic content, and in particular, its maintenance and layout, suggested it was a sedentary hamlet that was cared for by the everyday occupants. However, its superfluity of lithics suggested it might be "a bladelet and biface 'factory.'" Kozarek had the same choice. They both explained the very similar array of features, midden deposits, well-maintained common area, and so on, as the signature of the former, not the latter. I think they made the wrong choice.

ALTERNATIVE ACCOUNT

My choice is to treat these sites as specialized production locales occupied by age-grade cult sodality groups. The well-defined nature of the sites indicates the operation of some strict rules by which transient users ensured the maintenance of the zone so as to avoid polluting the production process. I have argued that one of the purposes of the bladelet was to ensure the use of a ritual tool that had not been previously used to mediate a prior ritual (Byers 2004; 2006b). Hence, it was easily and quickly produced and tossed when the ritual was completed and its use was no longer needed. Tossing it ensured that it would not be kept and mistakenly reused in a subsequent ritual. I have argued that this rule of avoiding mixing ritual implements was fundamental to maintaining the Hopewell ritual sphere and, in particular, avoiding mixing the tools used in the mundane domestic sphere with those used in the specialized Hopewell sphere. This avoidance of mixing would appear to have embraced the production facilities also. Hence, it was regarded as inappropriate to mix the debitage of a production episode with that of a preceding episode in the same spot. This rule obliged the producers to "clean up" the spot after the episode and, furthermore, to keep this debitage separate from the rest of the functioning zones so that the used debris was clearly identified as forbidden to use for further ritual. This would account for the type of maintenance practices that Kozarek identified and, in fact, that Dancey also identified. That is, while under the monistic modular polity community view, the only explanation that would seem to work is to postulate sedentary occupation such that the ongoing set of residents would avoid living in their own garbage, under the alternative model, the same patterning can be quite coherently accounted for as the result of ongoing but sequential transient occupation by age-grades organized into specialized age-set groups of a cult sodality having the task to produce a valuable superfluity of lithic objects to ensure that cult sodality ritual could be effectively served. I suggest that this is why there is so little in the way of actually used implements, despite the superfluity of production debitage. That is, for the most part the products were carried away for use in the ceremonial sphere.

Does this notion itself hold water, namely, that mixing production debitage counts as polluting the sacred production process? I think that a recent report by Frank Cowan (2005) on his analysis of the Koenig Quartz deposit, a major deposit of obsidian and crystal quartz debitage at the Barnyard site, which is adjacent to the Stubbs Works site, clearly substantiates this claim. When Cowan started his analysis of the deposit, it consisted of literally thousands of crystal quartz fragments that mapped the full range of reduction steps equivalent to those identified in the Wyandotte chert material at the Jennison Guard site. However, further analysis also revealed a significantly large quantity of obsidian reduction flakes. Once he was able to analyze a representative sample of the total deposit, while rock crystal quartz probably derived from western North Carolina was the dominant lithic (as he noted, this was likely also the source of much of the mica found in Ohio), obsidian was a substantial second lithic resource. Even more importantly, he was able to establish through flotation analysis that the mixed obsidian and quartz deposit included very small fragments of these materials, much too small to be the result of even careful collection following a production episode. His conclusion was that the producer must have worked on hides or bark surfaces sufficiently large to ensure that all or at least most debitage, even the smallest, would not fall on the exposed surface. This cover was then gathered up and, in all likelihood, the contents were spilled into a container or onto a larger sheet. The total would be wrapped up and preserved. At a certain point the accumulated debitage of these two valued resources was ritually buried.

Now it is true that this hyperavoidance treatment did not prevent but actually ensured the mixing of the debitage output of obsidian and quartz production. However, it is also clear that it prevented the mixing of this debitage with the earth or other materials that were in the immediate zone. Clearly, mixing obsidian and quartz was permissible, suggesting that these two were complementary and largely equivalent in their sacred nature. At the same time, however, this practice manifests strict rules of avoidance ensuring that this debitage would not be mixed with lesser debitage and residue. That is, production of ritual materials would be burdened by symbolic pragmatic rules that constituted the production as felicitous. The site maintenance practices that Kozarek and Dancey claim generated the patterning of these two sites could be and probably were the result of exercising non-domestic-based rules of production that would constitute the site as a specialized cult sodality type locale having a strong hostel-like habitation aspect and this would be characteristic of cult sodality sites in which seclusion in transient residency and regular long distant traveling was expected.

This completes the critical discussion part of the claim that these two sites, Jennison Guard and Murphy, and by extension any sites like them, were sedentary habitation sites. However, the hermeneutic spiral method entails that a critique is only completed when the alternative account is given and empirically grounded. I am obliged methodologically, therefore, to present the alternative account in terms of the Dual Complementary Clan/Cult Sodality Clusters Community model or, to be more specific, of its auxiliary Cult Sodality Cluster model, in order to demonstrate that these sites can be more coherently understood as part of a system of cult sodality heterarchies. I turn to this task in the next chapter, first summarizing the archaeological record of the Murphy Tract as this was described by Paul Pacheco. Following Dancey and Kozarek in this regard, he used these empirical data to claim that this tract manifested a dispersed sedentary hamlet community as postulated by his Hamlet Hypothesis. I think it is perfectly appropriate, therefore, to draw on these same data to ground empirically the Cult Sodality Cluster model.

9

The Murphy Tract

The Empirical Grounding of the Cult Sodality Cluster Model

Paul Pacheco expanded Dancey's research on the Murphy site by carrying out a series of intensive and carefully organized surface surveys of the larger 50 ha zone in which the Murphy site is located (Pacheco 1993, 110, figure 12). He refers to this as the Murphy Tract. It is located on an upper terrace of the floor of the lower Raccoon Creek about 2.5 km west of the very large, complex, and well-known Newark site (figure 3.2; see 1993, 96, figure 11). His point was to extrapolate from Dancey's interpretation of the Murphy site as a sedentary hamlet to argue that the patterning of the lithic data derived from his comprehensive surface survey of the Murphy Tract, particularly the presence or absence of what he terms a uninodal lithic refuse cluster, displays the signature of a series of such sedentary hamlets, thereby reinforcing and, indeed, for him confirming Prufer's initial "thesis" that the Middle Woodland community settlement pattern consisted of primarily two components, the civic-ceremonial earthwork center and the dispersed set of kinship-based domestic sedentary hamlets around it. Since I have already critiqued Dancey's claim that the Murphy site was a Middle Woodland period sedentary hamlet, as well as Kozarek's essentially identical claim for the Jennison Guard site, it is not necessary for me to critique Pacheco's claim in this regard. Therefore, if the Murphy site with its "bull's-eye" refuse deposit is not the residue of a Middle Woodland period sedentary hamlet, then it is reasonable for me to interpret the four additional surface lithic clusters displaying the signature bull's-eye refuse deposit as also not being sedentary hamlets. Indeed, this also means that the total set of lithic clusters dispersed across the Murphy Tract, with no single cluster being more than 200 m or 300 m from its nearest neighbor, cannot be properly characterized as manifesting a dispersed set of sedentary hamlets constituting a segment of a local residential community, as Pacheco claims to have demonstrated. However, the empirical data that he has gathered and presented are invaluable since I can use them to empirically ground the alternative Cult Sodality Cluster model. To do so will require summarizing Pacheco's data and critically assessing the way he interpreted them in the light of the premises of the Hamlet Hypothesis and its theoretical background, namely, the Vacant Center/Dispersed Hamlet model. This will enable me to show that the patternings and material nature of these data are generally not consistent with the type of dispersed habitation units that are postulated under the Hamlet Hypothesis, particularly because of the quantitative and qualitative nature of the lithic record. Like Pacheco I will rely on Dancey's detailed excavation and analysis of the Murphy site as a guide to interpreting the surface survey data of the rest of the Murphy Tract and argue that, in quantitative terms, the lithic record surpasses the instrumental needs of small residential units, whether sedentary or semisedentary, and the lithic record also surpasses in qualitative terms the symbolic pragmatic needs of this type of postulated residential social unit. Instead, my main argument will be that in both qualitative and quantitative terms the record is much more consistent with both the symbolic pragmatic and the instrumental needs of a cult sodality as it would be organized in the countryside, this being the organizational type and place postulated under the Cult Sodality Cluster model. I will first summarize Pacheco's Hamlet Hypothesis since, in fact, the categories of activity areas that this distinguishes are also important in operationalizing the range of key sites of the Cult Sodality Cluster model. That is, I will emphasize that rather than the content, variable size, and distribution of these sites fitting the notion of the hamlet and its subcategories as he defines them, they can be very easily and more coherently accommodated to the categories specified by the Cult Sodality Cluster model, as I intend to demonstrate.

THE HAMLET HYPOTHESIS

In the Hamlet Hypothesis, Pacheco specifically defined the hamlet as the core domestic unit of the Ohio Hopewell settlement system consisting of "one to at most a few household units . . . [and that] interacting clusters of hamlets in local regions form[ed] dispersed sedentary communities" (1993, 8). Based on this definition, he interpreted the lithic clusters of the Murphy Tract as constituting a cluster of dispersed hamlets with associated special purpose activity areas and, as such, it would be only one cluster of a dispersed set of such hamlet clusters, the total set of clusters constituting a local kinship-based community of the Raccoon Valley region. His model consisted of four main empirical criteria that should be present for a given locale to count as a hamlet. These were: "1. Hamlets will be small in size, with a uninodal size distribution. 2.

Hamlets will have functionally redundant assemblages, representing the general day to day activities of the domestic unit. 3. Hamlets will be structurally redundant, consisting of a repetitive pattern of maintained activity zones. Refuse dumps are characterized by sharply defined (uninodal) high density clusters of debris. 4. Hamlets will be spatially dispersed, but clustered around earthwork or burial mound complexes" (1993, 84). He then rounded out the Hamlet Hypothesis by defining three types of activity areas that would be part of the total range of locales associated with the dispersed sedentary hamlet community: the logistical activity area, the short-term activity area, and the specialized camp area. All three would reflect the type of activities conducted in them. The short-term and the logistical activity areas were differentiated primarily by the former being proximally "located between hamlets" (1993, 85), and the latter being distally located from any sedentary hamlet site. In effect, the "logistical activity" notion covers activity areas that were used by special, usually foraging or raw material procuring, task groups. These are assumed to be found generally in the uplands as short-term subsistence camps or in zones that served as specialized source locales for procuring Hopewellian material cultural raw materials, such as the Flint Ridge quarry zone that was about 20 km southeast of the Murphy Tract. Therefore, no particular upland logistical, short-term activity area could be matched to a hamlet or hamlet cluster.[1] However, the first type, the proximal "short-term activity areas," would be used for tasks serving the nearby hamlets. They would also be generally smaller than those nearby activity areas counting as hamlets, as well as having residue patterns that would differentiate them as specialized domestically related task areas.

In addition to these distal and proximal short-term activity areas, there was the above third category—the "specialized camp area." This could also be proximal or distal in relation to any given hamlet or hamlet cluster. In fact, this type is a bit of a catchall since it could vary in size. Pacheco specified that some might be larger than nearby hamlets. He ties areal size "to the size of the group participating in the activity and the locations of the camp, thus, some specialized camps will be relatively large when compared to hamlets, and some may be much smaller" (1993, 85). In fact, he specifically recognized subtypes of "specialized camps," for example, one that would include activity areas that "related to the production of Hopewellian paraphernalia, including a high frequency of blade-core industry usage and debris" (1993, 85). There was another specialized camp type since, while the former would be part of the cluster of hamlets, specialized camps also would appear at the "ceremonial centers" displaying "assemblages similar to hamlets, with evidence for multiple general domestic activities" (1993, 85). He finally notes that if found among the hamlet clusters this type of specialized camp displaying domestic residue could in some cases "represent temporary encampments of visiting domestic units. There should be little evidence of structural rebuilding, but feature overlap should be common, representing separate occupations of the camp" (1993, 86). However, these specialized campsites would differ from the hamlet proper in that "[d]ebris patterns should in general be scattered and light, because most camps are short-term" (1993, 86). Nevertheless, he follows this by stressing that specialized Hopewell assemblage workshop camps would be expected to build up "formal refuse deposits." As he puts it: "Formal refuse deposits may be expected to occur at non-habitation locations or structures permanently maintained in the settlement system for repetitive workshop functions" (1993, 86).

Pacheco then applied this model to interpreting the primary empirical data that he collected from the 50 ha Murphy Tract. These consisted of lithics collected by systematic surface surveying over the tract. The Murphy site data that Dancey's detailed surface survey and excavation revealed were also incorporated by Pacheco into his own data set. Since his own set consisted of only surface surveyed materials, that is, none of the clusters he noted were then excavated, he strongly relied on Dancey's noting the bull's-eye nature of the lithic midden deposit as a defining component of the sedentary hamlet. This midden deposit should show up on the surface as a distinct lithic clustering, which he termed the uninodal lithic cluster. Using this patterning, he assumed that the rest of the typical sedentary hamlet site would be revealed if, indeed, the locale was excavated. Of course, any lithic cluster that did not display this type of distinctive uninodal lithic clustering must be the manifestation of one of the other postulated activity areas, either a short-term special task area associated with a nearby hamlet locale or a specialized base camp associated with Hopewell ceremonial production, or, a domestic-like short-term base camp for visitors.

With the completion of the surface survey collection, he carried out a formal qualitative and quantitative comparison of the lithic categories and their distribution in each cluster. He identified 16 categories of chert production and combined them to generate nine main lithic artifact categories, and further subdivided them into Wyandotte and Flint Ridge cherts. The nine included different categories of formal artifacts, such as bifaces, bladelets (distinguished between single and multiple arris bladelets), and bladelet cores as well as different categories of debitage by size and usage. He then generated a series of bar graphs displaying the frequency distribution of these artifact and debitage categories for each cluster (e.g., figure 9.1, Murphy IV assemblage profile). He referred to the bar graphs of each cluster as delineating the artifact assemblage profile. Finally, he plotted the distribution for each cluster and its general makeup in order to establish the probable functional nature,

Table 9.1. Frequency Distribution of Wyandotte and Flint Ridge Cherts by Weight across the Murphy Tract Lithic Clusters

	Vanport	*Wyandotte*
Murphy I	4,535.9	18.2
Murphy III	6,137.2	7.3
Murphy IV	2,831.6	681.1
Murphy V	646.6	691.3
Murphy VI	4,432.7	125.4
Cluster 1	211.0	19.8
Cluster 2	209.5	63.4
Intercluster space	366.3	311.6
Total (in grams)	19,370.8	1,918.1

Source: Pacheco 1993, 212, table 13. By permission of Paul Pacheco.

divided between short-term activity area, specialized activity area, and hamlet area. These multiple analyses established quantitative but also, equally or even more importantly, qualitative variations in the plan and profile distribution of the lithic assemblages that, he claims, nicely fit what could be the expected types of locales postulated under the Hamlet Hypothesis with its auxiliary hypotheses: the hamlet type proper, proximal short-term activity areas, and the different types of specialized campsites.

The identified clusters all displayed multiple bladelets, whole and broken, as well as a rich assortment of manufacturing debitage, some bifacial tools and associated utilized flakes. Not surprisingly, given my earlier discussion on this matter, the lithic assemblages all displayed primarily two types of cherts, Flint Ridge and Wyandotte, although the Flint Ridge variety prevailed quantitatively overall. He also gave a summary of the total of Wyandotte and Flint Ridge cherts by weight for all the clusters he defined as hamlets, Murphy I, III, IV, V, and VI, as well as for two of the largest non-uninodal clusters, that is, Clusters 1 and 2, being activity areas, and for the intercluster space (table 9.1). He concluded that the Murphy Tract manifested "[f]ive hamlets, several possible logistical or short-term activity areas, and a specialized camp. . . . Based on these interpretations it is concluded that the Vacant Center Model is a productive organizational framework for understanding Ohio Hopewell domestic settlement patterns" (1993, 139).

CRITICAL DISCUSSION

Under the Cult Sodality Cluster model, the major sites that Pacheco is speaking of as hamlets would count as *age-grade site locales* and the auxiliary sites would count as *age-set site locales.* An interesting exercise, in fact, is to replace "hamlet" in the first four postulated criteria of the Hamlet Hypothesis with "age-grade locale" and then assess the data in these terms. Instead of the first postulate being "[h]amlets will be small in size, with a uninodal size distribution," it becomes "[age-grade locales] will be small in size, with a uninodal size distribution," followed by the second, namely, "[age-grade locales] will have functionally redundant assemblages, representing the general day to day activities of the [age-grade] unit." The third postulate becomes "[age-grade locales] will be structurally redundant, consisting of a repetitive pattern of maintained activity zones. Refuse dumps are characterized by sharply defined (uninodal) high density clusters of debris," and the fourth becomes "[age-grade locales] will be spatially dispersed, but clustered around earthwork or burial mound complexes." The benefit of doing this is that it enables us to comparatively assess the data in terms of the natures of the social organizations that each of these models postulates. Interestingly, there is considerable congruency. That is, with little modification both sets of criteria as listed could be "predicted" by both models. For example, while clearly just as the social nature of a family would tend to generate similar patterning in their locales such that there would be considerable qualitative and quantitative functional redundancy, so it could be expected for age-grade locales. The question is what criteria *in detail* would be consistent with the former but not the latter and vice versa? In fact, I have already made my case in this regard. I do not dispute that *sedentary domestic* hamlets would display site maintenance effects, for example, uninodal disposal areas, cleared common activity areas, storage and cooking features, and so on. However, I have argued that all this would be the case for age-grade components of cult sodalities also, and possibly with even more disciplinary control given the deontic imperatives that would be characteristic of a cult sodality itself, for example, careful separation of materials hinges on the avoidance of mixing residues of rituals and ritual production so as to ensure the felicity of the ritual material produced and the rituals performed there. And of course, there would be good representation of food preparation features, particularly earth ovens, since these would be ideal to prepare large quantities of food for group meals. This would be the case for the hamlets since, presumably, their occupants would also act as hosts for major get-togethers from time to time. In short, these two lists illustrate a primary problem with prediction based on deduction from basic premises. Opposing premises can be used that generate the same predictions. This means that the primary concepts of the two sets of premises that can be operationally tied to material patterning must be carefully explicated so as to serve as a sufficient means of discriminating among alternative possibilities. Therefore, the list of criteria must be detailed and this means having a very developed set of criteria for what will count as the type of site predicted. That is, if "prediction" is going to work, much more detail has to be added by which to differentiate between the two types. This is particularly the case for archaeology since the complexity of social systems is great and we have no experimental control by which to hold the multiple variables constant while varying only one or two.

There is another lesson in this comparison. It shows an important weakness in relying on the hypothetico-deductive method, particularly in archaeology where our ability to make detailed predictions is severely limited and where, in fact, by the very nature of the object studied, prehistoric society, our archaeological methodology cannot control the conditions that brought about the empirical data. This comparison shows that contrasting social premises can generate the same suite of fairly broadly delineated predictions. From this, two considerations should be recognized. First, a comparison of alternative models is required to establish the most adequate in accounting for the data. This is very important. Indeed, to rely on only one model to make empirical predictions is known as the fallacy of affirming the consequent. While it is demonstrable in experiment to show that X causes Y, this does not eliminate the possibility that several other quite causally different factors could also cause Y. This contingency is a problem even when experimental controls can be set up, as in the natural sciences of chemistry and physics. These controls ensure that only the postulated factor was the cause of the experimental outcome. However, it is effectively impossible to experiment with the social phenomena that were responsible for the archaeological record. Of course, I am not denying that archaeologists can work in sophisticated laboratories and can also experiment with the materials they find. However, typically this laboratory work draws on preexisting natural scientific knowledge to assist in interpreting the data when the latter have material properties that can be registered by tests, for example, radiocarbon dating, makeup of ceramic temper, and so on. Material sciences are unquestionably important to archaeologists. However, this type of laboratory work supplements and greatly assists the archaeologist as a *social scientist* in interpreting and explaining the archaeological record. It cannot be a substitute for this social scientific work. This is because as with all social systems, the past social systems were intrinsically open systems and this means that even if we had been present (per impossible, of course), we could not experimentally close them. Generating alternative models of the possible causal factors, therefore, is necessary and this enables the possibility of making a choice based on reasoned comparison.

This means much more theorizing of the social phenomena believed to be responsible must be done so that necessary distinctions can be made and tied to the postulated empirical data. Many archaeologists might despair over this process, saying that it is mere speculation that disconnects the models from the data so that the latter cannot be used to ground the former. I disagree, however. This theorizing depends on retroductive, not deductive, inference.

Given our current theoretical knowledge about traditional Native North American social systems, we can postulate what possible social conditions could have existed in the Ohio Middle Woodland period that would generate the domestic/ceremonial dichotomy, or what I prefer speaking of as the bifurcated settlement articulation modal posture. Indeed, this is how Prufer first constructed his Vacant Center thesis! However, since this was not the type of settlement pattern that existed when Europeans first encountered these communities, it must be that a different social arrangement existed, one that promoted the bifurcated posture pattern and which had the potential to transform it into the integrated posture pattern that was in place when Europeans arrived, and so on. I have even used retroductive inference to critique the current theoretical knowledge we have of the historic Native North American culture and society, arguing that we have underestimated the role of companionship and the nature and implications of their cosmology for understanding ecological behaviors, and so on.

In any case, this retroductive approach, taking (and modifying where necessary) what we already know was inherited from the past and modifying it to build theory by working back retroductively to postulate the possible social structural conditions that would have existed in the past given the tangible patterning we know was generated as indicated by the archaeological record, enables the archaeologists to postulate models of the social structural conditions that are not immediately perceivable in the archaeological record but that would explain the patternings of that record if these conditions existed at that time. Of course this is not God's-truth, but it does give rational grounds for choosing between or among alternative models by testing the explanations these alternatives can be used to give. The assumption is that the model that gives the fuller and more coherent explanation of the data must be the better approximation of the prehistoric social conditions that were the cause of the pattern than the alternative model or models. By recognizing that all are approximations, we avoid committing the fallacy of affirming the consequent. Hence, our models emerge from generally recognized theoretical knowledge of the phenomenon that would be responsible for the empirical data and they are also tightly and rationally tied to these data by means of explanation. Yes, the model goes beyond the data and so we can only ever assume that we have made an approximate characterization of the causal factors that were responsible. But all social science does this, particularly prehistory, since the tangible patterning of the archaeological record of human society is not to be conflated with that social process. Rather, the pattern is its material expression and material realization, not its summation. Of course, this is a restatement of hermeneutic spiral method. This method incorporates two primary interrelated steps: retroduction and abduction, and it also can rely on deduction and induction. Retroductive inference draws on our current theoretical knowledge to generate models that explicate the necessary conditions for the patterning to be explained; abduction is the comparative method by which models explicating different and alternative possible conditions are tested through interpreting and explaining the same data. Deduction and induction, then, allow for detailed comparison (Danermark et al. 2002, 163–64).

I have already argued that characterizing the social nature of such sites as Jennison Guard and Murphy as domestic habitation sites of kin-based groups is not reasonable on empirical and social theoretical grounds; and I did this by critically addressing the material criteria that would be consistent with such sites, given what we can reasonably know about the needs and practices of "sedentary hamlets." I pointed out the large quantities and broad range of the selected lithics and exotics that were found and these are not consistent with hamlets, sedentary or mobile; while they certainly are consistent with cult sodalities. I will now assess the patterning of these Murphy Tract clusters so as to establish the degree to which this patterning would be consistent with what we could expect the specialized components of cult sodalities would generate while, at the same time, generating fewer anomalies than does the Hamlet Hypothesis. If so, then the Cult Sodality Cluster model promises to be a useful interpretive and explanatory tool for expanding our understanding of the Ohio Hopewell episode.

DEMONSTRATING THE CULT SODALITY CLUSTER MODEL

As an initial step in this process, I think that it is important to reinforce the quantitative richness of this material record in which chert had such an important presence, particularly the Wyandotte and Flint Ridge varieties. Pacheco has recently given a summary quantitative overview of the lithic assemblage that characterized the Murphy Tract, emphasizing only the debitage and formal remains of what he called the expedient tools, namely the flake tools and bladelets.[2] "[T]he number of expedient tools in the assemblage is immense, since a conservative estimate of the flake debitage at Murphy I is about three-quarters of a million specimens. . . . The Murphy III assemblage is equally large . . . ; there may be 135,000 expedient tools in the assemblage (with hundreds of thousands of potential tools lying along side them)" (Pacheco 2010b, 53). Interpreting these in sedentary hamlet terms, he goes on to conclude that "[t]his vast reserve of available cutting edges explains why use-wear polish is not well developed in the Murphy I assemblage, and it is the hallmark of a sedentary residence utilizing an expediently organized lithic technology rather than a residentially mobile residence dominated by curated bifaces" (2010b, 53–54). While Pacheco is interpreting these lithics as reinforcing his sedentary hamlet thesis, the Cult Sodality Cluster model can account for these data as the outcome of ritual activity of transient but continually sequential age-grades and age-sets, as I do in more detail below, a type of usage that minimized the reuse of these tools. As I have also argued, I see these lithics as far surpassing either the instrumental or qualitative (symbolic pragmatic) needs or capacities of any domestic habitation social unit or set of social units, whether sedentary or mobile. As with the Jennison Guard site, this lithic record represents a superfluity of lithics that is quite inadequately accounted for in small domestic hamlet terms, whether sedentary, seasonally semisedentary, or fully residentially mobile. At the same time, it represents a quantitative mobilization of labor that would surpass the capacity of such sedentary habitation units.

Extrapolating from my characterization of the Jennison Guard and the Murphy sites (i.e., Murphy I) as cult sodality locales probably used by the age-grade group sectors of the sodality, I would simply extend this characterization to the other uninodal lithic cluster locales. The non-uninodal locale clusters would then be activity areas used by the constituent age-sets of the cult sodality. This claim can be reinforced by reassessing the distribution of Wyandotte chert that Pacheco's survey and analysis has revealed. Before doing that, however, I want it to be very clearly understood that I am not denying that the Middle Woodland period domestic component of the population of the Central Ohio Valley likely occupied dispersed habitation locales. I believe that there is plenty of evidence, albeit mostly negative, that this was the case (Church and Erickson 1997, 346–47). Furthermore, I have already postulated the Dispersed Kinship Habitation Cluster model and this is effectively what is meant by Pacheco's Hamlet Hypothesis, except that (1) it postulates that the kinship-based clan component of a complementary heterarchical community in the bifurcated settlement articulation modal posture would have its constituent families dispersed as multiple semisedentary/seasonally mobile and small domestic units, and (2) their size and operating deontics, namely, the "live-lightly-on-the-land" rule, would promote a near but not complete archaeological invisibility. Therefore, what I am claiming is that the Murphy Tract sites and other formally similar sites that have been used to represent a dispersed hamlet system are, in fact, more likely to be representative of the relatively autonomous cult sodalities of these complementary heterarchical communities. Therefore, I think that by his intensive survey Pacheco has unwittingly revealed the locales and their associated material residue of the age-set and age-grade components of a local cult sodality and it is these that were distributed across the landscape in a manner that can be described as dispersed clusters, and, therefore, the social relations that linked up contemporary neighboring sites were companionship- and seniority-based.

In short, while I disagree with the social characterization of the Murphy Tract sites as domestic, kinship-based habitation units with associated short-term task areas, whether sedentary or seasonally mobile/semisedentary, I do not disagree with the more general characterization that a major component of this regional social system would consist of multiple clusters of dispersed kinship-based habitation units. Some sites have been identified that would easily fit the parameters of this type of site, such as those identified by Church and Erickson (1997) in the Salt Creek Valley region south of Chillicothe. However, much more research is needed in order to reveal what are nearly archaeologically invisible signs of kinship/clan-based habitation sites (Cowan 2006, 48–49). I am not claiming that this archaeological "invisibility" is just a matter of the near absence or ephemeral nature of the material indicators, although this is the objective and technical part of the explanation. However, the invisibility is also related to the dominance of the monistic modular polity view, of which the Hamlet Hypothesis is a leading expression. When sites such as those on the Salt Creek are recognized, even though they lack the rich residue of the Murphy site, they are assimilated to this type and, therefore, they are interpreted as simply smaller versions of Murphy or Jennison Guard or, alternatively, they are somewhat grudgingly acknowledged as being the rare case of nonsedentary habitation locales, that is, as seasonal base camps. In that sense, the evidence that would support the existence of the complementary cluster of small habitations as postulated under the Dispersed Kinship Habitation Cluster model is systematically conflated to the Vacant Center model. Since my purpose here is to demonstrate the Cult Sodality Cluster model, I will now focus on grounding my claim empirically that the Murphy Tract data manifest a characteristic example of certain components of a cult sodality cluster by giving a detailed interpretive analysis of the Wyandotte chert distribution and its relation to the parallel but much denser Flint Ridge chert distribution of the Murphy Tract.

THE WYANDOTTE AND FLINT RIDGE CHERT DISTRIBUTION PATTERNS

Pacheco recognized that over 93 percent of the chert sample he gathered from across the Murphy Tract consisted of both Flint Ridge chert (of the Vanport variety) and Wyandotte cherts with the former being 81.2 percent and the latter 11.1 percent of the total (1993, 119). Extrapolated to the total potential chert usage, this means that the smallest percentage of the total flint content of the tract (7.7 percent) consisted of mostly local cherts and much of this lithic content was either pre– or post–Middle Woodland period deposition. As noted earlier, the large Flint Ridge chert quarries are found only about 20 km southeast of Newark. In contrast the Wyandotte chert quarries are found in southeast Indiana, about 350 km to the southwest of Newark. Also, although these two cherts made up the large bulk of the chert used on the Murphy Tract, Pacheco estimated that proportionally Flint Ridge chert was ten times by weight the quantity of Wyandotte chert. In fact, the total amount of Wyandotte chert brought into the Murphy Tract did not exceed 40 to 50 kg, in his estimation. He postulated that since Wyandotte chert was distinctly exotic in terms of distance, and 50 kg could be easily transported by a small party or even a single person, the presence of this resource was likely a one-shot deal. This singular procurement event was used by him as a chronological marker: the "presence and types of Wyandotte chert artifacts in assemblages . . . serve as time markers" (1993, 211). For him, therefore, the appearance of the Wyandotte chert was the result of an event (or possibly two closely sequential events), and, therefore, the distribution of the chert should be able to be used to structure the tract into two phases, the before and after Wyandotte event periods.

I have defined most or even possibly all the uninodal locales as specialized production locales of cult sodalities operated by the age-grade laity sectors. Now, as I noted earlier, the specialized campsite is postulated under the Hamlet Hypothesis model. However, because the uninodal locales are defined by Pacheco as sedentary hamlets, he has considerable difficulty identifying any specialized production sites at all in the tract, except for one. And this did not exist as a single cluster but as a dispersed set of clusters dominating the southern sector of the Murphy Tract. He calls this the South Block. It was about 4 ha in overall size and incorporated at least two clusters that, under his model, qualified as short-term sites, as well as a larger cluster site, which he termed Murphy IV (Pacheco 1993, 110, figure 12). However, using the Wyandotte event premise and further differentiations noted in the distribution of the Wyandotte and Flint Ridge chert in the South Block, he structured Murphy IV cluster into two chronological periods, Murphy IV-A and Murphy IV-B. The former was the pre-Wyandotte-event period and during this period Murphy IV, as interpreted by him, was a sedentary hamlet. Murphy IV-B marked the post-Wyandotte-event period and during this period, that is, after the Murphy IV-A hamlet had been abandoned, it was used as a specialized production campsite. He grounds this claim by contrasting the Wyandotte chert and Flint Ridge chert distributions in the same area. "The Wyandotte chert surface distribution in the South Block is generally concordant with Vanport chert distribution, but is considerably more patchy and scattered. . . . Wyandotte chert artifacts comprised about 18 percent of the total sample in the South Block, approximately 25 percent of which were bladelets. . . . The main concentration of Wyandotte chert is to the west of the potential Murphy

IV lithic refuse deposit. There is only slight overlap in these concentrations" (1993, 174).

Pacheco then specifies the significance of this patchiness of the Wyandotte chert and, in particular, the non-overlap of the latter chert with the Flint Ridge chert making up the uninodal cluster defining Murphy IV. "Non-overlapping distributions potentially stem from a lack of contemporaneity between the Vanport refuse deposit and the depositional events responsible for the disposal of the Wyandotte chert" (1993, 174–75). That is, this distribution pattern suggests to him not a disparity caused by the differences in quantity of the two cherts but a chronological structuring with the Flint Ridge chert being deposited to make up the major part of the uninodal cluster of Murphy IV prior to the activity that generated the Wyandotte chert distribution over the same cluster. He also emphasizes the differential patterning of the two cherts in the rest of the South Block, characterizing the distribution of the Wyandotte bladelets as a "scattered pattern over the entire South Block, including Cluster 2 and the intercluster area south, north, and west of Cluster 1. A majority of the Wyandotte bladelets are located in the southwest quadrant of Murphy IV, including a few within the high density Vanport node. There are only a couple of small concentrations of bladelets within the cluster, with the highest density concentration located on the northern margin of the Vanport chert nodal concentration" (1993, 175). From this contrast between the patterning of the two cherts, he argues that the Wyandotte chert distribution in the South Block was the result of use-and-toss depositional behavior while the majority of the Flint Ridge chert of Murphy IV was the result of careful cleaning up. "Hence within the South Block, Wyandotte chert and at least one concentrated area of Vanport chert in the Murphy IV cluster, probably represent different disposal patterns. The high frequency of scattered Wyandotte bladelets in the South Block points to an activity which relied heavily on bladelets. Following this activity bladelets were casually discarded as opposed to being cleared and deposited in a formal refuse zone like those observed in the other large clusters" (1993, 175).

Why all this in his view is important is that within the Murphy IV cluster, this disparity in distribution patterns of the two cherts marks both use-and-toss and clean-up-and-dump methods, with the former used with the Wyandotte bladelets and the latter with Flint Ridge bladelets, respectively, while in the rest of the South Block, pretty well only the use-and-toss method prevailed for both Wyandotte and Flint Ridge bladelets. He directly attributes the absence of the clean-up-and-dump method in association with Wyandotte chert distribution as "associated with short-term activities or occupations" and, he goes on to add, the "limited overlap in the distributions of Wyandotte and

Middle Woodland Vanport refuse deposit [of Murphy IV] was fortuitous" (1993, 176). He interpreted this fortuitous distribution, therefore, as indicating that the Murphy IV refuse deposit primarily consisted of Flint Ridge chert and this preexisted the use-and-toss deposition of the Wyandotte chert debitage. Hence, the "limited overlap in the distributions of Wyandotte and Middle Woodland Vanport refuse deposit" of the Murphy IV site indicates temporal priority to the presence of Flint Ridge chert over Wyandotte chert.

Since the Wyandotte and Flint Ridge chert bladelets were distributed in the same scattered manner across the South Block, with some concentration delineating Clusters 1 and 2, then the total block was structured in terms of the same Flint Ridge and Wyandotte dual components. The quantitative dominance of Wyandotte chert in Cluster 2 suggests that while it was used as a Flint Ridge–based activity area in pre-Wyandotte-event times, it was more extensively used in the same manner during the post-Wyandotte-event times. In contrast, Cluster 1 "is primarily composed of Vanport chert." Therefore, even though scattered Wyandotte bladelets are also associated with this cluster and its surrounding intercluster space, I think Pacheco would see its main usage period as occurring in pre-Wyandotte times (1993, 177). A similar structuring is apparent for most of the other clusters north of the South Block, except for Cluster 4, which seems to be predominantly Wyandotte chert. Cluster 7 has 26 percent of its lithics as Wyandotte chert, including two bladelets. "The Wyandotte and Vanport chert artifacts overlap in distribution with the cluster, but the scattered pattern is probably indicative of a short-term, single event, activity within the area" (1993, 179).

Using these data and the Wyandotte procurement event assumption, he proceeded to construct a postulated chronology of the Murphy Tract (Pacheco 1993, 223, figure 50). He demarcated the clusters that would appear to be contemporary, or at least had some overlapping occupation periods. As noted above, he first structured Murphy IV into two phases, A and B, or the pre-Wyandotte-event and post-Wyandotte-event phases, based on the more scattered and casual use-and-toss distribution of the Wyandotte bladelets compared to the greater gathered-and-dumped distribution of the Flint Ridge bladelets, and then suggested that Murphy IV-B and the rest of the South Block clusters displaying Wyandotte chert artifacts and Murphy V were probably largely contemporary, that is, belonging to the post-Wyandotte-event phase. However, because of the greater presence of Wyandotte chert in Murphy I than in Murphy III or VI, the former was placed as partly contemporary with the South Block and Murphy V, while Murphy III and Murphy VI came later in the post-Wyandotte-event period, marking the third phase as well as accounting for the low density of this chert, the premise being that since Wyandotte chert procurement was a single-shot deal, the passage of time would seriously reduce its availability to those occupying the Murphy Tract. In fact, he suggests that "the Wyandotte presence in these assemblages [was] a result of recycling of bladelets discovered [by the later occupants] while living in the study area" (1993, 213). However, Murphy V is a bit puzzling for him since the Wyandotte chert usage paralleled the way Flint Ridge chert was used in the other "hamlets" while "[e]verywhere else in the study area Wyandotte was channeled into the blade-core industry, but at Murphy V it is used as every day material" (1993, 214). He tries to resolve this puzzle by speculating that the occupants of Murphy V may have been responsible for the Wyandotte event itself, being the "household . . . that acquired the Wyandotte, either through exchange or as a result of an expedition to southern Indiana" (1993, 214).

In sum, he presents four maps marking the chronological development of the Murphy Tract (1993, 223, figure 50). The initial settlement was Murphy IV-A with Cluster 2. The implication here is that the former was a hamlet and the latter was a short-term activity site. Time 2, the immediate post-Wyandotte-event period, is correlated with Murphy IV-B, Murphy V, and Murphy I as contemporaneous hamlets, along with Cluster 1, Cluster 4, Cluster 5/8, and Cluster 7. He indicates Cluster 2 was abandoned. I find his placing Cluster 2 in the pre-Wyandotte-event time and Cluster 1 in the post-Wyandotte-event time puzzling since he earlier noted that Cluster 1 had a very low Wyandotte presence while Cluster 2 had a much higher Wyandotte presence. "Cluster 1 is primarily composed of Vanport chert, while Cluster 2 has a higher frequency of Wyandotte chert, including several bladelets" (1993, 177). This may be a simple mix-up and modifying his map would not make a substantive change in the number of clusters between the before and after Wyandotte event. Hence, the short-term activity areas per period would be the same number and both the relative positions and distances between these and the nearby postulated hamlets would be equivalent. That is, in Time 1, Murphy IV-A was the only hamlet and it had one nearby short-term activity cluster, whether it was Cluster 1 or 2; and in Time 2, Murphy IV still had one nearby short-term activity cluster (Cluster 1 or 2). Sometime during Time 2 and before Time 3, however, Murphy IV must have been abandoned and transformed into Murphy IV-B by becoming either a short-term activity area or a specialized production site, since in Time 3, Murphy IV and Clusters 1 and 2, as well as Murphy V, are shown to be abandoned. Instead only Murphy VI occupies this southern portion of the Murphy Tract and it is shown as contemporary with Cluster 4, the only short-term activity area still occupied across the total tract, while Murphy I and Murphy III are occupied in the northern reach of the tract. Time 4 shows the Murphy Tract as unoccupied (see Pacheco 1993, 223, figure 50, for details).

CRITIQUE

If we examine the differential distribution by weight of the uninodal chert deposits across the five main clusters, what Pacheco refers to as the residue of hamlets labeled as Murphy I, III, IV, V, and VI, a disparity is notable that would suggest that the differential distribution of Wyandotte and Flint Ridge chert assemblages was caused in part by the some factor or set of factors not related to chronology, per se. This would suggest that the use of the Wyandotte chert was part of the conditions that promoted the initial formation of the Murphy Tract clusters, meaning that it was there "from the beginning." If so, then its distribution cannot be used as a chronological marker but as a marker of one of the differences responsible for the variable quantitative distribution of the total chert assemblage across the Murphy Tract. In any case, the quantitative difference becomes apparent by comparing the five main clusters. For the moment, since Wyandotte chert is only 10 percent by weight of the total, I will compare only the Flint Ridge (Vanport variety) portion of the chert assemblage by weight (table 9.1). In terms of overall weight of Flint Ridge, two outliers are immediately revealed, Murphy V with about 650 grams of Flint Ridge chert and Murphy III with about 6,100 grams, almost ten times the amount. The other three, Murphy I, VI, and IV, make a loose "central" cluster by weight of about 4,500, 4,400, and 2,800 grams, respectively. Murphy I and VI are effectively the same in quantity and are separate from and greater than Murphy IV by about 1,700 grams, almost triple the total of the outlier Murphy V, and almost equal to the difference of 1,600 grams between these two and the upper outlier Murphy III (6,100 grams). This suggests that, in terms of Flint Ridge chert, these five clusters resolve into four categories, two outliers, one with a superfluity of this chert, Murphy III, and one with an impoverished quantity, Murphy V. Then there are two with an "average" amount, Murphy I and Murphy VI, and one with a "below-average-but-not-impoverished" amount, Murphy IV.

Now Pacheco argues that at Murphy V Wyandotte chert was used for everyday purposes much like Flint Ridge was used at the other "hamlets," and this would include Murphy IV, at least during its postulated pre-Wyandotte-event phase, the Murphy IV-A phase. I happen to disagree with his "everyday use" assessment, but I will address that later. More to the point, since I have suggested that the use of Wyandotte chert participated from the beginning of the formation of the clusters, that is, the activities its use constitutively mediated were part of the overall activities through time of the responsible group, namely, a cult sodality, it seems fair to incorporate the Wyandotte chert by weight across these five clusters (I am excluding the Wyandotte chert in the small clusters and the intercluster space). Does this change the above categories? In fact, the only significant change this makes is to the total aggregate chert by weight of Murphy IV and Murphy V since these two alone incorporate 86 percent by weight of the total Wyandotte chert in the five uninodal clusters. Adding these doubles the quantity of chert in association with Murphy V to about 1,300 grams. Since Murphy IV and Murphy V have almost the same amount of this chert, it also increases significantly the total chert of Murphy IV from 2,800 to about 3,500 grams. Now this alleviates but does not eliminate the impoverished status of Murphy V since, with the equivalent amount added to Murphy IV, the absolute difference between them remains the same. Does it lift Murphy IV from "below-average-but-not-impoverished" to "average" status compared to Murphy I and Murphy VI? I think not. It is still about 1,000 grams short of the average 4,500 grams of the latter. However, this difference is less than the difference between the "average" of Murphy I and VI and the bloated Murphy III, a difference between averages that is about 1,600 grams. Therefore, this means that the addition of the Wyandotte chert makes no significant difference in the four categories: one minimum and one maximum outlier, Murphy V and Murphy III, respectively, an "average" category of Murphy I and VI, and a "below-average" Murphy IV.

However, the qualitative difference marked by the Wyandotte and Flint Ridge distinction should also be considered. Pacheco has used it for chronological purposes. I will use it for initially grounding qualitative distinctions, the nature of which I will elucidate later. When the Wyandotte and Flint Ridge chert distinction is included, since in Murphy IV and Murphy V Wyandotte chert is effectively equal in both, then we can immediately lump these two into one category, suggesting in qualitative terms that they are more similar to each other than either is to the other three, all of which have very low Wyandotte chert content. Hence, while Murphy V retains its overall impoverished chert status quantitatively compared to Murphy IV, it seems clear that this status did not mean that it was qualitatively of lesser importance than Murphy IV. Indeed, it would seem that overall, in qualitative terms, Murphy V was somewhat unique. This is particularly likely since the Wyandotte chert was a costly resource suggesting that it served a critical need. Since it was concentrated equally in Murphy IV and V, it would appear that these two were critical in terms of how the Wyandotte chert was gained, used, and distributed. That is, since Murphy IV is second only to Murphy V in Wyandotte chert, then despite its quantitatively "below average" overall flint assemblage, it also played an important role in the procuring, using, and distributing of the Wyandotte chert. Finally, the quantitative difference in Flint Ridge chert between them suggests that each can be further differentiated. That is, while sharing the qualitative property that distinguishes them equally from Murphy I, III, and VI, these two, Murphy IV and V, are also qualitatively different from each other in that they strongly differ quantitatively in Flint Ridge chert.

A qualitative distinction is also the case for Murphy I, III, and VI. They share having a much lower amount of Wyandotte chert than Murphy IV and V, suggesting that they are qualitatively more like each other than any one is like Murphy IV or V. However, the quantitative difference in Wyandotte chert distribution across the three also seems to ground a qualitative difference among them suggesting that the Flint Ridge quantitative "average" and "above average" grouping has qualitative roots. In this case, Murphy VI and Murphy I, the "average," have 125 grams and 18 grams, respectively, of Wyandotte chert, while the maximum outlier Murphy III has a very small almost incidental amount of 7 grams. Given that Murphy III has 35 percent more Flint Ridge chert than the other two, if there were no qualitative differences in their social natures, it should also have at least 35 percent more Wyandotte chert than Murphy VI, or about 25 grams, or at least 35 percent more than Murphy I, or about 170 grams. That is, qualitative likeness should have generated between 25 to 170 grams for Murphy III. Since it does not, although Murphy III may still be more like the other two than it is like Murphy IV or Murphy V, given that all three share a very low Wyandotte chert content, it would appear that some type of qualitative difference, one that accounts for its impoverished Wyandotte content, does distinguish Murphy III from Murphy I and Murphy VI.

All this suggests that the qualitative distinction marked by the variable quantitative distribution of the Wyandotte and Flint Ridge chert assemblages organizes these five clusters into two major socially distinctive categories, Murphy IV and Murphy V, on the one hand, and Murphy I, III, and VI, on the other, and that internally, these two categories are qualitatively further distinguished. To anticipate a bit here, the conclusion of the analysis I make in the rest of this chapter suggests that Murphy I, III, and VI are probably of the same social nature, being the locales of age-grade sectors of the cult sodality that was historically responsible for the Murphy Tract archaeological record, while the quantitative differences may be a function of senior and junior age-grade difference. Also, Murphy IV and Murphy V share special social qualities that make them different from the other three. But they do so for different reasons. The former may have possibly been the ceremonial nodal locale of the cult sodality and the latter was likely a Hopewellian production camp specializing in Wyandotte chert tools, particularly the bladelet. I carry out the requisite analyses to ground these claims in the rest of this chapter.

Now, this brief analysis clearly makes a break with Pacheco's basic assumption about the relevance of the Wyandotte chert. There is a reason for this break, of course, and it is the different views we have about the nature of the bladelet. He treats it as simply one of two expedient tool types, the other being flake tools derived from the bifacial core industry. As I briefly commented in chapter 5, I treat the bladelet and its core industry as a formal mode by which a critically important symbolic pragmatic action cue of ritual was produced. As a tool, it certainly appears to be expedient. But this only mimics expediency since, as I argued with regard to the Wyandotte chert content of the Jennison Guard site, in fact, bladelet production entailed considerable and costly investment and time. These costs of procurement must be included in assessing the function and meaning of the bladelet. However, I am not going to deny that, in fact, Wyandotte chert was introduced into the Newark zone sometime into the Middle Woodland period occupancy history. But, as I argue later, the presence of the Wyandotte chert either occurred shortly after or, more likely, as I noted above, was there "from the beginning," or at least almost so, along with the Flint Ridge chert. For this reason, I postulate that both Flint Ridge and Wyandotte chert were procured by regularized processes, specifically by direct procurement of Flint Ridge chert from the Flint Ridge quarries and by long distance modes of intersodality Wyandotte chert transference, and that the usage of the two cherts at the Murphy Tract sites probably remained pretty well unchanged over the period during which the Ohio Hopewell episode played out in the Newark zone. This is because its appearance may mark the emergence of the ecclesiastic-communal cult sodality organizational structure in the Upper Muskingum zone—as I discuss later in my closing chapter. By this I mean to suggest that until the appearance of Wyandotte chert in this zone, the history of earthwork construction and usage in the Upper Muskingum area was not Hopewellian but Adenan. As I discuss later in the book, the usage of this Wyandotte chert was probably tightly tied into a specific ritual usufruct that was franchised into the Newark area, as I discuss below, and this franchise promoted the refocusing of earthwork construction to bring about the Ohio Hopewell component of Newark.

In this regard, it is also important to note that while Pacheco recognizes that the Wyandotte usage was introduced into the Murphy Tract sometime during the occupation period, he largely identifies the use of Flint Ridge chert at the Murphy Tract with the Middle Woodland period. He recognizes that some minor amount of Flint Ridge chert usage can be correlated with pre– and post–Middle Woodland period times. But he noted that most non–Middle Woodland period components of the tract used Upper Mercer and other types of localized cherts. That is, while Flint Ridge chert was certainly known and used at the site prior and subsequent to the Middle Woodland period (in fact, the Murphy IV locale had a Late Archaic component marked by Flint Ridge chert [Pacheco 2010b, 51]), this chert did not hold any special value for the users of those times in the way it did for the users during the Middle Woodland period. Pacheco also noted that Flint Ridge chert was commonly heat-treated in order, as he wrote, to make bladelets instrumentally equivalent to those produced with Wyandotte chert, which was not subjected to heat treatment. Thus, it seems that Flint Ridge chert, as colorful and attractive as it was, was not objectively the most effective chert available locally for tool production, including the Middle Woodland period bladelet. This suggests that there were factors involved that influenced its usage that were surplus to the particular objective instrumental properties it had. This is reinforced by the apparent fact that, as I noted earlier, Flint Ridge and Wyandotte cherts are found widely paired across the Ohio Hopewellian zone.

THE BLADELET AND FRANCHISING RITUAL USUFRUCT

I have already argued that the Middle Woodland bladelet cannot be accounted for in objective instrumental terms (Byers 2004, 230–39; 2006b, 66–73). Rather, it is best recognized as a ritual tool that was adopted in order to avoid its unwitting reuse in different ritual events. Since I have based my above and subsequent discussion on this premise, it is important now to give a more detailed argument to support this claim. It is widely recognized among Middle Woodland archaeologists that as a tool the bladelet (or the lamellar blade or lamellar flake—different terms have been used) appeared rather abruptly on the Middle Woodland period scene and, indeed, it is now generally regarded among Hopewell archaeologists to be a primary marker of the different regional Hopewell episodes. It did not replace previous expedient flake tools. Rather, its core technology, which was particularly designed to produce a range of elongated, cylindrical, and other similarly shaped cores from which the bladelet could be quickly and efficiently produced, was added to the traditional biface core technology that had its roots in the emergence of lithic technology in the Eastern Woodlands (Morrow 1987; Morrow et al. 1992; Odell 1994). Finally, both the bladelet and its core technology disappeared equally abruptly as they appeared (Yerkes 1994).

Hence, when found on sites, it is also often found in association with the biface tradition. Indeed, the flake tools that were traditionally produced as part of the bifacial core technology in addition to the symmetrical bifacial tools continued to be used in parallel with the bladelet, even though microwear analyses have demonstrated that both the bladelet and the flake tools were used to mediate the same range of material behaviors—slicing, cutting, and scraping of soft, medium, medium-hard, and hard materials—so that whatever materials the flake tools were used to modify were also modified by using bladelets (Yerkes 1994, 123–24). In short, using and retaining these two "expediently" produced tool types seems to be extraordinarily redundant. Eliminate the bladelet and all the material interventions that it was used to mediate could continue to be performed using the traditional expedient flake tools, with the added benefit of not having to produce a specialized core or, for that matter, needing to exchange or travel over hundreds of kilometers to procure such exotic material as Wyandotte chert!

Given all this redundancy and the extra costs of exotic or nonlocal chert procurement that seemed to be directly tied to the bladelet technology, it follows that explaining the continuing use of both flake and bladelet tools requires a symbolic pragmatic perspective. To say this means that as utilitarian as these two tool types were, it was their symbolic pragmatic meanings that made producing both of them necessary. In short, both the flake tool and the bladelet tool had important and probably contrasting action-constitutive functions. Performing a behavior mediated by a flake tool would constitute it as one type of social activity; performing the objectively same behavior mediated by a bladelet would constitute it as another type of social activity. This also suggests that the circumstances of usage would be a critical part of the action-constitutive process—where and when used, the purpose of the usage, and—most importantly—the social position the user occupied at the time of usage. The upshot of my argument is that the bladelet became empirically common not only because it was identified with and constitutive of Hopewell rituals, although this no doubt was a critical reason, but also because it became necessary as a means of avoiding the mixing of tools used for rituals produced in different contexts. I have argued that the expedient-like nature of the bladelet can be attributed to this avoidance rule. That is, each time the tool was required for the performance of a ritual, the agent could produce it from the bladelet core that he or she carried with him. Alternatively, he or she could make a packet of bladelets that could be conveniently carried, used as needed, and then tossed or dropped. All this is implicitly recognized by Pacheco when he argued above that both Wyandotte and Flint Ridge bladelets were subjected to two types of depositional behavior: clean-up-and-dump, on the one hand, and use-and-toss, on the other. Both methods manifest the same avoidance, namely, not mixing the tools across rituals. To do so would make the activity an infelicitous ritual of the type intended. Hence, flakes probably continued to be used as expedient tools to mediate material behaviors that were to be perceived and thereby constituted as having no particular ritual implication, while bladelet tools were used exclusively to mediate behaviors related to a ritual cycle, for example, preparing a wooden instrument such as a spear that was intended to be used as part of a sacred game constituting an animal renewal and regrowth rite.

Importantly, once the bladelet is recognized by the archaeologist as having this particular symbolic pragmatic meaning for the users and by which they could constitute felicitous rituals of the sort intended, then it is very easy to recognize that the same users would likely elaborate the bladelet by selecting contrasting attributes in order to refine the range of rituals that it would be used to mediate, or, for that matter, to govern the range of social persons that could use these different bladelets. That is, I claim that the preferential use of particular cherts, even when they were not easily available, arose from these ritual imperatives. Wyandotte chert and Flint Ridge chert would be used to constitute different rituals by mediating objectively similar behaviors, and this means that different social persons having particular ritual performative rights would use the different cherts.

It is at this point that the premises of the Ritual Usufruct Conveyancing and Franchising model can be applied. As I noted in elucidating this model, the particular "tools" that are defined and stipulated by the ritual usufruct that is being conveyed or franchised are not merely convenient. They are part of the usufruct practices and, therefore, stipulations defining the form and other properties that the requisite tools must have are among the rules and protocols that make up the ritual usufruct that is being transferred. That is, without having the custodial copyright of the ritual usufruct in which certain tool types are defined and stipulated (Flint Ridge or Wyandotte chert bladelets, ceramics, coppers, and so on), then both production and use of these tools is proscribed. The initial appearance of Wyandotte chert, therefore, would not be simply a chert procurement event, as Pacheco describes it. Since the chert was derived from a distant quarry and probably brought by representatives of a group that was one of the custodians of the ritual usufruct that stipulated its use, it is likely the result of a ritual franchising event. This initial event, however, would necessarily instigate an ongoing and continual process of Wyandotte chert procurement in order to ensure the continuity of performance of the ritual. By its nature, bladelet use was costly in chert since a given bladelet could not be reused for ritual purposes (it is possible, of course, that a tossed bladelet might serve as a convenient tool for a nonritual act, although this possibility could be debated). The procurement mode was part of the usufruct being transferred. Hence, it is very likely that complex rules governed the way by which Wyandotte chert could be procured, including who could procure it, who could distribute it, and who could use it!

Now this does not mean that the advent of Wyandotte use would not mark an important era in the zone. It certainly would since it would mark a ritual innovation in the sense that a new type of ritual usufruct was franchised and this would also add to the action prerogatives of only certain groups, the custodians of the new ritual, thereby endowing them with special relevance. Indeed, it is likely that its appearance was part of a wider process of ritual usufruct franchising that occurred across the Ohio Hopewell region, either occurring in some places in parallel with the prior and largely equivalent traditional Adena ritual usufruct sets, or in many other cases displacing this older set of ritual forms. The possibility that this raises, therefore, is that the appearance of Wyandotte chert marks a developmental stage of the Ohio Hopewell system, one in which a new set of rituals or a new symbolic pragmatic structuring of established rituals came into being and was diffused through ritual usufruct franchising. This also suggests that the differential proportion of Wyandotte to Flint Ridge was only contingently related to the greater distances of the sources of the former from the Murphy Tract. The important condition causing this difference would be limitations arising from the nature of the ritual usufruct itself. In this case, I suggest that while Flint Ridge chert bladelets were a constitutive part of the range of original Hopewellian rituals practiced, the Wyandotte chert was probably introduced as part of a new Hopewell ritual or as an innovation of an established ritual; and this could be performed only by participants in the sector of a cult sodality that had been the recipients of this new or newly modified ritual usufruct.

This immediately suggests why there was a 10:1 by weight differential in these two cherts. If this pairing was effectively part of the Murphy Tract occupancy from the beginning, then it is reasonable to suggest that this ratio indicates that the Wyandotte-mediated ritual was in the quantitative minority and, therefore, only a minority of the age-sets of a sodality would be warranted to perform the Wyandotte-mediated ritual. Given the minority proportion and the economic costs of procuring it, it is likely that this would be a special ritual performed by members of the more senior age-sets. Once the ritual usufruct associated with the Wyandotte chert was franchised to the first of the senior age-set (or age-sets), only members of these named groups would have the responsibility and privilege to use it for the associated ritual. Further implications of the distribution of Flint Ridge and Wyandotte chert debitage and tools in support of the Cult Sodality Cluster model are discussed below.

The upshot of this discussion is that Wyandotte chert demarcates a rather limited range of rituals, and a limited proportion of probably senior cult sodality members at any given time that could perform them. Even though these same senior persons could use the Wyandotte chert to perform clan-related rituals, they would tend to economize its use outside the Hopewell sodality ritual sphere. This economizing would arise from the costs involved in procuring it, both ritual as well as economic costs, and would partly explain why there was a much larger proportion of multiple-arris to single-arris Wyandotte bladelets than there was of multiple-arris to single-arris Flint Ridge bladelets (Pacheco 2010b, 52–53). Hence, its distribution, both in quantitative and qualitative terms, could be used to differentiate between those locales that were typically occupied by those initiated in the performance of Wyandotte ritual, usually members of senior age-sets, from those that were not, these usually being members of less senior and junior age-sets. In short, as postulated under the Cult Sodality Cluster model, the set of lithic clusters dispersed

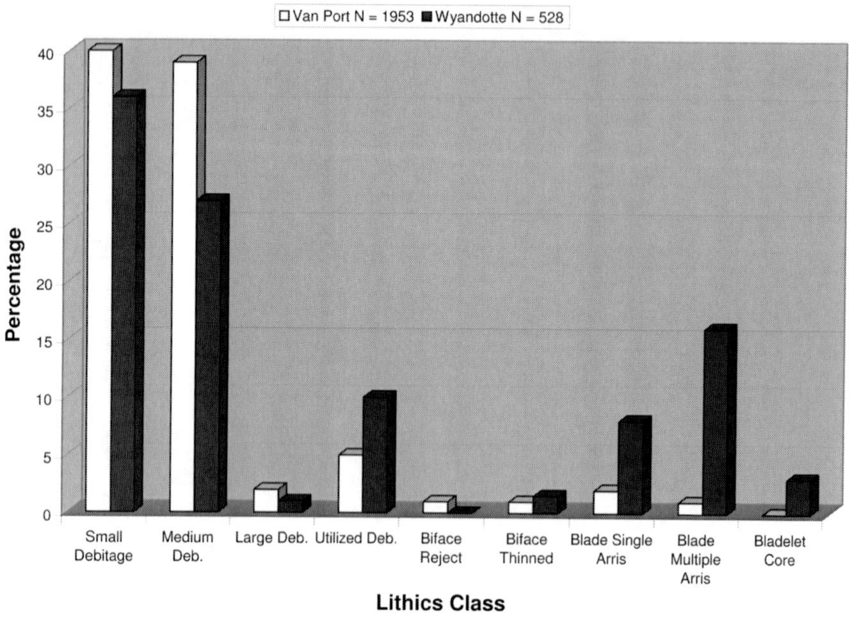

FIGURE 9.1
Murphy IV Assemblage Profile
Source: Pacheco 1993, 195, figure 40. By permission of Paul Pacheco.

across the 50 ha Murphy Tract should be structured in such a manner as to manifest the arm's-length relation between senior and junior age-grades and their respective age-sets. I believe that some of these clusters can be validly interpreted in these terms, in particular Murphy IV and Murphy V, the two clusters having the maximum proportion of Wyandotte chert debitage.

In sum, while I have set aside the chronological explanation for the distribution of the Wyandotte chert, I certainly do not deny that its distribution calls for an explanation. In this regard, I have proposed that the distribution manifests the franchising of a new ritual and/or new symbolic pragmatics of traditional rituals that called for and simultaneously constrained the usage of Wyandotte chert, followed by intra- and intergenerational conveyancing of this ritual usufruct as part of the normal promotional cycle of the cult sodality. I have also postulated that this Wyandotte–Flint Ridge dual pattern was likely a constituent part of the Murphy Tract occupation from the beginning, or almost so, a claim I will further discuss in the closing chapter. Since this usage was to mediate Ohio Hopewell ritual, it follows that the organization responsible would be a cult sodality in which Wyandotte chert–mediated ritual would be largely constrained by the seniority of the users in the enabling hierarchy of the cult sodality. Therefore, this distribution is likely the result of the monopoly of ritual mediated by Wyandotte chert by the senior age-grade sector of an ecclesiastic-communal cult sodality. Given the quantity of Wyandotte chert, this senior age-grade, or several of the age-sets that constituted it, would have regularly used at least one of the Murphy Tract sites, such as Murphy V. Because of the equivalent quantity of Wyandotte chert at Murphy IV (figure 9.1), it may also have been a senior age-grade cult sodality locale. However, it has special characteristics that suggest another possibility, as I noted above and will note again below, this being that it was the cult sodality ceremonial nodal site.

THE MURPHY TRACT AS A CULT SODALITY CLUSTER

I will now turn to elaborating the alternative account of the Murphy Tract as the manifestation of the individual autonomous ecclesiastic-communal cult sodality sector of the Ohio Middle Woodland period social system. Pacheco's careful surface surveying and his classification of this chert record is an excellent source of empirical data just for this purpose since he generated assemblage profiles for each cluster and used the distributions of these categories across each cluster plan for comparative purposes, particularly to distinguish between "hamlets" and other types of sites, for example, short-term activity and specialized production areas. For him, as I noted earlier, the primary attribute that defines a hamlet is a crisply distinct uninodal chert deposit representing a long-term refuse heap. However, for him, assessing Murphy V in these terms was largely due to the distribution of the Wyandotte chert, not the Flint Ridge chert. Why this must be the case is that the distribution pattern of the Flint Ridge chert component that he interpreted as part of the deposition zone can only with some special pleading be characterized in uninodal terms, since the main concentration in Murphy V, as he puts it, "is not as crisply defined as in Murphy I or III . . . yet the distribution is best described as uninodal in structure" (1993, 157). That is, the Flint Ridge chert distribution of Murphy V was rather diffuse. It might be fair to say that it only nominally delineated a crisp bull's-eye deposit. Furthermore, even though he also characterizes the Wyandotte component of the deposition zone of Murphy V as uninodal, he recognizes that it is clearly also more diffuse than the uninodal Flint Ridge chert deposits of Murphy I and III.

His bar graphs of the Murphy I and Murphy III artifact profiles did not distinguish between Wyandotte and Flint Ridge cherts since, as I noted earlier, these had very small quantities by weight of the Wyandotte chert, 18.2 grams and 7.3 grams. However, he specifies both the approximate or average density that the "uninodal" deposits that Murphy I and Murphy III had as well as the absolute density of the chert deposits in each. Murphy I had the uninodal or bull's-eye pattern with an average density of "7.25 artifacts per square meter" while its absolute density across the cluster was "3.86 artifacts per square meter" (1993, 153). Murphy III had a range between "7 and 21.65 artifacts per square meter" while its estimated absolute density was "3.58 artifacts per square meter" (1993, 154). Murphy V, however, had a very low absolute density, "almost six times lower on average at 0.66 artifacts per square meter" and, he adds, "Murphy V stands out as the cluster with the highest relative frequency of Wyandotte chert (80.3 percent of all recovered chert)" (1993, 157). However, he also commented above that for Murphy V the "main concentration is not as crisply defined as in Murphy I or III, especially on the southeastern edge of the cluster, yet the distribution is best described as uninodal in structure. . . . The peak density in the main concentration of Wyandotte chert has an average of 2.6 artifacts per square meter" (1993, 157).

This "peak density" of 2.6 for the Murphy V Wyandotte concentration must be compared to the average density of "7.25 artifacts per square meter" for Murphy I and Murphy III's peak density of "7 and 21.65 artifacts per square meter" and its absolute density of 3.58 artifacts per square meter. Given that the assemblage profile of Murphy V (figure 9.2) in both Flint Ridge

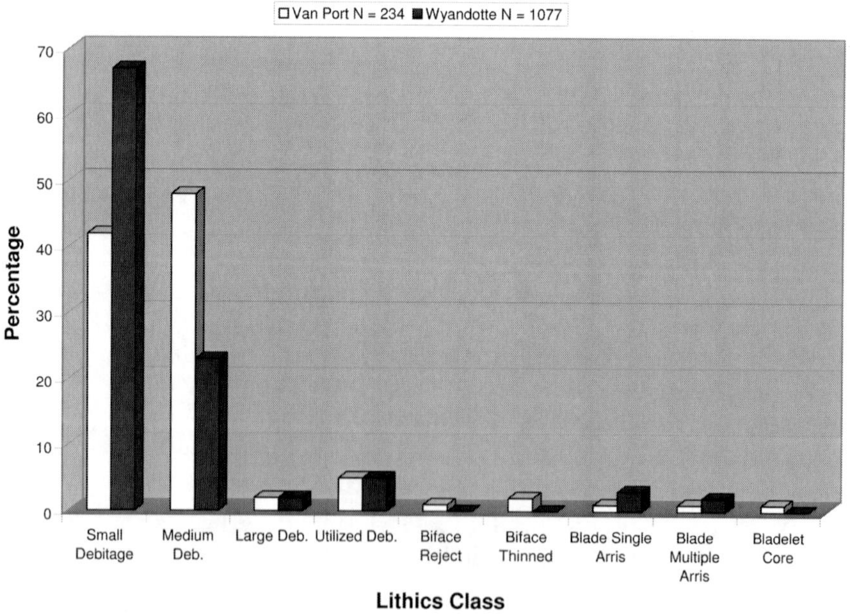

FIGURE 9.2
Murphy V Assemblage Profile
Source: Pacheco 1993, 192, figure 38. By permission of Paul Pacheco.

and Wyandotte cherts had a particularly low bladelet count, given that it had a very high percentage of small and medium debitage (about 85 percent of its Wyandotte chert and over 90 percent of its Flint Ridge chert), given that it had the largest concentration by weight of Wyandotte chert of all the sites in the Murphy Tract locale (and even larger than its Flint Ridge chert), and given the rather poorly defined uninodal concentration of its lithic deposit, all this suggests that Murphy V did not display a uninodal deposition as Pacheco defines it. Of course, I do not accept his interpretation that these Murphy Tract uninodal sites were hamlets. Instead, as postulated above, they were cult sodality locales largely dedicated to the age-grade components of these organizations. Since the latter as ecclesiastic-communal cult sodalities are postulated to have had their laity sector structured into senior and junior age-grade subsectors, each being further structured by age-set companions in terms of seniority, then these five uninodal clusters would probably be distributed between the senior and junior age-grades. This distribution could be the result of a single cult sodality going through intergenerational cycling.

However, while the group(s) responsible for Murphy V lithic cluster would be of the same social nature as the others, namely, age-grades, my above comments suggest that it deviates qualitatively in an important way from these other age-grade cult sodality locales, Murphy I, III, IV, and VI. Can the Cult Sodality Cluster model account for this distinctive patterning of Murphy V compared to the other uninodal clusters? I think it can. The patterned attributes would be consistent with its being a *specialized production area* in which the production of both Wyandotte and Flint Ridge bladelet cores was carried out. As Pacheco commented: "Bladelets are almost exclusively distributed in the area of the uninodal concentration, with none recovered from the northern half of the Murphy V collections blocks. . . . Two bladelet cores were recovered from the eastern fringe of the cluster, adjacent to units with multiple bladelets. Blade-core industry materials were apparently disposed of in the refuse dump with other lithic debris. Corresponding to the lower absolute artifact surface density, only 45 bladelets were recovered from the Murphy V cluster, 41 of which were made out of Wyandotte chert" (1993, 161). It should be remembered that this core production would itself be a form of ritual. Furthermore, as noted above, at any given time, those having the ritual usufruct prerogative to produce such cores would be a rather small group of core senior members of the local cult sodality having the right to use Wyandotte chert. Of course they would already have the right to use Flint Ridge chert. Therefore, the near equivalence in weight of both Flint Ridge and Wyandotte chert suggests that this was a specialized space used only for and by those who were warranted to perform the ritualized production of Wyandotte bladelet cores, as well as Flint Ridge bladelet cores, of course, although the latter could and would also be produced at other Murphy Tract locales. This would constitute Murphy V not only as a sodality locale dedicated largely to Hopewellian production, akin to the other four locales, especially the production of Wyandotte bladelet cores, but a locale that was used fairly exclusively by senior age-sets and, therefore, largely minimized domestic residency, suggesting that this was only used during the daytime and these senior age-set users retreated to another nearby site at the end of the day, possibly Murphy IV as I discuss below.

I am not claiming that the ritual requiring Wyandotte bladelets was performed there, although some may have been. This is because the latter bladelets were very low in overall proportion. Rather, the production of both Wyandotte and, possibly to a lesser degree, Flint Ridge bladelet cores would be performed here, and because the specialized production of Wyandotte bladelet cores would be itself a fairly exclusive form of ritual practice, possibly this group would have the sole prerogative in the sodality to produce the Wyandotte bladelet cores. From here, they would be taken to other locales for producing ritual bladelets or used for ritual in the nearby Newark earthworks.

Although Pacheco presents bladelet data relevant to Murphy I, III, and VI in order to ground his claim that these were sedentary hamlets, the same data can be used to support the claim that these were age-grade site locales used for specialized Hopewellian production, among other ritualized activities. In fact, and very relevant to this, Pacheco argues that the occupants of at least these three uninodal clusters had a bladelet "cottage industry" producing a surplus of bladelet cores for exchange—Flint Ridge cores, of course, since they had a very low quantity of Wyandotte chert.

> [B]ladelets are being produced in the proposed Murphy Tract households, with classic examples being exported, exchanged, or taken elsewhere . . . [and] several of the proposed Murphy Households, especially Murphy I, III, and VI, may have engaged in the production of bladelets as a craft or lapidary cottage industry . . . [and] this cottage industry may have included biface production too. The regional proximity of the Vanport quarries at Flint Ridge likely facilitated the development of this lapidary cottage industry by Licking Valley Hopewell households (2010b, 52).

Interpreted in terms of the Cult Sodality Cluster model, this strongly suggests that, indeed, these were specialized production locales of Hopewellian ritual items, particularly items that related to less senior age-sets. That is, as discussed above, I consider the bladelet core to be a ritual tool used to produce ritual tools (bladelets). His excluding Murphy V (and Murphy IV) from the specific "hamlets" devoted to this "lapidary cottage industry" simply reinforces my argument that Murphy V was different from the other age-grade locales by having a particular specialization related to the production of Wyandotte bifacial and bladelet cores while the others focused on Flint Ridge production. This would be consistent with my suggestion that while Murphy V was an age-grade locale, it was different from Murphy I, III, and VI, and this difference, of course, hinges on the Wyandotte specialization, implicating a senior age-grade in which only some of the age-sets were the specialists in this ritual usufruct.

It is also interesting that, as Pacheco (1993, 110, figure 12) notes, Murphy IV, which is about 200 m northwest of Murphy V, the two being separated by Murphy VI, displays a more defined uninodal pattern in its Flint Ridge chert distribution than is characteristic of the other uninodal sites while displaying a minor or, in Pacheco's view, a non-uninodal pattern in the dispersed Wyandotte chert distribution, a pattern that may be more akin to the minimally uninodal Wyandotte chert pattern of Murphy V. Pacheco assesses the primary uninodal refuse deposit as peaking at 2.3 artifacts per square meter. This is close to the peak density of 2.6 per square meter for the Wyandotte concentration of artifacts of Murphy V compared to the peak density of 7.25 artifacts per square meter for the Flint Ridge chert uninodal deposit of Murphy I and between 7 to 21.65 artifacts per square meter for Murphy III. That is, the Murphy IV peak density is more akin to that of Murphy V than to either Murphy I or Murphy III. And it should be noted again that Murphy IV and Murphy V share almost the same quantity by weight of Wyandotte chert, Murphy V having only a slightly greater quantity. However, overall, Murphy IV's assemblage profile (figure 9.1) is quite different from the profile of Murphy V (figure 9.2) and more akin to Murphy I (figure 9.3), Murphy III (figure 9.4), and Murphy VI. For example, while Murphy IV has about 65 percent debitage and 25 percent bladelets, Murphy V has 90 percent debitage and only about 5 percent bladelets. Also, in Pacheco's view, the Wyandotte bladelet distribution in Murphy IV was more similar to the other clusters of the South Block in that they were the result of use-and-toss deposition. He treats this pattern as marking a short-term activity area, and, as noted above, argues that Murphy IV should be structured into early Murphy IV-A, as a hamlet, and later Murphy IV-B, as a short-term activity area. However, this assessment overlooks both the 10:1 weighting of Flint Ridge to Wyandotte chert and the fact that its total Wyandotte chert by weight was effectively equal to Murphy V. The other South Block clusters, Clusters 1 and 2, had significant amounts of Wyandotte chert, 19.8 and 63.4 grams, respectively, higher than Murphy I and Murphy III, but certainly much lower than the amount of Wyandotte chert in Murphy IV. Furthermore, the overall Wyandotte assemblage profile (figure 9.1) of Murphy IV paralleled the assemblage

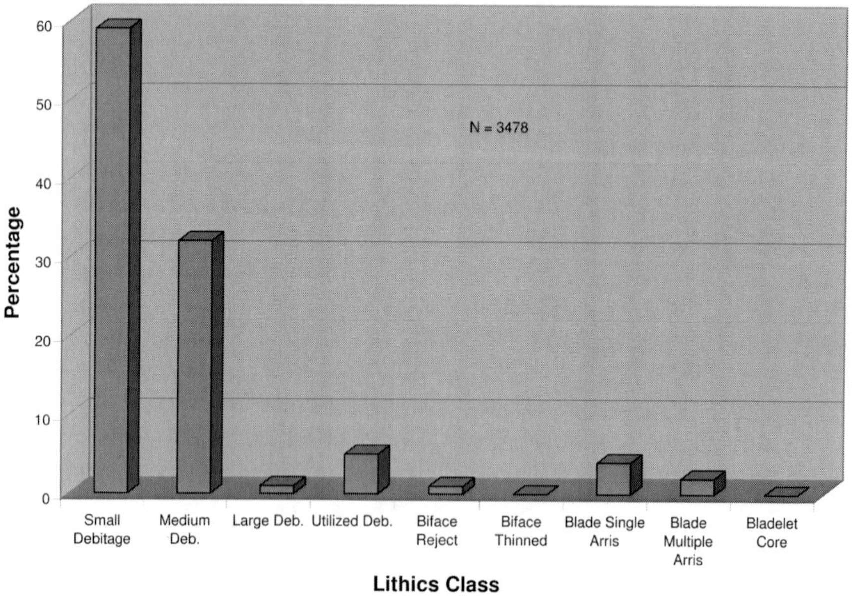

FIGURE 9.3
Murphy I Assemblage Profile
Source: Pacheco 1993, 189, figure 36. By permission of Paul Pacheco.

profile characteristic of the other hamlets (e.g., Murphy I, figure 9.3; Murphy III, figure 9.4). All this simply reinforces my claim that it is wrong to interpret the dual Wyandotte and Flint Ridge chert distribution in chronological terms. Instead, as postulated above, it was procured as part of the ritual interaction characteristic among cult sodalities whose age-grade components would be distributed in these uninodal locales. The variable distribution of Wyandotte and Flint Ridge chert results from the senior and junior age-grade structure and the likelihood that only age-sets in the senior age-grade component held the Wyandotte chert ritual usufruct.

To be specific now, Pacheco provides a set of surface distribution plan maps of the Flint Ridge and Wyandotte cherts of the South Block in order to support his conclusion that even though Wyandotte chert was found in the Murphy IV uninodal cluster, its particular distribution demarcates a use-and-toss disposal method that is characteristic of the short-term activity areas.[3] Therefore, he argues, its presence on the uninodal cluster of Murphy IV actually marks a later period after the Murphy IV "hamlet" was abandoned. As he states, in his opinion the "limited overlap in the distributions of Wyandotte and the Middle Woodland Vanport refuse deposit was fortuitous" (1993, 176). I have carefully studied these plan maps, particularly in light of the claim

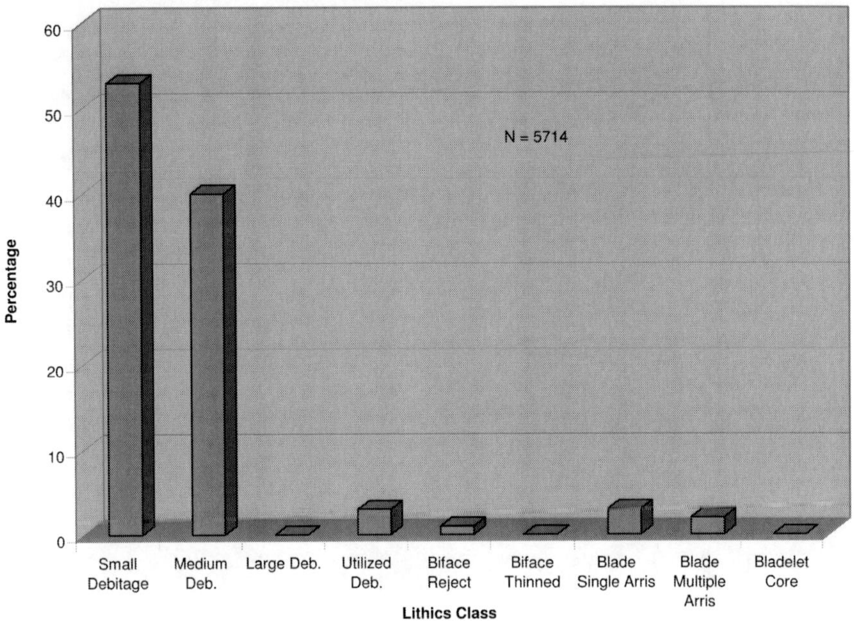

FIGURE 9.4
Murphy III Assemblage Profile
Source: Pacheco 1993, 190, figure 37. By permission of Paul Pacheco.

that there is only a slight overlap of the Wyandotte chert with the Flint Ridge chert deposit (Pacheco 1993, 169, fig. 26, and 170, fig. 27, respectively). In my view, and this is just as subjective an assessment as was his, while he is correct that the Wyandotte chert stretches farther to the west than does the Flint Ridge chert, the distributions of these two cherts work together to constitute a single uninodal deposition pattern of Murphy IV. It seems to me that the only fortuitous aspect of the uninodal distribution of the Wyandotte chert was that it "looked" like a use-and-toss disposal pattern outcome as seen in Clusters 1 and 2. Furthermore, it seems notable that the uninodal deposit of Murphy IV has a density level more akin to that of Murphy V, 2.3 and 2.6 artifacts per square meter, respectively. I noted above that the uninodal deposit of Murphy V is less dense than those of Murphy I, III, and VI and this applies also to Murphy IV, making Murphy IV and V more akin. In short, I *do not see* that these empirical data support his claim that the distribution of Wyandotte chert marks a Wyandotte procurement event.

To add to this, what Pacheco has noted about the Murphy IV patterning conforms only partly to the Murphy I and Murphy III pattern while also only partly conforming to the Murphy V specialized Hopewell production pattern.

This suggests, therefore, that while it certainly was a sodality site, it was not of the same type as Murphy I, Murphy III, or Murphy VI, although it would probably have had considerable domestic residency of a transient nature, as postulated under the Cult Sodality Cluster model. However, Murphy IV also does not appear to be the same type of specialized production locale as I claim was the case for Murphy V since its assemblage profile was similar to the profiles of the other uninodal locales, Murphy I, III, and VI. However, it had a much higher proportion of Wyandotte chert to Flint Ridge chert than did these three and, as I noted earlier, it had almost the same quantity of Wyandotte chert as did Murphy V. Indeed, together these make up 86 percent of the Wyandotte chert by weight for all five uninodal clusters of the Murphy Tract. The only other cluster locale that comes even close to Murphy IV and Murphy V in terms of Wyandotte chert is Murphy VI, having 125.4 grams, or 6.5 percent of the total. With this exception, however, Murphy VI displayed all the characteristics of Murphy I, III, and IV having the same uninodal deposit and assemblage profile distribution. In fact, possibly the most important common factor for these four clusters is that they all had large quantities of Flint Ridge chert. At the same time, however, with the exception of Murphy IV, they had even smaller quantities of Wyandotte chert than Clusters 1 and 2, interpreted by Pacheco as short-term sites.

All this enables me to lump Murphy I, III, and VI together as more akin to each other than any of them is to Murphy IV and V; while at the same time, noting that Murphy IV was "split" equally between, on the one hand, Murphy V, in terms of profile differences but Wyandotte chert similarities, and, on the other, Murphy I, III, and VI, in terms of similarities of assemblage profiles and Flint Ridge quantities but differences in Wyandotte chert. Hence, I am going to postulate Murphy IV was the common integrator of the sites of the Murphy Tract and it is why I suggested above that it may have been a cult sodality *ceremonial nodal locale.*

How well does this hang together? First Murphy V did not display the same profile as the other four, indicating a considerable amount of transient nondomestic (i.e., possibly daytime only) occupation. So I will set Murphy V aside as a specialized production locale of the senior age-grade, or of the age-sets of this senior age-grade that were custodians of the Wyandotte chert ritual usufruct. However, Murphy IV can also be distinguished from Murphy I, III, and VI since the latter ranged between 4,500 and 6,100 grams of Flint Ridge chert while Murphy IV had only 2,832 grams. Murphy IV also differs from the latter by its large Wyandotte assemblage. However, Murphy IV displays a uninodal disposal zone and an assemblage profile similar to Murphy I, III, and VI. Still, it is not the same type of sodality site as they are since its Flint Ridge total is too *low* and its Wyandotte total is too *high* (equal in quantity but different in formal content to Murphy V [see figures 9.1 and 9.2]). Of course, in noting that it had a uninodal deposition zone, this commits me to recognizing that a fair amount of activity would have occurred there. But this activity would not be as intense or as drawn out as at the other uninodal sites—given the lower overall quantity of chert deposition compared to the three other uninodal sites, Murphy I, III, and VI. Also a much higher percentage of activities mediated by Wyandotte chert tools, particularly bladelets, would have occurred here than in these other three clusters or, for that matter, in the Murphy V site, which had a low proportion of bladelets, high proportion of bladelet cores. In short, while these attributes of Murphy IV fit what we could expect of specialized area mediating Hopewell production *and* the ritual for which much of this production was used to mediate, its lower average quantity of Flint Ridge chert and its relatively high quantity of Wyandotte chert suggest that its transient occupation was lower than at Murphy I, III, and VI, and greater than at Murphy V. Finally, as a specialized camp displaying the same overall assemblage profile as Murphy I, III, and VI but with special ritual variation, Murphy IV would be consistent with the type of usage expected of a ceremonial nodal locale as characterized under the Cult Sodality Cluster model. What this means is that it may have been the primary gathering place of the ecclesiastic-communal cult sodality of one of the local complementary heterarchical communities in the bifurcated settlement articulation modal posture of the region. This would also explain its association with Murphy V where it is likely that many of the Wyandotte bladelet cores were produced that became the many Wyandotte bladelets at Murphy IV. Of course, given the presence of Wyandotte chert in Clusters 1 and 2, these also demarcate auxiliary sodality locales but clearly serving only particular age-set components of the cult sodality. The latter would likely be more senior age-sets, given the amount of Wyandotte chert, particularly Cluster 2, and would explain their spatial closeness to Murphy IV, the ceremonial nodal locale. If these clusters were dedicated to senior age-sets of the sodality, then they could be expected to be nearest to the nodal center.

However, there is also a significant amount of Wyandotte chert on Clusters 4, 5/8, and 7. Pacheco suggests that "Cluster 5/8 has a unique profile for Wyandotte chert, emphasizing finished products of both trajectories (bifaces and bladelets), and low frequencies of small to medium debitage . . . [while] Cluster 7 has a unique profile for both chert types . . . including a high frequency of Wyandotte biface rejects" (1993, 200). He interprets all these clusters as representing "short-term localized activity areas." The presence of Wyandotte chert, therefore, can be explained as the result of these age-sets calling on the assistance of members from the more senior age-sets when their tasks required this specialized Wyandotte chert–mediated intervention or, alternatively, it could be the result of some junior age-set having rights to using the Wyandotte chert for rituals as the auxiliary arm of a senior age-set that retained the Wyandotte ritual usufruct. None of this denies that these tasks would also serve the practical needs of the domestic base camps of the community or communities from which the cult sodality(ies) were derived (I am not overlooking the possibility that more than one cult sodality may have used and shared the Murphy site). I have already argued that the age-set sodality system was likely the primary medium for mobilizing community-wide subsistence labor. I have also argued that subsistence tasks, such as hunting and gathering, would have midwifery ritual built into them. The use of bladelets, both Flint Ridge and Wyandotte, therefore, could be expected since using these would realize the midwifery ritual aspect of such practical tasks as slicing, scraping, and dividing of floral and faunal resources among the companions of the age-set group so they could return with their equitable proportions to the not-too-distant domestic habitation base-camp locales of their respective kin groups, namely, families. In short, while Clusters 1, 2, 3, 4, 5/8, and 7 probably represent different cult sodality age-set sites, they also would have served dual duty as locales where the responsible age-sets could become secluded in order to perform rituals particular to their rank level in the sodality and also where they could carry out part of the subsistence tasks appropriate to their seniority.

In fact, what Pacheco has to say about the bifacial lithics in these clusters reinforces my claim that the uninodal and non-uninodal locales were dedicated spaces of the age-grades and age-sets, respectively. Of course, his argument was intended to support his sedentary hamlet thesis, but it can be even more coherently used to support the Cult Sodality Cluster model. He argues that the variation in the bifacial lithics in the uninodal and non-uninodal clusters is distinctly different such that the production of bifacial tools was carried out primarily in the uninodal clusters (the "hamlets" in his terms, "age-grade locales" in my terms), while the use of these tools was carried out primarily in the latter (in his terms, "short-term activity areas," in my terms, "age-set locales"). According to his analysis "bifaces are primarily produced in the proposed household but are exclusively used/broken in the small clusters and intercluster space in between the households. Dancey (1991:55) reports the same pattern in the excavated sample from Murphy I . . . [and] this is the kind of pattern of inter-assemblage lithic assemblage variability expected within a sedentary community. . . . The documented assemblages from the upland Middle Woodland rock shelters . . . are characterized by assemblages similarly skewed toward biface use (especially projectile points, supporting their use as logistical hunting camps" (2010b, 52). Of course, this can be reconstrued as age-grade locales and age-set locales. Under the Cult Sodality Cluster model, it would be consistent that the production of bifacial tools would occur in the former and, of course, used in the latter since these were primarily used by the junior age-sets for carrying out both sodality- and kinship-related subsistence tasks along with their ritual practices.

DISCUSSION

By taking a symbolic pragmatic view of the bladelet and the usage of selected and usually paired cherts, such as Wyandotte and Flint Ridge cherts, and invoking the postulated process of ritual usufruct franchising and conveyancing structuring rituals according to seniority, I have been able to resolve the lithic clusters of the Murphy Tract as having been produced by different sectors of an ecclesiastic-communal cult sodality. To this point, I have recognized four types of cult sodality locales (I think there were more, as I discuss later): (1) the *age-set* sodality site, or what has been termed under the Hamlet Hypothesis, the short-term activity area, represented by the Murphy Tract non-unimodal clusters; (2) the age-grade domestic-related site used both for ritual and carrying out the specialized Hopewell ritual tool production, represented by Murphy I, III, and VI; (3) a nondomestic age-grade-based site for the specialized production of Wyandotte and, in a less specialized manner, of Flint Ridge bladelet cores, represented by Murphy V; and (4) the ecclesiastic-communal cult sodality ceremonial nodal site, represented by Murphy IV. Since Murphy VI displays the same assemblage profile and plan distribution as Murphy I (figure 9.3) and Murphy III (figure 9.4), and it also has the largest quantity of Wyandotte chert of these three (as well as the largest overall quantity of Flint Ridge chert), it was probably occupied in a transient, short-term but regular manner by the senior age-grade of the cult sodality responsible for the Murphy Tract record. The age-sets of this age-grade would also have largely monopolized the right to perform ritual mediated with the Wyandotte chert bladelets, thereby explaining the presence of such a larger amount of Wyandotte chert compared to Murphy I and III, and likely the bladelets were produced from bladelet cores that one or two of the age-sets of the same age-grade produced at the nearby Murphy V site.

I believe that the above analysis and redescription of the Murphy Tract has demonstrated that the Cult Sodality Cluster model has invested the settlement data with greater coherence than has the Hamlet Hypothesis model. However, I am not totally convinced that Murphy IV is the ceremonial nodal locale site of the cult sodality of the local complementary heterarchical community. This is because too much evidence is unavailable. Only excavation of the site could demonstrate the validity of this claim. Currently, Murphy I is the only full excavation that has been done. As I noted in the previous chapter, Dancey claimed that the excavation of the Murphy site demonstrated what the basic components of a hamlet should be like: the uninodal refuse deposit, the in situ activity area beside the dwelling quarters, and so on. However, as Dancey recognized, the dwelling quarters were not defined by a clear pattern of wall posts. Only scattered posts were discovered. He suggests that the scattered nature of the post holes may obscure a more formal patterning that, however, has been plow damaged.

In a comprehensive reexamination of the radiocarbon dating samples of the Murphy I site, including one new sample, this same patterning is explained by Christopher Carr and Herbert Haas as the result of separate and discrete rather short-term occupations of domestic family-based groups. "Specifically, the site has six or seven spatially segregated clusters or features that could logically be attributed to several different periods of occupation of the site. Most of the clusters are functionally equivalent, containing one or more basins and earth ovens, with post molds nearby. . . . Each of these clusters could represent processing features with supplemental pole-supported racks of a kind" (1996, 29). In fact, they emphasize that the number of features was rather small and overall certainly too small to represent a long-term sedentary occupation. "The location of these several clusters of features in the same area need not be attributed to their functional interrelationships and contemporaneity, and to Murphy having been occupied once, as Dancey has concluded. Instead the total distribution could reflect simply the repeated location of very small, year-round habitations (or more temporary, seasonal or multi-seasonal special-purposes camps) within the same general areas, within the constraints of the topographic high on which Murphy sits" (1996, 29). Along these lines, they suggest that, as well as adding to the radiocarbon dating samples, their rereading supports the conclusion that the overall site was the result of either several short-term sedentary occupation periods over a span of about 200 years, cal A.D. 120–330, with a possible outlying occupation either sooner (about cal 40 B.C.) or later (about cal A.D. 450), or, while recognizing these may have been sedentary year-round occupations, they also suggest seasonal or multiseasonal occupations. "Our suggestion is that this well-dated occupation, somewhere between ca. A.D. 120 and A.D. 330 calibrated time, and the other possible one or two occupations of Murphy, were each brief, on the order of years. The number of pits found at Murphy is small: 20 basins, earth ovens, cylindrical pits, and hearths, and 17 post molds. Ceramics are scant: 858 sherds . . . and could reasonably be the product of 10 to 20 broken vessels" (1996, 29). Despite this claim, they reconfirm the basic premises of the Vacant Center/Dispersed Hamlet model (1996, 30).

Of course, Dancey's reading of the radiocarbon dates is different. However, it is important to note that he did not have available one of the dates that Carr and Haas had, this being ETH 4243, which is the basis for the late outlying date of about cal A.D. 450. However, I do not think that this is a real problem for my purposes since the differences in dating between Carr and Haas and Dancey would remain the same even if these data are excluded. For my purposes, either dating would be acceptable as a general overall period of usage. Where I specifically support Carr and Haas, however, is their claim that this was not an extended period of sedentary occupation. Where I disagree with them is their continued support of the notion that Murphy was a hamlet. While Carr and Haas claim that the distribution of the multiple features suggests that a series of individual and sequential occupations occurred, each marking a separate "hamlet" site that was used only for a rather short period, what they overlook is that, as Dancey notes, there was effectively no overlap among these features. Dancey notes 43 features and while several "are close to one another . . . overlap is found only in one case, where Feature 110B intrudes into Feature 110A" (1991, 43). This lack of overlap is one of the grounds that Dancey uses to argue for a long-term sedentary continuity. In contrast, I would argue that this lack of overlap of features suggests that the periods of transient occupation usually involved several simultaneous groups at any given time and these groups recognized the "appropriate" place of each. This does not mean that these features, for example, ten earth ovens and seven basins, were all generated and used simultaneously. Given the range of radiocarbon dates that Carr and Hass derived, these were likely developed over time. However, the collective memory of occupational spaces was largely intact and persisted, probably a result of arm's-length relations between sequential age-grades by seniority, so that when a new age-grade took up occupancy at the same site, they would respectfully locate their activity area slightly to one side of the area occupied by the previous age-grade. In fact, Dancey suggests that the earth ovens were likely reused basin pits, and if so this suggests that one age-grade group would carefully limit itself to the selected locale, preferring to cycle their own features rather than expand outside the area where they would possibly encroach on the site features of an earlier age-grade group. This careful avoidance of areas where prior age-grades had produced occupational features would explain the formation of a common activity area where most of the productive activity was conducted. This was also carefully cleaned, as in the case of the Jennison Guard site, suggesting that proscriptive rules applied so as to ensure that the waste materials of different sequential ritual production events carried out in the same area would not be unwittingly mixed. As I argued earlier, this type of rule would account for the formation of the bull's-eye refuse deposit. The tendency for several groups to occupy the site sequentially while carefully avoiding the particular usage areas of previous groups would also explain the scattering of the post molds that Dancey described.

Carr and Haas also overlook the extraordinary nature of the lithic record and the orderly state of the site, particularly the uninodal refuse deposit and the absence of overlapping features; and even their ceramic argument is problematic. With regard to the uninodal refuse deposit, since they reject the long-term sedentary occupation that Dancey's argument implicates while still recognizing the domestic hamlet-like nature of the site, they cannot invoke Dancey's explanation that these aspects of the patterning resulted from site maintenance practices since seasonal mobility would likely create a "messy" site, as Dancey and Kozarek both argue. And they cannot explain the absence of feature overlap since this would be expected of a series of short-term domestic occupations, even by the same families. While they would appear to be right to argue that a long-term sedentary occupation would generate a larger ceramic sample, their assumption that a series of short-term occupations, whether seasonal or sedentary, would generate such a small sample does not follow. It seems to me that a larger sample could be expected, particularly when the size of the ceramic assemblage is compared to the size of the lithic assemblage since, presumably, a series of short-term domestic household occupations that generated such a small ceramic sample would also generate a proportionately small lithic sample. That is, if Carr and Haas wish to maintain the position that a limited series of short-term seasonal occupations by a family-based residence group was responsible for the small ceramics sample, then it follows that they have not explained how this same sequential series of small group occupations would have generated such a spectacularly large lithic debitage assemblage, much of which was redeposited in a rather small, specialized refuse area, and much of which was a select chert, Flint Ridge, brought in by this "family" from a quarry that they seem to have regularly attended that was 20 km away. However, if Murphy I was, in fact, an age-grade sector locale of an autonomous cult sodality that occupied the site transiently as a Hopewellian specialized production activity area, then consistent with this type of occupation would be (1) a small ceramic sample, (2) a large and complex lithic deposit manifesting the total range of lithic *chaîne opératoire*, (3) earth ovens for collective group feasting, (4) poles and posts for temporary shelter and/or ritual offering posts, and, of course, as I argued earlier, (5) a carefully maintained work area respecting the proscriptions against mixing the residue of past ritual production with the residue of current ritual production.

CONCLUSION

The Cult Sodality Cluster model is an auxiliary of the more comprehensive Complementary Heterarchical Community model and the Ecclesiastic-Communal Cult Sodality Heterarchy System model. Just as the Hamlet Hypothesis model was designed to address the nonearthwork component of the Middle

Woodland period settlement pattern, the Cult Sodality Cluster model does also. In contrast to the former, however, it assumes that the ceremonial sphere would not be manifested only in the great earthworks but would also constitute a significant component of the settlement patterning of the countryside. The Complementary Heterarchical Community model postulates that clan and sodality organizations stood in a relatively autonomous arm's-length posture to each other and that this type of community embodied a potential to exist in different settlement patterns that collectively manifested what I termed the integrated-bifurcated settlement articulation modal continuum. Hence, this community model requires alternative settlement models, one to characterize the settlement pattern when the communities of a region were in the integrated posture and one to characterize the pattern in the bifurcated posture. The latter would be responsible for the domestic/ceremonial dichotomy, a dichotomy, however, that is now seen as much more complex than imagined under the Monistic Modular Polity model. The overall bifurcated settlement model I have termed the Dual Complementary Clan/Cult Sodality Clusters Community model argues that two parallel systems of site clusters would persist, one embodying the domestic kinship-based component of the complementary heterarchical community, namely, the clan system, and the other embodying the cult sodality component, the companionship-based component. I termed the former the Dispersed Kinship Habitation Cluster model and the latter the Cult Sodality Cluster model. Thus, the Complementary Heterarchical Community model entails a settlement pattern that manifests *two* complementary cluster spheres, kinship habitational and sodality ceremonial. Most of near-adult and adult members of any given complementary heterarchical community would actively participate in both, moving back and forth from the domestic family-based habitation locale to one or other of the cult sodality locales as their responsibilities in both spheres of their communities required.

I have not empirically grounded the Dispersed Kinship Habitation Cluster model in detail. However, I have noted that this aspect of the complementary heterarchical community in the bifurcated model posture would be small, almost archaeologically invisible, having modest bifacial and bladelet lithic and ceramic assemblages, small hearths, scattered post molds, and so on. This is because I consider these to be manifesting the principle of "living lightly on the land," that is, sustaining a strong proscriptive settlement practice while actually maintaining a fairly intensive prescriptive subsistence system. By this I mean that gardening as well as plant and animal foraging would be rather intense and would generate the perceived increase in sacred pollution of the land that was necessarily the outcome of growing populations pursuing biological survival, thereby promoting a strong deontic need for intensifying world renewal rituals. I suspect that very little of the Hopewell exotics would be found in these ephemeral seasonally based domestic kinship-based sites, whether warm season lowland sites or cold season upland sites. However, bladelets would not be uncommon. This is because of the Hopewellian proscription underwriting the bladelet usage and the tendency to use bladelets to mediate some of the midwifery ritual built into subsistence practices. This would legitimize and promote the use of the bladelet in family- and clan-based rituals simply to ensure that the tools used to constitute these rituals were not unwittingly pocketed and then used again in the sodality ceremonial context. Of course, the special requirements to use select cherts, Flint Ridge or Wyandotte (and a few others were apparently recognized as warranted), would not be entailed in the context of kinship-based ritual and, therefore, we could expect a range of chert types more responsive to local availability.

Having empirically grounded the claims of the Cult Sodality Cluster model of the Central Ohio Valley Middle Woodland period countryside settlement patterning, I now turn to part II of this book, which I have titled "Sacred Games, Death, and Renewal in Ohio Hopewell." This is a comprehensive discussion and empirical description of the data supporting the postulated ritual processes that generated the Ohio Hopewell episode and it requires some further theoretical elucidation, particularly focusing on sacred games and the role of mortuary ritual in the pursuit of world renewal. This will also develop the elucidation of the interactive processes that would have been responsible for the great Ohio Hopewell earthworks as explicated under the Ecclesiastic-Communal Cult Sodality Heterarchy System model. This discussion will further elucidate and empirically ground this model.

II

SACRED GAMES, DEATH, AND RENEWAL IN OHIO HOPEWELL

10

The Sacred Games *Tournée* of the Ohio Hopewell Cult Sodality Heterarchy System

I argued earlier that the Big Houses (or Great Houses) or, as I prefer to term them, the Edwin Harness (Liberty Works, figure 1.2) and the Seip-Pricer and Seip-Conjoined (Seip Works, figure 3.5) Renewal Lodges were the key world renewal locales of two sets of ecclesiastic-communal cult sodalities and, in fact, given the particular patterning of the differential distribution of the split-log and fire-clay rituals of the Seip-Conjoined Renewal Lodge, the latter likely mediated a dual or two-generational cycle of mortuary/world renewal ritual history (Byers 2004, 312–19). The larger rectilinear burial space, Locus 1, likely contained the mortuary residue of two sequential senior age-grades and the smaller rectilinear space, Locus 2, the deceased of the two sequential junior age-grades. I also allowed for deceased dependents of members to be processed by the postmortem ritual, thereby accounting for a small proportion of females (there were essentially no infants or children, a situation that the funerary paradigm cannot adequately explain). Building on the analogy of the age-set system of the Hidatsa and Mandan, I argued that when the senior age-grade retired the surviving members of the junior age-grade would become the new senior age-grade and would appropriate the mortuary space used by their predecessors. In turn, the former space, the smaller rectilinear room and the mortuary floor beneath it, would then be handed over to the new junior age-grade, and so on. I have postulated that a similar cycling was the case for the earlier Seip-Pricer Renewal Lodge covering possibly a five-generation period, and, of course, it is very likely that a parallel cycling would have occurred at Edwin Harness (Byers 2004, 565–67). In these terms, I have reasoned that each split-generation cycle would be about 25–30 years. The two cycles incorporated by Seip-Conjoined would equate to about 50–60 years and the four or five cycles of Seip-Pricer would be at least 100 years and likely closer to 150 years. Together then these two renewal lodges would incorporate close to two centuries of historic use as world renewal ritual locales, ca A.D. 150/200 to A.D. 350/400. Edwin Harness would probably largely parallel this history.

I also argued that only some of the deceased members of the cult sodality would be retained and subjected to the total postmortem human sacrificial *chaîne opératoire* process (Byers 2004, 314–21). Most would be only partially processed in this manner and then returned to their clans to be given terminal mortuary rites in a clan mortuary mound. There are many such mounds known to be dispersed across the countryside. Although many have been destroyed by agricultural practices, Mark Seeman and James Branch (2006, 116) have estimated that in Ross County alone there are about 98 known Middle Woodland period mortuary mounds. These manifest a deep tradition of countryside mortuary mounding since they also estimate that there are in Ross County at least 46 Early Woodland mortuary mounds. These are only estimates since they noted that there are 91 more mounds dispersed over the countryside and that these likely have mortuary contents, but they are unidentified as to period.

While the mortuary rituals that generated these lesser mound locales would have significant input from the clans of the deceased, I still consider the ritual process mediated at the embankment earthwork locales to be world renewal and not funerary in nature. As I discuss in this chapter, most if not all mortuary deposits were the outcome of cult sodality–based processing and it is also likely that many of the final remains of the deceased were returned to the custodial lands of their clans to serve as the media of the final release rites of the living souls, thereby enabling these sacred reproductive powers to return to the local land and its natural forms (animals, plants, waters, and so on) from which they were derived. Here I am drawing on my interpretation of the Huron Feast of the Dead as this type of world renewal ritual for analogical support of this claim. I discuss in more detail the actual process of the postmortem sacrificial mortuary *chaîne opératoire* in this chapter, arguing that it was itself a primary medium of a cyclic series of spirit-accumulating and spirit-releasing sacred games that were carried out at the great embankment earthwork locales—a very dynamic "pilgrimage" process (Lepper 2006, 128–31; 2010, 108–10, 116–19; Vickery and Sunderhaus 2004, 169–74).

However, given my earlier presentation of the Ecclesiastic-Communal Cult Sodality Heterarchy model and its auxiliary Cult Sodality Cluster model, I must make a modification to my interpretation that I made in my 2004 book. My initial modeling of the Ohio Hopewell episode identified an embankment earthwork with a single ecclesiastic-communal cult sodality. Clearly, my elucidation of the cult sodality heterarchy is an important modification of this earlier claim since I am now arguing that these sodalities allied into first-order, second-order, and third-order level heterarchies. In this scheme, I now argue that Seip, for example, was likely the site of a second-order cult sodality heterarchy and the major Seip-Pricer and Seip-Conjoined Renewal Lodges would have been sequentially built and used by all the affiliated cult sodality components that constituted this complex heterarchy through several generational cycles (possibly seven or eight). Despite this expansion of the size of the organizations that were responsible, however, the fundamental structural components and processes of generational cycling described above would be the same. That is, this more expansive view of the organizational dimension of the Ohio Hopewell episode does not require any fundamental change to the premises that age-grades were associated with specific burial locales. Rather, while I continue to recognize the mortuary floors as age-grade specific, it requires recognizing that, for example, the junior age-grades of the several allied cult sodalities constituting the heterarchy during a given generation would jointly use the same age-grade specific spaces, as would be the case for the senior age-grades of the same sodalities.

However, this claim requires reassessing the terminal steps of the mortuary *chaîne opératoire* that I initially presented. I argued earlier that only some of the deceased of the cult sodality were retained and their mortuary treatment was terminated with cremation and deposition on the floor of the renewal lodges. Therefore, I treated the in situ burials as the terminal deposits of the retained deceased that had accumulated over the generational use of a given renewal lodge, until it was decommissioned. While this is still a valid step to postulate, given the larger numbers involved in treating Seip as a second-order heterarchy, that is, as the affiliation of several first-order heterarchies, each of these consisting of an alliance of two or more cult sodalities, it is reasonable to assume that many more deceased would have been processed through the history of a given renewal lodge than I had initially estimated. Of course, correcting for this could be done simply by reducing the retention rate per cult sodality, possibly tenfold—from the 1:4–6 deceased I originally postulated were retained and suggest that this would more likely be 1 retention for each 40 to 60 deceased. This would mean, however, that the criteria on which retention was practiced would not be based on the wishes of the deceased being implemented as the duty of the survivors but would be contingent on the particular ritual needs of cult sodality heterarchy.

The former was my earlier suggestion, namely, that prior to death, when possible the deceased would express his or her wishes to be given terminal treatment by the cult sodality and buried on the floor. Under this modified view, this possibility might still occur; but given the much lower retention ratio of deceased of the average cult sodality, possibly 1 per 40 to 60, it is likely that some other factor was at work. I postulate, therefore, that the primary enabling factor at work was not the individual's personal wishes as expressed prior to death, but the particular ritual needs of the cult sodalities making up the heterarchy at that time.[1] Establishing what these needs might be and how resolving them would generate the terminal depositions makes up the primary goal of part II. What this does suggest, however, is that from the perspective of the total mortuary *chaîne opératoire*, while the mortuary-mediated rituals that occurred at these major embankment earthworks probably applied to the great majority of the deceased, only a small proportion of the total deceased that they were used to mediate the process came to be given terminal treatment there in the form of final burial. Logically, this means that the majority processed would be terminally buried in one of the many postulated clan-based mounds widely dispersed across the countryside.

I have already argued that the mortuary data nicely fit the requirements of an ecclesiastic-communal cult sodality structure with respect to the timing of death and the relative "richness" of the mortuary treatment across the mortuary loci, thereby explaining the "inverse pyramidal distribution of prestige." There are some further empirical data that can be interpreted as evidence to support this cult sodality view, in particular identifying certain components of the cult sodalities with particular groupings of deceased. N'omi Greber (1976, 73–77) has noted that the mortuary deposits on the floors of both Locus 1 and Locus 2 of the Seip-Pricer mound consist of four to five relatively discrete clusters of cremated burials. I suggested previously that these may represent the particular age-sets of the two age-grades, senior and junior, respectively (Byers 2004). Under this expanded view of the number of cult sodalities involved, however, another possibility is that each discrete burial group in these two loci represents only some of the deceased of the age-grades, senior and junior, respectively, of each of the multiple cult sodalities that constituted the first-order heterarchies that affiliated and generated this postulated second-order Seip cult sodality heterarchy. If so, the five clusters of mortuary deposits in the smaller rectilinear mortuary locus would represent an accumulation of the deceased of the junior age-grade sectors of at least five autonomous cult sodalities. The cluster of deposits in the larger locus would simply represent the deceased of the senior age-grade sectors of the same sodalities. Hence, this would translate into the second-order heterarchy of Seip being constituted of at least two first-order heterarchies, one consisting of two and the other of three autonomous cult sodalities. Speaking conservatively, if the average cult sodality consisted of about 100 active members (junior and senior age-grades plus clergy; later I increase this to 120), then these two first-order heterarchies could muster about 200 and 300 participants, respectively, or about 500 in the aggregate. Alternatively, given the factor of 10 by which I am reducing the retention rate, instead of the five discrete mortuary clusters representing two first-order heterarchies of two and three cult sodalities, respectively, these five discrete groups could represent the junior age-grade sectors of five first-order cult sodality heterarchies, each heterarchy consisting of between two to four cult sodalities, or, in total, between a minimum of 10 and a maximum of 20 autonomous cult sodalities. If so, using the same base of 100 participants per sodality, these five affiliated first-order heterarchies constituting the second-order heterarchy of Seip would be able to muster a minimum aggregate of participants of about 1,000 (five first-order heterarchies, each having two sodalities with 100 members each) to 2,000, or, to be more conservative, a mean of 1,500 active participants. For reasons I discuss later, I suspect that Seip consisted of five rather than two first-order heterarchies and, therefore, that it was able to muster on its own about 1,500 participants for major collective activities.

However, given the Ecclesiastic-Communal Cult Sodality Heterarchy model, a further modification from my earlier interpretation is needed, this being that the second-order heterarchy of Seip may have been affiliated with the second-order heterarchy of Liberty Works and, therefore, assuming some equivalence in the number of participating cult sodalities in each, together they could mobilize about 3,000 participants. This also suggests that it would be quite likely that equivalent age-sets in the different cult sodalities affiliated with Seip and Liberty Works shared their deceased across the two heterarchies. This echoes the premise of the Tripartite Ceremonial Alliance model since the latter also argued that the deceased of different unitary or monistic communities were distributed across at least three different and separate charnel houses. Of course, the mortuary practices postulated by the Ecclesiastic-Communal Cult Sodality model as being performed are quite different, being effectively postmortem world renewal sacrificial rituals of different types. And, as I noted above, the burials on the floors of the renewal lodges represent probably only a small proportion of the membership of the constituent sodalities since the majority of the deceased processed during the period of usage of these renewal lodges would be released to their clans for terminal burial in one of the multiple mortuary mounds dispersed over the valley. As I discuss in this and subsequent chapters, a significant number of the deceased that have been found on the floors of these major renewal lodges are likely the result of what I call truncation events, events that terminated the use of a renewal lodge, and, therefore, these numbers cannot be used to estimate the total number of deceased processed in these facilities. Also, at least for Seip and Liberty Works I will now argue that these floor deposits, which were for the most part cremations, were likely the final outcome of only one category of the range of world renewal ritual types that were carried out in this manner at these particular sites, and that in quantitative terms, the cremations may represent a minority of the types of rituals performed by these heterarchies. By minority I do not mean that they formed an unimportant category of world renewal ritual. In some senses, it may have been among the most important, not because of the deceased who were cremated but because of the likelihood that the cremations were part of the conveyancing transfer of the ritual usufruct for which the deceased had served as the primary custodians at the time of their deaths. I elucidate this transfer event in greater detail later. However, briefly stated, what many but not all of these cremations may mark would be the "decommissioning" of the ritual regalia that embodied the prerogatives to the performance of the particular rituals that they were normally used to constitute. These regalia were likely the set of well-known artifact types termed copper plates, copper headdresses, copper celts, and a few other critically important ritual warrants. As I noted above, I will return to this conveyancing ritual later since I consider it a critical aspect of the next step in my analysis and interpretation of the Ohio Hopewell earthworks.

What all this means, of course, is that sharing deceased members among affiliated alliances is not only possible, it makes a great deal of sense since the point of the mortuary practices was to resanctify the world and the point of the alliances was to enhance the resanctifying rituals. Sharing would be one means of doing this. Indeed, the most important modification of my earlier interpretation that this heterarchical view entails would explain why the circular mortuary space of the Seip-Conjoined Renewal Lodge has no burials. If mortuary rituals were shared between Seip and Liberty Works, then the most reasonable explanation for the absence of burials in the circular burial space at Seip-Conjoined (the formal space that I have argued was dedicated to deceased members of the clergy, shamanic-priests and their apprentices) is that the members of the clergy of this heterarchy were likely being buried in the circular space of the Edwin Harness Renewal Lodge at Liberty Works. This interpretation does not require modifying the social significance of my earlier claim arising from the absence of clergy burials at Seip-Conjoined. This original interpretation treated the absence of burials as a sign of increasing turmoil in the Seip-Conjoined cult sodality. This would still be a valid claim; only now it also solves the puzzle of where the deceased clergy were buried. It also reinforces my earlier claim that not only was Seip suffering; other sodalities were also, and the total system of cult sodality heterarchies was heading toward collapse through a chain-reaction-like process of disaffiliation of the affiliated cult sodalities.

In any case, if major earthworks and their associated features and facilities are interpreted as second-order heterarchies, that is, consisting of affiliations of first-order heterarchies, then the question of the material correlates of both individual autonomous cult sodalities and first-order heterarchies is raised. Indeed, this question is very important since it opens up considerable conceptual space to generate categories of sites and their empirical indicators that have been absent in the orthodox model. As I argued in the bottom-up view that I initiated in the previous chapter, the first level of the heterarchy system, represented in the Murphy Tract, would be the individual autonomous ecclesiastic-communal cult sodalities manifested typically in that aspect of the archaeological record I termed the ecclesiastic-communal cult sodality cluster structured into ceremonial nodal locales with spatially associated age-grade and age-set locale sites. The second-level would be the alliance of two or more of these cult sodalities, each with its own sodality cluster, into what I have termed a first-order ecclesiastic-communal cult heterarchy. These would be responsible for the relatively simple, small-scale or "lesser" earthwork sites. I postulate that many lesser earthwork sites that are found dispersed across the Ohio Hopewell zone of the Central Ohio Valley, for example, the Granville Works about 700 m west of the Murphy Tract, are the expression of first-order cult sodality heterarchies (figure 10.1). Importantly, treated individually, these lesser earthwork sites may not manifest the total range of earthwork locales of the first-order cult sodality heterarchies. There is growing recognition that spatially close but noncontiguous earthworks, such as the Pollock Works (figure 16.2) and the Bull Works in the Little Miami Valley, can be properly treated as intrinsically connected by being complementary components of a single first-order cult sodality heterarchy (Riordan 2004, 238–39; 2010, 13–27). Granville itself is actually a dual earthwork having an inner Sacred Circle and an outer C-Form. I have argued that, given their forms, particularly the complementary positioning of the "borrow" trenches of each, "inside" with regard to the circular embankment and "outside" with regard to the oblong embankment, these are chronologically sequential, with the former being associated with the Late Adena and the latter with the early Hopewell. However, they actually probably represent organizational continuity with the Sacred Circle representing the Below World and the lunar aspect of the cosmology and the C-Form representing the Above World and the solar aspect.

This pairing of two formally distinct earthworks would be a form of what I termed earlier the Sacred Dual motif. A formally more evolved expression of it is found in the Scioto region, and also at Newark. In fact, it is likely that the emergence of the second-order heterarchy level promoted the evolution of the "Chillicothe" type Sacred Dual motif, what I termed earlier the Sacred Dual C-R motif. That is, in the Central Ohio region, a second-order heterarchy apparently required material expressions of both the High Bank and the Paint Creek C-R motifs, or their equivalents, thereby constituting

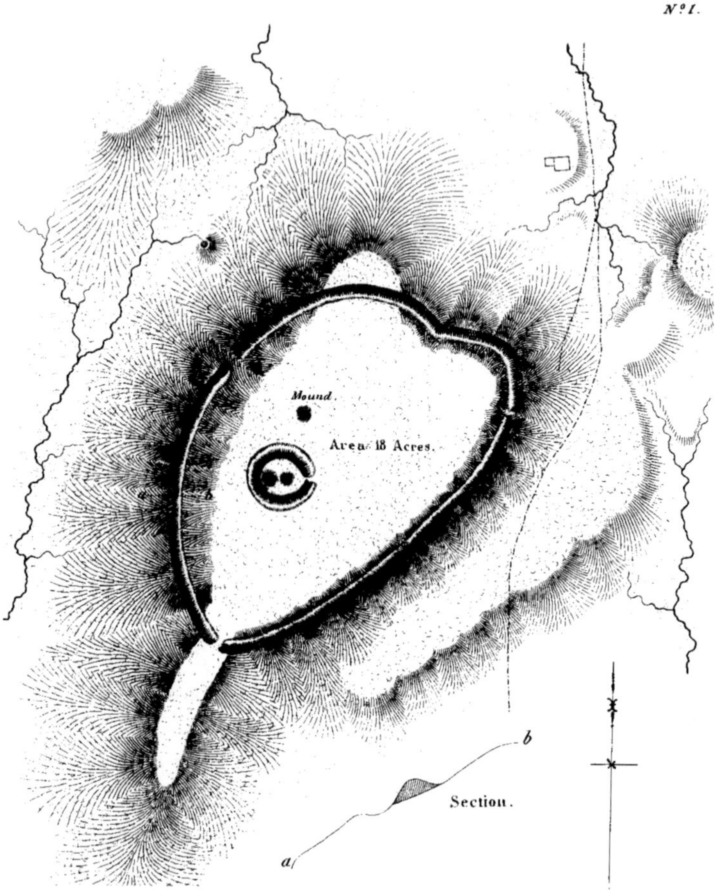

FIGURE 10.1
The Granville Site
Source: Squier and Davis 1848, plate IX, no. 1.

the Sacred Dual C-R motif version of the Sacred Dual motif. These would be monumental icons that in the collective understanding of the regional communities embodied the total sacred structuring of the cosmos as characterized by the traditional immanentist cosmology of the region. In these terms, the High Bank C-R motif (figure 3.4) manifests and participates in the *lunar aspect* of the cosmos, for reasons I give later, both the Above World (the circle) and the Beneath World (the octagon) aspects. Therefore, I have termed it the Lunar motif. The Paint Creek C-R motif (see Liberty Works, figure 1.2) manifests and participates in the complementary solar aspect, constituting it as the Solar motif, with the small circle on the periphery of the large "central" circular element representing the Above World under the solar aspect and the square representing the Beneath World under the solar aspect.[2] At Seip, Liberty Works, and Frankfort, since the Above World is represented by the small perimeter embankment circle, I have maintained that the large "inner" circle of this "tripartite" configuration, bracketed by the Paint Creek Square and the small perimeter Paint Creek Circle, is the *infix*, in my terminology. In my interpretation, it had a very significant symbolic pragmatic meaning in that it represented the Middle World, the world occupied by humans. This may be the reason that, when mortuary features and remains are found in embankment earthwork contexts, these are situated in the infix of the Paint Creek C-R motif, or its equivalent (Byers 2004, 46–51, 77–101; 1987, 343–69). This is where the most tangible aspect of the mortuary rites was typically carried out. This does not mean that the High Bank C-R motif was not used to contextualize a part of the mortuary *chaîne opératoire*. Rather the mortuary rites performed in the High Bank component probably simply did not normally involve terminal "burial" or other mortuary behaviors that would leave overt indicators.

Typically, these two motif configurations did not have to be present in one complex site, although I argue that the complexity of Newark arises largely from its combining them in the same site, as I describe in a later chapter. I have also argued that Hopeton and Mound City (figures 10.2 and 10.3), opposite each other on the central Scioto River and figuratively linked by a long set of parallel walls, which I refer to as the aggregation component or element, constitute another example of the Sacred Dual C-R motif and possibly its earliest known expression. These are probably all manifestations of second-order and, if the more distant Newark is included, possibly third-order heterarchies. Nevertheless, in principle, there is no reason why a first-order heterarchy, such as the cult sodalities responsible for Bull Works and Pollock Works, could not express a similar duality, if not the lunar and solar, at least the more fundamental spatial complementary opposition of Above World and Beneath World, that is, circle and square. It is also important to note that the High Bank site (figure 3.4) is itself unique in the central Scioto. It is paired with Liberty Works, only about 4 km to its south. It is probably emergent from the Mound City/Hopeton complex and was constructed as the replacement of the latter when the responsible second-order or, more likely, third-order cult sodality heterarchy abandoned or "decommissioned" the Mound City/Hopeton complex for which it was responsible. However, there is no High Bank motif site that can be identified with Seip on the Paint Creek. This is unusual since consistency would argue that just as Liberty Works and High Bank conjointly manifest the Dual Sacred C-R motif in the Paint Creek–central Scioto confluence region, it would be consistent for a similar High Bank

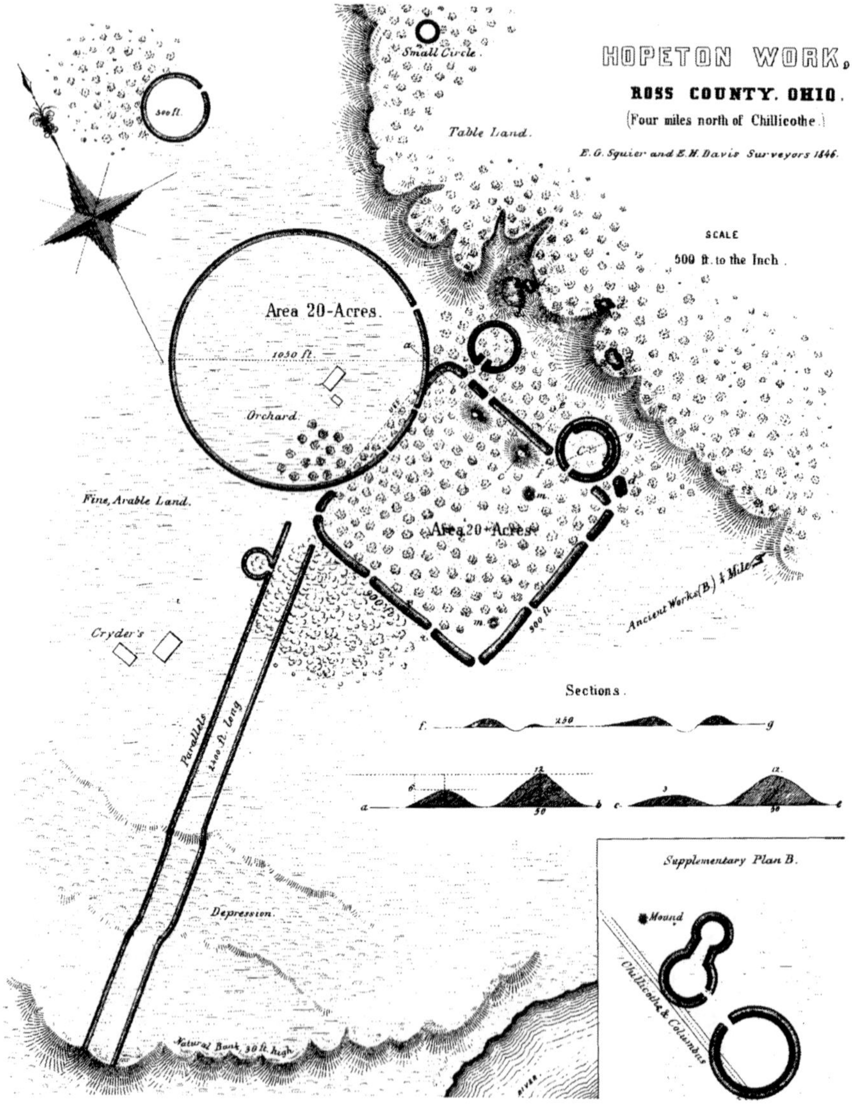

FIGURE 10.2

Hopeton Earthworks

Source: Squier and Davis 1848, plate XVII.

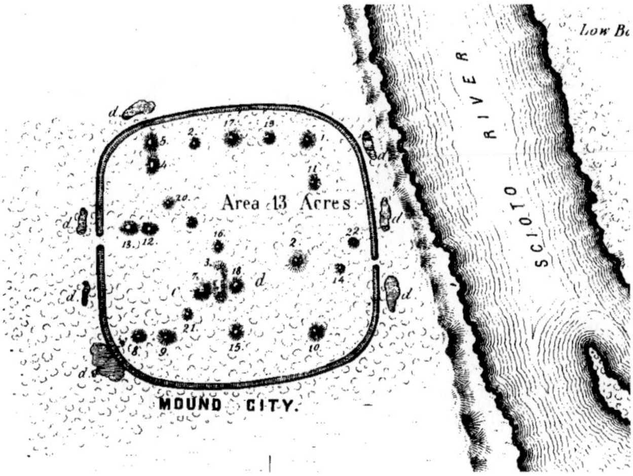

FIGURE 10.3
Mound City
Source: Squier and Davis 1848, from plate XIX.

C-R motif site to complement Seip. Later I will argue that, in fact, Seip does have a complementary High Bank C-R motif. However, it is likely to be the High Bank site itself. That is, as noted above, Seip and Liberty Works, the two second-order heterarchies of the Paint Creek–Scioto confluence region, were likely allied and part of their alliance required joint responsibility for the operation of the High Bank site, and this would have constituted these central Scioto embankment earthwork sites as the core of a third-order cult sodality heterarchy, which also likely came to include Newark and this inclusion, in all likelihood, was constituted by the building of the Newark Circle-Octagon, among other components of this very large and complex site. All this I discuss in more detail later. In any case, the bottom-up view now includes, at the highest level, what I refer to as the third-order heterarchy, the result of the affiliation of two or more second-order heterarchies and this affiliation can, indeed, link multiple ecclesiastic-communal cult sodalities across drainages, as I claim was the case when the second-order heterarchies in the Chillicothe and Newark regions affiliated.

I will now briefly return to the basal level of the Ohio Hopewell cult sodality heterarchy system, this being the individual autonomous cult sodality. This may be basal, but it is in fact the power of this core component that was responsible for the total system. This is because it was autonomous and, therefore, decisions at each level were by consensus. In such a system, a great deal of consultation would occur. Despite this basic social power, however,

I postulate that a cult sodality not only would not usually construct a local embankment earthwork, it would not necessarily have a mortuary component that would be archaeologically visible.[3] By this I mean that it would still participate importantly in the mortuary sphere of a region but most of the mortuary rituals held in the ceremonial nodal locale would mediate the earlier steps in the mortuary *chaîne opératoire* process. Hence, scaffolding and temporary curating of the deceased in the site would be an important part of the ritual that would occur there. Following the latter steps, it is likely that the age-set companions of the deceased would wrap his or her body in the appropriate mortuary shrouds and carry it on a litter to the first-order heterarchy earthwork. Here postmortem mediated rituals involving body reduction might occur, for example, long-term curating in specially built crypts, a series of spirit-release rites mediated by body part burial, cremation and burial, while other deceased might be further curated and then, at the appropriate time and in order to participate in important centralized rituals, the several curated remains would be taken on litters in sacred procession to be given penultimate treatment at the second-order heterarchy. Importantly, therefore, mortuary treatment at the ceremonial nodal site would tend to leave no major archaeological residue.[4] But each subsequent step might involve incremental postmortem manipulation, first in the earthworks of the first-order heterarchy entailing, followed by body or bone bundles carried in procession to the second-order heterarchy to mediate the incremental series of mortuary rituals there. Some of these—relatively few—would terminate in final mortuary deposition at the second-order site. However, as I noted above, it is also likely that significant numbers of the deceased might be returned to the clan locale where they would be given terminal rites in a local clan mound. I will discuss this in more detail shortly and present empirical evidence in support of this claim.

I noted in the preceding chapter that, as it now stands, while Murphy IV may be a cult sodality ceremonial nodal locale site, there are insufficient empirical data to confirm this. However, I cannot see at this point any particular reason that the ceremonial nodal locale of a sodality cluster could not be located away from the cluster of auxiliary age-grade and age-set sites, particularly if the cult sodality cluster was near the second-order or even third-order cult sodality heterarchy in which the organization participated. The Murphy Tract, of course, is only 700 m east of Granville and less than 2 km west of Newark and, therefore, it is possible that the postulated cult sodality constructed its ceremonial nodal locale lodge near the former, or even the latter, particularly if these two earthwork sites were not contemporaneous. Only future research can resolve that question. For example, magnetic geophysical surveying of the Murphy Tract could be carried out to see if anomalies can be discovered that might indicate the residue of a currently unknown timber structure (see note 4), somewhat akin to the recent discovery of two major timber structures at the Brown's Bottom #1 site and Lady's Run site, about 1.5 km west of Liberty Works (Pacheco et al. 2005, 2009a, 2009b).

Human mortuary practices would not exhaust the range of world renewal rites performed by the cult sodalities. Historically we know that Native North American communities performed a range of animal and plant rebirth and increase rites and there is no reason that these known world renewal ritual types would not have historically deep roots. That is, world renewal rituals to enhance the growth of the deer herd or the proliferation of the gardens would be performed using appropriate elements of the animals and plants that were exploited. I have argued that even everyday practical exploitative activities would have a built-in series of renewal rites, what I have termed midwifery rituals (Byers 2004, 136–39). Typically, foraging peoples characterize their hunting and gardening as a form of renewal of the species that they exploited (Ingold 1987, 246–47). Very often spirit-release and species increase rituals are an inbuilt part of the actual subsistence practice. I have already argued that the style of material cultural gear mediated the warranting imperative. This style constituted the instrumental tools as symbolic pragmatic warrants that transformed the destructive moment of species exploitation and killing into the legitimate activities of hunting, gathering, and harvesting. Without tools displaying these styles, the same behaviors would count as forms of poaching and pilfering, and poaching and pilfering would be particularly disliked because these behaviors fail to participate in the reproduction of the species being exploited and, therefore, they are polluting rather than sanctifying the sacred natural order.

It takes very little extension of the notion of the midwifery ritual to assume that when the ecclesiastic-communal cult sodality congregated at its ceremonial nodal locale, many of both its informal and formal activities would be experienced as having important world renewal aspects, quite independently of any human mortuary practices, although these would also occur and probably be used to enhance the world renewal moment of their activities. Therefore, while the world renewal ritual sphere of the cult sodalities would not be exhaustively constituted by human mortuary practices, the latter would be the most important form of ritual by which the cult sodalities realized their sacred purposes. Often these congregations could involve fairly extensive residency, even though many of the members may have their domestic habitations nearby. Once the cult sodality went into its "retreat" posture, it would probably sustain a voluntary seclusion and its members would be encouraged not to leave the site until the termination of their ritual practices, unless off-site tasks were required as part of the successful retreat. Hence, transient residency could be expected, but a residency that could also be drawn out for several weeks or even months. For example, as discussed earlier, ritual usufruct franchising events by which the cult sodality incorporated new rituals would probably occur at this ceremonial nodal site. Visiting cult sodalities, or their appropriate representative age-set groups acting in their capacity as the ritual usufruct franchisers, would expect to be housed and fed for the duration and they would also be very active in instructing their hosts in the details of the ritual, the constitutive myths, the imperatives and taboos that must be respected, and so on. They would also require the particular material resources for producing the required iconic warrants and to guide their hosts in properly producing as well as using and storing them.

The first performance of the ritual might, in fact, require the total sodality and its guest sodality to move to the first-order or even second-order heterarchy where the ritual was given its first local public performance. This performance would count as both the successful transfer of the ritual usufruct to the franchisee host sodality and the public acknowledgment by its cult sodality alliance that they were now the local custodians of this new ritual and, therefore, responsible for both its being among the suite of rituals that the heterarchy could and would perform and for performing it on behalf of the total heterarchy. This ritual would now be used to reinforce established alliances at the second-order heterarchy level or to establish new alliances with other second-order heterarchies. It also would reinforce the need to procure the necessary raw materials to produce these new iconic symbols that were critical constitutive media of the ritual, even if these raw materials were in distant regions.

All these demands required of a ceremonial cult nodal site would translate into a locale that would be rather distinct from the specialized production age-grade and age-set sodality locales. Transient residency would tend to produce domestic residue, but not fully typical of the seasonal base camp of a kin-based domestic habitation site. For example, residency at the sodality ceremonial nodal locale would involve major cooking events as part of the series of feasts that would be intrinsic to world renewal rituals. Therefore, as noted earlier, we could expect earth ovens, fancy ceramics, and a fair quantity of faunal residue. However, caution is required. The sacred nature of the locale would probably promote careful clearing of residue and, in fact, dumping that would not disturb the environment. As I have also suggested, even though it was the ceremonial nodal locale of the total cult sodality, it would also have a respectable amount of Hopewellian production debitage since it could also be used to some degree for this purpose. The use of a nearby creek might be promoted as a form of returning the sacred properties of the faunal residue to the natural order. Because of the need for segregation and seclusion, for example, both conveyancing and franchising require teaching esoteric knowledge and know-how that is treated as secret. Therefore, permanent structures would usually be required, as well as screens to block "curious eyes." Some residue of the production of symbolic icons would be typical and even broken icons would not be unusual since both learning to produce and use these would be part of the ritual activities performed. The permanent timber features would take on forms that would echo if not replicate the permanent timber features found at the major earthwork sites, particularly the second-order cult sodality heterarchy earthworks, such as Seip and Liberty Works. Therefore, the typical Ohio Hopewell rectangular structures would prevail.

Importantly, the ceremonial nodal locale could evolve into a first-order heterarchy locale simply by being selected by the two to four cult sodalities that were allying to be used for the purpose of this emergent heterarchical organization. However, this would likely encourage the more distant ecclesiastic-communal cult sodalities to build secondary nodal locales at or near the emergent first-order heterarchy while maintaining their primary ceremonial nodal locales. They would use these secondary locales in much the same way as their primary nodal locales while in transient residency at their first-order cult sodality heterarchy. However, respecting the autonomy of their allies, they would likely build the secondary locale a little distant from the embankment earthwork. Hence, these secondary ceremonial nodal sites would probably form a well-spaced set located one or more kilometers from the earthwork site and from each other. As secondary ceremonial nodal locales, they would probably not be used for intensive Hopewellian production. Rather, they would serve as a type of hostel, a way station for the cult sodalities traveling from some distance, and they would have only the range of debitage appropriate for minor repairs and preparation for ritual to be performed at the nearby first- or second-order heterarchy. Of course, careful site maintenance would be in order so that defined middens would be typical but extensive and dense debitage with a uninodal refuse deposit of the type found at the Murphy Tract age-grade sites would not be expected.

As briefly noted above, a similar pattern would occur for second-order heterarchy affiliations. Only now, given my estimated number of sodalities involved, this might require some tighter clustering while maintaining arm's-length distance from the earthwork itself. Indeed, as the second-order heterarchy affiliation developed, nodal sites that had been initially built nearby may be abandoned and the space they occupied incorporated into new extensions to the embankment earthwork. In some cases, particularly for second-order heterarchies, some of the autonomous cult sodalities would be quite distant from their primary ceremonial nodal locales and, therefore, they would not only build a replication of the main feature of this locale but also recognize the need for the component age-set sodalities to have access to separate sites, thereby enabling the formation of auxiliary age-grade or age-set sodality sites.

While the previous chapter elucidated and empirically grounded the Cult Sodality Cluster model, because the surface survey of the Murphy Tract was insufficient to establish if the Murphy IV uninodal lithic clusters marked a ceremonial nodal locale site, as such, the latter site type is still not empirically demonstrated. I plan to do this as part of my shift of focus from the cult sodality cluster of the countryside to the sodality locales associated with the major embankment earthworks, postulating that these served to mediate the intersodality relations constituting the Ohio Hopewell cult sodality heterarchy system. I initiate this project below by reexamining the relation among the major sites of the central Scioto region and the Little Miami Valley, treating this relation as mediating two major third-order transdrainage cult sodality heterarchies.

THE SACRED GAME *TOURNÉE* MODE

Earlier I critiqued Carr's Tripartite Ceremonial Alliance model by showing that, in its own terms, it inadequately explained the patterning of the tripartite mortuary spaces of the Seip-Pricer Renewal Lodge, and by extension, of the comparable mortuary patterning at the Seip-Conjoined and the Liberty Works Renewal Lodges. I would include in this assessment the Hopewell Renewal Lodge complexes at the Hopewell and Frankfort sites. However, no critique is complete until an alternative account is presented and empirically grounded. I now want to complete this earlier critique by presenting a different model of the nature of the interaction among these same earthwork sites. However, as implied in my brief discussion of the Ohio Hopewell cult sodality system of heterarchies as organized at multiple levels, I will have to go beyond these four main mortuary-related sites—Hopewell, Frankfort, Seip, and Liberty Works—in order to incorporate a number of other sites that were not part of Carr's model. I have already referred to this alternative as the Ohio Hopewell Cult Sodality Heterarchy System model. However, for this model to be used dynamically to account for the content of the embankment earthwork sites, an auxiliary model characterizing the social mechanism that was responsible for the interaction among these earthworks is needed in order to tie the system of heterarchies to the empirical data that demonstrate it, that is, to the mortuary and related artifactual data. I consider the social mechanism to be a complex process of intersodality sacred games and I call this the Sacred Games *Tournée* model. Following its elucidation I am going to argue that, along with a number of other major embankment earthwork sites, the same sites that Carr treated as constituting a unitary tripartite alliance were central to the interaction of two autonomous networks of dispersed third-order cult sodality heterarchies and that the juncture zone of the North Fork–Paint Creek Valleys constituted their interface. To be specific, I will treat the Hopewell site as the easternmost extension of the dispersed third-order Little Miami Valley cult sodality heterarchy, which I will refer to as the Fort Ancient–Turner–Hopewell heterarchy, while I will treat Seip as the westernmost extension of the dispersed third-order Chillicothe-Newark cult sodality heterarchy. Hence, while Carr explains the Hopewell site and its wealth and complexity of the mortuary sphere as a measure of the wealth of the Tripartite Alliance being concentrated here, I treat the site and this wealth and complexity as the result of its being a primary interface of the two third-order heterarchies that linked southwest Ohio to central Ohio. I have referred to these previously as the Turner-Hopewell and the Chillicothe-Newark axes, respectively. I will now refer to them in the above terms as the dispersed third-order Fort Ancient–Turner–Hopewell cult sodality heterarchy and the dispersed third-order Chillicothe-Newark cult sodality heterarchy.

MORTUARY PRACTICES AND THE OHIO HOPEWELL SACRED GAMES *TOURNÉE*

These two dispersed third-order cult sodalities transcended drainage systems with the Fort Ancient–Turner–Hopewell heterarchy minimally linking the Little Miami and possibly the Great Miami River Valleys with the North Fork tributary of the Paint Creek–central Scioto drainage and the Chillicothe-Newark heterarchy minimally linking the Licking River valley of the upper Muskingum drainage with the Paint Creek–central Scioto drainage. This means that the region where the North Fork flowed into the Paint Creek served as the interface zone of these two dispersed third-order heterarchy systems with the Hopewell site and the Seip site as the two primary reciprocal "gateway" sites bridging this interface zone.[5] With the earthworks of these two regional drainages interpreted under the same Ohio Hopewell Cult Sodality Heterarchy model, I will then extend its premises to examine a similar patterning in three neighboring regions that, however, have a strong representation of Late Adena contemporary with the Ohio Hopewell during the first half of the Middle Woodland period: the classic Adena zone of the central Kentucky region, the central-east Indiana region, and the central Muskingum Valley region. It will turn out, however, that I will also have to reexamine the Licking-Newark region as extending into the central Muskingum, thereby manifesting a complex history of Adena-Hopewell transformation. The purpose of this final exploration is to demonstrate the validity of the Ritual Usufruct Conveyancing and Franchising model. In this case, its validity will be supported by both indicating where ritual usufruct franchising largely failed, Kentucky and the Hocking Valley, implicating serious resistance on the part of local cult sodalities anchored to the traditional Adena rituals, and where it succeeded in at least a partial manner, central-east Indiana, and where it succeeded in an outstanding manner, Newark. However, before addressing this problem, I will use the model to explicate the formation of the above two major third-order cult sodality heterarchies, particularly focusing on the Hopewell site, by arguing that the extraordinary nature of its mortuary record was largely the result of its serving as a primary monumental iconic locale of the dispersed Fort Ancient–Turner–Hopewell third-order heterarchy where among the many "regular" postmortem sacrificial rituals that were performed I postulate that the focusing of the primary conveyancing rituals by which the transfer from the deceased of the custodial leadership positions of the multiple cult sodalities of this third-order heterarchy to their descendent custodians was carried out and this was likely the primary cause for the great build up of major Ohio Hopewellian regalia, such as copper plates, copper celts, copper headdresses, and so on, since these were the formal symbolic pragmatic warranting devices of these rituals. This is the hypothesis that I will now devote the next several chapters to demonstrating.

I want to stress that, as used here, the Ritual Usufruct Conveyancing and Franchising model is designed only to explain the Hopewellianization process as it proceeded in the Central Ohio Valley, both in terms of successes and failures. In a later book, I intend to apply it to the larger Hopewellianization process of the Eastern Woodland that generated the Hopewell Interaction Sphere. Therefore, while this is an important model, that is, it presents the social mechanism by which the cult sodality heterarchies and their material assemblages were generated and reproduced over space and time, it only makes sense in this context as an auxiliary of the Ecclesiastic-Communal Cult Sodality Heterarchy model. Furthermore, presupposing this model is the more basic substantive model that characterizes the primary activity of these cult sodalities and why they actively pursued ritual usufruct conveyancing and franchising. This is the view that they performed a complex of world renewal rituals, many mediated by postmortem human sacrifice, in order to reverse the polluting effects that everyday settlement and subsistence practices had. In the eyes of the prehistoric populations, some of these polluting effects may have been manifested as major flooding events (Van Nest 2006, 403–4, 419; Van Nest et al. 2001). These effects may have been becoming particularly intensive as the Middle Woodland communities became more reliant on gardening. This intensification of gardening also meant deliberate and increased intervening into the sacred natural order and, therefore, the need to increase the intensity and efficacy of large-scale world renewal ritual. I have already fully articulated this view in what I term the World Renewal model of Ohio Hopewell arguing that the primary medium of these world renewal rituals was the mortuary sphere (Byers 2004, 1999, 1996, 1992, 1987). This sphere was constituted as a complex process of incremental postmortem sacrificial rituals in which the deceased were the primary sacrificial offerings. I have articulated this as the Mourning/World Renewal Mortuary model and earlier I suggested that the process can be analytically conceptualized as a mortuary *chaîne opératoire* that unfolds as the realization of an incremental series of differential mortuary intentions, some of which we might adequately describe as funerary intentions, mourning intentions, spirit-release intentions, memorial intentions, name-transfer and name-renewal intentions, group renewal intentions, species renewal intentions, earth renewal intentions, and so on.

At this point, it is important to elucidate the social mechanism by which this complex sacrificial mortuary *chaîne opératoire* unfolded and that also was used to effect the postulated ritual usufruct conveyancing of custodial leadership from the deceased to the living replacement custodians, and this means adding another layer of complexity to this process, what I called above the sacred games *tournée*. This *tournée* introduces another critical sacred power into the mortuary-mediated world renewal process, this being the energies of the living participants themselves. That is, the world renewal rituals that the *chaîne opératoire* articulates cannot be exhaustively described only in mortuary terms. While human deceased played a critical constitutive role in the spirit-release sacrificial renewal rituals, the most important of the rituals, or at least the most public and active aspect of these rituals, involved multiple numbers of the living as the primary participants. I am postulating here that many of the world renewal rituals performed in the embankment earthwork contexts were of the order of sacred games reenacting the unfolding of the different world creation events as these would have been narrated in the creation stories. Therefore, not only were the deceased the primary source of powers released back to the cosmos in sacrificial ritual, they also served as the constitutive "counters and embodiments" by which the energies of the living were formally "fed" to the cosmos through the renewal ritual. The energies of the players may have been experienced as feeding their material items, their warrants of games activity, the earspools, their necklaces and bracelets, and so forth, that they wore. Those who won received these from the losers and, combining these gains with their own potent action cue materials (e.g., their earplugs and bracelets), they gave them as offerings to the deceased, who thereby added these energies to their own sacred powers, as I describe later. Hence, the primary renewal rituals were large-scale collective mortuary events that had competitive *sacred games* as their critically important medium; and "winning" and "losing" of the deceased and/or the important regalia for which they had been the custodians in life were the rewards for the winning cult sodalities and the penalties for the losing ones. It then became the winners' responsibility to be the collective "soul keepers" that cared for these sacred bones and the accumulated artifacts and, of course, this committed them to participate even more deeply in the next ritual step. Hence, winners at one set of games would be responsible to bring their custodial burdens, the deceased and their regalia, to the next and "defend" their "soul keeper" positions, in which case they could also lose it and be required to pass the burden of souls to the winners, and so on.

Thus, the game did more than decide who the (temporary) soul keepers might be. The games were a means of investing the animating energies of the players into the sacred bones and artifacts that were intended as the postmortem sacrificial offerings, thereby intensifying the sacred powers of these materials; and although there were both winners and losers, the recognition that the sacred energies of both were invested in these bones and artifacts simply enhanced the honor and worth for both. The winners would receive the prestigious task of being the soul keepers, the custodians of the bodies, bones, or ashes of the deceased and, therefore, would have primary responsibility for the performance of the subsequent mortuary-mediated ritual in the chain until the final or terminal rites were performed. I postulate therefore that, ultimately, the point of the games was to lead to terminal mortuary-mediated world renewal spirit-release rituals and the peer leaders of those cult sodalities who were the (winning) custodians had the honor and obligation to act as the leading postmortem sacrificers in the offering rites while acting of course on behalf of their cult sodality, thereby bringing honor to this group.

I have used the term "postmortem sacrificer" deliberately. Although I will not deny that some lethal human sacrifice may have been involved, I have argued that postmortem sacrifice was the most prevalent form of "feeding the gods" in Hopewellian practice. I have already argued that, for the most part, traditional Native North American mortuary practices served as media of postmortem human sacrifice. I suggest that, unless evidence can be forthcoming supporting the practice of lethal human sacrifice, the Ohio Hopewell episode is most reasonably characterized as the unfolding of a complex postmortem human sacrificial process and that the sacred games were the primary active social mechanism whereby this process was developed. Sometimes the terminal ritual would occur in the same locale following the end of the sacred games, for example, in the great C-Form embankment of the Hopewell site. In some cases, however, the winners would carry the remains of the deceased back to their own first-order embankment earthworks where they might either curate them in order to use them in "return matches," or, with the losing team as their guests, perform other terminating world renewal rituals there. Indeed, as I suggested above, the "counters" in the games would not only be the bones of the deceased but also the important custodial regalia of the more prestigious of the deceased. Since the accompanying deceased were the custodians of these regalia during their lifetimes, they may have been perceived as continuing as custodians in their death, and not only was the free soul of the deceased required to be present for the release of his or her living souls to the intended recipient gods, the same spirit-release rite would return the powers of the sacred regalia to these gods, who were conceived as the original givers.[6]

Hence, I am postulating that a part of the significance of the sacred games was not simply that the mortuary remains of the deceased served as counters to determine who "won" and who "lost" the games, but the games were themselves an important mode of regenerating of sacred energy. That is, the reenactments of the world creation events that they mimicked, reenactments that occurred in the iconic context of the great earthworks, thereby presencing the relevant gods and transforming the games into the acts of re-creating the world, would also invest the players' energies expended in the games into the deceased and their regalia. Furthermore, as suggested above, winners and losers would likely gamble personal items, such as copper earspools, favored pearl and shell necklaces, and so on, and these would end up as mourning gifts to the deceased. That is, these items would be deposited with the deceased for whom the winners had become or had maintained their position as the "soul keepers" in order to transfer the energies the players had built up in them during their game playing to the deceased through the medium of these personal gifts. In this way the players participated directly in the sacrificial offering aspect of the rituals by enlivening the bones and the regalia of the deceased with their own sacred energies expended in the games. Hence, through the medium of the mortuary remains the participating players of the games directly contributed their own energies to the world renewal sacrifices.

Of course, some readers are now saying to themselves: "This is a Just-So story that cannot be proven. How are we ever to know that the Ohio Hopewell archaeological record, including the mortuary deposits, is a product of such activity? Is this not simply flying high, quite disconnected from the empirical data? Pure speculation and imagination!" or thoughts to this effect. Let me first counter such criticism by dismissing the term "'just-so' story." Dismissing a narration of events in the social world by speaking of it as a "just-so" story, that is, as merely a fairy tale, is hardly a valid criticism in itself since it begs the very question that the story presupposes. That is, it actually is a refusal to engage with claims about the nature of the social world responsible for this tangible record by dismissing the story as about a "pretend" world, an "unreal world." Well, of course the social world that the above story presupposes does not exist now! However, this certainly does not mean that it never did exist. I think archaeologists can agree that the empirical evidence presupposes the prior existence of a particular type of social world, one that is quite outside their cultural experience. Therefore, what this narrative raises is whether, given our current theoretical knowledge of human social systems, the story is plausible in its wider and broader themes, rather than in its specific details, and, most importantly, if empirical evidence can be marshaled that can be used to give credible support to this story such that it makes more sense than *alternative* stories, or than *no story at all*!

I think that as archaeologists of prehistoric societies our primary purpose is to give the interpretation and explanation of the archaeological record in social action terms, namely, in terms requiring interpreting the material cultural patterns as the outcome of social activities, these being humanly generated social events. The only access we have to these events is via the material things themselves and how their use modified the tangible world and reproduced or transformed the social world that generated them. If this is the case, then we are necessarily involved in narrating stories that presuppose the social systems that made it possible for the responsible prehistoric agents to act in ways as described by one or another narrative that, if these ways were carried out, would necessarily generate this type of tangible archaeological record. But this means that *all archaeological interpretations* are based on stories and to dismiss a story simply by labeling it as a just-so story is to refuse to engage in the scientific process whereby we can reconstruct past social systems, even though, and possibly especially since, the participants in these social systems may have engaged in social activities that would be considered beyond the normal range of possible activities in our own social world. The social scientific process entails real critical examination by asking how valid, reasonable, and relevant is one story compared to alternative stories and which of the different theoretical models that each story presupposes is the most reasonable given the explanation of the empirical evidence it enables? Does the Sacred Games *Tournée* model enable a more coherent and consistent account of the empirical data compared to the alternative models and the stories that they presuppose? In retroductive terms, given the theorization of the prehistoric social system, do the activities that this story claims would occur explain the patterns that are manifested in the empirical data? Of course, even if it is a good explanation, this does not guarantee that such activities occurred. In fact, no story should be treated as privileged such that it can be used as the catch-all default account since no one living now could claim to have observed and participated in the responsible social system so as to attest that the model is privileged. A model has to be tested by comparison with alternatives and the theories that presuppose them in order to achieve this privileged state. Of course, this is simply a restatement of the hermeneutic spiral method, which consists of critically comparing alternative "just-so" stories and choosing the one that endows the patterning with greatest coherence and that accounts for the widest range of data making up that pattern.

However, as I have emphasized before, absolute surety that the model that is chosen is true is not possible, even if its explanatory power has been demonstrated as superior to the alternative models. This is not because a true story is impossible to narrate (if this was the case then there would be no point to the scientific process). I am committed to the position that telling a story that is true is possible and likely happens fairly frequently, although no story can ever describe the totality of past activities since any story is always from a particular perspective and there are too many perspectives that must be ignored or not fully appreciated. The problem, however, extends beyond the multiple perspectives that can be taken. The problem is that even should a story be true, we can never "absolutely" know that it is. We can only know its truth value by judging its adequacy to "fit" the empirical data in terms of how the other stories explained the same data and in terms of the adequacy of the theories that these use. Certainly, I was not a witness to the events of the story that I narrated based on the Sacred Games *Tournée* model; and, for that matter, no one alive today could have witnessed the events that generated the embankment earthworks and their associated mortuary data and, as far as we know, even the traditional Native peoples of the region when first encountered by Europeans had no stories of this sort. So, in that sense, all those who want to tell stories to explain the same empirical data start their work from a "level playing field."

However, we know that historic Native North Americans certainly played different games that had sacred implications. For example, lacrosse was a game played in the Northeast and many witnesses compared it to a war-like battle between villages (Fogelson 1985, 330–31). The men of different villages formed teams and challenged each other. Much as if going to war, they would congregate as a team, often organized as linked age-sets, in a special locale outside their village where their peer leaders would check that they had all exercised the behavioral avoidances that were necessary prior to going to engage the opposition, much like the taboos that warriors had to respect prior to leaving for battle and while at war. The leaders would emphasize the importance of their being dressed appropriately, this manifesting their action intentions (whether going to war or going to play a sacred game) and the group would comply with the advice of their shaman whom they specially contracted to lead them in the best way he could to follow the best game pathway to the locale where they were to confront the opposing team. The shaman was charged with performing protective magic to counter the damaging powers of the opposing team's shaman. Confronting the opponents on the game field led to a daylong "battle" and after the game the men retreated to count their wounds. They could not reenter their village immediately but had to subject themselves to a series of cleansing rituals in order to dispel the potent forces that their game playing had built up.

It appears to be the case that oral histories of these villages did not include a representation of a deep historical practice of such games. However, this does not mean that there were no such games practiced in this deep historical time; and certainly, the size of the spaces embraced by the major Ohio Hopewell embankment earthwork sites implicate that these were fulfilling requirements that might only be able to be served by the symbolic pragmatic nature of such large material forms. The labor involved in building them, the mortuary evidence, both in terms of variety and quantity, and the likely ceremonial nature of the behaviors that these data would mediate, when given a symbolic pragmatic reading, would suggest that these were material conditions that were eminently suitable for enabling large groups to congregate regularly in order to perform collective behavioral interventions requiring expansive areas embodying special symbolic pragmatic meanings. Games of the type witnessed historically would certainly be plausible. Also, the complex patterning of the associated mortuary data would certainly suggest that any games of this sort in these contexts would not be simply incidental to the complex of mortuary features, facilities, and deposits. That is, there is a causal nexus of mortuary practices, large expanses of deliberately designed spaces enabling group interaction requiring expansive areas, and variable distribution of facilities and artifactual materials that is implicated by all this. Indeed, we know that the Mississippian period platform mound locales probably were used for these purposes, among others, and, according to recent research, it appears that the most likely games that were played were intended to replicate the conditions of world creation in which the gods of the Above World, the Thunderbirds, and the gods of the Beneath World, the Giants, namely, the Great Serpent, repeatedly battled one another to the death, only for the dead to be resuscitated magically, requiring rematches (Brown 2007a, 2007b, 2007c; 2004a; Brown and Kelly 2000; Kelly et al. 2007; Knight 2007; Knight et al. 2001; Reilly 2007, 2004).

The game of chunkey recruited one of the most important skills of the active generation, particularly of the males, this being the skill of spear throwing. The precise rules of the chunkey game are not known now. However, the tools are well recognized and they involved the competitive targeting of a moving object, the chunkey stone, as teams of men threw their spears. The game was interpreted as originated by the creator gods, the Above World Thunderbirds and the Beneath World gods, and reenacted in their lethal struggles against each other. This was a time, of course, when the standard hunting weapon was the bow and arrow and, therefore, the use of the spear was probably treated as a sacred skill rooted in deep time and associated with the gods themselves. In fact, Robert Hall has suggested the chunkey game was the precursor of the Plains Indian spear-and-hoop game, which he notes was, in fact, a ritual performed by the warriors of the community in order to enhance and renew the fertility of the animal species they hunted (Hall 1979, 265). Importantly, it is likely that the chunkey game would not have been the only game undertaken. While it would have been a competitive game between more-or-less equivalently matched teams, based on historical analogy, there probably was a type of ball game that involved competing groups, such as the game of lacrosse or a type of sacred ball game akin to the classic and postclassic Mesoamerican cultures. Very germane to this is a recent interpretation of the traditional Eastern Woodland game of lacrosse as expressing and realizing world renewal themes. Jay Toth (2009, 2) has noted that the Iroquoian Great Panther, a creator god, is directly associated with lacrosse. "Like all religions people carry their religious symbolism into battle and native warriors did as well by brandishing a woodland club in the image of the panther. This war instrument in turn becomes the wonderful woodland sport known as Lacrosse. Lacrosse being known as the 'game of the creator' by its participants as this game is played with the lacrosse sticks held up and is the reverse of that of the falling comets and meteorites."

The Mayan ball game, for example, was interpreted as a world renewal rite replicating the battles between the gods of the Underworld and the original god-like humans of the Middle World. Furthermore, given the size of aggregations that could be accommodated by the great earthworks, there would probably be a parallel series of different types of challenging competitions, from foot racing to strength assessing, all of which were tied into the main purpose of the sacred games, namely, to effect the release and transfer of the sacred energies of the active human players back into the deceased and through them into the cosmos.

What empirical evidence is there that such games actually were performed? Clearly, ball games could have equipment in the form of hide-produced balls and these would likely not survive in the archaeological record. However, some of the instruments that were used to play the games or were used to produce the game items would survive. Several classes of artifacts that have survived from Ohio Middle Woodland times would strongly suggest that at least one major form of sacred game was carried out. This period was probably the time of the apex of the atlatl-spear hunting complex and correlated with this time is the well-known Hopewell platform pipe complex. Robert Hall has argued that there is more than a formal relation between the Hopewell platform pipe and the Hopewell spear and atlatl complex. I have already noted that foraging peoples, particularly those bearing an immanentist cosmology, characteristically treat their subsistence practices as having a dual moment of death and rebirth. That is, hunting is a sacrificial process that not only provides the nutritional and other resources necessary for reproducing the economic needs of the community but, in the understanding of the hunters, when done properly it also reproduces the species that they exploit. Hence, their subsistence practices have a built-in midwifery ritual aspect and the style of the hunting gear is experienced as the primary symbolic pragmatic warrant by which such killing behaviors are constituted as hunting activity mediating a dual sacrificial renewal—of the human community and of the species exploited.

In this regard, Hall (1977, 510) has pointed out that the atlatl and spear complex bears for the traditional Native North American peoples the dual meaning of life destroyer and life creator and that the act of penetration of the spear is also experienced as akin to an act of sexual penetration and reproduction, thereby ensuring the rebirth of the animals (also see Turner 1993, 67–69, 75). Hall has also drawn a direct parallel between the formal properties of the Middle Woodland atlatl and the Hopewell platform pipe. The atlatl was probably made of some form of hardwood that was carefully shaped having a carved handle for the hand to grip, sometimes with holes for the thumbs and fingers, and a carved hook-like horn, shell, or stone item attached to the distal end in order to be a secure anchor for the butt end of the spear or dart. The hand grip was often carved as an effigy animal, not unusually representing one of the spiritual guardians of the animal species. Most importantly, Hall has noted that the well-known Hopewell effigy platform pipe was modeled after this spear thrower grip and was attached to a long piece of wood, such as cedar, that was split lengthwise in order to enable its core to be gouged out and then glued back together, thus becoming a hollow pipe stem with the platform pipe simulating the handle grip of an atlatl (Hall 1997, 119–20). He suggests that the effigy platform pipe was a figurative elaboration of the same representation of the atlatl transformed into a ceremonial pipe. In fact, he interprets the Ohio Hopewell platform pipe-stem complex as an early form of the Calumet-like pipe that mediated the Calumet ceremonialism I discussed fully in chapter 4. Also, of course, the pipe complex was tightly tied to ritual invoking the presence of powerful spiritual forces, the type of invocation that mortuary practices would require. All this ties a major ceremonial item of the Hopewellian assemblage to the atlatl-and-spear subsistence hunting complex and the conceptualization of this practice as a sacrificial process by which humans both hunted and reproduced the very species they exploited. It also ties this complex to the ritual practice of smoking as the medium of spiritual interaction of the smoker with the gods. Hence, the atlatl-and-spear complex and the platform pipe complex suggest atlatl-and-spear complex games as an important part of the mortuary ritual of the Ohio Hopewell world renewal ritual ceremonialism.

If this is the case, then we could expect that everyday spears and spear throwers might not have been adequate. Instead, there would be a formally parallel set of gear specially produced using selected resources that were recognized as having particular sacred powers identified with the gods. Hence, these "ceremonial" tools would be produced and used as constitutive warrants of the sacred games. I have already commented extensively on the use of selected dual cherts, such as the Wyandotte and Flint Ridge cherts, as well as the dual usage of rock crystal quartz and obsidian. In fact, bifacial projectile points would be standard for the spears and the use of blank disks of these different selected lithic resources would clearly be the expression of symbolic pragmatic rules governing the formal sacred properties of the spears' projectile points that were required for them to serve as media of the sacred games. Not only are all these resources in the form of blanks and debitage well represented at key great earthwork sites, for example, Stubbs Works, the Hopewell site, Fort Ancient, and so on, elaborately formed obsidian and flint points have been found, the so-called Ross Barbed point. These appear to have been unused in the instrumental sense; however, they probably would serve as an excellent model of the range of points that could serve for this and related purposes. That is, some of these could serve as points for the spears used in a sacred game, others as blades would serve to mediate slicing and cutting entailing a range of game-related activities, including mediating the manipulation of the deceased as a postmortem sacrificial rite, and, of course, in preparing animal bodies for ritual feasts.

If it is accepted that an atlatl-and-spear throwing competition having ritual spirit-release powers is implied by the objective evidence of the platform pipe and atlatl-and-spear complex, along with the complex of ceremonial obsidian, quartz, and selected chert blades, then at least one possible sacred game is evident in the archaeological assemblage. If we add the likelihood that the size of great earthworks presupposes games involving large aggregates of players moving quickly across the open spaces, then these earthworks can serve as empirical evidence that they were the monumental symbolic pragmatic locales of sacred games, that is, not only competitive spear throwing but also some form of team ball-game playing using ball throwers that may have copied the atlatl, such as lacrosse (Toth 2009). Some recent research on the effectiveness of bladelet usage has demonstrated that one type of skillful use for which it was probably ideal was the carving of wood and, if properly softened, antler and possibly bone. In particular, the authors comment that bladelets made it "easy to clearly strip bark off of a branch. The bladelet ably eliminated any problematic knots or curvature in the wood. This use of a bladelet would have been useful in the production of wooden objects like shafts, handles, and utensils" (Snyder et al. 2008, 56–57). These types of materials would have made excellent spear shafts as well as atlatls, both for the spear-mediated games and for ball games of the lacrosse type, suggesting, of course, bladelets were used as ritual tools for making and repairing these game tools. The superfluity of bladelets made of select cherts found at such sites as the Murphy Tract and the Jennison Guard site may attest to their important use in preparing the game tools necessary for the postulated sacred games. And, of course, the select nature of the cherts used would be fully consistent with the notion that the felicity of these tools was perceived as largely governed by using only those cherts that were collectively believed to be appropriate for producing such sacred game items.

Of course, as noted above, I fully recognize that we can never be absolutely sure that a sacred game mediated by what I will term the dual ritual atlatl-and-spear-and-Hopewell platform pipe complex, as well as other sacred games, actually occurred and, of course, even if it is accepted, I cannot be absolutely sure that a suite of games, such as atlatl-and-spear target games, and sacred ball games, racing games, and so on, was regularly performed as central components of the ritual programs that were mediated by the mortuary sphere. However, historical analogy, the range of ceremonial items (e.g., Ross Barbed points, elaborate platform pipes, bladelets), and the material size and layout of the earthworks suggest that some form of activity of this order was of critical importance. Furthermore, as I note shortly, the actual distribution across a set of formally interrelated embankment earthwork sites of the mortuary-related materials, including the deceased, the facilities used, and the associated artifact assemblage, can be explained most coherently in these terms, namely, ongoing sacred games *tourneés* that were mediated by progressively modified human remains. That is, for the patterning of the data as we know it now to exist, the most reasonable explanation is that it was the context, medium, and ongoing outcome of a complex system of interembankment earthwork sacred games *tournées*.

Importantly, while the details concerning the postulated games are being imagined here, and may have to be left as imaginary, the principles that would promote the use of such games are not imaginary. We have good analogy to this effect. As I noted above, there is good theory about the nature of Native North American beliefs and practices in the sacred nature of such games and the relation of this sacredness to world renewal. I have directly tied mortuary practices to world renewal carried out by historical Native North American peoples who, indeed, did play competitive games as world renewal and rebirth rituals. There is scattered but irrefutable evidence that traditional Native North American peoples considered human bones and even human hair to embody the living souls of the deceased and these materials are known to have been used to form sacred mortuary bundles that were under the custodial care of soul keepers. As Hall (1997, 27) has noted, these soul keepers were under strict taboos while undertaking the task of caring for the bones of their deceased. Most importantly, the institution of the soul keeper supports the view that the practice of carrying the deceased in the form of sacred bundles that were systematically transformed from being deceased carried on litters to being bundles of bones and other related items, particularly hair, is an ancient practice in Native North American mortuary traditions. What I have added here is the claim that this carrying was not simply a passive form of caring for but an active part of transferring the deceased from place to place and, indeed, of exchanging the deceased or material components of the deceased and/or their associated artifactual kits through the medium of sacred games. This is an important claim to the effect that sacred games were an intrinsic part of the system of Ohio Hopewell cult sodality heterarchies and, as I noted above, I will shortly demonstrate the likelihood that such sacred games occurred by interpreting the mortuary evidence as not only manifesting the systematic transformation of the mortuary remains as media of postmortem sacrificial offerings, but that this transformation process entailed major transportation of the mortuary remains and their associated artifactual materials. Such evidence would reinforce and be fully consistent with this claim that a system of sacred games *tournées* was responsible.

CONCLUSION

By developing the implications to the Ohio Hopewell archaeological record of the symbolic pragmatic view I have argued that earthworks were monumental media of mortuary-mediated world renewal rituals and, drawing on Hall's interpretive work, I have also argued that the Hopewell platform pipe and atlatl-and-spear complexes were probably deliberately produced in the forms that they were in order to serve as a dual kit of sacred as well as instrumental tools to mediate these rituals as part of a suite of sacred games. Most importantly, the Sacred Games *Tournée* model immediately forces us to extend our interpretations of the embankment earthworks beyond the spatial boundaries of these monumental constructions themselves and of the zones that immediately surrounded them. That is, the playing of such games in a major embankment earthwork identified with a rich mortuary residue would not be limited to just the earthwork where these remains were found. If this is a competitive process, then any given set of games at one earthwork site would be simply part of a complex interembankment earthwork *tournée* process. I now develop the implications of this model for understanding and explaining the relevant empirical data.

11

The North Fork–Paint Creek Interface Zone and the Terminal Conveyancing of Custodial Regalia

The Sacred Games *Tournée* model expresses the range of social conditions that must have existed in order to account for the patternings in the archaeological record of the Ohio Hopewell episode as we currently know them. These empirical data—in the form of monumental earthworks, mounds, their mortuary content, complex features, and artifactual assemblages—were not self-generated. They were generated by real social groups producing and using them as the symbolic pragmatic media and context of the activities that realized their raison d'être. What kinds of groups must these have been? I have proposed characterizing them as autonomous world renewal ecclesiastic-communal cult sodalities integrated into a complex system of mutualistic heterarchies, as postulated under the Ohio Hopewell Cult Sodality Heterarchy System model. I have also proposed characterizing the primary social mechanisms that were responsible for these data as a complex mortuary *chaîne opératoire* process piggybacked on a system of sacred games *tournée*s that promoted intersodality competition that simultaneously enhanced the sacred powers immanent in the deceased. This chapter will be dedicated to answering this question.

I first turn to the same set of sites that the Tripartite Ceremonial Alliance model interpreted, these being the paired sites of Hopewell and Frankfort in the North Fork valley of the Paint Creek drainage, Seip and Baum of the central and lower Paint Creek, and Liberty Works and Works East of the Paint Creek–Scioto juncture. As noted earlier, this model treats these six as constituting three autonomous local symbolic communities in an alliance and it claims the Hopewell site was the civic-ceremonial center of the wealthiest and largest of these three local symbolic communities. In contrast, under the Ohio Hopewell Cult Sodality Heterarchy System model, I consider the Hopewell site and the Frankfort site, the latter postulated as being occupied after the former was abandoned, to be the easternmost locales of a major third-order world renewal cult heterarchy that had its roots in the Little Miami Valley and, possibly, in parts of the Great Miami Valley (although this region may have embodied a separate dispersed third-order cult sodality heterarchy). In the previous chapter, I termed it the dispersed third-order Fort Ancient–Turner–Hopewell cult sodality heterarchy. The Hopewell site, therefore, was the collective responsibility of this heterarchy and either it was established by the Little Miami Valley heterarchies founding it directly or, alternatively, it is possible that the component affiliates of this heterarchy initially franchised the ritual usufruct to possibly a first-order cult sodality heterarchy in the North Fork of the Paint Creek that enabled it to construct the C-Form/SL-Profile embankment earthwork and, in cooperation with its western allies, the latter heterarchy built the Hopewell site. Either is possible, particularly since through the mechanism of alliance a cult sodality heterarchy can and usually did transcend its local region.

In any case, the Hopewell site became a conduit through which the Fort Ancient–Turner–Hopewell heterarchy could both franchise and be franchised of the different ritual usufructs that came to constitute the repertoire of world renewal rituals for which they were responsible to perform. The original goal was likely to franchise their ideological strategy of world renewal ritual as expressed in the version of the Sacred Dual motif particular to the Miami Fort tradition, what I have called the Sacred Dual C-Form/T-Form motif, the equivalent of the Sacred Dual C-R motif. The term "T-Form" is an acronym I coined for "topographical form" and this form of earthwork is often referred to as the "fortification" or ridge-top earthwork. Fort Ancient (figure 1.1) is the best known example. However, there are many others primarily but not exclusively in the southwestern region of Ohio. I discussed the C-Form briefly in the previous chapter. It is an embankment earthwork feature that has tended to be assigned sometimes to the "geometrical" and sometimes to the "fortification" types. However, I maintain that it constitutes a separate type. It is usually located on an upper terrace overlooking a valley bottom. It consists of a single embankment in the form of a large C with the ends of the embankment terminating at the terrace edge. Typically it is associated with an external "borrow" ditch. I have described this as the C-Form/SL-Profile embankment earthwork. The main embankment feature of the Hopewell site displays this classic C-Form/SL-Profile (figure 3.7). The Sacred Dual C-Form/T-Form motif is prevalent in the southwestern sector of Ohio, the Great and Little Miami Valleys. However, there are examples of both earthwork types in the central Scioto and the upper Muskingum regions (see Byers 2004, 1–62, for a comprehensive description and analysis).

It is likely that the attraction of the North Fork that promoted the establishment of the Hopewell site as an easternmost expression of the Little Miami heterarchies stemmed from its nearness to the emerging Mound City heterarchy. This central Scioto region was probably the origin of much of the Ohio Hopewell assemblage (Greber 1991, 18–21), particularly what I have referred to as the custodial regalia of copper plates, copper axes, copper headdresses, and possibly trophy skulls (Byers 2004, 336–42)—as well as other well-known artifact categories, such as the use of Flint Ridge chert for bladelet production, along with the range of rituals that these bladelets mediated. I also suspect that even the right to produce and use the well-known Hopewell platform pipe, or at least certain styles, would be among the ritual usufructs transferred by the Mound City heterarchy, and, if I am right that this pipe and its complex was part of the sacred game itself, then the custodial copyright governing the producing and using of the pipe was part of the ritual usufruct of the postulated sacred spear game itself.

Indeed, I have argued that it was likely the interaction between the central Scioto heterarchy based in the Mound City area and the Hopewell site as the representative of the third-order heterarchy based in the Little Miami Valley of southwestern Ohio that generated the dynamism that promoted the activity processes that constituted the Ohio Hopewell episode (Byers 2004, 518–20). Initially, the Mound City/Hopeton heterarchy focused on renewal lodge construction while continuing to use its Adena-based embankment earthwork tradition of building Sacred Circles (figures 10.2 and 10.3). However, it quickly incorporated the C-Form mode from the Hopewell site by building a classic C-Form/SL-Profile embankment earthwork, the Cedar Bank Works (figure 11.1), on the east bank of the Scioto River and facing the renewal lodges being built and used on the west bank, as well as building a modified or, as I have termed it, a constrained C-Form embankment earthwork immediately to the southwest of these renewal lodges on the west bank. This is termed the Shriver Works (figure 11.2). Building embankment earthworks displaying the exterior ditch attribute would be a major ritual commitment and, of course, building and using such a material component entailed franchising the ritual usufruct from the cult sodality heterarchy responsible for the Hopewell site. The reciprocation process between the Little Miami heterarchy as represented locally at the Hopewell site and the Mound City heterarchy would quickly develop. The large deposit of Wyandotte chert disks at the Hopewell site, over 8,000 individual disk-shaped blanks generated by multiple small deposits of several blanks each, suggests that even at this initial stage of Hopewell–Mound City interaction, the ritual franchising of the Wyandotte chert ritual usufruct may have occurred. This chert-mediated ritual was likely quite quickly transferred to Newark, although possibly via a

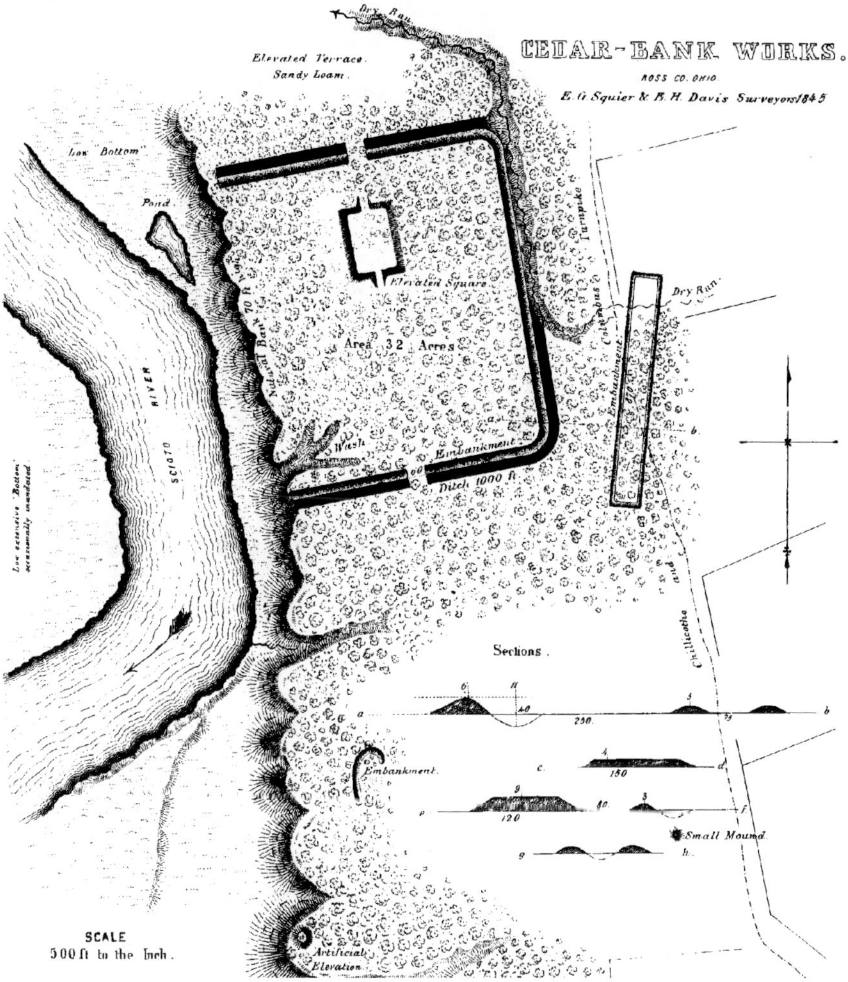

FIGURE 11.1
Cedar Bank Works
Source: Squier and Davis 1848, plate XVIII.

more direct route connecting the upper Great and Little Miami drainages to Newark in the upper Muskingum drainage, thereby marking its introduction into the upper Licking Valley and the Murphy site quite early in the Ohio Hopewell episode. It is not accidental, therefore, that the Granville site, a constrained C-Form/SL-Profile embankment earthwork (figure 10.1), is only 700 m west of the Murphy Tract.

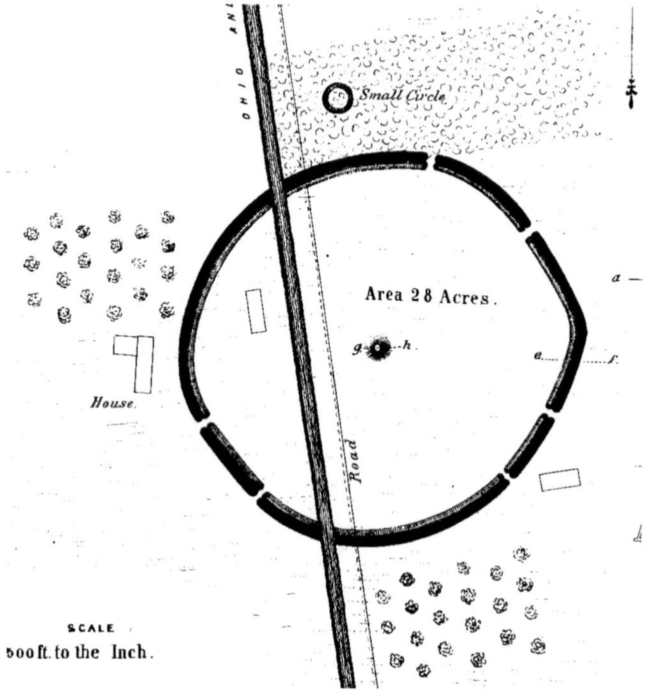

FIGURE 11.2
Shriver Works
Source: Squier and Davis 1848, from plate XIX.

Of course, I will present empirical data in support of these assertions later. For now, however, I maintain that while the Hopewell site certainly was established early in the episode, it did not form an alliance with Mound City. The two cult sodality heterarchies that these sites represented and in which they were major participants likely maintained an arm's-length relation characteristic of mutualistic heterarchies that are regionally distinct but are at the same time interdependent. As I noted in the previous chapter, the Seip and Liberty Works sites, as I have construed them, are simply among the later "descendants" of the Mound City/Hopeton heterarchy and this historical development is marked in the Scioto Valley by the emergence of the expression of the Sacred Dual C-R motif, namely, the Paint Creek C-R motif and the High Bank C-R motif. In my view, it is very germane, therefore, that the two primary components of the C-R motif, the rectilinear and the circle, are found directly associated with but *added to* the C-Form/SL-Profile embankment of the Hopewell site. I have interpreted this addition as occurring sometime after the construction of Seip and Liberty Works and, given that the Hopewell site C-R additions are "miniature" circle and square versions of the C-R components of a full-scale Paint Creek C-R configuration, I have suggested that their being constructed was the result of an expedient decision by the Fort Ancient–Turner–Hopewell heterarchy that was thought necessary to sustain the important relations with the emerging Chillicothe-Newark heterarchy (2004, 546–47). Hence, the latter heterarchy, probably at this time consisting of Seip and Liberty Works (as well as Newark and possibly Portsmouth, as I discuss later), would have franchised the ritual usufruct of the Paint Creek C-R motif to the neighboring Hopewell site. Subsequently, when the Fort Ancient–Turner–Hopewell cult sodality heterarchy abandoned the Hopewell site on the North Fork, the affiliation moved upstream and built the Frankfort site. The fact that the latter was a full-fledged Paint Creek C-R motif site suggests that by this time the heterarchy had fully recognized the felicity of this form and the ritual it mediated.

That is, Seip and Liberty Works constituted two of the earthworks of the third-order Mound City/Hopeton heterarchy, although at this time the Mound City/Hopeton complex, as such, was probably abandoned; and these two were affiliated possibly with the Newark heterarchy to constitute another third-order heterarchy.[1] As I noted earlier, to mark the nature of the relation between these two major third-order heterarchies, I will speak of the spatial zone incorporating the Hopewell site and the Mound City/Hopeton complex as the North Fork–Paint Creek interface and this interface continued to be respected when the Mound City/Hopeton complex was abandoned and replaced by the Liberty Works/Seip/High Bank complex of sites. Hence, this interface would have manifested an arm's-length relation existing between these two major third-order heterarchy networks and probably most of the exchange between them would have occurred in the most important of the embankment earthworks at any given time, for example, Mound City/Hopeton and Hopewell in the early period of interaction and the Hopewell site and the Liberty Works/Seip/High Bank sites in the middle period; and when the Hopewell site was probably "decommissioned" in the later period and the cult sodality moved to Frankfort, these two third-order heterarchies continued their interaction. Similarly, Seip built Baum and Liberty Works built Works East, each site being the anticipated new locale of these two second-order heterarchies, respectively. I have argued, however, that these two heterarchies went into crisis and experienced a rapid disaffiliation and this would not leave Frankfort and its Miami Valley–based third-order heterarchy untouched. In fact, I suspect that the total system of Ohio Hopewell heterarchies rapidly dissolved as the cult sodalities disaffiliated and thereby dissolved these heterarchies and the Ohio Hopewell episode fairly abruptly terminated as the total region shifted into the integrated settlement articulation modal posture marking the emergence of what is generally termed the Late Woodland period.

Besides the contrast between the two versions of the Ohio Hopewell Sacred Dual Motif, namely, the Sacred Dual C-Form/T-Form motif and the Sacred Dual Paint Creek/High Bank C-R motif, the main empirical data that suggest to me that these sets of sites constituting the dispersed third-order Fort Ancient–Turner–Hopewell and Chillicothe-Newark heterarchies stood in this arm's-length relation was the radical differences in the mortuary programs of the Hopewell site, on the one hand, and of the Seip and Liberty Works sites, on the other. I do not have to do an exhaustive description of these sites since the summary description I made in my earlier critical analysis of the Tripartite Ceremonial Alliance model should be sufficient. The main difference I noted then was that the mortuary program of the Hopewell site had a very low incidence of cremation and, in contrast, a high incidence of extended burials (2004, 370–71). In contrast, extended burials were almost absent at Seip and Liberty Works, with the exception of a few off-floor burials that were placed on ancillary earth platforms or, more often, on the surface of the mantles that were used to build the mounds. At Hopewell, many of the extended burials were placed in log cribs built on the floors of the mortuary structures and most of these log cribs, in fact, were built with vaulted roofs so that each constituted a type of crypt. While log cribs containing mortuary deposits were also built on the floors of the Seip and Liberty Works Renewal Lodges, apparently they did not have any vaulted roofing. That is, these were open log cribs covered with puddled clay and the cremations were not performed in these cribs but were performed elsewhere and deposited in the cribs, usually two or more in a crib. Then, as I described earlier, the mortuary ritual would be terminated by one of two rites, either the split-log rite or, alternatively, the fire-clay rite. In both cases, the log crib with its mortuary deposit would be covered with earth forming the primary mound. At the Edwin Harness Renewal Lodge, only the fire-clay terminal ritual was performed. At the Seip-Pricer Renewal Lodge, only the spilt-log terminal ritual was performed. At the Seip-Conjoined Renewal Lodge, the split-log terminal rite was exclusively performed in the large rectilinear mortuary space and in ten of the cribs in the smaller rectilinear space, while the fire-clay rite was used for the other nine in this latter space.

As I noted earlier, Carr does not comment on the different split-log and fire-clay terminal rituals of the cremations at Seip and Liberty Works. But he does recognize the prevalence of extended burials over cremated burials at Hopewell and the inverse at Seip and Liberty Works. He explains it in funerary terms claiming the cremated and extended burials manifested different degrees of prestige and wealth with the extended burials marking greater prestige than the cremated burials. He argues that this must be the case because of the greater wealth on the average found with the extended deceased at Hopewell compared to similar burial goods associated with cremated deceased at Seip and Liberty Works. However, this is not convincing since, in fact, in terms of actual wealth objects, the same range was found in association with the burials at both sites. And even if there was a greater proportion of wealth items in association with some extended deceased at Hopewell, there were a number of deceased at the other two sites that probably had an equal range and the same or even more numerous such items than at the Hopewell site. Therefore, they ought to have been extended in burial, and yet they were cremated.

Since almost the same range of artifact categories was used at the Hopewell, Seip, and Liberty Works sites and certainly, for most burial deposits containing one or two individuals, the same proportional quantitative variation of such material was deposited (I will set aside for the moment the several large deposits of copper plates and celts at Hopewell and Seip), I have argued that the difference in extended and cremated burials was unrelated to social standing at the time of death, the latter principle being grounded on the universal generalization used under the funerary paradigm in order to explain such variation. Rather, it was very much related to differential mortuary ideological strategies. The mortuary *chaîne opératoire* is the unfolding product of the mortuary ideological strategy as a sequence of rituals, each having a different ritual action quality. The purpose, as I have argued, was world renewal; its methods and outcomes when their behaviors were performed felicitously constitute the material conditions that fulfill and satisfy the collective mortuary intentions that the group exercised in acting. The representational contents of these collective mortuary intentions consist of the rules and protocols that specify what form the collective behaviors and their material forms and outcomes must manifest to count as the intended ritual activity and, thereby, ensure that their primary goals were achieved, namely, world renewal goals and fulfilling their sacred duties. Since I have postulated that the burials were both the media and outcome of world renewal rituals that were themselves characterized in a major manner as being sacred games, this large number of extended compared to cremated burials at the Hopewell site simply means that the responsible groups either had a more varied range of world renewal ritual usufruct copyrights than did those at Seip and Liberty Works, or else, the mortuary program at the Hopewell site was only partly realized there. In my view, the latter was the case. That is, the Hopewell site mediated only a portion of the total mortuary *chaîne opératoire.* The rest of the process was performed and terminated elsewhere. Another way of putting this is to suggest that the terminal outcome of some of the sacred games at the Hopewell site generated an allocation of the deceased that served to mediate the performance of another round of sacred, mortuary-mediated games at another cult sodality heterarchy locale. Alternatively, the difference in the mortuary features, in the case of the Hopewell site, the individual vaulted crypts compared to the collective renewal lodges at Seip and Liberty Works, the upper level of which probably served the same purpose as the crypts at the Hopewell site, resulted in generating these differential extended-to-cremated burial outcomes. I suspect that both these reasons operated.

I have argued that the mortuary crypts on the floor of Mound 25 of the Hopewell site served as laying-in period facilities. The deceased were placed in these while being used as the media of an extensive sequence of rites (Byers 2004, 370–406; also Mound 23 had mortuary crypts). This laying-in period would entail a series of spirit accumulation and spirit-release rituals in which the deceased were probably used as the major but not exclusive symbolic pragmatic media. While the free soul may have already been released during funerary-like rites in the clan habitation locale, it could still be recalled by his or her companions when further mortuary rites were performed, a practice that is known to have been performed by a number of traditional Native North American peoples. I suggested earlier that following the clan-based mortuary rites, the deceased would be carried in procession by his or her age-set companions to their ecclesiastic-communal cult sodality ceremonial nodal locale and, following further rites, from there to the first-order heterarchy earthwork. Even here there was likely a laying-in period, possibly using an open-air scaffold during which the companions would possibly transfer the spirit name of the deceased as used in the context of his or her sodality context to another member or else return it to the custodian of names for the sodality, who would subsequently use it to initiate a companion into the position now vacated by the deceased member. This might particularly be the case if the deceased had achieved some peer group leadership standing as manifested by a copper plate or some other custodial regalia item that served as one of the symbolic pragmatic warrants of the group's major ritual performances. I have argued that these custodial regalia were, in fact, recognized as autonomous agents in their own right, representing and presencing the action-constitutive powers of their sacred sources. Therefore, it is reasonable to assume that these items were named, that is, they had spirit names, and the custodian would take on this name as his or her source of action-constitutive powers. If such were the case, with the death of a custodian of one of these sacred regalia items, another companion may have been selected by his or her peers to occupy the leadership position and this would mean having the spirit name of their deceased companion's custodial regalia item transferred to him or her, who would then be the new peer group leader. This transfer ceremony could be characterized as a conveyancing ritual whereby the transfer of usufruct powers and responsibilities from the deceased companion to the living replacement companion was effected. This also would likely mean that a new copper plate would need to be commissioned and made and, at the appropriate time, the spirit name of the old sacred copper plate would be transferred to the new one and the latter would then count as endowing the selected leader of the age-set as the new custodian. However, until the newly commissioned plate was completed, the conveyancing ceremony would be postponed and, in the meantime, the original plate in its sacred bundle would likely accompany the deceased to the next stage.

As noted above, this would require her or his age-set to bear the deceased companion in procession from the first-order to the appropriate second-order or even third-order heterarchy locale. Since I have already focused on the Hopewell site, I will set the following scenario there, the point being that I postulate that the Hopewell site was a major locale where this conveyancing event regularly was undertaken. Here the deceased, wrapped in the appropriate shroud and accompanied by various personal items (e.g., earspools, necklaces, and so on), as well as his or her sacred copper plate or copper celt bundle, would be placed in one of the available vaulted crypts and further and very important laying-in rites would be performed (Byers 2006c, 131–32). Sometime later, when a large gathering of cult sodalities occurred at the Hopewell site to perform sacred games as part of the world renewal cycle, the deceased in the laying-in crypts would be recruited as part of the process. As noted earlier, the sacred games called for waging of valuables and winners would usually contribute the artifacts they won from the losers, for example, copper earspools or pearl necklaces, as sacrificial gifts to their deceased "laying-in period" companions, thereby transferring to these deceased the energies stored in the artifacts as a result of the game playing. Also, if the new copper plate or celt was completed, then this would be the opportunity for his or her companions to gather around the crypt to complete the transfer of the sacred name of the old copper plate or celt accompanying the deceased to the new copper plate or celt bundle that would serve as its replacement as the symbolic pragmatic warrant of the new age-set peer leader. As I noted above, I postulate that this spirit name may have also been the name of the sodality leadership position that the deceased had occupied in virtue of being the custodian of the copper plate or celt bundle and the ritual usufruct it mediated. This rite of conveyance, then, would count as the final transfer of the custodial ritual to the deceased's living companion and the latter companion became the deceased's age-set "namesake." Such a ritual also would probably require the summoning of the deceased's free soul from the land of the Dead in order to approve and warrant the transfer. At this time, when the free soul of the deceased was presenced in the event, he or she might be given more mourning gifts, sets of copper earspools, for example, or a necklace of bear's teeth, and this giving would be performed by placing them with the body. The spiritual essence of the gift placed on the body would then be transferred to the free soul and he or she would be thanked and asked to return back to the land of the Dead, and so on. Therefore, the end of this ritual would see the constitution of a new copper plate or copper celt sacred bundle and the decommissioning of the old one. The latter would be retained with the body of the former custodian until the end of the laying-in period. In fact, the conveyancing rite may have been used to mark the imminent end of the laying-in period and the deceased and his associated artifacts would be subjected to a further ritual process, which I review shortly.

However, this only accounts for those mortuary deposits at Hopewell that have several copper earspools, necklaces, and only one copper plate or one copper celt, and so on. There are a good number of extended burials that, while also accompanied by several pairs of earspools, sets of bead, pearl, or animal teeth necklaces, and so on, are also accompanied by two or more copper plates or two or more copper celts (a similar pattern occurred at Seip and Liberty Works). If these two artifact categories are among the custodial regalia, and if each deceased who is accompanied by one of them is so because he or she was the custodian at the time of death, then why would more than one of the same category of custodial regalia be present? With regard to the several copper plates with one deceased, these were typically placed at different positions on or under the body. For example, one plate might be on the chest, but another might be under the head, another under the feet, and so on. As critical symbolic pragmatic warranting media of the rituals the users performed, it is possible that each item of the same regalia category (e.g., two or three copper plates) was a warrant of a different ritual usufruct that the deceased as custodian had accumulated during her or his sodality career. An alternative possibility is to return to the notion that the deceased associated with custodial regalia had originally received the plate or celt by means of either a conveyancing or a franchising ritual event. It will be remembered that conveyancing is an absolute transfer of a ritual usufruct from the current custodian to the new custodian. The custodian doing the transfer extinguishes his or her own ritual usufruct rights and I suspect that most transfers over the body of the deceased would entail conveyancing. As I noted earlier, franchising is a form of transfer by which the franchiser transfers rights in a given ritual usufruct to a new recipient while retaining his or her own rights to the ritual usufruct, including the sacred bundle that embodies it. In the former or conveyancing case, therefore, the transfer occurs once, as noted above usually from a peer leader of a senior age-set to the new peer leader of the receiving junior age-set, or in the case of death, from the dead custodian to her or his replacement in the same age-set. In the franchising case, the transfer is carried out by social equals so that the peer leader of an age-set having a custodial ritual usufruct can transfer the rights to perform this ritual to the peer leader of another cult sodality having the same or equivalent seniority. The franchiser, therefore, retains the age-set sodality's right to the ritual usufruct and can subsequently transfer it to equivalently positioned peer leaders of other cult sodalities. This franchising transfer, I argued earlier, was a primary mechanism by which the diffusion of the Hopewellian ritual usufructs during the Ohio Middle Woodland period occurred, and, of course, this would apply to interregional Hopewellianization and the establishment and development of the Hopewell Interaction Sphere.

Now, in the case of ritual franchising, it is also possible that the franchised sacred bundle may have continued to be perceived and experienced as deriving its power through the still-living custodian who had transferred a newly commissioned copper plate bundle and its ritual usufruct powers to the new custodian of the franchisee age-set sodality. That is, while the peer leader of the franchiser age-set sodality transfers the *ritual usufruct* of that particular copper plate bundle through attaching and sharing the name soul of the original copper plate to the new copper plate, the latter is treated as only "temporary" or "contingent" and is treated as retaining an intrinsic link with the original copper plate and its custodian. When she or he dies, that sacred copper plate bundle (or bundles, if the deceased had performed a series of franchising events with different sodalities) may have been seen as then having to be returned to her or him so its spirit name could be permanently conveyed to the replacement copper plate bundle (or bundles) that the franchisee(s) who initially received the plate(s) would commission just so that she, he, or they would be able to both return the plate(s) constituting the franchise transfer and have the sacred name of that plate conveyed finally to the replacement plate(s). Hence, this rite by which a ritual usufruct franchise was transformed into a ritual usufruct conveyance would also involve two warranting items, the plate or celt that was used for the original franchising rite and the new plate or celt that would receive the spirit name permanently, thereby completing the original franchising event as a conveyancing ritual. In either case, the same ritual of spirit-name transfer would occur as described above. That is, each of the regalia items being returned for burial with the deceased would have its spirit name formally and finally transferred to the newly produced replacement(s). Hence, at the end of the ceremony, there would be a new set of same-name copper plates or copper celts that would be carried away by those who had attended the spirit-name transfer ritual held in or beside the laying-in period crypt and there would be the set of old franchising copper plates or celts and these sets would be positioned at different parts of the body of the deceased, on the forehead, under the back, on the chest, according to some code that defined the proper position of each plate in the franchising history of the ritual usufruct that this deceased had undertaken.

In sum, a singular deposit of one of these items indicates that the deceased had originally been the recipient in a conveyancing ritual; multiple items of the same type would indicate that the deceased, who in his or her capacity as the recipient of a conveyancing ritual of his or her own copper, had subsequently acted on behalf of his or her cult sodality to perform a series of franchising of this custodial ritual usufruct to other cult sodalities. These were returned to the deceased who was the original custodian; and the spirit name of his or her own sacred copper or celt bundle was formally and permanently transferred to the specially produced replacements. Hence, the deceased has both the copper that he or she was originally conveyed when installed as peer leader and the coppers he or she subsequently franchised deposited with him or her, one for each prior franchising event, thereby generating this accumulation of several of a given category.

Now I do not see these two explanations as mutually exclusive. That is, in some cases, it may be that the deceased with two or three copper plates located at different parts of the body had accumulated the custodianship of these plates through conveyancing different rituals over time as his or her age-set was promoted up the enabling hierarchy of the cult sodality, and each was used to mediate the ritual for which it served as the warrant. In other cases, they may have been the result of the same ritual usufruct being franchised by this deceased to other cult sodalities with the custodians of these franchised rituals returning the original plates or coppers that they had received and presenting replacements in order to have their spirit names permanently transferred, or conveyed. Further research will be required to verify this possibility. For example, it might be that if two or more copper plates are found in the same location, for example, on the chest, this might be a clear indicator of the multiple franchising of the same ritual usufruct. However, if two or more copper plates are found in different locations, one on the chest and one under the hips, then this could indicate that the same individual had accumulated at least two copper plate ritual usufructs of different natures.

However, the explanation of the multiple deposits is still not complete. This is because there are several very large deposits of copper plates and copper celts, what I will call the megadeposits, as well as other regalia that make the above multiple deposits look puny. Analyzing and explaining these requires postulating another step in this mortuary process and I will develop the latter shortly.

As noted above, probably shortly following this rite of transfer by which the spirit name of the sacred custodial regalia ritual bundle(s) was(were) conveyed to the new item(s), the laying-in period of the individual deceased would be terminated. The total range of materials deposited would be sorted out according to the type of burial categories they represented, as I discuss below (Byers 2006c, 132–40). Then the deceased might be given final cremation and buried, either in the renewal lodge or in his or her clan CBL (collective burial locale), this latter rite transferring the rest of the living souls to the various recipient gods of the cosmos. However, as noted above, while cremation certainly was one terminal trajectory at the Hopewell site, given the limited number of cremated burials, it was not as common as at Seip and Liberty Works. This suggests that, with the termination of the laying-in period and its associated sequence of rituals at the Hopewell site, the deceased were normally removed and taken in procession possibly back to their second-order or even first-order heterarchies to be given further, in some cases, final mortuary rites. Again, I discuss this possibility in more detail below. In any case, by being removed from the vaulted laying-in crypt, possibly as a result of a sacred game in which the winners were endowed with soul keeper responsibility for this body—or the bones if advance decay had occurred by this time—this crypt feature would have been freed up to be used to mediate the laying-in period of another deceased. Therefore, I postulate that many deceased could have been and likely were cycled through each crypt during its usage history, suggesting that the "stray" items found in these crypts were the result of systematic reuse. This means that at any given time, many of the crypts would be filled, some would be empty and, of course, since "natural" death is not something that can be scheduled, the deceased across the crypts could be at different stages of the laying-in period process. Also, since bodies were removed and replaced by new deceased, for the most part the Hopewell site was not the scene of the completion of the individual mortuary processes.

In principle, this cycling processual use of the crypts could continue indefinitely. But I postulate that it was abruptly terminated and it is this termination that generated the states in which the "final burials" were found. That is, rather than "winding down" the process by not reusing the individual crypts as each was emptied at the end of the laying-in rites for each deceased, all the deceased in the crypts were abruptly "frozen" in place, no matter at what stage they were in their individual laying-in periods (Byers 2004, chapter 16; 2006c). This rather sudden abandonment would require some ritual performances that would not be part of the regular mortuary *chaîne opératoire* process. Therefore, we could anticipate outstanding deposits of materials that, while certainly clearly part of the range already manifested in the laying-in crypts, would be unique in some sense. Indeed, I postulate that this truncation event is the reason that we find several megadeposits of such custodial regalia as copper celts and plates, along with other distinctive copper symbols. These were the accumulated custodial regalia of prior deceased that had been removed in the normal course following the termination of their laying-in rites and were curated, as I discuss shortly. These accumulated and curated regalia came to form the copper megadeposits.

In fact, I have postulated that there were probably two truncations or abandonment events, one marking the abandonment of the mortuary complex on the floor of Mound 25, along with the mortuary complexes on the floors under the lesser mounds that were associated with the mortuary process occurring in the main Mound 25 complex, and possibly a generation or more later, another similar truncation event froze the mortuary process on the floor of the Mound 23 complex and on the floors of the other lesser mounds associated with the complex on the floor of Mound 23. This means that the mortuary contents of the vaulted crypts are in a sense unfinished individual mortuary trajectories. Another way of putting this would be to say that their individual postmortem sacrificial processes were transformed en masse into a collective terminal rite as the final offering to the cosmos of the spiritual contents of the total mortuary complex. Therefore, the destruction of the mortuary complex and the construction of Mound 25 over it constituted the terminal steps of a massive world renewal ritual event and this event was likely part of constituting a major promotion cycle of the many cult sodalities that were constituent components of the third-order heterarchy in which the Hopewell site played such an important part. The newly promoted sodality components would immediately build a second mortuary complex as the likely replacement for the complex under Mound 25, this being the new prepared floor and building that came to be under Mound 23, and in its turn, possibly a generation or so later, it was also likely subjected to a replay of the truncation event that generated Mound 25 when this mortuary complex was abandoned. The second truncation event also likely marked the abandonment of the Hopewell site and its replacement with the building and occupying of Frankfort, as I noted earlier.[2]

I have demonstrated the validity of this claim of truncation of the laying-in process by hypothetically reconstructing that part of the mortuary *chaîne opératoire* process performed at the Hopewell site, particularly focusing on the artifactual patterning found in the various deposits of this site (Byers 2006c, 132–40). It must be remembered that according to the Sacred Games *Tournée* model, the mortuary complex of the Hopewell site was itself an important context of the total set of sacred games that served as the most dynamic action component of the postmortem sacrificial world renewal mortuary *chaîne opératoire* process. Hence, the accumulated buildup of mortuary artifacts during the laying-in period would be largely the result of winners and losers transferring the highly spiritually enlivened artifacts that they had worn to mediate their game activities as sacrifices to accompany the release of the living souls of the associated deceased, and so on. This mortuary process—involving bearing the deceased in sacred procession to the Hopewell site, installing them in the crypts, adding mortuary artifacts, removing the deceased and their associated artifacts, sorting these, and so on—would be part of the sacred games and the total would be a complex unfolding of incremental rituals.

I have postulated the ongoing active addition and accumulation of four categories of artifactual items with the deceased during this laying-in period: the personalty of the deceased, these being his or her personal artifacts at the time of death; the mourning gifts, the latter being presented by companions and kin to honor the deceased, in many cases resulting from the outcome of waging on one or another of the sacred games that the companions would play; the custodial regalia, such as copper plates, trophy skulls, copper pan flutes, copper headdresses, and copper celts, as described above; and a fourth category I termed the laying-in shroud and its associated decorative components, if any. The latter would be some type of covering, possibly made from a woven textile or animal fur, and these shrouds could range from being quite elaborately decorated to being rather plain. It is also possible that these shrouds would be changed at some time to mark a stage in the laying-in process. With the termination of the laying-in period rites and the complex of parallel sacred games, the deceased would be removed and transferred to the next and possibly final series of rites to occur at Hopewell for these deceased. These would probably occur on the floors of the lesser mounds in the complex. Some of these, following further processing, would be redeposited on small, specially prepared areas of the main complex. However, the termination of this post-laying-in ritual period may not have, and for the Hopewell site, in most cases did not lead to burial at this site. As I noted above, the deceased that were found in Mounds 23 and 25, and the lesser mounds, were for the most part the result of unique truncation rites. Normally, therefore, following the laying-in period, the deceased would be removed from the Hopewell site, probably without any associated artifacts, as I noted above and discuss in more detail shortly.

Why would they be removed from the Hopewell site without any associated artifacts? I have argued that the actual rite of removal of the body from the laying-in crypt would lead to the post-laying-in period rite. This would involve sorting out the four artifact categories and storing these at the site. I have argued that the mourning gifts and the laying-in shrouds would be removed from the bodies and curated for planned use during the (future) truncation ritual event. Only the personalty items, such as bead and pearl necklaces, copper earspools, platform pipes, personal dress, and the like, as well as any custodial regalia, would accompany the deceased during the next stage of post-laying-in period rites at the Hopewell site, which probably occurred on the floors of auxiliary renewal lodges, those now covered by the lesser mounds. The regalia items, at this stage, would have been "decommissioned," since their spirit names would have been transferred to the replacement regalia items during the laying-in period and, indeed, this transfer may have marked the end of the laying-in period. However, these regalia would still be required to be buried since, while the spirit names were transferred, the regalia were themselves still potent icons of the powers of the cosmos and these powers would need to be returned to the source powers from which they were derived. The termination of the post-laying-in period would involve removing *all* the personalty items and custodial regalia, if any, and the deceased would probably be wrapped in a new shroud and prepared for being returned by his or her age-set companions to his or her second-order cult sodality heterarchy locale. In effect, the deceased was left "naked," except for a second simple shroud, and all their "wealth" was accumulated and curated to serve as media of the complex set of rites that constituted the truncation event, as I discuss below.

In this regard, it is important to note that the Hopewell site had three major contexts of artifact deposits: deposits associated with the deceased on the floors of the major mortuary complexes, for example, the floors of the Mound 25 and 23 complexes; the mass of artifacts making up the several burnt deposits (Shetrone Mound 17 and Mound 25); and those artifacts associated with the deceased buried on the floors of lesser mounds (there was a fourth unique megadeposit called the Great Copper Deposit that I discuss later). As noted above, the burials in the laying-in period crypts would have been the deceased who had their processing truncated by the abandonment of the complex. However, the cremated burials on the floor of the complex but not in a crypt would likely have been terminal burials. In overall numbers these would represent a very small proportion of all the deceased processed through the Hopewell site. I postulated that those on the floors of the lesser mounds had probably been removed from the crypts and were in midstage of being given post-laying-in period rites when the truncation event occurred. Therefore, their processing was also "frozen." Finally, I postulated that the burnt offering deposits were likely the mass remains of the curated burial shrouds, the personalty, and the mourning gifts of the multiple prior deceased who had been subjected to the complete process at the Hopewell site, as noted above, and then removed to their source cult sodality site. Of course, this means that by the time they were removed from the site they would likely be simply a bundle of bones without any associated artifacts. The above curated noncustodial regalia items then were used to serve as sacrificial offerings mediating collective memorial rites of the deceased as part of the truncation event. I will add here, of course, that these memorial rites would be part of the multiple sacred games that had ensured their accumulation. If I am correct, then each type of deposit should display a different mix of the four categories of artifacts, for example, the burnt deposits should display massive amounts of personalty, mourning gifts (accumulated as offerings arising from the sacred games), and the residue of laying-in shrouds, while displaying no custodial regalia, the latter having been curated and, of course, they would not be subjected to deliberate destruction. The laying-in crypt deposits should be rich in all four categories since these deceased were at different stages in their individual laying-in periods when the truncation event occurred. The lesser mound burials should have custodial regalia but be somewhat skimpy on mourning gifts and shrouds since the latter would have been removed when their laying-in periods had terminated. I carried out a comparative analysis of these three contexts and found that they conformed to my expectations, thereby reinforcing the credibility of my claim that, in fact, the mortuary pattern of Mound 25, and probably Mound 23 also, was the result of at least two truncations of the complex incremental mourning → spirit-release → world renewal *chaîne opératoire* mortuary ritual process that I have postulated under the Mourning/World Renewal Mortuary model (Byers 2004, 377–85; 402–3, tables 16.1, 16.2, 16.3; 2006c, 132–40).

What this analysis also showed is that we cannot assess the prestige or standing of the deceased in a burial, whether extended or cremated, simply on the basis of the quality and number of associated artifacts or overall postmortem treatment. This is clear since if we compare the two sets of extended custodial regalia burials under Mound 25 and under the lesser mounds, each set displaying the same range of regalia, only those under Mound 25 have a superfluity of personalty, mourning gifts, and shroud-related decorative materials while those under the lesser mounds, equally endowed with custodial regalia, have about the amount and variation of personalty items that we could expect an individual to have. If the custodial regalia items control for prestige, then this suggests that the difference in the quantity and distribution of personalty, mourning gifts, and mortuary shrouds between these two sets of custodial regalia associated burials is a consequence of the stage at which these deceased were given terminal rites. The same can be argued for the variation between cremated and extended burials. It is clear that cremation was not often performed at the Hopewell site; while, in contrast, it was pervasive at Seip and Liberty Works. However, this difference is also unrelated to differential prestige. Rather, it was a matter of timing and, more important, the low proportion of cremated to extended burials suggests that cremation was only one of several possible mortuary trajectories and probably one that was the least common at the Hopewell site. I can say this because, it must be noted, almost all of the few cremated burials were found on the Mound 25 floor. If Mound 25 was the result of truncation rituals such that most of the deceased in the laying-in crypts were "frozen" in place, then the cremations were also already in place prior to this abandonment event.

I want to stress here that cremation was only one of possibly two or three mortuary trajectories at the Hopewell site. This is clear simply by considering the shear quantity and variety of curated goods making up the contents of the Ohio Hopewell burnt deposits. There were literally thousands of shell and pearl beads, as well as hundreds of copper earspools carefully strung into hoops, and many other items. However, given the rather few extended burials (there are only 102 burials in the Mound 25 crypts, including the few cremations), the size of the burnt offerings, that is, the curated and cumulated artifacts retrieved after the laying-in periods, suggests that many other deceased had been processed at the Hopewell site but were not buried there. In some rather few cases, this phase may have terminated in cremation. In the vast majority of cases, including the custodial deceased, as I noted above, various rites would be performed and then the bodies, likely wrapped in (plain) shrouds as bone bundles, for the most part, would be returned without embellishment in procession back to their first-order or second-order cult sodality heterarchy.

This means that the removal of the deceased to another locale also involved the retention and curation of the custodial regalia at the Hopewell site. This retention was the consequence of the Hopewell site laying-in period rites being the context of the terminal conveyancing of ritual usufruct to those living agents replacing the deceased custodians. That is, the deceased with custodial regalia would have the latter removed and curated at the Hopewell site, along with the mourning gifts and the laying-in shrouds that had been removed following the laying-in period. Once the custodial regalia of these deceased had been removed, they would be treated like the other deceased and returned to their first- or second-order cult sodality for further mortuary processing.

This is a complex description and interpretation of what is undoubtedly one of the most complex mortuary-related assemblages in Native North American archaeological sites. It requires further elucidation and empirical grounding, particularly relating the custodial regalia to the copper megadeposits, which I do in the next chapter. I will then complete the grounding of this view of Ohio Hopewell in terms of third-order cult sodality heterarchies by linking the mortuary spheres of Turner, Hopewell, and Fort Ancient. With this completed, I will return to the elucidation of the range of site categories that such a complex system of world renewal ecclesiastic-communal cult sodality heterarchies would entail and show that, in fact, recent excavations and reviews of old excavations have significantly confirmed my earlier comments on the Cult Sodality Cluster model.

12

The Ohio Hopewell as Dispersed Third-Order Cult Sodality Heterarchies

Probably the most outstanding aspect of the artifactual record of the Hopewell site is the custodial regalia, primarily consisting of copper plates, copper celts and headdresses, as well as conch shells, copper earspools, copper and silver flute covers (called pan pipes), and so on. In fact, the largest known deposit of two categories of custodial regalia, copper celts and copper plates, was found positioned above and covering the log crib containing the paired Burials 260–261, which was located toward the center of the floor of the Mound 25 mortuary complex. Carr and his colleagues report on this deposition. "Ninety-four or ninety-five copper breastplates and 66 copper celts were found above the [Burials 260 and 261] skeletons, tightly fitted together, forming a rectangular area 5 × 7 feet. It is likely that this deposit was placed within the limits of and above a rectangular log-surrounded tomb, similar to the ones that Shetrone . . . had recorded for most of the burials he excavated. . . . The two skeletons may have lain partially exposed within the big tomb, after their rites of separation, and before the layer of breastplates and celts was placed down. If so, the celts and breastplates would probably constitute the remains of a rite of liminality, offered by leaders and prestigious sodality members whose roles were marked by these items" (Carr et al. 2005, 500). In fact, as they also noted, the largest known Ohio Hopewell copper celt was among the 66 celts.

Carr and his colleagues actually cite Shetrone (1926, 75–76) as the source of their claim that "ninety-four or ninety-five copper breastplates and 66 copper celts were found above the skeletons, tightly fitted together, forming a rectangular area 5 × 7 feet." They repeat these numbers in table 13.2, pp. 486–88, summarizing the major deposits. They are correct with regard to the 66 celts. However, Shetrone, who is actually quoting Moorehead (1922), reports only

23 copper plates "mostly fragmentary." Possibly Carr and his colleagues derived their extraordinary number of plates by actually analyzing the "mostly fragmentary" plates, although they do not specify this. However, Moorehead also comments on the advanced state of corrosion that this deposit suffered and specifically states there were "twenty-three copper plates, mostly fragmentary, and a great number of pieces . . ." (1922, 110). By this I take him to mean that the 23 plates were still in sufficiently good condition to count them, even though many were fragmented, and *in addition* there were many other pieces that clearly were the residue of a "great number" more. He goes on a few pages later to estimate that on the floor of Mound 25 there were "[a]t least fifty more or less perfect examples . . . and counting the many fragments, it seems probably that over a hundred were originally placed with the various burials and deposits" (1922, 119). If so, this would mean that there were 50 plates in reasonably good condition and an estimated 50 in fragmented condition. Given this proportion, then his reported 23 plates in presumably complete if poor condition, along with the many other fragments with Burials 260 and 261, might amount to no more than an additional 25 to 28, or about 48 to 50 in total as making up the copper plate component of this copper megadeposit. In contrast, Carr and his colleagues apparently calculate that the "great number" amounted to almost three times Moorehead's estimated 25 to 28, or about 72 to 73 in addition to the 23 plates that everyone seems to agree upon. It may be in this way that they come to their estimated total of 95 or so plates in this megadeposit. This would also boost Moorehead's estimate for the total set of copper plates on the floor of Mound 25 from 100 plates to about 148. In either case, this would be a substantial number and far surpasses any other known Ohio Hopewell copper plate deposit.

Of course, Carr and his colleagues have handled interpreting this mortuary deposit as a funerary rite of passage, a rite of liminality, and, therefore, they suggest that the megadeposit of copper celts and copper plates were mourning gifts added to accompany these two deceased sometime after their initial placement in the crypt. "The two skeletons [Burials 260 and 261] may have lain partially exposed within the big tomb, after their rites of separation, and before the layer of breastplates and celts was placed down." Besides highlighting the funerary treatment they make of the mortuary record, this interpretation of the megadeposit is of considerable interest in that it clearly reveals the referential perspective they have with regard to the nature of the symbolic meaning of material items. Why can I make this assessment? Note that they comment that "the celts and breastplates would probably constitute the remains of a rite of liminality, offered by leaders and prestigious sodality members whose roles were marked by these items." Presumably the givers being themselves possessors of the objects could do this because these items were used by them as merely referring to and not being constitutive of the roles they occupied as leaders. If it was otherwise, that is, if the items were used expressively as critical symbolic pragmatic devices endowing their custodians with the powers that enabled them to carry out the associated rituals, then in giving away the items as rites of liminality gifts they would also be surrendering their positions and these powers. Since this seems improbable, it must be that Carr and his colleagues are treating symbolic material items as making reference to the roles the givers occupied and, therefore, these items were not intrinsic constituents of these roles. The use of the term "marked" is revealing in this regard. To mark something, this something must preexist the act of marking itself. For example, it is to enable us to find the entity being marked; and this means the mark is used to "refer" to what already exists and, presumably, would still exist even if the mark was removed. That is, unless given a figurative twist, marking expresses the conventional sign–referent relation and, as I argued earlier, the referent, on the one hand, and the sign, on the other, are independent objects. We express this ontological distinction by the figurative use of the term *stands for*, as in the word "stands for its referent."

Under the referential perspective, since this means that there is no socially and culturally constituted intrinsic relation between the user of the material symbol and his or her social position, only a contingent "marking" relation, then there would seem to be little point to the exercise of giving "liminal" gifts. However, if there is an intrinsic relation, as this relation is characterized under the expressive symbolic pragmatic view, then an en masse gifting of this nature would eliminate the capacity of the givers to continue as leaders and, moreover, pretty well cripple the capacity of the cult sodalities to sustain their ritual activity—since under this interpretive scheme these custodial items are, in fact, the warrants of such activity. Of course, a mass extinguishing of ritual usufruct sets in this manner is not impossible; but it is certainly implausible. Therefore, when treated in symbolic pragmatic terms, it is more reasonable to interpret this megadeposit of custodial regalia of copper plates and celts as the curated decommissioned custodial regalia resulting from the multiple conveyancing rites I postulated earlier, namely, conveyancing the ritual usufruct from the deceased peer-chosen leaders to their replacements. In these terms, for every one of these items there would have been a replacement that was commissioned to be produced by those having the ritual power to do so and then endowed with the spirit name of the item it was replacing. Hence, it would have been the duty of the cult sodalities of the deceased custodians to care for these decommissioned items, still potent icons, and, under proper conditions, return them to the permanent care of the sacred powers that they represented and in whose powers therefore they participated.

Which is the more valid interpretive approach is quite important. Carr and Case use the referential view as the basis of their interpretation of the Ohio Hopewell assemblage and Carr, in particular, uses it as an important empirical support of the Tripartite Ceremonial Alliance model. He claims that the Hopewell site was the special "cemetery" for burial of the most prestigious of the deceased from the postulated three allied "symbolic communities" located in these three valley regions; and, of course, while the overall numbers and sizes of deposits of custodial regalia found on the floor of Mound 25 form the empirical base for this case, this megadeposit is specified by him as a strong confirmation of this "fact." My characterization of the Mound 25 mortuary-related custodial regalia deposits, of course, is quite different and also serves as an important empirical support for my claim of the Hopewell site as a specialized mortuary locale that, among other rites, also served for conveyancing the world renewal ritual usufruct to those taking over the responsibility and leadership from the deceased custodial leaders.

Is there a relevant body of empirical data that might be marshaled to adjudicate between these two claims? In fact, there is and it happens to be the rest of the custodial regalia found on the total floor of Mound 25 distributed across the various deceased, plus another set that I have only alluded to but will also address below. As carefully elucidated in the previous chapter, I have claimed that the custodial regalia items found in association with many of the other deceased on the floor were, in fact, the result of conveyancing rites. However, the floor mortuary deposits would have been the result of the laying-in period rites to which all the deceased—custodians of regalia or not—were treated and, therefore, each deposit represents only a particular ritual stage in the total normal mortuary *chaîne opératoire* and, in the normal course of this process, each deceased would have been removed at the termination of her or his laying-in period and, probably shortly after, a new deceased would be put in place to repeat the cycle. This means that at all times there would be a mix of some deceased with and without custodial regalia, some vaulted crypts that were empty, some that may have been a bit "tightly" filled with two or more deceased, and of course, all these could be at different stages in their laying-in periods.

I postulated in the previous chapter and demonstrated through the distribution of the artifact categories across the three major contexts of artifact deposition that the truncation event occurred and was a massive collective decommissioning of the mortuary complex itself! This "freezing" of the normal diachronic unfolding of the mortuary *chaîne opératoire* process would leave in the laying-in crypts all those deceased, both those unassociated and those associated with custodial regalia that were only partway through their individual laying-in periods. Of course, the mortuary-associated custodial regalia would be only a part of the total regalia that had passed through the process, since I have argued that with the termination of the laying-in period of each deceased, those with regalia had it removed and curated. This means that the cult sodality heterarchy would have built up a "treasury" of decommissioned custodial regalia that it was curating. As I have suggested, they would still be potent items and, clearly, these could not simply be destroyed or, for that matter, used in the burnt deposits since they directly participated in the sacred properties of the immanently sacred cosmos. Their being decommissioned would also be the reason they were withdrawn from their deceased custodians when the latter were returned to their second-order heterarchy, for example, the Turner site, after the conveyancing ritual (as I discuss more fully below). Therefore, the truncation event not only required the performance of a collective mourning rite in order to sacrifice the multiple curated mourning gifts, personalty, and laying-in shrouds accumulated from the multiple deceased over a generation or possible more, these being *action cue* items, that is, nonfocal artifacts, equally or even more importantly was the need to return the powers immanent in the curated custodial regalia to the sacred powers of the cosmos from which they were derived. Therefore, I postulate that it was this truncation event that was responsible for the ritual that was constituted by this megadeposit of copper celts and copper plates and its being carried out *by being added on top of and independent of the ritual depositing of Burials 260 and 261 constituted the closing of this very sacred mortuary complex.* Building the mound to incorporate its sacredness then proceeded, as demonstrated by an additional megadeposit of sheet copper icons that was placed on one of the mantles partway through the construction, as I discuss below.

There are several lines of evidence embedded in the custodial regalia and their distribution to support this claim. I will note first that Carr et al. make it clear in the above quotation that this megadeposit was placed over Burials 260 and 261 only after the latter two had already been in place for some time period since they specify this as a rite of liminality. This type of mortuary rite terminates a period of time during which the social "separation" of the relatives and companions of a deceased was required. They go on to note that the total deposit was made as a single event in that these multiple items were "tightly fitted together, forming a rectangular area 5 × 7 feet" and that they were "placed within the limits of and above a rectangular log-surrounded tomb." This description essentially paraphrases Moorehead's earlier comments in this regard and Moorehead's recapitulation of the discovery of the megadeposit reinforces the likelihood that the generation of these two components, *Burials 260 and 261 with their associated artifacts*, on the one hand, and the *megadeposit of copper plates and celts* placed over then, on the other, can be reasonably treated as two chronologically separate events. In this regard, Moorehead reported not only that this megadeposit on top of the burials formed a "rectangle 7 feet long and 5 feet wide" and their placement was separate from these burials, but he also specifically noted that when the earth was being removed by the horse-drawn "dragger" shovel, it "caught and turned over several of the [copper] plates, but a careful examination indicated that they were not placed in any special position, being simply put down *after* some interments below had been placed" (1922, 110, emphasis added). This was followed by his unordered list of the rest of the mortuary-related objects.

Moorehead is known to be somewhat undersystematic in his reporting and quite general in describing formal patternings of things. However, in this case, he might have had an excuse since he was describing from memory what was excavated under his direction 30 years earlier. Therefore, his description is particularly unstructured, except for the order of discovery. That is, he *first* described the megadeposit of copper, and then noted that these had been "simply put down after some interments below had been placed," that is, Burials 260 and 261. He then aggregated together the megadeposit, the skeletons, and everything else, but in a distinct order. First he described the megadeposit and its particularly careful fitting together of the plates; he then repeated himself but now gave the contents of the deposit, pointing out that "[t]he objects covering the two skeletons were as follows: Sixty-six copper celts, ranging in length from 1 1/2 to 22 1/2 inches; one stone celt, 11 inches long; twenty-three copper plates, *mostly fragmentary, and a great number of pieces.*" He then immediately added the rest of the items, presumably those *under* the copper plates and celts and directly in association with the two burials, "one very large jaw, a curious copper head-ornament, a broken shell; some very fine pearls, pearl and shell beads, and teeth; carved bones and bone fragments; effigies; meteoric iron, partly worked copper, etc.; and colored earth" (1922, 110). Several of these last items I would suggest were residue left over from laying-in periods of deceased *prior* to the terminal deposit of Burial 260 and Burial 261, particularly the "bone fragments" and "colored earth." In any case, analytically separating the burials from the copper plates and celts, which I think is the appropriate way to interpret them, the rest of the assemblage associated with the burials (less the "bone fragments" and "colored earth") is quite impressive in its own right: a stumpy-antlered copper headdress in quite good condition (apparently on the skull of Burial 260), a large jaw (presumably human), a broken (presumably) marine shell container, a large stone celt, some "very fine pearls," pearl and shell beads, as well as other materials, including meteoric iron and copper. He also notes later in his book that 30 to 35 copper anklets, bracelets, and disks were associated with these burials (1922, 122).

I suggest that the parsing of this list reflects a certain order in Moorehead's memory reinforcing the claim that the megadeposit of copper celts and plates is distinct from the rest of the artifact assemblage. This is certainly clear from his wording of the description of the headdress and the many copper bracelets, anklets, and disks; and, of course, marine shell containers were an important category of custodial regalia. When found these were usually placed beside the upper body. That is, if Burials 260 and 261 are examined minus the copper megadeposit, their overall patterning would be akin to the many other mortuary deposits associated with custodial regalia on the Mound 25 floor. In counterfactual terms, this suggests that, but for the truncation event occurring, Burials 260 and 261 would have been removed and the directly associated artifacts would have been curated with their two or three custodial regalia items separate from the rest of the artifactual assemblage as described in the above procedure. However, the truncation event did occur and, along with all the other deceased who were only partway through their individual laying-in period ritual trajectories, Burials 260 and 261 were "frozen" in the state that was subsequently revealed in excavation. The position of their crypt was toward the center of the main mortuary structure. Therefore, being conveniently placed, the space—rather than the two deceased—was probably recruited to serve as the altar by which the spiritual powers of these multiple custodial regalia items could be sacrificially returned to the cosmic sources from which they came.

As I noted above, Moorehead estimated that there were about 100 copper plates in total on the floor of Mound 25, at least 23 of which were included in the megadeposit. As I also noted, Carr and his colleagues have suggested that this was an underestimation and, presumably by carefully analyzing the fragments, they have specified 94 or 95 copper plates for this deposit. The quantitative difference is not relevant for my immediate purposes. What is relevant, however, is that the total number of copper plates deposited on the floor of Mound 25 can be divided into two groups based on condition: those in good condition and those in very poor to fragmentary condition. These two groups are pretty well congruent with the plates found in the megadeposit, on the one hand, and those found in the floor burials unassociated with this deposit, on the other, these being the "fifty more or less perfect examples" (1922, 119) to which Moorehead makes reference. He also comments on the high degree of deterioration of the 66 copper celts found with the megadeposit, and the much less degree of deterioration of copper celts with the other burials. "One would like very much to know why the heavy axes and adzes over the skeletons 260 and 261, and the thick copper plates and eagle effigies, were often badly oxidized, while the thin sheet-copper designs of the other deposits were (for the most part) well preserved" (1922, 119). That is, the copper plates and celts of the megadeposit are generally in very poor condition while apparently most of the copper plates and celts deposited with individuals distributed across the floor are in quite good condition, *including* the copper headdress found with Burial 260. Many of the latter copper plates often still had remains of their wrappings, indicating that the coppers were the central artifacts of carefully constructed bundles, probably of the same symbolic nature as sacred bundles of many historically known Native North American communities. These bundles were crucial enabling warrants that endowed their custodians with the ritual usufruct powers that constituted them as shamans or other important persons. What this suggests is that the majority of the 66 copper celts, and the majority of the copper plates, a small majority if Moorehead's estimate is accepted, and a very large majority if the estimate by Carr and his colleagues is accepted, were in very poor condition, while copper celts and plates, as well as copper headdresses, and so on, in association with individual burials were generally in much better shape than those in association with the megadeposit.

As I noted above, not only were many of the individual copper plates in good condition, the copper helped preserve the wrappings and even some of the costumes of their associated deceased. If these coppers had such preservative powers, why were so many in the megadeposit in fragments? Moorehead was puzzled by this, even though he did not resolve the puzzle. In fact, he enhanced it by commenting on the remarkable condition of "the thin sheet-copper designs of the other deposits." In this case he is referring to a second megadeposit of copper sheet custodial regalia that I will comment on below. However, given that the greatest number of badly deteriorated copper plates and celts seems to be those that made up the megadeposit over Burials 260 and 261, the very type I am suggesting were accumulated and curated, what this suggests is that copper custodial regalia, both celts and plates, were truly cared for by their living custodians and the material handling, the regular replacing of the coverings—a common practice historically known was for these to be changed with every conveyancing or franchising event—and possibly constant bodily contact ensured that the copper item itself was in good condition when the custodian died. Once it was removed at the end of the laying-in period and curated, however, it would be "stashed" with other similarly curated copper plates and celts and, while certainly given some careful storage to prevent loss, probably the total deposit would be regularly exposed to temperature and moisture variation of the seasons. These plates and celts were manufactured through annealing and hammering of native copper nuggets and this would ensure the brittling of the copper and the formation of multiple fine cracks. Thus, once no longer subject to continual care, these cracks and brittle edges would be the source of rapid deterioration by weathering relative to those plates and celts that they replaced, the latter being actively cared for and used by their custodians. While the plates and celts may have been still in moderate condition when used to constitute the final megadeposit, rather than the earthen cover protecting them it would simply ensure that deterioration would proceed much more quickly than it would for those associated with the deceased who had simply been "frozen" in place as a result of the truncation ritual itself.

To confirm this, it should be noted that there is a significant contrast between the condition of the copper celts and plates making up this megadeposit placed over Burials 260 and 261 and the "curious copper head-ornament" directly associated with Burial 260 (or possibly 261). This is actually one of the well-known copper-effigy antler headdresses, in this case displaying the "stubby" base of the antlers as they initiate regrowth. This headdress was in good condition. The coppers in the megadeposit immediately on top of the copper headdress were in poor condition. Now, if the megadeposit in fact consisted of the copper items given by colleagues of one or both of the deceased constituting Burials 260 and 261 as Carr and his colleagues argue, it certainly is strange that the headdress of thin copper sheet was in good order while the thicker copper plates and heavier copper celts were in such poor condition. After all, under the funerary view they would have been actively part of the givers' personalty until these were deposited by them on top of Burials 260 and 261 and, therefore, they should also have been in pretty well the same condition as or even in better condition than the copper headdress and the other many similar items distributed among the deceased on the floor of Mound 25, such as the 50 or so copper plates that Moorehead noted above were in good condition. Clearly, then, this suggests that many of the items making up the megadeposit had been curated possibly for many years before being deposited and that Burials 260 and 261 were, in fact, only partway through their laying-in period rituals, possibly having been initially placed only a few months before the megadeposit was placed.[1]

Strengthening this interpretation is a second megadeposit of custodial regalia artifacts in Mound 25 that I only briefly alluded to above. This deposit was not found in association with any mortuary remains on the floor under Mound 25. Rather, it may have been intended to "embrace" all of them. It is in fact probably the most impressive deposit in the total Ohio Hopewell assemblage, not in terms only of size, although in terms of bulk and weight the former megadeposit is the largest, but in terms of its formal makeup and variety. It is sometimes termed the Great Copper Deposit and consists of a large and complex number of copper sheet "cut out" items shaped as swastikas, crescents, exotic animal forms, and so on, and many with small holes drilled in them likely serving to sew them to garments. As I noted above, Moorehead was puzzled about the very good condition of these items, particularly since they were made of sheet copper that was considerably thinner than most if not all copper plates. He suggests that this deposit's being carefully wrapped in bark may be partly why it was in such good condition (1922, 119). Just as with the megadeposit of copper celts and plates, these were carefully deposited and did not display any deliberate damage (although they also displayed some deterioration). In this case, they were carefully placed on wood and enveloped top and bottom by layers of bark, an excellent form of protection. It was placed at the midpoint of Mound 25 about 4 feet above the floor surface and 16 feet below the top of the mound. "[Four] feet from the base line, were found one hundred and twenty pieces of copper . . . all laid flat, and occupying a space 3 feet long by 2 feet wide, with layers of bark above and below. There were no skeletal remains connected with the deposit nor was any altar found near it" (1922, 109). That is, the deposit was put in place after the mortuary complex on the floor of Mound 25 was abandoned and during the construction of the covering mantles and, therefore, it was unrelated to any particular mortuary deposits. I count them as another megadeposit of special custodial regalia items. Instead of being accumulated and curated during the life history of usage of the mortuary complex on the floor of Mound 25, as were the decommissioned celts and plates, they were conveyed at the death of their custodians and then used by their new custodians. I would interpret them as examples of what I have previously termed "group custodial items," these being important warrants of action that were believed to embody spiritual powers immanent in the group rather than in the natural sectors of the cosmos itself (Byers 2004, 337–38). This would explain the limited deteriorated nature of these items, in contrast to the copper plates of the megadeposit just discussed above.

To clarify this, it is necessary to briefly note that in my view there were two types of custodial regalia: (1) usufruct custodial regalia, these being the standard celts and plates and these are termed this since they are viewed as being "borrowed" from the powers of the cosmos and embody these powers; and (2), as in the above case, group custodial regalia. Group custodial regalia embody the spirit or different spiritual aspects of the group itself and, therefore, the group sustains them, passing them on from one custodian to another. This would account for their rather better material condition. That is, they were being constantly used as the relevant ritual usufruct powers were conveyed from age-set to age-set, until the final age-set of the ecclesiastic-communal cult sodalities that had preserved and used these items died. At this time these were likely buried with the cult sodalities whose spirit names they embodied. That would mean that the items making up the contents of this Great Copper Deposit would not have been curated and set aside in "dead" storage but, instead, were actively used and accumulated over 50 years (two generations, junior and senior), finally being deposited when the truncation ritual closed the floor of Mound 25, thereby honoring and transferring the spirits of these generations to the land of the Dead (Byers 2004, 337).

This means that there are two megadeposits, one that can be definitively argued as being unrelated to any particular deceased burials at all, the Great Copper Deposit, and one that, while in spatial association with Burials 260 and 261, because of the deteriorated state of many of the items can be coherently interpreted as being deposited after the mortuary rites of Burials 260 and 261 had been performed. Therefore, it is more reasonable to treat the Great Copper Deposit and the megadeposit of copper celts and plates as the sequential result of the terminal rituals constituting the truncation event rather than to argue that the latter megadeposit was part of a uniquely large set of multiple celts and plates deposited with two extended burials while the former megadeposit was a uniquely large copper accumulation that was made with no mortuary associations. Furthermore, treating the events generating the two large copper deposits, on the one hand, and the event generating Burials 260 and 261, on the other, as independent and separate rituals eliminates what is arguably the single largest mortuary anomaly in the known Ohio Hopewell assemblage; at least this would be the case if Burial 260 and Burial 261 were treated as being intrinsically associated with the megadeposit of copper celts and plates. Remove these, and instead of the two burials forming a major anomalous mortuary deposit, they become assimilated to the many other very respectable custodial regalia burials found across such major sites as Mound City, Seip, and Liberty Works.

While all this explains the great concentration of custodial regalia at Hopewell, it does not explain why there was such a greater concentration at the Hopewell site than at the nearby Seip and the slightly more distant Liberty Works sites. Added to this are several other differences between these two sets of sites, such as the absence of major burnt deposits at Seip and Liberty Works and the prevalence of cremations at these two sites compared to the prevalence of extended burials at the Hopewell site. Part of the explanation of this disparity is simply that even though all three sites were used to mediate conveyancing rites, Seip and Liberty Works would have cooperatively shared the conveyancing rites of the total mortuary *chaîne opératoire* process of their dispersed third-order cult sodality heterarchy, namely, the Chillicothe-Newark heterarchy, while the Hopewell site was the sole locale for mediating these rites, being spatially distant from but socially integrated into the main set of cult sodality locales that made up its third-order heterarchy whose most participating components were located in the Little Miami Valley. It should also be noted that the excavation history of the Edwin Harness mound is such that a great deal of its contents has been lost or unrecorded so that even important deposits such as curated custodial regalia and burnt offerings of curated shrouds and mourning/mortuary gifts could have suffered this fate. That is, much of the mortuary contents of the Edwin Harness mound may have been lost as a result of its being subjected to a series of erratic and poorly conducted and archived excavations. Finally, the absence of equivalent burnt deposits at these two sites may be the result of a rapid disaffiliation of the heterarchy.

With regard to the cremation/extended burial differentiation between Hopewell and Seip and Liberty Works, I suggest that this is related primarily to the fact that the renewal lodges of Seip and Liberty Works were two storied. Why should this make a difference with the Hopewell site? As I noted above, the Hopewell trajectory was divided into the laying-in period and the post-laying-in period. The former was carried out on the floor of Mound 25 while the latter was carried out on the floors of what I will term the auxiliary renewal lodges. These were probably the renewal lodges of the first- or second-order heterarchies that constituted the total third-order Fort Ancient–Turner–Hopewell heterarchy. Now there were some cremations carried out at the Hopewell site, as I noted earlier. However, the cremations were a minority of the mortuary deposits and most of these were deposited on prepared spaces on the floor of Mound 25. These cremated deposits probably had been given laying-in period rites as full bodies, following the normal pattern. However, their post-laying-in period treatment involved their being recruited as postmortem sacrificial media of special world renewal rites requiring cremation and subsequent deposition on the floor of Mound 25. In contrast, I have suggested that most of the deceased processed at the Hopewell site were removed from the site and forwarded back to their first-order or second-order heterarchies in the Little Miami Valley, as I describe shortly.

In any case, I would suggest that the equivalent bifurcation of laying-in period and post-laying-in period rites occurred at Seip and Liberty Works. However, the upper floor of the renewal lodge was probably used for the laying-in period rites and the lower floor for the post-laying-in period rites, the equivalent set of rites being performed on the floors of the renewal lodges under the lesser mounds at the Hopewell site. Following the latter rites, it is probable that many of these deceased—uncremated—were returned to their first-order cult sodality heterarchies and, ultimately, the majority of these to their clans for terminal burial in one of the many lesser burial mounds scattered over the valley (Seeman and Branch 2006, 113–14). However, as at the Hopewell site, some of the deceased were recruited for the post-laying-in period crematorial trajectory and were finally deposited in one of the log cribs on the floor of the renewal lodge. This is indicated by the fact that, as I discussed earlier, they would be given terminal burial rites, either the split-log or the fire-clay rite. It is also highly likely that the actual cremations would have occurred in a facility outside the renewal lodge since it is clear that the log cribs where the cremations were deposited were not themselves the place of cremation. However, since effectively all the floor burials in the great renewal lodges of Seip and Liberty were cremations, while only about one-third of the floor burials on the floor of Mound 25 were cremations, how did this disproportion of cremated deposits between the two sets come about?

The difference, I suggest, was in the manner that the truncation events at Seip and Liberty Works were carried out compared to the same type of events at the Hopewell site. That is, the design of the Seip and Liberty Works renewal lodges did present a "problem" that was not experienced at the Hopewell site since the truncation events at Seip and Liberty Works, for example, entailed burning the main renewal lodges and this would mean indiscriminately burning the deceased on the upper floor. Therefore, I postulate that they were not left in situ, as at the Hopewell site, but were removed and most were likely given terminal cremation and then deposited in the appropriate floor locale where the terminal split-log or fire-clay rites were performed. When all these were completed, the renewal lodge was "cremated" and a great mounding of strata was carried out, generating Seip-Pricer, Seip-Conjoined, and Edwin Harness. Of course, we now know that Seip-Conjoined was never given its final gravel stratum.

Hence, just as at the Hopewell site, probably the majority of the cremated deposits on the floors of the Seip and Liberty Works great renewal lodges was the result of the three truncation events recruiting those deceased only partway through their laying-in period rites on the upper floor to serve the special ritual needs of this event, namely, being cremated to serve as special postmortem sacrificial offerings to accompany the spiritual powers accumulated in the renewal lodge and directed back to the cosmos. Of course, this verges on speculation. However, I suspect that some special deviation from the normal number of cremations occurred as part of the truncation event and this would explain the rather larger number of cremations on the floors of these renewal lodges than at the Hopewell site. I postulated, therefore, that many of the multiple cremations on these floors were the result of the exceptional demands of the truncation events. This also means, however, that for most of the history of usage of the great renewal lodges at Seip and Liberty Works, most of the deceased processed were given the type of post-laying-in period treatment that I am going to outline was the case for those processed through the Hopewell site, that is, those deceased who had completed their post-laying-in period rites, and, therefore, my following description of the post-Hopewell site mortuary *chaîne opératoire* trajectory of the third-order Miami Valley cult sodality heterarchy largely applies to the third-order Chillicothe-Newark cult sodality heterarchy also—although this claim will have to look forward to future empirical research since the current mortuary data related to this latter heterarchy are unlikely sufficient to confirm it (i.e., Liberty Works, Seip, Newark, and possibly Portsmouth).

In sum, the apparently excessive wealth of the mortuary deposits at the Hopewell site and the lesser wealth of the neighboring and contemporary sites of Seip and Liberty Works dissolves these anomalies and both can be considered as largely equivalent. The only major difference is the prevalence of cremation at Seip and Liberty Works compared to extended interment at the Hopewell site and although this seems to be a real difference, as I postulated above, it may relate to the difference in the architecture of the renewal lodges in that those at Seip and Liberty Works had two vertically related mortuary spaces, on the ground and on the upper floor, while the Hopewell site had only floor spaces for their mortuary processes. These were spatially separated to accommodate the laying-in period and post-laying-in period mortuary trajectories.

THE FORT ANCIENT–TURNER–HOPEWELL MORTUARY *CHAÎNE OPÉRATOIRE* PROCESS

A striking contrast between the above central Scioto embankment earthwork sites and the equivalently sized earthworks in the Great and Little Miami Valleys is that, as described above, in terms of their Hopewellian artifact assemblages, the former were extremely rich and the latter were exceptionally impoverished. However, if the earthworks in the two drainages are treated as a form of "wealth" independently of the Hopewellian artifacts, it is clear that there was no disparity of labor and commitment to the Ohio Hopewellian "mission." As Greber has recently pointed out, "The Great Miami Valley . . . contains more walls than remarkable artifacts. The Muskingum contains a remarkable suite of walls. Local communities used economic and social resources that produced different types of cultural remains reflecting a mosaic of selective participation in the Hopewellian worldview." She continued by asking "in sharing this [Hopewellian] view, what was the 'catchment area' for the labor that constructed Newark, Portsmouth, and the Hopewell site? Concomitantly, who provided the thousands of artifacts deposited at Hopewell and the hundreds at Turner?" (2006, 88). Although she comments on the superfluity of embankment earthworks in the Great Miami Valley compared to the artifacts, the same assessment could be extended to the Little Miami (figure 12.1). In fact, one of the largest single embankment earthwork sites in Ohio is Fort Ancient (figures 1.1 and 12.3), a major ridge-top site overlooking the deep Little Miami Valley and about 50 km from its confluence with the Ohio River. Its mortuary remains are extensive, but they are largely in the

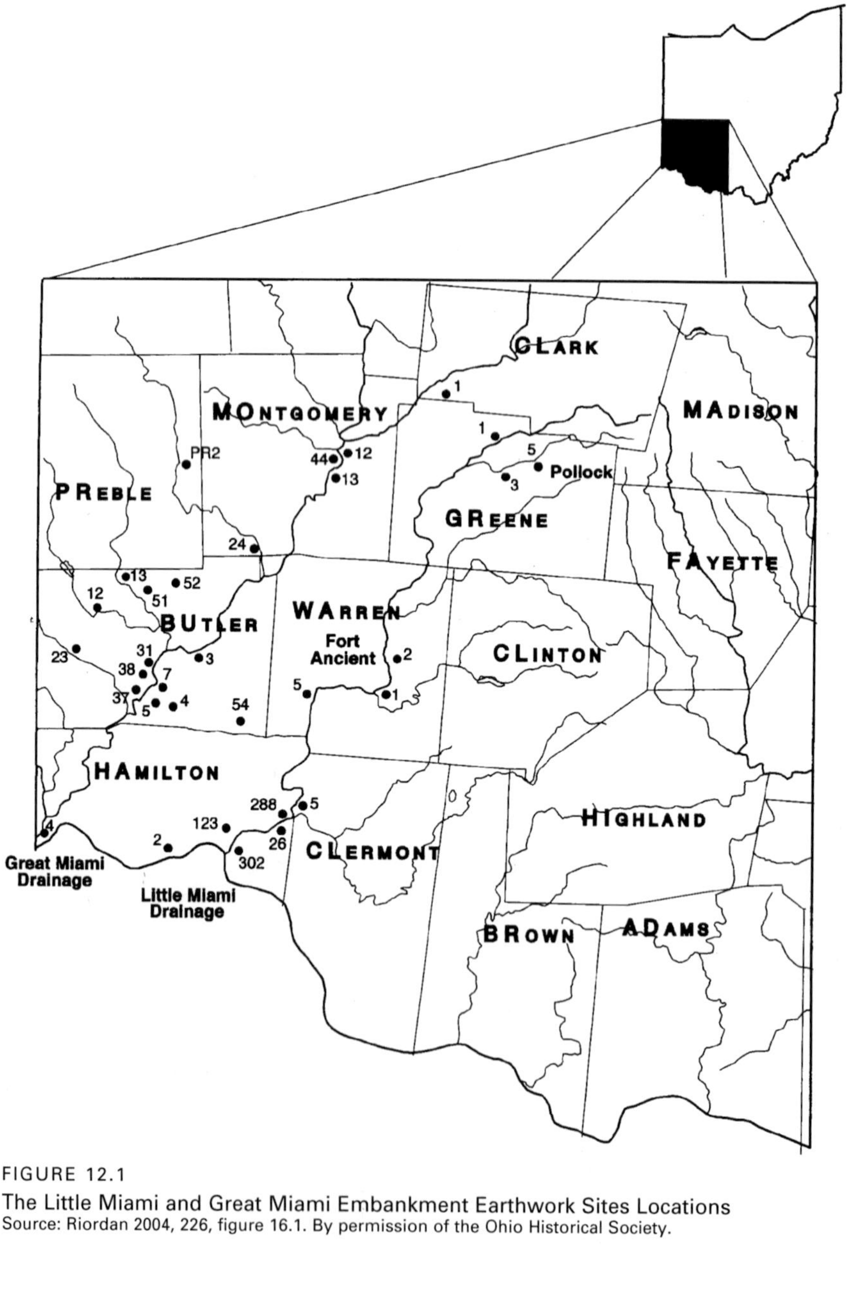

FIGURE 12.1

The Little Miami and Great Miami Embankment Earthwork Sites Locations

Source: Riordan 2004, 226, figure 16.1. By permission of the Ohio Historical Society.

form of loose and broken bones, and there are very few mortuary-associated artifacts.

It is notable that the assumption framing the observations Greber makes and the questions she asks is that the groups responsible for this disparate distribution of earthworks and elaborate artifacts were "local communities." That is, clearly implied here is that whatever the human resources that enabled this erratic distribution of both earthworks and artifacts to be produced and used, they were tied to local valleys. This is recognized as axiomatic, even though many of the material resources used to produce such exotic artifacts as copper plates and celts, obsidian blades, and ocean shell containers were from disparate regions distant from Ohio. That is, Greber explicitly raises these questions from within the perspective of the civic-ceremonial center version of the Monistic Modular Polity Community model and the latter is tied to the notion of the local communities having exclusive territories. This perspective makes the disparate nature of the archeological distribution of earthworks and artifacts very puzzling indeed. How can the same types of communities in spatially separate river drainages, clearly sharing similar ways of life and the cultural background that made these ways possible, generate such major differences of material assemblage? If the communities in the central Scioto and the Great and Little Miami valley zones could produce equivalent monumental earthworks and include major mortuary residue in some of them, then why did only the former produce such elaborate and quantitatively large and qualitatively varied artifactual assemblages to accompany the deceased while the deceased found in the latter were buried with little and often without any such materials?[2]

Of course, I am in the process of answering these questions, and the first step I have taken to make it less puzzling is to work with a different set of theoretical assumptions. While the agents responsible for the labor and commitment were members of local communities, that is, local complementary heterarchical communities, the groups that were responsible were not these communities but the cult sodality heterarchies that integrated multiple cult sodalities from different regions. It was these groups that mobilized their members to generate the commitment to provide the necessary labor and material resources! Therefore, labor mobilization was not tied to local communities in these disparate drainages but was a function of the cult sodality heterarchy system and, as I argued above and in the previous chapter, the labor that built these earthworks was able to be mobilized by the systems of cult sodality heterarchies that were distributed across and between regions. I have already postulated the third-order Chillicothe-Newark (probably including Portsmouth) cult sodality heterarchy, on the one hand, and the equivalent third-order Fort Ancient–Turner–Hopewell cult sodality heterarchy, connecting the Little Miami and the North Fork of the Paint Creek–Scioto valleys, on the other. Of course, in the spirit of interheterarchical cooperation, the participating cult sodalities of these separate networks may have reciprocally shared labor across these networks. The primary social mechanism that both made the labor mobilization possible and promoted this mobilization would be the sacred games *tournée*/world renewal mortuary-mediated sacrificial *chaîne opératoire* process.

It is also notable that in asking "who provided the thousands of artifacts deposited at Hopewell and the hundreds at Turner" that Greber has touched on a major quantitative contrast while noting a significant qualitative equivalence. The observation that the Hopewell site had thousands and the Turner site had hundreds of artifactual items consisting of *almost* the same range of artifactual categories is particularly germane since it immediately invokes not two different sets of cultural practices but the same set organized so as to make a significant difference in the quantitative distribution. At the same time, however, in quantitative terms, the magnitude of the embankment earthworks in all these regions remains equivalent. It is this strong quantitative difference in artifacts and artifact categories, particularly those associated with mortuary practices, and the strong quantitative equivalence of the embankment earthworks that I particularly find important for empirically grounding the Ohio Hopewell Cult Sodality Heterarchy System model. I will initiate this grounding by focusing on the Turner site (figure 12.2) since it is particularly relevant, given my earlier claim that the Hopewell site was the recipient of the burden of custodial regalia and associated mourning gifts from the many cult sodality heterarchies of the Little Miami Valley. My central thesis is that the primary route or routes connecting the Turner and Hopewell sites was or were the primary processional pathways connecting the Little Miami Valley and the North Fork of the Paint Creek drainage where the Hopewell site is located, and both the similarities between the two earthworks of Turner and Hopewell and the similarities and disparities in the mortuary record of the two is precisely a function of this processional pathway. It is now time to examine the Turner site in some detail.

THE TURNER SITE

Turner (figure 12.2) is a major embankment earthwork on the Little Miami River and it is downstream from Fort Ancient. It also has the distinction of containing the *second* richest Hopewellian artifactual assemblage in Ohio west of the Hopewell site, which has the richest, as Greber effectively notes.[3] I suggest, therefore, that it displays precisely the patterning that this explanation of the Hopewell pattern would require. Why is this? As I argued earlier, the Hopewell site is uniquely rich in custodial regalia that were curated from

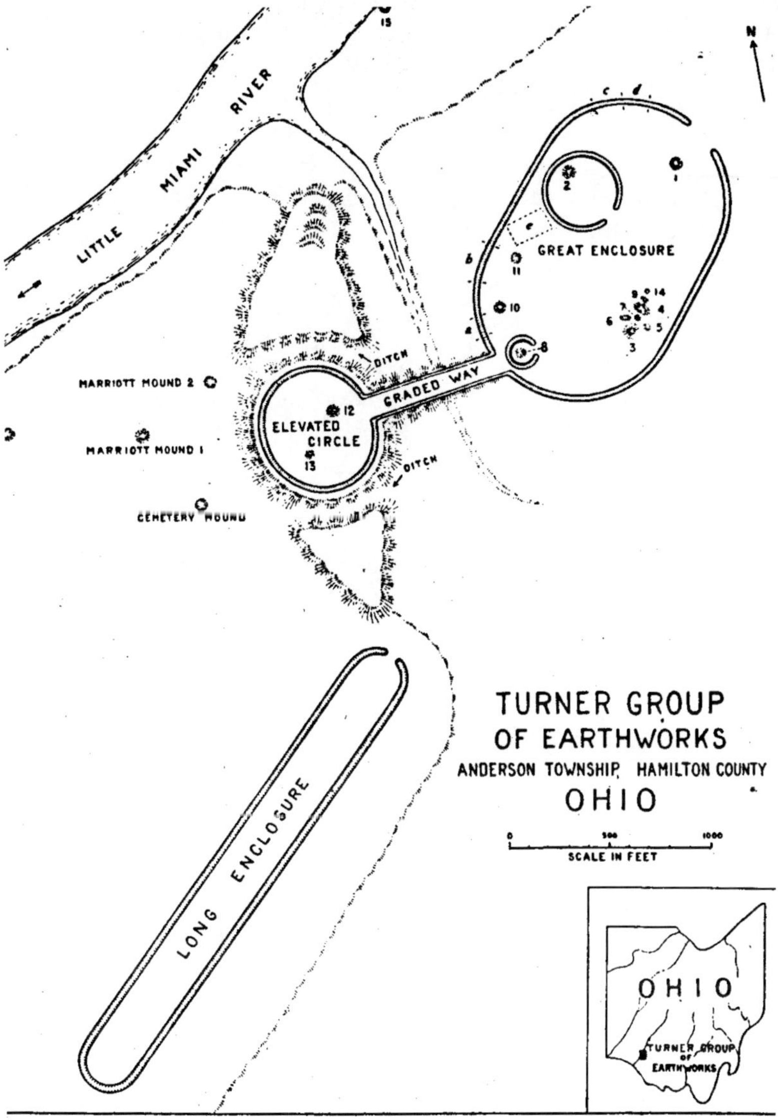

FIGURE 12.2

The Turner Site

Source: Willoughby and Hooton 1922, plate 1. Peabody Museum.

many deceased who were given laying-in mortuary rites there. Therefore, there should be one or more major Ohio Hopewell embankment earthwork sites that display attributes that echo those found at the Hopewell site but that *lack the normal range of custodial regalia.* As noted above, Seip and Liberty Works do not fulfill these criteria since I have already argued that they had a rich representation of these custodial regalia artifacts, even though each had a lesser amount than found at the Hopewell site. Besides, the earlier Mound City also incorporated significant numbers of the same categories of custodial regalia found at the Hopewell site. Therefore, despite being only a few kilometers from the Hopewell site, all three can be excluded as possible sources from which these materials, in all their superfluity, were generated at the Hopewell site. Of course, we know that the group responsible for the Hopewell site was very much involved with the groups of these other sites and that, as I noted earlier, some time during the history of this interaction, Hopewell added two key embankment earthwork components to its original C-Form embankment, namely, a small circle and a small Paint Creek square. As I noted then, this addition reinforces the view that the relation between Hopewell site and its near-neighbor Paint Creek C-R motif sites of Liberty Works and Seip was somewhat arm's length in social interaction nature.

Turner, however, does fulfill the above criteria. There is no question that Turner has a rich variety of Hopewellian artifacts. However, its quantity is much less than at the Hopewell site. As noted above, Greber speaks of the *hundreds* of artifacts that were found at Turner in contrast to the *thousands* that were found at the Hopewell site, even though the overall number of burial deposits at Turner was about equal to the number on the mortuary floor covered by Mound 25. In fact, the vast majority of the Turner artifact assemblage made up the contents of several well-known burnt offering rituals, two inside the main renewal lodge of the cult sodality heterarchy, and one found under the main embankment of the earthwork. These deposits manifest the same patterning and much of the same variation of artifact materials as those found in the two great burnt deposits at the Hopewell site, although consisting of a fraction of the quantity of the latter deposits. However, the form and variety are sufficient, in my view, to interpret them as the equivalent to those at the Hopewell site and, therefore, these also were the result of mortuary *chaîne opératoire* truncation events in which curated mourning gifts, personalty, and elaborately decorated laying-in shrouds served as a mass sacrificial offering mediating a collective mourning and spirit-release rite. Given these burnt deposits, one might be warranted to assume, therefore, that there should also be deposits of deceased accompanied by custodial regalia of the type that are so well represented at the Hopewell site. That is, if Turner corresponds so closely to the Hopewell site in terms of the burnt deposits, then there should also be three main forms of artifact deposits equivalent to those at the Hopewell site. However, while there are roughly similar burnt artifact deposits at Turner and Hopewell, what is clearly absent from Turner is anything similar to *either* mortuary deposits in association with custodial regalia as found prolifically at the Hopewell site (there is one exception), *or*, even more puzzling, anything in the form of megadeposits of copper custodial regalia that were found at the Hopewell site. Another difference is very apparent. While a number of the deceased at the Turner site were accompanied by noncustodial artifact materials, in stark contrast to the richness in noncustodial regalia of the Hopewell deceased, that is, personalty, laying-in shrouds, and mourning gifts, the Turner deceased were impoverished having only the odd associated artifact. In fact, not only were there few artifacts, there were no custodial regalia artifacts fitting the major categories of copper celt, copper plate, and copper headdress in the major burial locale (the one exception was "trophy skulls," which I discuss shortly).

These differences constitute a major puzzle that most Hopewellian archaeologists recognize. Despite the richness and variety of its burnt deposit contents, effectively replicating the variety if not the quantity of materials in the burnt deposits at the Hopewell site, and despite having a good representation of deceased, about 100 deposits, most of them as extended or loose bone bundles (there are also a small number of cremations and highly fractured bones, usually infant), custodial regalia, either deposited with individual deceased or as large deposits of the type found at the Hopewell site, are essentially absent. In fact, Turner is not even the major embankment earthwork site of the region. Without a doubt, in terms of size, complexity, and history, Fort Ancient would be the primary earthwork site, situated about 25 km north of Fort Ancient on the east bank of the same river. However, this is another puzzle. Despite the massive size of Fort Ancient, it has an even lesser, indeed a much lesser, representation of the Hopewellian artifactual assemblage than Turner, as I discuss below. In line with my earlier comment, therefore, it seems quite reasonable to postulate that the multiple items of custodial regalia that "should-be-at-but-are-missing" from Turner, and for that matter, that "should-be-at-but-are-missing" from Fort Ancient, are in fact the ones that we know are located at the Hopewell site.

Although being about 100 km from the Hopewell site raises questions of validity for this claim, I should point out that equivalent distances separate Liberty Works and High Banks from Newark and the formal similarities in the earthworks grounding the claim that there was a dispersed third-order Chillicothe-Newark heterarchy are also equivalent to the formal similarities to the earthworks that constitute what I claim was a dispersed third-order Fort Ancient–Turner–Hopewell heterarchy, as I discuss in more detail shortly. I need hardly argue that long distant relations among earthwork groups were common, given the widespread sharing of Hopewellian material themes, and that formal patterns and alignments played as important a role in these relations as did the mortuary contents. I postulate that the Turner site probably held the standing of being the core locale of a second-order sodality heterarchy that was part of the dispersed Fort Ancient–Turner–Hopewell third-order heterarchy. If this is correct, then it may actually have been the "home" site of a second-order heterarchy incorporating earthwork sites south of Fort Ancient, such as Foster's. That is, as I argue shortly, while the Hopewell site was a very impressive earthwork in the Scioto region, the first-order sodalities that affiliated into a second-order heterarchy treated Turner, not Hopewell, as their primary second-order site. In turn, Turner and several other second-order heterarchies located to its north in the Little Miami Valley, affiliated to form a third-order heterarchy with its main locale being Fort Ancient. In addition, Turner held an important position in this third-order heterarchy by being the primary site through which many of the deceased of this set of affiliated cult sodalities were "funneled" to the Hopewell site where the heterarchy-wide conveyancing rites were held and then returned to the Little Miami Valley, probably also via Turner. Further, as I argue below, the Hopewell site was likely the complement of the Fort Ancient site built to constitute the Sacred Dual C-Form/T-Form motif characteristic of the southwestern sector of Ohio. Turner, therefore, held an important position in this third-order heterarchy by being the primary second-order heterarchy site through which many of the deceased of this third-order cult sodality heterarchy were "funneled" to the Hopewell site and then returned to Turner, and probably from there many were taken in procession to serve as symbolic pragmatic media in world renewal rituals at Fort Ancient and terminated in mortuary deposits in the South Fort sector of Fort Ancient.

Above I postulated that the Hopewell site also served as the complementary site with Fort Ancient to constitute the two as a dispersed Sacred Dual C-Form/T-Form motif. This may explain the accumulation of over 8,000 Wyandotte chert disks at the Hopewell site. That is, piggybacked on the mortuary processions of deceased from the Little Miami Valley to the Hopewell site would be loads of Wyandotte chert that would serve as gifts and offerings. For example, each procession of cult sodality age-sets would be required to make a small deposit of such disks as a rectification of the polluting effect on the sacred powers of the Fort Ancient–Turner–Hopewell world renewal mortuary pathway caused by the mortuary/sacred games *tournée* processions. These sacrificial deposits would make up only a small part of the total amount of Wyandotte chert transported along with any given mortuary procession. No doubt the majority of this select and special chert would serve as gifts to representative participants from the cult sodalities belonging to third-order Chillicothe-Newark cult sodality heterarchy who were invited participants in the sacred games performed at the Hopewell site as part of the mortuary process. These Wyandotte chert gifts would probably be reciprocated with the participants from the Chillicothe-Newark heterarchy offering Flint Ridge disks that they had similarly carried from Newark and the Flint Ridge chert quarries. Hence, correlated with these two dispersed third-order cult sodality heterarchies would be the distribution of Wyandotte chert into the Newark zone, as witnessed by the Murphy Tract survey, and Flint Ridge chert into the Miami Valley zone, as witnessed by the very large amount of Flint Ridge chert debitage at the Turner Workshop site. "Thousands and thousands of blades were produced at the Turner Workshop, a small site immediately adjacent to the Turner Earthworks" (Nolan et al. 2007, 321). The content of this workshop site and its spatial relation to the Turner site, separated by about 300 m (Nolan et al. 2007), is very reminiscent of the relation between the Murphy Tract and Newark or, alternatively, the Granville C-Form earthworks. Specifically, it bears similarities with Murphy V and may have been the reciprocal counterpart at Turner with regard to specialized Flint Ridge production that I postulated was the case for Murphy V, as the specialized workshop for the production of Wyandotte bladelet and bifacial cores.

The Turner Site Configuration

Possibly the best way to approach demonstrating the above claims is first to analyze the configuration of the Turner site embankments and relate this to the Hopewell site since, even though on first appearance they seem very different, in my view the architectural attributes they display clearly structurally link these two sites. This will be followed by an analysis of the mortuary patterning, showing where it was similar and where it differed and that the most important difference was the conspicuous absence at Turner of the artifactual category I have termed custodial regalia. As I noted earlier, the main Hopewell site embankment manifests the C-Form/SL-Profile configuration. C-Form refers to its bird's-eye view plan, being a large fairly straight-backed "C" with its two arms terminating at the terrace edge overlooking the valley bottom. Notably, the "back" of the Hopewell C-Form actually was built on an upper terrace and the embankment arms were built from this upper terrace down onto the lower terrace and terminated at the edge overlooking the creek bottom. I consider this double level to be an important attribute. I also consider the SL-Profile of the C-Form to be a critical attribute of this configuration and the reason I term it the SL-Profile is simple. Assume you are an observer standing on top of the upper embankment of the Hopewell C-Form. This embankment runs east–west so to your right would be the lower terrace and to your left would be the external ditch, that is, on the "outside." If you were to cut through the embankment with a straight north–south trench, the profile of the embankment and "external" ditch would form a sine curve or S-profile with the "outer" ditch on your left. This is characteristic of almost all C-Form embankments and, hence, I term it the SL-Profile. Since these two embankment attributes, C-Form plan and SL-Profile, are correlated, I have interpreted it as an intrinsic, rule-governed pattern, that is, a real embankment earthwork category. I have also treated this configuration as marking the early Middle Woodland period. Certainly most such configurations are found in the Great and Little Miami Valleys. This is why I noted earlier that the Hopewell site is probably a "foreign" intrusion in the central Scioto region and marks the introduction of a new ritual embankment usufruct into this area, as indicated by the building of not only the Hopewell site itself but also the Shriver and Cedar Works earthworks that bracket the Mound City site. Because of its prevalence in the Great Miami and Little Miami Valleys, I have treated the classic C-Form/SL-Profile configuration as part of what I term the Miami Fort tradition.

Having said all this, it is germane that the Turner embankment earthwork does not display this C-Form/SL-Profile and I explain this by claiming that its embankment system is a late development. However, a careful examination of the other components of the Turner embankments clearly supports attributes that can easily relate it to the Hopewell site itself and, of course, the generic Fort Miami tradition. First, the Turner site is a complex earthwork having a small circle and a large oblong or oval embankment (figure 12.2). The latter is often referred to as the Great Enclosure. The two components are linked by a parallel-wall passageway (there is also a southern linear oval-rectilinear that was probably an even later addition). Most importantly, the smaller circular embankment component is constructed on the highest land in the immediate area and overlooks the Great Enclosure, replicating the dual-leveled arrangement of the Hopewell C-Form. The embankments are also what I call K-Profile forms. That is, they do not have either inner or external ditches. Instead, the earth fill was derived from borrow pitting or surface earth scraping. Indeed, it is likely that most of the earth fill was derived by cutting around the remains of the small high bluff on which the smaller circle was constructed and, at the same time, by narrowing the drop-off step from the bluff top to the lower terrace where the large oblong or oval embankment component was built. This careful shaping produced a ramp lined with two embankments. In short, the site consists primarily of an upper small circle, the sacred ramp, and the large oblong embankment combination and displays what I term the K-Profile attribute (k = cone), which I consider to be a middle to late Ohio Hopewell embankment construction attribute.[4]

I have called this total layout the C-O motif configuration and I treat it as a late variant of the Paint Creek C-R motif and claim that it is an imported but modified expression of the latter motif at the Hopewell site that it emulated. In the latter case, as I noted earlier, the Hopewell site added a small circle inside the main C-Form and a small Paint Creek Square attached to the east wall of the C-Form. For all these reasons, I have postulated that the Turner earthwork is a late Ohio Hopewell construction and it is an innovated design by selectively synthesizing attributes of both the Paint Creek C-R motif and the C-Form/SL-Profile motif. Just as the Hopewell C-Form incorporates the highest land overlooking the lower terrace, so the Turner C-O Form incorporates the highest land overlooking the lower terrace. Just as the Hopewell site incorporates a modified Paint Creek C-R motif, so the C-O motif of Turner is a unique innovation of the latter. Just as mortuary deposits when found are usually associated with the Paint Creek C-R motif, not the complementary High Bank C-R motif, so Turner incorporates multiple mortuary deposits, suggesting that in symbolic pragmatic terms it is the equivalent of Seip and Liberty Works. Finally, as I stated above, this innovative combination strongly suggests that the Turner embankment earthwork was built rather late in the Ohio Hopewellian episode, probably shortly after the Paint Creek C-R motif components were added at the Hopewell site (Byers 2004, 482–86; 2010b).

Therefore, the overall layout of the Turner embankment earthworks can be seen to be incorporating both basic upper/lower attributes of the traditional C-Form/SL-Profile configuration and variant attributes of the Paint Creek C-R configuration. However, to reinforce this claim, I will note that there are other important attributes of the Turner site that are variants of those found at Hopewell, in this case manifested in the mortuary features themselves. The primary location of the Turner mortuary deposits is what is termed the Burial Place located in the south-central sector of the Great Enclosure (figure 12.2). This is actually a low mound that covers multiple stone-lined burial deposits. I have argued that these stone-lined features were the symbolic pragmatic equivalent of the Hopewell vaulted chambers. That is, they both served as laying-in period features by which the postmortem manipulation of the deceased would count as world renewal rituals of different types and as post-laying-in period features. Although these stone-lined mortuary features strongly depart formally from the log crib and vaulted chambers at Hopewell, I see greater similarity than differences. Using limestone in order to construct ritual features is the norm in the Little Miami Valley; it is not in the Scioto region.[5] However, from the Turner perspective, mediating their deceased in the vaulted chambers at the Hopewell site would be seen as quite acceptable since, in fact, given my earlier analysis, this ritual treatment was not intended, in general, to be terminated there. Rather, as I have postulated, following the laying-in period at Hopewell, the deceased would be *returned to Turner* to be given a further series of postmortem ritual treatments in the stone-lined crypts that served for both initial laying-in period rites and post-laying-in period rites. In local tradition, this dual usage is probably what made these the proper symbolic pragmatic media for such rites.

In fact, there is quite abundant evidence that these features were used in a manner similar to the vaulted chambers at the Hopewell site. I have carefully analyzed the contents as reported by Putnam and his colleagues of the Peabody Museum in the late 19th century and the early years of the 20th century, particularly relying on the work of Willoughby and Hooton (1922) as well as Greber's work (1976, 124–30). There is a great deal of evidence to support the claim that these were not "graves" in the sense of terminal burial locales and that the burials found in many of them were the result of truncation of the mortuary *chaîne opératoire* equivalent to the same type of events at the Hopewell site. These mortuary features, as noted above, had dual uses as stone-lined laying-in and post-laying-in crypts. They were provided with stone covers and served to process a multiple series of (usually) individual deceased. The features were often modified during their usage history, being added to or subtracted from, sometimes by the adding of stone slabs to the floor, sometimes by dividing the crypt in half. The bones of prior deceased were returned and covered with ash and dirt, only to have another series of deceased processed on top, and so on. I suspect that each stone-lined feature had a complex history of sequential postmortem processing (Byers 2004, 432–42). Probably in all cases an initial laying-in period was performed in these features. These would then be temporarily covered with stone slabs. At the appropriate time, these would be lifted, the deceased would be removed, and their mourning gifts, personalty, and shrouds curated. Then the deceased would be wrapped in new shrouds, *along with custodial regalia*, if any, and taken in mortuary processions to different locations. If my earlier scenario is correct, many would have been taken by their companions to the Hopewell site, where they were then given a second laying-in period series of rites. The termination of this series, as I described earlier, would then mean that the deceased, possibly with new shrouds, were returned to Turner where they were once more placed in the stone-lined crypts for further extended post-laying-in period rites. Alternatively, they were carried to a different locale, possibly Stubbs Works and from there a little farther north to Fort Ancient, where they served as media of terminal spirit-release sacrificial rites, as I discuss below.

This dual laying-in/post-laying-in period process, once before removal to the Hopewell site and once when returned, and the truncation of the process, at least twice, would explain the two very large burnt deposits containing a similar range of artifact categories as found in the Hopewell site burnt deposits. However, they also contain some very unusual artifacts suggesting a type of ritual sacrifice that was not quite the same as at the Hopewell site. The presence of these in the burnt deposits suggests that the laying-in process at Turner was different and this difference could well relate to the variation in the contents of the burnt deposits at the Turner and Hopewell sites. The above scenario would also account for another difference between the mortuary deposits of the two sites. Given the large quantity of multiple copper earspools, beads, pearls, animal paws, and so on, at the Turner site, similar in makeup if not as quantitatively large as the contents of the Hopewell site burnt deposits, it has puzzled many archaeologists that effectively no copper plates, copper celts, or copper headdresses accompanied the deceased in the Burial Place at Turner.

However, there is one form of custodial regalia at the Turner site that constitutes the single largest known deposit of this type, this being a burial in association with a set of 16 "trophy skulls." These 16 were all placed at the bottom of a specially constructed crypt dug into Mound 3 after it had been built to cover one of the rooms constituting the Turner Renewal Lodge. Two extended burials were found in the center of the floor of the crypt and the 16 skulls were placed in a circle around them. I consider this deposit to be of the same order of importance as the megadeposit of copper plates and celts over Burials 260 and 261 in Mound 25 and that these were the consequence of a major decommissioning event with the abandonment of the site (Byers 2004, 479–82). No doubt the free souls embodied in the skulls were given release as an important part of this decommissioning ritual. Importantly, however, given their good condition, these skulls would not have been curated over many years but were probably actively passed from one custodial caretaker to another. That is, I do not consider them to be usufruct custodial regalia. Instead, like the Great Copper Deposit, they were probably group custodial regalia. Finding these 16 "trophy skulls" (a term that is a serious misnomer, in my view) suggests that two or more generations of cult sodalities constituting the second-order heterarchy responsible for the Turner earthworks were responsible for this large Turner Renewal Lodge. Indeed, as I argued in the previous chapter, since group custodial regalia were typically conveyed from one to the next age-set, sustaining and accumulating the sacred name powers of the cult sodality itself, only with the abandonment of Turner, and possibly the disaffiliation of the third-order Fort Ancient–Turner–Hopewell heterarchy itself, was it possible and necessary to release the free souls that they embodied.

In radical contrast, the deceased in the stone-lined laying-in crypts were almost bereft of associated artifacts. A few had a pair of earspools, possibly an extra pair in their hands, some scattered bladelets, and some formed in small clusters beside deceased, and so on. There were also lumps of galena, broken earspools, and other exotic materials in some of the features. However, given the erratic nature of their distribution and in a number of cases their broken state, I have argued these were residue of items placed with deceased during prior laying-in periods that were unwittingly left in the crypts when the deceased were removed and new deceased were deposited. Many of these stray items are found in the corners, some are under floor stones on which the terminal deceased was laid, indicating that the feature had an earlier history of mortuary use, and so on. However, it is also notable that there are not very many burials at Turner, about the same as found on the floor of Mound 25. Again, given the size of the burnt offerings, this suggests that many more deceased were processed through the stone-lined crypts than were actually found in them. Therefore, these large numbers were likely given terminal burial elsewhere. That is, as in the case of the vaulted chambers at the Hopewell site, those that were found in the stone-lined crypts of Turner were simply partway through the normal processing that individual deceased received when the particular operating portion of the Burial Place locale was abandoned. I consider the abundant evidence of a serial process of usage of the stone-lined laying-in crypts; the absence of custodial regalia; the paucity of artifacts; the relatively low number of actual in situ human deceased, the bones of which were often in considerable disorder; the large burnt deposits containing a rather rich concentration of mourning, personalty, and laying-in shroud artifacts; and, in contrast, the absence of custodial regalia, as confirming my claim that the Turner site was the source of the excessively rich concentration of custodial regalia at the Hopewell site. That is, given the numbers of deceased being processed, the reason for the absence of custodial regalia at Turner arises not from the artifactual poverty of the cult sodalities in the region but from their custodial regalia wealth being given final deposition at the Hopewell site. This concentration at the Hopewell site of custodial regalia that was produced and used in the Little Miami Valley, according to my interpretation, could only have occurred as a result of ritual mortuary-mediated processions being regularly carried out between these two major sites. In order to continue the story I now turn to the remarkable site of Fort Ancient, about 25 km north of Turner.

THE FORT ANCIENT SITE

Fort Ancient (figure 12.3) is recognized by Ohio Hopewell archaeologists as a compound feature consisting of three major and one minor embankment earthwork components. The major components are referred to as the North Fort, the Middle Fort, and the South Fort (Connolly 2004, 1996; Connolly and Sunderhaus 2004; Cowan et al. 2004; Lazazzera 2004; Riordan 2004,

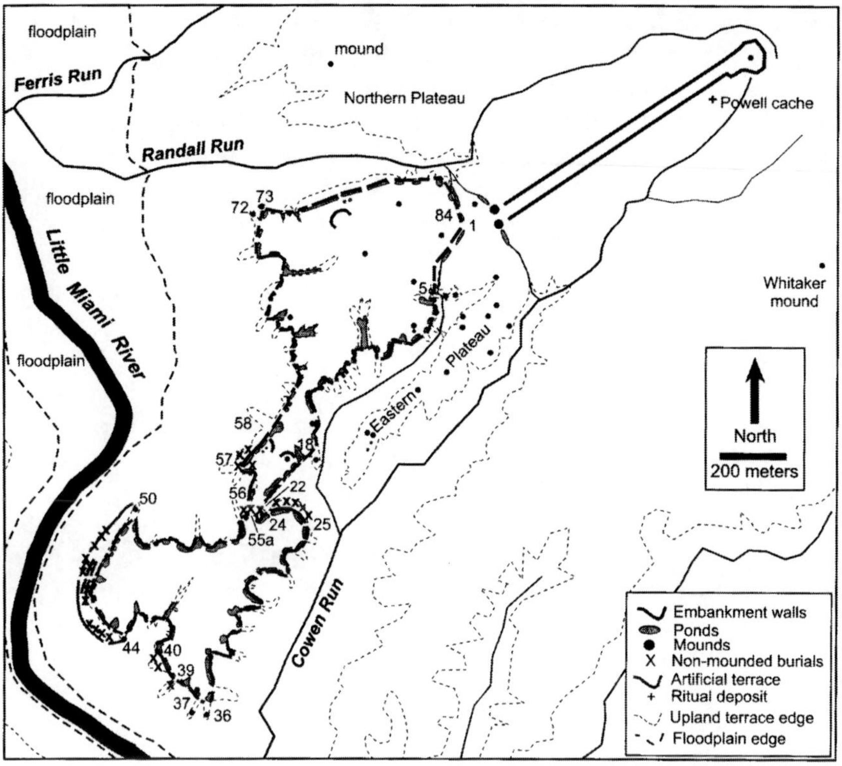

FIGURE 12.3
Fort Ancient, Schematic Diagram
Source: Cowan et al. 2004, 108, figure 8.1. By permission of Frank Cowan.

2010; Sunderhaus 2004; Vickery and Sunderhaus 2004). The minor component is the long set of parallel embankments leading northeast from the main gateway of the North Fort, Gate No. 1. It also has a Middle Woodland period mortuary component. However, almost all of the burials are reported to be located in association with the South Fort. A few have been reported in association with the Middle Fort but near the entranceway to the South Fort. Effectively none have been reported for the North Fort component. A very germane fact for my purposes is to note that the many mortuary remains are generally bereft of artifacts. There have been a few extended burials found, one of which was associated with a "mask"-like copper plate. However, by far most mortuary remains were deposited as bone bundles, or even as separate bones from unrelated deceased, and all seem to have been deposited at critical locations in the Fort Ancient site, most of these being in association with primary and secondary gateways of the South Fort, as well as the exterior terraces level with and below the embankments of this component. Many of the known mortuary deposits were revealed in the late 19th and early 20th centuries. Moorehead (1890, 37–38) recorded excavating what he estimated to be about 18 to 20 individuals under the southern ramp of Gateway 55a complex, while reporting many more finds of scattered and broken human bones mixed with prolific quantities of stone on the lower terraces that were external to and "surrounding" the embankments of the South Fort.

According to Robert Connolly's classification of the various features of Fort Ancient (Connolly 2004, 44–45; Connolly and Sunderhaus 2004, 53–54), Gateway 55a (figure 12.3; see also figure 12.4), the primary entrance between the Middle and the South Forts, figures as a key architectural complex. In Connolly's taxonomy, being a primary gateway would mean that normally it was the point of entry into and exit from an *autonomous* or stand-alone hilltop embankment earthwork. As noted above, however, the South Fort is now treated as simply one of three major embankment earthwork components of the larger Fort Ancient earthwork system. Connolly resolves this matter by characterizing Fort Ancient in historical developmental terms, arguing that the South Fort was originally built as a "stand-alone" hilltop embankment earthwork, what I have referred to generically as a T-Form embankment. Therefore, according to Connolly's interpretation, the South Fort was the first embankment earthwork component to be built and, as such, it manifested the critical attributes of other known hilltop sites. Probably the Gateway 55a complex was rather modest at that time. In fact, it would appear that the "gateway," as such, was the result of first building the initial embankment and

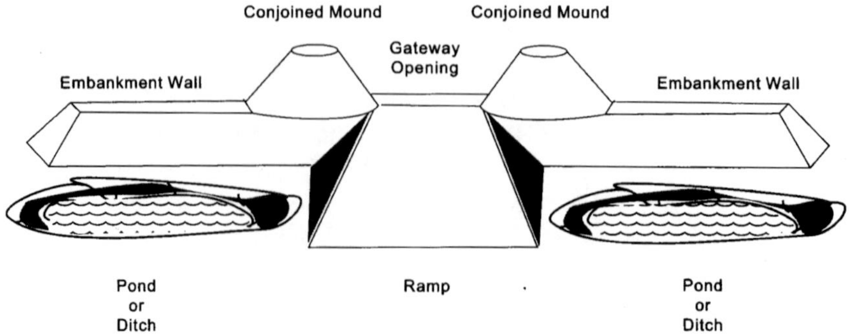

FIGURE 12.4
Ideal Primary Gateway Schematic
Source: Connolly and Sunderhaus 2004, 52, figure 5.1. By permission of the Ohio Historical Society.

then building these two mounds on top of the embankment about ten feet apart, while leaving the original embankment between the mounds exposed. That is, no fill would have to be removed from the embankment. Instead, soil was placed on top and, indeed, one earthen ramp was added on the north side and connected the embankment bracketed by the mounds to the slightly lower isthmus, and another ramp was added on the south or interior side to connect to the interior plateau of the South Fort, which was slightly higher than the level of the northern isthmus. The two ramps from the embankment sector bracketed by the two mounds generated a walkover pathway and, of course, gave the two mounds the appearance of being conjoined. The ramp leading into the South Fort was also bracketed by two ponds, one built on the east side and the other on the west side of the ramp.

At a currently unknown time, but well after the construction of the South Fort and into its initial history of usage, the "isthmus" sector north of Gateway 55a had embankments built along its bluff edges. This set of embankments and the isthmus they incorporate are now referred to as the Middle Fort (Connolly 2004, 44–46). More embankments were constructed leading from the Middle Fort along the perimeter of the broad northern plateau of the ridge top. This plateau area with its incorporating perimeter embankments and "gateways" constitutes the North Fort, that is, the third and northernmost major component of Fort Ancient. The main Gateway 1 complex (figure 12.3) is at the most northeastern sector of the North Fort and it is marked by an elaborate combination of two major mounds (the Twin Mounds), complementary twin ponds, artificially extended creeks, ramps, and so on. According to Connolly, part of the completion of the Gateway 1 complex included the addition of the parallel northeast walls enclosing a small mound at their distal end. "Without the twin mounds and parallel walls, no primary gateway complex marks the northeast end of the enclosure therefore creating a form anomalous to other hilltop enclosures. Therefore, this study assumes that the construction of the Middle and North Forts, along with the Twin Mounds and parallel walls, were conceived and initiated as a single expansion of earth work architecture" (Connolly 2004, 46–47).

I think that Connolly is right to claim that the 840 m long set of parallel walls "connect" with Gateway 1 and, therefore, the Gateway 1 complex and the walls constitute an important symbolic pragmatic form. However, given the finding of a rich distribution of locales displaying prolific specialized lithic production (including selected cherts, obsidian, crystal quartz, and so on), Cowan and his colleagues (2004, 113–20) have established that the eastern plateau outside Gateway 1 was occupied prior to the building of the parallel walls by a range of what I would define under the Cult Sodality Cluster model as specialized Hopewell production base camps, the type occupied and used by age-grade sectors of cult sodalities while undertaking ritual and related tasks at the earthwork site. Cowan and his colleagues may even have revealed evidence of a more permanent structure, the type that I will argue later would serve as a ritual way station, a hostel-like structure, for the members of some of the cult sodalities responsible for the nearby earthworks. They note that a number of these sites were then superimposed by the parallel wall embankments (2004, 113), and this suggests that there was a period prior to or following the completion of Gateway 1 when this eastern plateau was used by transient members of the various cult sodalities participating in the third-order Fort Ancient–Turner–Hopewell cult sodality heterarchy for specialized production of ritual materials. Then the parallel walls were constructed. This would mean that the latter walls were built late in the history of Fort Ancient, during a time when the influence of the third-order Chillicothe-Newark cult sodality heterarchy was possibly at its maximum, given that the parallel wall motif is a major hallmark of the middle to late period of the Chillicothe tradition. Therefore, this assertion by Cowan and his colleagues is strongly supported by the evidence. "Fort Ancient is not a single earthwork enclosure. Instead, it is like an onion, . . . [a] layered series of symbolically enclosed spaces, each deliberately bounded by natural and artificial, earthen and aqueous architectural elements between which users of the site had to pass upon going into or out from ritually important spaces" (Cowan et al. 2004, 107).

The total Fort Ancient configuration was not only unique in the extent and size of the embankments required to incorporate the topographical form of the ridge-top plateau, slightly over 5 km of embankments averaging about 2–3 m high, it was unique in having multiple sectors rather than a single sector that was standard for the ridge-top T-forms. Only the South Fort component fits the standard T-Form configuration, according to Connolly, a point he makes quite explicit. "The North Fort marks an elaboration and departure from the basic hilltop enclosure form of the region. No other Middle Woodland hilltop site encloses two distinct spatial zones. Also, the North Fort incorporates a more rigid application and evolution of the original design grammar rules for the South Fort" (2004, 45–46). Connolly also quite specifically attributes this overall development as being instigated with the addition of a human ossuary deposition to the South Fort, a form of deposition that is unknown at any other hilltop embankment earthwork and, therefore, was also unknown at the South Fort until the development and construction of the Middle and North Fort components. Therefore, he sees this process of ossuary deposition as remarkable; an assessment with which I am in full accord. "The overwhelming majority of Middle Woodland burials at Fort Ancient are reported from an ossuary deposit within a small earthen mound south of Gateway 55a on the interior of the South Fort, and along the exterior terraces of the South Fort. Notably, burials are not recorded along the exterior terraces or spurs of the North Fort. No other hilltop enclosure contains a similar mortuary program" (2004, 47). It also appears that not only did the initial South Fort enclosure manifest the standard T-Form, it also mediated the standard ritual, which did *not* include making any mortuary deposits. Therefore, the establishment of mortuary deposits would definitely mark a transformation of the symbolic pragmatic nature of the South Fort.

As noted above, Moorehead reported finding the human bone ossuary as the content of the south ramp of Gateway 55a. Connolly reports that these bones were placed onto the preexisting ramp of Gateway 55a and then covered with a limestone pavement, clearly constituting the transformation of the South Fort into its new function as an ossuary locale. "The ossuary in the ramp and gateway is immediately beneath the ground surface . . . suggesting that the south ramp was enlarged to accommodate the placement of the burials after the initial construction events [and] . . . most of the limestone slabs that capped the elevated sections of Gateway 55a's conjoined mounds overlay the ossuary deposit as part of a construction event after the original embankment wall was built" (2004, 47). However, this ossuary was simply the initial step in the transformation. According to Connolly's interpretation, following the initial deposition of the human bones and the expansion of the south ramp of Gateway 55a into the South Fort, multiple mortuary bundles were buried under stones inside the Gateway 55a complex and these burial and stone depositions apparently generated a large stone mound. Then multiple and cumulative stone-and-bone bundle burials were also deposited on the exterior periphery of the South Fort, usually on terraces. Some of these terraces were expanded for this purpose. Connolly concludes that the "Gateway 55a ossuary deposit legitimized the placement of burials in the South Fort. . . . The mortuary program on the South Fort terraces is uncharacteristic [of T-Form earthworks] and perhaps unique for the Middle Woodland in southern Ohio" (2004, 47).

DISCUSSION

I reported above that most of the depositions were bone bundles or even dispersed bones of multiple humans. I have made this as an interpretation of Moorehead's description. His initial report of these burials is far from clear. Indeed, as Connolly noted, he does not even state "whether the terrace burials were primary or secondary deposits" (2004, 48). However, the various descriptions Moorehead makes enables concluding that, in most cases, these consisted of multiple discrete deposits of human bone bundles that were accumulated rather than being generated as a single event of deposition of individual bundles. This suggests that many discrete and probably sequential groups of "soul keepers" were responsible, each group with its set of bone bundles. In reporting on a large burial zone on the exterior terrace east of Gateway 55a, Moorehead estimated 18 to 20 individuals making up the content. Possibly this was because of the high degree of degradation of the bones. However, as he excavated deeper, bone degradation significantly reduced, and still, he speaks as if these were "scattered" among the stones with many bones being broken. This suggests, therefore, that the majority of the "burials" he reports were the accumulation of discrete "loads" of scattered and broken bone bundles. "There were decayed bones scattered all through this stone pile, and pottery fragments in large numbers. These were under the first layer of stone and very much decayed. They were not over 10 inches deep, most of them, but the larger and better preserved bones were about two feet deep. From the number of bones found, there must have been 18 or 20 individuals interred in this place" (Moorehead 1890, 37–38).

He goes on to describe another "mass of bones," also apparently on the exterior eastern terrace near Gateway 55a, having "several very fine knifes [probably bladelets] made of long curved flint flakes. . . . These skeletons had bones heaped over them, not laid regularly. The bones were broken in small fragments, about two bushels in quantity . . . not longer than six inches and most of them less than four inches" (1890, 38). This aggregate deposition would seem to be structured, possibly marking several sequential mortuary events, in that the lower ones were placed such as to maintain some skeletal order, but the others were "dumped." I noted above that the Turner Burial Place also had similar depositions, extended but disturbed skeletons (including deliberately broken arm or leg bones still connected to the body and carefully placed on it) along with bone bundles of disarticulated deceased. Other descriptions of "graves" that Moorehead makes also implicate the deposition of bone bundles, some bones being unbroken, others broken, and often mixed with the limestones that were used to accompany them. Reading this descriptive material clearly suggests that the term "grave" that Moorehead constantly used is extremely inappropriate. Of course, these deposits were certainly the material conditions of collective mortuary intentions, but characterizing these mortuary intentions in funerary terms is hardly illuminating.

In any case, as I noted above, while I am in full agreement with Connolly's claim that the ritual purpose of the South Fort was transformed by the addition of the south ramp and the mortuary component it covered, I do not agree with his claim that prior to this the South Fort was used for nonmortuary purposes and only became a context of mortuary ritual following the transformation. Rather, I see its original symbolic pragmatic meaning as mortuary in nature and that its mortuary meaning transformed into a new mortuary meaning. As I noted in the previous chapter, I interpret the T-Form as the equivalent of the High Bank C-R motif configuration and, as I argued in the latter case, this likely mediated a part of the mortuary *chaîne opératoire* process, but the part that did not entail deposition of mortuary remains. Connolly comments that, with the exception of Fort Ancient, typically T-Form earthworks have no mortuary depositions. I would explain the latter in terms of the symbolic pragmatic equivalency of the T-Form motif configuration earthwork and the High Bank C-R motif configuration earthwork. Therefore, before the "conversion," South Fort served as a symbolic pragmatic device for initial spirit-release mortuary ritual, possibly mediated by scaffolding, and when this scaffolding period ended, the body was removed to another site, possibly Turner, where it was given further postmortem treatment, as discussed above. However, as Connolly notes, a new regime was introduced to this site, marked by the deposition of the ramp ossuary at Gateway 55a, and this also entailed the construction of the Middle Fort and the North Fort. Therefore, while the symbolic pragmatic purpose of the South Fort was modified, this transformational construction program probably represents a redistribution of the sequential stages of the world renewal rites of the preexisting mortuary *chaîne opératoire* process rather than the innovation of a radically new trajectory.

Since there is very little mortuary residue associated with the North Fort, it is likely that this area was transformed into the standard T–Form component to carry out the tasks that had previously been performed in the South Fort. Here are found multiple stone pavement circles and stone rings. No doubt these also played an important role in the mortuary *chaîne opératoire* process, as well as, probably, the range of sacred games that were carried out as part of this process. These games were probably terminated in the multiple bone bundle depositions on the terraces surrounding the South Fort. Hence, the mortuary residue of the South Fort was deposited only after the Middle and North Forts were added and the latter constructions were probably critical to the felicity of these terminal sacred games-as-world-renewal-rites. What this implies is that, in symbolic pragmatic-meaning terms, the South Fort initially would have been the equivalent of the High Bank C-R motif type embankment earthwork in the Chillicothe tradition of south-central and central Ohio and, as I noted above, the High Bank C-R motif type certainly would have been involved in mortuary practices. These would have involved the deceased in a series of rituals, probably characterized as different sacred games. However, these games did not involve any terminal burials. Rather, the deceased would have been removed, possibly new artifacts added as contributed by the "losers" and "winners," and the deceased initiated into their laying-in period at a nearby site that manifested a symbolic pragmatic meaning equivalent to the Paint Creek C-R motif site, such as Liberty Works or Seip. If this is the case, then the ritual mortuary process that the stand-alone South Fort earthwork had mediated must have been continued elsewhere. As I commented briefly above, this "elsewhere" may have been Turner. This means that this transformation constituted Fort Ancient as a *Sacred Dual C-Form/T-Form motif earthwork complex*, the equivalent of the Sacred Dual C-R motif complex of the Chillicothe tradition. The C-Form was the South Fort, associated with mortuary remains, and the T-Form was embodied in the Middle and North Forts in which no mortuary remains were deposited.

Therefore, like the Mound City/Hopeton complex, the Fort Ancient embankment earthwork complex may have come to combine both the solar and lunar aspects of the cosmos as well as the vertical Above World–Middle World–Beneath World aspects. This would explain the formation of the four earth mounds in the north-central sector of the North Fort that embody alignments marking both the lunar and solar azimuth event cycles. It is very relevant, therefore, that these four mounds are also spaced from each other such that they constituted a square area having sides displaying a half OCD unit on which the Newark Circle-Octagon is based, the latter being a classic expression of the High Bank C-R motif (Romain 2004, 74–78). Also, according to Romain (2004, 70) the "virtual" square, as marked by the relative positioning of the four mounds, is oriented such as to incorporate the summer solstice sunset; and the set of northeastern parallel walls extending from Gateway 1 are oriented such that they align with the winter solstice sunset. The major axis of orientation of the Fort Ancient embankment as mediated through the four mounds constituting the above square orients on the maximum northern turning point of the 18.6-year lunar cycle, the same orientation that the main axis of orientation of the Newark Circle-Octagon has, as I discuss later. In short, these solar and lunar azimuth alignments mark some of the same lunar and solar azimuth turning points as found combined in the Sacred Dual C-R motif constituting the core earthwork configuration of the Chillicothe tradition. Hence, while prior to the addition of the dual Middle Fort/North Fort complex, the South Fort operated in terms similar to those of the High Bank C-R motif and probably passed on the deceased to Turner; after the construction that brought the Fort Ancient to its unique form, the South Fort was transformed and came to be the recipient of deceased from Turner (and possibly other sites, such as Stubbs Works) when the latter locales had completed their mortuary laying-in crypt rites. As I argued earlier, many of the latter likely were transferred to the Hopewell site, then returned to Turner (without their custodial regalia); and then many of these were given final terminal rites at the South Fort.

What is important about the Fort Ancient mortuary deposits is their particular state, primarily scattered and, in many cases, shattered human remains mixed with limestones and, in the case of the south ramp of Gateway 55a, covered by limestone slabs. The prolific use of limestone was also found at Turner. In fact, both infant and adult bones covered with limestone slabs were found. However, there is also a specific difference between the Turner mortuary program and the Fort Ancient program. The majority of the human remains at Turner were found in the stone-lined crypts (although many if not almost all of these were in a disturbed order), and only a small proportion of the mortuary deposits at Turner was identified as scattered bones covered by limestone. In contrast, at Fort Ancient, the latter type of bone distribution was standard and, as far as we currently know, very few depositions were made such that the bones retained some of their skeletal order.

Why I find this of considerable interest is the mix of similarities and differences between the treatments at Fort Ancient, Turner, and Hopewell. It

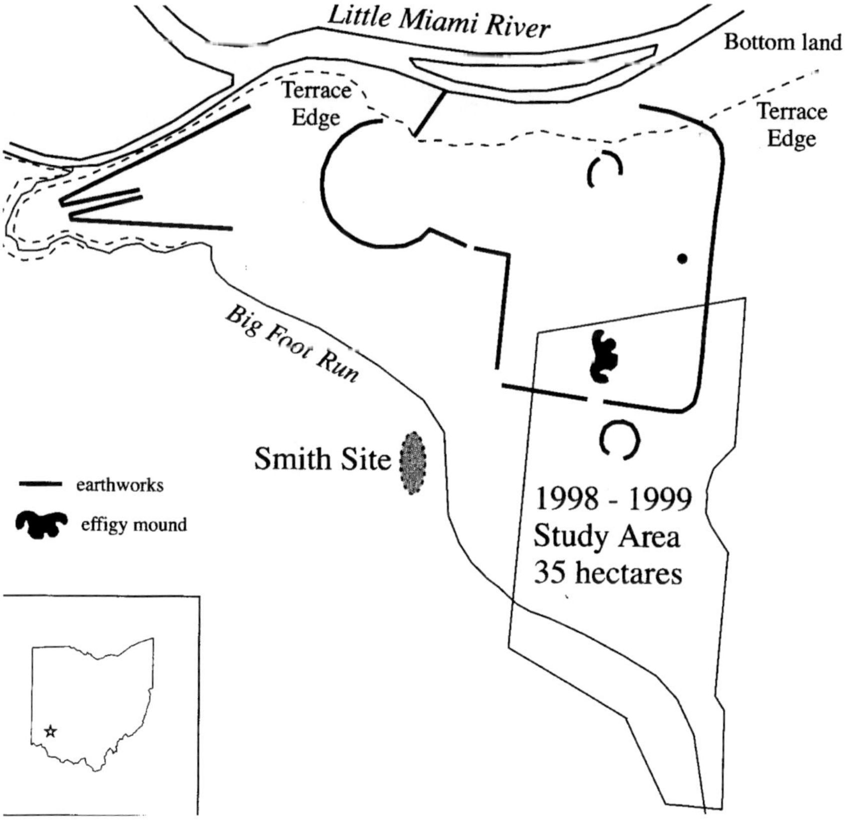

FIGURE 12.5
Stubbs Works
Source: Sunderhaus et al. 2001, figure 1. Courtesy of the Ohio Archaeological Council.

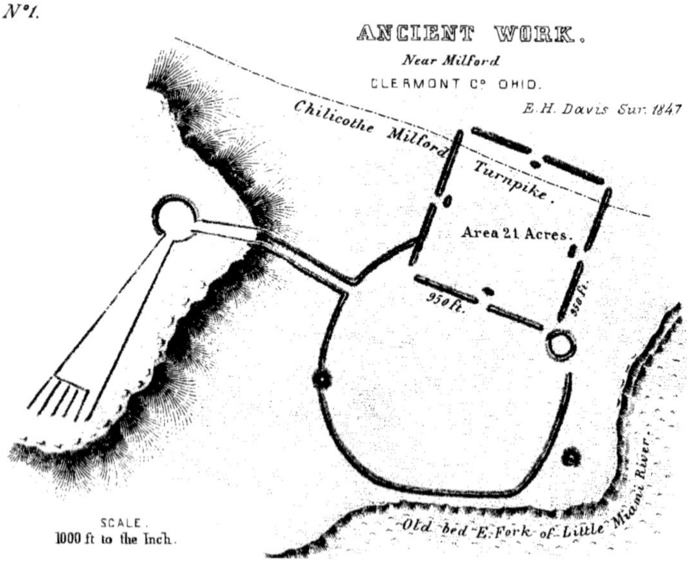

FIGURE 12.6
Milford Works
Source: Squier and Davis 1848, plate XXXIV, no. 1.

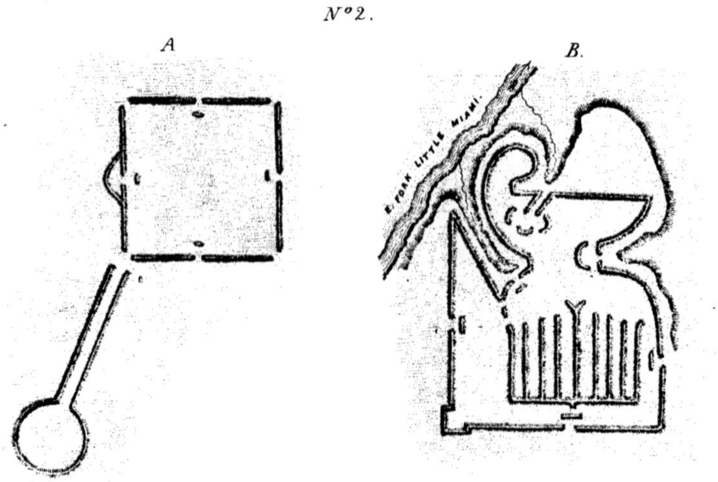

FIGURE 12.7
Camden Works (A)
Source: Squier and Davis 1848, plate XXXIV, no. 2a.

would appear that even though Turner both "fed" human deceased to the Hopewell site and received many of them back, in both cases the mortuary processing proceeded through the mediation of mortuary crypts—the vaulted log cribs at the Hopewell site and the in-ground stone-lined crypts at Turner.[6] It would appear that, with the extension of the South Fort by the building of the dual Middle Fort/North Fort complex, many of those who were returned to Turner, therefore, were once more passed on at the appropriate time as loose bundles of bones to be deposited at Fort Ancient. All this suggests not only a very complex, historically changing mortuary program linking Fort Ancient, Turner, and the Hopewell site, as well as other ancillary sites, such as the Stubbs Works, as I discuss below and in a later chapter, but a program that interfaced via the Hopewell and Seip sites with an equivalent mortuary program of the Chillicothe tradition sites.

CONCLUSION

Only recently has serious attention been paid to the Stubbs Works. This is a major earthwork that is only about 7 km downstream from Fort Ancient. This large and important site is under strong threat of being destroyed through residential development. Several archaeologists have jointly carried out important work during the last decade that has revealed that this was a significant embankment earthwork site (Cowan et al. 1999; Genheimer 1996, 1997; Sunderhaus et al. 2001). The actual plan form of the embankment earthworks cannot be fully reconstructed at this time and the illustrative map is only the best approximation at this time (figure 12.5). Nevertheless, if this is even a rough rendition of its form, then it was clearly modeled on the Paint Creek C-R motif, albeit one that looks significantly different from the standard. However, there are several other Paint Creek–like C-R motif earthworks in the same region, such as Milford and Camden (figures 12.6 and 12.7), and each of these is also a variant of the classic Paint Creek C-R motif as represented by Seip and Frankfort. In any case, there is another deviation that Stubbs has in terms of its usage. In this case, no mortuary deposits have as yet been found and, given the lack of any mounding, it might well be that this is because, while manifesting the Paint Creek C-R motif configuration, as I noted above, it was used only as an important *way station* for the sacred procession and sacred games in the move from Turner to Fort Ancient. That is, it appears to have been a major point of aggregation of cult sodality teams where they would stay as transient occupants while pursuing a cycle of sacred mortuary-mediated game playing. I will return to discuss Stubbs Works more fully later in the book since I believe that the work in this region has revealed important features and subsites that suggest strong representation of several cult sodality clusters, as indicated by the concentration of discrete locales marked by dense lithic scatters, particularly rich in bladelets.

It should be noted that my discussion up to now has clarified my position that the Sacred Games *Tournées* model postulates a major mechanism by which systems of cult sodality heterarchies were generated and sustained. That is, the games that it postulates are not to be treated as simply "add-on" events. Rather, they would serve as key mortuary-mediated ritual performances by which the human remains were being continually revitalized. It postulates that the games probably replicated the battles between the Above World Thunderbirds and Beneath World Serpents, the two sets of creator gods, these battles representing and participating in the ongoing cycling of life and death. A similar process would have occurred between the cult sodalities constituting the dispersed third-order Chillicothe-Newark cult sodality heterarchy. In the active experience of the cult sodalities, these games were an intrinsic part of their activities by which the primary raison d'être of the cult sodality heterarchies was realized and, indeed, organizing and conducting them, along with the associated mortuary events such as the laying-in period and the total mortuary *chaîne opératoire* process, including the long distance expeditions for producing resources (in some cases, these may have been more sacred bone bundles procured from distant areas as gifts for the franchising of important Hopewellian ritual usufruct), probably drew on the total organizational capacity of the third-order cult sodality heterarchy and its affiliated first- and second-order heterarchies. Many of the custodial regalia and auxiliary ceremonial artifacts served to endow the peer leaders and ordinary participants of these cult sodalities with the social action powers enabling them to constitute their behaviors so that they counted as the types of ritual activities by which the sodalities realized and fulfilled their ongoing duties. Therefore, the two major interacting networks, Fort Ancient–Turner–Hopewell, on the one hand, and Chillicothe-Newark, on the other, may also have sponsored sacred games directly between each other with teams cycling from one of these major sites to another according to a complex seasonal schedule. The winning teams might be rewarded with bundles of the sacred bones of the deceased from the cult sodality heterarchies of the losing teams, thereby rewarding them by transferring to their cult sodalities a greater abundance of sacrificial offerings than when they had left on their competitive rounds. The question this analysis raises is whether there is any other similar or equivalent patterning in the Ohio Hopewell site assemblage that could confirm it. I think there is and answering this question requires addressing the empirical ties that link Tremper and the Mound City/Hopeton complex together. To demonstrate this and further support the Ohio Hopewell Cult Sodality Heterarchy System model and the sacred games *tournées*/world renewal mortuary-mediated ritual process it postulates, I refocus my attention in the next chapter on the central Scioto region.

13

The Development of the Ohio Hopewell Cult Sodality Heterarchy System

I argued in the previous chapters that the earthworks of the Chillicothe region manifest a pattern that was formally different from, but the equivalent to, the formal pattern of the earthworks of the Great and Little Miami Valleys of southwest Ohio. I have referred to this generically as the Sacred Dual C-R motif. This motif combined formally complementary contrasting earthwork types that embodied the range of symbolic pragmatic meanings required for a heterarchy to perform its total suite of sacred games *tournées*/world renewal rituals. One of the best known expressions of the Sacred Dual C-R motif, of course, consists of the two complementary sites of (1) Liberty Works, manifesting the Paint Creek C-R motif aspect, and (2) High Bank, manifesting the High Bank C-R motif aspect and only a few kilometers north of Liberty Works on the same east bank of the Scioto River. This is also why I argued earlier that I consider these two sites as constituting a second-order cult sodality heterarchy. I also argued, however, that it is likely that the High Bank site also served to complement the Paint Creek C-R motif of the Seip site. Hence, to ensure access to an earthwork complex embodying the Sacred Dual C-R motif, these two second-order cult sodality heterarchies probably jointly built and used High Bank. I have argued that this is probably a historical result of the Seip and Liberty Works heterarchies being the organizational descendants of what was in my view the earliest formal expression of the Sacred Dual C-R motif that can be currently recognized, this being the complementary sites of Mound City and Hopeton. Building on earlier work by N'omi Greber and James Brown, I have reconstructed the likely historical development of the Mound City and Hopeton complex. The Mound City embankment incorporates 23 to 25 mounds that cover the residue of Hopewellian structures with prepared floors on which major ritual events of the mortuary *chaîne opératoire* of this site were carried out. These buildings were probably the renewal lodges of the set of first-order cult sodality heterarchies that were collectively responsible for these earthworks. Given the number of mounds, each covering the material remains of at least one, and sometimes two sequential renewal lodges, I think it is safe to say that Mound City constituted a major cult sodality heterarchy. I argue below that, in fact, it served one of the dispersed third-order cult sodality heterarchies in Ohio where, as at the Hopewell site, custodial regalia ritual usufruct conveyancing rites were performed.

As I have already argued for other mounds incorporated into major Ohio Hopewell embankment earthworks, such as the Hopewell, Seip, and Liberty Works sites, the Mound City mounds likely represent the residue of truncation events. Each mound was likely the particular responsibility of a first-order cult sodality heterarchy that abandoned the old renewal lodge structure and initiated a new one. The first-order cult sodality heterarchy would move laterally to a new space and start a new renewal lodge and all this probably marked a reproductive/renewal cycle of the age-grade promotions within the sodalities making up the heterarchy. The fact that several of these mounds actually cover two floors, one superimposed on the earlier and lower, suggests that, at least in the early times, instead of a mound being required to complete the truncation ritual, a renewal lodge was simply dismantled, the floor repaired and built up, and a new lodge constructed (some were initially dug into the ground and with their being abandoned, the huge pit had to be filled). While this replacement process occurred, the renewal lodges of the other first-order cult sodality heterarchies would be continued and rituals would be uninterrupted. Twenty-three or 24 mounds suggest that possibly at least five or six renewal lodges were being used simultaneously. However, it is important to note that some of these lodges were paired, suggesting a single second-order heterarchy required two or three at the same time. This suggests that the five or six (or more) first-order cult sodality heterarchies were affiliated into at least two second-order heterarchies incorporated in this site, thereby making Mound City the equivalent of the Hopewell site, being the place where a dispersed third-order cult sodality heterarchy performed the conveyancing of the ritual usufruct associated with the custodial regalia of the deceased custodians of all the cult sodalities of the heterarchy, and these conveyancing rites, of course, counted as decommissioning these potent items. In fact, the purpose of this chapter is to demonstrate the hypothesis that what I have termed the Mound City/Hopeton complex and Tremper, as well as other associated sites, constituted a dispersed third-order heterarchy equivalent to the dispersed third-order Fort Ancient–Turner–Hopewell heterarchy. I will term it the dispersed third-order Mound City/Hopeton–

Tremper cult sodality heterarchy. After the Mound City/Hopeton complex and the Tremper sites were abandoned, rather than disaffiliating, it further developed into the dispersed third-order Chillicothe-Newark cult sodality, with the continuation realized in the nearby Liberty Works/High Bank/Seip complex of earthwork sites along with, possibly, the complex Portsmouth embankment earthwork site as the continuity of the earlier Tremper site. This chapter demonstrates the former claim, that is, that Mound City/ Hopeton–Tremper constituted an early dispersed third-order cult sodality heterarchy, and the second claim is demonstrated as part of the development of the rest of this book, this second claim being the emergence of the Chillicothe group of Seip/High Bank/Liberty Works in the Chillicothe region with, possibly, Portsmouth manifesting the continuity of the earlier heterarchy; and then the addition of Newark to this complex forms the dispersed third-order Chillicothe-Newark heterarchy.

MOUND CITY AND HOPETON

As James Brown (2004b, 155–59) notes, many of the structures covered by the Mound City mounds, probably at least half, were built, used, abandoned, and mounded over prior to the building of the embankment earthwork that now surrounds them. Drawing on Greber's reconstruction of the ceremonial structures of this region immediately north of Chillicothe, he argues that, prior to building these cult sodality renewal lodges (I am using my terminology for them, not his), there were several other large renewal lodges constructed, constituting what Greber (1991) has referred to as the Northwest Chillicothe group. The two most prominent are found under the Miller–Carriage Factory mound and the Worthington mound. In fact, Brown's summary of Greber's data persuaded me that these structures were probably the expression of a second-order cult sodality heterarchy emerging more or less directly out of the cult sodality heterarchy responsible for the Adena mound, which is one of the better known mounds of this Northwest Chillicothe group. Hence, as Greber has suggested, most of the fundamental religious themes and practices, as well as the range of artifactual materials and motifs that make Ohio Hopewell so unique may have been innovated in this zone. "Some groups, in a relatively restricted area, greatly elaborated upon and possibly changed what had been wide spread, common ritual/ceremonial themes and left behind what we know as Ohio Hopewell. The (Adena) mound . . . appears to represent people who participated in the exceptional rather than the more common trajectory of cultural expression. William Mills' recognition of these people as separate from their apparent cultural descendants is quite valid in the Central Scioto. Stretching the name, without modification, to cover very different cultural histories, has, I believe, abetted confusion" (Greber 1991, 22).[1]

Brown has noted that during this very creative post-Adena and early Ohio Hopewell time, two examples of a new embankment form were constructed, one to the southwest and one to the northeast. I noted these in chapter 11. The northeast earthwork is the Cedar Bank site (figure 11.1) and the southwest embankment earthwork is the Shriver site (figure 11.2). Although their plan forms were different, both earthworks manifest the SL-Profile. Furthermore, Cedar Bank displays another classic attribute of the C-Form/SL-Profile motif, namely, having its open side overlooking the lower terrace of the Scioto River. The Shriver site, I have suggested, constituted a constrained C-Form/SL-Profile site. Definitely, it was unique in that instead of an open side overlooking the lower terrace, it formed a roughly circular embankment that had several wide entry and egress gates. As I postulated in chapter 11, these two SL-Profile embankments were the result of franchising world renewal ritual usufruct to the Northwest Chillicothe group by the group responsible for the contemporaneous Hopewell site on the nearby North Fork. Hence, the Northwest Chillicothe cult sodality heterarchy prior to the emergence of the Mound City embankment earthwork site consisted minimally of the Shriver site, the Cedar Bank site, and one or more major renewal lodge complexes in between, probably initially just west of where Mound City is now located. When these were abandoned, their replacements were built where Mound City is now. Notably, however, as I pointed out above, Brown claims that the Mound City embankment, a K-Profile embankment, was only built after many of these mounds were already in place. Most importantly, for my immediate purposes, it may also have had close relations with Tremper, an early embankment earthwork and mound site near the mouth of the Scioto River also displaying a K-Profile embankment with the same overall subrectilinear form (figure 13.1).

About the same time as the building of the Mound City embankment earthwork, it is likely that the Shriver site and the Cedar Bank site were abandoned and the Hopeton site across from Mound City with its new embankment earthwork was constructed (Byers 2004, 537–43). As I noted in chapter 10, the Hopeton C-R probably constitutes the earliest known expression of the High Bank C-R motif and, at the same time, Mound City with its rectilinear embankment was the earliest known expression of the infix component of the Paint Creek C-R motif (figure 10.3). Brown specifically postulates that the Mound City embankment form was strategically built so as to replicate the rectangular form of the renewal lodges found under the many mounds that it came to encircle. This suggests to me that the total complex was constructed to embody the powers of that part of the cosmos occupied by humans—that is, the Middle World. I have noted that a set of parallel walls built from the juncture of the Hopeton C-R southwest toward the bank of the Scioto River

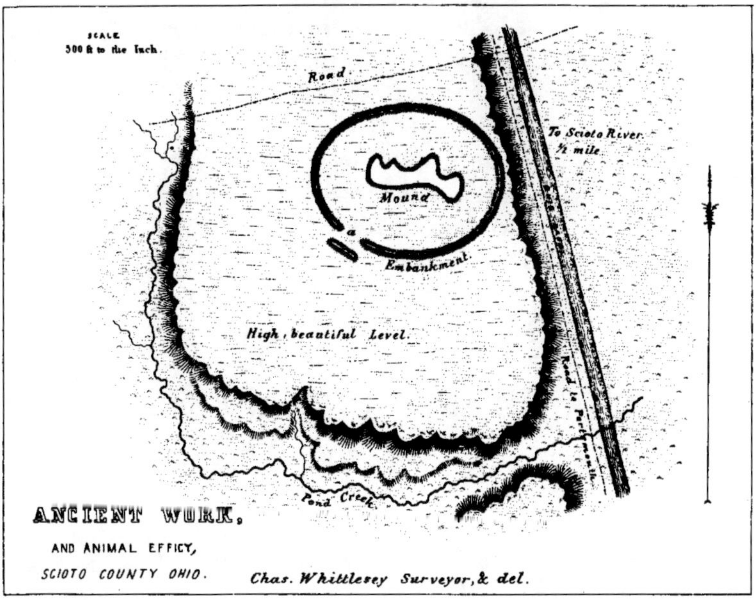

FIGURE 13.1
Tremper Site
Source: Squier and Davis 1848, plate XXIX.

stops at a point that is diametrically opposite a "sacra via" cut from the eastern gate of the Mound City embankment to the riverside, a position that Brown has also reiterated (2004b, 163, n13). Hence, rather than the parallel walls "targeting" Mound City (as some have claimed I have said), they target the spot on the east bank of the Scioto that is diametrically opposite the "sacra via" ramp constructed leading from the riverbank into the eastern gateway of the newly built Mound City embankment enclosure.[2] I have interpreted this arrangement as expressing the particular design intention to use the parallel walls in order to "collapse" the spatial separation of Hopeton and Mound City (figures 10.2 and 10.3) and, simultaneously, to represent Mound City and its embankment earthwork as being "inserted" *between* the C and R components of Hopeton (Byers 2004, 46–50). If the total complex is treated as a monumental icon and is given a symbolic pragmatic interpretation, this would effectively constitute Mound City as the "infix" component "inserting" its essential properties at the juncture of the Hopeton Circle and Square, thereby constituting the latter as the C and R components of the Paint Creek C-R motif earthworks. There is reason to support this possibility. As I noted earlier, when mortuary mounds are found in association with a Paint Creek

C-R motif site, they are located in the infix component, as exemplified at Seip and Liberty Works. Therefore, as I commented in chapter 10, the "sacra via" and the parallel walls constitute Mound City and Hopeton as the earliest known expression of the Paint Creek C-R motif. The fact that the "infix" and the circle and rectilinear are separated by the Scioto River does not preclude my claim. Indeed, it is now being recognized by a number of Hopewellian archaeologists that the interplay of water, earthworks, and mortuary practices was likely the outcome of a ritual strategy that specified this combination in order for the world renewal ritual to be felicitous (Cowan et al. 2004, 107–8).

What seems to be lacking is the complementary High Bank C-R motif. However, if the parallel embankments are conceptually "erased," then the main components of Hopeton proper, the Hopeton Circle and the Hopeton Rectilinear, embody the primary attributes of the High Bank C-R motif, making it probably the earliest known expression of the High Bank C-R motif, as such.[3] Incorporating the aggregation element, Mound City is once more positioned, that is, "fixed," between the Hopeton Circle and Rectilinear, constituting it as the earliest known expression of the Paint Creek C-R motif. Hence, in a gestalt-switching manner, this total configuration of the Mound City/Hopeton complex embodies the earliest known expression of the *Sacred Dual C-R motif.* As I argued earlier, if this is the case, then the Mound City/Hopeton complex participated in and presenced the powers of the two basic components of the cosmos that this dual motif represents. In this case, I have claimed that the Paint Creek C-R motif represents and participates in the solar aspect of the cosmos conceived as stratified into the Above World (the small circle), the Middle World (the large infix circle), and the Beneath World, the rectilinear, and, in like fashion, the High Bank C-R motif represents and participates in the lunar aspect (Byers 2004, 101, 221).[4] The presence of powers of both aspects may have been required because they operated in a complementary manner to mediate the total suite of postmortem human sacrificial offering rites. Of course, as noted in the previous chapter with regard to the South Fort of Fort Ancient prior to its conversion, embankment earthwork sites manifesting the Lunar motif such as Hopeton usually lack overt representation of deceased human remains. This does not mean, however, that deceased humans were not processed in these contexts. It simply means that following the mortuary rites performed in them, the bodies were removed to the renewal lodge in the nearby Paint Creek C-R motif site—or its equivalent—where the more extensive laying-in rites would be performed as described previously. This is likely why Mound City is so rich in mortuary remains while just across the river in the contemporary Hopeton embankments mortuary remains are absent. The fact that two extended burials have been found at the southwest end of the parallel wall aggregation element does not vitiate but enhances the validity of this conclusion (Romain

2004, 118–19). The mortuary depositions were likely deliberately not placed in the context of Hopeton embankments but in the context of the juncturing element that "inserted" Mound City as the "infix" component into the place that it should be conceptualized as occupying in order to embody the powers of the Middle World and it is in this infix unit that the mortuary depositions were traditionally made. As Romain also comments, the parallel walls or, as I call it, the aggregation element incorporates the winter solstice sunset, further reinforcing the notion that the earthworks served as monumental icons presencing relevant powers of the cosmos that thereby transformed mortuary behaviors to count as critically important world renewal rituals. Of course, it should not be ignored that while Mound City has little in the way of open areas where sacred games could be effectively carried out, Hopeton embodies two very expansive zones where many such games could be accommodated and, of course, as embodying both the Solar and Lunar powers, the total suite of games required as part of the world renewal mortuary process could be performed there.

If this is the case, then any monumental site that can be unequivocally identified as Hopewellian but has no demonstrated mortuary residue is likely the symbolic pragmatic expression of the High Bank C-R motif or its equivalent. Near Mound City is the site referred to as Spruce Hill (Ruby 2009, 61–62). It is built on the high plateau ridge overlooking the juncture of the Scioto River and the Paint Creek and could well serve this purpose. Hence, Spruce Hill may have been the complement not of the Mound City/Hopeton complex but of the Hopewell site itself. What is the basis for my claim? As I also noted earlier, initially the Hopewell site was constructed as a standard C-Form/SL-Profile embankment earthwork and only later in its occupational history were the small versions of the Paint Creek Circle and Paint Creek Square added, thereby constituting the C-R components of the Paint Creek C-R motif. I interpret these additions as demonstrating that for the responsible groups, the C-Form/SL-Profile configuration and the infix of the Paint Creek C-R configuration were equivalent in symbolic pragmatic meaning, both taken to be embodying the powers of the Middle World under the solar aspect. It is not surprising, therefore, that there is a strong representation of the mortuary sphere at the Hopewell site. The equivalent representation at Mound City would suggest that both sites were used in the equivalent manner, as Solar motif sites.

Remember, however, that the original Hopewell site was built as a typical C-Form/SL-Profile site. As I noted in the previous chapter, this site is typically paired with a ridge-top site, the latter representing the Lunar motif. Spruce Hill may have served this purpose for the Hopewell site. Also as I noted earlier, the C-Form type is built on a higher terrace or, if a terrace is not available, even a hilltop. Its single SL-Profile (an external ditch) linear embankment is formed into a C shape with an open side overlooking the valley bottom. Sometimes it will have several asymmetrically spaced entryways. Now this may have had a "practical" purpose in that the external ditch of the embankment would then contain any rainwater and this would drain out at the two ends where the embankment terminated at the terrace edge. Again, the importance of water is noted. In fact, several reports of the external ditches of such sites have been made and it is noted that the external ditch was itself more than simply the source of earth for the contiguous embankment since, in fact, once the earth was removed, the exposed earth was covered with a layer of clay, suggesting the intent was to form a waterproofing or sealing layer to encourage ponding (Cowan 2007). A similar intention may have been expressed in the formation of the two lateral ponds that defined the typical gateway in the T-Form earthwork like Fort Ancient (Connolly and Sunderhaus 2004, 53–54; figure 12.4). These ponds were also typically lined and sealed such as to retain the water that drained into them. The Hopewell C-Form/SL-Profile embankment certainly conforms to all these criteria. Assuming that the C-Form was the symbolic pragmatic equivalent of the infix component of the Paint Creek C-R motif, then the Hopewell site and the Paint Creek C-R motif sites of the Chillicothe region have the same symbolic pragmatic meaning for their respective heterarchies such that both were critical monumental symbolic pragmatic devices by which the mortuary behaviors performed in their contexts were transformed to count as the type of mortuary rituals intended.

This simply reiterates the point I made earlier that there are two formal expressions of the Sacred Dual motif, the version that forms the core of the Chillicothe earthwork tradition and the version that serves the same purpose for the Fort Miami earthwork tradition of the Great and Little Miami Valleys. Hence, I have concluded that there are two equivalent Sacred Dual Motif earthwork configurations in the Ohio Middle Woodland period and these form the core of the two embankment Hopewell earthwork traditions in Ohio: the Sacred Dual C-Form/T-Form motif that is the core of the Miami Fort tradition, which probably emerged originally in the Little and Great Miami River Valleys; and the Sacred Dual Paint Creek /High Bank C-R motif, which is the core of the Chillicothe tradition that emerged in the Scioto region. Clearly, the North Fork–Paint Creek region was a dynamic interface where these two traditions interacted.

THE THIRD-ORDER MOUND CITY/HOPETON–TREMPER CULT SODALITY HETERARCHY

I postulated above that the Mound City/Hopeton complex constituted a type of site equivalent to the Hopewell site, which as I discussed fully earlier was where, along with the full range of rituals, the specialized conveyancing of the ritual usufruct rites occurred. This would mean that, in fact, it played a ritual role equivalent to the Hopewell site for a second equally extensive dispersed third-order cult sodality heterarchy. I postulate that this is the dispersed third-order Mound City/Hopeton–Tremper cult sodality heterarchy. I now want to address the empirical data that will demonstrate this claim.

The mortuary record of Mound City (figure 10.3) is well known to have a rich representation of custodial regalia in the form of copper plates, copper headdresses, large quantities of mica sheets, and so on. It also has an interesting burnt deposit on the floor of Mound 8 containing the largest known set of Hopewell platform pipes, close to 200, both animal effigy and plain types, as well as pearl and shell beads, copper and silver items, and so on. This large burnt deposit was almost equaled by a similar burnt deposit at Tremper (figure 13.1), which is located on the lower Scioto River just a few kilometers north of the confluence of the Scioto-Ohio Rivers at the city of Portsmouth. There is a major burnt deposit on the floor of the Tremper mound, Feature 5, which was found not in but beside a large depository basin on the floor of the central eastern room of the large Tremper Renewal Lodge. The deposit included 136 platform pipes, both effigy and plain, along with a large quantity of small items: gorgets, copper items, pearl and shell beads, cones of quartz and galena, animal jaws, and so on, typical of the residual remains of what I have classified as personalty, mourning gifts, and laying-in shrouds (Mills 1916, 285–86). The contents of both the Feature 5 burnt deposit in the Tremper Renewal Lodge and the great pipe deposit beside a crematory basin in the Mound 8 renewal lodge deposit at Mound City had been broken and burned.[5] The pipes in both displayed the same style, as well as the same range of effigy animals. For long it had been assumed that these artifacts were produced from material procured at the Feurt Ohio pipestone quarries, these being only a few kilometers east of the Tremper site. However, it is now known that this was not the case. According to Sarah Wisseman and her colleagues, "many artifacts thought to have been produced from Ohio pipestone were in fact made from northern Illinois pipestone or Minnesota catlinite. Another surprise was our discovery that Hopewellian craftsmen working at Tremper Mound, Ohio, did not produce all of their pipes from the nearby Feurt Hill pipestone quarries. In fact, only about fifteen percent of the production was from local stone; eighty-five percent of the pipes were made from pipestone from northwestern Illinois and Minnesota catlinite. On the other hand, 97 percent of the pipes found at Mound City National Monument only miles away were revealed by analysis to be made from local stones" (2008, 3).[6] The similarities in representation suggest that possibly the same persons carved the pipes that made up both deposits at Mound City and Tremper.

However, just as the Hopewell and Turner sites differed in important ways, so too Mound City/Hopeton and Tremper differed in significant ways. At Mound City proper, each of the renewal lodges at the base of the mounds discussed above had carefully placed cremated burials (Byers 2004, 346–68). There were several deposits in every lodge consisting of cremated human remains (there were no extended burials), and these were easily differentiated into two categories. There were the elaborate cremated mortuary deposits usually centered if a single cremation, or if several, these were symmetrically spaced across a large burial platform altar. The cremated human remains were usually carefully deposited on or scattered across one or more major custodial regalia items—copper plates, a copper axe, an example of copper mushroom effigy, copper headdresses, and so on. There also were a number of cremated human remains, typically deposited on small prepared surfaces and also usually mixed with these remains were burnt and broken artifacts that clearly had been part of the cremation. These two categories of cremations makes it clear that it was not the humans who were being given differential treatment, since in both cases the human remains were cremated, but the artifact categories. Artifacts of one set of categories were systematically subjected to burning and breakage along with the humans being cremated; and those of another set were deliberately not subjected to such destructive treatment, although the humans that accompanied them were cremated. The above cremations make this differential treatment clear and a careful examination of the categories of artifacts being cremated showed that these were what I earlier referred to as personalty, mourning gifts, and laying-in shrouds. Those that were not subjected to destruction typically fell within the custodial regalia category of copper plates, headdresses, marine shells, exotic copper symbols, and so on. Indeed, the relative positioning of the human cremated remains on top of the custodial regalia suggests that the latter were primary and the former were auxiliary or supplemental (Byers 2004, 337–42). That is, the custodial regalia were placed with great care, usually very symmetrically and properly on the puddled clay floor of the log-crib altar. Then the cremated human remains were either scattered over the deposit of (undamaged) custodial regalia or were placed as a pile on top of a central copper custodial regalia item, such as a copper plate. It is from this differential treatment of human remains and artifactual remains at Mound City that I inferred the special nature of what I have been calling the custodial regalia. Interestingly, if only the Hopewell site Mound 25 deposits were available for analysis, since these were for the most part extended burials, the structural distinction of personalty, mourning gifts, laying-in shroud, and custodial regalia would have been largely unnoticeable since there would be no way of noting from the Hopewell site mortuary remains alone that human and custodial regalia items were subject to different sacrificial rules.[7]

Indeed, overall there is a surprisingly small number of cremations on the floor of any given renewal lodge at Mound City, often no more than eight or ten individual cremations, and only a few of these were associated with custodial regalia. Besides the cremated burials in association with custodial regalia deposits and the small number of "ordinary" mixed burnt artifact/human remain deposits that were placed on simple prepared floor spaces, these multiple Mound City renewal lodges also included large crematory basins displaying signs of multiple uses. However, they also were usually empty and carefully cleaned of any ashes. Careful repairs of cracks caused by heavy usage indicated that many more cremations occurred in these basins than can be accounted for by the rather few of the above cremated deposits. Indeed, the long-term and repeated intensive burning to which most if not all of the crematory basins were subjected appears to be far in excess of the actual number of cremated deposits found on the floors of these renewal lodges. If this is the case, then where are all these cremated burials? Recalling the answer to the similar question with regard to the Hopewell and Turner sites, I postulate that many of them ended up on the floor of another renewal lodge, in this case the large Tremper Renewal Lodge. Here, in stark contrast to the carefully performed and, in general, small number of Mound City cremations, most of them richly accompanied by custodial regalia, the floor of the Tremper mound incorporated one large multiroomed complex renewal lodge and it contained four collective depositories of cremated humans, one very large 10 × 5 foot rectangular depository built into the floor of the central of three eastern rooms, and three lesser depositories on prepared clay areas of the central main room. None of these had artifacts in association and, in particular, there was a complete absence of the type of custodial regalia that was associated with the cremations of Mound City. Since almost all the Tremper cremations were "dumped" into one of these four depositories, and also many human ashes were scattered across the surrounding floor space, Mills could only make a calculated estimate of about 375 individual cremations making up the contents of the major depository. He admitted, however, that this was probably overly conservative. Mills also noted that there were two below-floor cremated burials, the only ones he noted.

Of course, the key puzzle is the fact that Tremper had such a large quantity of mass-deposited cremations compared to the much smaller number of individually deposited cremations at Mound City. This is particularly puzzling since Tremper had only twelve crematory basins while the much smaller multiple single-roomed renewal lodges at Mound City had usually three or four crematory basins each. An equally important puzzle, of course, is the conspicuous absence of any custodial regalia at Tremper and its proliferation at Mound City. These puzzles, however, are easily resolved if the contrasts between Mound City and Tremper mortuary deposits are viewed as the result of a type of sacred games *tournées*/mortuary *chaîne opératoire* process similar to that postulated as linking the Hopewell, Turner, and Fort Ancient sites. That is, if the similarities are substantive, then the Mound City/Hopeton complex and Tremper constituted major sites of an early Ohio Hopewell dispersed third-order cult sodality heterarchy. The deceased of the participating cult sodalities may have first been brought in sacred procession from their first-order and second-order cult sodality heterarchies to converge at Mound City. Here they were curated in the renewal lodges that the autonomous first-order cult sodality heterarchies built and used at Mound City. Appropriate sacred games were played, likely at Hopeton, and many of the bodies and sacred bones were then cremated at Mound City in the renewal lodge of the appropriate first-order cult sodality heterarchy. Others may have been curated and ultimately constituted as sacred bone bundles to be carried in procession to Tremper where final cremation occurred and deposition in one of the four depositories. The custodial regalia of course, following my earlier interpretation of similar items at the Hopewell site, would have served to mediate the conveyancing rituals by which the spirit names of these critical items were permanently transferred to the replacement custodial peer-group leaders and the original regalia items were curated at Mound City to serve as a sacrificial offering for the anticipated truncation events.[8] The human cremations, as well as the bone bundles of those not yet cremated, were then removed to Tremper, where the former were deposited in one of the four depositories and the latter were cremated in one of the twelve basins and also deposited in one of the depositories. This removal of the cremations from Mound City is clearly indicated by the fact that its many crematory basins were carefully cleaned of any ashes and, in fact, when necessary repaired and not reused prior to the truncation ritual that led to the construction of the mound over the total floor. However, it is possible that when one or more of the renewal lodges at Mound City was scheduled to be abandoned by its cult sodality heterarchy, the most recently curated deceased would be cremated and, instead of being taken to Tremper for deposition in the collective depository, they were deposited as mixed burnt deposits of human ashes and bones with their accompanying burnt artifacts, as described earlier. In short, the reason the crematory basins display heavy use and repairs while there were actually very few cremated burials at Mound City is that during the life history usage of the renewal lodge, most deceased cremated there were transported to Tremper for final deposition in one of the cumulative depositories, itself a form of spirit-release sacrificial ritual, of course.

Given this empirical evidence, therefore, I would suggest that the Mound City/Hopeton–Tremper complex constituted an early Middle Woodland period dispersed third-order cult sodality heterarchy similar to the ones I have already described with regard to both Fort Ancient–Turner–Hopewell and Seip–High Bank–Liberty Works. It must be kept in mind there are likely other sites involved in the postulated dispersed third-order Mound City/Hopeton–Tremper cult sodality heterarchy. I would postulate Fort Hill, in this case. This is a major hilltop embankment earthwork that is only a few kilometers northwest of Tremper. Finally, the fact that Portsmouth displays a variant of the C-R motif patterning suggests that this may have been constructed by the "descendants" of the second-order cult sodality heterarchy that was initially located and responsible for Tremper and, therefore, it was a significant part of the later Middle Woodland period Chillicothe-Newark cult sodality heterarchy. Indeed, Greber has commented that the Cincinnati museum has a map of Portsmouth in its archives that shows what might be the core of a Sacred Dual C-R motif configuration. "A nineteenth century map curated at the Cincinnati Museum shows both a square and an octagon in the southern areas of the Portsmouth Works . . . [but] it has not been field tested to my knowledge" (Greber 2006, 103). However, if they were, then we would have to consider terming the Chillicothe-Newark nexus as the dispersed third-order Portsmouth-Chillicothe-Newark cult sodality heterarchy. However, it is also possible that with the abandonment of Tremper and the establishment of Portsmouth, instead of retaining its connection with Chillicothe, this heterarchy shifted its interaction up the Ohio to incorporate Marietta in an autonomous Portsmouth-Marietta second- or possibly third-order cult sodality heterarchy.

THE MORTUARY/NONMORTUARY RITUAL DICHOTOMY

There is a critical dimension of the dispersed third-order cult sodality heterarchy model and its associated sacred games *tournées*/postmortem human sacrificial *chaîne opératoire* view that stands in considerable contrast to most interpretations of the Ohio Hopewell. In most cases, while the mortuary practices of Ohio Hopewell are widely acknowledged to have been an important aspect of this episode, most archaeologists strongly resist attributing to them the significance that I have. Many argue that while mortuary ritual was performed in the earthwork context, it was only a small proportion of the overall ritual performed and this was generally nonmortuary in nature. The thinking appears to be that the time, effort, and organization invested into building these earthworks cannot be intelligibly explained if the only ritual performed there was funerary in nature! And it is typical that those who make this assessment assume that, indeed, the mortuary practices express what I have termed the funerary paradigm. Therefore, just as in societies embodying a Euro-American cultural sphere where funerary ritual makes up only a small set of the rituals held in a religious complex, such as a church or synagogue, so it is assumed that, as basically a complicated set of funerary rites, these would make up only a small set of the total range of rituals held in the embankment earthworks. Hence, informed by this view, the ceremonial sphere is treated as strongly sectoring the ceremonial activity areas in the typical embankment earthwork or facility, such as the Big House or auxiliary structures, as being dichotomized between funerary (i.e., mortuary) and nonfunerary (i.e., nonmortuary), and assessing which type was expressed in any particular ceremonial context largely depends on the presence or absence of human remains. If there is a large burnt deposit of artifacts in a basin and if there are no human cremated remains that can be associated with these, then this deposit is treated as the residue of a nonmortuary ceremony because the absence of human remains makes it count as a nonfunerary ritual. Even if the burnt artifacts consist of categories that are well represented in human burial deposits that may be only a few feet away from the burnt deposit, only the deposits directly associated with human remains, not those that lack them, are treated as the residue of a mortuary rite, and this rite is reductively treated as a funerary rite.

This bias underwrites what might be called the mortuary/nonmortuary ceremonial dichotomy. This dichotomy extends to the embankment earthworks themselves. Hence, an earthwork displaying the High Bank C-R configuration or its equivalent lacks human remains. Therefore, the ritual purpose and symbolic pragmatic meaning excluded funerary practices and, of course, a similar view has been expressed by Connolly toward the T-Form ridge-top earthworks. When built and used as a stand-alone ridge-top earthwork, the South Fort component lacked associated mortuary residue and, therefore, it was not part of the funerary ritual sphere, and so on. Christopher Carr also has strongly advocated this mortuary/nonmortuary dichotomy and, of course, he is a strong advocate of treating the mortuary practices as primarily funerary in nature. However, he is prepared to recognize that some mortuary residue may have been the result of nonfunerary practices since he comments that "some gatherings at Hopewell ceremonial centers may have occurred to renew the world and/or to initiate youngsters to adulthood, and these *may have been integrated within mortuary ceremonies*" (Carr 2005a, 475, emphases added). Nevertheless, in any major mortuary gatherings, apparently the funerary characterization would prevail, particularly related to ancestor ritual, and world renewal purposes might simply be conveniently piggybacked on mortuary behaviors that were performed primarily as funerary rites. "Any mortuary ceremonies that involved rites of reincorporation or ancestor worship on a large scale could have had world renewal rites and group (age-set) initiation rites intertwined with them" (2005a, 476). Carr has recently expanded on his reason for downgrading the relevance of world renewal ritual to Ohio Hopewell ceremonialism in general and the mortuary sphere in particular and it appears that one source of difference we have depends primarily on how we define world renewal rituals. He notes that Robert Hall advanced the notion that some regions identified mortuary practices with world renewal ritual, particularly the reenactment of the world creation stories, and spirit-adoption rites, such as fictive kinship Calumet ceremonialism.

Interestingly, while recognizing that all this is an important insight, Carr considers that this mortuary/world renewal connection does not account for the elaborate complexity of Hopewellian ceremonialism. His argument for this is based on analogy with historic Native American communities, who he quite rightly argues performed a broad range of rituals dealing with increasing the fertility of both animal and plant species, as well as rites of human reproduction, social rites of passage, and so on. In his view, these were not mortuary rites, even though they were *world renewal practices.* "Also not considered by recent researchers in their ethnohistorical analogies are the many themes and practices that comprise world renewal rites of Woodland and Plains Native Americans, beyond rites of re-creating the cosmos through reiteration of creation myths by oratory, drama, and material construction. These additional elements of ceremony include: petitioning for the fertility of animal and plant species; renewing day length and maintaining the seasons" (Carr 2008a, 632). He goes on to emphasize the importance of funerary rites.

I think that his interpretation of Hall's identification of mortuary practices with world renewal and spirit-adoption rites is overly narrow and all it does is enable Carr to sustain his claim that the mortuary sphere was largely identical to the funerary sphere. Certainly, I would not accept this construal of world renewal ritual as applying to my approach. I have treated the mortuary sphere of Ohio Hopewell as clearly playing a major constitutive role in the reproduction of the sacred order of nature and, therefore, it figures as central to the social concerns of the communities and to their investment of time and labor. It would easily accommodate the many species-specific and species-general fertility rituals, and so on, that Carr has specified. Indeed, it would go well beyond his specifications by including the need to reduce sacred pollution and reverse perceived deterioration of the environment. I have consistently tied subsistence, settlement, and ceremonialism together as causally integrated and I have treated the mortuary sphere as the primary core of this ceremonialism. Furthermore, this does not ignore the funerary aspect. However, it treats the latter as only a small part of the total mortuary *chaîne opératoire* process and, for my purposes, little of the funerary aspect actually relates to the Ohio Hopewell mortuary sphere, as such. However, this does not deny the relevance of the funerary ritual for Ohio Middle Woodland communities since it would make up a greater aspect of the clan-based mortuary sphere. It is in this context, as I argued earlier, where the major funerary rites were primarily carried out. My approach also insists on the critical importance of the symbolic pragmatic meaning of the material context of collective human behaviors. Major contexts, such as the embankment earthworks, entail treating all lesser associated components—the features, facilities, and even artifacts—as taking on their particular symbolic pragmatic meanings in virtue of the major contexts in which they are regularly used (Byers 2004, 342–44). Hence, if the Hopewell site is recognized as a monumental context by which behaviors directly mediated by human remains are constituted as world renewal rituals of *different sorts*, there is no necessity to have mortuary remains directly associated with all features in order for these features to have symbolic pragmatic mortuary/world renewal meaning. Hence, the burnt deposits at the base of Shetrone Mound 17 and Mound 25 that have no cremated human remains are no less mortuary media by which the collective burning behaviors that were carried out in them were constituted as sacrificial mortuary rites than were the vaulted chambers where human remains *were* found. Indeed, the Mound 25 burnt deposits were surrounded by these chambers. A contextualist symbolic pragmatic approach entails treating these burnt-deposits-without-human-remains as part of the mortuary sphere and the ritual that they mediated would not be funerary but world renewal in nature. Again, in somewhat stark contrast, Carr has argued that the reason ritual that did not have mortuary remains directly related would, nevertheless, be performed in such contexts would be in order to have it enhanced by the sanctity of the mortuary facilities. "First is the distinction between ceremonies that were concerned directly with the recent dead and social adjustment and that were necessarily tied to the mortuary setting versus ceremonies that had other purposes such as world renewal, initiation, and thanksgiving yet were enacted in mortuary settings. The latter kinds of ceremonies were choreographed in charnel houses or near burial mounds perhaps to enhance their potency, or to ensure inclusion of the dead as well as the living members of the society in the ceremony"(2008c, 255). As I noted above, this view assumes a sharp separation of rituals into funerary (mortuary) versus nonfunerary (nonmortuary) and is forced to account for copresence on the facile claim that the sanctity of mortuary practices and the associated facilities, such as "charnel houses," would have a "spill-over" effect on the "potency" of the nonmortuary ritual. In my view, this is unacceptable. Rather, the rituals without direct involvement of human remains are a critical part of the mortuary *chaîne opératoire* process and the reason they were performed in association with the embankment earthwork facilities was that the latter had the intended constitutive effect, this being that only in that context would the rituals making burnt offerings of mortuary-associated artifacts count as having a world renewal nature.

CONCLUSION

The Ohio Hopewell Cult Sodality Heterarchy System model does not stand alone. It operates in tandem with a number of models to constitute a theoretical framework: the Sacred Games *Tournées* model, the important Ecclesiastic-Communal Cult Sodality model, and the latter has also generated its associated settlement pattern model, which I have termed the Cult Sodality Cluster model, and so on. This presupposes the general settlement model that is auxiliary to the Complementary Heterarchical Community model that addresses the settlement pattern of these communities when in the bifurcated settlement articulation modal posture. I have termed it the Dual Complementary Clan/Cult Sodality Clusters Community model and it has two complementary subsidiary settlement models, of course: the Dispersed Kinship Habitation Cluster model, addressing the everyday domestic-based clan component, and the Cult Sodality Cluster model. This framework of interrelated models has generated a further need to develop the conceptual framework articulating the range of relevant site types since, in fact, there are two gaps that need to be filled, one postulating the site modes that linked the cult sodality clusters bottom up to the sodality heterarchies, and the other postulating the physical structures that would be part of the major embankment earthwork complexes themselves. I already have discussed the renewal lodge category, as exemplified by the great timber structures of the Seip and Liberty Works sites. However, if this renewal lodge category actually served an affiliation of autonomous first-order heterarchies, then these latter alliances and their component cult sodalities would probably also have separate locales for their in-house rituals and meetings at the embankment earthworks of the second-order cult sodality heterarchy constituted by their affiliation. I address these important matters in the next chapter.

14

Embankment Earthwork and Way Station Facilities

If it is accepted that the Ohio Hopewell features, facilities, artifacts, and mortuary deposits are the material expression of the cult sodality sphere and this material assemblage was primarily, although not exhaustively, the set of complex symbolic pragmatic devices by which the sacred games *tournées*/mortuary-mediated world renewal ritual program was realized, then this sphere of material cultural ceremonialism must be treated methodologically and substantively as structurally autonomous of the kinship-based domestic habitation sphere. This is in virtue of my theoretical claim that the Ohio Middle Woodland community was based on the deep kinship-companionship social structure. This means that these two social components stood to each other as reciprocally constitutive and relatively autonomous. Hence, the domestic/ceremonial dichotomy that is so strongly developed in the Ohio Middle Woodland period is a regional manifestation of the system of complementary heterarchical communities in a fairly radical bifurcated settlement articulation modal posture. This arm's-length relation is manifested at the local level by distributing the countryside sites into clusters of complementary locales, the almost archaeologically invisible kinship-based semisedentary seasonal (warm and cold) base-camp habitations and the significantly more visible clusters of cult sodality ceremonial nodal sites and their auxiliary associated age-set and age-grade specialized production locales. The arm's-length relation manifested by these two complementary categories of site clusters was critical to ensuring that individuals could freely exercise their obligations in the positions that they occupied in both spheres. Individuals would move back and forth between the locales of these two clusters, acting in the capacity as kin when in their seasonal base-camp habitation locales and as companions when in one of the sites making up the sodality cluster of the community.

Clearly, in these circumstances, the patterning of a seasonal base-camp habitation site would tend to manifest the practical needs of a semisedentary but rather everyday intensive mixed gardening and foraging way of life—shelters, cooking and heating facilities, garbage refuse, special activity areas, storage pits, and so on. In terms of material facilities and features, this patterning can easily be assimilated to the notion of domestic behavior. Of course, as I argued earlier, living lightly on the land would be a primary deontic principle of a people having a custodial-squatter ethos and immanentist cosmology and, therefore, the seasonal basis of these camps and the likelihood that in each season a kin group would occupy a base locale slightly displaced from the previous season would tend to generate a minimalist distribution of daily living material residue, the very point that, as I noted earlier, was argued by both Kozarek (1987, 127; 1997, 135–39) and Dancey (1991, 66) should mobile (or semisedentary, if you wish) seasonal occupation be practiced. However, caution is required since the kinship-based habitation locale site would not monopolize domestic facilities. As I noted earlier, it is now generally recognized that at least around if not in the embankment earthworks there is considerable residue that manifests domesticity since those attending to centralized ritual practices would need to fulfill their practical daily life needs. Furthermore, it is clear that the locales for the performing of ritual were much more stable in terms of spatial continuity than those of the domestic habitation. The latter would be deliberately shifted seasonally; the former were anchored as traditional sacred locales where ritual was required to be performed since the material forms, orientation, and contents of these locales were part of the symbolic pragmatics that transformed the collective behaviors carried out there to count as the ritual practices that were intended.

Of course, the critical factor that most recognize now is that the quantity of domestic residue associated with embankment earthworks is insufficient to support the claim that these also sustained permanent, nucleated villages. This is an important conclusion that is generally recognized. However, for most archaeologists this conclusion is made within the perspective of the monistic modular polity community view. It is also generally assumed, therefore, that whatever the nature of the occupational patterning, including the domestic residue (if any), it was generated by some form of kinship-based grouping making up the proprietorial corporate community or alliance of communities responsible for the earthwork. In short, under the orthodox view, the groups that occupied the earthworks, however temporarily or otherwise, and the groups that occupied the habitation locales, whether sedentary or mobile, have been treated as being of the same social nature—kin groups.

Therefore, even when sodality groups are recognized under a monistic modular polity community view, these are typically treated as simply a subsumed aspect of the dominant kinship-structured community, a point clearly emphasized in Carr's interpretation of the tripartite mortuary patterning of the Seip and Liberty Works Big Houses in which he contrasted the copper headdresses and celts as marking "community-wide" leaders while the copper earspools and plates marked the deceased as having only prestige in one of the sodalities of the community. The "leadership roles [were] indicated by headplates and celts and membership or achievement in sodalities [were] marked by breastplates and earspools" (2005b, 267–68); and although earspools and plates "are widely enough distributed among persons at Seip-Pricer and Edwin Harness to have symbolized sodalities, they are not segregated by cluster" (2005b, 292). In the latter case, he presented the lack of "segregated" distribution as grounds to reject the possibility that the tripartite mortuary patterning, as such, manifested sodalities. Hence, under this unitary or monistic community view, characterizing the groupings that occupied the earthworks meant speaking of different permutations of kin groups, for example, two or more nuclear families belonging to the same clan, or several families from different clans cooperating to carry out a ritual, and so on, such that, while carrying out activities in the embankment site, they were assumed to reproduce to the degree necessary the domestic aspect of the home "hamlet" in that locale (Greber 1997, 210–11, 214–15).

In strong contrast, under the complementary heterarchical community view, while many of the individuals occupying semisedentary seasonal base camps in the vicinity of local earthworks would also be the same individuals who participated in the rituals at these nearby earthworks, many probably were not since they would have come from cult sodality clusters that were quite distant. As I carefully stressed earlier, the differences that make the difference between these two views reside at the social structural level. Under the complementary heterarchical community view, those who might occupy nearby seasonal base camps and also participate in the local earthwork activities would deliberately do so while wearing different "hats"—and wearing these different hats also meant that the two social organizations, clans and sodalities, while sharing and pursuing common interests also had and pursued interests that were not always congruent. That is, the interests of both groups would only partly correspond. While some might argue that the distinction I am making between these two views is no distinction at all, after all it would only exist in the collective understanding of those making up the regional population, no matter which version, I would respond and say that this difference defines the critical difference between my complementary heterarchical community view and the monistic modular polity view. Even the proponents of the latter view would have to admit that variation in kinship structures makes a critical difference between the forms and practices of the communities having these different structures and this is easily demonstrated if we compare the operations of a community based on matrilineality to those based on patrilineality and how these two structural contrasts condition marriage alliance, postmarital residency, and land tenure in the respective social systems. If differences in kinship structures generate differences in forms of conduct, it cannot be denied that a complementary heterarchical community would embody opportunities, constraints, and enabling powers that would not be congruent with those embodied in a monistic or unitary kinship-based community. Delineating what some of these differences might be is what this book is about.

Under the sedentary hamlet version of the monistic perspective, part of the definition of a domestic habitation site is that it was *not* spatially associated with an embankment earthwork, at least not directly. Exactly what is going to count in this regard as "not directly" is somewhat problematic if the Hamlet Hypothesis interpretation of the Murphy Tract is taken as exemplary. As noted earlier this set of locales is right between two major sets of earthworks, Newark to its east and the Granville Works to the west, and it is only about 700 m from the latter. In any case, this view notes that since domestic residue found in the context of an earthwork is the residue of people who came from their (sedentary) hamlets to participate for a short period in embankment earthwork activities, finding the same domestic residue pattern in a locale "relatively" distant from an embankment earthwork is usually assumed to be the result of its marking a domestic-based family habitation site, not a ceremonial site. In a significant way, this sedentary hamlet position radically dichotomizes the patterning of sites and their features (huts, buildings) and other facilities into two types according to whether they are associated or not associated with embankment earthworks. Those that display domestic-like residue and are associated with or are quite near (next to?) earthworks typically count as manifesting kinship-based domestic activity in a kinship-based ceremonial context. If domestic residue is found in a locale distant from any embankment earthworks, then, by default, this is treated as a sedentary kinship-based habitation, no matter if it also displays attributes that suggest significant investment of time and effort in the ceremonial sphere. This dichotomization is clearly illustrated by Kozarek (1987, 1) when she emphasizes the significance of the Jennison Guard site as being distally located from any embankment site, thereby definitively constituting it for her as a domestic sedentary kinship-based habitation site. In short, this view reduces the settlement pattern to the domestic habitation/ceremonial earthwork dichotomy that is itself very "flexible." Hence, a locale displaying domestic facilities and residue in the absence of any explicit ceremonial features, such as earthworks, is treated as a kinship-based domestic habitation unit, even when there are important material attributes that would suggest the expressive exercise of a major and ongoing concern for ceremonial practices (Blosser 1996; Dancey 1991; Kozarek 1987, 1–3; 1997, 132; Whitacre and Whitacre 1986). If there are two or more such "hamlets," then they simply represent a cluster of related sedentary families also "involved" in some way with Hopewellian ceremonialism. Only if the cluster was actually contiguous to an embankment earthwork, or even better, surrounded by the embankments, is it unproblematically considered to be primarily part of the Ohio Hopewell ceremonial sphere.

This problematic dichotomizing of the settlement pattern is, of course, directly related to the problematic characterizing of the community structure itself. If it is characterized in terms of the monistic modular polity community view, then effectively only two different types of locales are allowed: the ceremonial earthworks and the domestic habitations, whether sedentary or seasonal camps. This results in lumping all those sites that are not directly in association with embankment earthworks, the prima facie examples of ceremonialism, into the single category of domestic habitation, either an actual hamlet or a related task activity area, and it also results in a very mixed bag of ceremonial sites from mortuary mounds having rich contents to small earthwork embankment sites with no mounds, to moderately sized embankment earthwork sites, some with and others without mounds, to massive embankment earthwork sites associated with multiple small and massive mounds, such as the Hopewell site itself. I contend that this monistic modular polity view generates a domestic/ceremonial dichotomy that obscures and confuses much more than it clarifies. Sites with significant ceremonial residue but displaying domestic residue are lumped into the category of sedentary habitation sites. Ceremonial sites that should be differentiated and split in ceremonial terms into a system of locales are all classed as equivalent; and, of course, there is the "third" order, those sites that are identified with major resource areas but seem to have no significant domestic or ceremonial attributes. In short, I contend that this dichotomization generates an Ohio Middle Woodland period settlement patterning that verges on being incoherent.

In contrast, I consider the dichotomization of the settlement pattern under the Complementary Heterarchical Community model as generating a much more coherent system of site categories, as summarized above. However, there are two areas that require further refinement, as I noted in the last chapter: the type of settlement locus that would serve to enable the regularized travel between the great earthworks of the sacred games *tournées* and the possible range of loci that would be auxiliary to the renewal lodges of the major second-order or third-order cult sodality heterarchies. To pursue characterizing and identifying examples of these, it would be useful first to give an overview of how the division of labor would be generated in conformity with the bifurcated settlement pattern of this type of community. This will then be followed by a critical account of two new sites locales that I believe are needed to "fill in" the bottom-up linkage between the cult sodality cluster level consisting of the ceremonial nodal site and the associated auxiliary age-set and age-grade sites and the cult sodality heterarchy level. These two new site locale types are what I call the Sacred Way Station site locale, and the auxiliary cult sodality renewal lodges of a major embankment earthwork site. I specifically speak of these as "auxiliary renewal lodges" in order to distinguish them from the large collective renewal lodges of the type found on the floors of such major mounds as Seip-Pricer and Edwin Harness. The auxiliary renewal lodge type, I will argue, serves the second- and third-order heterarchy levels; while the former, the way station type, serves the first-order heterarchy level within the context of the second-order earthwork. I will address and illustrate the way station category first by summarizing and critiquing two sites that have been reported and treated as sedentary hamlets by Paul Pacheco, Jarrod Burks, and DeeAnne Wymer. They have referred to these as the Brown's Bottom #1 and the Lady's Run sites and they have interpreted them as substantial hamlets. The second type, the auxiliary renewal lodge type, will be derived from the recent overview report of the Seip auxiliary structures (Greber 2009a, 4–5) and the fairly recent salvage work at the Stubbs Works site and its immediate surroundings.

LABOR MOBILIZATION

By treating the Middle Woodland period dichotomization of the Ohio region settlement pattern in terms of the Complementary Heterarchical Community model, it immediately emerges that there are two largely mutually exclusive classes of sites generated: kinship-based and sodality-based. I have argued that both types of locales will have domestic and ceremonial aspects, although differently organized and manifested. Earlier, I did not become involved in the question of the degree of mobility of the habitation component, simply suggesting that this could vary in time and space. While this no doubt is the case, I think the variation occurred only toward the termination of the Middle Woodland period and that, for the most part, the habitation component of the Ohio Middle Woodland period was realized in semisedentary seasonal base camps and, therefore, they likely were organized on the basis of a dual warm season lowland and cold season upland schedule. However, this is not the residential mobility strategy that is traditionally claimed in archaeology, which assumes that the community is a unitary kin group. This is a semisedentary or seasonally mobile residential mobility in which parallel kin and sodality group schedules occur year-round. Therefore, both the kin and sodality schedules run during the warm and cold seasons. This may not be so difficult to model since, as I argued earlier, for the most part the age-sets operate as the logistical task groups for both kin and sodality groups. Two junior age-sets of a community might cooperatively split sodality and kin task responsibilities, one age-set participating in sodality rituals at the ceremonial nodal site while the other goes foraging for the domestic kin groups to which both severally belong. The companions of the latter share their procured resources among the kin groups of the age-set attending rituals. Then the two groups could reciprocally reverse their roles.

Besides reciprocally sharing a division of labor between kin and sodality groups, another key advantage of the cult sodality system in the bifurcated posture is that it can generate large logistical task groups made up of cooperating age-sets from the member cult sodalities drawn from many dispersed communities. This network-based aggregating of labor that a cult sodality heterarchy can carry out can then rather easily organize specialized allocation of labor, specialized according to the age-sets ranked by seniority, so that separate tasks demanding mutually exclusive labor can be performed in parallel, each group producing a surplus that then is distributed equitably according to the needs of both kin and sodality. That is, as noted above, while the practical requirements of kin and sodality groups can be understood as demanding mutually exclusive labor, namely, the individual autonomous agent could not go hunting while cooperatively participating in the building of an earthwork, the freeing up of the sodalities that the principle of clan-sodality autonomy enabled would not mean that the sodalities stole labor from the clans, or vice versa. I think most would recognize that the level of labor capacity immanent in the total population of a human community can produce much more than the community needs for its own survival. The question is how to expand production output in the absence of dominance and exploitation. The relative autonomy characterizing kinship and companionship relations does this since, when the community moves into a bifurcated posture, sodalities can ally, thereby consensually amassing a labor force that can produce surplus labor that can be allocated equitably by the participants for both of their shared spheres of responsibility, clan and sodality. The age-set that is preparing and performing rituals for its sodality knows that an age-set of "*irakúu* brothers" is foraging for their families. Hence, each will consensually generate a surplus output, ritual and subsistence, in order to ensure that their labor will maintain the autonomy of their sodality and families.

Furthermore, this capacity to expand surplus labor consensually and distribute its products equitably between kin and sodality applies to the ceremonial sphere of the clan as well as to the ceremonial sphere of the sodalities.

Most clan ceremonialism will be performed at the seasonal kinship-based base camp cluster level and, most likely, at the warm-season base camps of the local clan leaders, and, of course, at the nearby clan collective burial locale where many of the deceased of the clans, returned by the sodalities, will be buried (Byers 2004, 503–13). However, the scope of clan ceremonialism will be constrained to the interests of the clans, for example, reproduction rites—marriages, birth rites, kin-based naming rites, other rites of passage, and so on. In general, the ritual aspect of clan life will be largely invisible, with the possible exception of the bladelet. The arm's-length relation between clan and sodality would make the presence of even production residue of Hopewell exotica unlikely. Instead, the presence of this material in the form of mica, copper, exotic cherts, and so on, will be largely limited to the sodality locales, from the auxiliary age-set and age-grade locales in the sodality clusters to the intermediate sites I note shortly, and to the embankment-related sites.

THE SACRED WAY STATION AND THE AUXILIARY RENEWAL LODGE

I have already elucidated the Cult Sodality Cluster model articulating the lowest and primary constituent component structural level of the system. The bottom-up formation out of these primary autonomous cult sodality constituents of the heterarchy system as manifested in the complex development of the lesser and greater earthworks would probably require another type of locale that would be used and occupied by transient groups in transit from the ceremonial nodal locales of their respective cult sodalities to the different earthworks of the heterarchies in which these participated. Since we are exploring the ceremonial sphere of prehistoric Native North American communities, it is likely that some set of fairly widespread imperatives and taboos existed and were exercised in governing the mode by which cult sodalities aggregated in major sacred second-order earthwork locales of a dispersed third-order cult sodality heterarchy. Typically, participants in historic Native North American sodalities that were on ritual travels along sacred pathways would make a series of regular stops, often divided into units of four, where they would perform rituals by which they were warranted to proceed to the next stage. These stopping places were known and recognized as "shrines" or what I will refer to as sodality transient *way stations*. I postulate that while these would be spaced along recognized paths connecting major earthworks, the terminal way stations would actually be within easy walking distance of the major second-order earthwork sites where the travelers intended to participate in the great sacred games/mortuary-mediated world renewal rituals. Therefore, a party would "pause" at their penultimate stop, the local way station of their first-order heterarchy, send a messenger on to announce its expected arrival, for example, on the fourth day following their ritual cleansing at the way station, and so on. Of course, historic Native North American communities were for the most part in the integrated settlement articulation posture and, therefore, transient guests would attend the integrated (i.e., nucleated) villages where the rituals were to be held. Their penultimate stopping places might be near these villages; but these final way stations would not be materially substantial since the groups would then reside as guests in the host village. However, when communities are in the bifurcated posture, there is no substantial integrated village in which to reside and, therefore, the terminal way stations near the earthworks would need to serve as transient residents for the duration of the rituals. Hence, they would become rather permanent structures displaying a range of attributes combining significant accumulation of residency residue, as well as an accumulation of ritual materials, since these locales would be used sequentially. As way stations serving as transient residences for cult sodalities of the first-order heterarchies from the surrounding regions, it could be expected that several such sites would be located within easy walking distance of a major embankment earthwork, each located in a different direction by the nearby embankment earthwork so as to be convenient to the member cult sodalities coming from outside the immediate region. It is unlikely that these stations would display any earthworks themselves, since the relevant earthwork would be nearby. Instead, they would likely be rather permanent timber structures where the different components of the cult sodalities of the responsible first-order heterarchies could reside while performing their cleansing and preparatory rituals. Since these would be used for mediating sacred processions of "soul keepers," they would *not* manifest quantities of the type of debitage associated, for example, with specialized age-grade production sites such as those established at the Jennison Guard and Murphy Tract sites. Since bearing the remains of sacred deceased and their associated artifacts would be part of the ritual procession, there would likely be a set of outdoor scaffolds or indoor charnel platforms where the deceased could be temporarily placed. Earth ovens, hearths, some storage pits where supplies would be set up in anticipation of transients, separate refuse zones, and so on, could be expected since, of course, considerable day-to-day activity would be carried out during the sacred game/mortuary periods.

That is, as ritual way stations used by groups involving multiple days of sacred game and mortuary rituals and even preparatory cleansing, and so on, these locales would have the facilities necessary to enable them to serve as hostels of transient occupants who, however, would anticipate regular return-runs. They would be built so as to house and provide for the domestic and ritual needs of the sodality members who were on a given ritual pathway, what some archaeologists have spoken of as pilgrimages (Lepper 1996, 238; 1998,

132–33; 2006, 129–33; Vickery 1996, 120–23). I prefer to speak of these sojourns as sacred games *tournées*. Residue of Hopewellian exotica would be expected since these way stations would be the places where last-minute repairs on custodial and other ceremonial artifacts could be made prior to the group of soul keepers making their processual entrances to the nearby embankment earthworks. At any given time, there might be one or two cult sodalities, or components of sodalities constituting first-order heterarchies, such as several age-sets or even full age-grades, using the facilities for ritual preparatory to the final procession and its subsequent sacred games/mortuary rituals at the embankment earthwork only a short distance away. Furthermore, as I noted above, this proximal sacred way station type presupposes distal types, those that were used as short, possibly only four-day ritual stops on the sacred pathway to the embankment earthworks. These also would be cult sodality structures, and, therefore, they would display a range of forms appropriate to the possible sodality rituals and groupings. It is likely of course that these would be less formal since the ritual stops would be short. Indeed, it is possible that age-grade locales of those cult sodalities on or near one of these soul keeper/*tournée* pathways would double up to host these transient sodality groups and then join them when they left the next day on the next stage of their sacred games *tournée*/mortuary-mediated world renewal passage.

The terminal sacred way station sites near the great earthworks, therefore, would likely consist of the residue of above features and contents: permanent timber structure, earth ovens, a mix of Hopewellian exotica, but the absence of major production refuse, and so on. Now, even though the buildings were used for transient residency, it would be a mistake to think that they would be physically ephemeral shelters. I suspect that these buildings, as well as the category of structure associated with the ceremonial nodal locale of the local cult sodalities, and the auxiliary cult sodality buildings in direct spatial association with the earthworks, as I discuss shortly, would be substantially built, better than the domestic habitation residences, even though they might be occupied for only a relatively minor part of the year by any specific sector of a given sodality of the ecclesiastic-communal cult sodalities that made up a given mutualistic heterarchy. However, while the whole set of cult sodalities of the heterarchy may be in collective attendance for only several brief periods annually, since the constituent components of each sodality, the different age-sets and shamanic-priestly groups, would have different duties to perform at different times, a staggered form of transient residency would be the norm. There probably would only be the rare relatively short period when these sites were left unoccupied.

Furthermore, there would be those structures in more or less direct association with the earthworks, either being contiguous to the walls or actually inside the embankments. These would be used for different ritual-related purposes, including curating ritual items (such as the decommissioned custodial regalia) and for ritual performance, and when honors might be distributed publicly, and so on. Finally, I would add one unique structure category separate from these latter two. It has been termed in the literature as the "Big House" or "Great House." I have preferred speaking of it as the "Renewal Lodge" since it apparently mediated the major world renewal postmortem mortuary spirit-release rites. These structures would be particular in that they are marked by mortuary remains resulting from truncation event rituals. There would be other, lesser renewal lodges that might mediate renewal rituals in which the deceased may have participated but were not deposited there. Both of these types would likely be located within the context of the sacred embankments themselves, one set in the infix component of the earthwork (or its equivalent), and another set of lesser structures, such as scaffolds, located in the High Bank C-R earthwork, or its equivalent, such as the stand-alone hilltop T-Forms.

With regard to the terminal way stations, I can postulate two possible types. Since the ecclesiastic-communal cult sodality was based on senior and junior age-grades hierarchically related by seniority, there could be some "hostels" built that incorporated both senior and junior age-grades or there could be separate structures built for each. In either case, these would be rather large structures in association with heating and cooking facilities, inside and outside, as well as specialized facilities, such as ritual cleansing loci, for example, sweat-lodge facilities. These hostels would probably be more substantially constructed than the seasonal base-camp family habitations since they would have to be able to withstand considerable wear and tear as different groups serially moved in, stayed briefly, and moved out. As I noted above, in general these would be set up about one or two kilometers from the embankment earthworks and probably be separated from each other as a result of being under the responsibility of the different participating cult sodalities.

I consider the above discussion of ancillary settlement loci that I have termed the cult sodality ceremonial nodal locale and the ritual way station locale, as well as the set of specialized earthwork-associated structures, to be an extension and enrichment of the Ohio Hopewell Cult Sodality Heterarchy System model. These categories "fill in" the range of settlement types that would link the cult sodalities of the typical complementary heterarchical community to the great embankment earthwork sites. To demonstrate the validity of these postulated ancillary settlement loci, I will now turn to the relevant empirical data. First I discuss the Brown's Bottom #1 site and the Lady's Run site, two complementary sites that I postulate were penultimate ritual way stations of the type I described above, although as I noted earlier the excavators have interpreted them as substantial hamlets. In the course of analyzing and interpreting these, I also compared them with and discuss the structures associated directly with Seip. I terminate the full analysis with a discussion of equivalent structures at the Stubbs Works.

Empirical Demonstration

I consider that probably the best known sites that could stand as examples of the cult sodality ritual way station type are the Brown's Bottom #1 and the Lady's Run sites currently being excavated as part of an intensive, ongoing project by Paul Pacheco, Jarrod Burks, and DeeAnne Wymer (Pacheco et al. 2009a, 2009b, 2005). As I noted, they characterize these as forming a cluster of two hamlet farmsteads and emphasize that their presence on the floodplain of the Scioto, 1.5 and 2 km west of Liberty Works, is strong evidence of the adequacy of the Vacant Center or Dispersed Sedentary Community model. "Our work at Lady's Run and BB#1 has identified two discrete, yet spatially clustered, Ohio Hopewell household settlements located on the prime bottom land within 2 km of a major Hopewell earthwork. . . . These sites appear to provide solid confirmation for the settlement model of Ohio Hopewell that we have promoted over the years based on Prufer's earlier work at McGraw and our work in Licking County [the Murphy Tract]. . . . Indeed, we would argue that our work on the Harness Farm represents an independent test of the general settlement model, because prior to this project we did not have Hopewell settlements with *complete structural patterns*" (2009b, emphasis added).

There is no question that these two sites constitute an exceptionally important advance in Ohio archaeology and the excavators are to be commended for their discovery and ongoing work on them. However, it should be clear that my reason for attributing the importance I do to these sites is not the same as the reason they do. It is noticeable that in the above quotation, no question is raised concerning possible alternative social natures of these sites. It simply asserts that these are "two discrete, yet spatially clustered, Ohio Hopewell household settlements." Of course, if this is the case, then they would be right to conclude that these "sites appear to provide solid confirmation for the [Prufer] settlement model of Ohio Hopewell." Although these are recent discoveries and little time has lapsed for counter views to come forward, some have. Richard Yerkes, for example, has expressed skepticism. He has commented to Kelli Burton (2006, 37) that, while "[i]t's not impossible that . . . [Brown's Bottom #1 is] some kind of big family dwelling . . . you can't rule out that it might have been some kind of ceremonial structure." Unfortunately Burton does not include the empirical data that Yerkes would highlight to support this assessment. However, I believe that Pacheco and his colleagues describe and list the major components of the Brown's Bottom #1 site that can easily be used to support Yerkes's latter assessment, and in my view the reports that Pacheco and his colleagues have subsequently published (2009a, 2009b; also see Pacheco et al. 2005) strengthen this claim. To show why this is the case, I will first give a summary of their description of the layout and content of the two sites, as well as the mutual spatial relations these two sites had. I will then critique their claim that these sites "provide solid confirmation for the settlement model of Ohio Hopewell" by arguing that the content, spacing, form, size, and patterning of these two sites can be more coherently understood as characteristic of what could be expected of ritual way stations of the type postulated above. My main argument will be to show that while the two sites are clearly spatially distinct from the nearby Liberty Works embankment earthwork, they nevertheless combine physical attributes that have only been observed up to now in structures that have been found in the direct context of these types of earthworks. Just as these directly associated earthwork structures, such as the Edwin Harness Renewal Lodge, are widely recognized to be ceremonial in nature, by extension, this is sound reason to interpret the structures of the nearby Brown's Bottom #1 and Lady's Run sites as also ceremonial in nature.

Site Descriptions

Two structures have been exposed through excavation, one each at Brown's Bottom #1 and at the nearby Lady's Run site. These two sites are about 100 m from each other with Brown's Bottom #1 to the southeast of Lady's Run. As the excavators Paul Pacheco, DeeAnne Wymer, and Jarrod Burks (Pacheco et al. 2009a, 2009b, 2005) point out these sites were originally discovered by Olaf Prufer, who named them Brown's Bottom #1 and #2. Prufer also established a third nearby site, calling it Brown's Bottom #3. John Blank (1965), Prufer's colleague, partly excavated Brown's Bottom #1. Pacheco and his colleagues have now renamed Brown's Bottom #2 the Lady's Run site. The three sites appear lined up with respect to each other in a northwest–southeast manner.

To initiate their work in this zone, Jarrod Burks applied his expertise in geomagnetic surveying methods and he was able to delineate a rich set of potential features for excavation. Of particular importance is the finding of these two structures, one in each site. The Brown's Bottom #1 structure was the first that they exposed. It formed a square having sides of about 13.7 m × 13.7 m (188 m^2), with the corners apparently aligned to the cardinal directions. About 6 m south of the southeast wall they exposed a second parallel line of wall posts. It was initially thought that this was possibly part of a second structure. However, their subsequent excavation demonstrated that this was a screen-like line of posts, possibly screening the central entryway in the southeast wall of the Brown's Bottom #1 structure (Pacheco et al. 2009a). The Lady's Run structure, also square, was slightly smaller than the former, in this case being about 11.8 m × 11.8 m (about 140 m^2). They note in their overall assessment of these individual structures in the two separate sites that, except for these size differences, they were similar in form, layout, and content. "In 2008 the remainder of the wall posts at the Lady's Run structure were excavated and mapped. The post holes mimic the BB#1 posts in all respects, with each containing small cobbles and gravel that appear to have been acquired from nearby Dry Run. Similar to BB#1, the structure posts were apparently pulled and then the post holes were purposefully backfilled. The forty wall posts excavated in the Lady's Run structure had an average diameter of 22.6 cm and an average depth of 42 cm below the base of the plowzone. This average size matches the posts of the BB#1 structure remarkably well, where the average diameter of the forty-seven excavated wall posts is 22.2 cm and the average depth is 33.2 cm below plowzone" (2009b). They also noted the two different types of internal thermal features that each structure had, hearths indicating in situ burning, and fire-cracked rock features indicating heating purposes. "The [Brown's Bottom #1] structure includes three sets of paired thermal features (F13, F135, F16, F91, F155, & F167) along each wall but the southeast wall, which includes the probable doorway. These features contain FCR [fire-cracked rock] and cultural debris but no evidence of in situ burning" (2005). They suggest that preheated rocks would have been placed in the thermal feature so as to give off ambient heat within the structures. They summarize the significant degree to which the two structures were alike. "Though feature placement, wall length, and corner post configuration of the Lady's Run structure are not identical to the BB#1 structure, the two structures are very similar in overall architectural design and orientation; both are square with large center posts and have interior hearths, other thermal features, and a possible storage pit. Likewise, both structures have a number of smaller interior posts suggesting possible benches or partitions" (2009b). As I commented above, there is also a row of post holes parallel to the southeast side of Brown's Bottom #1 structure and they suggest that this is some sort of screen for the entranceway.

There are equally interesting features external to the two structures. To the south and southwest of the Brown's Bottom #1 structure there was an arc of earth ovens not unlike those found at the Murphy I and Jennison Guard sites (Dancey 1991; Kozarek 1987, 1996). At least two earth ovens were also found southeast of the structure of the Lady's Run site, except these were smaller and had a lower quantity of fire-cracked rock than those at Brown's Bottom. A large discrete refuse pile was separate from the Lady's Run structure. Brown's Bottom #1 may also have a similar discrete refuse deposit, although if so it has not as yet been found (Pacheco et al. 2009a, 2009b). As with the Lady's Run site, most of its features, particularly the earth ovens, had secondary refuse. Brown's Bottom #1 also had several interesting burials, both human and dog. In fact, there were at least three full-bodied domestic dog burials placed inside apparently abandoned earth ovens. As the excavators point out, such dog burials have not been recorded in other Ohio Middle Woodland period sites. The mode of deposition of the dogs suggested to them that the dog burials were not a result of their being butchered or eaten. Rather, as full-full bodied "extended burials," they were deposited in a manner mediating a ritual. Two human burials were also revealed, one male and one female, about 35–40 and 45 years of age, respectively. Although they had no mortuary artifacts in association, both are considered to be unique since, according to the excavators, they are the only "documented Hopewell burials . . . from domestic sites in Ross County" (Pacheco et al. 2009a, 5; 2005).

The artifact contents of these sites are also very interesting. Unlike the quantitatively large lithic debitage record of the Murphy Tract and the Jennison Guard sites, indicating the full range of the Ohio Hopewell lithic *chaîne opératoire* of both bifacial and bladelet core production trajectories of select cherts derived from the distant quarries, there is actually only a sampling of the finished tools of these two traditions, and not many of these. A total of 541 lithic artifacts were reported with no major indication of lithic production. There were the ubiquitous Flint Ridge bladelets, of course. In the 2005 report, 72 were found, 69 of Flint Ridge chert and 3 of Upper Mercer chert. Therefore, rather than a significant level of lithic production occurring here, there appears to have been only significant refinement of preexisting lithic tools, refurbishing and so on. A similar pattern of bladelets, but no bladelet cores, was found in several features of the Lady's Run site. Also, very interestingly, a broken platform pipe was found in the large undisturbed midden deposit at this site. The excavators report that it was probably broken in the process of being made (2009b). A worked bear canine was found in a separate feature (F403), also broken in the process of being modified. The same feature also contained a small limestone bowl, broken in manufacture, along with a dense amount of paleobotanical residue displaying the whole range of cultivated and domesticated seed crops.

Ceramics was probably the most abundant artifact category found in both sites, although overall somewhat limited in quantity. The excavators note in their 2005 report that 2,877 sherds were found in the various features of Brown's Bottom #1—the earth ovens, refilled post holes—representing a minimum of 47 vessels. Decorated sherds were rare but those that were present, particularly stamped ware, suggest association with the Southeastern series, often identified as "ceremonial." In fact, they reported the base of a tetrapodal vessel, a classic representative of this series. It was also found in the same earth oven feature as a fragment of a copper awl (2009a). However, the majority of the ceramics was McGraw Cordmarked plain, standard Ohio Middle Woodland period vessels. Most interestingly, however, was the finding of several classic examples of Ohio Hopewell exotics. There was the broken platform pipe made of Ohio pipestone from the quarries near Tremper that I noted above. Also found inside the Brown's Bottom #1 structure was a mica cutout displaying a form that may have been an effigy of a projectile point effigy; and other items were recovered (Pacheco et al. 2009a).

Critical Discussion

Pacheco and his colleagues have particularly emphasized the clarity of the patterning of the post hole features and the fact that no post holes were apparently missing. Each indicated that the original posts were removed and the holes carefully filled, a point that I find extremely interesting, as I comment in detail shortly. Now, given that this patterning of post holes is supposed to represent sedentary homesteads modeled after the type revealed by Dancey's excavation of the Murphy site, it is very interesting that only a few scattered post holes were found at the Murphy I site and, as I noted earlier, no clear patterning could be identified that might reasonably be attributed to timber structures of the above sort. Dancey accounted for this paucity of post holes and the absence of any structural patterning as likely being attributable to destruction caused by the long history of plowing to which the Murphy Tract was subjected. However, Pacheco and his colleagues note that the current and equally long-term plow zone of the Brown's Bottom #1 and Lady's Run sites was effectively the same depth as the plow zone of the Murphy Tract and, furthermore, the multiple and clearly patterned post holes of the former structures penetrated 32 to 42 cm *below* that plow zone! Pacheco and his colleagues are quite aware of the question of the depth of the post hole pattern since they take some care to explain the differences in post depth between Brown's Bottom #1 and Lady's Run. They note that the "difference in post depth between Lady's Run and BB#1 is likely a product of the Lady's Run structure being partially buried, while the BB#1 structure has been somewhat truncated by plowing." In any case, this difference in post hole patterns alone suggests that the Murphy I site is not of the same order as these two sites and, therefore, if the latter is going be treated as a sedentary hamlet, then both the Lady's Run and Brown's Bottom #1 structures are not of the same sedentary nature as the Murphy site. Of course, I have already argued that I consider the Murphy site to be a specialized production camp operated by one of the age-grade sectors of the associated cult sodality. I also consider the Brown's Bottom #1 and Lady's Run sites to be cult sodality sites but distinctly not of the same order as the Murphy site, since I postulate that they are way stations.

It is important to further compare the Brown's Bottom #1 and Lady's Run structures to other known structures, in this case, structures that are widely recognized to have ceremonial functions. In quantitative and qualitative terms (number of posts, post holes, sizes, areas, formal spaces, and so on) these structures can be easily placed into the same category as the structures in the nearby Liberty Works, in particular, the individual components of the Edwin Harness Renewal Lodge, only 1.5 to 2 km southeast of these two sites. First, as noted above, the structure in the Lady's Run site was 11.8 m × 11.8 m. Altogether it had 40 wall posts having an average of 22.2 cm diameter and set to an average of 33.2 cm below plow zone. The Brown's Bottom #1 structure was even larger, 13.7 m × 13.7 m (188 m^2; 2005). It had 47 wall posts comparable in size and depth to those making up the structure on the Lady's Run site. As I described the Edwin Harness Renewal Lodge earlier, it actually had three large floor spaces, two rectangular and one circular. The two rectangular floors are the largest of the three. The larger of these two, which I have attributed to the senior age-grade laity sector of the responsible cult sodality heterarchy, is about 14 m north–south × 11.9 m east–west. That is, its area size is about 167 m^2, a good deal smaller when compared to the area of Brown's Bottom #1, about 188 m^2. In contrast to the larger of the floor spaces, the smaller rectilinear floor of the Edwin Harness Renewal Lodge, which I have attributed to the junior age-grade laity sector of the responsible cult sodality heterarchy, is a square space, like Lady's Run, and has about the same area. The post diameters of all these structures are in the same size range (Greber 1983, 27).

Each of these two large floor areas of the Edwin Harness Renewal Lodge is delineated by 48 large posts set in a careful checkerboard pattern of 7 × 7 rows. Greber suggests that these were used to support an upper platform. Although some of the posts were extracted when this large tripartite structure was abandoned, most were left and burned in situ. As Greber has noted, one of these posts was only partially burned, leaving about a 10-foot unburned extension. It would be reasonable to add at least 2 feet to this above-ground extension, suggesting that the upper level defined by these multiple support posts may have been about 12 feet above the floor. This is actually a good height for curating bodies out of reach of larger animals, such as bears. However, since she also noted that a line of wall posts surrounded these large support posts, it is possible as I noted earlier that the whole area, including the third set of posts delineating the circular and smallest of the three areas, was incorporated into one roofed building. My own inclination is to treat the structure as having a roof so that, in effect, a single large crypt-like building existed that enabled the performance of the range of laying-in rituals equivalent to those conducted in the multiple vaulted chamber crypts on the floors of Mounds 23 and 25 at the Hopewell site on the North Fork. In either case, the total structure, whether an open complex scaffold or a roofed complex laying-in crypt, would serve very well for curating the dead, some of which ended up on the floor of structure as cremations.

Most notable is that the two structures of the Brown's Bottom #1 and Lady's Run sites parallel in size the two main rectangular floors of the Edwin Harness Renewal Lodge. Also they required about the same number and size of posts to make their walls. They differ from the Edwin Harness Renewal Lodge, of course, in that these posts were to construct walls and not to create a checkerboard set of support posts for an upper floor or scaffolding. Nevertheless, the amount of labor that was required to build the Brown's Bottom #1 and Lady's Run structures would not be that much less than the labor involved in building the two largest portions of the Edwin Harness Renewal Lodge. Finally, not only are the forms similar, the features and contents of the Brown's Bottom #1 and Lady's Run structures could also easily be interpreted in ritual terms. For example, each had an internally placed thermal feature near the wall that would serve very nicely as a localized sweat-lodge-like area. They also had inner post hole rows that could easily have been used as internal scaffolds or supports for bone bundles, and so on. However, not only do the attributes and sizes of the Brown's Bottom #1 and Lady's Run structures correspond to those of Edwin Harness Renewal Lodge, these same attributes allow them to fit into the range of wooden structures found directly associated with several Ohio Hopewell embankment earthworks. For example, as I discuss shortly, Seip has at least seven structures incorporated on the west side of the large infix element about halfway between the central Seip-Pricer mound and the western circumference of the infix embankment. These seven structures, possibly more, are closely spaced. They contain multiple features, including deep post pits that had multiple internal steps enabling the insertion and removal of large posts. There is no evidence that these were used for everyday habitation and, in fact, their floors are remarkably "clean." There are considerable amounts of debris in the fill used to build the low strata covering the floors. However, this material was caught up in the midden and other fills that were procured apparently from outside the earthwork and used to build the low stratified mounds over the structures as part of their being abandoned. Several of the structures may have been occupied contemporaneously, or at least partly contemporaneously, and then when abandoned, they were covered by these low mounds of humus, midden, pea gravels, and sand. One or more new structures were then built and used, presumably for the same or similar ritual purposes as the prior structures (Greber 2009b, 47).

In terms of areal size, however, these ritual structures are much smaller than the Brown's Bottom #1 and Lady's Run structures. While the latter range in size between 11 m and 14 m per side, the Seip structures range about 3 m to 4 m per side. Importantly, although smaller, the same mode of abandonment was carried out for both sets. That is, the wall posts and all the nonwall posts were removed and the holes were backfilled in a similar manner. Typically earth, gravel, and river cobbles were procured and carefully placed in layers (Burks and Greber 2009, 143–70). Where the two sets differ, of course, is that the Seip structures were covered with low mounds while, after dismantling the walls and filling the post holes in the careful manner described, the groups responsible for Brown's Bottom #1 and Lady's Run structures apparently left them unmounded. At least there is no reported indication of mounding.

With the latter exception, the above comparison suggests that the Brown's Bottom #1 and Lady's Run structures have much more in common with the known ritual structures of both the Liberty Works and Seip than they do with the type of structure postulated as a sedentary hamlet or homestead. Both the Jennison Guard and the Murphy Tract sites are recognized by Pacheco and his colleagues to be, in a sense, model hamlets. However, as noted above, neither of these sites has any indication of having structures of the size revealed at the Brown's Bottom #1 and Lady's Run sites. In particular, the Murphy I site, the only fully excavated site of the Murphy Tract, had nothing that could be compared to the latter. As I noted above, Dancey has suggested that the scattered post holes happened to be the deepest below the plow zone and that there could have been many other post holes that were probably destroyed, along with any likely floor of a structure. The problem with this explanation as I noted is that the plow zone depth of the Murphy I site was equal to the plow zone depth of both the Brown's Bottom #1 and the Lady's Run sites. However, the depth of the latter post holes was quite distinct and went 20 or more centimeters further below the plow zone compared to Murphy I. If Murphy I was a site like the other two, then we could expect a similar set of deeply entrenched post holes. Interestingly, Brown's Bottom #1 shares the practice of human burials with the Jennison Guard site. Each had two burials. However, the former also had three domestic dog burials. With regard to Ross County, Ohio, the excavators consider both types of burials to be unique.

Strangely, however, while recognizing that these burials were unique, this did not seem to raise any red flags concerning the adequacy of their primary claim that these were sedentary domestic hamlets. Since they recognize such burials are not characteristic of "hamlets" in Ross County, I find it puzzling that they did not reflect critically on their original claim. Of course, little published feedback is available on their research. Still, reflection seems to be lacking. This is particularly the case in that the contemporaneous Edwin Harness Renewal Lodge, containing one of the richest sets of Ohio Hopewell mortuary depositions, is only 1.5 to 2 km east of Brown's Bottom #1. Furthermore, the large majority of these human mortuary deposits were cremated while the two human burials and three dog burials were extended. All this suggests a puzzle to be explored, namely, why were these two human deceased buried at Brown's Bottom when, under the premises of the Hamlet Hypothesis, as participants in the community responsible for Liberty Works, many of their kin would have been buried there? In another way, a similar puzzle is raised concerning the absence at these two sites of the type and quantity of lithic data that were found in abundance at Murphy Tract and the Jennison Guard sites. If the latter are hamlets and Brown's Bottom #1 and Lady's Run are also, it seems anomalous that there were no comparable lithics given that these have been postulated to be hamlets like those at the Murphy Tract. Indeed, the Murphy Tract sites were equivalently close to several major embankment earthwork sites, Granville and Newark, as Brown's Bottom #1 and Lady's Run were to Liberty Works, suggesting that "hamlets" near earthworks should have quantitatively and qualitatively equivalent lithic materials.

THE ALTERNATIVE RITUAL WAY STATION ACCOUNT

Of course, I have already argued that neither Murphy I nor Jennison Guard was a hamlet, sedentary or otherwise. Instead, I have postulated that these were cult sodality sites occupied transiently by age-grades undertaking specialized production of Hopewell lithics, in particular, the full range of production of Flint Ridge chert lithics and Wyandotte chert lithics, respectively. Clearly, Brown's Bottom #1 and Lady's Run were cult sodality sites also, but not of the same type as Murphy and Jennison Guard. I postulated above, however, that there should be a category of cult sodality site that links the cult sodality clusters in the countryside to the embankment earthworks and that these were used to enable the performance of properly constituted ritual processions by which the cult sodalities discharged their sacred duties to the cosmos through participating in sacred games *tournées*/mortuary-mediated world renewal rituals. In this regard, as noted above, not only are these two sites close to Liberty Works, the presence of Hopewell exotics, human burials, dog burials, and the excessive size of these structures, as well as their formal spatial similarities to the major rooms of the Edwin Harness Renewal Lodge, argues for treating them not in domestic habitation terms at all but in cult sodality terms. As ritual way stations, it is here that members of the cult sodalities of first-order heterarchies would make their penultimate pauses on their sacred procession to the Liberty Works. They would likely be bearing deceased and these would be placed on one of the "benches" that the excavators argue were built in these structures. It is here that last minute repairs and preparations for the sacred games to be played at Liberty Works would be carried out.

Empirical support for this claim is considerable. For example, not only do these two structures exceed in size any other known "hamlet," their floor plans replicate the form of most structures found at such earthworks as Mound City and Seip. As I noted above, in terms of areal size they are actually slightly larger than the two rectangular floors of the renewal lodges at Liberty Works and Seip. Interestingly, the spatial orientation and differential size that the structures at Brown's Bottom #1 and Lady's Run have toward each other almost replicate the spatial orientation and differential size of the two rectangular floors with their upper levels at Edwin Harness. Besides their size, their internal features and external features would fit the needs of a cult sodality whose members would require a hostel for transient residency that was located close to the major cult heterarchy locale, Liberty Works. As I argued earlier, traveling to the ritual center was itself a form of polluting to the members and they would wish to pause before participating in the rituals at the earthworks. This would enable them to perform cleansing rituals and also to perform mortuary rituals for the deceased whom they were bearing. Temporary burial of deceased may have been one important possibility. The use of abandoned earth ovens could have been standard. Typically the bodies would be disinterred at the appropriate time and cremated, possibly in the same feature. Such interment could be treated as a form of curating and, therefore, buried bodies could be left for later use when the responsible soul keepers who had brought the bodies of their companions returned the next year. Under these circumstances, it is quite possible that one or two bodies were overlooked and not retrieved. This would not be a particularly heinous act since their burial at the ritual way station was itself a type of postmortem sacrificial ritual. Alternatively, these burials could have been deliberately performed as either foundation rites constituting the initial construction of the site as a way station or as decomissioning rites by which the responsible sodality left an offering of their own members' living souls to the ongoing sanctification of the locale.

As I noted earlier, the thermal features found in both structures could well serve as sweat lodges, a classic feature used for ritual cleansing. Also, the structures had internal platforms that could have served as laying-in altars where the deceased could also be placed prior to their being subjected to further rituals at the earthworks. Earth ovens, of course, suggest collective meals, indeed, feasts, and not small-scale family meals. While it seems clear that site maintenance was regularly and consistently performed, rather than this supporting the claim that the sites were domestic habitations, it strongly supports the view that prescriptions were in force that made it imperative that transient occupants cleaned and maintained the area so that it would be in good order and well purified for the next group that would be following them in short order. As I also noted above, the labor that was invested in procuring the timber and setting the posts of these two structures was of the same magnitude as the labor required to build most of the Edwin Harness Renewal Lodge. However, it was not only the raw labor that suggests that the Brown's Bottom #1 and Lady's Run sites drew on an organizational capacity akin to a cult sodality system; the actual authority and warranting required for cutting this timber and bringing it to the sites would be characteristic of the ritual authority of the cult sodalities. That is, this construction labor was as much ritual as it was practical and its performance was probably embedded in a set of traditional labor tasks that only certain age-sets would be empowered to carry out.

The mode of abandonment is particularly telling. As I noted above, the removal of the posts and the filling of the post holes was characteristic of decommissioning the seven structures excavated at Seip. I think that there is no serious doubt that these latter structures were ceremonial in nature. They were built within the infix of Seip. They were mantled with low mound stratification that was of the same structural nature as the mounds covering the major renewal lodges. They were not used for productive purposes but for ritual practices associated with the Hopewell ceremonial sphere. Indeed, a major plaza was revealed to exist next to this complex, the type of plaza that would be ideal for carrying out different types of sacred games. Above all, when these ritual structures were abandoned, rather than being burned, the posts were carefully extracted, including the large posts that required stepped sides, indicating probably several cycles of inserting and extracting posts. This treatment and the fact that they consisted of a spaced series that was placed in line suggests that these were a type of ritual post, for example, sacrificial offering posts, posts representing the axis mundi, a solar post, and so on, rather than wall posts, as such. The possibility that these posts participated in and presenced the sacred powers of the axis mundi by which the Above, Middle, and Beneath Worlds were integrated would explain why the open post holes were carefully filled with strata of earth, gravel, and stones.

As I stated, with the exception that post holes were not stepped, this was the same pattern used at Brown's Bottom #1 and Lady's Run. If we were to treat these two structures as hamlets, this careful extraction of the posts and filling of the post holes would be indeed puzzling, even anomalous. After all, if the purpose for removing these posts was to save labor by reusing them, then the careful procuring of cobbles and gravel seems to contradict the labor-saving claim. The labor invested in procuring cobbles could have been avoided simply by scraping in the immediately available surface earth, or simply leaving them unfilled. If labor saving was not the motive for removal of the timber posts when the structures were abandoned, it might well be that the purpose was unrelated to recycling the posts but to eliminating the structures from the landscape. This purpose, of course, could easily have been done by simply burning down the structures. However, such burning was clearly not among the conditions of satisfaction of the collective intentions being exercised in bringing about their being abandoned. Burning was permissible only in some cases, such as the burning of the Edwin Harness Renewal Lodge. However, the seven ceremonial structures at Seip described above were not burned down. Rather, their posts were also carefully removed and the holes filled with cobble stones and other carefully procured fills. Therefore, it would seem that the Lady's Run and Brown's Bottom #1 structures were somewhere between being equivalent to the lesser ritual structures or, as I have called them, the lesser renewal lodges of Seip, on the one hand, and the major renewal lodges of Seip and Liberty Works, on the other. Their size and orientation to each other replicated the Edwin Harness rectangular spaces, but their abandonment did not warrant burning and mounding. However, they were twice the size of the lesser renewal lodges of the Seip site and were abandoned in the same manner with regard to the extraction of their posts and the filling of the holes. In any case, the most reasonable conclusion arising from this comparative analysis of these structures is to place them categorically in the cult sodality sphere and, as I suggested above, they would neatly fit the expectations of the Ohio Hopewell Cult Sodality Heterarchy System model as being an example of ritual way stations of the type that participating cult sodalities of a first-order cult sodality heterarchy would require to ensure active participation in the world renewal rituals and sacred games that would be performed in the context of the sacred embankment earthworks and sacrificially mediated by the deceased that the living members bore in sacred procession.

In an important sense, the mode of abandoning the structures by removing the posts and filling them with select materials suggests that the total structure was experienced by the users as participating in the powers of the cosmos. Hence, the abandonment activities would appear to be the conditions of satisfaction of collective ritual "decommissioning" intentions. I have characterized the representational contents of collective intentions of this sort as ideological rules, specifying the conditions and tangible outcome that collective behaviors must display in order for the purposes of the performers to be achieved. These purposes presuppose and invoke an immanentist cosmology, that is, collective world beliefs that characterized the world as immanently sacred, making the representational contents of these collective intentions constitutive rules and regulatory and moral protocols suggesting that the removal of the posts would be akin to removing the great axis mundi by which the stratification of the cosmos was sustained. And yet, these posts could not be permitted simply to rot for this would likely be taken as doing greater harm to the sanctity of the cosmos than if they were removed. That is, removal of the structures was imperative and the mode of removal was equally imperative. This must be the case since it required not only considerable labor to remove these quite large posts; this removal had to be done carefully so as to minimize any further damage to the surrounding earth. And, of course, the closing or "sealing" of the post holes had to be done by the use of stone cobbles and gravel procured with some labor.

All this means that we can best understand the dismantling of the structures in deontic terms. This would further strongly suggest that the symbolic pragmatic meaning of these structures could not be characterized in simple domestic hamlet terms, even though both domestic habitations and major timber structures of this type presuppose the same cosmology-ethos complex. Given an immanentist cosmology with a complementary custodial-squatter ethos, the central logic arising from this complex was that humans had a moral burden that obliged them to "live lightly on the land." I have already noted that the habitation component would manifest this complex by practicing a dispersed semisedentary seasonal base-camp settlement system, minimizing the disordering of the sacred natural world that their pursuit of everyday survival necessarily brought about. However, the cult sodality component also practiced the same cultural traditions, in this case by the sodalities rectifying the disorder that the everyday pursuit of organic survival by gardening and foraging brought about. They did this through carefully controlling the patterning of the material facilities that they produced. Even though the construction of these material facilities entailed major intervention into the sacred order, they were required as monumental icons of the cosmos to constitute the complex behaviors performed in their context as the type of sacred games and mortuary-mediated world renewal ritual they intended, thereby enhancing the desired renewal and world rebalancing effect of these performances.

Seen in these terms, it is clear that the large structures constituting the focus of these two sites would not be domestic habitation units and, instead, would be cult sodality units. Hence, it becomes clear that the ideological strategy of construction and usage would also include rules of abandonment, the latter being carried out so as to reverse and rectify the disturbance to the natural order that their earlier construction generated. It is almost as if the careful retrieval of the posts requiring the filling of the post holes with cobbles was intended to seal "wounds" to the land created by the building. The notion of "sealing wounds" is even manifested in the earth ovens and other large and deep pits that were built. In all cases, cobble stones were left either in situ or put back into the pits before final burial with surface scraped earth. The fact that the post holes were filled with cobbles and gravel from the nearby

Dry Run suggests that this latter natural feature had particular meaning to the Ohio Hopewell. This was a passageway that regularly directed the flow of water across the floodplain as the floods retreated and exposed the cobbles and gravel. It is possible that the latter materials were interpreted as part of the natural order separating the surface stratum earth from the deep stratum earth and, therefore, it was a "natural" material that could be properly used to seal any deep wounds in the land surface caused by human construction. The initial depth of these holes may have been required just to "tap" the sacred powers of the deep stratum earth so that this sacredness could pervade the structures as part of the powers by which the activities performed there were constituted as sacred rites of the intended type. However, when abandoned, the posts had to be removed and the holes sealed in order to stop the flow of this sacred power. Allowed to continue in an uncontrolled manner would lead to great pollution of the landscape.

Is this a God's truth claim? Can I now claim to have characterized the precise nature of these structures? No. I am sure that this story is not the absolute truth nor is it the complete story. However, what I can claim is to have articulated the general category of collective intentionality that must have existed and been exercised for these post hole patterns to exist in the way we now know they do. The fact that the same pattern is found in other major earthwork sites grounds my claim that this is a strongly rule-governed practice and not simply the practical exercise of a universal need to conserve labor through recycling posts. However, if all this is the case, then it certainly falsifies the view that the Brown's Bottom #1 and Lady's Run sites are adequately characterized in terms of being domestic habitations. Rather, when the presence of Ohio Hopewell exotics, burials, and the other attributes listed above are taken into account, and when these attributes are demonstrated to be characteristic of recognized ceremonial structures, it is more reasonable to conclude that these structures would be associated with the ceremonial sphere. I have postulated that ritual way stations would be part of the Ohio cult sodality heterarchy system and I claim that the Lady's Run and Brown's Bottom #1 structures can be quite adequately treated in these terms.

Discussion

Under the Ohio Hopewell Cult Sodality Heterarchy System model and its theoretical framework, the Complementary Heterarchical Community model, I have been able to generate a range of possible types of site categories that could not even be contemplated under the Vacant Center/Dispersed Hamlet model and its monistic modular polity premises. The contrast is nicely illustrated by how proponents of these two perspectives have approached the interpretation of the same empirical evidence constituting the

Brown' Bottom #1 and Lady's Run sites. Informed by the latter perspective, Pacheco and his colleagues were faced with an either/or situation when they exposed these two structures. Either these were sedentary hamlets or they were ceremonial locales comparable in size and quality of construction to the nearby Edwin Harness Renewal Lodge with its multiple and artifact-rich mortuary deposits. However, treating them in the latter terms would seem to fly in the face of "common sense," in the face of the theoretical presuppositions of the model, since this would mean building and using major ritual locales that were only 1–2 km from an embankment earthwork locale that is a classic expression of the ceremonial aspect of the community (or allied communities). Why would a monistic modular community double up on its ceremonial construction in this way and, instead, simply build much nearer to the embankment earthwork? Therefore, under this unitary view, the only reasonable explanation appeared to be to treat these as sedentary hamlets, even if no other sites recognized as displaying the combination of attributes have been exposed by excavation.

As I noted earlier, the model that presents the most coherent set of categories that enables the avoidance of lumping or splitting is the more reasonable model, even if it is the more complicated and unfamiliar, since it is able to explain the basic data with the least number of anomalies. I claim that my "sacred way station" interpretation has accomplished this goal—for now. In effect, the Ohio Hopewell Cult Sodality Heterarchy System model postulates from the "bottom up" a range of cult sodality sites—from the cult sodality cluster of nodal ceremonial site with its associated age-set and age-grade sites, to the ritual way station sites that served as transient hostel-like sites for the cult sodalities participating in the sacred games *tournées*/mortuary *chaîne opératoire* process of Ohio Hopewell system of cult sodality heterarchies, to the large embankment earthworks that served, along with their associated major and lesser renewal lodges, as the primary monumental iconic symbolic pragmatic devices that enabled this complex process to be felicitously performed. Of course, I recognize that the nodal ceremonial site type has still not been *clearly* represented in the current archaeological record. When it is identified empirically, I suggest that it would be very much like the Brown's Bottom #1 and Lady's Run sites; but it would also have a strong representation of the type of debitage associated with the specialized production camp. As I noted in chapter 9, if it were excavated Murphy IV might turn out to be a cult sodality ceremonial nodal locale site displaying one or more structures similar to the two at the Brown's Bottom #1 and Lady's Run sites, in addition to the known uninodal refuse deposit displaying the total range of lithic production dominated by two select cherts, Wyandotte and Flint Ridge. Indeed, with the wonderful advances in geomagnetic surveying that have been made and that were responsible for finding the Brown's Bottom #1 and Lady's Run sites, there is good reason to return to the Jennison Guard site, and even to the Murphy Tract for this purpose.

The Lithic Clusters, Stubbs Works, and the Smith Site

I will immediately qualify my above comment to suggest that there may already be a known example of a cult sodality ceremonial cult nodal locale with associated ceremonial materials, as well as a uninodal refuse deposit—except that it has not been identified as such by its surveyors. It is listed as Site 33WA362 and the archaeologists also referred to as the Smith site (Sunderhaus et al. 2001). It actually overlooks the Stubbs Works (figure 12.5) and is situated on a bluff immediately southwest of and overlooking this earthwork. I earlier noted that the Stubbs Works site is a major embankment earthwork on the floodplain of the Little Miami River about 7 km south of Fort Ancient and about 30 km upstream from the Turner site. I also suggested then that it may have participated in the dispersed Fort Ancient–Turner–Hopewell third-order cult sodality heterarchy.

Robert Genheimer carried out a series of surface surveys and collections in the zone outside the embankment earthwork itself and has established that there were 28 discrete lithic clusters that he refers to as the Stubbs Works Clusters (1996, 97, figure 6.3; also 1997, 298, figure 11.3). He notes that these 28 lithic clusters can be subdivided into two subclusters, which he refers to as the north and south subclusters. They are spatially very distinct. The north subcluster consists of 11 discrete lithic scatters on the north bank terrace of the river and about 1 km downstream from the Stubbs Works. The south subcluster is immediately south of the embankment earthwork, on the same side of the river, and consists of 17 discrete lithic scatters. Genheimer surface collected all these clusters and found that each had a solid representation of Middle Woodland period lithics, in particular bladelets. However, he found that the discrete lithic cluster components of the south subcluster were generally richer and denser than those of the north subcluster.

He and his colleagues subsequently conducted intense surveys of three of the larger components of the south subcluster, specifically 33WA256, 33WA257, and 33WA290. Following these controlled surface surveys they had the opportunity to excavate several transects in the southern sector of the Stubbs Works, both inside and outside the embankment circle. Here they revealed a rich complex of post holes clustered for the most part outside the southern sector of the embankment. Unraveling the pattern revealed multiple timber structures displaying a range of different forms: rectangular, circular, single-pole walls, even a series of superimposed wall-trench structures. One major feature that Cowan et al. (1999) revealed in their excavation was a large "woodhenge" circle constituted of regularly spaced and large posts. It had a 73 m diameter and was constructed of 172 posts averaging between 20 and 35 cm in diameter. Eventually when abandoned, the posts were extracted and the holes carefully filled. The whole set of post holes was covered by earth derived from other areas of this large site, thereby generating a circular embankment. This large wooden post circle is reminiscent of the large circular woodhenges built and used between A.D. 1050 and A.D. 1200 at Cahokia, the major Mississippian period world renewal cult sodality heterarchy on the American Bottom (Byers 2006a).[1] The associated structures, particularly the eight (and possibly more) wall-trench structures, are also reminiscent of the Cahokia structures. However, except for the eastern sector of 33WA256, this area of multiple structures is not part of the south subcluster and, in fact, the whole area was largely devoid of lithics or any artifacts, being predominantly covered by the floors of these structures and the floors were remarkably clean.

> It is evident that this portion of the Stubbs Earthwork complex was a very busy place some 1,600 to 2,000 years ago. But it is also clear that these building remnants are the accumulation of repeated building and use episodes that took place over significant periods of time, as indicated by structure overlap (Structures 15 and 21) and by the direct superimposition of Structures 18 and 19. In addition, the extremely close proximity of some other "houses" (e.g., of Structure 15 with both Structures 17 and 19) suggests that those structures probably were not strictly contemporary. Nevertheless, the scant artifactual evidence indicates that all are products of Hopewellian period construction and use. Also intriguing are the apparently common orientations of many of these structures. Structures 15, 17, 18, 19, and 20 are identically oriented, and Structures 14 and 21 share the same northeasterly orientation. Structure 16 exhibits an orientation intermediate between the two more common alignments. It is conceivable that the principles that may have governed structure orientation in this portion of the site changed through time. (Cowan et al. 1999)

I have summarized the above to ground my suggestion that the Stubbs Works embankment earthwork zone itself must be looked at separately from the north and south subclusters. Given its size and form, there is no doubt that the earthwork, a version of the Paint Creek C-R motif, can be treated as the context of probably a second-order cult sodality heterarchy, and that the complex of timber structures, single post and wall-trench types, were ritual renewal lodges akin to the Seip structures discussed above. There was also the sacred "woodhenge" of this heterarchy. It is likely that in late Turner times it came to be a transfer point where the sacred bone bundles being borne in procession from Turner to Fort Ancient were probably used to serve as "counters" for sacred games performed there, the point being to reenliven these bundles by being endowed with the sacred life energies from the strenuous competitive gaming efforts of the participating sodalities. It is unlikely, however, that artifacts would be added at this stage since there is no indication, for now, that there were laying-in crypts of the sort already described for Turner and Hopewell. Hence, these games may have been more of a mode of enhancing the sacred powers immanent in the bones themselves in preparation for final burial disposal at Fort Ancient, only 7 km north on the Little Miami River.

In any case, if the two subclusters as they were mapped by the surface surveying are analytically separated from the Stubbs Works site, and indeed, there was no physical overlap, the former look remarkably similar to the Murphy Tract lithic clusters. Each cluster of both subclusters can be defined as relatively discrete; some are clearly larger and have more dense lithic debitage and artifacts, others are less dense. In particular, as I noted earlier, lithic cluster site 33WA362 turned out to be exceptional. Recently, Ted Sunderhaus, Rodney Riggs, and Frank Cowan (2001) were able to carry out salvage excavations at this site and they have renamed it the Smith site. It is actually located on a relatively high bluff that is southwest and overlooking the Stubbs Works. Although they did not have the opportunity to excavate fully, they were able to establish that it had at least three zones. The most southerly zone was dominated by Structure 1 (figure 14.1) that displayed the characteristic Ohio Hopewell rounded-corner rectangular form. It had a large central post and the northwest and northeast corners had dual posts. The floor was about 8 m × 8 m, much smaller than Brown's Bottom #1, and it had two entrances, a smaller northeast corner entrance and a large southern entrance. Very little in the way of internal features or cultural materials was found, although they did retrieve scraps of mica in the post hole fill. Apparently, the structure was burned when abandoned.

They exposed an area about 30 m north of Structure 1 that displayed a complex set of post holes, pits, and assorted features, up to 100, most of which they had no opportunity to excavate. They termed this the Sandy Knoll sector (figure 14.2). Those features that they did excavate indicate Middle Woodland lithics and artifacts, although they noted that Genheimer's earlier surface survey had revealed some lithics of an earlier period. About 30 m north of this zone and near the bluff edge they exposed a large pit that they termed Feature 37. The pit was straight sided, about 1.5 m in diameter and close to 1 m deep. It contained an extremely dense and rich range of cultural materials in three strata. The uppermost stratum was dominated by fire-cracked rock and other lithics, including about 70 or more bladelets and fragments. Also, two of these

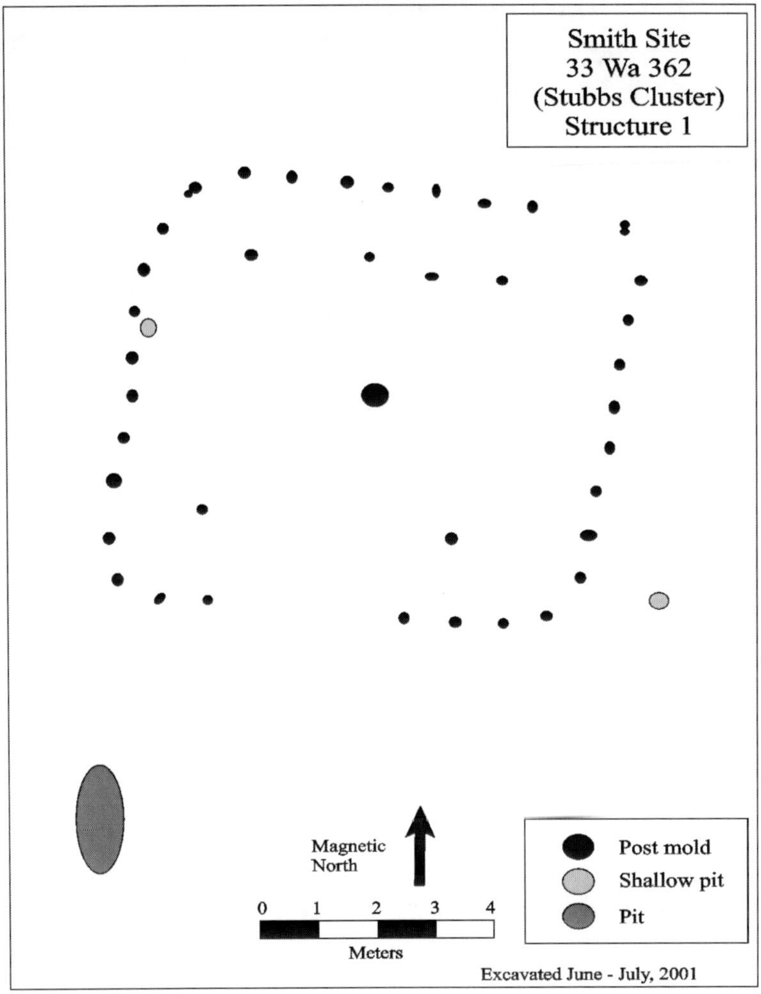

FIGURE 14.1
The Smith Site Structure 1
Source: Sunderhaus et al. 2001, figure 2. Courtesy of the Ohio Archaeological Council.

were obsidian bladelets and a small obsidian flake. They commented that local cherts were "sparse to non-existent." The second stratum was dense, including fire-cracked rock, burnt earth, as well as a significant quantity of cut mica fragments, broken ceramics in relatively large quantities, displaying a variety of exotic styles, including tetrapod vessels. The third and bottom stratum was less impressive in content, being primarily fire-cracked rock and some

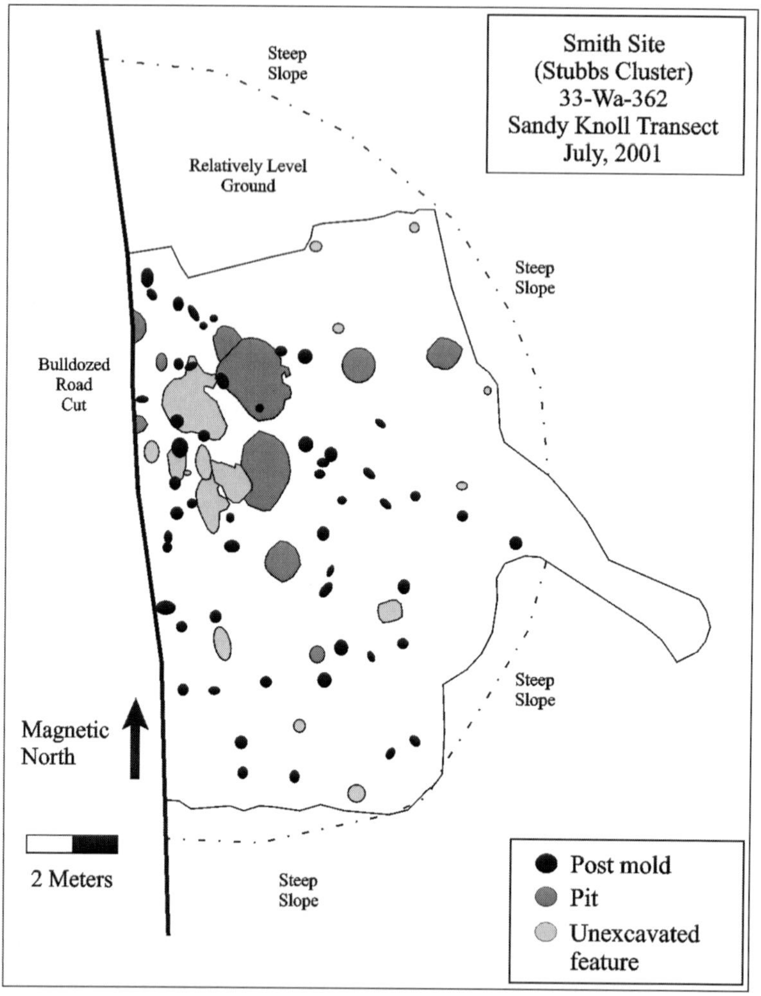

FIGURE 14.2
Sandy Knoll Sector, Smith Site
Source: Sunderhaus et al. 2001, figure 3. Courtesy of the Ohio Archaeological Council.

ceramics and wood charcoal. They conclude that Feature 37 was the result of careful and ongoing cleaning of the surrounding site but that the contents were not indicative of everyday life. Rather, in their view the Smith site was "an earthwork-focused site with 'ritual' overtones" (Sunderhaus et al. 2001).

Critical Discussion

I think they are being overly conservative and quite modest here. I certainly agree with them that the Smith site displayed a range of attributes that would be characteristic of the cult sodality sphere. However, their speaking of it as "an earthwork-focused site" may be another example of identifying ceremonial attributes with embankment earthworks. If it is assumed that, along with most of the other discrete sites of the south subcluster, the Smith site actually predated the Stubbs Earthworks, how would it be characterized—now that there would be no earthwork in spatial association? As I suggested earlier, the lithic clusters are very similar to the lithic clusters of the Murphy Tract. I have already argued that these represent a cult sodality cluster consisting of specialized Hopewell production age-grade base camps and age-set task areas. I have postulated that because of the special nature of the uninodal lithic refuse deposit Murphy IV may be the ceremonial nodal locale of that cult sodality cluster. However, excavation is required to establish this. I would suggest, given what we know of contents of the Smith site, as well as its location overlooking the other lithic clusters, it would be consistent with what could be expected of the type of patterning a *cult sodality ceremonial nodal* locale would display. Indeed, the north subcluster may be another cult sodality cluster and these two clusters may have been contemporary, maintaining their spatial integrity as part of maintaining their mutual autonomy.

This suggests that the north subcluster should also have a site equivalent to the Smith site. However, they likely also cooperated and, in fact, may have been important components of a first-order heterarchy. However, I suspect that this occurred only later in their history. Initially as a first-order heterarchy, rather than these two cult sodalities building a smaller local earthwork, they allied with several other first-order heterarchies upstream and downstream and constituted a large second-order heterarchy that cooperatively constructed the Stubbs Works and, along with other second-order heterarchies, further cooperated to build what we now refer to as the South Fort sector of Fort Ancient and, possibly, the Turner earthworks. In short, I postulate that these two clusters existed prior to Stubbs Works. These two sodalities may have allied to form a first-order heterarchy, which in turn affiliated with several other first-order heterarchies of the region to the south of Fort Ancient. This second-order heterarchy, affiliated probably to one or more second-order heterarchies north of Fort Ancient, was responsible for constructing and using Turner and Fort Ancient, as well as the Hopewell site. Then, possibly when the Turner site was abandoned, the first-order heterarchy constituting the above north and south clusters promoted the second-order heterarchy with which it was affiliated to build the Stubbs Works. The abandonment of Turner not only led to the building of Stubbs Works but also the building of several other equivalent embankment earthwork sites on the Little Miami River between Turner and Fort Ancient that display variants of the Paint Creek C-R motif, Milford and Camden (figures 12.6 and 12.7). Stubbs Works, as the nearest of the three to Fort Ancient, possibly became effectively a large ritual station partly replacing Turner in the sacred games *tournée*/mortuary *chaîne opératoire* cyclic process and this would explain the proliferation of the above wooden structures that Cowan and his colleagues exposed (1999).

Clearly, this is only suggestive. Much more work is required to demonstrate that the Smith site represents a cult sodality ceremonial nodal locale that preexisted Stubbs Works. Unfortunately, of course, given the current state of suburban expansion and development, it may be impossible to do so. However, this "just-so" story does alert us to what we could expect to find along these lines. It is incumbent on archaeologists to be attuned to this possibility. The Jennison Guard site, for example, would seem to be another excellent candidate for finding a cult sodality ceremonial nodal locale.

OVERVIEW

I initiated this description and analysis of the Ohio Hopewell embankment earthworks in terms of the sacred games *tournée*/mortuary-mediated world renewal ritual process by first noting Greber's recognition of the differential distribution of mortuary residue, artifact assemblage, and great embankment earthworks across central and southern Ohio. I have attempted to explain this distribution through developing the Sacred Games *Tournée* model in tandem with the notion of the mortuary-mediated world renewal ritual process. In the process of developing this explanation, I have added several new categories of structural features that could be expected to be generated by the type of organizational system postulated under the Ohio Hopewell Cult Sodality Heterarchy System model and I have demonstrated that there are such features that conform to these categories. One category that constitutes a site in itself I have termed sacred way stations. These would be ritual hostels for the cult sodality parties traveling to the earthworks and they would be deliberately located spatially separate from them. The second category includes at least two component features that would be spatially embodied by embankment earthworks: the major renewal lodges and the auxiliary or lesser renewal lodges—some of which, however, might be immediately adjacent to rather than embodied by their associated embankment earthworks. The major renewal lodges are the mortuary-associated structures found under the largest mounds at such sites as Mound City, Tremper, Turner, Hopewell, Seip, and so on. The ancillary renewal lodges, sometimes with associated plazas, are represented by features such as the seven structures at Seip that I noted earlier in the chapter, and, as I noted above, similar such structures found at Stubbs Works and Fort Ancient. The ancillary lodges are all characterized by the absence of mortuary residue and, indeed, in general, they had no ritual residue, the latter apparently being carefully avoided or at least cleared away when the structures were abandoned. I suggest that the Seip ancillary renewal lodges, along with their nearby plazas, would be the "in-house" ritual locales of the constituent first-order heterarchy components of the second-order heterarchy. Hence, these renewal lodges would be the places where mortuary-mediated rites by the cult sodalities of the constituent groups would be conducted, including the performance of rituals mediated by the series of large posts that were systematically raised, removed, and reinserted into the stepped post holes (Burks and Greber 2009, 147–49, 152–55). The role of trees or posts is particularly interesting. Hall (1997, 102–8) has long argued that the procuring and cutting of special trees, and the carrying and "planting" of them by companions of selected age-set sodalities figured centrally in the material configuration of the world renewal rituals of many historic Native North American woodland communities and this is because trees figured centrally in the cosmology of many of these cultures. "The Milky Way has been seen as a trail for the spirits of the dead quite widely in the world. . . . The Algonquian-speaking Potomacs of Virginia believed that spirits ascended into the sky by climbing a tree . . . , and to the Potomacs could be added the Winnebago, so seeing the Milky Way as a tree must have required no great leap of logic for ancients pondering their world. Pole climbing in the Feast of the Dead among Great Lake Algonquians and in that of the Aztecs can be easily interpreted as being in the nature of imitative magic to aid the spirits in their ascent. . . . Poles once figured in mortuary ritual from coast to coast and could thus have had a logical role in any Sun Dance prototype conducted as a mourning ritual" (1997, 162). I would add that the large stepped post holes in association with several of these auxiliary renewal lodges of Seip could also have figured centrally in mortuary-mediated renewal rituals.[2]

Overall, therefore, the analyses of this and the preceding chapter would suggest that it is reasonable to treat the large renewal lodges, such as those found under the Seip-Pricer and Seip-Conjoined mounds and Mounds 23 and 25 of the Hopewell site, and the activities that occurred there as the collective responsibility of these two dispersed third-order heterarchies. It is important to note that I am not claiming that Seip, Liberty Works, or the Hopewell sites were the central locales of third-order heterarchies. I am saying that these major renewal lodges were the collective responsibility of the dispersed third-order heterarchies with which the sites were affiliated. In my view, as with all major embankment earthwork locales, these were the direct responsibility of second-order cult sodality heterarchies and, therefore, each of these sites, Hopewell, Seip, and Liberty Works, was the locale of an autonomous second-order heterarchy. And, as I noted earlier, since their forms count as Solar motifs, they also manifest and presence the same aspect of the cosmos, the Above World–Middle World–Beneath World in the solar aspect.

To complete this analysis, it is important to clarify this point. In organizational terms while major renewal lodges are distinguished from lesser or auxiliary renewal lodges by the rich presence of mortuary and other ritual residues in the former and their absence in the latter, the major renewal lodges can also be internally distinguished into two types, which I will simply speak of as Type A and Type B. The major renewal lodges of the Seip, Liberty Works, and Hopewell sites would be examples of Type A, while those of Turner and Tremper would be Type B. The primary distinguishing attribute is that Type A served to mediate laying-in and post-laying-in period rituals that incorporated the conveyancing rites by which custodial regalia of critical ritual were decommissioned, while Type B renewal lodges lacked this important conveyancing rite. It is for this reason that I argued that Turner and Tremper display no or almost no custodial regalia, and I will not repeat that explanation, except to say that I have argued that the laying-in periods performed at Turner were both before and after with the conveyancing rites of its deceased being performed during the laying-in period at the Hopewell site, as was the case for Mound City as the locale for conveyancing rites, leaving no custodial regalia to be deposited at Tremper. What the Type A and Type B major renewal lodge categories clearly highlight, therefore, is that the third-order heterarchy cannot be located in a particular embankment earthwork. That is, this is a *dispersed* third-order organizational structure and what is dispersed are its major components, which are second-order heterarchies and, therefore, the third-order level does not have a single locale. Rather, it has a network of second-order locales and among these locales one is typically used to perform the very important conveyancing rite whereby all or at least most of the custodial ritual usufructs of the cult sodality components of the third-order heterarchy are transferred from the deceased custodians to their replacements. The embankment earthwork in which this typically occurs will be simply the locale of *one* of the affiliated second-order heterarchies, such as the Hopewell site, as in the case of the dispersed Fort Ancient–Turner–Hopewell cult sodality heterarchy, or, as in the case of the dispersed third-order Chillicothe-Newark cult sodality heterarchy, of both Seip and Liberty Works, the two second-order heterarchies that were jointly responsible for the High Bank site. That is, I postulated that an Ohio Hopewell dispersed third-order cult sodality heterarchy is constituted of multiple second-order heterarchies (each of which is in turn constituted of several first-order heterarchies) and among the locales of the second-order heterarchies, at least one serves as the focal locale for performing the standard laying-in period rites that *incorporate the conveyancing rites* of the custodial usufruct rituals.

Above I have asserted, cased on my careful empirical demonstration of the distribution of the custodial regalia, that the Hopewell site was the focal locale for the dispersed third-order Fort Ancient–Turner–Hopewell cult sodality heterarchy and I suggest that Seip and Liberty Works operated as the cofocal sites of the dispersed third-order Chillicothe-Newark cult sodality heterarchy. I have already argued that Seip and Liberty Works were second-order heterarchies that affiliated through sharing the High Bank site, composing the full complement of sites constituting the Sacred Dual C-R motif. In the same way, the Hopewell site was likely paired with the Spruce Hill site, a local expression of a ridge-top T-Form overlooking the Paint Creek–Scioto confluence, thereby constituting together the Sacred Dual C-Form/T-Form motif. Indeed, the Hopewell site might be unique in that the set of first-order heterarchies that originally affiliated and built it may have been transient migrants from the Little Miami Valley who deliberately established themselves on the North Fork in order to franchise the C-Form/T-Form ritual usufruct copyright to the cult sodalities that were responsible for the renewal lodges that formed what Greber (1991) refers to as the Northwest Chillicothe Group. In any case, I think it is important to note that the system of heterarchies, first-order, second-order, and third-order, should not be conceptualized as a hierarchical structure but as a network of autonomous cult sodality components organized from the bottom up, and each level and each component at each level sustained agentive autonomy, so that the focal site is simply the locale of the second-order heterarchy of the dispersed third-order heterarchy that takes on the important task of enabling the performance of the conveyancing ritual. This ensures that it becomes the focus of all the cult sodalities constituting the third-order heterarchy while not being in any way a dominant locale.

CONCLUSION

In the next chapter I particularly address the most appropriate approach to take concerning the interpretation of the Ohio Hopewell features. Should this be done objectively, that is, in terms that focus on formal attributes and which we define in functional rather than intersubjective terms? This distinction is often spoken of in anthropology as the etic and emic perspectives. I have a particular interest in this question since the social realist approach I take is firmly committed to the intersubjective perspective. I do not think that this is simply a matter of taste since I take the position that the cultural traditions of a people are partly constitutive of the nature of the social system in which they live and which makes the activities they carry out possible, a position I lay out in the next chapter.

I then illustrate the importance of the intersubjective perspective by addressing the meaningful construction and use of the paths and pathways that must have pervaded the Ohio Middle Woodland period communities since clearly the sacred games *tournée*/mortuary-mediated world renewal ritual process hinged on a complex of mobility strategies and their constitutive rules by which participants were warranted to travel from one drainage to another, a process that effectively presupposes such cultural principles as inclusive territorialism. How did the symbolic pragmatic meanings of the Ohio Hopewellian archaeological assemblage figure in the use of this set of transdrainage paths and pathways by both the mutualistic cult sodalities and the kinship-based domestic habitation groups that constituted the complementary heterarchical communities of a given region that were their primary custodians? Finally, I demonstrate that the principles implicated in this usage of the paths and pathways can be found to be expressed in the siting of spatially distant earthworks such that they were integrated into a network of pathways that transcended the local limits and by which the heterarchies could share and distribute the sacred powers that were regularly released into the cosmos through the collective sacred games *tournée*/mortuary-mediated world renewal ritual process they cooperatively and collectively performed. The subsequent and final chapter then leads into addressing relations that the Ohio Hopewell cult sodality heterarchies had with the neighboring Adena heterarchies. This will be addressed in order to show how the conceptual scheme I have developed, and in particular, the Ritual Usufruct Conveyancing and Franchising model, can resolve significant puzzles about how the Adena system, what might have been the first cult sodality heterarchy system to emerge definitively in the prehistory of the region, could persist side by side with the later Ohio Hopewell in subregions of the same Central Ohio Valley at least for the first half of what I have been calling here the Middle Woodland period.

15

The Structuring of Ohio Hopewell Sites and Pathways

As I argued in the overview of the preceding chapter, it seems clear now that most major embankment earthwork sites with a central mound covering what I have termed a major renewal lodge, that is, a structure displaying a range of features and facilities used to process the dead and, in most cases, including mortuary remains, also have auxiliary structures in which there is an absence of the latter, but a presence of other features, such as hearths, large posts, and so on. It is perfectly reasonable to assume that the types of activities these different types of locales mediated were related since they share the same embankment earthwork context. This would entail that the nature of the activities in one type of structure is partly constituted by the nature of the activities in the other type(s). In short, these structures were intrinsically related as symbolic pragmatic devices in that they mediated activities that constituted the "way of life" that the earthworks made possible. Therefore, it is important to start developing terminology that might enable us to speak of these structures in terms that would be relevant to the groups that produced and used them.

In this regard, I consider terminology to be the expression of the relevant concepts that form the core of the theory used to elucidate the nature of the phenomenon being studied. The adequacy of the concepts is measured by the coherence with which they can be used to order and explain the empirical data. This usually means minimizing lumping under one term empirical phenomena that display formal properties that suggest they are different kinds or, alternatively, minimizing splitting, that is, minimizing treating empirical phenomena that vary formally in minor ways as if this variation makes a difference in their nature. This avoidance of lumping and splitting applies to both the natural and the social sciences. However, concept-construction has a particular dimension that is unique to the social sciences, in general, and prehistoric archaeology in particular in that these concepts must have an emic core since it is this core that is partly constitutive of the social phenomena that social scientists study. The conceptual schemes of the natural sciences, of course, must confront the same problem of making these concepts "fit" the reality they are studying. However, if they get it wrong, the natural world that they study does not change (only the way we experience it changes) since the scientific concepts and the objects of the world are ontologically unrelated. However, in the communities that the social sciences study there is an internal relation between the social nature of the communities and the concepts that are expressed in their symbols, verbal and nonverbal form, and this means that this relation is constitutive in nature; that is, the deliberate use of the symbols is important to the makeup of that social world. As Charles Taylor (1985c, 275–77) has put it, in the social world of classical Athens (his chosen example), the self-description the Greeks had as "equals" was not simply a description of an objective phenomenon. It was an affirmation of and commitment to the very social world it was about, the Athenian world. That is, the expression in symbols of this Athenian Greek concept, along with the total paradigm of concepts it entailed, was a critical constitutive factor of the social world it described. "[A] term like 'equals' had to be articulated in the polis, because it carried this sense of mutually non-subordinated agents who are nevertheless part of the same society, who owe allegiance to the same laws and must defend them together. Equals, likes (*isoi, homoioi*), we are bound together, and yet also not hierarchically. Equals is the right term; and it had to be *articulated* in the society, because this kind of society, based on pride in this kind of ideal, could only exist if it was seen as an achievement, the avoidance of an alternative to which lesser peoples fell prey—the Persians in one context; in Pericles' exaltation of Athens, the comparison is with the Spartans. This is why there is no such society without some term like 'equals'" (1985c, 277). For this reason, archaeology cannot ignore the constitutive meaning when it uses formal properties to develop taxonomies of the material cultural patternings that are the objective data on which its analyses are founded.

Therefore, it is clear that a strenuously objectivist taxonomy in prehistory will likely fail to lead to adequately describing the social reality that was responsible for the archaeological record, simply because the symbolic pragmatic meaning of the material culture that the people made and used was a constitutive medium of this social reality, and therefore, to describe the data correctly it is necessary to use a vocabulary that adequately captures the responsible community's likely "emic" meaning. I have argued that the stylistics of material culture are among the primary media of this constitutive moment.

I have made this point in the analogy of the warrant and this can be extended to even everyday activity such as hunting and gathering. The term *hunting* does not describe a basic "act." It describes a social action in which material behavior involving the killing of animals is constituted by the symbolic pragmatic meaning of the tools used, and this meaning is manifested in the stylistics of the hunting gear. These styles mediate the warranting moment by which the behavior of animal killing is constituted as a social act of hunting, a warranted, that is, legitimate, appropriation of the life and its embodied material value by the hunter. This means that as with all social actions, hunting is an emergent phenomenon, as I noted in chapter 5. This is easily illustrated by pairing hunting with poaching. These terms define behaviors that are perspicuous contrasts only at the emergent, warranting, or action-constitutive level since, objectively, poaching and hunting entail the same killing behavior. What makes the difference is the use of the "warrant"; and this is a symbolic moment that operates at the deontic level of rights and duties. Hunting and poaching; gathering and pilfering; storing and hoarding. All three pairings are objectively equivalent while deontically they perspicuously contrast, each being diametrically opposite. In each case, we can speak of diametrically opposite positions, for example, hunter/poacher, gatherer/pilferer, and saver/hoarder, and in each case the person occupying the position defined by the left-hand term is admired while the person occupying the position defined by the right-hand term is strongly condemned. Clearly, while the behaviors that occupants of pairs of opposed position perform may be objectively the same, the action natures of these behaviors are radically opposed. I have asserted that in a nonliterate social system, since written warrants and authoritative constitutive documents are by definition nonexistent, a critically important way that this moment is mediated is by the stylistics of the material weapons and tools that are characteristically used in any given society for these specific instrumental tasks. As social scientists, therefore, while certainly archaeologists must respect the objective recording of the data, in constructing material taxonomies, we cannot ignore the emic perspective. This is the perspective of the understanding of those who were responsible for these data. It is the meaningful media by which this collective intentionality was expressed and manifested in the very moment of usage. In sum, these stylistics were not simply descriptive of the social world in which they participated; they were also an important constitutive factor of this social world.

Some may criticize my promoting the importance of generating terms and their relations that have possible emic relevance and validity since it could be claimed as leading to accomplishing the opposite of its purpose. While intending to reconstruct an emic taxonomy we may effectively project a meaning that would be foreign to those who were responsible for the range of building structures I have suggested above since, of course, no archaeologist lived or participated in that life! Therefore, pursuing the intersubjective action-constitutive (i.e., symbolic pragmatic) meaning of these constructions may simply lead to distorting the real functions they actually served. Hence, the objectivist counter argument could be made that it is better and more "scientific" to present as culturally and meaningfully neutral a taxonomy as possible, one that would simply focus on the major formal tangible properties and could be described in quantitative terms, such as "big house" or "long house," and the more accurately these data are measured, the better.

Of course, I agree that this type of formal naming and classifying certainly is important, but only as the initial stage of collecting and describing the data. Unless a deliberate and strategic move is made to establish possible emic meanings, that is, their substantive meanings, then, as the process of collecting and description and elaboration proceeds, what started as a formal objective taxonomy imperceptibly transforms into an intersubjective, namely, emic, social structural taxonomy. That is, the taxonomy takes on an emic meaning without the deliberate intention of the archaeologist. But, being done imperceptibly, it is more than likely that this emic meaning would be only for the archaeologist and not for those who built and used them. That is, since this move from the objective to the intersubjective occurs in an intuitive manner, it is pretty well guaranteed to be simply the projection of his or her own intersubjective, cultural meanings. Taking an objectivist stance will likely generate the very outcome that the critic claims would be avoided by this stance! To avoid this, we have to *explicitly* pursue the plausible intersubjective collective meanings relevant to those who built them. In a basic way, this is what I have been doing throughout this book and the method is by perspicuous contrast, setting up alternative possibilities and testing them against each other by showing which gives the most coherent account of the empirical data with the fewest anomalies. This technique cannot guarantee "perfection," that is, there will still likely be some misfit between the real prehistoric emic meanings and the archaeologist's constructed "emic" meanings, but it initiates a spiraling process of critical examination and correction that is rational.

I would suggest that, in fact, the uncritical application of "objective" concepts to the archaeological record is illustrated by the Vacant Center/Dispersed Hamlet model in all its versions. This model simply and largely without self-critique imposes the traditions of Euro-American culture on the archaeological settlement pattern. Two examples of this I have suggested is the modular polity perspective, which, in fact, is explicitly modeled on the modern European notion of the classical Greek *polis* or city-state. A second perspective, of course, is the funerary paradigm and why I consider it as the *funerary fallacy*. What is taken by the archeologists as an objective measuring and counting of mortuary data has all along been an unwitting imposition of the Euro-American funerary perspective on the mortuary sphere of the prehistoric Native North American communities, the latter being universalized largely on the assumption that the only relevant aspect of a mortuary sphere is the funerary aspect. Of course, this cannot be completely avoided since the "objective" approach to delineating a data set entails an initial interpretation. We cannot assume an acultural or universal category of meaning for culturally produced objects and only subsequently interpret them. The archaeologist's cultural background is there "from the beginning" and inevitably as the process of collecting and organizing the data proceeds in terms of formal categories, the taxonomic terms shift from the assumed objective formal to the archaeologist's intersubjective structural. If this transformation is not recognized, then rather than explicitly presenting and warranting the theorization of the meaningful social and cultural nature of the phenomena being studied, an implicit process occurs and, equally inevitably, the objective category described in formal terms, for example, "big house" becomes the substantive intersubjective object, "the Big House," which is interpreted as pretty well like the Euro-American church or cathedral or the Islamic mosque that are understood as the sacred centers of Euro-American and Islamic polities, social systems firmly wedded to transcendentalist cosmologies; and the long distance activities linking these "Big Houses" in their embankment earthworks become much the same as Christian or Islamic "pilgrimages" in which personal salvation in a future transcendent heaven is the goal of such religious practices. In a way, of course, there are parallels between the latter pilgrimages and what I am calling the sacred games *tournées*. But in their essential ways, they are quite perspicuously different and the result is to mischaracterize the nature of both the intra- and interembankment earthwork activities and distort the social nature of the groups that were responsible.

To prevent this unwitting emergence of the archaeologist's cultural meaning that ends up projecting Old World social and cultural structures onto Native North American societies, I believe that the hermeneutic process should be made explicit, informed by an adequate theory of the symbolic meaning of material culture that can invest intelligibility and coherence into the construction of monumental earthworks by a people who apparently had no significant dominance-based class structure that could be the source of control power enabling the exploitation of the majority by the minority. Having an adequate theory of the symbolic meaning of material culture is critical since this enables the interpreter to be explicit in elucidating a relevant theory of the social and cultural nature of the objects making up the patterning of the archeological record, namely, the earthworks, mounds, the material structures and the contents that they covered (i.e., the facilities, features, mortuary residue, and artifactual contents), and so on. Of course, I have characterized these as the expressive and constitutive symbolic pragmatic devices of cult sodality heterarchies and I have explicitly postulated this pragmatic symbolism as a universal tendency for humans in society. However, the hermeneutic spiral method promotes an ongoing critical process of verifying such claims and this means it promotes an ongoing critique of such specific claims to show where they have fallen short. But showing where they fail or fall short is not sufficient since to leave the matter there is to promote nonknowledge rather than knowledge. It is necessary to present an alternative account, which is then shown to explain the same data more coherently than the one it replaces. Of course, even should this alternative be agreed upon as the more coherent, it must also be subjected to the same critical hermeneutic spiral process.

Some may fear that this becomes an endless pursuit of truth claims about the past and, in fact, they would be right—it is. However, this does not mean that we can never achieve a truthful characterization. What it means is that we can never (absolutely) know when we do. The best we can do is to say that, at this point in the spiral, this or that explanation is the better and, therefore, we will accept it as a contingent truth, that is, the best approximation currently available. Now, even though recognizing that it is the better of the different explanatory models on tap, some will likely reject accepting it and opt to accept one of the runner-up models on the grounds that this or that one is "more familiar" or "simpler," and so on. I would consider this to be a profoundly irrational choice; just as irrational as considering rejecting both since, as noted above, to reject all models means preferring nonknowledge over knowledge and the former means that we accept what we already know as preferable to knowing something in a better way. Certainly I will accept that in some cases we can come to a real impasse in that two contending and quite contrasting models seem to have equivalent rational reasons for acceptance. This simply means, of course, that we have a lot of work ahead of us since, in the ontology I accept, the world is only one way and if there are contrasting understandings of it, the problem is in us and not the world. Only in the social world can we change it to conform to our preferences. But if the changes will be successful it is because we have an adequate view of the way the social world was prior to that process of change we brought about. And this means two types of work: empirical and theoretical. An authentic standoff can be beneficial for the discipline since it promotes greater effort to resolve the problems and, most often, the solution is a synthesis and modification of both models with a positive outcome of real knowledge growth—for now. This synthesis does not change the prehistoric world. This stays the same while we change and improve our understanding of it.

I believe that much more work must be devoted both to elucidating the intersubjective nature of these facilities, features, mortuary residue, and artifactual contents, that is, their cultural meaning and social purpose, as well as to recovering the patterning of these ancillary features within the embankment earthwork sites. This is important work since it will enable us to carry out a more complete characterization of the range of social groups that existed and the criteria by which to identify them. This differs from organizing a taxonomy, since this is based on formal patterns. Rather, it draws on the taxonomies by moving beyond them to reconstruct the substantive social worlds that generated these patterns. I call this task the *structuring* of the archaeological record, in this case referring explicitly to that part of the record I have spoken of as cult sodality locales, and this structuring amounts to reconstructing the nature of the abstract social relations that linked and the cultural structures that characterized these locales. For example, first-order and second-order heterarchies may have a different qualitative and quantitative range of ancillary features in their sites. I suggested the latter likelihood when discussing the empirical data of the Stubbs Works. The post hole structure exposed at the Smith site has certain formal characteristics making it similar to the Brown's Bottom #1 structure, but it also has major formal differences and its ancillary zones are also different. I have moved to the substantive level to explain these differences by suggesting that the Smith site was a cult sodality ceremonial nodal locale while the Brown's Bottom #1 and Lady's Run sites were penultimate sacred way stations. The Smith site claim immediately raises historical developmental issues since it implies that both the Smith site and also the nearby cluster of discrete surface lithic scatters, the south subcluster in Genheimer's terms, marked occupations that preexisted the Stubbs Earthworks, or at least most of them did; and, in fact, the cult sodality that was responsible for the Smith site, interpreted as a ceremonial nodal site, may have been a major player along with the postulated and as yet unknown cult sodality(ies) responsible for the northern subcluster in building this large embankment earthwork. Hence, it may turn out that the patterning of the ancillary feature sites of first-order cult sodalities will significantly differ from the patterning of the ancillary feature sites of a second-order cult sodality heterarchy locale, even though in terms of sizes of earthworks they are very similar.

Each site will be the product of a unique history and each must be interpreted in its own terms and within the context of its likely interaction with other earthwork sites. This will be a difficult task. However, it is important in order to empirically ground and substantively develop our understanding of the Ohio Hopewell episode. I have claimed, of course, that the Ohio Cult Sodality Heterarchy System model best develops this understanding. Therefore, an important form of developing this model is to reconstruct the history of a given site in relation to the history of other relevant sites. That is, the model postulates a dynamic interaction among these sites through the participation of the autonomous components, the cult sodalities that had their own clusters consisting of ceremonial nodal locales and auxiliary age-grade and age-set locales. In this regard, for example, it is relevant that recent systematic surface surveying and collecting of the interior and exterior of the Hopewell site has revealed many scattered ancillary feature sites but limited in range of variety, suggesting multiple short-term occupations (Burks and Pederson 2006, 401). This strongly contrasts with the richness of the mortuary deposits on the floors of Mounds 25 and 23, as well as most of the other lesser mounds. This might suggest that, despite the critical importance of the Hopewell site in the lives of those who used it, its occupation seemed to be almost superficial, suggesting that the groups responsible for it hardly ever attended for any length of time or in large numbers. However, this cannot be since the monumental nature of the earthworks and the superfluity of exotic Hopewellian artifacts and features that were cumulatively generated clearly indicate otherwise. Not only was it an important locale, it was the focus of major aggregations of participants. I see two conclusions that can be drawn from this, therefore. The actual presence of those participating in the range of tasks entailed by this site practiced some very strict avoidances ensuring that, with the exception of the floors of the mounds themselves, their occupational signature was minor. That is, attendees practiced the principle of living lightly on the land even when attending the earthworks. Given the intensity of surface surveying that has been carried out within and outside the great C-Form embankment, it would appear that most of the transient residency in which domestic matters played a role occurred apart from the site, say 1 km or so away, as I suggested may also be indicated by the Brown's Bottom #1 and Lady's Run sites near Liberty Works. Possibly other sites bearing the signature of the penultimate ritual way station similar to the Brown's Bottom #1 and Lady's Run sites are located in this slightly more distal region and the scattered but multiple remains located inside and immediately adjacent to the embankment earthwork are in the nature of "daytime" sojourns undertaken from the more substantial sites in the nearby-but-distal zone.

The other and more substantive theoretical conclusion is that the size of the earthworks and the special artifactual content of the mortuary sphere of the Hopewell site suggest, as I noted in the closing discussion of the previous chapter, that it was treated by the cult sodality heterarchy as a "campus" that was largely devoted to the *conveyancing* of the primary ritual positions from the deceased to their successors of the ecclesiastic-communal cult sodalities that constituted the heterarchy. This purpose is what made it so critical to all the cult sodalities that constituted this dispersed third-order Fort Ancient–Turner–Hopewell cult sodality heterarchy. Without the appropriately conducted mortuary-mediated conveyancing rituals that generated the accumulation of this custodial regalia, the custodial ritual usufruct rights would lapse. These ritual usufruct rights and prerogatives and, I would add, obligations constituted the social powers that enabled the sodality to perform the suite of postmortem-mediated world renewal rites that was its raison d'être. These social powers are deontic in nature, that is, they are endowed rights and duties that the legitimate holders have, and these rights and duties, obligations and privileges make up the symbolic pragmatic meaning of the custodial regalia. The ritual transfer of these items to a custodian ensures that the subsequent behaviors of these agents are transformed into the types of social actions (rituals) they intended.

PATHS AND PATHWAYS

An important symbolic pragmatic question I want to address is how inclusive territorialism and the practice of inclusive custodial land usufruct would influence the mode of traveling that would be required for the complex practices to be undertaken constituting the earlier described sacred games *tournée*/mortuary-mediated world renewal ritual process. The trails and paths, both water-based and land-based, that the cult sodality members would necessarily have to take in order to participate in these activities would be needed to link distantly separated earthworks into extensive cult sodality heterarchy networks. This question needs to be addressed before I continue since I have characterized the paths that connected the locales of a local population to be part of the custodial domains of the complementary heterarchical communities that habitually occupied and exploited the surrounding region. These communities did not control the land, but they did control the use of the paths and places that they habitually used in moving across the landscape from habitation site to habitation site and from these to the associated gardens and into the foraging territories that they habitually used. Access to the two-dimensional extension we call the land was controlled through controlling the locales (zero-dimensional extension) and the connecting paths (one-dimensional extension), and groups from other communities required permission from the neighboring local custodial communities to use these paths (Ingold 1987, 147–54).[1] In his discussion of the Huron paths and territory Heidenreich (1978, 378) puts it this way. "Travel between villages was primarily in the fall, after the harvest, for social and political activities, and then mainly with neighboring villages. This pattern is reflected by the trail network, which shows that every village was connected to its neighbor but that a wider regional trail network integrating distant parts of Huronia was absent. In view of the self-sufficient economic, social, and political nature of Huron villages this is to be expected." However, he goes on to note that, nevertheless, this intervillage network of paths was in fact part of a system of interregional routes such that for neighboring tribal groups to the east of Huronia to travel to tribal groups west of Huronia, they had to request permission of the Hurons to transit through these intervillage paths, and this was a jealously guarded privilege. In effect a form of temporary ritual usufruct had to be "franchised" to those requesting it so that they could access the Huronian intervillage routes. "In protecting their trade from members outside their confederacy the Hurons were quite ruthless. They would permit neither the Petun nor the Neutral to cross Huron territory or routes under Huron control to trade on the St. Lawrence with the French. . . . Similarly, they did everything in their power to discourage the French from making permanent contacts with these tribes. In this practice the Huron were simply following trade conventions set up in eastern Canada. To cross the territory of another group, permission had to be sought. Such permission was often refused if it was deemed to be against the interest of the group. Disregard of these conventions would cause a war" (1976, 384).

Of course, Heidenreich is unproblematically interpreting the trade routes in monistic modular polity terms, effectively projecting Euro-American cultural concepts onto the Huron sense of territory. I think it is clear, however, that the Huron social power hinged not on control of territory, in the sense of proprietorial domain, but on exclusive usufruct of the paths and locales, including the waters that crisscrossed the Huron "territory." In complementary heterarchical community terms, inclusive territorialism means that habitual occupiers of a region, namely, the custodians, cannot deny others in need access to the resources of the territory simply on the grounds that they, the habitual occupiers, use these resources. This would count as hoarding and such practice was distinctly taboo among the Huron, an attitude that is in conformity with the notion of inclusive territorialism and agentive autonomy. Heidenreich makes this very clear in this comment: "Hoarding goods and stinginess met with strong village disapproval and could lead to accusations of witchcraft and expulsion, while liberality was highly valued and received strong social approval" (1978, 383). Since the habitual community of users of an inclusive territory are the responsible custodians of the land, their power extends to the exclusive usufruct of the paths and locales of the community and not to the land. This is sacred and is available to everyone. However, if the custodians, in this case the Hurons, have *justifiable reason* to refuse access to the paths, then they certainly can refuse those who approach them. In the above justifiable case, refusing outsiders access to the paths would not be transgressing custodial obligations since, of course, the purpose these outsiders had did not relate to subsistence needs that the land could supply. Instead, request for such passage would count as their intending to break preexisting relations of exchange between themselves and the Huron who, of course, would have traditionally been the source of the goods transshipped across the Huron region via the pathways that connected the Huron villages. Hence it is the need for these nonsubsistence goods and not the resources of the Huron area that the outsiders were pursuing. Clearly, any such request would be perceived by the Huron as counting as the intention of the outsiders, even if neighbors, not to continue in the reciprocal trade relationship that they had with the Huron. To break reciprocal relations, or to act so as to suspect that these relations were not being honored, would be grounds of mistrust and, therefore, those who would use "our paths" are probably also going to transgress the rituals that must be performed in the using of the paths, and so on. In short, whether a community system is in a bifurcated or integrated settlement articulation modal posture, use of paths would be governed by ritual usufruct prerogatives and responsibilities.

It is very important to distinguish between the material path itself and its symbolic pragmatic meaning. This is because the same physical path can be used for multiple types of activity-usages, some of which were themselves of complementary nature (Ingold 1987, 153). To express this difference I will speak in terms of the path/pathway duality with "path" referring to the tangible aspect of a trail and "pathway" referring to its intangible and constituted (emic) nature. Hence, every path is linked to other paths and the total makes up an indefinite network of one-dimensional paths. This network is constitutively sectored into many pathways that are constantly changing in accordance with the particular purposes of those using the paths. This means that two groups could use the same network of paths while traveling different pathways. The pathways would likely be named, at least those that would constitute the sacred games *tournée* pathways. These would likely use the names of the heterarchy locales that were linked by the particular set of sacred games/mortuary-mediated renewal ceremonies that these two or more locales were designed for, as I discuss in more detail shortly.

This path/pathway duality takes on a different character depending on the settlement articulation modal posture of the communities of a region. When these are in the integrated settlement articulation modal posture, as exemplified above by the historic Hurons, the network that links their multiple integrated villages together is an important part of the custodial domain of these separate villages and they cooperatively undertake the necessary rituals to ensure the sanctity of their pathways. If outsiders want to transit the territory to go elsewhere, for example, if they were traveling the fur trade pathway, they would have to attend to the different villages and arrange the necessary permission. When the regional communities are in the bifurcated posture, in principle use of the paths for foraging would also require the same protocols of requesting permission. However, this would likely apply only to foraging groups that were from more distant regions, and even these might not require gaining permission since, as I pointed out earlier, the foraging required to supply the subsistence needs of the dispersed kinship-based domestic groups would be carried out as part of dual tasks of the age-sets of the cult sodalities. These age-sets would undertake subsistence hunting and they would share the game among themselves in order that each could return to their respective kinship-based habitation base camps with the food required by their resident groups. Since most of the companions making up a given age-set would also be kin to each other, permission to use local paths to go on the foraging pathway by these groups would be unproblematic. Furthermore, most age-sets of one community would regularly visit those of another and, therefore, compound foraging groups would cooperatively operate and among themselves they would have members from a set of communities whose paths linked to each other. Therefore, by bearing the standard subsistence gear with its typical stylistics of the region the groups would have unproblematic access to a large and effectively inclusive foraging territory.

However, a different situation would arise for the use of these same paths as cult sodality pathways, that is, as sacred games *tournée* pathways. In this case, I postulate that permission from the communities would not be required since the cult sodality was autonomous and their purpose would be unrelated to foraging, as such. However, a traveling age-set sodality group would be required to display the sodality warrants, in this case operating as a form of passport and visa.[2] Having these warrants enabled the use of the paths as the *tournée* pathways and the source of this enabling action power was the ritual usufruct that is a constitutive aspect of the custodial regalia itself. These regalia would include the sacred mortuary bundles and their contents so that bearing these bundles would serve as passports as well as constitutive devices transforming the material behaviors of the bearers into sacred processions licensed by the presence of the sacred powers of the gods for whom these burdens were to serve as sacrificial offerings. Still, it is likely the spirit guardians of the paths would require sacrificial offerings that would reverse any polluting effect that the physical use of the pathway would cause. As I noted above, the different interheterarchy sacred games *tournée* pathways would likely be named, for example, using the name of the cult sodality heterarchy locales that were the origin from which the travelers with their sacred bundles started and the place they were going, such as the "Turner-Hopewell" pathway or the "Wyandotte-Hopewell" pathway.

SACRIFICIAL PATHWAY OFFERINGS

The objects that served as offerings to the guardian spirits of the pathways being traveled could include some of the deceased or their body parts or actual exotic resources from the source region that were being brought by travelers as part of the task to be performed on arrival. The great deposit of Wyandotte chert disks found on the base of Mound 2 was carefully accumulated through multiple depositions of sets of 10 to 15 disks; and each deposition was probably a sacrificial ritual by a particular party of travelers in order to thank the spirit guardians of the pathway for safe passageway. Each set was carefully added beside the previously accumulated deposits and covered with a small mound of sand. Moorehead (1892, 190) reports 8,185 disks were retrieved from this mound (some scattered on the surface surrounding the mound). According to his report, the average deposit would have been 12 to 13 with a range of 10 to 15. Therefore, these 8,135 disks would mark about 680 to 690 separate offerings by those travelers attending the Hopewell site and, of course, most of these groups would be from the Little Miami Valley or points farther west since the primary Wyandotte chert quarries are about 150 km west of the mouth of the Great Miami River. Moorehead also reports that this megadeposit consisted of two discrete strata of multiple disks accumulated over the history of its depositions. If each stratum was about equal in size, each would consist of between 340 to 345 deposits of about 12 disks each.

I have already argued that the mound constructions of the Hopewell site were the result of two postulated truncation events, probably separated by several generations. If each stratum is assumed to have been approximately equal in content, then each would consist of the accumulated residue of minimally about 340 sacrificial offerings. Of course, we cannot know precisely what the numerical relation would be between a given deposit and the size of the offering group. However, if the validity of my argument that the Ohio Hopewell embankment earthworks were the symbolic pragmatic contexts of cult sodality heterarchies is accepted, then it may be reasonable to assume that the travelers were undertaking a cult sodality task and that a set of about 12–13 disks would represent minimally the equal number of cult sodality groups. Since the basic constituent group of a cult sodality is the age-set of companions, and this would probably be about 10 persons each, then a deposit of 12–13 disks represents the same number of age-sets, or a total of about 120 to 130 persons. These could be representative age-sets from several allied cult sodalities or, less likely, they could be all the age-sets of a given ecclesiastic-communal cult sodality. I would suggest that the most active participants of a given cult sodality would total about 100 to 120 and, characteristic of rituals at a major heterarchy center like the Hopewell site, as many as possible of the most active participants of a cult sodality would participate. In any case, each deposit, between 10 and up to 15 disks, would represent one cult sodality with a total of between 100 and 120 arriving together.

As I suggested above, each stratum may have been produced as an accumulation of such sacrificial offering deposits during the period up to a truncation event. I estimate that at least one and more likely two generations would be involved prior to any truncation event. Since I have postulated two truncation events, one generating Mound 25 and the other Mound 23, therefore, I will assume a two-generation accumulation per stratum, that is, about 50 years per stratum and 100 years for the total dual deposit. Over each 50-year period about 340 to 345 depositions would have occurred. If each deposit involved an average of 120 persons, then between 40,800 to 41,400 individuals visited the Hopewell site over the two generations. The 50 years for these 340 to 345 depositions to accumulate would average an accumulation of about 6.8 to 6.9 deposits per year (340/50 = 6.8 per annum; 345/50 = 6.9 per annum). If the annual number is rounded to 7, this would entail about 840 persons per year (7 deposits × 120 per person each). However, this number of persons involved in sacred games *tournée* visitations per year seems excessively small, given the areal size of the Hopewell site. It would accommodate aggregations for games that would be much larger, not to mention the labor required to build the great mounds. Of course, instead of two generations, possibly only one generation was involved per stratum, although the overall period of occupation of the Hopewell site would seem to preclude such a short period. Besides, this single-generation-period of accumulation would still mean only about 1,680 persons per year. Since it is likely that at least two major ritual events were held per year, then again, this reduces to only about 840 persons per ritual event. I consider this number to be much too low, particularly for the sacred games *tournée* and, furthermore, for the overall amount of labor involved in the building and using of the Hopewell site. Also, I am speaking of the ritual usage of a major path/pathway that connected the Hopewell site to its associated Little Miami Valley constituent heterarchies and, therefore, pretty well all the rituals, and even tasks required to prepare for these rituals, including construction tasks, would involve many persons traveling this path/pathway and such travel would necessarily have required sacrificial offerings of Wyandotte chert as part of the constitution of the travels as fully felicitous.

Therefore, I have no hesitation returning to the two-generation accumulation per stratum and leveraging upward the quantitative relation of the chert disk deposit to the group responsible. Since such travel would be quite dense in numbers of persons, the offerings would be real but treated as nominal in the sense that each was simply the "down payment" of the total ritual renewal that would follow with the sacred games *tournée*/mortuary-mediated world renewal rituals that this travel on the "Wyandotte-Hopewell" pathway enabled. Also, since the Hopewell site was the focus of conveyancing rites of all the second-order heterarchies constituting the dispersed Fort Ancient–Turner–Hopewell cult sodality heterarchy, these individual deposits are more reasonably interpreted as the sacrificial offerings not of individual cult sodalities but of second-order cult sodality heterarchies. A second-order heterarchy could easily include two or three first-order heterarchies; and each of these would consist of an alliance of two or three autonomous cult sodalities. Again, assuming 100 as the average number of active members of a cult sodality attending the sacred games and the associated mortuary rites, including the critical decommissioning of custodial regalia through the conveyancing rites, what would the total numbers attending be as represented by these deposits? If a second-order heterarchy consisted of three first-order heterarchies, and each of these would average three or four cult sodalities or about 300–400 active participants, then the second-order heterarchy consisting of about nine to twelve cult sodalities of 100 participants each would muster about 900 to 1,200 participants. Each deposit, then, represents a sacrificial offering by a second-order heterarchy to the spirit guardians of the "Wyandotte-Hopewell" pathway, probably performed prior to their return trip to the Little Miami Valley. There would be 6 or 7 of these per year, probably split into two seasonal *tourneés*, or 3 and 4 each. This means that each second-order heterarchy was responsible for at least two deposits per year, one per season. Given two sets of 3 and 4 deposits each year, it seems reasonable to suggest that the dispersed third-order Fort Ancient–Turner–Hopewell cult sodality heterarchy was constituted as an affiliation of two second-order heterarchies mobilizing about 18 to 24 cult sodalities (given the above estimate of three to four cult sodalities per first-order heterarchy). It also means that most sacred games *tourneés*/mortuary-mediated world renewal ritual gatherings involved between 1,800 to 2,400 persons. I will average that to about 22 cult sodalities and 2,200 persons per aggregation. I suspect that the maximum 2,200 size might last only a few days during particularly critical rituals with subsequent days involving a reduced number as many groups or many participants of the many groups would leave to perform other duties.[3]

Of course, all this hinges on ballpark estimates of the relation between the numbers of cult sodalities in relation to the Wyandotte chert megadeposit and, therefore, requires some further independent evidence to cross-check. Since I have argued that the Hopewell site was the specialized locale for conveyancing of ritual usufruct from a deceased custodial regalia leader to his or her replacement, this means that the megadeposit of copper celts and plates on top of Burials 260 and 261 would represent the accumulation of these important custodial regalia. If I am right that there were about 22 cult sodalities, then this copper celt and copper plate megadeposit and those copper celts and plates in association with the crypt burials in total represent a two-generation accumulation of these regalia from deceased age-set peer leaders. The estimated 148 copper plates (combining Moorehead's estimate of about 100 with Carr and Case's additional estimate of 48) would represent about 74 copper plates per generation. This means about 3 copper plates per cult sodality. There were probably an equal number of copper celts in total, adding another 3 per cult sodality per generation. Add copper headdresses, "trophy skulls," and possibly several other items, such as obsidian Ross Points, and the average number of custodial regalia per cult sodality would be about 10, possibly constituting the peer group leaders and holders of critical ritual usufruct prerogatives of the age-sets of both the senior and junior age-grades. So the two estimates, the megadeposit of Wyandotte chert and the megadeposit as well as crypt deposits of custodial regalia, give some mutual support to the claim that there were two second-order heterarchies each consisting of nine to twelve first-order heterarchies affiliated to constitute the dispersed third-order Fort Ancient–Turner–Hopewell ecclesiastic-communal cult sodality heterarchy. Alternatively, if the second-order heterarchies had fewer first-order heterarchies, then there would be three or four second-order heterarchies. I do not think it really matters since the same overall numbers of autonomous cult sodalities are involved.

THE SACRED GAMES *TOURNÉES* AS CONTROLLED INTERSODALITY FEUDING

While the Wyandotte chert deposits would be the source of sacrificial offerings of thanks to the spirit guardian of the "Wyandotte-Turner-Hopewell" *tournée* pathway, the actual travel on the path would require that the peer leaders of the age-sets wear their sodality warrants of leadership while traveling since these would warrant the use of these paths and the absence of any need to approach the local communities for permission. However, this immunity of the cult sodalities also required that the cult sodality group avoid to the degree practical interacting with the kin groups of the communities who also used the same paths as their foraging pathways. This avoidance pattern is part of the arm's-length relation emergent from the relative autonomy of the clan and sodality structures. It also means that should there be hostile relations between the cult sodalities whose communities are located along a *tournée* pathway they all use in common, these hostilities cannot be expressed against those occupying the habitation locales linked by these paths, even if those living in these locales were also members of the hostile cult sodalities. Even if a sodality was having a feud with one or more of the local cult sodalities, those cult sodality members on the *tournée* pathway cannot attack the isolated and dispersed habitation locales of the members of these feuding sodalities. In general such hostilities would be expressed in the sacred games themselves.

I have already suggested that the sacred games would be conducted much as if the cult sodalities were going to war so that, in an important way, the groups using the paths as sacred games *tournées* pathways would be organized as teams almost as if on vengeance expeditions—and in some cases, they would be. The confrontations between these teams, however, would be regulated by the protocols of the sacred games and in most cases vengeance would be achieved by winning the sacred bones of the deceased of the "hostile enemy" sodality, a winning that would also see the two sides as temporarily allied in order to complete the mortuary-mediated rituals. However, the losers would likely be eager to reciprocate at the next round, regaining their honor by overwhelming the opposing side. If these games were played using some sort of stick and ball equipment, then inevitably there would be many injuries and some deaths. Even the Robbins-point-mediated spear and hoop games that I discussed earlier may have involved careful targeting of the opposition with the point being to "miss" as closely as possible. Such types of games could well lead to "unwitting" wounding and killing of members of "feuding" sodalities, leading to significant mourning gifts to assuage the dead and his kith and kin, and, of course, further vengeance-like rematches.

Another source of "hostility" that the sacred games could regulate and simultaneously feed would be suspicion between third-order cult sodality heterarchies over the formal design of their respective monumental earthworks and facilities. These differences in design manifest differences in the rules and protocols among cult sodalities. They could be adequately termed doctrinal or ideological differences of considerable import since the rules and protocols specifying how sacred games and mortuary-mediated world renewal rites are to be fully felicitously conducted include the form and allowable variation of the earthworks and these rules could vary across regions, thereby being a source of considerable inter- and intraregional disagreement and opposition. This would be a particular source of mutual disagreement between regional cult sodality heterarchies, such as the Adena and Ohio Hopewell, as I discuss later.

DISCUSSION

Addressing directly the social role of paths in the Middle Woodland period of the Central Ohio Valley has been sparse by archaeologists, in general, and the cultural aspect of paths as pathways has almost been ignored. This is strange since, in the monistic modular polity view, paths would seem to be a particularly sensitive area to address, as illustrated by my earlier discussion of the Huron relations with their neighbors in regard to transiting their paths. In particular, under the monistic modular community polity view, paths are problems and sources of danger since they cross the community's exclusive-marking boundaries; therefore, their use would be subject to significant controls by the polity. Paths and their use as pathways would be a real issue that would impact strongly on the relations that polities would be able to develop and sustain. In fact, it could very reasonably be suggested that the typical attitudes toward its paths that monistic modular polities would make impossible the magnitude and intensity of intra- and interregional travel that is implicated in the great earthworks. For that matter, even if travel protocols were somehow agreed upon between land-jealous polities, how could the permission be gained to appropriate the required land from the local polity or, for that matter, the amount of labor be mobilized from far afield to build them, problems that I raised in my earlier analysis of the Mapuche? These particular problematics of paths and pathways arise directly from the monistic modular polity perspective but have not been adequately addressed, except to invoke local alliances, as exemplified in the case of Carr's Tripartite Ceremonial Alliance model. This model addresses the problem by recruiting the mortuary sphere both as the warranting source of exclusive territorialism and as the solution to the problem that exclusive boundaries generate. That is, the now largely standardized view is that the collective burial locales, generally referred to as "cemeteries," serve as a politicomaterial mode of legitimizing the exclusive control of the land through presencing the ancestors, thereby emphasizing that it was from these deceased that their descendants inherited their exclusive land rights. However, this legitimization generates the problem of seriously constraining a community's mobility, despite its reliance on foraging of wild and mobile species, and this means the same communities must innovate some institutional practice that enables them to gain access to each other's exclusive territories! The proposed solution to this fundamentally model-generated contradiction between foraging and exclusive territorialism is to propose that neighboring polities allied, these neighbors being the same persons who are expected to transgress the boundaries. This is not to deny that some such alliances could occur. But given these are small-scale monistic modular polities, the alliances would be mediated by marriage practices and not practices that would entail monumental earthworks! Furthermore, such alliances would entrench rather than dissolve boundary maintenance since the point of the alliance was to gain access to neighboring resources. In achieving this, the principle of exclusive territorialism is entrenched, and so on.

The Tripartite Ceremonial Alliance model, of course, weds these contradictions together by claiming that several contiguous "symbolic communities" based on exclusive territorialism shared cemeteries for their ancestors just so as to ensure the mobility and access that their own exclusive territorialism would otherwise deny them. I will not repeat my critique and falsification of this model. But I will repeat that the widespread nature of the Hopewellian assemblage implicates the view that pretty well socially unconstrained access to different regions was the rule and not the exception. That is, the Complementary Heterarchical Community model easily enables resolving this problem of accessibility. Of course, it raises another. While access to paths would be socially unconstrained, this access would be governed in another way, depending on the type of pathway being followed. Those following the foraging pathway, as noted earlier, would seek permission from the local custodial community, a permission that could not be unreasonably withheld. Those who followed a sacred games *tournée* pathway, of course, would need only to seek permission from the spirit guardians of the pathways, particularly when crossing an immanently sacred natural division in the landscape. As I noted above, they would likely unproblematically address this problem by wearing their sacred warrants, thereby manifesting to the guardians their sacred intentions and, of course, by regularly pausing to carry out the necessary sacrificial rites. In terms of human-to-human intercommunity relations, therefore, the use of paths and passing from region to region would be largely unproblematic. Distance from home did not put a crimp on the use of paths. This reinforces the notion that paths were bifurcated and were the shared responsibilities of the clans and sodalities of the complementary heterarchical communities practicing a form of inclusive custodial territorialism; and the Hopewellian artifactual materials were recognized as intraregional and interregional "passports" of the deities (Seeman 1995, 123–24).

While the role of the path or trail as the medium of interconnection among Middle Woodland period Ohio communities is implicit in most work of Ohio archeologists of this time period, I know of only two who address it specifically, each differently. N'omi Greber (2006, 103–4; 2010, 345–46) has addressed the intercommunity path as a set of natural paths that probably followed the edges of the uplands skirting the long valleys of the Ohio tributaries (figure 15.1). Bradley Lepper (1996, 1998, 2006, and 2010; Lepper and Yerkes 1997) has taken a different tact, treating the most desired type of paths linking earthworks as part of the monumental construction process itself. In fact, his approach is very amenable to the dual path/pathway perspective that I have raised here, although he does not use these terms. Lepper has promoted what he terms the Great Hopewell Road. He specifically argues that Newark and Chillicothe, approximately 100 km from each other as the crow flies, were connected by a parallel set of embankments that extended from the Newark Circle-Octagon in an apparent straight line southwest toward the sister

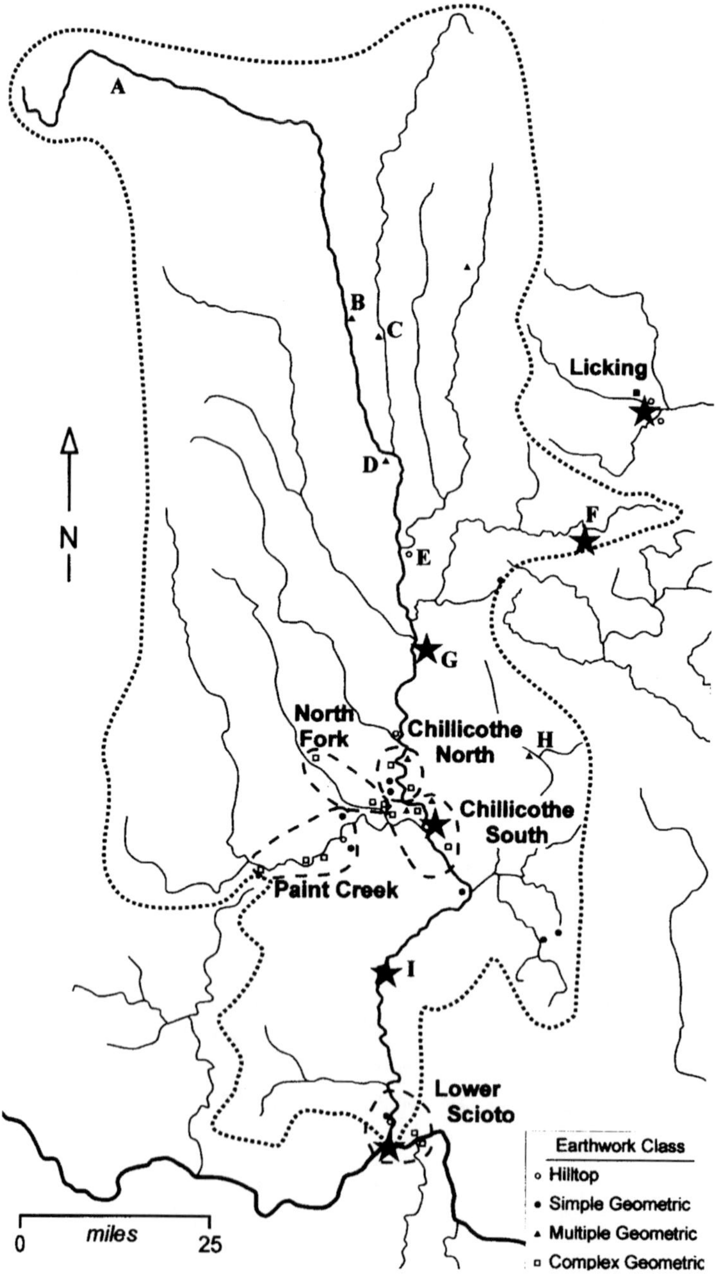

FIGURE 15.1

The Scioto Drainage and Greber's Five Modular Polities
Source: Greber 2006, 101, figure 5.11. By permission of N'omi Greber.

earthwork of the High Bank Circle-Octagon just north of Chillicothe (1998, 130–33; 2006, 124–26; 2010, 116). He is the first to acknowledge that he has not been able to map out the residue of this path except for short lengths of parallel embankments at several different locations along his postulated route. He claims that each of the slight traces of these parallel embankments is located such that if the stretches separating them were connected, a single straight-line parallel set would result.

Greber suggests a "natural" route, tracing the route in line with crests of the uplands overlooking the Scioto Valley and argues that this route was actually the path used by historical Native North American communities of the region (figure 15.1).

> The paths along which persons walked from the Little Miami to the central Scioto during the Hopewell era were most likely a part of intersecting trails that joined areas of the Eastern Woodlands in a manner similar to those traveled in 1751 by Christopher Gist, a frontier guide. These trails tended to follow the uplands along waterways, likely using the rivers as maps but avoiding the marshes and other obstructions along the river banks. Traveling westward from the upper Ohio, Gist took parts of trails that intersected at Maguck, an Indian settlement near present-day Circleville, Ohio, less than 20 miles north of Mound City. From Maguck, trails went north to Sandusky on Lake Erie, westward to the Great Miami and passing near the headwaters of the Little Miami, southward along the east side of the Scioto to the Ohio River, and east toward Newark and beyond (Greber 2006: 101). Gist took the southward trail from Maguck toward Portsmouth at the mouth of the Scioto, where the Portsmouth Earthworks stretched for many miles along the Ohio River. Perhaps if he had continued westward he would have passed near the site of the Manring Mounds. (2010, 345–46)

She suggests that it had deep historical roots and most likely was used by the Middle Woodland period communities of the Scioto Valley, which she treats as "mitigated" monistic modular polities.[4] She argues that there were at least five of these, each anchored by its respective civic-ceremonial center: the North Fork polity at the Hopewell site, the Paint Creek polity at Seip and its descendant Baum site, the Chillicothe North polity at Mound City and its associated Hopeton, the Chillicothe South polity based on Liberty Works (and presumably High Bank), and the Lower Scioto polity based on the Portsmouth complex. She argues that each of these locales hosted a multiple set of events of different kinship-related groups. "Individuals and groups who planned, supported, and participated in these endeavors formed the community associated with a given enclosure at a given point in time" (2006, 77). She estimates that these five "polities" incorporated most of the 17,000 square kilometers of the Scioto drainage and that the "general areal extent of these major divisions was likely stable throughout the Hopewell era, but the borders were not concrete walls, and hegemony changed. Each polity formed at least part of the community associated with the earthworks built within its borders" (2006, 100–102).

I find it very interesting that, despite her accepting the assumptions of the civic-ceremonial polity view, she remains open about the precise nature of how these polities defined their limits and, furthermore, how entrenched they were in terms of settlement and subsistence. She comments that "in general, the communities identified as Hopewell lived lightly on the land. Also, the localities identified as having Hopewell domestic debris are often multicomponent. This set of circumstances may suggest that we may not really know what a 'Hopewell' settlement looks like" (2006, 104). Her comments suggest to me that despite her long-term interest in characterizing the Central Ohio Valley social system of the Middle Woodland period, she is only lukewarm in her commitment to the monistic modular community polity view. In fact, her position could easily be assimilated to the complementary heterarchical community view since, indeed, she is right that such a community would be stable in terms of its occupation of a region. This is because it would be the recognized custodian of the land and its members would be primarily responsible to sustain the paths that connected its dispersed habitation locales in as unpolluted a state as practically possible. One way would probably be by continually moving and shifting. As she very insightfully comments, "We may not really know what a 'Hopewell' settlement looks like." Maintaining the sanctity of the pathways means ensuring that they were properly used and that the midwifery rituals of visiting groups were being performed, while these same custodial communities, including their own clans, treated the locales where they camped with proper respect, including "living lightly on the land" by frequently moving their base camps from season to season. Her argument that the primary paths that connected these communities probably ran along the edges of the uplands overlooking the valleys is particularly apt and, indeed, the primary reason these were used is that, even though local communities and their neighbors would use these as part of their everyday subsistence pathways, the cult sodalities would probably consider them particularly valuable. For this reason, they would likely be perceived as being the special responsibility of the cult sodalities of the third-order (Portsmouth?)-Chillicothe-Newark cult sodality heterarchy and very useful in that they would probably circumvent most of the clan-based seasonal camps. Also, the upland paths may have been experienced as having special sanctity. The sector separating the lowland and upland zone would likely be interpreted as a liminal zone representing the sacred upper–lower sectoring of the cosmos and, therefore, moving along this zone would require wearing the appropriate warrants and conducting oneself according to the strict rules and protocols of the sacred games *tournées*/mortuary-mediated world renewal ritual pathways.

Let me pause here for a moment. I can endorse much of Greber's discussion of the way a "Hopewell" community related to its land and, in fact, I have also commented that we can characterize this relation as "living lightly on the land." For me this latter mode of living was totally compatible with a custodial or squatters ethos, which effectively addresses a fundamental existential contradiction of a people who have an immanentist cosmology. Since the world is immanently sacred and human subsistence and settlement entails regularly intervening into the sacred natural order, such intervention always has the potential of reducing the sacred powers that sustain this world. This experienced contradiction promotes a community response that is complex and, in fact, requires a whole region of communities to coordinate. But, with regard to everyday life, the method is to establish fundamental proscriptions promoting an ongoing process of avoidances, including spacing domestic habitations well apart and ensuring that they occupy the zone only in a transient manner. This minimizes intervention and maximizes land recuperation. Living lightly on the land, therefore, entails a mobile way of life, even when this mobility seems to contradict the imperatives of the subsistence system itself. In this case, as effectively all Ohio Middle Woodland period archaeologists now recognize, gardening of indigenous domestic seed crops significantly intensified from the Early Woodland into the Middle Woodland period and I have postulated that this intensification brought a perception that the integrity of the sacred natural order was being reduced by human communities themselves. Therefore, I have interpreted the subsistence and settlement practices as being performed by a mobile population that at the same time recognize that their exploitation methods demanded serious increases in world renewal ritual. Hence, for me the complementary heterarchical community system in a bifurcated settlement articulation modal posture is the strategic accommodation of the population to their perceived existential contradiction and for them this way of life was a serious attempt to minimize and actively rectify the rising levels of pollution that their own intensifying pursuit of survival entailed.

Therefore, while I recognize that intensive gardening seems to contradict the notion of living lightly on the land, and added to this the massive production of major earthworks that required serious intervention also seems to contradict the principle of minimizing pollution levels, I recognize that this apparent skein of contradictions really is a complex, emically engineered social adaptation to resolving in an ongoing manner what was unavoidable—the pollution that human social life entailed. This pollution was recognized as having to be minimized through living lightly on the land, while being rectified by recycling the living souls of the members of the community at their death, thereby returning this sacred power back to the sources, the land and its resources. This recycling was perceived as being enabled and enhanced by means of the sacred game *tournée* system in tandem with the postmortem human sacrificial mortuary *chaîne opératoire* process. Ultimately, of course, this complex adaptation failed and those who were responsible dismantled it, unwittingly thereby bringing to an end this Ohio Hopewell episode.

This relates me back to Lepper's modeling the dual path/pathway phenomenon. While Greber's notion of the path/pathway nicely fits the above domestic-based form of minimizing pollution, and also can nicely accommodate to the needs of the cult sodalities to travel along sacred pathways connecting earthworks, as I note below, Lepper's view presents another strategy to enhance the rectification and lowering of the pollution levels that the cult sodality heterarchies pursued and whereby sacred energies are recycled. Therefore, I am also inclined to support his Great Hopewell Road thesis, treating it as modeling an innovative alternative ritual pathway strategy by which the felicity of the sacred games *tournées*/mortuary-mediated world renewal could be enhanced. That is, it is consistent with the symbolic pragmatic perspective that I have been applying to interpret the sacrificial action-constitutive meaning of the great embankment earthworks. Of course, much more empirical work must be carried out to reveal as much of the roadway as possible. The few stretches that Lepper has exposed up to now can be dismissed by skeptics as quantitatively inadequate to validate the model. However, this skeptical treatment does not, in point of fact, deny his claim that these empirical data exist. Therefore, rejecting the claim on quantitative terms is quite inadequate. According to the hermeneutic spiral method, the skeptic must present an alternative model that explains the same data more persuasively. If this is not done, then Lepper's claim stands as a hypothesis that can be invoked to promote further empirical research. In doing so, it may turn out that new data emerge that make the original model a poorer explanation and that demand and, indeed, suggest an alternative model. In any case, discovering and also excavating a few more stretches would likely advance our knowledge of this important sphere. Therefore, the first step is to demonstrate sufficient stretches to establish the validity of the claim itself or, if necessary, the validity of a new claim.

Most importantly, however, is to elucidate a convincing rationale for building such a monumental pathway. As I suggested above, it is here that Greber's and Lepper's approaches can be mutually supportive rather than mutually exclusive. Networks of sacred games *tournées*/mortuary-mediated world renewal ritual pathways are presupposed by the Ohio Hopewell Cult Sodality Heterarchy System model. Therefore, dealing with the paths would be an intrinsic aspect of the world renewal ritual strategy. For example, as noted earlier Fogelson reminds us that in historic times, the Southeastern sacred games were not only a form of managed warfare, that is, intercommunity feuding, there was a complex, warlike protocol for teams to follow when converging on the chosen playing field. The shamans of each team had to scout ahead and decide where to invoke powers that could cripple the good-fortune powers of the other team. As sacred game pathways, these paths were critically assessed and prepared in advance. As Fogelson puts it "the players marched in military fashion to the site of the game. This march was interrupted at four resting places where additional rituals were performed. The team usually took a devious route to the ball field in order to avoid the 'trail magic' of the enemy conjurer" (1985, 331). The ideological strategy of any particular sphere of endeavor of a given organization should be treated as internally structured into alternative and somewhat contrasting sets of symbolic pragmatic rules and protocols articulating and defining the preferred ways of behaving in order for the organization to constitute and carry out its activities so as to fulfill its duties and achieve its ongoing goals. If these alternatives are to persist, they must attract and maintain factions within the organization and the factions will compete to promote their alternative preferred ways of proceeding in a given sphere of activity. Of course, if the organization is going to be sustained despite the factionalism, compromise must also occur. Sometimes the compromise results in one collective procedure that all factions can agree upon, for the time being. Another possibility, however, is for two or more procedures to be recognized, possibly with special conditions defining the conditions in which one or the other procedure will be followed. The need for the latter type of compromise is particularly acute in heterarchies since these are organizations that respect the autonomy of its component parts; and, therefore, collective activities hinge on consensus. It is quite plausible that the third-degree Chillicothe-Newark cult sodality heterarchy could have achieved through debate and finally consensus an agreement on two forms of sacred games *tournées*/world renewal mortuary pathways, each conditioned for example by being treated as appropriate for different seasons, one to be used for the spring *tournée* and the other for the fall/winter *tournée.*

I am inclined to this factional view because I assess the Great Hopewell Road to be an expression of a profound commitment by this third-level cult sodality heterarchy to enhance long distance modes of sacred connection. Just as one important faction supported and pushed for the Great Hopewell Road pathway while another promoted the ridge-top pathway, another important faction, and possibly the same ones, pushed for integrating the azimuth alignments of the embankment earthworks with interembankment earthwork alignments since it appears that this dual process of alignment was actively pursued in both the Chillicothe and the Newark zones of this heterarchy. I turn to this interesting problem in the next chapter.

16

Embankment Earthwork Site Alignments and Relations

Ray Hively and Robert Horn (1982, 1984) have noted that the patterning of the great earthworks can be correlated with the turning points of both the lunar and solar cycles. They have published several papers using different statistical methods to demonstrate that this patterning is not accidental or simply the result of chance. William Romain has pursued the same course and has been able to reinforce the nonrandom nature of the earthwork patterns by correlating these with celestial cycles as marked by the rise and setting of both solar and lunar azimuth events corresponding to the well-known cycles: the winter and summer solstices, the maximum and minimum turning points of the 18.6-year lunar cycle, and so on. Of course, demonstrating that these alignments are not random and, therefore, that deliberation and planning was involved, does not alone either explain the earthworks or characterize what the content of this deliberation was. To do this requires retroductive inference and this means a theory that would elucidate why building such monumental constructions would make sense to those who were responsible. With this theory elucidated, then the theorist could use it to explain the significance of the nonrandom correlations of the sort that Hively and Horn have inductively established. Of course, the explanation would be only one approximation of the conditions that brought about these empirical data. What is desirable is to avoid committing the fallacy of affirming the consequent. It could be that another theory could explain the same data. Testing the two models these theories generate is a matter of assessing the models in the light of the plausibility of the theories that generate them and, of course, applying the models by explaining the same set of empirical data. Because these are monumental forms requiring time and labor to build, a particularly apt part of the explanation would be to reconstruct the steps that were undertaken that resulted in the forms and layouts they have. These steps would also include addressing any features that appear to be anomalous. It is certainly rational then to accept the model that invests our understanding of the data with greater coherence, the fewest anomalies, and so on, and actually expands our empirically based knowledge of the range of material patterning that relates to the alignments. Of course, this is only a contingent "truth," acceptable until such time that it in turn is critiqued and improved or even replaced with a more adequate model generated by new theorizing of the nature of the phenomenon being studied.

Again, of course, there is the important proviso that the validity of the theory that informs the model hinges on its being an intersubjective and not an "objective" theory. As I noted in the previous chapter, an "objective" approach encourages the theoretical, that is, cultural perspective of the analyst and, therefore, the emic meaning-based necessity that informed the original construction can easily be and, in fact, will likely be largely oblivious to the archaeologist as he or she uses his or her own "objective" cultural framework to reconstruct the construction steps. This framework "takes over" the interpretation process. Hence, the reverse-engineering procedures of the archaeologist might rather easily generate an "objective" complex of technical steps and procedures that the builders must have physically exercised in bringing about the alignments. However, establishing these steps independently of the cultural context of the builders not only cannot reconstruct the meaning that the constructions had for those who built them, the process of reconstruction may well overlook critical empirical patterns that implicate the real purposes and meanings for the builders. That is, the "objective" theory would not allow us to establish why building the earthworks would have been important to them and, therefore, why they would be motivated to produce them. Motivation and the cosmology and ethos that made the particular type of motivation possible constitutes what I call the intelligibility factor. As I have argued, to establish the intelligibility factor of material culture requires developing a theory of the symbolic meaning of material culture that explains such monumental constructions and I have referred to this as the symbolic pragmatic view of material culture.[1]

Presupposing this view of course is the assumption that premodern human cultures use symbolic forms of material culture as icons, which I have defined as material symbols that are taken by their users to participate in the essential powers of what they represent. Hence, explicitly recognizing that such symbols would be experienced by the builders/users as icons is part of the theory so that the deliberate construction of the earthworks and especially aligning different components of the works with the turning points of the various celestial cycles can be interpreted as realizing an ideological strategy by which the immanently sacred powers of the cosmos were invoked and presenced in the earthworks themselves. This presencing thereby transformed the behavioral processes carried out in their context into the types of social actions intended, which I have postulated were a complex of world renewal rituals. The recipients of the benefits of these renewal rites would be the gods themselves, and so on, as I have fully discussed.

Given the expressive relation that connects the celestial cycles with the earthworks, it would be reasonable to assume that the earthworks were also experienced as relating to each other in the same manner. That is, if the Newark Circle-Octagon (see figure 3.2) was built so as to presence the sacred powers of the cosmos under the lunar aspect, would it not be rational for builders to also understand that these monumental icons could relate in a similar manner to each other over distance? Certainly, presupposed by the Ohio Hopewell Cult Sodality Heterarchy System model is an assumption that these locales mediated linkages among social groups. Greber (2006, 77) has certainly made this argument, suggesting the similarity of form relates to such connections: "Patterns of spatial distributions of enclosures at both local and regional scales may offer suggestions for definitions of associated communities, as may patterns in other attributes of design and construction." She later implicates the symbolic moment when she tentatively raises the possibility that formal patterning of the earthworks might be treated as a clue to the social relations of those who built them.

> The design of embankments as "artifacts writ large" appears to share similar architectural canons contrasting shape and fill of polygons and circles at High Bank and apparently Hopeton. What were the relationships among the builders and users of these two complex enclosures? The similarities in ground plan suggest shared views on a symbolic design, perhaps "complementary," with the Hopeton Polygon reflecting the High Bank Great Circle. The contrast in apparent use of the environs appears similar to the contrast suggested for Seip and Baum. However, the probable close association of users of Mound City and Hopeton suggests stronger ties to this local region than to the area of High Bank and Liberty. (2006, 97)

This is a very promising way to go. However, for it to be fully effective, it is important to be more comprehensive. I have always treated the monumental forms as mediating both social and temporal relations. Just as we use pottery as a form of relative dating, so formal patterning of monumental architecture also deserves to be treated in the same way. Of course, just as relative dating by means of artifact form must be subjected to forms of chronometric dating such as radiocarbon dating when possible, this would also be the case for monumental architecture. The symbolic pragmatic approach in fact gives good reasons why the formal variation in artifacts and features can be used with some confidence for chronology since this variation maps changes in the stylistic modes by which material actions were constituted. That is, symbolic pragmatics gives a theoretical basis to the *necessity* of style continuity over time and space, embedding this necessity in the constitutive moment by which actions emerge from the behaviors agents perform. It is the style and not the instrumental moment that is action constitutive. The instrumental moment operates at the behavioral level, making it possible for certain changes to be brought about that serve as among the conditions of satisfaction of the action intentions of the agent; but these conditions always need to conform to the action-constitutive rules and protocols. Without the proper style the agents' killing of an animal counts as the condition of satisfaction of a poaching intention (misappropriation of life); with the proper style, it counts as the condition of satisfaction of a hunting intention (rightful appropriation of life). Therefore, both continuity and modification in style ties directly into social processes. This means that changing styles mark negotiations among groups over alternative symbolic expressive forms that would ensure the greatest felicity of the material actions performed. Not only does the behavioral moment remain the same, but the action-constitutive moment does too, that is, the behavior still counts as hunting, not poaching. All that has changed is the symbolic form that expresses the deontic constitutive moment. By recognizing that changing styles requires consensual negotiation, it becomes clear that the continuity of style is itself explained as arising from the importance of symbolic pragmatic imperative. Do the gods want our sacrificial actions to be mediated by X or by Y, by obsidian knives or Flint Ridge knives or by both types but varied according to the intended recipient god? The intelligibility of stylistic continuity and change arises from this view that style is an action-constitutive medium and, therefore, it is also a constitutive medium of social structure. Those who radically modify their styles are going to bear the onus of demonstrating why these changes are correct and advance the goals of the group rather than being retrogressive and counterproductive.[2]

In any case, if it is accepted that formal patterning of the embankment earthworks expressed, manifested, and presenced the spiritual powers immanent in the cosmos, and if alignments are treated as the mode by which these powers were invoked and presenced, then we could expect that the groups responsible for the embankment earthwork sites would explore how to enhance the powers of a particular earthwork site by materially constructing them so as to participate in the powers of related but spatially distant earthworks. I have already argued that Hopeton and Mound City were deliberately "connected" by the parallel embankments and Lepper has pointed out that a similar series of parallel embankments likely linked monumental features within the Newark complex. I noted in the preceding chapter that he has promoted the Great Hopewell Road thesis and such a material feature would be a logical extension of this principle of the iconic nature of the embankment earthworks. Therefore, it is not implausible that the embankment locales separated by miles may also have been built in some manner so that some of their features were aligned with each other. This would be possible if, in fact, what Hively and Horn (2010, 132) have spoken of as zero-altitude azimuth planning was carried out. This type of planning relies on a location that is in a raised zone such that a number of embankment earthworks that are not visible to each other at "ground level" are simultaneously visible from this raised location. Alternatively, it also allows laying out a geometrical embankment earthwork, such as the Newark Circle-Octagon, so as to align it with the locations on the ambient horizon marking points where important celestial rising and setting events occurred, for example, the summer and winter solstice points. Hively and Horn argue that selecting a location of this nature may have been done at Newark.

> The zero-altitude hypothesis asserts that the key lunar alignments found in the Circle-Octagon Earthworks were designed to fall along lunar lines which had been determined by observations conducted from high points with distant horizons and not by observations made from the valley floor where the earthworks are located. If the intent of the builders was to accurately record the "true rise and set points" as they would be seen unobscured by local topography, then it is plausible that these astronomically significant lines would be determined from observations made from high hilltops in the region rather than from positions within the Octagon structure itself. (2010, 132–33)

They came to this conclusion when they reexamined their earlier work on the lunar alignments of the Newark Circle-Octagon (figures 3.2 and 16.1). They noted that the northern maximum lunar set marked by embankment EF was actually the least accurate of the total set of lunar cycle alignments when these were observed from the ground level of the octagon itself (figure 16.1). As they noted there was a 1°.7 error of alignment. They considered this to be anomalous and therefore reconsidered their original approach, coming up with the zero-altitude hypothesis, as they call it.

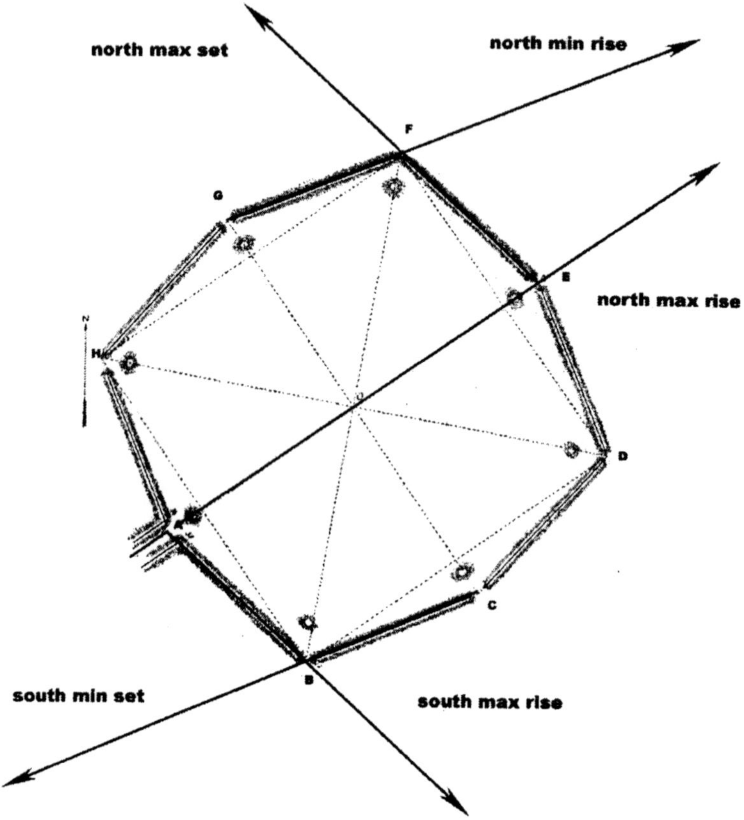

FIGURE 16.1
Side EF among Selected Lunar Turning Point Alignments
Source: Hively and Horn 2010, 130. By permission of Ray Hively and Robert Horn.

The 1°.7 error results from a local hill on the azimuth of wall EF 1.9 km from octagon vertex E. If the intent of the builders had been to mark the northern maximum moonset with high accuracy as observed from vertex E, it would seem strange to choose a location where the distant horizons were obscured by local obstructions. Moreover, the local hill forming the visible horizon does not appear to distinguish itself in any way as being particularly useful as an astronomical foresight. If a primary priority of the designers had been to conduct precise observations of the lunar maximum north set point along wall EF, it would appear to have been better *to move the octagon farther south, away from obstructing hills north of Raccoon Creek.* The alignment error of wall EF

> relative to the moonset as it would appear on a zero-altitude horizon for lower limb tangency is negligible (0°.2). These considerations led us to formulate a zero-altitude hypothesis which we now believe gives a better explanation of the astronomical alignments at the site. (2010, 132, emphases added)

It is this accuracy that convinces them that the zero-altitude horizon method was used. Through a type of "reverse engineering," that is, a careful search for high prominent topographical features that would enable clear identification of lunar and solar alignments of the current embankments of Newark, as well as other characteristics that would indicate likely deliberation, they selected a local prominence referred to as H1.[3] "One site, the most prominent hill (H1) southwest of the earthworks, fits these criteria in an impressive fashion. From the highest elevation on H1 the azimuth to the north maximum moonrise passes through the long axis of the Observatory Circle-Octagon, and the azimuth to the north minimum moonrise passes through the centroid of the Great Circle. . . . Samuel Park, in fact, noted that in 1870 a 'circumvalation' (enclosure) and mounds near the H1 location site afforded a clear view of Cherry Valley and the Newark earthworks" (2010, 133–34).[4]

In fact, they also claim that another prominence played an important role. This is locally termed Coffman's Knob and by combining these two local prominences with other prominences in the hills surrounding the Raccoon/Licking River juncture, they were able to establish all the necessary zero-altitude alignments. For example, while H1 enabled the north maximum moonrise through the Circle-Octagon main axis, with regard to the north maximum moonset, they looked for a prominent highpoint that could be used as a backsight for embankment EF and found one (H3), thereby giving an explanation of how a zero-altitude alignment made this accuracy possible.

> Seen from a zero-altitude horizon vantage point, octagon wall EF is aligned accurately with the north maximum moonset. This suggests that this wall may have been carefully constructed to fall on that line as observed from high hilltops. When moonset is viewed over the local horizon from vertex E of the octagon, wall EF misses the north maximum . . . by nearly four lunar diameters. Consistent with the roles we have suggested for H1 and Coffman's Knob in the layout of Newark, it is pertinent to look for a hill on the bearing of wall EF which could serve as a backsight for wall EF and allow a zero-altitude horizon for moonset observation. Across the valley to the southeast, a small prominence (H3) in the first range of hills 4,300 meters distant from vertex E allows a zero-altitude view of the north maximum moonset on the line of octagon wall EF. . . . The local topography affords comparable locations for long-distance backsights

> associated with the three remaining lunar oriented walls of the octagon. (2010, 136–37)

To verify their claims they suggest that a similar zero-altitude method may have been used in the Chillicothe zone, particularly since it also has a Circle-Octagon that replicates the form of the Newark Circle-Octagon. However, their reexamination of the High Bank Circle-Octagon convinced them that the method was not used for laying it out. "There is no evidence on the [High Bank] Circle-Octagon that the alignments to lunar and solar extremes are made from high zero-altitude horizon locations. All of the alignments are along local horizons" (2010, 159).[5] They go on to qualify this claim by arguing that an equivalent method was used at Chillicothe but in a different manner and, as I argue shortly, it seems reasonable to conclude that the zero-altitude method used at Newark was, in fact, a modification of this method as it had apparently been initially developed and used at Chillicothe, as I discuss in some detail shortly.

SPIRIT PATHWAYS AND THE CONGRUENCY OF STRUCTURAL AXES

My earlier elucidation of the path/pathway duality is grounds for interpreting the zero-altitude azimuth alignments as a mode of iconic congruency and by this I mean to say that the earthworks, their forms, and their positioning were designed and laid out so as to embody the sacred powers of the cosmos and these powers were conceived as congruently structured in a series of strata: the Above World, the Middle World, and the Beneath World. In an important nonfigurative sense, by using the zero-altitude method, the builders may have taken themselves to be projecting onto the surface of the earth the spirit pathways in the sky. That is, they chose to use the highest hills of the local region to map the azimuth alignments and then project and materialize them on the surface of the earth. In this regard, there is a widespread recognition by historical Native North American peoples that the celestial patterns in the night sky embody the sacred powers of the cosmos and that humans can incorporate these powers into their material features on the surface of the Middle World by constructing them so as to be congruent with the sacred patterns and pathways that these celestial patterns constitute. The Algonkian cosmology, for example, warrants the building of the Medicine Lodge in a pattern that the Mahican-Munsee [Delaware] take to replicate the Big Dipper, which is perceived by them as the dwelling place of the Great Bear, one of the creator gods. "The house in which the ceremony took place was regarded as a projection of the constellation Big Dipper (Great Bear) upon the earth. When the Big Dipper is seen as a bear in American Indian mythology, it is only the four stars of the dipper bowl that are seen as the bear; the three stars of the handle are considered to be hunters following the bear" (Hall 1997, 107–108; also see DeBoer 2010, 192–93). Hall treats the Medicine Lodge as a material iconic symbol of the Big Dipper by noting that the central pole of the Medicine Lodge would have the fur skin of a sacrificial bear attached, thereby presencing the spirit of the Great Bear. "The skin from the sacrificed bear was hung on the large centerpost of the house, where it represented the sacrificed bear as the earthly counterpart of the Sky Bear, renewed each year by the sacrifice, just as the Sky Bear rises in the sky each spring, seemingly renewed, and the earthly bears emerge from the hibernation each spring, seemingly reborn from the earth" (1997, 108). Hall makes very clear the nature of what I have called iconic congruency when he goes on to state that "[t]he post itself was imagined to project upward into the heavens straight to the hand of the Creator. . . . [T]his centerpost . . . [was] a material symbol of the imaginary axis around which the stars of the night sky revolve, then the projection of this post would lead directly to Polaris, the north star" (1997, 108).[6]

I would suggest that these spirit pathways are particular to a specific stratum of the complementary cosmic components of the Above World and Beneath World. That is, many traditional Native North American peoples conceptualize the Above World and Beneath World sectors as subdivided into concentric strata and each stratum is the particular "home" of different gods—immanently sacred celestial objects—such as the Polar star, the Sun, the Moon, and so on. Hence, it is quite possible that the development of a new modal style, such as the Sacred Dual C-R motif as embodied in the Paint Creek and High Bank C-R motifs, is more than simply a new way of expressing the solar and lunar aspects of the vertically structured cosmos. It may have been used as a mode of expressively articulating and invoking/embodying the powers of those gods occupying particular strata of the cosmos, for example, those in which the sun and moon traveled in the Above World and the Beneath World. This new motif, therefore, would not contradict other formally different monumental symbolic motifs of the cosmos, either older or contemporary but regionally variant. Rather, it would be simply a new way of articulating particular aspects of the cosmos that possibly had been recognized but not previously expressed in earthwork monumentalism since these were treated as bundled with other strata. Of course, this does not mean that the new monumental forms would be embraced by those groups in other regions. In fact, it could be expected that these might resist recognizing this expressive innovation, while certainly recognizing it for what the builders intended it to be. Therefore, they would also resist any interaction with those promoting these new forms just because they considered them to be unacceptable material expressive articulations of the cosmos, for example, unacceptable in that such highlighting of particular strata may lead to "dismantling" an integrated world. Importantly, while new modes of expression of deep structural understandings could become sources of interregional contention, it should also be noted that each new mode would have "attached" to it a complex ritual usufruct that would need to be transferred to any groups who recognized the validity of this notion and this means a major ritual usufruct franchising event in order for these groups to build and use these new icons also. Part of the contention that these new modes could generate then could be within neighboring regions, since here splits could occur within established cult sodalities over the benefits and dangers of emulating the symbolic pragmatic modes of their neighbors.

Hence, I would add another important reason to Hively and Horn's explanation that the zero-altitude horizon azimuth method was used to enhance accuracy of the layout of earthworks, this addition being that it was used to enhance and clarify precisely what *aspect* of the cosmos was being articulated and expressed by the C-R motif earthworks. Therefore, specifying particular azimuth locations with greater accuracy may have been necessary in order to enhance the congruency factor. As I illustrated above, by this notion of congruency I am suggesting that as iconic symbols embankment earthworks were experienced by their builders/users as participating in the properties and powers of those aspects of the cosmos that they represented and this entailed material and engineering modes by which to "fit" the tangible earthwork properties to the particular cosmic objects the sources and movements of which constituted the ongoing life of the world. Therefore, the zero-altitude horizon method would be valued precisely because it was promoted as ensuring the desired expressive "fit" of the earthwork to the azimuth points relevant to presencing the powers of the sun and the moon as they traveled their celestial spirit pathways in their recognized strata. Of course, as noted above, I am not claiming that this new form was the expression of a new world belief. Rather, it was simply a mode of articulating more specifically what the traditional cosmology as manifested in the older monumental forms had simply subsumed to the larger cosmos. If Hively and Horn's analysis is valid, then the builders understood that by mapping the land through the use of a region's highest points, they were able to embody most effectively in the earthworks the spiritual powers of the targeted celestial object or objects in their proper celestial strata, and, as a result, fine-tune and thereby enhance the symbolic pragmatic powers of the embankment earthworks.

However, as I also noted above, they have concluded that the zero-altitude method was not used to lay out the High Bank Circle-Octagon, as such, and, instead, apparently its particular lunar alignments were laid out from the valley floor. However, having recognized this, they go on to show that, prior to the application of the zero-altitude horizon method at Newark, it had been used, and likely first developed, in the Chillicothe zone—but its mode of usage was different. In this case, it had been used to integrate spatially distal earthworks in relation to each other and the local topographic features so as to participate in the same sacred pathways, thereby adding to the immanent powers of any single earthwork the sacredness of the others. This differential use of the zero-altitude method in the Newark and the Chillicothe zones to refine the postulated articulation of the solar and lunar cycles in their appropriate strata as embodied in the Sacred Dual C-R motif can be used to reconstruct the chronological development of these two sets of earthworks that are many kilometers separate.

In their discussion of the zero-altitude horizon at Chillicothe, Hively and Horn have suggested that Mount Prospect was the high observation point that was used to orient the positions of the many earthworks relative to each other and the common sacred celestial pathways. Mount Prospect is a raised table-like zone on the west bank of the Scioto River overlooking the sites of Mound City/Hopeton, High Bank, the Shriver Circle, Liberty Works, and so on. In fact, Mount Prospect incorporates the Northwest Chillicothe zone where the Adena mound was constructed. Hively and Horn refer to the postulated position in this table plateau as Prospect Point. Their argument is that this location was particularly suitable since it enabled the systematic placement of a number of embankment earthworks such that they were both spatially aligned to each other and along a celestial turning point alignment (i.e., what I am calling a sacred celestial pathway), and along the lay of the land of the local region, even though the individual earthworks were not observable from each other. "[S]outh of High Bank, the Scioto abandons its meandering course to hug the west wall of the Teays Valley on a straight bearing of 143.4° for more than 10 km . . . ; the 143.4° bearing from . . . the High Bank Circle bisects the large circle of the Liberty Works 6.3 km to the south . . . ; the opposite 323.4° bearing from . . . the High Bank Circle bisects the large circle of Works East 3.5 km to the north . . . and . . . the north lunar maximum rise (53.4° tangent to the local horizon) occurs at a 90-degree angle to the major axis of the Circle-Octagon" (2010, 139–40). This means that not only are these three earthworks congruent with each other on the same alignment parallel to the local lay of the Teays Valley, they are tied into the north lunar maximum rise through sharing their alignment with the High Bank site. Importantly, this also means that even though the High Bank and Newark Circle-Octagon embankment earthworks are separated by 100 km, their main axes are tied into the maximum northern lunar rise, but in a complementary manner. The central axis of the Newark Circle-Octagon is directly on this azimuth and the central axis of the High Bank Circle-Octagon is 90 degrees to the same azimuth. As I note below, Warren DeBoer (2010, 167, 193) has argued that such intersite alignments may have a significant historical dimension to it. On the one hand, long distance alignments of this order may manifest the collective intention of the cult sodality heterarchies to sustain sacred connections with the old earthwork when this was abandoned and they constructed a new one. On the other, a first-order cult sodality heterarchy (using my terms) might use this method to enhance its participation in the local regional second-order heterarchy, doing so by aligning its new locale with the more distant and established earthwork locales of the second-order heterarchy.[7]

If it is assumed that this difference in usage of the zero-altitude horizon method is valid, being applied in the Chillicothe zone to link spatially distal embankment earthworks on common celestial turning point azimuth alignments parallel to the local lay of the land and being applied in the Newark zone to enhance the accuracy of actual celestial turning point azimuth alignments in the confluence of the Raccoon and Licking Rivers, this suggests a historical development of the Sacred Dual C-R motif. Furthermore, as I also noted above, the application of this innovation of the zero-altitude azimuth method in the Newark zone suggests the introduction of a new and major ritual usufruct and, therefore, the likelihood is that the Chillicothe and Newark groups responsible for the two expressions of this method would need to be related as franchiser–franchisee. Since the franchiser–franchisee relation is the basis of alliance between autonomous groups of the same social nature, if the groups responsible for these two expressions of the same ritual usufruct practices were themselves part of separate cult sodality heterarchies, then these two heterarchies would also be allied. In this regard I have already argued that the High Bank site was likely jointly built and used by the two second-order cult heterarchies, Seip and Liberty Works.[8] If this compound second-order heterarchy was allied to the Newark second-order heterarchy, and the above discussion certainly supports this likelihood, then these two distal complexes constituted a dispersed third-order cult sodality heterarchy. Indeed, the specialized nature of the zero-altitude horizon ritual usufruct suggests that there would have been a particular sector of the franchising cult sodality responsible for this transfer, this being a distinct esoteric ritual group, that is, a specialized set of shamanic-priests belonging to the clergy sector.

Now, as I suggested above, the conceptualization of the High Bank Works site was probably emergent from the original notion as expressed in the Hopeton component of the Mound City/Hopeton C-R complex and, therefore, High Bank would have been the next step, the "refined" expression, in the development of this C-R motif configuration. As I argued earlier, subsequently the Paint Creek C-R motif was developed to complement the High Bank C-R motif. I also argued that the Paint Creek C-R motif was probably first constructed at Seip and, while the Seip version was being constructed, the same motif was initiated and emulated by the Liberty Works cult sodality heterarchy. If the next generational stage in developing the Sacred Dual C-R motif configuration occurred at Chillicothe and emerged from the original Mound City/Hopeton C-R configuration, it seems reasonable to conclude that the construction of the Newark Circle-Octagon version of the High Bank C-R motif would have emerged as a result of the franchising of the Sacred Dual C-R motif from the compound second-order Seip–Liberty Works cult sodality heterarchy.[9] It is also reasonable to assume that transferring the zero-altitude horizon ritual usufruct was part of this franchising event and that the building of the Newark Circle-Octagon was the third-generational stage of this motif and, indeed, was the first public manifestation of this stage of the ritual usufruct in this zone. My reason for asserting this hinges on my further claim that initially only the High Bank C-R motif ritual usufruct was franchised to the Newark region and it was in the first stages of the initial building of the Newark Circle-Octagon that the Paint Creek C-R motif ritual usufruct was *also* transferred by means of performing another intersodality ritual usufruct franchising event. That is, in my reconstruction, there was a historic hiatus at Chillicothe between the building of the High Bank site as the embodiment of this second-generational development of the Hopeton C-R motif and the innovation and building of the Paint Creek C-R motif. It was during this hiatus and fairly shortly prior to the innovation of the Paint Creek configuration that the franchising of the ritual usufruct of the High Bank C-R motif to Newark occurred. Then, shortly into the construction of the Newark Circle as the first step in constructing the Circle-Octagon, the Paint Creek C-R motif was newly innovated and constructed in Chillicothe, first at Seip and then at Liberty Works (probably the latter started even before Seip had completed its own large Paint Creek C-R embankment earthwork). With these two construction events at Chillicothe, either the Newark group realized and requested or the Seip and Liberty Works heterarchies realized and promoted the franchising of this ritual usufruct also, as a necessary completion of the Sacred Dual C-R motif at Newark. The need for the Newark group to build this new motif even before completing its own Circle-Octagon as the expression of the High Bank C-R motif caused the Newark builders to make an abrupt change of plan in the way that the Circle-Octagon was to be completed. I will detail this claim shortly with a close analysis of the Newark site.

In any case, all this suggests that the Newark Circle-Octagon postdates the High Bank Circle-Octagon, and the former was laid out to incorporate the lunar cycle turning points using the zero-altitude horizon method but the latter was not. Hence, sometime after the High Bank site was completed and before the Newark Circle-Octagon was laid out, this new application of the zero-altitude azimuth method was developed. Since Hively and Horn's recent work has grounded the claim that this method was likely used to align Seip and Liberty Works and both of these with High Banks, then not only was the Sacred Dual Paint Creek/High Bank C-R motif configuration first emergent at Chillicothe but the zero-altitude method was also and this was innovated between the construction of High Bank and the construction of Seip and Liberty Works. This should not be surprising since as I postulated above it would appear that the development of the zero-altitude method was the result of the innovation of the lunar/solar articulation, that is, the desire to enhance the presencing of the sacred powers of those celestial Above World and Beneath World strata particular to the lunar- and solar-related gods. This means that the Sacred Dual Paint Creek/High Bank C-R motif was a refined articulation of the congruency construction method by which the powers of the gods of these strata would be particularly presenced in the earthworks themselves. Hence, once the geometrical adequacy of the layout became a desired method for enhancing the presencing of these powers, concern with "fitting" the earthworks to the cosmos by means of laying out the embankments so as to align with azimuth turning points of the solar and lunar cycles would drive further construction refinement. However, since the High Bank site was already constructed, and given the sacred earth principle, the method could not be retroactively applied to this site but could be applied to aligning the Seip and Liberty Works embankment earthworks, both in terms of aligning with High Bank and with the solar turning points, at least in this case, the Paint Creek Squares.[10]

In a sense, then, the Newark Circle-Octagon was the "first" opportunity to apply the method to ensuring the layout of this earthwork so as to optimize embedding the lunar turning points in its formal geometric plan. Hence, I postulate that the construction of the Newark Circle-Octagon was a critically important process by which the preexisting cult sodality heterarchy of this major site came to be integrated into the Chillicothe heterarchy. The construction of the Newark Circle-Octagon was particularly important since it would constitute a successful ritual usufruct franchising of both the High Bank C-R motif and this new ritual usufruct of zero-altitude azimuth site layout.[11] Out of this may have developed the motive for the emergent third-order cult sodality heterarchy to construct, or at least initiate the construction of, what Lepper has referred to as the Great Hopewell Road. Save for the latter claim, which requires further empirical grounding, all of the above can stand as a hypothesis that I will now empirically ground.

THE CONSTRUCTION OF THE NEWARK CIRCLE-OCTAGON

As Hively and Horn have demonstrated, the current layout of the Newark Circle-Octagon Earthwork has the main axis oriented southwest–northeast with the circle constituting the southwest component and the octagon the northeast component and this orientation ensures that the axis delineates the maximum northern moonrise turning point in the 18.6-year lunar cycle (figure 3.2). They also cogently argued for the use of the zero-altitude horizon method in the layout of the octagon precisely because the orientation of side EF of the octagon is such that taken from the valley bottom perspective, this alignment failed to incorporate the maximum northern moon set of the lunar cycle because with the northern positioning of the octagon a low hill obscures the northwestern azimuth horizon. However, when seen from the zero-altitude horizon azimuth vantage point, EF is effectively directly aligned to the lunar maximum north set point. In fact, in an almost offhand manner, Hively and Horn make another suggestion by which the builders could have resolved this EF alignment problem, this being by simply moving the octagon farther south along the same southwest–northeast axis. "If a primary priority of the designers had been to conduct precise observations of the lunar maximum north set point along wall EF, it would appear to have been better to move the octagon farther south, away from obstructing hills north of Raccoon Creek" (2010, 130). Their observation is very germane for my purposes since it notes that, indeed, if the octagon had been built to the southwest of where the circle is now located, then not only would all the alignments be accurate, the wall EF alignment could have been made accurate *without the use of the zero-altitude* horizon method. That is, the primary purpose for the method, they argue, was to overcome the problem of obscuring the EF alignment, given the position of the octagon as we see it, that is, immediately northeast of the circle. Therefore, the ground level method could be used for all the alignments, if the whole octagon had been moved "farther south, away from obstructing hills north of Raccoon Creek."

I consider their observation and assessment in the position of the Circle-Octagon relative to the "obstructing hills north of Raccoon Creek" to be very important for they raise the issue of why, if it was simply a matter of a rather minor repositioning of the octagon, this was not done. Hively and Horn do not pursue this question and, although I cannot speak for them, I would hazard to suggest that this may be simply because they are operating from the basic assumption that the current layout of the Newark Circle-Octagon as we see it just *is* the concrete realization of the original plan. If so, this would mean that it was only while in the process of building the earthwork that the builders discovered the EF alignment problem, and by then it would have been too late to start over. Therefore, the builders decided to use the zero-altitude method to achieve accuracy. However, there is another scenario worth looking at. Given the above discussion, it is quite reasonable to assume that the builders intended to incorporate the lunar cycle alignments in the layout of the octagon because achieving this would have been a critical condition of satisfaction of the overall construction strategy. This follows from my summary of Hively and Horn's views about the deliberation involved in achieving such alignments at Chillicothe with regard to the High Bank and related sites. Therefore, it is also reasonable to assume that the builders were perfectly aware that they would have to build the octagon farther south than it is now just so as to avoid the EF alignment error that Hively and Horn have insightfully noted. Therefore, why would they not have done what Hively and Horn observed should have been done, namely, start at the beginning of the construction by building the octagon "*farther south, away from obstructing hills north of Raccoon Creek*"? In fact, I think that they did. Notice, there would be two ways to ensure this positioning of the octagon. Either the total Circle-Octagon earthwork could be built exactly as it is now but removed farther (some might say too much farther) to the southwest as Hively and Horn commented; or the Circle-Octagon could be built in the "inverse" order of the positioning it now has. I suggest that the reader perform the following mental experiment. Imagine "flipping" the order of circle and octagon relative to each other. Keep the same axis orientation and keep the circle precisely where it is now but "flip" the octagon to the southwest side of the circle. This would mean that the main axis would still be oriented southwest–northeast but now instead of being the southwest component the circle would constitute the northeast component and the octagon would constitute the southwest instead of the northeast component. Now, whether the repositioning of the octagon was done through en-masse southwestern displacement or through the "flipping" of relative position, the octagon would be positioned so as to ensure all of its lunar alignments would be accurately carried out, in particular, the wall EF would target the maximum northern lunar set point without the intervention of the local prominence.

As I noted above, Hively and Horn seem to assume that the en-masse move would be necessary to achieve their suggested repositioning; and therefore, in effect they appear to assume that the Circle-Octagon was planned to be built precisely as we see it now, except that the zero-altitude method needed to be applied when the alignment problem was recognized. I postulate that the original plan was the second layout, that is, if the original plan had been completed, then the octagon would constitute the southwest component; and, while the circle would be in the current position as we see it now, it would actually constitute the northeast component of the completed High Bank C-R motif configuration. This would certainly be consistent with the knowledge and planning capacity implicated by the Chillicothe constructions. This raises a pressing question, therefore. What happened? I postulate that, shortly into the initial construction schedule, a special set of circumstances confronted the builders that made it imperative to change this original plan, and that the least costly way of doing this was to decide not to build the octagon to the southwest of the circle but to "flip" its position by building it to the northeast, *even though this would be costly in terms of requiring applying the zero horizon method* to overcome the EF alignment problem, which they would have anticipated if the change of plan was to be effected. The application of the zero-altitude horizon method, therefore, would have been an *expedient* solution to resolving the EF alignment problem that this change of plan caused, just as Hively and Horn suggest. In counterfactual terms, but for the use of the zero-altitude horizon method, a change of plan of the magnitude I am speaking of would have resulted in a major misalignment of side EF.

Now Hively and Horn's demonstration that a zero-altitude horizon method was used to lay out the Newark Circle-Octagon does not confirm my claim that there was a change of plan of the above magnitude. But it does confirm that the builders had a method that gave them the flexibility to make such a change of plan if required. A separate argument, along with relevant empirical evidence, then is needed to confirm the claim that this postulated change of plan occurred. I have already made that argument and presented the evidence and I will summarize both here (Byers 1987, 346–69; 2004, 77–123). In brief, I have postulated that the initial construction of the Newark Circle-Octagon was radically modified early into the initial construction of this monumental earthwork. In these terms, the initial stage of construction started with the Newark Circle and well before the Newark Octagon construction had started. I have claimed and argued in considerable detail that the first step in construction started with the building of a short set of parallel walls. I commented earlier that, when used, parallel walls constitute the aggregation element or "neck" of the High Bank C-R configuration. This aggregation neck element is not always clearly indicated, but it is at High Bank where it connects the circle and octagon (figure 3.4). Another example of it, of course, is clearly indicated at the Newark Circle-Octagon, being the set of parallel walls in the northeast sector of the Newark Circle that connects it to the Newark Octagon (figure 3.2). However, in my view this was not the original but the second aggregation component to be built. To see what was intended as the original neck it is necessary to shift attention to the unique Observatory Mound. This is the large mound approximately 50 m long and 5 m high at a tangent to and partly covering the southwest sector of the Newark or Observatory Circle. At the southwest or exterior base of this mound there is a set of low (1 m) parallel embankments that extends about 30 m in a southwest direction. I have called this Feature A. I consider this to be the aggregation neck component of the original planned earthwork and that its construction initiated the building of the Newark Circle of the Newark earthworks.

To understand this claim, it is helpful to treat the Observatory Mound and Feature A as a related complex. I have called it the Observatory Mound/Feature A complex and it stands as a major construction anomaly. I interpret it as being anomalous because no other C-R motif configuration embankment earthwork has an equivalent feature distorting its symmetry. I have interpreted the Observatory Mound/Feature A complex to be the tangible result of the exercise of a proscriptive symbolic pragmatic construction rule: "Do not dismantle or disturb the fill of an embankment earthwork." This rule presupposes the Sacred Earth principle, and this principle, of course, is the content of the collective cultural belief that the world is immanently sacred. As iconic symbols of the cosmos, embankments embody this sacredness and, therefore, to willfully dismantle an earthwork is to "dismantle" or pollute the sacred powers of the cosmos. To explain this anomaly, therefore, I have argued retroductively that Feature A was built as the first step in construction of the Newark Circle-Octagon. That is, under the original plan if properly completed Feature A would have been the aggregation component linking the circle and the octagon. Or course, since it is on the southwest sector of the circle, this means that completion according to the original plan would have seen the octagon attached to the southwest end of Feature A and the circle to the northeast end. As I noted above, in this way the octagon would be well south of the obscuring hill that would have misaligned EF. It also means that only with the completion of the circle would they have then built the octagon. It is for this reason that I argue that Feature A was the first step. With Feature A completed, they extended it as two large semicircular embankments, the intention probably being to close these diametrically opposite Feature A, thereby completing the Newark Circle. If this had been done, then they would have moved to the southwest end of Feature A and built the octagon. However, before the circle could be completed, this change of plan occurred. That is, the change occurred after the beginning of the construction of Feature A and *before* the two semicircular embankment extensions of this feature making up the perimeter of the Newark Circle were closed since, if they had been closed, then according to the Sacred Earth principle, the newly formed embankment could not have been dismantled. This timing is important in order to explain the layout of the Newark Circle-Octagon as we see it now. Since they were not yet connected this enabled the builders to leave a gap and simply add a second aggregation neck that I have termed Feature B and, of course, this became the aggregation neck that now connects the octagon to the northeast sector of the Newark Circle.

The builders were then faced with what to do with Feature A, the original aggregation neck. The simplest method—seen in terms of a Euro-American engineer resolving a reverse engineering task—would be to remove these two low embankments and simply fill in the gap in the southwest sector of the Newark Circle. However, I have cautioned that it is important to take an emic attitude and even though we cannot live the life of a participant in the social system of the Ohio Middle Woodland period, we can reasonably assume, as noted above, that they had an immanentist cosmology and, therefore, they would have acted in accordance with the Sacred Earth principle. In these circumstances the principle would have sanctioned a proscription against dismantling earthworks. Therefore, to respect the rule, the builders could not simply remove Feature A. The pragmatic solution was to leave Feature A in place while covering the gap in the Newark Circle by building the first of several stages of what is now termed the Observatory Mound. Subsequent additions to this mound, which no doubt now that it was built was recruited as a ritual observatory station, resulted in its becoming a major monumental feature in its own right, namely, the large Observatory Mound we now see.

This emic-centered retroductive reconstruction of the Newark Circle-Octagon layout, of course, relies on the actual existence of the Sacred Earth principle as the core of the cosmology of the builders; and this cosmology would have to be immanentist in nature. Of course, this is a basic premise of all the analyses that I have carried out in this book. Therefore, implicating the Sacred Earth principle is simply an extension of the basic assumptions I have made in order to characterize the nature of Ohio Hopewell. In my original articulation of this reconstruction argument, I empirically confirmed the prehistoric existence of the avoidance rule by noting several other instances of what I considered to be construction anomalies, given the normative patterns of the earthworks that I had summarized, and showed that these could also be explained in terms of being the result of deliberately avoiding dismantling preexisting embankment earthworks. For example, there is the lobed circular embankment addition at Liberty Works that incorporates a small incomplete circular embankment. This lobed form is situated between the Paint Creek Square and the small perimeter circle, which I define as the actual C component of the Paint Creek C-R motif configuration. An equivalently located distortion of the Seip infix embankment connecting its large Paint Creek Square and small perimeter Paint Creek Circle occurs, also incorporating a small but completed circular element. Other patternings at different earthwork sites could be noted and explained in similar terms, namely, as the result of avoiding dismantling prior embankment construction components.[12]

In sum, the builders had to respect some major symbolic pragmatic avoidance or proscriptive rules (taboos) and, therefore, they were faced with a rather limited set of design options for continuing the construction of the Circle-Octagon. First, the decision to suspend the use of Feature A as the aggregation neck meant that a new neck had to be constructed. However, according to the proscription, this was only possible if the circle was not completed at that time. Second, to respect the primary axis, the only possibility was to build the second neck diametrically opposite Feature A. In effect, the change of plan required "flipping" the original layout plan, which would have had the octagon southwest of the circle if no change of plan was made. However, by reversing this plan, the octagon was placed northeast of the circle. As suggested above, this move presented the problem that Hively and Horn may have observed since being positioned in the northeast sector of the circle, it would be farther north than originally planned and, hence, the alignment of embankment EF had to be effected by the application of the zero-altitude horizon method. The full retroductive argument by which I established the necessity of this sequence can be found in *The Ohio Hopewell Episode* (Byers 2004, 78–123).[13]

Of course, this simply notes that a change of plan was required and what this change entailed—which was quite a bit, in this case. However, it does not clarify the reason for this change of plan. As noted above, it must have been a very pressing reason since the above modification required breaking several lesser rules, for example, tolerating the asymmetry of the Observatory Mound/Feature A complex, and also it required increased labor costs, for example, the need to apply the zero-altitude horizon method, and several other possibly linked changes that Hively and Horn have articulated (1982). To characterize the possible condition that would have made the change of plan necessary, I postulated that sometime between the initial construction of Feature A, which committed the builders to building the Circle-Octagon, and prior to the completion of the initial circle component, a new and very important necessity arose from the franchising of a new ritual usufruct calling for the construction of further major features. These further major additions likely entailed enhancing the range of world renewal rituals to which those involved in building the Circle-Octagon had already committed, as indicated by their being in the midst of building the Newark Circle, starting first with the Feature A aggregation neck. I argued that this new imperative entailed building an earthwork configuration that manifested the Paint Creek C-R motif configuration, this being a newly innovated symbolic pragmatic medium required to complement the High Bank C-R motif that was already being built as the circular component of the future Newark Circle-Octagon. That is, up to this point, the Paint Creek C-R motif configuration, as such, had not been part of the repertoire of symbolic constructions at Newark. Clearly, the idea was immanent in the earlier Mound City/Hopeton C-R complex. But as I noted above, I postulate that the notion of a "stand-alone" Solar motif (i.e., the Paint Creek C-R motif configuration) emerged at Chillicothe only *after* Newark had already committed to building the Newark Circle-Octagon in conformity with the custodial ritual usufruct expressed by the High Bank C-R motif that had been franchised to the Newark heterarchy. Until this time, it is likely that the two second-order cult sodality heterarchies of Seip and Liberty Works were jointly using only the High Bank C-R motif while jointly using the last renewal lodges at Mound City for terminal mortuary/world renewal ritual burial. They had already constructed their own new renewal lodges, the Seip-Pricer and Edwin Harness structures, but they had not committed themselves to building separate embankments around them. It is at this time that the relatively new High Bank C-R motif ritual usufruct was probably franchised to Newark and this initiated the construction of the Feature A aggregation element, as described above. However, I maintain that shortly on the coattails of the franchising of the High Bank C-R motif to Newark, and even before the Newark builders had the opportunity to complete the construction of the first stage of the circle, the need to build a Paint Creek C-R motif configuration to complement the High Bank C-R motif rapidly, possibly one could say abruptly, emerged.[14]

I argued earlier that the Sacred Dual C-R motif was probably a new articulation of an old conceptual scheme that characterized the cosmos as consisting of multiple levels and once the High Bank C-R Lunar motif was innovated, there would have been a disposition toward thinking in complementary terms, suggesting that a complementary earthwork design would enable the invoking and presencing of the same type of specific powers for the solar-related rituals as the High Bank C-R motif was invoking for the lunar-related rituals. The new ritual usufruct, forged and manifested in the newly constructed Seip and Liberty Works earthworks during the time that the initial construction of the Newark Circle was being carried out, was then quickly franchised to Newark. I propose that it was this new ritual usufruct franchise that entailed their making the above change of plan. Indeed, this change of plan turned out to require major reconfiguration of the overall construction forms of the Newark site arising from the need to construct an earthwork configuration that would serve as the equivalent of the Paint Creek C-R motif earthworks of Seip and Liberty Works.

Given the Sacred Earth principle, an examination of Newark in chronological terms, as defined by embankment earthwork styles, immediately shows that building a Paint Creek C-R configuration would present problems of spacing. The preexisting Adena-style earthworks could not be removed. These would be the Sacred Circles, that is, the circular embankment earthworks with SR-Profiles. According to the Sacred Earth principle, these monumental earthworks could only be avoided by being built around or possibly incorporated into new constructions—but without modification of the original earth fill. But incorporation was likely only if the symbolic pragmatic meanings of the old Adena Sacred Circles and the new Ohio Hopewell earthworks were consistent or compatible. The most important and pressing problem, therefore, was to suspend temporarily the construction of the Circle-Octagon until the spatial problems arising from these new ritual demands could be resolved. I have argued that the primary resolution required recruiting the Newark Observatory Circle, when completed, to do double duty as the iconic representation of the Above World for both the High Bank Lunar motif, as initially planned, but also to serve as the icon of the Above World in the solar aspect, thereby doing dual service as the circle component for both. However, I have postulated that this could be possible only if the octagon was not built according to the initial plan, which was to locate it as the southwest component of the Newark Circle-Octagon. Instead, it would have to become the northeast component.

Again, my argument is complex. The primary problem was to fit in an earthwork in this circumscribed area of the Newark site that would conform to the Paint Creek C-R motif configuration and, at the same time, because of its overall size, which was large, could be accommodated to the preexisting embankment earthworks. The Paint Creek C-R motif has three critical components: the large Paint Creek Square, which I have argued is the icon of the Beneath World; the large infix, which I claim is the icon of the Middle World; and the small circle on the perimeter of the infix, representing the Above World. As I noted earlier, I called the Middle World component the infix because it fits "between" the Above World circle and the Beneath World rectilinear (the Paint Creek Circle and Paint Creek Square, respectively), holding these together but also separating them, much like the great tree that acts as the axis mundi that embraces the triple strata of the cosmos: Sky or Above World, the Earth or Middle World, and the Underworld or Beneath World. I have also noted that the infix is the focus of mortuary residue in that when mortuary residue in the form of burial mounds is found in a "geometrical" earthwork, it is always in the infix component, or its equivalent.

Seen in these terms, I argued that the Wright Square (also sometimes termed the Newark Square), which most closely conforms to the Paint Creek Square, was constructed as the Beneath World component of the newly innovated Paint Creek C-R motif (figure 3.2). The Cherry Valley embankment incorporating the preexisting burial mounds was built and counted as the infix, or the Middle World component; and, as I noted above, the Newark Circle was recruited to serve as the Above World component, doing double duty for both the High Bank and Paint Creek C-R motifs. The Newark Circle, the Cherry Valley infix, and the Wright Square were integrated into a single Paint Creek C-R motif by the use of three sets of parallel walls, as seen in figure 3.2. For all this compromising of the layout to "work," however, it was necessary to place the octagon on the northeast sector of the Newark Circle so that, as the Beneath World in its lunar aspect, it could be figuratively placed "under" the Cherry Valley infix, the Middle World. The two sets of parallel walls linking the Cherry Valley infix and the Wright Square to the Newark Circle actually circumvent the Newark Octagon, that is, they are not physically attached to it. As I noted earlier, the use of parallel walls or extended aggregation elements meant "collapsing" the space separating two earthworks, as in the case of Hopeton and Mound City. In a similar manner, I have argued that the two sets of parallel walls were intended to "collapse" or "dissolve" the space separating the Cherry Valley infix/Wright Square from the Newark Circle. In your imagination, assume that the Newark Circle-Octagon remains fixed, constituting the classic example of a High Bank C-R motif, and these two sets of parallel walls are treated as drawing both the Cherry Valley infix and the Wright Square in tandem from the eastern to the western sector of the site with the real but nonfigurative collective intention being that the Cherry Valley infix be recognized as being "fitted over" the octagon and the Wright Square as being "fitted" to the southeast of the Cherry Valley infix where it is located "over" the octagon. In effect, the Cherry Valley embankment earthwork with its mortuary mound contents, serving as presencing the powers of the Middle World in its solar aspect, would be positioned "above" the octagon, manifesting the Beneath World in its lunar aspect, and, manifesting the Beneath World in its solar aspect, the Wright Square would be positioned to one side of the Cherry Valley infix. Hence, the Wright Square–Cherry Valley–Observatory Circle complex would take up the same formal configuration equivalent to the Paint Creek C-R motif configurations of Seip, Liberty Works, and Frankfort (as well as Baum and Works East). In this way, the builders of Newark would take their earthwork site to embody in the same large embankment earthwork complex the Sacred Dual C-R motif in that the Newark Circle-Octagon constituted the Lunar motif and the Newark Circle–Cherry Valley–Wright Square plus aggregation walls constituted the Solar motif. Except that the geometry is more precise, it would replicate the patterning of the Mound City/Hopeton complex, embodying in one complex site a Sacred Dual C-R motif, a monumental icon of the cosmos. At the same time, the sacred games *tournées*/mortuary-mediated renewal rituals appropriate to both the lunar and solar aspects of the cosmos could be performed in the separate monumental embankment features with the lunar aspect rituals performed in the octagon and the solar aspect rituals performed in the Cherry Valley infix and the Wright Square.

It is interesting to note that while the Newark earthworks are very complex, our knowledge of its contents in terms of mortuary and artifactual deposits is rather skimpy. Of course, one of the problems is that most of the mounds were badly damaged as a result of the expansion of Newark during the 19th century and the building of the canal. However, newspaper reports indicate that when bones were found in a mound that was being razed to clear the way for construction, it was rare that any artifacts were found. No doubt many cremations were also destroyed without the construction crews even noticing the destruction they were causing. Hence, while speculative at the moment, I would suggest that a similar pattern in mortuary ritual that linked Turner to the Hopewell site also linked Newark to Chillicothe. That is, in keeping with the notion of the dispersed third-order cult sodality heterarchy and the specialized nature of the component embankment earthwork locales that manifest it, Seip and Liberty Works may have been specialized to serve as the locales where the conveyancing of custodial regalia and the ritual usufructs that they mediated occurred such that the copper plates, copper celts, copper headdresses, and other forms of custodial regalia were curated and finally terminally deposited with the ashes of deceased custodians in the Edwin Harness and the Seip-Pricer and Seip-Conjoined Renewal Lodges, following truncation event rites similar to those at Hopewell. This would explain the relative impoverishment of Newark in regard to these important artifactual categories and their relative concentration at the Chillicothe sites. This likelihood is reinforced in the light of my earlier argument that Mound City mediated the same type of conveyancing ritual in the third-order Mound City/Hopeton–Tremper cult sodality heterarchy system that preceded the Seip and Liberty Works sites. Indeed, as I noted earlier, one of the puzzles when comparing Seip and Liberty to Hopewell is the much greater concentration of this type of artifactual regalia in the latter compared to the former and, for this reason, I suggested that possibly the Seip and Liberty Work deposits include only part of the total conveyancing ritual of the associated third-order cult sodality heterarchy.

In this regard, therefore, we may have a missing factor. If Newark was incorporated into the Chillicothe system that descended from the earlier Mound City/Hopeton–Tremper cult sodality heterarchy, is it possible that, in fact, this heterarchy retained the cult sodalities of the Portsmouth-Tremper region? Portsmouth is a major earthwork locale. Greber (2006, 103) has reported that the archives of the Cleveland Museum of Natural History display a map indicating a set of Paint Creek C-R motif and High Bank C-R motif embankment earthworks. She notes that these earthworks have never been properly confirmed in the field. Nevertheless, it is not implausible to postulate that the older Mound City/Hopeton–Tremper cult sodality heterarchy persisted by transforming into the Chillicothe-Portsmouth cult sodality heterarchy and that Newark was then added with the construction of the Newark Circle-Octagon embankment earthwork, thereby constituting the dispersed third-order Newark-Chillicothe-Portsmouth cult sodality heterarchy. This will stand as a hypothesis for further research and investigation.

This claim that it was the building of the Newark Circle-Octagon, along with the local version of the Paint Creek C-R motif, that marks the alliance of Newark with Chillicothe does not deny that interaction between these two regions has a deep history. Granville, for example, is just 2 km west of the Newark Circle-Octagon and its internal Sacred Circle combined with its constrained C-Form/SL-Profile embankment suggests that this has Late Adena–early Ohio Hopewell cult sodality roots. However, what I am claiming is that any interaction between the more southerly cult sodality heterarchies of Upper Muskingum during this pre–Newark Circle-Octagon era was not the basis of an alliance. The attributes of the Granville site suggest significant intensity of interaction with the earlier stages of the third-order Fort Ancient–Turner–Hopewell cult sodality heterarchy and, of course, the presence of Wyandotte chert in the Murphy Tract also suggests such contacts. At that time, I would suggest that Newark was maintaining its Late Adena identification and that many of its participating cult sodalities had their constituent ceremonial nodal locales farther east, for example, in the middle Muskingum drainage where they sustained a Late Adena material assemblage (Carskadden 2008, 252–53). This possibility is examined in more detail in the final chapter. In any case, this means that prior to the Newark Circle-Octagon construction event, Newark was already a major second-order cult sodality heterarchy and serving as a conduit linking the Ohio Hopewell *ecclesiastic-communal cult sodality* system, possibly through the Hopewell site, and the Adena *communal cult sodality* system. The construction event of the Sacred Dual C-R motif may have marked two major transformations therefore: the emergence of an ecclesiastic-communal cult sodality structure out of the preexisting Adena communal cult sodality structure, and the formal alliance with the Chillicothe-based heterarchy, thereby bringing into existence this dispersed third-order heterarchy I have referred to as the dispersed third-order Chillicothe-Portsmouth(?)-Newark cult sodality heterarchy.

The claim that the reconfiguration of Newark into a Sacred Dual C-R motif site corresponds to its formally transforming into a heterarchy based on the ecclesiastic-communal cult sodality structure arises from my earlier claim that this particular motif presupposes a specialized shamanic-priestly organization that served as the custodial group of the C-R ritual usufruct and, therefore, part of the franchise transfer would entail the formation of just such an organization at Newark. This would probably have occurred by means of special training of those local persons who, as shamans of the middle Muskingum and Licking Valley region, had been traditionally called upon by local Late Adena communal cult sodalities when required. This group would now be formally trained and incorporated into the Sacred Dual C-R motif ritual usufruct know-how and recognized as a specialized priestly group directly integrated into the Newark cult sodality heterarchy, thereby transforming this into a major second-order *ecclesiastic-communal cult sodality* heterarchy. This new order would probably rather quickly be emulated by the rest of the constituent communal cult sodalities of the Newark heterarchy, who would also transform themselves into local autonomous ecclesiastic-communal cult sodalities.

Setting the latter aside for further discussion in the next chapter, the possibility that Portsmouth continued as part of the Chillicothe heterarchy is strengthened by Warren DeBoer's (2010) recent analysis, published in the same volume as the above analysis by Hively and Horn. Again, he has explored the same notion that they did, namely, that long distance "spirit pathways" connecting earthworks were materially mapped through the positioning of distally spaced embankment earthworks in respect to each other. He particularly focuses on the possible linkages deliberately mapped in the positions of embankment earthwork sites in the Chillicothe zone, and he extends this zone down the Scioto to the Seal site. He terms the total area the Scioto Ceremonial Zone (CSZ) and makes the argument that it developed over time with a progressive "abandoning" of one earthwork and a movement to its replacement. However, the replacement was typically positioned so that the main axis of its rectangular component would bisect the prior earthwork, even if this earthwork was not within ground level view of the new earthwork. He marshals support for this claim by carrying out two steps (2010, 183–84). First, he argues that any alignment pattern that he established would not be the result of the fact that these earthworks shared the same river system. That is, the fact that the upstream site A was aligned with the downstream B site would not be simply because they were sharing the same floodplain and orientation to the lay of the land. As he notes, "There is little correlation between the distribution of river bearings sampled at kilometer intervals and the orientation of riverside earthworks. Furthermore, six of the 19 alignments crosscut river drainages, while only four of the interdrainage alignments meet the requirement that an aligned embankment also parallel the course of the neighboring riverbank. In addition, all but one of the intradrainage alignments (Anderson to Hopewell) are directed downstream. This asymmetry would not be generated randomly. Entrainment does not afford a general explanation for the observed alignments" (2010, 185–86). He then used all the major earthworks of the zone, a total of 19. For statistical purposes, he treated the orientations of these as if they were individually and randomly rotated a full 360 degrees, asking what the likelihood would be for sites to end up targeting each other. In fact, he noted that 12 of the 19 sites did target at least one other site in the manner he postulated above. He calculated that the probability that these 12 "hits" out of the 19 sites would occur randomly would be less than 0.01 percent. "The probability of obtaining 12 hits for 19 site-spinners is less than .01. This result, obtained mechanically through the binomial theorem, is matched when the observed frequency is assessed against 100 randomly generated distributions. This significance of this patterning, however, remains moot until it sheds light upon the workings of the Scioto Ceremonial Zone" (2010, 186).

He then explores the possible reasons for this. Because the Ohio Hopewell sites are so closely linked to mortuary practices, he discusses the notion that these "timelines" as he terms them may have been to invoke the ancestors. Interestingly, he rejects this as a relevant explanation since many of the sites that figured in his analysis did not have any overt burial associations. Instead, he prefers speaking in terms of the alignments being designed to ensure that the sacred powers of the targeted embankment earthwork, that is, presumably previously occupied by those who built the targeting earthwork, were presenced in this latter earthwork. Very interestingly he specifically postulates that the Hopewell builders may have conceived that the sacred powers embodied in the earthworks were derived from the Above World/Beneath World structuring of the cosmos and that these powers were conceived as flowing downstream. He also concludes that the earthworks were probably built for reasons directly related to what I have termed the sacred games *tournées*, although he does not use this term. However, he directly addresses the function of the structures found at such earthworks as Seip and Liberty Works, and suggests that they served as hostels for travelers who came from distances in order to participate in feasts and dances. "These structures can be viewed more adequately as hostels for local visitors or foreign pilgrims drawn to the Scioto to witness or otherwise participate in ceremonial spectacles designed to set the cosmos right, to feast, dance, and socialize with other congregants, to outdo the performances of competing congregations, to be committed movers of earth when collective labor was required, to bury the dead, or, long after the heyday of a particular monument had passed, to revisit ancestors interred there" (2010, 197). This view is largely consistent with my own interpretation, of course, and nicely fits into the notion that the earthworks were the iconic contexts of sacred games mediated by mortuary practices serving as world renewal rituals.

He raises some interesting formal points that I wish to dwell on briefly. He notes the taxonomy of the earthworks that I had earlier developed but chose not to use it on the grounds that it is too closely tied to my overall view of the Ohio Hopewell. This is interesting since the above view that he develops is largely consistent with my own, although he has retained a significant commitment to the earthworks as civic-ceremonial locales. In any case, rather than speaking of the earthworks in terms of C-R motifs, he decided to categorize the earthworks as dyads and triads. His "dyadic" embankment earthwork is what I have termed the High Bank C-R motif configuration and his "triadic" earthwork, of course, is the Paint Creek C-R motif configuration. He then notes that with the exception of Circleville all the circles of the dyads that he includes in his study are oriented upstream and, of course, this means that the rectilinear components, the octagons, are oriented downstream. He then notes that for the triads, this orientation is split. Only Frankfort and Seip have their (large) circles oriented upstream while Liberty Works, Works East, and Baum have their (large) circles oriented downstream. He finds this puzzling. His conclusion is that "[t]he upstream, unbroken circles of Scioto dyads are worlds apart from the large, perforated circles of later triads. The metaphorically disposed might even sense an unfolding cosmic drama in which these ruptured circles mark the last gasp of what some archaeologists call the Hopewell 'climax'" (2010, 197).

While his observation is interesting, I find his analysis to be confusing and this confusion would be immediately dissolved if he used my taxonomy. In his taxonomy, by the circular component of his dyads and triads he means the large circle in each case. This is made clear in the above quotation when he speaks of the dyadic circles as unbroken and the triadic circles as "ruptured." Identifying these two as "equivalent" forms is the only reason he can say that, with one exception, the "unbroken" circles of the dyads are oriented upstream while only two of the five equivalent but "broken" circles of the triads are oriented upstream, the other three "broken" circles being oriented downstream. Clearly, he assumes that all the "large" circles should be oriented upstream and, therefore, he defines the failure to do so as a puzzle of his scheme. However, this is a false puzzle. In my scheme, the large "unbroken" circle of his dyadic earthwork, which I term the High Bank C-R motif, is *not* the equivalent of the large "ruptured" circle of his triadic earthwork, what I term the Paint Creek C-R motif. The "ruptured" circle *is* the infix of the latter, and, as I noted above, in my scheme it represents the Middle World in the solar aspect. As the infix it is "grammatically" a junctural component that "links" the *small peripheral circle* and the large rectilinear of the Paint Creek C-R motif configuration and, therefore, is formally, functionally, and meaningfully the equivalent of the aggregation neck of the High Bank C-R motif. In meaningful terms, therefore, the small peripheral circle of the Paint Creek C-R configuration and the large "unbroken" circle of the High Bank C-R configuration are equivalent (also notably both are "unbroken" save for where they connect to the juncture component) and represent and participate in the powers of the Above World—in its dual complementary solar and lunar aspects, respectively. The Paint Creek Square and the octagon then represent and participate in the powers of the Beneath World—also in its complementary solar and lunar aspects, respectively. Now, if the layout of the embankment earthworks that he classes as triads, namely, my Paint Creek C-R motif configuration earthworks, are reexamined, it turns out that *all* the small unbroken circles are oriented upstream. In fact, this applies to the Hopewell site also since its small unbroken single-entrance circle is oriented upstream relative to the positioning of its associated small Paint Creek Square. Finally, Seal also has its small unbroken circle oriented upstream. Hence, with the exception of Circleville, as DeBoer notes, all the equivalent circular components of the earthworks he examines are oriented upstream. With the Circleville exception, DeBoer's puzzle is resolved. However, this also suggests that the unique nature of Circleville may be resolved. It has a dual circle component, with the circles fitting one inside the other. They are on the downstream side of the rectilinear. This suggests that the fitting of one circle into the other is an alternative expression of representing the stratification of the cosmos. The rectilinear represents the Beneath World, as in all the other cases, and the concentric circles represent the Middle World and Above Worlds. Of course, which circle represents which stratum would require further empirical data. For example, if the two circles consist of different earth fills, one derived from the deep stratum and one from the surface stratum, then one could speculate that just as the latter is "above" the former, so the circles are intended to replicate the same stratification of the powers of the Middle World and Above World. However, this is only speculation at this point.

DeBoer also addresses Hively and Horn's alignments of the earthworks that they examined, commenting that they addressed a different interearthwork alignment process. In this case, for them the question was the alignment of at least three locales on a common azimuth. They note that there were at least three such alignment sets. Are these two patterns mutually contradictory, suggesting that we would be better to recognize one and ignore the other or ignore both? I believe that these two approaches are not incompatible. Indeed, both presuppose the same intelligibility, except that one set of alignments, DeBoer's, enables the invoking of the sacred powers that were incorporated in both the targeted and the targeting site; while Hively and Horn's approach suggests that a similar interaction was ensured, only in this case, by the mutually aligned sites participating in the same azimuth alignment. I interpret DeBoer's intersite alignments as linking the sacred pathways connecting the earthworks as they were positioned on the surface of the Middle World while I interpret Hively and Horn's intersite alignments as mediating the sacred pathways as these existed in the Above World and Beneath World. Hence, in the latter case, the sites are located so that the linking alignments trace Above World and Beneath World Spirit Pathways, while in the former case, the sites are located so as to invoke and presence the sacred powers of the earthworks in each other through the mediation of the Middle World Spirit Pathways.

Both Hively and Horn and DeBoer have made cogent arguments that clearly implicate the significance of the builders' plotting linear alignments as being a major, although not the only, congruency strategy by which the sets of embankment earthworks that are the material symbolic pragmatic media of what I have been calling ecclesiastic-communal cult sodality heterarchies expressively embodied the sacred powers of the cosmos in the earthworks themselves. I have considered these congruency strategies to be a critical factor in the overall ritual strategies responsible for the formation and development of the Ohio Hopewell landscape. Possibly a good way to terminate this discussion is to come full circle and reexamine the earthwork patterning of the Little Miami Valley cult sodality heterarchy system. In this regard, Robert Riordan (2010, 2004) has addressed what I consider to be an equivalent congruency strategy of the Great and Little Miami Valley cult sodality heterarchies. However, this region generated its own unique strategy for constituting expressive linkages of spatially separate earthworks, although no doubt having the same intended effect. In particular, he has noted several instances of what he has referred to as complementary pairs of earthworks. By complementary, he is referring to their contrasting in terms of form, circular and rectilinear, and location, both linearly and vertically relative to each other. When two formally complementary embankment earthworks are near but spatially distinct from each other, the rectangular earthwork is typically located on the valley floor and is oriented toward its more distal circular neighbor, which is also located on the highest point in the immediate region, usually a large plateau. He specifically interprets the sites of Pollock (figure 16.2) and Bull Works in these terms and treats them as representing a single unit, and I would characterize this as the embodiment of a first-order cult sodality heterarchy.

> A mile to the west of Pollock there is a second enclosure known as the Bull Works (33GR3), which was depicted by Squier and Davis (1848: Plate 34, No.3) as a rectangle with outlying arcs and mounds. . . . It was built in the first location downstream that offered a spot wide enough to hold a figure that large (it enclosed about 8 acres), and it is in a section of the valley that is over 15 m lower in elevation than the highest point within the Pollock hilltop. This same earthwork could as easily have been built on expansive uplands to the north, south, or west of Pollock, which are all about equal in elevation or higher than the Pollock plateau, but the builders instead selected the lower valley. I think that this was intentionally done, that Pollock and Bull were temporally contemporaneous, and that they constituted a linked pair of earthworks that was always intended to be considered together rather than in isolation. (Riordan 2010, 222)

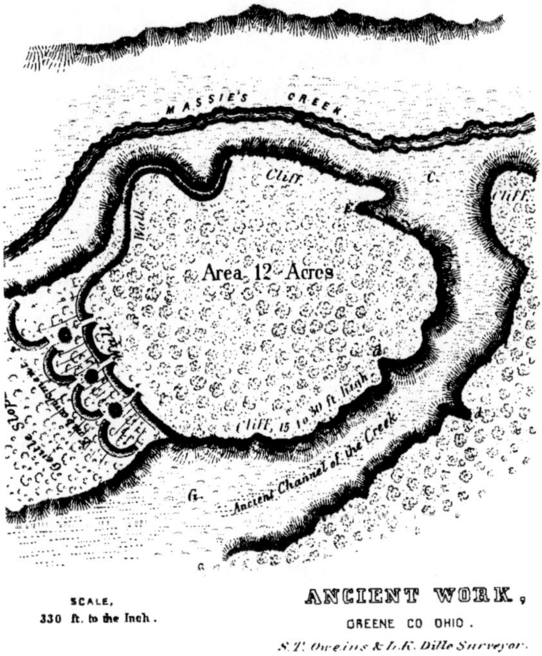

FIGURE 16.2
The Pollock Earthworks
Source: Squier and Davis 1848, plate XII, no. 3.

These two sites are separated about 1.6 km and flank the same valley of Massie's Creek, a small tributary of the Little Miami (figure 12.1). Riordan has further suggested that this upper/circular and lower/rectilinear pairing may be expressing the structure of the cosmos as it existed in the collective understanding of the builders. In these terms he suggests that the complementary duality represents and (I would add) presences the sacred powers of the Above World and the Middle World, respectively. I would also add on analogy with Newark and Chillicothe that they represent the lunar aspect of the cosmos. To claim this would be consistent with Riordan's noting that mortuary remains are conspicuously absent. As I argued earlier the Lunar motif earthworks displaying the High Bank C-R motif in the Chillicothe-Newark heterarchy complex would certainly be an important context for world renewal ritual and, of course, would be ideal for conducting sacred games particularly identified with the lunar aspect of the cosmos, for example, the Milky Way, and furthermore, that the actual mortuary-mediated rituals occurring in this context would not result in mortuary deposits in the forms of burials, whether extended or cremated. Rather, the bodies would probably be exposed on scaffolds and when the games were completed they would be removed and relocated in the laying-in altar crypts, such as at Turner.

Importantly, Riordan has recognized the special value that stone had for the peoples of this region since his argument of the sacred duality of form hinges on his interpreting the use of stone as a major mode of constructing the western facing of the Pollock embankment, thereby—as I would construe them—constituting it as embodying the sacred powers of the cosmos. This would explain why the complementary paired earthworks that Riordan has noted do not have any known mortuary deposits. It suggests that these would serve as the locale of a first-order cult sodality heterarchy and that this heterarchy would actively maintain alliances with several other neighboring first-order heterarchies in order to cooperatively construct at least one other earthwork that would embody the solar aspect of the cosmos. I have suggested that Turner represents this type. Indeed, even though the main representative examples of this southwestern Ohio complementary pairing of earthworks that Riordan (2004, 238–39) has presented are in the upper Little Miami Valley and the Great Miami Valley (for example, in Butler County he postulates a similar pairing of the Fortified Hill site and the Pleasant Run Works [2010, 221–22]), it could well be that those in the middle-to-upper reaches of the Little Miami Valley were actively involved in the dispersed third-degree Fort Ancient–Turner–Hopewell cult sodality heterarchy, particularly because the Turner-Hopewell axis provided the critically important Solar motif for those stages of the world renewal rituals entailing the conveyancing rites of the custodial regalia ritual usufructs. Therefore, following the sacred games and world renewal rituals mediated by earthworks manifesting the Lunar motif, the deceased would be taken in sacred procession to the Turner site in order to move into the later phase of the postmortem human sacrificial *chaîne opératoire* mortuary trajectory, as described earlier.

The Pollock Works presents a particularly intriguing feature. As Riordan has described it, this earthwork was developed in several building stages. In each case, the same basic forms were preserved. However, the fourth stage involved the building of a palisade-like wall of large timber posts along the top of the embankment and extended along both sides of a plateau. He has argued that this palisade-like feature was in existence for only about a decade when it was burned. This burning was deliberate, in his view, and probably mediated a ritual since the thoroughness of the burning required the addition of tinder to ensure that the fire would penetrate the mud daubing that had apparently been used to cover the lower part of the timber structure. He has postulated that the construction represents a period of instability in the region and suggests that, while Pollock was decidedly a ceremonial locale, for a brief period, it also served as a defensive locale with a palisade (2010, 224).

In my 2004 book I expressed skepticism related to this latter possibility, but I am now inclined to accept his claim as quite valid. My reason arises from my delineation and description of the sacred games *tournées*/mortuary-mediated world renewal *chaîne opératoire* process. I suggested then that the sacred games *tournées* component promoted strong intersodality competition for honor and fame and, furthermore, some of the games would entail violent albeit regulated confrontations among and between participating groups. Thus underwriting the process would be the largely unintended promotion of intersodality feuds and while these would be played out in the sacred game arenas, sometimes they might well have generated such hostility between competing cult sodalities that a defensive posture would be a wise tactic for a heterarchy to exercise. Of course, such feuds would endanger the integration of the second- and third-order heterarchies to which the hostile and competitive sodalities belonged and, no doubt, there would be active peacemaking overtures that participating allied groups would carry out. Most often these would result in mutual accommodations and truces among feuding parties. Such successful interventions would probably be marked by shared renewal rituals. Such a scenario may be suggestive of the events that both motivated the construction of the timber palisade and, after several years of hostility and intermediaries acting as peace activists, led to its ritual destruction as a medium of peace and the honorable resolution of the feud.

Therefore, it is not that Pollock ceased to be used as a ceremonial locale for the first-order cult sodality heterarchy that constructed it. Rather, I would suggest that this palisade manifests a period when this heterarchy continued to use it as its ritual locale while experiencing a particularly sharp escalation of a chronic feud with another first-order cult sodality. If we examine the Pollock–Bull Works dual complex in the context of the region, it is somewhat unique in form. Such uniqueness may have been interpreted by other cult sodalities as an infelicitous context for proper world renewal ritual and, indeed, they may have perceived such ritual and the sacred games that would be an intrinsic part of this ritual as not only polluting to the locale but to the region in general. I have argued that radical deviation in form could be the source of antagonism and hostile confrontations. The Pollock situation may be an example of this. However, even though the feud was probably long-standing, it would have been largely controlled and regulated by participation in the regional sacred games *tournées*/mortuary-mediated world renewal ritual as performed through the second- and third-order cult sodality heterarchy levels. However, even the latter may have been unable to prevent an escalation and for a short time Pollock may have had to withdraw from the system or shift to participating in another system, while defending itself as the feud escalated. Since the palisade was only in place for a rather brief period, and was removed through a ritual burning followed immediately by the addition of the fourth and final embankment stratum, it seems that the cult sodality heterarchy system was able to prevail and reestablish less aggressive relations between the Pollock cult sodality heterarchy and its affiliated allies of the Fort Ancient–Turner–Hopewell cult sodality heterarchy.

CONCLUSION

Now that I have completed my structural analysis of the Ohio Hopewell cult sodality heterarchy system, I want to address one of the most puzzling aspects of the Central Ohio Valley Middle Woodland period archaeological record, this being the partly simultaneous existence of two complex archaeological records in this same region. These have traditionally been referred to as the Late Adena and Ohio Hopewell. I turn to this task in my next and concluding chapter by arguing that both were systems of cult sodality heterarchies largely differentiated by the former being based on a complex system of communal cult sodalities structured into two mutually autonomous senior age-grade and junior age-grade sodalities and by the latter being based on the more structurally complex ecclesiastic-communal cult sodality type. In both cases, the systems of communities of which they were the sodality components were of the same order, being complementary heterarchical communities of their respective regions in the bifurcated settlement articulation modal posture. Characterizing these two earthwork/mortuary-mediated traditions in this manner and treating the two corresponding systems of communities in the same manner, as dispersed complementary heterarchical communities, will highlight the potential these had for interrelating and cross-fertilizing. At the same time, it is rather easy to understand why each was able to sustain continuity in the context of the other since, of course, the critical importance of material culture as symbolic pragmatic media constitutive of social lives would both impede and promote as well as color the quality of social interaction. As I suggested above, it is likely that the most complex unfolding of these interrelations occurred in the upper and middle Muskingum drainage and resulted in the great Newark earthwork locale.

17

The Ohio Hopewell and Adena as Neighbors and Strangers

One of the outstanding characteristics of the Central Ohio Valley Woodland, and possibly one of the most interesting of the many puzzles of the Eastern North American Woodland region, is the fact that it embodies two of the most impressive Native North American prehistoric archaeological records generally referred to as the Adena and the Ohio Hopewell. Each of these has similar mortuary patterning and their associated settlement patterns display strong expressions of the bifurcated settlement articulation modal posture. Prior to chronometric dating techniques these two assemblages were interpreted as sequential with the Adena being first and widespread throughout the Central Ohio Valley, even spilling over into borderland regions, and then followed by Ohio Hopewell, having a much more restricted distribution limited largely to southwestern, south-central, southeastern, and central Ohio. With the development of dating methods, this rather neat sequential ordering has come to be seen as not being so neat. It is still generally recognized that Adena-like mortuary features and bifurcated settlement patterns preexisted Ohio Hopewell and many still refer to these as Early Adena, dating from about 500 B.C. While the Ohio Hopewell, with its significantly different mortuary features and variant bifurcated settlement posture, is still recognized as emerging later, ca 100 B.C., instead of Adena "disappearing" with the entrance of Ohio Hopewell it is now generally recognized that the Adena-like practices continued in full swing into the Middle Woodland period, albeit primarily only in those areas where the Ohio Hopewell assemblage was largely, but not exclusively, absent. This continuity of Adena into the Middle Woodland period is now usually referred to as the Late Adena. While the Late Adena mortuary sites, consisting of mortuary mounds, paired-pole circles, and Sacred Circles (circular embankments usually with one "gateway" and displaying what I have termed the SR-Profile), were still quite extensive and partly surrounded the zone where Ohio Hopewell emerged, they dominated in Kentucky and West Virginia, persisted in the Hocking Valley of southeast Ohio, and also continued in the central Muskingum and, as discussed in the previous chapter, were well entrenched in the Licking River Valley. This valley may have started its Ohio Hopewellian phase quite early with the construction of Granville. This does not mean, however, that it abandoned its preexisting Adena ritual practices since, given that the Adena and Ohio Hopewell assemblages are the symbolic pragmatic media of particular ritual usufruct practices and not the manifestation of mutually exclusive monistic modular polity communities, these two sets of practices could have persisted in parallel, with the Adena features of the nearby pre-Hopewellian Newark site continuing in use. Hence, both types of rituals, Adenan and Hopewellian, likely occurred in the Licking Valley prior to the emergence of the Newark Circle-Octagon, possibly in the first half of the third millennium, ca A.D. 250. Of course, this possibility raises the issue of the degree to which the two sets of ritual usufruct practices were compatible or incompatible. Is it possible that certain zones of the Central Ohio Valley saw a type of eclecticism prevailing while other zones sustained a type of intolerance on the part of both mutually exclusive neighboring complexes? I believe that the archaeological record supports this claim and, of course, this raises the issue of why these contradictory attitudes could emerge.

If the building of the Newark Circle-Octagon was initiated around or shortly before A.D. 250, then I would argue that the neighboring middle Muskingum Valley Late Adena, spatially a mere 20 km east of Newark, probably persisted to at least this time, and, indeed, probably Adena practices continued to be manifested in the middle sector of the valley for some time thereafter. This claim pushes the Late Adena practices in this region beyond the time that Jeff Carskadden has most recently suggested for the "ending" of Late Adena in the central Muskingum, which is ca A.D. 100 (2008, 253). While I recognize his expertise in this area, I think that he is being overly conservative. Indeed, his conservative dating might be largely a function of the monistic modular polity view since, as I noted above, this promotes the notion that these two social phenomena are constituted by sets of unitary communities, and the Adena and Ohio Hopewell complexes constitute their social identities. Therefore, a community has to be either Late Adena or Ohio Hopewell. It cannot be both. However, seen in terms of the complementary heterarchical community perspective, these two phenomena are the expression of the relatively autonomous institutional structures characteristic of complementary heterarchical communities when these are in the bifurcated settlement articulation modal posture. Indeed, both assemblages, as I noted above, can be interpreted as constituting a complex of ritual usufruct practices and, in principle, these could be distributed independently of each other. An autonomous cult sodality having Adena ritual usufruct practices prevailing could incorporate some Hopewellian practices, if the group interpreted the latter as a valued addition to its ritual repertoire while, at the same time, recognizing that there was no essential contradiction between this new ritual usufruct and their traditional practices.

Berle Clay has presented a view of the Adena that is *almost* consistent with the above in that he has argued that the Adena assemblage manifests a specialized ritual organization and he has also extended this characterization to the Ohio Hopewell (1986, 589; 1991, 32, 35). However, he has not characterized the precise relations between these ritual organizational types and the Early "Adena" community, except to deny that the latter was organized in what he termed the "bull's-eye" manner, which is his favored term to refer to the civic-ceremonial interpretation of what I have called the monistic modular community polity view. Despite his criticism of the latter view, he has himself used the term "Adena" interchangeably to speak of both a community social system, as such, and the assemblage that marks the specialized ritual organization and, of course, this is precisely what I have resisted when speaking about the Ohio Hopewell.

As I noted in the opening chapter, it is critically important to keep the Middle Woodland period community and the Ohio Hopewell organization of this period as distinct, albeit related social systems. The relationship, as I have stressed, is characterized as relatively autonomous such that any given autonomous cult sodality can forge its social identity independently of the social identity of the common set of community clans from which its members are drawn. It is this relative autonomy of the clans and sodalities of a given complementary heterarchical community that makes it possible for the bifurcated settlement articulation mode to exist as a stable system and, therefore, makes it possible for the cult sodalities to constitute intersodality alliances, namely, cult sodality heterarchies, each with its repertoire of ritual usufruct practices. However, treating Ohio Hopewell and Late Adena as defining contemporary cult sodality heterarchy systems in the same Central Ohio Valley region does raise the issue of whether the systems of complementary heterarchical communities to which the cult sodalities of the Ohio Hopewell and Adena heterarchy systems belonged should also be given separate names. Unfortunately, the term *Adena* has been used to refer to both the communities and to the cultural tradition. However, the cultural tradition of the Middle Woodland period communities whose sodality components constituted the Ohio Hopewell cult sodality heterarchy system has been termed the "Scioto tradition"; and therefore, these communities could be called the Scioto complementary heterarchical community system. But it does not follow that the cult sodalities of all these communities would practice only Ohio Hopewell rituals. This is also the case for the complementary heterarchical communities whose cult sodalities practice Adena rituals. This is because, in principle, both "Ohio Hopewell" and "Adena" define constellations of custodial ritual usufructs and, in my view, these constellation are only contingently rather intrinsically related.

This distinction is important, in my view. Intrinsically related rituals would come as a structured package: to practice one ritual entails commitment to the total package of rituals. In contrast, contingently related rituals would be a package constructed through historical processes of accumulation. I believe that it is more appropriate to speak of the Ohio Hopewell as a historically constructed system of rituals and, therefore, while many would be related and a core of rituals would be common, this core would itself be contingently related. Hence, cult sodalities having primarily Ohio Hopewellian types of rituals could and might very likely accumulate and practice a mix of Hopewellian rituals that is not precisely matched by another cult sodality. Indeed, this is the basis of the distinction I have made in speaking of the Miami Fort (C-Form/T-Form) and Chillicothe (C-R Forms) traditions of embankment earthworks. And this contingent relation could "bleed" over the Ohio Hopewell and Adena "boundary." That is, since cult sodalities are autonomous, some of the cult sodalities that constitute a first-order heterarchy in which Hopewell rituals prevail could also practice one or two Adenan rituals. This could also be the case for Adena-type cult sodalities. This overlapping would likely not happen too often or to any great degree; but its possibility would enable "crossbreeding" to occur—a practice I postulated in the previous chapter as being responsible for the emergence of the Sacred Dual C-R monumental earthworks constituting the Newark site. Furthermore, this "bleeding" applied to the nonsodality sector as well. Hence, it is quite possible, and indeed, I think very likely, that many of the complementary heterarchical communities to which Adena cult sodalities belonged practiced cultural traditions that could comfortably fit the "Scioto" tradition. All this raises the issue of what to call this Central Ohio Valley Middle Woodland period system of communities. However, I will not resolve this issue. I only raise it to indicate that while the symbolic pragmatics, the assemblages, of the two social phenomena that have been traditionally termed "Ohio Hopewell" and "Adena" seem to perspicuously contrast, almost as if they were mutually exclusive, the social organizations were not "closed shops" to each other and, therefore, cross-fertilization could and probably did occur, although differently in different regions of the Central Ohio Valley. Therefore, as I noted in the previous chapter, while there is no question that the material assemblages that have been labeled as Adena and Ohio Hopewell contrast in significant ways, as symbolic pragmatic media of ritual practices, this does not mean that the cosmology and ethos differed that presupposed these practices and their different material symbols. The cosmology and ethos are deep structures and the ideology constitutes surface structures of rules and protocols that define the form that behaviors must take to count as the ritual intended. Therefore, while the Adena and Ohio Hopewell pragmatic symbols can differ, the two sets can and most likely will share the same cosmology and ethos.[1] There is no necessity, therefore, that the ritual practices of Adena and Ohio Hopewell be mutually exclusive, although it would likely require a deliberate action strategy to convince an Adena-oriented group to become franchisees of an Ohio Hopewell ritual usufruct and, of course, there would likely be a reactive action strategy on the part of a significant proportion of the Adena cult sodality heterarchy that may have been the target of such a franchising attempt.

I have also already prepared the grounds for why the Newark Circle-Octagon could be built by a complex cult sodality heterarchy known for its Adena ritual usufruct. As I suggested in the previous chapter the Sacred Dual C-R motif is a particular monumental iconic symbolic articulation of an aspect of the regional cosmology that, while this expression was likely innovated in the Chillicothe zone, did not contradict the expressive meanings of the earlier and regionally different earthwork types. Of course, commitment to particular ideological practices is itself commitment to the formal symbolic pragmatic modes and it often is the case that these modes are identified by their users as necessary for constituting authentic rituals; and those so committed perceive that using alternative formal modes would count as significantly infelicitous icons of ritual such that performing the ritual in these icons probably will do more damage to the sacred order than it does good. This sort of attitude is an exemplification of a resistant action strategy. Hence, groups using these different forms may stand as hostile and mutually exclusive to each other, somewhat equivalent to the long-standing historical hostility between the Protestant and Roman Catholic Christian ecclesiastical cult organizations. However, such hostility is a contingent and not a necessary social condition. Therefore, it is also possible that action strategies could be developed, that is, propagandistic forms of action promoting ritual usufruct franchising, such that the two different symbolic pragmatic expressive materials can come to be seen by the two different groups as simply articulating different aspects of the same cosmos and, therefore, they are noncontradictory expressive specializations. If this is understood, then it is perfectly reasonable to find that an initially resistant group can come to accommodate to this innovation through becoming ritual usufruct franchisees while maintaining their old practices, possibly by modifying a site to constitute it as the specialized locale for the performance of the newly franchised ritual usufruct. This would be accomplished in ways that would be consistent with my discussion in the previous chapter of the building of the Newark Circle-Octagon and the modification of this process so as to incorporate the second, complementary ritual usufruct manifested in the Paint Creek C-R motif configuration.

I suggest that one way to modify a site to effect this type of specialization is to modify one of the traditional sites to incorporate the material needs of the franchised ritual usufruct while maintaining the established ritual usufruct practices in the older sites. Another way would simply be to add new sectors to the older sites by building earthworks that would "fit" the symbolic pragmatic needs of the newly franchised ritual usufruct while maintaining the older sectors for the traditional ritual. No doubt other modes of accommodation could be innovated. For example, in the first possible case noted above, the traditional Late Adena practices may be the responsibility of alliances of local autonomous cult sodalities constituting first-order heterarchies. The same first-order heterarchies may ally with more distant first-order heterarchies to form a second-order cult sodality heterarchy that does so precisely to specialize in the Ohio Hopewell practices. These could then select one of the traditional second-order cult sodality heterarchy sites, such as Newark, and modify it overall in order to accommodate to the imperatives arising from the ritual usufruct that called for the Sacred Dual C-R motif configuration, as described in the previous chapter. In time, a reverse flow of ritual influence from this innovated second-order Newark heterarchy locale to the first-order heterarchies located in the older sites can occur, promoting the replacement of Late Adena practices at the more localized level with the equivalent Ohio Hopewell practices.

I postulate that the material continuity of Late Adena and Ohio Hopewell in the Central Ohio Valley can be understood in these terms. In some regions, however, the interaction was a form of hostile standoff and, therefore, resistance was effective. Indeed, the Hocking Valley may have been the most resistant, despite being spatially closest to the core Ohio Hopewell Chillicothe tradition. In other areas, such as the Upper and Middle Muskingum Valley, it was an ongoing trade-off and specialization. In others, such as south-central Indiana, an interesting synthesis developed.

DISCUSSION

Clay (2005, 109–10) has pointed out that the terms *Adena* and *Hopewell* have tended to impede our understanding of the archaeological records they are used to name. He sees these terms as expressing cultural historical concepts and, for this reason, they have pushed archaeologists to think of Adena and

Ohio Hopewell as delineating separate, mutually exclusive, and to one degree or another, coherent sets of communities. As I noted above, he has partly rejected this view by arguing that Adena (and Ohio Hopewell) must be treated as a particular organizational type, one in which mortuary practices are the primary common factor. "I have focused on how ritual space was defined and deployed in mounds and earthworks. . . . With this approach, 'Adena' loses importance as a culture historical term and becomes an organizational type, with possible wider utility in eastern United States. . . . I examine Adena as a *ritual organization* to provide some substance to an *organizational type* and to indicate its developmental trajectory in the Ohio Valley" (1991, 30). It is also clear that he treats the Adena archaeological record, and by extension the Ohio Hopewell record (2002, 109–10; 1991, 35), as specialized organizational components mediating the mortuary-religious process of a multiple set of individual but interacting communities.

While I strongly endorse this view, as I suggested above, Clay has an overall commitment to treating the community in monistic modular polity terms and, as such, leaves problematic how to characterize the relation between the community, as such, and the ritual organization, whether Adena or Ohio Hopewell. To do this he specifically argues against the civic-ceremonial center view, referring to it as the "bull's-eye" view (1998, 16). Nevertheless, he argues that these locales are the expression of alliances *among* communities and not among organizational groups. Therefore, while the earthworks are not directly coincident with monistic communities in the way they are under the orthodox bull's-eye view, the groups that used them were components that cooperatively shared "joint" civic-ceremonial locales on the "edges" of their respective territories and the social nature of these groups was left uncharacterized by Clay. "Reconstructed, the Adena mound occupied an 'edge' location with respect to the groups that used it and, because of this placement, it is difficult to interpret from the mound and its burial population what groups used it" (1991, 32). He is quite specific in this regard since he argues that the primary purpose of the Adena mortuary locales was to constitute alliances by which member *communities could gain access to the resources of one another's territories* (1991, 36). However, if I focus specifically on his treatment of Adena as an organizational type, his approach to the Adena and my approach to the Ohio Hopewell are quite compatible. Indeed, he treats Ohio Hopewell as simply an organizational type of the same order as the Adena except that the former was more complex and manifested a formally different range of features, facilities, and artifacts. Hence, I contend that what Clay's modeling lacks is a commitment to something akin to the complementary heterarchical community structure.

> I interpret Hopewell as an extension of the complexity that developed in Adena, and the discussion of Adena as a ritual type should lead logically into a consideration of Hopewell. Importantly for the Adena concept, the three subdivisions used here are both *temporal stages* and *levels* of organization. The early and middle levels persisted into Late Adena [A.D. 1–250]; they were replaced by a Wright mound level. By extension, the three levels probably persisted into Hopewell together with the even greater complexity reflected in distinctively Hopewell facilities (such as conjoined earthworks, great houses, and effigy mounds). Artifact styles associated with Adena and Hopewell burials and ritual contexts changed and have been used with variable success to separate the two in time and space as if they were simply traditional culture historical entities. I submit, however, that there is very little difference in ritual organization between the Fischer mound of Early Adena and any one of many small, late Hopewellian mounds. (1991, 35)

He has given considerable empirical detail so as to argue how the Adena system operated. He notes the likely cycling of different types of Adena locales, what I have termed the Sacred Circle, the paired-pole circle, and the Adena mortuary mound (1991, 34). He recognizes that in the Late Adena mound, a type of crypt-mediated cycling of the deceased was undertaken, and this clearly indicates that our approaches overlap to a considerable degree. In a most interesting manner, as noted in the above quotation, the development of Adena was not a matter of changing organizational types but of adding organizational levels. Early Adena involved rather simple mounds; Middle Adena maintained the latter and added more complex mortuary patterning, and Late Adena adds the complex mortuary-crypt cycling. Hence, this way of characterizing the development of Adena would suggest initially a first-order level, with a second-order level emerging, and finally the most complex or third-order level.

However, where we differ is in the differential characterization of the structural organization of the community itself. In particular, despite his "edge" model, and despite his rejection of "chiefdom" and "big men" models (1992, 78–79), he seems quite committed to the exclusive territorial perspective and, for him, the community was apparently monistic, or, kinship-dominant (1992, 80). This also means that, as I noted above, he leaves responsibility for the sphere of mortuary locales somewhat vague. Other than being in areas that were a type of no-man's-land, not claimed as part of the territories by any of the users of the mortuary locales, he does not explicate the nature of the organization that was responsible for them and how this organization would relate to the communities. Therefore, I see a contradiction between his characterization of Adena (and by extension Ohio Hopewell) as organizational types and his commitment to the community as a kinship-based territorially defined polity, albeit one that was highly flexible and mobile. Indeed, these latter attributes that he highlights (Clay 2002, 184) in particular require a firm characterization of the Adena organizational type. If I am right, then this contradiction clearly indicates that the "Adena/Hopewell problem" he has identified as rooted in the cultural historical approach is actually rooted in the inadequacy of the modeling of the type of social systems, that is, the systems of communities that would be the key structural components of this cultural history.

The problem that he is highlighting, in my view, is not taxonomic or cultural historic. Rather, it is ontological. That is, it is rooted in the way archaeologists have typically characterized the possible nature of the social systems that must have existed in order for this record to have been generated. The term *Adena* has become well entrenched in the archaeological literature, of course, and it has articulated this record as having properties that distinguish it from the records of other regions and times. This suggests that the social reality that this concept is about existed and was a major force in the prehistory of the Central Ohio Valley, and beyond. As I argued earlier, the standard assumption is that the terms *Adena* and *Ohio Hopewell* can be used to label communities, and typically the community, whether called "Adena" or "Ohio Hopewell," has been treated in monistic modular polity terms. Clay's notion that the social groups responsible for Adena locales transcended any given "Adena" community is well motivated and it echoes the conceptualization underwriting the Multiple Community model presented by Ruby and his colleagues (2005) that I fully discussed in chapter 2. However, his "edge" model suffers from the same problem; and I attribute this to his being too closely wedded to the monistic modular polity view. Therefore, he is unable to treat the Adena component of the assemblage as manifesting a system of relatively autonomous organizations that, as such, were able to sustain continuity over the generations, even though the face-to-face residential groups were highly mobile and, as he notes, ephemeral in their way of life, largely because "the attractions of hunting, gathering, and foraging seem to have tugged the Heartland Native Americans toward a resolutely dispersed and dispersing way of life" (2002, 184).

As I have emphasized in this book and previous books, social organizations are real and not simply epiphenomenal structures. They are structures of social relations that have temporal and spatial reach through the collective intentionality of the agents that occupy the positions that constitute the relations. These social positions have a deontic ontology, that is, an intersubjective ontology. Their nature entails reflexive understanding by the occupants of the rights, duties, and obligations, that is, the social powers and liabilities they have in virtue of their social positions. These social powers exist only because of the collective intentionality they have. I have termed the latter the cultural traditions of a people and the core of these traditions is the set of ethos standards and values that ground the deontic structure of rules and protocols. These rules and protocols can be articulated as rights, duties, and other deontic standards, values, preferences, prescriptions, and proscriptions, as the representational content of the group's ideological strategies. The latter embody these deep cultural structures of cosmology and ethos that make the formation of collective intentions possible and these formations just are the ideological strategies "at work." Hence, the groups *act* and the Adena and Ohio Hopewell material records were both the meaningful contexts and outputs of this activity.

The absence from Clay's model of the likely organizational structure that would be manifested in Adena material cultural patterning is particularly telling in that, as noted above, he claims the Adena-type organization evolved so that later Adena complexes in the bluegrass prairie of Kentucky, contemporary with the early and middle periods of the sites of Fort Ancient, Hopewell, and Mound City, also developed regional-type mortuary locales in which major earthwork embankments and cumulative mounds with laying-in crypts developed. In short, I would class these as drawing in and cycling participants in a manner equivalent to although not as spatially embracing as I outlined in my discussion of the dispersed third-order Fort Ancient–Turner–Hopewell cult sodality heterarchy. However, without articulating a possible social structure for this Adena organization, and instead remaining somewhat ambiguous by speaking of the "community" in dispersed residential terms that were such as to maintain spatial separation of the mortuary ceremonialism from the everyday locales, it is hard to explain how the continuity and expansion of such a major mortuary-mediated process could occur and be sustained.

In sum, what I take Clay to mean when he speaks of Adena as an organizational type tied to mortuary-mediated ritual is a system of cult sodality heterarchies and this system would entail the same type of community that I have already postulated for the Middle Woodland period in the region where the Ohio Hopewell episode unfolded. That is, Adena is the sodality component of a regional system of complementary heterarchical communities in the bifurcated settlement articulation modal posture that prevailed in the later Early Woodland period of the Central Ohio Valley and persisted in a more limited fashion into the Middle Woodland period. Indeed, he has cogently argued that this dispersed settlement pattern is characteristic of the "heartland" and persisted for two thousand years, terminating only at the end of the Late Woodland period in this region (2002, 184).

Clay has promoted shifting the internal temporal boundaries of the Woodland period by identifying the Middle Woodland period of this region with the emergence of mound building and the termination of the period would correlate with the termination of this mound building and its replacement with "cemeteries." I prefer to retain the more traditional dates and simply accept that the Adena cult sodality system bridged the later Early Woodland and the early-to-middle sector of the Middle Woodland periods. This is because I think that while the Ohio Hopewell organizations, where they emerged, were definitely the transformation and continuity of the earlier Adena organizations, they were marked by a fairly distinct, possibly unique departure from the Adena organizations, this being the emergence of the ecclesiastic-communal cult sodality as an organization, and this deserves reserving the use of the notion of the Ohio Middle Woodland period to the times when the Ohio Hopewell episode unfolded. As I noted above, I suspect that many Adena cult sodalities resisted both any shifting of the traditional structural makeup toward the ecclesiastic-communal sodality posture and the franchising of any of the "newfangled" Hopewellian ritual usufruct, and these two refusals probably constituted a single resistance action strategy on the part of many—but certainly not all—Adena organizations. In short, while I quite agree with Clay that Adena is a ritual organization, I also think that Adena and Ohio Hopewell organizations were structurally different. This means that I agree with him that Adena locales were alliances of ritual organizations similar in that regard to Ohio Hopewell. However, I postulate that "classic" Adena organizations, per se, are best characterized as *communal cult sodalities* in a social world consisting of complementary heterarchical communities maintaining a strong bifurcated settlement articulation modal posture, a posture, as Clay has noted, that was likely sustained as the norm for two millenniums.

To be clear here, what I am claiming distinguishes the Adena as a ritual organizational type from the Ohio Hopewell is that the former manifested a formal *communal cult sodality* structure while the latter manifested a formal *ecclesiastic-communal cult sodality* structure, one that emerged from the preexisting background of Adena communal cult sodalities. Indeed, I have argued that what was unique about Early Adena (and, in fact, may have been characteristic of Late Adena also) was that it was sustained by arm's-length relations between two complementary communal cult sodalities distinguished by relative seniority. I have termed these the senior and junior age-grade communal cult sodalities. This means that these sodalities would not constitute a permanent congregation of the type I claimed for the Ohio Hopewell, that is, one based on the laity-clergy structure, and this means that organizing the labor for ritual construction and even for performing ritual would likely be of a more limited nature than it would be for the ecclesiastic-communal cult sodality type. The senior age-grade sodality, of course, would consist of an aging group having limited physical abilities while the junior age-grade, of course, would tend to have many more members in their twenties and early thirties. In any given region, these two sets of sodalities would stand at arm's length to each other and this posture would likely make labor distribution and sharing more limited in comparison to the division of labor implicated by the ecclesiastic-communal cult sodality structure. This organizational difference between Adena and Ohio Hopewell alone might go some distance to explaining the lower quantity of labor investment in the former compared to much greater in the latter, as well as, respectively, the lesser and greater geographical scope of long distance expeditions. Now, my purpose in this closing chapter is not to characterize the Late Adena but to empirically demonstrate the complex unfolding of the Late Adena–Ohio Hopewell interaction, as exemplified, for example, by the emergence of Newark as a second-order Ohio Hopewellian cult sodality heterarchy in alliance with the Chillicothe second-order cult sodality heterarchy, thereby constituting what I termed earlier the dispersed third-order Chillicothe-Newark cult sodality heterarchy. To this end, I will give a brief summary of my characterization of Adena since I consider the existence of the latter to be among the critical social conditions that made the emergence of the Ohio Hopewell ecclesiastic-communal cult sodality possible.

ADENA COMMUNAL CULT SODALITY HETERARCHIES

I have argued that in the Adena case, a local region would consist of a complex senior age-grade communal cult sodality responsible for one set of Adena features and rituals, and a complex junior age-grade communal cult sodality responsible for another complementary set (Byers 2004, 255–68). I refer to them as "complex" communal cult sodalities for two reasons. First, there were two mutually autonomous but relatively exclusive (i.e., arm's-length) age-grade sodalities in a given region. By relatively exclusive I am speaking in terms of generational structure, one consisting of the age-sets making up the senior age-grades among the communities of a region and the other of the junior age-grades. Therefore, each complex senior age-grade sodality and junior age-grade sodality would consist of four or five age-sets. I also characterize both as complex because, for example, the junior age-grade sodalities of the regional communities would ally with each other, constituting a complex, possibly first-order heterarchy, as would the senior age-grade sodalities. Hence, the junior age-grade cult sodalities of the complementary heterarchical communities of a local region would establish ritual locales appropriate to the range of rituals for which they were traditionally responsible, and the senior age-grade cult sodalities of the same communities would also.

Of course, the rituals were of the same order as I have discussed for the Ohio Hopewell, being mortuary-mediated world renewal practices that were geared into rectifying the increased pollution levels that both traditional foraging and the emerging gardening practices were perceived to be generating. The two sets of sodalities, junior and senior age-grade, would cooperate but sustain arm's-length relations and this relation was manifested in the production and distribution of spatially separate and socially arm's-length ceremonial nodal locales.

Clay has argued that, at least for the Late Adena in the Kentucky and West Virginia regions (Clay 1986, 1991, 1992; Clay and Niquette 1992), there were three characteristic ceremonial nodal sites: the paired-pole circle, the Adena burial mound, and the Adena Circle.[2] He has given a processual discussion of these three primary Adena features. He recognizes the paired-pole circle as a "mortuary camp," the mortuary mounding as an accretional cemetery, and what I have termed the Sacred Circle as an earthwork mediating a nonmortuary form of ritual. His reason for the latter was that this large feature rarely had any empirical evidence of mortuary practices in the form of human bodily remains while both the paired-pole circle and mortuary mound did. He also recognized that the paired-pole circle may have been used for an indefinite time for nonmortuary ritual and then only became a mortuary camp in the last stages of its use. At this point mortuary evidence in the form of cremated burials occurred and, he argues, this marks its transformation in ritual meaning. After being used as a mortuary camp for depositing cremations, it was then transformed into a mortuary mounding, an accumulative (i.e., "vertical") cemetery. He particularly notes that the Late Adena crypts with portable covers were used so as to enable a series of mortuary rites of different deceased to occur. When the crypt-based rites of a given deceased were terminated the body would be removed, often buried on a prepared platform to one side of the crypt, and the emptied crypt used to process another deceased. However, he also suggests that rather than the removed bodies being given burial in the sides of the mound, in many cases they could have been given terminal burial in one of the many small burial mounds dispersed across the landscape. In such a case, he argues that ceramic-mediated rituals were performed beside the deceased. In any case, with regard to the crypt, at a certain point its use for this purpose would be terminated and it was appropriated as the burial crypt of the last deceased person to be processed. Often the total mound would be covered with a thick earth stratum and then a new crypt was usually started by being dug into the newly placed upper mantle. He argues, therefore, that the Adena ritual sphere was a complex set of sequential rituals, only some of which were given terminal burial rituals in the mound, while others were subjected to terminal rites in separate small mounds. He particularly emphasizes that the most complex development of the Adena ritual organization occurred in Late Adena, contemporary with the early to middle Ohio Hopewell (ca A.D. 1–A.D. 250) and it is at this time that the cycling of deceased through the great crypts was carried out. He specifically notes that the Wright Mound (Kentucky) would be a good example of this. However, as I noted above, the other components, particularly the mortuary camp, the paired-circle, and the dispersed small burial mounds, emerged earlier and persisted in parallel into the Late Adena. In other words, this mortuary processing underwent a historical development.[3]

I can accept the latter claim. However, I would add and modify several points. First, I would add that what is manifested in the Late Adena is a type of cult sodality heterarchical system that was akin to that of the Ohio Hopewell, that is, it involved multiple Adena cult sodalities with their own sacred games *tournées*. However, I would also modify this claim by arguing that, in contrast to the Ohio Hopewell system of heterarchies, which was based on *ecclesiastic-communal cult sodalities*, the Adena system likely consisted of two systems of mutually arm's-length but cooperating autonomous senior and junior age-grade *communal cult sodalities*. This structural difference means that there would be no laity-clergy structure and the two systems of junior and senior communal cults would have to make ad hoc arrangements with local shamans should the need arise, as it no doubt would, to apply specialized ritual usufruct know-how. I suspect, however, that this "external" need was rather limited since most of the ritual usufruct know-how and capacity would be part of each communal cult sodality so that only special cases would require shamanic assistance.

I would also modify his claim that the Adena ritual sphere can be usefully structured into mortuary and nonmortuary ritual; and this claim requires a restructuring of the social nature and relations of the groups associated with the three Adena features. In contrast to Clay's view, I have argued (2004, 255–68) that all the Adena rituals were mortuary-related, even those performed in the Sacred Circle. However, each mediated a different sphere of world renewal rituals. One sphere was performed in the context of each of the three major nodal locales: the paired-pole circle, the Sacred Circle embankment earthwork, and the mortuary mound. The first in this order, the paired-pole circle, was likely the ceremonial nodal locale under the custodianship of the complex senior age-grade cult sodality heterarchy of the region; the second, the Sacred Circle embankment earthwork, was likely the ceremonial nodal locale under the custodianship of the complex junior age-grade communal cult sodality heterarchy. The third, the Adena mortuary mound, was likely the equivalent of the Ohio Hopewell Paint Creek C-R motif embankment earthwork and was under the joint custodianship of both complex communal cult sodalities. Because of joint custodianship, I have suggested that the mortuary mound was internally divided into senior and junior age-grade sectors, similar to the sectoring of the great renewal lodges found under the Seip-Pricer, Seip-Conjoined, and Edwin Harness mounds, and the cycling of usage would lead to a split-generational mortuary population.

The above allocation of ritual spheres between the two age-grade sodalities would suggest a specialized religious sectoring. I have suggested that the same lunar/solar structuring as found in the Ohio Hopewell also prevailed in the Adena and that this was a deep structural component of the cosmology. Hence, lunar-related and solar-related rites were performed and the deceased typically served for both suites of rituals. In this regard I have suggested that the senior age-grade sodality heterarchy was identified with the solar suite, and the junior age-grade sodality heterarchy with the lunar suite. The paired-pole circle, what Berle refers to as the mortuary camp, therefore, would have been the locale for the performance of the specialized solar-related mortuary-mediated renewal rituals. It is for this reason that I have suggested that it might be appropriately termed the Solar Circle. Here initial scaffolding was probably carried out with some mourning-mediated release rites. Indeed, release of the free soul may have been performed here. The deceased would then be passed over to the complementary junior age-grade sodality heterarchy to be taken in procession to their nearby Sacred Circle. The lunar suite of renewal rituals would be performed there. However, it usually did not involve any postmortem dismemberment of the bodies. Rather, the deceased were subjected to scaffolding and possibly the addition of artifactual materials resulting from sacred games played on their behalf and in order to release some of their living soul spiritual powers. With the solar- and lunar-related rituals completed, the deceased would then be taken to the jointly used mortuary mounding and placed in one of the actively used laying-in period crypts. As I noted above, I have suggested that this mounding was sectored according to age-grade seniority. Hence, there may have been at least two laying-in crypts at any given time, one for the senior age-grade deceased and one for the junior age-grade deceased. Here laying-in rites would be performed, addition and subtraction of artifacts would be made, much as I discussed for the Ohio Hopewell; the conveyancing rites of custodial regalia—if any—could also be performed, and with the termination of the laying-in rites, the body would be removed and either buried to one side of the crypt in association with the decommissioned custodial regalia or removed and buried in a small burial mound.

This is a particular articulation of a cycling of religious contexts that Clay has argued would be typical of the Adena organization. However, rather than identifying these nodal locales with particular groups, he identifies them with different rituals divided into mortuary and nonmortuary types. This might be seen again as an expression of the mortuary/nonmortuary dichotomy. I prefer seeing the cycling as an early version of the same type of processual cycling that I outlined earlier for the Ohio Hopewell. In this case, the cycling was tied into the conveyancing of ritual usufructs of the age-sets of both the complex senior communal cult sodality and the complex junior communal cult sodality. The terminal burials in the laying-in period crypts probably marked the retirement of the senior and promotion of the junior age-grades, along with the conveyancing of the necessary ritual usufructs. Hence, the mantling of the mounding of burials would be the equivalent of the Ohio Hopewell truncation events. That is, this mounding may have marked the retirement of the senior age-grade and the promotion of the junior age-grade sodality to the senior age-grade level. In some, possibly many cases, with the completion of the mantle, new crypts could be dug into it to initiate a new cycle. Now this means that, just as in the Ohio Hopewell case, the deceased members of an age-grade came to be split between two separate mortuary sectors. The deceased members of the prior complex junior age-grade cult sodalities would be buried in the appropriate sector of the older and physically lower part of the joint mound and their surviving companions who were promoted to the senior age-grade level came to be buried in the senior sector of the new and upper stratum.

This conveyancing process and age-grade cycling would also involve modifying the usage of the two ceremonial nodal locales, the Solar Circle (paired-pole circle) and the Sacred Circle (the SR-Profile embankment circle), either by transferring custodianship from the senior to the junior age-grade cult sodality heterarchy as the latter was promoted to senior status, or by the abandonment of one or more of the locales and the creation of new ones. As Clay points out, very often the only reason we know that a paired-pole circle structure existed is that it was found on the floor of an Adena mound when the excavation of the latter was completed. This clearly suggests that the circle was used by a group until it became the floor of a new mortuary mounding locale, which would accumulate to become an Adena mound. Clay (1991, 33) describes this transformation in considerable detail, noting that shortly prior to the abandonment of the circle, initial cremations may have been deposited. Then, with its abandonment, a central crypt was built and the above described process unfolded, thereby generating a mounding of mortuary deposits with two or more central laying-in crypts. I have postulated that the transformation of the paired-pole structure into the mortuary locale was instigated by the retirement of the senior age-grade cult sodality heterarchy and the appropriation of the locale by the newly promoted senior and junior age-grade sodalities to serve as their joint world renewal mortuary-mediated ritual context. This also means that the newly promoted senior age-grade cult sodality heterarchy would need to establish nearby a new paired-post circle (i.e., Solar Circle) while abandoning their old Sacred Circle. Alternatively, rather than abandoning the latter, they could formally transfer it to the newly promoted junior age-grade communal cult sodality heterarchy. Different variations of cycling space and cult sodalities could apply. Indeed, as I argued above, a major Late Adena mound could have grown by accretion through the split-burial cycling of several generations of mortuary deposition. Each cycle could be terminated with a mantle covering the total set of prior burials and then a new accumulation would be initiated with new laying-in crypts built, and so on. This process of promotion, transfer, abandonment, rebuilding, and addition would explain the accumulation of clusters of Sacred Circles, Adena mounds, and Solar Circles.

If Adena and Ohio Hopewell are, in fact, cult sodality heterarchies each practicing equivalent sacred games *tournées*/mortuary-mediated world renewal ritual cycles, then there may have been only two factors that distinguished and separated them. First, as I noted above, it is likely that Adena was based on paired and complementary senior and junior age-grade *communal* cult sodalities that maintained arm's-length relations, each focusing on its own rituals and the material media that was required, possibly cooperating only to exchange deceased and to place earth mantles on the shared mortuary moundings. The Ohio Hopewell contrast, of course, in that it developed beyond the communal cult sodality level to what I termed earlier the ecclesiastic-communal cult sodality level. The second was the form of the material media that each was committed to using. If this is the case, then explaining the parallel existence of the two and the differences they had has to be done in social structural and symbolic pragmatic ideological terms. In social structural terms, apparently the ecclesiastic-communal cult sodality structure was the much more efficient organization of the two in terms of mobilizing labor, organizing long distance expeditions and exchanges, large-scale sacred games *tournées*/mortuary-mediated world renewal rituals, and so on. However, at the same time the two maintained possibly equal population levels per area while differently dispersed. The participants in the Ohio Hopewell, apparently, dispersed to the uplands in the cold season and focused on the lowland gardening-based semisedentary habitations during the warm season.

I suspect that the ideological differences, however, were not limited to the variation in material cultural forms. The Ohio Hopewell had larger and more complex monumental forms and features and, certainly, overall, a more complex artifactual assemblage. I suspect that this greater variation not only flows from the greater efficiency of labor mobilization but also the greater need to refine the symbolic pragmatic media of the enabling-based hierarchical organization in order to constitute and distinguish between leaders in the junior and senior age-grades, as well as constitute the clergy sector. This is because they belonged to the same ecclesiastic-communal cult sodality organization. Even though the Adena would also have senior and junior age-grade leaders, these would not be marked as distinct from each other since, being members of separate and mutually arm's-length autonomous organizations, the leaders of these two age-grades did not have to distinguish themselves symbolically from each other in this way. Also, of course, they had no permanent priestly group. Instead, shamans would be "contracted" when needed. Therefore, the greater variation of artifact assemblage of the Ohio Hopewell compared to the Adena could well be related primarily to the more complex social structure, including the incorporation of a priestly group. Importantly, except in the latter case, the social powers of the two types of cult sodalities were the same.

The social structural differences could also partly explain the continuity of Adena in parallel with Ohio Hopewell. The two recognized each other as different and, in some regions, did not mutually recognize these differences as "good." That is, while formal variation in artifacts and features is an ideological difference that makes no substantive meaning difference, that is, the same type of leaders having the same range of social powers constituting the same range of ritual activities, simply being expressed in formally different symbols, as I suggested above, these formal differences are often taken by the two parties as substantively significant. It would not be surprising, therefore, that in many cases the Adena cult sodality heterarchies were motivated to resist tendencies to emulate the Ohio Hopewell heterarchies. Of course, if they were tempted to emulate them, they would then need to gain the Ohio Hopewell ritual usufruct prerogatives to do so and this would include taking on the Ohio Hopewellian stylistics. To do this, however, would mean inviting an Ohio Hopewell cult sodality to franchise these ritual usufruct rites to them or, alternatively, being invited by the relevant Ohio Hopewell sodality so that the latter could franchise them to their guests. However, along with this ritual usufruct franchise would be the need to rationalize this ritual usufruct.

There appear to have been several attempts by Adena cult sodality heterarchies in Kentucky to carry out this type of franchise transfer that, in fact, failed to take root. For example, Clay (2002, 171) discerns a pattern of rectangular post holes under the Landing Mound in northern Kentucky. This pattern distinctly contrasts with a paired-pole circle and a "spiral fencing" under the same mound and, as he argues, these were sequentially constructed, one being abandoned before the next was built. The rectangular structure strongly suggests that an Ohio Hopewell ritual usufruct transfer occurred involving the need to use a standard rectangular structure for its performance. However, being the only one built and used suggests that when the communal cult sodality was promoted and the new sodality became the custodians of the locale, the latter resisted taking on the custodianship of the ritual usufruct implicated in the rectangular structure and it was allowed to lapse. A similar example is reported by Eric Schlarb for the Bullock Mound and its immediate environs.

> Analysis of the materials and field records from the Bullock Mound . . . suggests that it is a late Adena site reflecting interaction with Hopewellian groups originating north of the Ohio River. The rectangular structure beneath the mound, which may have served as a charnel house, represents variation in the Woodland period mound use and construction. The Bullock Mound may also reflect the presence of more than one social group contemporaneously within the Bluegrass region during this time period. In any case, the Bullock Mound is unique among the earthen mounds of Kentucky's Bluegrass region and challenges our concept of Woodland period mound building cultures in the Middle Ohio Valley. Indeed, the Bullock Mound should be regarded as a physical manifestation of the taxonomic conundrum with which the archaeological community must continue to contend. (2005, 62)

It is interesting that he sees this combination as the "manifestation of the taxonomic conundrum" with which archaeologists must contend. However, as I noted above, by treating Adena and Ohio Hopewell ontologically as cult sodality systems rather than as monistic modular polity communities, this presence of a typical Ohio Hopewell rectangular structure no longer represents a "taxonomic conundrum." Rather it suggests that there was a drawn-out performance of a franchising event in which the complex ritual usufruct involving the construction and use of a typical rectangular Ohio Hopewell ritual structure occurred. However, since this structure remains as the sole attribute of its type in the context of an apparently ongoing use and construction of typical Adena paired-pole circles, this suggests that, as in the above Landing Mound case, the franchise failed to become established, probably as a result of resistance from opposing factions within the Adena communal cult sodality heterarchy. Another example in which successful resistance to Ohio Hopewell ritual usufruct franchising seems to have occurred would be the maintenance of Adena practices in the Hocking Valley. There are instances of some Ohio Hopewellian attributes, such as bladelets, but in general, and despite the close proximity of the two organizations, the Adena retained strong resistance to what were likely rather strong Ohio Hopewell ritual usufruct franchising efforts (Abrams and Freter 2005, 184). In short, we can start to understand how it is that the Adena and Ohio Hopewell could persist in time to perform complex rituals in neighboring sectors of the same region.

Largely contemporaneous with these examples of Adena communal cult sodality resistance to the franchising transfer of Ohio Hopewell ritual usufructs, however, are several examples in which transfers were successful. This is how I would interpret the analyses made by Cochran (1992, 26–27, 40; 1996, 349) and McCord and Cochran (2008, 357–58) with regard to the indicators of ritual usufruct franchising carried out in east-central Indiana. With regard to the classic New Castle site, Cochran comments that it "can more accurately be classified as a multicomponent ceremonial site containing both Adena and Hopewell materials and demonstrating continuing use through time. To classify the site as a 'Hopewell Ceremonial Complex' . . . ignores the data for an equally important Adena component" (1996, 345). His summary overview of the Anderson site also highlights the rich cross-fertilization that occurred apparently between the southwestern Ohio Hopewell cult sodality heterarchies and their southeast and east-central Indiana Adena cult sodality neighbors. The Anderson Mounds site "consists of an assemblage of circular enclosures at the south end and three rectangular enclosures at the north end of the site. The two groups are about 800 m apart. The southern circular group contains one large enclosure (the Great Mound), a panduriform enclosure (Fiddleback Mound) and at least two smaller enclosures" (1996, 345). These sites would be an example of how continuity of the old practices would be sustained in one sector while the new practices would be performed in an area reserved for this purpose but still considered as part of the total locale of the responsible heterarchy. Indeed, the only comparable Adena–Hopewell interaction, one that may have surpassed the above, would be the Newark site itself, a case exemplifying successful cooperative interaction mediated by a fairly intense process of Ohio Hopewell ritual usufruct franchising.

CONCLUSION

This completes my structural analysis of the Ohio Hopewell cult sodality heterarchy system. It also completes my characterization of the range of relations between the Late Adena and Ohio Hopewell organizations. I have argued that both systems were cult sodalities largely differentiated by the former being based on a complex cooperative arrangement among mutually autonomous complex senior age-grade and junior age-grade communal cult sodalities and by the latter being based on the more structurally complex ecclesiastic-communal cult sodality type. In both cases, the social systems of which they were the sodality components were of the same order, being complementary heterarchical communities of their respective regions in the bifurcated settlement articulation modal posture. Characterizing these two earthwork/mortuary-mediated traditions in this manner and treating the two corresponding systems of communities in the same manner, as dispersed complementary heterarchical communities, highlights the potential these social formations had for interrelating and cross-fertilizing. At the same time, it is rather easy to understand why each was able to sustain continuity in the context of the other since, of course, the critical importance of material culture as symbolic pragmatic media constitutive of social lives would both impede and promote as well as color social interaction. As I have argued, it is likely that the most complex unfolding of these interrelations occurred in the upper and middle Muskingum drainage and resulted in the great Newark earthwork locale. Overall, the set of social cultural models that I have developed in this book has now prepared me to advance the hermeneutic spiral by moving to the next major step, interpreting and explaining the widespread distribution of the Hopewell assemblage as manifesting what has been termed the Hopewell Interaction Sphere. This is the next challenge that I plan to undertake.

Notes

CHAPTER 1: INTRODUCTION

1. I will maintain that while these deep complementary cultural traditions of transcendentalist cosmology and proprietorial ethos are presupposed by the Monistic Modular Polity Community model, they actually contradict the dual complementary cosmology/ethos of the known traditional historic Native North American culture, a point that the anthropology of Native North American peoples has demonstrated. I emphasize this in my counterproposal. This alone would suggest that the above model is a serious distortion of the social nature of the prehistoric communities of the Middle Woodland period of the Central Ohio Valley.

2. In my earlier publication on the Ohio Hopewell (Byers 2004) I referred to this dual structure as the dual clan/cult structure. I now wish to modify it to the dual clan/sodality structure and when treating it in cultic terms, I will refer to it as the dual clan/cult sodality structure. Of course, the notion of clan is to be understood in the general sense of kinship-based groups and sodality as any companionship-based group, as defined above; therefore, this change from the use of the term *cult* to *cult sodality* makes no basic change to my original characterization.

3. I originally spoke of this as the squatter ethos. I chose the term *squatter* because it connotes an agent who recognizes the temporary nature of land use and occupancy. However, custodianship is an important concept in my modeling of the Ohio Middle Woodland period community system and therefore I have decided to refer to it as a custodial ethos and, in fact, I could as correctly speak of its as the custodial-squatter ethos.

4. When the meaning is clear from the context, I may sometimes shorten the full descriptive term to simply saying "first-order heterarchy" or "second-order heterarchy." Clearly, these affiliations must be understood as pertaining to

mutualistic cult sodality heterarchies and these contrast with the complementary heterarchical communities. This is why I have used the nominal form "heterarchy" for the cult sodality alliance and the adjectival form "heterarchical" for the communities.

CHAPTER 2: THE DOMESTIC/CEREMONIAL DICHOTOMY

1. A similar open U-formation of the central plazas of the Inca capital of Cuzco and those of their major prehistoric predecessors has been recognized as having the same symbolic meaning, effectively presencing the sacred powers of the cosmos (Conrad and Demarest 1984, 116–121, see Cuzco plan, 117, figure 21; Moseley 1992, 137–40).

2. While Faron (1968, 24–25) notes that age-set "buddies" and "companions" were part of Mapuche life, he makes it very clear that these were always patrilineal relatives, and seniority prevailed so that the senior "buddy" was the leader and dominant over the junior buddy. Interaction between unrelated same-age/same-gender persons or groups was typically discouraged or occurred only in formal contexts through the mediation of the chiefs of the lineages to which these same-age/same-gender persons belonged. He also notes that all collective labor was organized within the lineal system and according to seniority (1964, 20; 1968, 22).

3. I consider this to be a form of custodial usufruct, albeit an exclusive form. This is because for the Mapuche, part of the rationale for their ceremonialism was to perform world renewal rituals. That is, the patrilineage recognized the obligation to care for the land they regularly used and this entailed actively undertaking the obligatory world renewal practices.

CHAPTER 3: THE TRIPARTITE CEREMONIAL ALLIANCE MODEL

1. The Ater mound site on the North Fork also figured in his model, although it is not associated with an embankment earthwork.

2. This dual patterning should not be confused with the Sacred Dual C-R motif. In this case, the patterning is simply the iteration of the Paint Creek C-R configuration while the Sacred Dual C-R motif is constituted by the proximal pairing of complementary embankment earthworks embodying the Paint Creek and High Bank C-R configurations. It would certainly be "convenient" if the High Bank C-R configuration were repeated in the same manner, the High Bank site itself and another one in the Paint Creek Valley, and a third in the North Fork. However, this is not the case. Importantly, as I note later, the Sacred Dual C-R motif is only one of possibly two variants of the Sacred Dual motif, the other being what I refer to as the Sacred Dual T-Form/C-Form motif. More on this later.

3. The exceptions were the Ater charnel house, which had only two rooms with associated mortuary residue, and Seip-Conjoined, one of the two charnel houses of the Seip site (Seip-Pricer being the other), which, although having three spaces, lacked burials in its third circular sector.

4. Typically in the archaeological literature locales that consist of aggregations of multiple burials (what I refer to as collective burial locales, see below), are specified as cemeteries and the latter are assumed to be the accumulated consequences of terminating multiple funerals of a given community. However, the terms *cemetery* and *funeral* express concepts that, while having great relevance for understanding Euro-American mortuary practices, may have much less relevance for understanding the mortuary practices of either historic or even prehistoric traditional Native North American communities. As I discuss later, I prefer using the generic term *collective burial locale* or CBL to refer to locales consisting of aggregations of human mortuary deposits and leave open more culturally specific characterizations for later interpretive clarification. Indeed, in my view, most CBLs of prehistoric Native North American communities probably are the outcome of mortuary-mediated ceremonial behaviors that are least adequately characterized as funerals and, therefore, aggregations of mortuary deposits cannot be reductively characterized as cemeteries.

5. This was the same conclusion I made with regard to Greber's ranked group thesis (Byers 2004, 289–91).

CHAPTER 4: THE NATURE OF OHIO HOPEWELL MORTUARY CEREMONIALISM

1. Of course empirical generalizations of this sort are simply correlations disguised as causal mechanisms. What should always be asked is what is the social mechanism that causes the patterned correlation and is it possible that there could be different mechanisms causing the same patternings? That is, the Euro-American mortuary patterning is the result of both mortuary ideology and political structures while Native North American mortuary patternings may have quite different ideological and social causes and, therefore, actually be the conditions of satisfaction of a host of mortuary actions that simply do not exist in the Euro-American mortuary sphere.

2. I am also pleased to see that James Brown has started to question the funerary paradigm and he is doing so in a manner very close to my own approach, namely, that mortuary behaviors can be different forms of sacrificial activities (2006, 204–9). He likes to refer to them as performances and I have no problem with this term—as long as we do not identify it with the notion of a theatrical performance. In Euro-American practice, the theater is where facsimiles of real events are carried out, whether these are fictional or historical. In Native North American communities, the mortuary performances, even when "mimicking" well-known mythical events, such as the great battles of the Above World and Beneath World gods, are not facsimile performances in this sense. Rather, they are humanly produced re-creations by which the community takes itself to be participating in these great world creation and re-creations. Their rituals are real-world renewal events—at least that is my claim and shortly I develop the symbolic theory to elucidate this view.

3. In fact, some of the steps I outlined actually are some of the important steps of the traditional historic Hidatsa mortuary process as outlined by Alfred

Bowers (1965, 75–76). I will return to the Hidatsa traditions later for analogical support of the notion that traditional Native North American mortuary spheres incorporated strong elements of various renewal rituals, in particular, world renewal ceremonialism.

4. Postmortem human sacrifice means, of course, a sacrifice that occurs *after* death so that, in this case, the mode of death does not figure in as part of the condition of satisfaction of the sacrificial intention. The person died "naturally" and then, following the initial spirit-release rites, the deceased is recruited to serve as sacrificial offerings of different types. This means that postmortem human sacrifice differs significantly from lethal human sacrifice in that in the latter case the mode of death is part of the condition of satisfaction of the sacrificial intention. While I focus on characterizing Ohio Hopewell mortuary practices as particularly postmortem sacrifices, I do not deny that some lethal human sacrifice could also be among the instituted forms of world renewal sacrifice; although I suspect that if this were the case it would be a severely limited practice.

5. I emphasize this mixing in order to note my earlier cautionary remark about the problematic nature of the "universal generalization" or "mortuary law" that Peebles asserted, namely, that the "crucial assumption which links burials with social organization is that individuals who are treated differentially in life will also be treated differentially in death," and that this treatment "will carry on into his burial and, in most societies, beyond" (1974, 38). Clearly, the Huron were equal opportunity communities since this mixing process ensured that all the deceased, no matter what their status in life, would be equitably treated. Of course, this also suggests that this treatment cannot be characterized in funerary terms.

6. Heidenreich (1978, 375) notes that the recently deceased were also part of the Feast of the Dead. In this case, their bodies were left intact and they were neatly laid on the base of the ossuary pit. The bundles of cleaned bones were then deposited over them and the total set of bones was mixed.

7. It is likely that the young men chosen for this task would have been selected because they were "boon companions" of the deceased or sons of the "boon companions" of these deceased, although Trigger (1969, 103–5; 1976, 52) does not make any comment in this regard. However, the fact that the parents of the deceased chose those who undertook the task suggests that it was performed by non-kin or by those kin who, in addition to their kinship, were recognized as having a special non-kinship-based relation with the deceased, that is, being boon companions or related to boon companions. The importance of boon companions in myths and mortuary practices has been noted by Robert Hall, although he often uses the term "fictive kin" (1997, 42, 61–62, 65, 80, 94, 149–50). In my view, treating these as companions is much closer to the real nature of these relations, as I discuss in considerable detail in a subsequent chapter.

8. In fact, Heidenreich makes the postmortem sacrificial practice of the Huron quite specific noting that the Huron periodically used a deceased human as a postmortem

sacrificial offering to the sky-world deity. "Feasts were given in [the Sky Oki's] honor, tobacco and on occasion the body of a dead man was burned as a sacrifice" (Heidenreich 1978, 372).

9. Concerning the reliance Carr has on treating mortuary rites as mechanism to enhance social integration, I think it should be noted that, according to Heidenreich (1978, 378), the village did not simply leave the immediate area following the Feast of the Dead; it also often bifurcated, each part reestablishing itself spatially separate from the other. It is almost as if, despite internal stresses, solidarity of the village was deliberately maintained for eight to twelve years until the Feast of the Dead could be performed. If so, this would suggest that the collective duty to the deceased and to the land motivated suppressing any tendencies to village fissioning until sufficient numbers of deceased had been accumulated, along with help from neighbors, to carry out the Feast of the Dead world renewal ceremony. Importantly, it is also notable that rather than this ritual being performed with sadness for the deceased, or reluctance, given the likelihood that the village would split, it was performed with joyfulness, probably expressing a combination of having fulfilled their sacred duties both to the land and to the dead. Such joyfulness also hints that the ceremony was experienced as finally enabling the community to split into two separate villages, thereby eliminating internal tensions that had built up and avoiding the most serious of all crimes for the Huron, the murder of one villager by another! None of this suggests that mortuary practices were performed to enhance actual social integration.

CHAPTER 5: THE SYMBOLIC MEANING OF MATERIAL CULTURE

1. This objectifying of the abstractions of material symbols, constituting them as icons, can also apply to word symbols. However, it does not mean that the reified words, such as the sacred names of gods, can be used to make reference to the gods in the same way as using words to refer to unreified independent objects. Typically, there are always heavy restrictions of a normative kind that operate on these word icons, for example, taboos against uttering the "sacred" terms of "god," and when they are uttered it is taken to actually presence the god or one of its powerful properties to the detriment of the well-being of the "sinful" speaker; for example, it is assumed that this person will be struck down with disease or some other catastrophe brought on by this unwarranted referential use of the iconic word. Of course, at the same time, typically those warranted to use the material symbols of the god are also warranted to use "his or her" sacred name, However, again, this usage is taken to be invocative, as calling on and addressing rather than referring to the god(s). Hence, the essential expressivity of abstract symbols even transforms their referential usage into a type of everted expressivity in the sense that the uttering of the words is actually taken to presence the objectified abstraction.

2. Terms of address are probably better characterized in expressive than referential terms since addressing a person entails expressing the intention to do so. In this

case, it is by using the term *sheriff* in the presence of the actual sheriff that I express my intention to communicate with this person as the sheriff and not, for example, as the man for whom I voted to be sheriff or the man who happens to be my backdoor neighbor.

3. For those who may be concerned that I am denigrating reference as an important part of speech communication, let me say that it is critical. For example, it is imperative in making a promise to express one's intent. However, promising by way of expressing an intention always entails specifying, that is, referring to what course of action the speaker intends to follow to fulfill the promise. This aspect of the speech is propositional meaning and in expressing the proposition I am making reference to a future action of my own. For example, I promise to X (and "to X" could be quite elaborate, for example, to meet you downtown tomorrow at the corner of Main and Sweet at such and such a time). So speech acts usually entail both expressing and referencing. However, I am claiming that while words are used both expressively and referentially, material symbols are usually used only to express the abstract properties and social powers that transform the behaviors into the intended actions.

4. In fact, a number of archaeologists claim that mica and small residues of copper and other esoteric materials are not unusually found in domestic hamlets, along with multiple bladelets. However, another way of thinking about this distribution is to ask whether these locales are kinship-based domestic habitation sites at all, despite some "domestic" residue. Instead, they may be cult sodality locales. This raises a difficult problem of how to identify "domestic hamlets" as opposed to specialized sodality locales that were transiently occupied by groups of companions preparing for rituals to be held in their cult sodality locales. I will address this very important question later.

5. To preclude confusion, when I speak of collective beliefs (cosmology) or collective values (ethos) as shared beliefs and values, I am not claiming that my belief X and your belief X are in some sense one "joined" mental state. Rather, I am making a distinction between beliefs as actual intentional states (thoughts) and beliefs as ideas. The "idea" is what Searle refers to as the representational contents of a belief. Collective beliefs are ideas that are held by a people, and part of a collective belief includes the idea that "everyone knows this." Hence, my beliefs as mental or intentional states are mine and yours are yours; but we can share the ideas that are the representational contents of these beliefs. These shared contents plus the idea that "everyone has this idea" constitutes a collective belief (Archer 2007, 24–26).

6. What is immediately clear here is that my above discussion of symbolic pragmatic meaning of material cultural items ties in very nicely with this notion of intentionality. This is not surprising, of course, since Searle has used his theory of intentionality to address speech actions as intrinsically meaningful forms of communicative behaviors by which we constitute our behaviors as social actions. S(r) applies to speech acts in parallel to forms of intentionality. Promises express intentions, assertions express beliefs, and directives or commands express wants.

CHAPTER 6: THE ECCLESIASTIC-COMMUNAL CULT SODALITY MODEL

1. It is notable that Alford had to rely figuratively on the English term *kinship* to characterize the emotional state that participation in the name group afforded its members. This is probably because we have no social grouping in the modern Anglo-American social structure and cultural traditions that fully captures the nature of the name group. The terms *friend*, *companion*, and *pal* are all used in English to specify personal relations and not social groups having community tasks to perform, namely, sodalities. The latter term, of course, is "manufactured" by anthropologists in order to refer to important groups that are bound by deontic structures unrelated to those of kinship. In Old English these were often referred to as one's "kith" in contrast to one's "kin." However, by Alford's time the term *kith* had dropped out of common use in Anglo-American culture and so he had to use the kinship term figuratively. Its figurative use is clearly indicated by his combining "kinship," "intimacy," and "fellowship" in his description of the name group as thereby enabling "a kind of fellowship which afforded much merriment and innocent fun among both old and young." This is clearly a figurative combination to express the emotional state since we know that kin relations of the 19th and early 20th centuries, particularly the "Victorian"-type family, were far from "intimate" or "innocent."

2. I will present more detail on how an ecclesiastic-communal cult sodality might emerge from a set of preexisting shamanic and age-set sodality cults when I discuss the known social structure of the historic Hidatsa and Mandan communities of the Plains in the next chapter. Most importantly, however, this modeling presumes that the initial settlement state was an integrated posture. In fact, this is likely not the case for the Ohio Hopewell since it emerged out of the preexisting Adena complex, which was itself the manifestation of a bifurcated posture. This means that a modification of this model will be needed and I do this later when I address the Adena–Hopewell relation.

3. The junior and senior age-grade sectors would probably each be internally structured by age-sets. An age-set is a group of companions of the same age range such that the age difference between the youngest and the oldest of a given group would be no more than four to five years. If a generation is estimated as 25 years, then each age-grade would consist of about four to five age-sets organized hierarchically by age seniority and the set of tasks and prerogatives traditionally performed by the age-grade would be distributed across the age-sets, again in terms of the traditional rules and standards according to relative age (see Byers 2006a, 122–32, for greater detail).

4. By "posture" I mean the group collectively forefronts the relevant aspect of their social identity that constitutes them as a religious group, namely, as a communal cult. It does this by exercising the representational contents of its ideological strategy by which to achieve its religiously defined purposes. These contents consist of the rules and protocols that define the timing, gathering, and interacting of the sodality participants along with their displaying the range of material warranting symbols

necessary to transform their interactive behavioral streams into the type of rituals by which to achieve the collective purpose, and so on. When the collective task is completed the group shifts out of its communal cult religious posture and takes on its "everyday" posture. This would see some of the age-sets disperse as members returned to their respective kin lodges; other age-sets remain behind to store equipment, repair, and clean up; other age-sets going out to hunt or gather food for a planned follow-up feast the next day; and so on.

5. This is not always the case, since intervening factors could operate that discouraged the formation of companionship-based sodalities at all, as I discussed earlier with regard to the Mapuche.

6. I noted earlier that not all deceased would need to be full members of the sodality. The deceased children or spouses of surviving members could be incorporated into the mortuary record since the treatment they would receive would count as living soul release rites, that is, later stages of the postmortem sacrificial process. The earlier stages would have ensured the release of their personal souls and any name souls that belonged to clans would be reincarnated when endowed on newborns of the clan. Interestingly, the vastly greatest proportion of burials is adult in any case. Of course, the paucity of infants has been a puzzle for many archaeologists and the reason for this puzzlement is that the funerary view assumes the monistic or unitary community view. Hence, all demographic components of the community ought to be proportionally represented. However, when this same mortuary record is perceived in sodality terms, we would expect an underrepresentation of infants and children as many of these would probably be retained under the mortuary responsibility of their kin groups.

7. In his 1909 report Mills referred to the mound he excavated as the Seip mound. Following Greber's (1976, 1979) practice, I refer to it in this book as the Seip-Conjoined mound. As I note shortly, its immediate neighbor, the Seip-Pricer mound, was excavated and reported on some years later by Shetrone and Greenman (1931, 343–509).

8. I will also argue that, in fact, the historical base of this cult sodality heterarchy was likely an early Mound City–Tremper complex and out of this emerged the larger third-order Chillicothe-Newark cult sodality heterarchy.

CHAPTER 7: THE HIDATSA AGE-SET SYSTEM AND THE RITUAL USUFRUCT CONVEYANCING AND FRANCHISING MODEL

1. A number of archaeologists have recently collaborated through collections of articles to develop Hall's insights (Reilly and Garber, eds. 2007; King, ed. 2007). They have recognized the iconography of the Mississippian artifactual assemblage in which this maskette figures centrally as originating in the American Bottom region, particularly. James Brown (2007b, 57–58) refers to this iconography as the Generalized Braden style and agrees with Hall that the Long Nosed God maskette

probably depicts the Red Horn god among the Winnebago and other peoples; it is also referred to as Morning Star among the Pawnee, Osage, Omaha, and so on. He specifically argues that out of this Generalized Braden style (ca cal A.D. 900 to ca A.D. 1200) emerged the Classic Braden, ca cal A.D. 1200 to ca A.D. 1300; and finally the Late Braden, ca cal A.D. 1300 to about A.D. 1400/1450 (Brown 2007c, 243). In effect, the Red Horn and different culture hero-god variants form an important component of the Mississippian assemblage, generally referred to as the Southeastern Ceremonial Complex (SECC).

2. I stress here that "most archaeologists" assume that the Hopewellian and Mississippian communities were of different orders in that the latter were dominance based and the former were not. In fact, I believe that they were largely similar types of social orders, both being constituted as non-dominance-based systems. However, arguing this point needs to be left for another book.

3. More accurately stated, Hidatsa persons relating as *irakúu* were explicitly not relating as kin, even though, given the type of face-to-face villages the Hidatsa had, it is likely that every person could relate to every other in more than one kinship position. This is a point that Bowers also stresses (1965, 71). This simply reinforces the notion that the kinship and companionship groups were relatively autonomous and special steps would likely have been taken to ensure that the proper etiquette was followed. Wearing particular symbols would probably serve to assist here so that two or more persons relating and interacting as companions could bring this relation to the fore and constitute their mutual standing by the particular action cue costuming they wore. As we say, they wore the "right hats," and even brothers who were in mutually autonomous senior and junior age-sets but were attending to joint rituals would probably assume the proper conduct as symbolically evoked and cued by the "hats" they were wearing. That is, they would likely carefully eschew the kinship posture.

4. Hall does not ignore the companionship relation but he seems to limit it to a warfare vengeance ritual. Among the Iowa and Fox, for example, the favored adoptee is a close or boon companion of a young man killed in war. In being adopted by the dead man's parents, the boon companion also takes on the obligation to kill an enemy in order to revenge the death of his deceased boon companion/adopted brother (Hall 1997, 42).

5. While these males would relate agnatically through having fathers of the same matriclan, since their clan affiliation is determined by their mothers they would not be in the same matriclans. Also, if they had immediate brothers through the same mother, their cognatic brothers, these would be in a different age-set, either senior or junior, depending on the order of birth.

6. While the senior-to-junior age-set conveyancing is a "one-shot deal," there are examples where serial conveyancing can occur. When the ritual usufruct is the custodial copyright of an individual, such as a shaman or a specialist artisan, the latter can usually retain personal custodial usage while transferring the copyright

usufruct on usually four of five separate occasions to four or five separate "apprentices." After that, the shaman or artisan recognizes that while she or he still possesses the knowledge and know-how, she or he no longer has any sacred performative powers so that even if they were to exercise and perform the ritual usufruct in the normal way, this would be ineffective. This applies to the artisan also. Even if the "decommissioned" war shield artisan made a shield in the normal way, it would not protect its user; that is, it would not count as a real war shield.

7. While Bowers speaks of this transferring of ritual rights in terms of "buying and selling," in my view, it is more appropriate to speak of the material exchanges that mediated the transfer as reciprocal gift exchange and I will use terms emphasizing this gifting. This is particularly the case because the types of rights and prerogatives that are being transferred are not proprietorial but custodial.

CHAPTER 9: THE MURPHY TRACT: THE EMPIRICAL GROUNDING OF THE CULT SODALITY CLUSTER MODEL

1. It is notable that these distal sites are assumed to be related more to the hamlets than to the ceremonial locales, even though the latter would include specialized camps used to procure exotic materials, such as Flint Ridge chert, and so on. In a sense, both the distal logistical sites and the earthwork sites could be subsumed to the same category, differentiated simply by ceremonial and nonceremonial functions. This is because, under the monistic modular polity view, the clusters of dispersed hamlets constitute the core of the community and the earthworks and the distal locales are simply specialized functional sites subsumed to this residential core of the community.

2. His purpose here was in order to marshal data against the claim by Frank Cowan (2006) that Ohio Hopewell communities were based on seasonal mobility (in contrast to the basic premise of the Hamlet Hypothesis that these were part of dispersed fully sedentary communities that used logistical task group mobility). His particular purpose is not immediately relevant here since it is the quantitative data themselves that are important in grounding my alternative, namely, that these were not hamlets associated with short-term task areas but age-grade and age-set locales.

3. Pacheco (1993) produces specific lithic distribution plans of Murphy III (155–56, figures 17 and 18), Murphy V (158–59, figures 19 and 20), and Murphy VI (162–64, figures 22, 23, and 24). There is no equivalent for Murphy I and Murphy IV. However, he does provide a series of 4 × 4 m unit plans of the South Block, indicating effectively Murphy IV and Clusters 1 and 2 (168–73, figures 25, 26, 27, 28, 29, and 30).

CHAPTER 10: THE SACRED GAMES *TOURNÉE* OF THE OHIO HOPEWELL CULT SODALITY HETERARCHY SYSTEM

1. Of course, making these changes could be used by skeptics to argue against the validity of the hermeneutic spiral method itself. After all, this simply proves that we

cannot operate at such abstract levels to reconstruct the social system. My response, of course, is to point out that this is precisely the strength of the method. By noting that no model is "God's truth" but simply the best we can postulate and reasonably demonstrate at this time with the current knowledge resources and empirical data through critical comparative explanation, the process enhances our knowledge through self-critique.

2. However, it is not simply that these two complementary C-R motif configurations represented, embodied, and manifested the totality of the cosmos. They may have been intended to emphasize a particular aspect of the cosmos, possibly the Above World and Beneath World strata that were particular or "home" to the Sun and Moon, the solar and lunar bodies whose movements constituted the cycling of the creative energies of a certain aspect of the cosmos. This point I will explore in more detail in a later chapter, particularly focusing on Newark as possibly the primary exemplification of this notion.

3. I want to qualify this statement by leaving open the possibility that, at least in the central region of Ohio, many individual autonomous cult sodalities may have constructed very small geometrical embankment earthworks that are invisible to normal observation techniques as a result of the massive modification to the landscape that has occurred with the expansion of the American settlement with its modern farming and industrial methods. Jarrod Burks reported at the 2010 Society of American Archaeology's 75th annual meeting that his careful geomagnetic and ground penetrating surveys of a number of separate valley zones revealed in each case anomalous geometrical formal patterns that were not observable with visual inspection. He admits that verification of these anomalies as small embankment earthworks still awaits. But if he is right, then these forms will have to be incorporated into our models of the Ohio Middle Woodland period settlement system. I look forward to the publication of such work hopefully in the near future.

4. However, mortuary deposits at the ceremonial nodal local would not be prohibited and I believe that the two burials at the Jennison Guard site might indicate that there was a nearby ceremonial nodal locale site that has been overlooked. There are other examples I will raise later. Clearly, with much of the mortuary-oriented archaeological attention having been focused on the main earthwork sites, we have to remain very open to the possibility of such depository behaviors in other sodality locales.

5. Later I qualify this claim by suggesting that another, possibly secondary bridge connected through the upper Great and Little Miami drainages to the upper Muskingum via the upper Scioto drainage. N'omi Greber (2006, 103) has noted an extensive network of historically known Native North American trails that linked the upper Scioto to both northern and southern sectors of Ohio. Therefore, there is relatively easy access between the head waters of upper Muskingum, Scioto, and the Great and Little Miamis. If this network is interpreted as having deep historical roots (and given the Hopewellian assemblage demarcating significant intra- and

interregional Middle Woodland period travel, this seems to be a reasonable assumption), then it is quite possible that there was an early linkage between the cult sodalities via the headwaters of the Miamis and the upper Muskingum and that this likely connected with Newark on the Licking River. However, I think the trail connecting the lower Miamis and the central Scioto drainages via the North Fork–Paint Creek interface mediated the more intensive level of interaction in the early Middle Woodland period and may have largely displaced the more northern interdrainage trail with the construction of High Bank, Seip, and Liberty Works, as I discuss in the closing chapters.

6. This association of custodial artifacts with the sacred gods immanent in the cosmos is figuratively expressed in the characterization that many historic Native North American peoples give of raw materials from which these artifacts were produced. For example, native copper nuggets are often treated as the cast-off parts of the skin of the Underworld God, the Horned Serpent, and the copper nuggets mined from the Keweenan Peninsula of Michigan and the islands of Lake Superior were treated as gifts from this god. "The metaphorical conception is that the Great Serpent bestows power as gifts of his own body. The three major forms the gifts take are horns, bones, and scales (which were considered manifest in the Middle World as shells or copper)" (Lankford 2007a, 119; also 2007c, 28).

CHAPTER 11: THE NORTH FORK–PAINT CREEK INTERFACE ZONE AND THE TERMINAL CONVEYANCING OF CUSTODIAL REGALIA

1. Later I suggest that the initial Chillicothe-based third-order cult sodality heterarchy of which the Mound City/Hopeton complex was a major component included Tremper and shortly following the abandonment of the complex and its replacement by Seip, Liberty Works, and High Banks during the middle of the Middle Woodland period, Newark was incorporated into this third-order heterarchy, possibly constituting the Chillicothe-Newark heterarchy. Although Tremper was probably also abandoned when the Mound City/Hopeton complex was abandoned, it is possible that the original heterarchy maintained a presence in the Portsmouth zone just south of Tremper, as I discuss later.

2. The validity of this chronological sequence claim hinges on the earlier discussion I made about the initial transformation of the Hopewell C-Form into a variant Paint Creek C-R motif configuration with the addition of the "nominal" C-R components, followed by the adoption of the standard expression of this motif at Frankfort. The former, I argued, was an expedient means of "fitting into" the region where the Paint Creek C-R motif configuration was "born." The emergence of Frankfort, I suggested, recognized the validity of this configuration and actually replaced the older C-Form mode. I also suggest that the Chillicothe influence on the Little Miami Valley Ohio Hopewell heterarchies was probably mediated through the Hopewell site as versions of the Paint Creek C-R motif configuration started to appear in this southwestern sector, as I note later. I have also noted that Mound 23 is actually

located between the small circle to its west and the small Paint Creek square attached to the eastern embankment of the C-Form. This places it in a relative C-R position equivalent to Seip-Pricer and Seip-Conjoined at the Seip site. Of course, the validity of this claim can be further tested by radiocarbon dating, when the requisite samples are found.

CHAPTER 12: THE OHIO HOPEWELL AS DISPERSED THIRD-ORDER CULT SODALITY HETERARCHIES

1. Of course, this tendency for exposed native copper items to deteriorate more quickly when not handled and directly cared for on an everyday basis is only a hypothesis and it certainly could be tested experimentally. I think that it would be worthwhile doing so. Until that time, however, the important point is that interpreting the megadeposit in these terms explains an important aspect of the material assemblage that was not explained by the funerary-referential perspective.

2. I am perfectly aware that Turner had respectable artifact deposits in terms of variety and size and that, in many ways, they replicated those at the Hopewell site, being burnt deposits. However, as noted by Greber in the above quotation, the contents could be counted in only the tens and hundreds while at the Hopewell site equivalent materials were counted in the hundreds and thousands. Also, it was those categories of artifacts that were superfluous at Hopewell while effectively absent at Turner (i.e., copper plates and celts) that mark a particularly important difference. Recognizing this difference is just as important as recognizing that, setting Turner aside for the moment (I address its content in detail shortly), the rest of the Hopewellian artifactual assemblage content of the Little Miami Valley earthworks is miniscule.

3. In fact, we now know of a Hopewellian mortuary mound west of Turner that is much richer in Hopewellian artifactual content than Turner and, in fact, it rivals or possibly even surpasses Mound 25 in the Hopewell site. This is the Mount Vernon mound, also called the General Electric (G.E.) mound, near the mouth of the Wabash River in Posy County, Indiana. In overall size this mound is effectively equivalent to Mound 25. Unfortunately, very little is known of the internal features, facilities, and artifactual assemblage and their overall organization since it was very badly damaged by looters, almost destroyed (Tomak 1994, 9; Seeman 1995, 129–30). However, experience has shown that despite the best efforts of looters the foundations of such major architecture are usually in very good order and careful excavation can recover very important data. This major site is also only a few kilometers west of the Mann site, probably the largest Hopewell embankment earthwork site outside Ohio. There are so many known parallels between the better known contents of Mound 25 and the residual artifactual assemblage we have of the Mount Vernon mound that I am tempted to argue that it served the same broad range of purposes as did the Hopewell site, particularly being a locale of multiple terminal conveyancing rites. If this is the case, then it also entails a contemporaneous existence of another dispersed third-order cult sodality heterarchy

primarily located in south-central, southwestern, and possibly southeastern Indiana. When I look at the interregional unfolding of the Hopewell episode in another book, I may explore this possibility.

4. Again the term “K-Profile” is straightforward in sense. If an embankment is constructed without a contiguous ditch on either side, the fill would have been the result of surface scraping or borrow ditching. If a K-Profile embankment was cut through from one side to the other, it would generate a cone-shaped or conical profile. I had already used the “C” in C-Form so I chose to render it phonically as the K-Profile. As I noted, since this attribute is found as part of the embankment forms added to preexisting SL-Form or SR-Form embankments, I concluded that it was a chronologically later attribute. This is why I consider the High Bank C-R and Paint Creek C-R configuration sites as middle Ohio Hopewellian in time, following and built from the earlier SL-Profile and SR-Profile earthwork sites (Byers 1987, 2004). I have no problem using formal earthwork attributes as the basis for relative dating since such constructions are public and are the result of deploying ideological strategies that have strong public commitment. Therefore, changing the formal properties would be a rather rare occurrence and, in itself, an important chronological and social systems constitutive marker. The Ohio Hopewell earthworks are particularly useful in this way because of their formal patterns.

5. In fact, it is interesting that the only stone-lined pit at the Hopewell site is on the floor of Mound 2 and this mound also covers the megadeposit of Wyandotte chert disks that I commented upon above and about which I will have more to say later. This association of the stone-lined feature and Wyandotte chert with the similar features at Turner and, of course, the large debitage collection of both Wyandotte and Flint Ridge chert at the Turner Workshop site reinforces this argument of the social relation of the Hopewell and Turner sites.

6. As I noted earlier, the prevailing laying-in crypt at the Hopewell site was the vaulted chamber built of timber. Clearly, as a laying-in crypt the symbolic pragmatic meaning of this feature was different from the symbolic pragmatic meaning of the stone-lined crypts that dominated the Turner Burial Place. Indeed, the use of timber at the Hopewell site and stone at the Turner site may have been deliberate in that it constituted what were formally very similar mortuary *behaviors* at the two sites into two different types of mortuary *rituals* with the intention being that deceased in the crypts at the Hopewell site be returned to the Turner site. As I noted earlier, there was one stone-lined crypt at the Hopewell site and it was on the floor of Mound 2, which also contained the megadeposit of Wyandotte chert blanks that I analyze in greater detail later.

CHAPTER 13: THE DEVELOPMENT OF THE OHIO HOPEWELL CULT SODALITY HETERARCHY SYSTEM

1. As I fully commented earlier, part of the confusion arising from extending such terms as *Adena* or even *Ohio Hopewell* is the operating assumption that these

terms delineate cultures defined in the traditional kinship-based community sense and, therefore, identifying the somewhat disparate distribution of the "defining" characteristics of these "cultures" induces confusion. Is this site that displays half of the key Adena attributes the expression of a real Adena community? What about the few Ohio Hopewellian traits that it also has? Does this make it a "mongrel" community, neither Adena nor Ohio Hopewell? Treating these attributes as the symbolic pragmatic media manifesting specific ritual usufructs by which autonomous cult sodality organizations are enabled to perform core ritual practices makes understanding the distribution of these attributes rather easier since no cult sodality necessarily must commit to the same range of rituals as its more distant cult sodality neighbors.

2. It has been commented by some colleagues that I have claimed that the set of walls, that I have formally termed the aggregation element, actually points at Mound City on the opposite side. This is not correct. As I put it, "Hopeton has a long aggregation element at the point where the Hopeton Circle and Rectilinear are conjoined. The southwest end of this aggregation element leads to the bank overlooking the Scioto River. If the aggregation element were extended straight across the Scioto River and at this angle, it would terminate at the base of a walkway that extends from the riverbank to the eastern 'gate' of the . . . embankment of the Mound City Cluster" (Byers 2004, 48). However, I will also note that in my dissertation, the way I expressed the same idea could be construed as my saying that the full aggregation element was pointed at the Mound City embankment earthwork (Byers 1987, 215). This is clearly not the case.

3. Much of the recent surveying and excavating work carried out at the Hopeton site by Mark Lynott and his colleagues (Lynott 2009) seems to confirm the overall chronological order of the building of the Hopeton Circle and Rectilinear that I have outlined. Lynott and Mandel (2009, 171) present a suite of radiocarbon dates derived from the various sources found at the base and in the embankments of the Hopeton Square that bracket the construction at A.D. 150–250, and agree with the dates that Bret Ruby derived in earlier research. This certainly is minimally within my own, stylistic-based estimate of ca A.D. 150 for the emergence of the Mound City/Hopeton complex (Byers 2004, 535, table 22.1). I have suggested that the fully developed geometrically "accurate" Paint Creek and High Bank C-R configurations evolved from this initial complex. This would suggest that the High Bank configuration would have emerged about A.D. 200 and the Paint Creek configuration a short time later, possibly only a few years or one or two decades later, about A.D. 210–220. My reasons to suggest this quick progression are presented later.

4. By definition, there is no infix linking the C-R of the High Bank C-R motif. Rather, there is the rather short aggregation neck. In a sense this means that the Middle World is not represented in the High Bank C-R motif. On the other hand, since this is also the Lunar motif, it could be argued that the narrow and rather short

aggregation neck actually does represent the Middle World in its lunar or nighttime phase, a time when human activity is not properly undertaken and, therefore, the Middle World is only nominally represented in the configuration, its main purpose being to represent the basic triple stratification of the cosmos: Above World, Middle World, and Beneath World.

5. Mills (1916, 285–86) insists that this was not a "burnt offering." He admits that there were many bone and wood items that showed burning and that all the pipes as well as copper and stone items were broken and showed some apparent burning, but the total deposit was not subjected to burning. He is equally skeptical that the large deposit of platform pipes and associated items on the floor and beside a well-used burnt basin of Mound 8 at Mound City was itself burned, although he also admits that he never examined the pipes that were derived from that deposit. Finally, he also notes that there was a second deposit of nine effigy platform and tubular pipes at Tremper. However, none of these were broken and they apparently were carefully placed as an offering on the surface of the earth mantle during the construction of the Tremper Renewal Lodge mound. A similar pattern of offering deposits placed while the mounds were being constructed was found at Mound City and, of course, this placement is also akin to that of the Great Copper Deposit of Mound 25.

6. While the nonlocal source of many of these pipes is now evident, it was surprising to learn, given that the Feurt quarries are so near to Tremper and Mound City. However, discovering that the pipes or at least the pipestone raw material was derived from distant places is quite consistent with the Ohio Hopewell artifact assemblage being of nonlocal resources, such as native copper, silver, mica, obsidian, and so on. What is particularly intriguing in the case of the two deposits at Mound City and Tremper is the differential makeup of their respective platform pipe content—both local and nonlocal—and the distribution between these two sites closely reflecting this division, that is, the majority of the Tremper pipes being derived from Illinoisian quarries while the majority of the Mound City pipes being derived from local quarries (Emerson et al. 2008, 7). Whether this marks temporal variation or ritual variation is an opportunity for future research on the nature of the interregional exchange that underwrote and was generated by regional social systems experiencing and generating Hopewell episodes and will not be pursued here.

7. Only at Mound City did it become clear that deliberate destruction of a set of artifacts was avoided, what I have termed the custodial regalia, and I was able to reconstruct this avoidance because destruction by burning applied equally to both humans and artifacts, the only exception being these unusual artifacts I have termed custodial regalia. When I interpreted the Hopewell data, even in the absence of large-scale human cremation, it became clear that a similar avoidance rule was being applied to the custodial regalia since none of these appear in the two burnt deposits although all of the categories that do appear there are also prolifically represented in the extended burials alongside the custodial regalia artifacts.

8. As I noted earlier, unlike the mortuary complex at the base of Mound 25, which was given a single truncation ritual after possibly two generations of usage, about 50 years, the renewal lodges were truncated individually and probably used for a briefer period, 20 or 25 years. The copper regalia were generally in good condition and, therefore, may not have been curated at all. Rather, the completion of the conveyancing rite entailed constructing a primary mound over the deposit, which was typically focused on the regalia itself, as I noted earlier, while the cremated human remains were scattered over or carefully place on them, suggesting the latter were sacrificially accompanying the regalia. This might also explain why most of the renewal lodges had several such deposits with low primary mounds. Each marked a conveyancing transfer of ritual usufruct carried out within that first-order heterarchy. This more immediate process would explain the good condition of these deposits since they were not exposed to conditions that would tend to deteriorate them.

CHAPTER 14: EMBANKMENT EARTHWORK AND WAY STATION FACILITIES

1. I describe Cahokia as a world renewal cult sodality heterarchy, in fact a third-order heterarchy, because I have interpreted Cahokia in the same terms that I have applied to Ohio Hopewell. The orthodox interpretation of Cahokia is that it is the capital seat of some type of centralized polity based on a dominance hierarchy, for example, a chiefdom society (Emerson 1997a, 1997b, 1997c; Milner 1998, 2003; Muller 1997; Pauketat 1993, 1994, 1997, 2000, 2004, 2005, 2007). Many Mississippian archaeologists interpret it as a paramount chiefdom, some as a "primitive" city, and so on. I interpret it as probably a *nucleated* third-order cult sodality heterarchy. I think of it as "nucleated" in the sense that, unlike the dispersed nature of the Fort Ancient–Turner–Hopewell third-order cult sodality heterarchy incorporating communities along the middle and lower Little Miami and over to the North Fork of the Paint Creek in the Scioto drainage, Cahokia as a cult sodality heterarchy was more spatially centralized including the large multiple-mound sites of St. Louis and East St. Louis, which bracketed the west and east banks of the Mississippi where the Cahokia Creek entered it, and the 102-plus mounds of Cahokia proper. All these platform and burial mounds with their plazas, woodhenges, and timber structures were incorporated into a rather small zone of the northern American bottom, stretching east to west and across the Mississippi about 30 km and north–south only a few kilometers on either side of the Cahokia Creek.

2. For example, the Cheyenne considered trees as embodying the axis mundi by which the different strata of the cosmos were maintained in their order. Indeed, the different structural parts of trees both delineated and held the world strata in place. The tree roots interlace and anchor the middle and deep earth strata and the branches reach up to upper strata of the Above World (Schlesier 1987, 6–7).

CHAPTER 15: THE STRUCTURING OF OHIO HOPEWELL SITES AND PATHWAYS

1. Ingold has theorized the perceptual experience characteristic of foraging peoples, noting that, in virtue of their immanentist cosmology and custodial-squatter ethos, they perceive the use of paths for access to resources as much a religious as a technical-subsistence activity. "From their point of view both moral and physical movement, the religious journey and the economic quest for food, are part of the same process: namely, living" (1987, 153).

2. Mark Seeman is certainly implicating this symbolic pragmatic perspective when he speaks of Hopewellian items as serving to express a particular ideological structure that was widely shared. However, his tendency to treat material symbols as descriptive rather than constitutive devices, as referring to beliefs rather than as constituting actions, limits the impact his insight has on interpreting the Hopewell material culture and its distribution.

> The circulation of distinctive Hopewell valuables no doubt functioned to maintain cooperative and competitive social relations; however, it is important to emphasize that these artifacts were also and fundamentally symbols, and their variety suggests the conveyance of multiple meanings. A major context across much of eastern North America for the validation of these beliefs was the public mortuary ritual. A need for systemic "redundancy" in interregional transactions does not capture the essential character of Hopewell as symbolic system(s). (1995, 123–24)

3. In his earlier book, *Primitive Man in Ohio*, Moorehead reports that the clusters of disks consisted of about 12 to 15 each (1892, 190). This book was published about the same time that he was supervising the excavation of Mound 25 and, therefore, he would have had these data fresh in his mind. It was in this book that he also reported that each set of disks was covered by a separate sand deposit. However, 30 years later, he relied on a report by Dr. Thomas Wilson of the Smithsonian with whom he was working on Mound 2 in the 1890s. Wilson commented in his report that the deposits making up these two strata consisted of about "a half dozen, more or less, in each pile, or handful and were arranged after the fashion of herringbone masonry" (1922, 95–96). No comment was made about depositing sand over each. While I am arguing that each deposit identifies the number of groups that were participating, the discrepancy between "a half dozen" and a dozen disks per group does not make the overall number of second-order heterarchies different.

4. I suggest qualifying her modular polity approach as mitigated because, as noted later, she seems to recognize some of the problematic nature of wedding exclusive territories with monumental earthworks and suggests that the firmness and permanence of the polity territories was, as I said, mitigated. Unfortunately, she does not precisely clarify theoretically how this mitigation would operate.

CHAPTER 16: EMBANKMENT EARTHWORK SITE ALIGNMENTS AND RELATIONS

1. I illustrate how this could happen later when I argue that the pattern of a particular empirical component of the Newark Circle-Octagon should not exist, given the cultural rules for the layout of this type of earthwork that I independently established. This complex component was an anomaly generated by the practice of an avoidance rule that overrode the application of the standard rules and the very existence of this avoidance rule necessarily presupposed that the builders were exercising an immanentist cosmology and custodial ethos. Without the emic perspective, the significance of this complex component for reconstructing the cultural perspective would likely not be noted because it would be seen by the archaeologist as simply a bit of random engineering and construction "noise."

2. Of course, I am claiming here that style is neither an inexplicable nor an ephemeral or largely irrelevant property of material culture. Rather, it is the core attribute by which those responsible for a given material cultural assemblage generate and sustain their social systems in their regular usage of it, although regularly using it is not typically done in order to sustain the social systems. Rather, it is regularly used because that is how the people constitute their social actions and fulfill their intentions, achieve their wants and desires, and discharge their duties, and so on.

3. Their "reverse engineering" assumed that accuracy was a pursued value. They have not imposed this value, however, since they came to this conclusion empirically by noting that the other seven alignments were more accurate. Only establishing the value of accuracy as a social fact was important to them and they did not explore why this was a value. As I noted above, this requires postulating in some depth the cultural structures.

4. They list their criteria for warranting their selection of a particular high-point location. "We have used three criteria in looking for sites which may have played a role in the planning and layout of the earthworks: (1) the site can serve as a backsight which allows a zero-altitude horizon view of a lunar (or solar) extreme over the length of an octagon wall, or along the symmetry axis of one or more geometrically regular constructions, such as the Circle-Octagon, the Great (or Fairground) Circle, the Wright Square, the Salisbury Square; (2) the site is prominent among the many eligible hill sites, affording an optimum view of the earthworks; and (3) the site may show evidence of Hopewell or Early Woodland activity" (Hively and Horn 2010, 133).

5. However, in an endnote they equivocate and suggest that evidence may be forthcoming that, in fact, "[o]ur work at High Bank since this paper was accepted for publication lends some support to the conjecture that high zero-altitude vantage points did play a role in the layout of the High Bank works, and other Chillicothe sites as well. This will be discussed in forthcoming papers" (2010, 163, n6). Notably they make a new distinction here between "zero-altitude" and "high zero-altitude"

azimuth readings and, apparently, by this addition they are suggesting that "high zero-altitude" was the type applied to lay out the High Bank Circle-Octagon and related earthworks, while "zero-altitude" was the type applied at Newark. Of course, all this hinges on their publishing these further findings. In the meantime, I will assume that the high zero-altitude method they claim was applied in the Chillicothe region was for a different purpose, as I discuss shortly.

6. I pointed out in chapter 14 that, according to Hall (1997, 162), traditional Native North American peoples identified the tree as a major icon by which the ground level and celestial level were related in this congruent manner, in this case using the sacred pole to assist the free spirits to ascend to the Milky Way, the Path of Souls, in order to embark on their travels to the land of the Dead. In this case I drew a parallel between this historically known practice and the great poles associated with the auxiliary renewal lodges at the Seip site.

7. In keeping with my claim that the earthworks were cult sodality sites, I have characterized the groups responsible as cult sodality heterarchies. DeBoer (2010) does not use this term nor does he specifically characterize the social nature of these groups.

8. This claim is reinforced by Hively and Horn's zero-altitude horizon hypothesis since, as I noted above, they argue that these three earthworks are aligned with each other and through a common turning-point alignment.

9. I have characterized the Seip–High Bank–Liberty Works complex by calling it a compound second-order heterarchy. In fact, this is simply a term of convenience to note the particular coresponsibility of two second-order heterarchies for the same High Bank Lunar motif. I earlier argued that Seip and Liberty Works were probably the "descendants" of the Mound City/Hopeton complex and I have argued that this was a second-order heterarchy that also was the focal site for the conveyancing rites of the custodial regalia with Tremper as the allied second-order heterarchy at Portsmouth. Hence, the Mound City/Hopeton complex would have been the focal site of the dispersed third-order Mound City/Hopeton–Tremper heterarchy. I suspect that this third-order heterarchy persisted after the Mound City/Hopeton complex and Tremper sites were abandoned, being replaced by compound second-order Liberty Works–High Bank–Seip and the postulated second-order Portsmouth cult sodality heterarchies. Therefore, the alliance with Newark would simply expand this third-order heterarchy by the addition of Newark. I suspect, however, that Newark itself was affiliated with a complex of "Adena" first- or second-order heterarchies in the central Muskingum, as I discuss in the next chapter. In any case, all this must stand as a hypothesis that requires much further elucidation and empirical grounding, a task that is well beyond the scope of this book.

10. The Sacred Earth principle is the core premise of an immanentist cosmology, namely, the natural order is immanently sacred and, therefore, physically intervening in the natural order necessarily intervenes into the sacred order. Such a principle does not mean that intervention, as such, was to be avoided. Rather

it meant that whenever interventions were performed they had to be designed to either enhance the sacred order or at least minimize its disordering, as I discussed briefly in the closing of the previous chapter. This premise arises from the deontic ecological perspective that would be presupposed by a social world based on a strong immanentist cosmology, which I claim in this and prior books was the basis of the emergence and development of the Ohio Hopewell episode.

11. Possibly a bit facetiously, Hively and Horn make the same point when they go on to suggest: "One is tempted to believe that the builders at High Bank decided to go to Newark and 'do it right,' to build a circle-octagon which displayed the symmetry of the octagon and the 18.6-year cycle of the moon unambiguously on its walls and long axis" (2010, 159).

12. Many other examples could be given. Earlier in my discussion of Fort Ancient I noted that Connolly argued that Gateway 55a was the result of *adding* to a preexisting embankment in order to build the crossway. Even the two mounds that delineated the form of the entryway were *added* by being built on top of the preexisting embankment. I believe that a careful analysis of the Fort Ancient "gateways" will indicate that they were formed by adding earth onto the preexisting embankment leaving an opening for the crossway. Other anomalous patterns can be explained in the similar avoidance terms.

13. The zero horizon method is an addition to this argument, of course, since Hively and Horn have noted it only recently. However, it is fully consistent with my original argument that the Observatory Mound/Feature A complex is the consequence of a major change of plan.

14. It may seem strange that I can make such a specific statement concerning timing. However, this logically follows from my above discussion since, in fact, if the circle had been completed according to the original plan the Octagon would have been added to the southwest end of Feature A and, of course, there would have been no possibility to make the modifications I have postulated were done since this would have required the removal of the Octagon! Retroductive logic is quite precise in inferring necessary, not sufficient, conditions; and since it addresses material patterns that are observable, then the conclusions they lead to can be quite compelling if these enable an explanation of the patterns themselves that is better than any other explanation that has been presented.

CHAPTER 17: THE OHIO HOPEWELL AND ADENA AS NEIGHBORS AND STRANGERS

1. Of course, the formal differences are also partly related to the organizational differences I have claimed were in place. As I noted at the close of the previous chapter and as I argue shortly, in contrast to the sodalities practicing the Ohio Hopewell ritual usufructs, which were constituted by ecclesiastic-communal cult sodalities, the Adena sodality organizations were probably characterized as a system

of communal cult sodalities, that is, sodalities that did not have the laity-clergy structure. Also, I have argued and empirically linked Adena to the persisting of two complementary and mutually autonomous communal cult sodalities differentiated as senior and junior age-grade sodalities. As I will argue, like the Ohio Hopewell, a local junior age-grade sodality would be promoted to the senior sodality level when the surviving members of the latter retired. Unlike the Ohio Hopewell, however, these two levels maintained a strong arm's-length relation.

2. I have called the paired-pole circle the Solar Circle and the Adena Circle the Sacred Circle, that is, the SR-Profile embankment circle.

3. Clay characterizes the mortuary sphere in the standard funerary manner and, indeed, argues that it was recruited by these dispersed communities in order to constitute their alliances for economic subsistence purposes. Therefore, what is lacking from his overview of the mortuary practices is a rationale for their complexity and development. What selective mechanism was in place that would generate the distribution of burials, some in the mound, some in the smaller mounds, and so on? None of this is addressed, to my knowledge.

References Cited

Abrams, Elliot M., and Ann Corrine Freter

2005 Tribal Societies in the Hocking Valley. In *The Emergence of Tribal Societies in Southeastern Ohio*, edited by Elliot M. Abrams and Ann Corrine Freter, pp. 174–95. Ohio University Press, Athens.

Alford, Thomas Wildcat

1936 *Civilization* (as told to Florence Drake). University of Oklahoma Press.

Archer, Margaret S.

2007 The Ontological Status of Subjectivity: The Missing Link Between Structure and Agency. In *Contributions to Social Ontology*, edited by Clive Lawson, John Latsis, and Nuno Martins, pp. 17–31. Routledge, London.

Bhaskar, Roy

1978 *A Realist Theory of Science*. The Harvester Press, Hassocks, Sussex.

1979 *The Possibility of Naturalism*. Humanities Press, Atlantic Highlands, N.J.

Blank, John

1965 The Brown's Bottom Site. *Ohio Archaeologist* 15(1): 16–21.

Blosser, Jack K.

1996 The 1984 Excavation of 12D29s: A Middle Woodland Village in Southeastern Indiana. In *A View from the Core*, edited by Paul J. Pacheco, pp. 56–68. The Ohio Archaeological Council, Columbus.

Bowers, Alfred W.

1965 *Hidatsa Social and Ceremonial Organization*. Smithsonian Institution, Bureau of American Ethnology, Bulletin 194. Washington, D.C.

2004 *Mandan Social and Ceremonial Organization.* Foreword by Gerard Baker. University of Nebraska Press, Lincoln. Originally published, University of Chicago Press, 1950.

Brown, James A.

1986 Food for Thought: Where Has Subsistence Analysis Gotten Us? In *Foraging, Collecting and Harvesting: Archaic Period Subsistence and Settlement in the Eastern Woodlands,* edited by Sarah W. Neusius, pp. 315–30. Center for Archaeological Investigations, Occasional Paper 6, University of Illinois at Carbondale.

2004a The Cahokian Expansion: Creating Court and Cult. In *Hero, Hawk, and Open Hand: American Indian Art of the Ancient Midwest and South,* edited by Richard F. Townsend and Robert V. Sharp, pp. 105–23. The Art Institute of Chicago. Yale University Press, New Haven, Conn.

2004b Mound City and Issues in the Development of Hopewell Culture in the Ross County Area of Southern Ohio. In *Aboriginal Ritual and Economy in the Eastern Woodlands: Essays in Memory of Howard Dalton Winter,* edited by Anne-Marie Cantwell, Lawrence A. Conrad, and Jonathan E. Ryan, pp. 146–68. Illinois State Museum Scientific Paper Vol. XXX, Illinois State Museum, Springfield, Kampsville Studies in Archaeology and History, volume 5, Center for American Archeology, Kampsville, Ill.

2006 Where's the Power in Mound Building? An Eastern Woodlands Perspective. In *Leadership and Polity in Mississippian Society,* edited by Brian M. Butler and Paul D. Welch, pp. 197–213. Center for Archaeological Investigations, Occasional Paper No. 33. Southern University of Illinois at Carbondale.

2007a The Chronological Implications of the Bellows-Shaped Apron. In *The Southeastern Ceremonial Complex: Chronology, Content, Context,* edited by Adam King, pp. 38–56. University of Alabama Press, Tuscaloosa.

2007b On the Identity of the Birdman within Mississippian Period Art and Iconography. In *Ancient Objects and Sacred Realms: Interpretations of Mississippian Iconography,* edited by F. Kent Reilly III and James F. Garber, pp. 56–106. University of Texas Press, Austin.

2007c Sequencing the Braden Style Within Mississippian Period Art and Iconography. In *Ancient Objects and Sacred Realms: Interpretations of Mississippian Iconography,* edited by F. Kent Reilly III and James F. Garber, pp. 213–45. University of Texas Press, Austin.

Brown, James A., and John Kelly

2000 Cahokia and the Southeastern Ceremonial Complex. In *Modoc, Mounds, and Mesoamerica: Papers in Honor of Melvin L. Fowler,* edited by Steven R. Ahler, pp. 469–510. Illinois State Museum Scientific Papers, Vol. XXVIII, Springfield.

Buikstra, Jane E., and Douglas K. Charles
1999 Centering the Ancestors: Cemeteries, Mounds, and Sacred Landscapes of the Ancient North American Midcontinent. In *Archaeologies of Landscape: Contemporary Perspective*, edited by Wendy Ashmore and A. Bernard Knapp, pp. 201–28. Blackwell Publishers, Oxford.

Burks, Jarrod, and N'omi B. Greber
2009 Exploring Features Found During the 1971–1977 Excavations. *Midcontinental Journal of Archaeology* 34(1): 143–70.

Burks, Jarrod, and Jennifer Pederson
2006 The Place of Nonmound Debris at Hopewell Mound Group (33RO27), Ross County, Ohio. In *Recreating Hopewell*, edited by Douglas K. Charles and Jane E. Buikstra, pp. 376–401. University Press of Florida, Gainesville.

Burton, Kelli Whitlock
2006 Putting Down Roots? *American Archaeology* 10(3): 33–37.

Byers, A. Martin
1987 *The Earthwork Enclosures of the Central Ohio Valley: A Temporal and Structural Analysis of Woodland Society and Culture*. Ph.D. dissertation. State University of New York at Albany. University Microfilms International, Ann Arbor, Mich.
1992 The Action-Constitutive Theory of Monuments: A Strong Pragmatist Version. *Journal for the Theory of Social Behaviour* 22(4): 403–46.
1996 Social Structure and the Pragmatic Meaning of Material Culture: Ohio Hopewell as Ecclesiastic-Communal Cult. In *A View from the Core: A Synthesis of Ohio Hopewell Archaeology*, edited by Paul J. Pacheco, 174–92. The Ohio Archaeological Council, Columbus.
1998 Is the Newark Circle-Octagon the Ohio Hopewell "Rosetta Stone"? In *Ancient Earthen Enclosures of the Eastern Woodlands*, edited by Robert C. Mainfort Jr. and Lynne P. Sullivan, 135–53. University Press of Florida, Gainesville.
1999 Intentionality, Symbolic Pragmatics and Material Culture: Revisiting Binford's View of the Old Copper Complex. *American Antiquity* 64(2): 265–87.
2004 *The Ohio Hopewell Episode: Paradigm Lost, Paradigm Gained*. University of Akron Press, Akron, Ohio.
2005 The Mortuary *Laying-In* Crypts of the Hopewell Site: Beyond the Funerary Paradigm. In *Interacting with the Dead: Perspectives on Mortuary Archaeology for the New Millennium*, edited by Gordon Rakita, Jane E. Buikstra, Lane A. Beck, and Sloan R. Williams, pp. 124–41. University Press of Florida, Gainesville.
2006a *Cahokia: A World Renewal Cult Heterarchy*. University Press of Florida, Gainesville.

2006b The Earthwork/Habitation Dichotomy: A Central Problem of Ohio Hopewell. In *Recreating Hopewell*, edited by Douglas K. Charles and Jane E. Buikstra, pp. 62–73. University Press of Florida, Gainesville.

2006c The Mortuary "Laying-In" Crypts of the Hopewell Site: Beyond the Funerary Paradigm. In *Interacting with the Dead: Perspectives on Mortuary Archaeology for the New Millennium*, edited by Gordon F. M. Rakita, Jane E. Buikstra, and Lane A. Beck, pp. 124–41. University Press of Florida, Gainesville.

2010a The "Heartland" Woodland Settlement System: Cultural Traditions and Resolving Key Puzzles. In *Hopewell Settlement Patterns, Subsistence, and Sacred Landscapes*, edited by A. Martin Byers and DeeAnne Wymer, pp. 274–94. University Press of Florida, Gainesville.

2010b The Turner-Hopewell Axis: Exploring Interaction through Embankment Form and Mortuary Patterning. In *Hopewell Settlement Patterns, Subsistence, and Sacred Landscapes*, edited by A. Martin Byers and DeeAnne Wymer, pp. 228–42. University Press of Florida, Gainesville.

Callendar, Charles

1978 Shawnee. In *Handbook of North American Indians*, edited by Bruce G. Trigger, pp. 622–35. Vol. 15. Smithsonian Institution, Washington, D.C.

Carr, Christopher

2005a Scioto Hopewell Ritual Gatherings. In *Gathering Hopewell: Society, Ritual, and Ritual Interaction*, ed. Christopher Carr and D. Troy Case, pp. 463–79. Kluwer Academic/Plenum Publishers, New York.

2005b The Tripartite Alliance among Scioto Hopewellian Communities and the Questions of Social Ranking. In *Gathering Hopewell: Society, Ritual, and Ritual Interaction*, edited by Christopher Carr and D. Troy Case, pp. 258–338. Kluwer Academic/Plenum Publishers, New York.

2008a Coming to Know Ohio Hopewell Peoples Better. In *The Scioto Hopewell and their Neighbors: Bioarchaeological Documentation and Cultural Understanding*, edited by D. Troy Case and Christopher Carr, pp. 603–90. Springer, New York.

2008b Settlement and Communities. In *The Scioto Hopewell and their Neighbors: Bioarchaeological Documentation and Cultural Understanding*, edited by D. Troy Case and Christopher Carr, pp. 101–50. Springer, New York.

2008c Social and Ritual Organization. In *The Scioto Hopewell and their Neighbors: Bioarchaeological Documentation and Cultural Understanding*, edited by D. Troy Case and Christopher Carr, pp. 151–288. Springer, New York.

Carr, Christopher, and D. Troy Case

2005a The Gathering of Hopewell. In *Gathering Hopewell: Society, Ritual, and Ritual Interaction*, edited by Christopher Carr and D. Troy Case, pp. 19–50. Kluwer Academic/Plenum Publishers, New York.

2005b The Nature of Leadership in Ohio Hopewellian Societies: Role Segregation and the Transformation from Shamanism. In *Gathering Hopewell: Society, Ritual, and Ritual Interaction*, ed. by Christopher Carr and D. Troy Case, pp. 177–237. Kluwer Academic/Plenum Publishers, New York.

Carr, Christopher, Beau J. Goldstein, and Jaimin D. Weets

2005 Estimating the Sizes and Social Composition of Mortuary-Related Gatherings at Scioto Hopewell Earthwork-Mound Sites. In *Gathering Hopewell: Society, Ritual, and Ritual Interaction*, edited by Christopher Carr and D. Troy Case, pp. 480–532. Kluwer Academic/Plenum Publishers, New York.

Carr, Christopher, and Herbert Haas

1996 Beta-Count and AMS Radiocarbon Dates of Woodland and Fort Ancient Period Occupations in Ohio 1350 B.C.–A.D. 1650. *The West Virginia Archaeologist* 48(1–2): 19–36.

Carskadden, Jeff

2008 Observations on the Early Woodland Cultural Landscape in the Central Muskingum Valley of Eastern Ohio. In *Transitions: Archaic and Early Woodland Research in the Ohio Country*, edited by Martha P. Otto and Brian G. Redmond, pp. 232–70. Ohio University Press, Athens.

Charles, Douglas K., and Jane E. Buikstra

1983 Archaic Mortuary Sites in the Central Mississippi Drainage: Distribution, Structure and Behavioral Implications. In *Archaic Hunters and Gatherers in the American Midwest*, edited by James L. Phillips and James A. Brown, pp. 117–45. Academic Press, New York.

Charles, Douglas K., Jane E. Buikstra, and Lyle W. Konigsberg

1986 Behavioral Implications of Terminal Archaic and Early Woodland Mortuary Practices in the Lower Illinois Valley. In *Early Woodland Archaeology*, edited by Kenneth B. Farnsworth and Thomas E. Emerson, pp. 458–74. Kampsville Seminars Vol. 2. Center for American Archeology Press, Kampsville, Ill.

Church, Flora, and Annette G. Ericksen

1997 Beyond the Scioto Valley: Middle Woodland Occupation in the Salt Creek Drainage. In *Ohio Hopewell Community Organization*, edited by William S. Dancey and Paul J. Pacheco, pp. 331–60. Kent State University Press, Kent, Ohio.

Clay, R. Berle

1986 Adena Ritual Spaces. In *Early Woodland Archaeology*, edited by Kenneth B. Farnsworth and Thomas E. Emerson, pp. 581–95. Center for American Archaeology, Archaeological Seminars Vol. 2. Center for American Archaeology Press, Kampsville, Ill.

1987 Circles and Ovals: Two Types of Adena Space. *Southeastern Archaeology* 6(1): 46–56.

1991 Adena Ritual Development: An Organizational Type in a Temporal Perspective. In *The Human Landscape in Kentucky's Past: Site Structure and Settlement Patterns*, edited by Charles Stout and Christine K. Hensley, pp. 30–39. Kentucky Heritage Council, Lexington, Ky.

1992 Chiefs, Big Men, or What? Economy, Settlement Patterns, and Their Bearing on Adena Political Models. In *Cultural Variability in Context: Woodland Settlements of the Mid-Ohio Valley*, edited by Mark F. Seeman, pp. 77–80. *Midcontinental Journal of Archaeology* Special Paper No. 7. Kent State University Press, Kent, Ohio.

1998 The Essential Features of Adena Ritual and Their Implications. *Southeastern Archaeology* 17(1): 1–21.

2002 Deconstructing the Woodland Sequence from the Heartland: A Review of Recent Research Directions in the Upper Ohio Valley. In *The Woodland Southeast*, edited by David G. Anderson and Robert C. Mainfort, Jr., pp. 162–84. The University of Alabama Press, Tuscaloosa.

2005 Adena: Rest in Peace? In *Woodland Period Systematics in the Middle Ohio Valley*, edited by Darlene Applegate and Robert C. Mainfort Jr., pp. 94–110. The University of Alabama Press, Tuscaloosa.

Clay, R. Berle, and Charles M. Niquette

1992 Middle Woodland Mortuary Rituals in the Gallipolis Locks and Dam Vicinity, Mason County, West Virginia. *West Virginian Archaeologist* 44(1–2): 1–25.

Cochran, Donald R.

1992 Adena and Hopewell Cosmology: New Evidence from East Central Indiana. In *Native American Cultures in Indiana: Proceedings of the First Minnetrista Council of Great Lakes Native American Studies*, edited by Ronald Hicks, pp. 26–40. Minnetrista Cultural Center and Ball State University, Muncie, Indiana.

1996 The Adena/Hopewell Convergence in East Central Indiana. In *A View from the Core: A Synthesis of Ohio Hopewell Archaeology*, edited by Paul J. Pacheco, 340–52. The Ohio Archaeological Council, Columbus.

Connolly, Robert P.

1996 Middle Woodland Hilltop Enclosures: The Built Environment, Construction and Function. Ph.D. dissertation, Department of Anthropology, University of Illinois at Urbana-Champaign.

2004 The Evolution of Fort Ancient Embankment Wall Form. In *The Fort Ancient Earthworks: Prehistoric Lifeways of the Hopewell Culture in Southwestern Ohio*, edited by Robert P. Connolly and Bradley T. Lepper, pp. 35–50. Ohio Historical Society, Columbus.

Connolly, Robert P., and Ted S. Sunderhaus
2004 Rules for "Reading" Fort Ancient Architecture. In *The Fort Ancient Earthworks: Prehistoric Lifeways of the Hopewell Culture in Southwestern Ohio,* edited by Robert P. Connolly and Bradley T. Lepper, pp. 51–65. Ohio Historical Society, Columbus.

Conrad, Geoffrey W., and Arthur A. Demarest
1984 *Religion and Empire: The Dynamics of Aztec and Inca Expansionism.* Cambridge University Press, Cambridge.

Cowan, Frank L.
2005 Black and White and Buried All Over. Paper presented at the Midwest Archaeological Conference, Dayton, Ohio.
2006 A Mobile Hopewell? Questioning Assumptions of Ohio Hopewell Sedentism. In *Recreating Hopewell,* edited by Douglas K. Charles and Jane E. Buikstra, pp. 26–49. University Press of Florida, Gainesville.
2007 The Shriver Circle Earthwork, Ross County, Ohio. Ohio Archaeological Council Meeting, Reece Center, Newark, Ohio.

Cowan, Frank L., Ted S. Sunderhaus, and Robert A. Genheimer
1999 Notes from the Field, 1999: More Hopewell "Houses" at the Stubbs Earthworks Site. *Current Research in Ohio Archaeology 1999,* http://www.ohioarchaeology.org/joomla/index.php?option=com_content&task=view&id=19&Itemid=32, accessed July 15, 2009.
2004 Earthwork Peripheries: Probing the Margins of the Fort Ancient Site. In *The Fort Ancient Earthworks: Prehistoric Lifeways of the Hopewell Culture in Southwestern Ohio,* edited by Robert P. Connolly and Bradley T. Lepper, pp. 107–24. Ohio Historical Society, Columbus.

Dancey, William S.
1991 A Middle Woodland Settlement in Central Ohio: A Preliminary Report on the Murphy Site (33LI212). *Pennsylvania Archaeologist* 61(2): 37–72.

Dancey, William S., and Paul J. Pacheco
1997 A Community Model of Ohio Hopewell Settlement. In *Ohio Hopewell Community Organization,* edited by William S. Dancey and Paul J. Pacheco, pp. 3–40. Kent State University Press, Kent, Ohio.

Danermark, Beerth, Mats Ekström, Lisolette Jakobsen, and Jan Ch. Karlsson
2002 *Explaining Society: Critical Realism in the Social Sciences.* Routledge, London.

DeBoer, Warren
2010 Strange Sightings on the Scioto. In *Hopewell Settlement Patterns, Subsistence, and Sacred Landscapes,* edited by A. Martin Byers and DeeAnne Wymer, pp. 163–96. University Press of Florida, Gainesville.

Dillehay, Tom D.
1992 Keeping Outsiders Out: Public Ceremony, Resource Rights, and Hierarchy in Historic and Contemporary Mapuche Society. In *Wealth and Hierarchy in the Intermediate Area*, edited by Frederick W. Lange, pp. 379–422. Dumbarton Oaks Research Library and Collection, Washington, D.C.

Dragoo, Don W.
1963 *Mounds for the Dead: An Analysis of the Adena Culture.* Annals of Carnegie Museum Vol. 37, Pittsburgh, Pa.

Emerson, Thomas E.
1997a *Cahokia and the Archaeology of Power.* The University of Alabama Press, Tuscaloosa.
1997b Cahokian Elite Ideology and the Mississippian Cosmos. In *Cahokia: Domination and Ideology in the Mississippian World*, edited by Timothy R. Pauketat and Thomas E. Emerson, pp. 190–228. University of Nebraska Press, Lincoln.
1997c Reflections from the Countryside on Cahokian Hegemony. In *Cahokia: Domination and Ideology in the Mississippian World*, edited by Timothy R. Pauketat and Thomas E. Emerson, pp. 167–89. The University of Alabama Press, Tuscaloosa.

Emerson, T., K. Farnsworth, S. Wisseman, and R. Hughes
2008 The Power and Lure of the Exotic? Re-examine the Place of Distant Pipestone Quarries in the Hopewellian Interaction Sphere. World Archaeological Congress, 6. Dublin, Ireland.

Faron, Louis C.
1964 *Hawks of the Sun: Mapuche Morality and Its Ritual Attributes.* University of Pittsburgh Press, Pittsburgh, Pa.
1968 *The Mapuche Indians of Chile.* Holt, Rinehart and Winston, New York.

Fogelson, Raymond
1985 The Cherokee Ballgame Cycle. *Ethnology of the Southeastern Indians: A Source Book,* edited by Charles Hudson, pp. 327–38. Garland Publishing, New York.

Galloway, Patricia
1995 *Choctaw Genesis: 1500–1700.* University of Nebraska Press, Lincoln.

Genheimer, Robert A.
1996 Bladelets Are Tools Too: The Predominance of Bladelets among Formal Tools at Ohio Hopewell Sites. *A View from the Core: A Synthesis of Ohio Hopewell Archaeology*, edited by Paul J. Pacheco, pp. 92–107. The Ohio Archeological Conference, Columbus.
1997 Stubbs Cluster: Hopewellian Site Dynamics at a Forgotten Little Miami River Valley Settlement. In *Ohio Hopewell Community Organization,*

edited by William S. Dancey and Paul J. Pacheco, pp. 283–309. The Kent State University Press, Kent, Ohio.

Goldstein, Lynne
1980 *Mississippian Mortuary Practices: A Case Study of Two Cemeteries in the Lower Illinois Valley.* Northwestern University Archeological Program, Scientific Papers, No. 4. Evanston, Ill.
2000 Mississippian Ritual as Viewed Through the Practice of Secondary Disposal of the Dead. In *Modoc, Monuments, Mesoamerica: Papers in Honor of Melvin L. Fowler*, edited by Steven R. Ahler, pp. 193–204. Illinois State Museum Scientific Papers, Vol. XXVIII. Springfield.

Greber, N'omi B.
1976 *Within Ohio Hopewell: Analyses of Burial Patterns from Several Classic Sites.* Ph.D. dissertation, Case Western Reserve University. University Microfilms International, Ann Arbor, Mich.
1979 A Comparative Study of Site Morphology and Burial Patterns at Edwin Harness Mound and Seip Mounds 1 and 2. In *Hopewell Archaeology: The Chillicothe Conference*, edited by D. S. Brose and N. Greber, pp. 27–38. Kent State University Press, Kent, Ohio.
1983 *Recent Excavations at the Edwin Harness Mound, Liberty Works, Ross County, Ohio. Midcontinental Journal of Archaeology* Special Paper No. 5. Kent State University Press, Kent, Ohio.
1991 A Study of Continuity and Contrast Between Central Scioto Adena and Hopewell Sites. *West Virginia Archaeologist* 43(1&2): 1–26.
1997 Two Geometric Enclosures in the Paint Creek Valley: An Estimate of the Possible Changes in Community Patterns Through Time. In *Ohio Hopewell Community Organization*, edited by William S. Dancey and Paul J. Pacheco, pp. 207–29. The Kent State University Press, Kent, Ohio.
2006 Enclosures and Communities in Ohio Hopewell. In *Recreating Hopewell*, edited by Douglas Charles and Jane Buikstra, pp. 74–105. University Press of Florida, Gainesville.
2009a Preface. *Midcontinental Journal of Archaeology* 34(1): 4–5.
2009b Stratigraphy and Chronology in the 1971–1977 Field Data. *Midcontinental Journal of Archaeology* 34(1): 19–52.
2010 Coda: Still Seeking Hopewell. In *Hopewell Settlement Patterns, Subsistence, and Sacred Landscapes*, edited by A. Martin Byers and DeeAnne Wymer, pp. 333–46. University Press of Florida, Gainesville.

Greber, N'omi B., and Katharine C. Ruhl
1989 *The Hopewell Site: A Contemporary Analysis Based on the Work of Charles C. Willoughby.* Investigations in American Archaeology, Westview Press, Boulder, Colo.

Hall, Robert L.
1977 An Anthropocentric Perspective for Eastern United States Prehistory. *American Antiquity* 42(4): 499–518.

1979 In Search of the Ideology of the Adena-Hopewell Climax. In *Hopewell Archaeology: The Chillicothe Conference*, edited by D. S. Brose and N. Greber, pp. 258–65. Kent State University Press, Kent, Ohio.

1980 The Two-Climax Model of Illinois Prehistory. In *Early Native Americans: Prehistoric Demography, Economy and Technology*, edited by David L. Browman, pp. 401–62. Mouton Press, The Hague.

1991 Cahokia Identity and Interaction Models of Cahokia Mississippian. In *Cahokia and the Hinterlands: Middle Mississippian Cultures of the Midwest*, edited by Thomas E. Emerson and R. Barry Lewis, pp. 3–34. Published in cooperation with the Illinois Historic Preservation Agency. University of Illinois Press, Urbana.

1997 *An Archaeology of the Soul: North American Indian Belief and Ritual.* University of Illinois Press, Urbana.

Heidenreich, Conrad E.

1978 Huron. In *Handbook of North American Indians: Northeast*, edited by Bruce G. Trigger, pp. 368–88. The Smithsonian Institute, Washington D.C.

Hively, Ray, and Robert Horn

1982 Geometry and Astronomy in Prehistoric Ohio. *Journal for the History of Astronomy, Archaeoastronomy Supplement* 13: S1–S20.

1984 Hopewellian Geometry and Astronomy at High Bank. *Journal for the History of Astronomy, Archaeoastronomy Supplement* 15: S85–S100.

2010 Hopewell Cosmography at Newark and Chillicothe, Ohio. In *Hopewell Settlement Patterns, Subsistence, and Sacred Landscapes*, edited by A. Martin Byers and DeeAnne Wymer, pp. 126–62. University Press of Florida, Gainesville.

Hurt, R. Douglas

1987 *Indian Agriculture in America: Prehistory to the Present.* University Press of Kansas, Lawrence.

Ingold, Tim

1987 *The Appropriation of Nature: Essays on Human Ecology and Social Relations.* University of Iowa Press, Iowa City.

Kelly, John E., James A. Brown, Jenna M. Hamlin, Lucretia S. Kelly, Laura Kozuch, Kathryn Parker, and Julieann Van Nest

2007 Mound 34: The Context for the Early Evidence of the Southeastern Ceremonial Complex at Cahokia. In *Southeastern Ceremonial Complex: Chronology, Content, Context*, edited by Adam King, pp. 57–87. The University of Alabama Press, Tuscaloosa.

King, Adam, ed.

2007 *The Southeastern Ceremonial Complex: Chronology, Content, Context.* University of Alabama Press, Tuscaloosa.

Kirchhoff, Paul
1959 The Principles of Clanship in Human Society. In *Readings in Anthropology*, edited by Morton H. Fried, Vol. II, pp. 259–70. Thomas Y. Crowell, New York.

Knight, Vernon James, Jr.
1990 Social Organization and the Evolution of Hierarchy in Southeastern Chiefdoms. *Journal of Anthropological Research* 46(1): 1–23.
2007 An Assessment of Moundville Engraved "Cult" Designs from Potsherds. In *Southeastern Ceremonial Complex: Chronology, Content, Context*, edited by Adam King, pp. 151–64. The University of Alabama Press, Tuscaloosa.

Knight, Vernon James, Jr., James A. Brown, and George E. Lankford
2001 On the Subject Matter of Southeastern Ceremonial Complex Art. *Southeastern Archaeology* 20(2): 129–53.

Konigsberg, Lyle W.
1985 "Demography and Mortuary Practice at Seip Mound One." *Midcontinental Journal of Archaeology* 10(1): 123–48.

Kozarek, Sue Ellen
1987 *A Hopewellian Homestead in the Ohio River Valley*. M.A. thesis, Department of Anthropology, University of Cincinnati.
1997 Determining Sedentism in the Archeological Record. In *Ohio Hopewell Community Organization*, edited by William S. Dancey and Paul J. Pacheco, pp. 131–52. Kent State University Press, Kent, Ohio.

Lankford, George E.
2007a The Great Serpent in Eastern North America. In *Ancient Objects and Sacred Realms: Interpretations of Mississippian Iconography*, edited by F. Kent Reilly III and James F. Garber, pp. 107–35. University of Texas Press, Austin.
2007b The "Path of Souls": Some Death Imagery in the Southeastern Ceremonial Complex. In *Ancient Objects and Sacred Realms: Interpretations of Mississippian Iconography*, edited by F. Kent Reilly III and James F. Garber, pp. 175–212. University of Texas Press, Austin.
2007c Some Cosmological Motifs in the Southeastern Ceremonial Complex. In *Ancient Objects and Sacred Realms: Interpretations of Mississippian Iconography*, edited by F. Kent Reilly III and James F. Garber, pp. 8–38. University of Texas Press, Austin.

Lazazzera, Adrienne J.
2004 Hopewell Household Variation at the Fort Ancient Site. In *The Fort Ancient Earthworks: Prehistoric Lifeways of the Hopewell Culture in Southwestern Ohio*, edited by Robert P. Connolly and Bardley T. Lepper, pp. 84–106. Ohio Historical Society, Columbus.

Lepper, Bradley T.
1996 The Newark Earthworks and the Geometric Enclosures of the Scioto Valley: Connections and Conjectures. In *A View from the Core: A Synthesis of Ohio Hopewell Archaeology*, edited by Paul J. Pacheco, pp. 226–41. The Ohio Archaeological Council, Columbus, Ohio.
1998 The Archaeology of the Newark Earthworks. In *Ancient Earthen Enclosures of the Eastern Woodlands*, edited by Robert C. Mainfort Jr. and Lynne P. Sullivan, pp. 114–34. University Press of Florida, Gainesville.
2006 The Great Hopewell Road and the Role of the Pilgrimage in the Hopewell Interactions Sphere, edited by Douglas K. Charles and Jane E. Buikstra, pp. 122–33. University Press of Florida, Gainesville.
2010 The Ceremonial Landscape of the Newark Earthworks and the Raccoon Creek Valley. In *Hopewell Settlement Patterns, Subsistence, and Sacred Landscapes*, edited by A. Martin Byers and DeeAnne Wymer, pp. 95–125. University Press of Florida, Gainesville.

Lepper, Bradley T., and Richard W. Yerkes
1997 Hopewellian Occupation at the Northern Periphery of the Newark Earthworks: The Newark Expressway Sites Revisited. In *Ohio Hopewell Community Organization*, edited by William S. Dancey and Paul J. Pacheco, pp. 175–205. Kent State University Press, Kent, Ohio.

Lynott, Mark J., ed.
2009 *Footprints: In the Footprints of Squier and Davis: Archaeological Fieldwork in Ross County, Ohio*. Midwest Archaeological Center, Special Report No. 5. National Park Service, Midwest Archaeological Center, Lincoln, Neb.

Lynott, Mark J., and Rolfe D. Mandel
2009 Archaeological and Geoarchaeological Study of the Rectangular Enclosure at the Hopeton Works. In *Footprints: In the Footprints of Squier and Davis: Archaeological Fieldwork in Ross County, Ohio,* edited by Mark J. Lynott, pp. 159–77. Midwest Archaeological Center, Special Report No. 5. National Park Service, Midwest Archaeological Center, Lincoln, Neb.

McCord, Beth K., and Donald R. Cochran
2008 The Adena Complex: Identity and Context in East-Central Indiana. In *Transitions: Archaic and Early Woodland Research in the Ohio County*, edited by Martha P. Otto and Brian G. Redmond, pp. 334–59. Ohio University Press, Athens.

Mills, William C.
1907 Explorations of the Edwin Harness Mound. *Ohio Archaeological and Historical Quarterly* 16: 113–93.
1909 Explorations of the Seip Mound. *Ohio Archaeological and Historical Quarterly* 18: 269–321.
1916 Exploration of the Tremper Mound. *Ohio Archaeological and Historical Quarterly* 25: 263–398.

Milner, George R.
1998 *The Cahokia Chiefdom: The Archaeology of a Mississippian Society.* Smithsonian Institution Press, Washington D.C.
2003 Archaeological Indicators of Rank in the Cahokian Chiefdom. In *Theory, Method, and Practice in Modern Archaeology,* edited by Robert J. Jeske and Douglas K. Charles, pp. 133–48. Praeger, Westport, Conn.

Moorehead, Warren K.
1890 *Fort Ancient: The Great Prehistoric Earthwork of Warren County, Ohio.* Robert Clarke and Co., Cincinnati.
1892 *Primitive Man in Ohio.* G. P. Putnam's Sons, New York.
1922 *The Hopewell Mound Group of Ohio.* Field Museum of Natural History. Publication 211, Anthropology Series, vol. 6, no. 5:75. 1980. Reprint, AMS Press, New York.

Morrow, Carol A.
1987 Blades and Cobden Chert: A Technological Argument for Their Role as Markers of Regional Identification during the Hopewell Period in Illinois. In *The Organization of Core Technology,* edited by Jay K. Johnson and Carol A. Morrow, 119–49. Westview Press, Boulder, Colo.

Morrow, Carol A., J. Michael Elam, and Michael D. Glascock
1992 The Use of Blue-Grey Chert in Midwestern Prehistory. *Midcontinental Journal of Archaeology* 17(2): 166–97.

Moseley, Michael E.
1992 *The Incas and Their Ancestors.* Thames and Hudson, London.

Muller, Jon
1997 *Mississippian Political Economy.* Plenum Press, New York.

Nolan, Kevin C., and Jacob E. Deppen
2006 Experiments in Hopewell Blade Production: Lessons for Archaeological Interpretation. *Current Research in Ohio Archaeology 2006*, http://www.ohioarchaeology.org/joomla/index.php?option=com_content&task=view&id=176&Itemid=32, accessed January 4, 2010.

Nolan, Kevin C., Mark F. Seeman, and James L. Thaler
2007 A Quantitative Analysis of Skill and Efficiency: Hopewell Blade Production at the Turner Workshop, Hamilton, Ohio. *Midcontinental Journal of Archaeology* 32(2): 297–330.

Odell, George H.
1994 The Role of Stone Bladelets in Middle Woodland Society. *American Antiquity* 59(1): 102–20.

Pacheco, Paul J.
1993 *Ohio Hopewell Settlement Patterns: An Application of the Vacant Center Model to Middle Woodland Period Intracommunity Settlement.* Ph.D.

dissertation, Ohio State University. University Microfilms International, Ann Arbor, Mich.

1996 Ohio Regional Settlement Patterns. In *A View from the Core: A Synthesis of Ohio Hopewell Archaeology,* edited by Paul J. Pacheco, pp. 16–35. The Ohio Archaeological Council, Columbus, Ohio.

1997 Ohio Middle Woodland Intracommunity Settlement Variability: A Case Study from the Licking Valley. In *Ohio Hopewell Community Organization,* edited by William S. Dancey and Paul J. Pacheco, pp. 41–85. Kent State University Press, Kent, Ohio.

2010a Why Move? Ohio Hopewell Sedentism Revisited. In *Hopewell Settlement Patterns, Subsistence, and Symbolic Landscapes,* edited by A. Martin Byers and DeeAnne Wymer, pp. 37–55. University Press of Florida, Gainesville.

2010b Commentary on Lauren Sieg and Jarrod Burks's "The Land between the Mounds: The Role of 'Empty' Spaces in the Hopewellian Build Environment." In *Hopewell Settlement Patterns, Subsistence, and Symbolic Landscapes,* edited by A. Martin Byers and DeeAnne Wymer, pp. 87–90. University Press of Florida, Gainesville.

Pacheco, Paul J., and William S. Dancey

2006 Integrating Mortuary and Settlement Data on Ohio Hopewell Society. In *Recreating Hopewell,* edited by Douglas K. Charles and Jane E. Buikstra, pp. 3–25. University Press of Florida, Gainesville.

Pacheco, Paul J., Jarrod Burks, and DeeAnne Wymer

2005 Investigating Ohio Hopewell Settlement Patterns in Central Ohio: A Preliminary Report of Archaeology at Brown's Bottom #1 (33RO21). *Current Research in Ohio Archaeology 2005,* http://www.ohioarchaeology.org/joomla/indexphp?option=com_content&task=view&id-103&Itemid=32, accessed August 25, 2009.

2009a The 2006 Archaeological Investigations at Brown's Bottom #1 (33RO1104). *Current Research in Ohio Archaeology 2009,* http://www.ohioarchaeology.org/joomla/index.php?option=com_content&task=view&id=268&Itemid=32, accessed August 24, 2009.

2009b The 2007–2008 Archaeological Investigations at Lady's Run (33RO1105) *Current Research in Ohio Archaeology 2009,* http://www.ohioarchaeology.org/joomla/index.php?option=com_content&task=view&id=281&Itemid=32, accessed August 24, 2009.

Pauketat, Timothy R.

1993 *Temples for Cahokia Lords: Preston Holder's 1955–1956 Excavations of Kunnemann Mound.* No. 26, Museum of Anthropology. University of Michigan, Ann Arbor.

1994 *The Ascent of Chiefs: Cahokia and Mississippian Politics in Native North America.* University of Alabama Press, Tuscaloosa.

1997 Cahokian Political Economy. In *Cahokia: Domination and Ideology in the Mississippian World,* edited by Timothy R. Pauketat and Thomas E. Emerson, pp. 30–51. University of Nebraska Press, Lincoln.

2000 Politicization and Community in the Pre-Columbian Mississippi Valley. In *The Archaeology of Communities: A New World Perspective*, edited by Marcello A. Canuto and Jaron Yaeger, pp. 16–43. Routledge, London.

2002 A Fourth-Generation Synthesis of Cahokia and Mississippianization. *Midcontinental Journal of Archaeology* 27(2): 149–170.

2003 Resettled Farmers and the Making of a Mississippian Polity. *American Antiquity* 68(1): 39–66.

2004 *Ancient Cahokia and the Mississippians.* Cambridge University Press, Cambridge.

2005 The Forgotten History of the Mississippians. In *North American Archaeology*, edited by Timothy R. Pauketat and Diana DiPaolo Loren, pp. 187–211. Blackwell, Oxford.

2007 *Chiefdoms and Other Archaeological Delusions.* AltaMira Press, New York.

Peebles, Christopher S.

1974 *Moundville: The Organization of a Prehistoric Community and Culture.* Ph.D. dissertation, University of California, Santa Barbara.

Peebles, Christopher S., and Susan M. Kus

1977 Some Archaeological Correlates of Ranked Societies. *American Antiquity* 42(3): 421–48.

Penney, David W.

1989 *Hopewell Art.* Ph.D. dissertation, Columbia University.

Peters, Virginia Bergman

1995 *Women of the Earth Lodges: Tribal Life on the Plains.* Anchor Books, North Haven, Conn.

Prufer, Olaf H.

1964 The Hopewell Complex of Ohio. In *Hopewellian Studies*, edited by Joseph R. Caldwell and Robert L. Hall, pp. 35–83. Scientific Papers Vol. XII. Illinois State Museum, Springfield.

1965 *The McGraw Site: A Study in Hopewellian Dynamics.* Scientific Publications. Cleveland Museum of Natural History, Cleveland, Ohio.

1996 Core and Periphery: The Final Chapter on Ohio Hopewell. In *A View from the Core: A Synthesis of Ohio Hopewell Archaeology*, edited by Paul J. Pacheco, pp. 406–25. The Ohio Archaeological Council, Columbus.

Reilly, F. Kent, III

2004 People of Earth, People of Sky: Visualizing the Sacred in Native Art of the Mississippian Period. In *Hero, Hawk, and Open Hand: American Indian Art of the Ancient Midwest and South*, edited by Richard F. Townsend and Robert V. Sharp, pp. 125–37. The Art Institute of Chicago. Yale University Press, New Haven, Conn.

2007 The Petaloid Motif: A Celestial Symbolic Locative in the Shell Art of Spiro. In *Ancient Objects and Sacred Realms: Interpretations of Mississippian*

Iconography, edited by F. Kent Reilly III and James F. Garber, pp. 39–55. University of Texas Press, Austin.

Reilly, F. Kent, III, and James F. Garber, eds.
2007 *Ancient Objects and Sacred Realms: Interpretations of Mississippian Iconography*. University of Texas Press, Austin.

Riordan, Robert V.
2004 Fort Ancient and Southwest Ohio. In *The Fort Ancient Earthworks: Prehistoric Lifeways of the Hopewell Culture in Southwestern Ohio*, edited by Robert P. Connolly and Bradley T. Lepper, pp. 223–49. Ohio Historical Society, Columbus.
2010 Enclosed by Stone. In *Hopewell Settlement Patterns, Subsistence, and Sacred Landscapes*, edited by A. Martin Byers and DeeAnne Wymer, pp. 213–27. University Press of Florida, Gainesville.

Romain, William F.
2000 *Mysteries of the Hopewell: Astronomers, Geometers, and Magicians of the Eastern Woodlands*. University of Akron Press, Akron, Ohio.
2004 Astronomy, Geometry, and Cosmology at the Fort Ancient Enclosure. In *The Fort Ancient Earthworks: Prehistoric Lifeways of the Hopewell Culture in Southwestern Ohio*, edited by Robert P. Connolly and Bradley T. Lepper, pp. 66–83, Ohio Historical Society, Columbus.

Ruby, Bret J.
2009 Spruce Hill Earthworks: The 1995–1996 National Park Service Investigations. In *Footprints: In the Footprints of Squier and Davis: Archaeological Fieldwork in Ross County, Ohio*, edited by Mark J. Lynott, pp. 49–66. Midwest Archaeological Center, Special Report No. 5. National Park Service, Midwest Archaeological Center, Lincoln, Neb.

Ruby, Bret J., Christopher Carr, and Douglas K. Charles
2005 Community Organization in the Scioto, Mann, and Havana Hopewellian Regions: Comparative Perspective. In *Gathering Hopewell: Society, Ritual, and Ritual Interaction*, edited by Christopher Carr and D. Troy Case, pp. 119–76. Kluwer Academic/Plenum Publishers, New York.

Sayer, Andrew
1984 *Method in Social Science: A Realist Approach*. Hutchinson, London.

Schlesier, Karl H.
1987 *The Wolves of Heaven: Cheyenne Shamanism, Ceremonies, and Prehistoric Origins*. University of Oklahoma Press, Norman.

Schlarb, Eric J.
2005 The Bullock Site: A Forgotten Mound in Woodford County, Kentucky. *Woodland Period Systematics in the Middle Ohio Valley*, edited by Darlene Applegate and Robert C. Mainfort Jr., pp. 52–63. The University of Alabama Press, Tuscaloosa.

Searle, John R.
1983 *Intentionality: An Essay in the Philosophy of Mind.* Cambridge University Press, Cambridge.
1995 *The Construction of Social Reality.* The Free Press, New York.

Seeman, Mark F.
1995 When Words Are Not Enough. In *Native American Interactions: Multiscalar Analyses and Interpretations in the Eastern Woodlands,* edited by Michael S. Nassaney and Kenneth E. Sassaman, pp.122–43. The University of Tennessee Press, Knoxville.

Seeman, Mark F., and James L. Branch
2006 The Mounded Landscape of Ohio: Ohio Patterns and Placements. In *Recreating Hopewell,* edited by Douglas K. Charles and Jane E. Buikstra, pp. 106–21. University Press of Florida, Gainesville.

Shetrone, Henry C.
1926 Explorations of the Hopewell Group of Prehistoric Earthworks. *Ohio Archaeological and Historical Quarterly* 35: 1–227.
1930 *The Mound Builders.* D. Appleton and Company, New York.

Shetrone, Henry C., and Emerson F. Greenman
1931 Explorations of the Seip Group of Prehistoric Earthworks. *Ohio Archaeological and Historical Quarterly* 40(3): 343–509.

Smith, Bruce D.
1992 *Rivers of Change: Essays on Early Agriculture in Eastern North America.* Smithsonian Institute Press, Washington, D.C.

Smith, M. Estellie
1983 Pueblo Councils: An Example of Stratified Egalitarianism. In *The Development of Political Organization in Native North America,* edited by Elizabeth Tooker, pp. 32–44. 1979 Proceedings of the American Ethnological Society.

Snyder, Daniel, Michael Powers, Paul J. Pacheco, and Jarrod Burks
2008 The Brown's Bottom #1 (33RO1104) Bladelet Assemblage: A Double-Blind Experiment in Use-Wear Analysis. *Pennsylvania Archaeologist* 78(1).

Squier, E. G., and E. H. Davis
1848 *Ancient Monuments of the Mississippi Valley.* Smithsonian Contributions to Knowledge 1. Smithsonian Institution, Washington, D.C.

Sunderhaus, Ted S.
2004 Patterning in the Distribution of Surface Exposed Architecture and Artifacts at Fort Ancient: Result of an Intensive Pedestrian Survey. In *The Fort Ancient Earthworks: Prehistoric Lifeways of the Hopewell Culture in*

Southwestern Ohio, edited by Robert P. Connolly and Bradley T. Lepper, pp. 137–46, Ohio Historical Society, Columbus.

Sunderhaus, Ted S., Rodney Riggs, and Frank S. Cowan
2001 The Smith Site: A Small Hopewell Site Overlooking the Stubbs Earthworks. Ohio Archaeological Council 2001, http://www.ohioarchaeology.org/joomla/index.php?option=com_content&task=view&id=27&Itemid=32, accessed September 30, 2009.

Tainter, Joseph A.
1977 Modeling Change in Prehistoric Social systems. In *For Theory Building in Archaeology: Essays on Faunal Remains, Aquatic Resources, Spatial Analysis, and Systemic Modeling,* edited by Lewis R. Binford, pp. 327–51. Academic Press, New York.

Taylor, Charles
1985a Language and Human Nature. In *Human Agency and Language: Philosophical Papers I,* pp. 215–47. Cambridge University Press, Cambridge.
1985b Theories of Meaning. In *Human Agency and Language: Philosophical Papers I,* pp. 248–92. Cambridge University Press, Cambridge.
1985c Social Theory as Practice. In *Philosophy and the Human Sciences: Philosophical Papers 2,* pp. 91–115. Cambridge University Press, Cambridge.
1985d Understanding and Ethnocentricity. In *Philosophy and the Human Sciences: Philosophical Papers 2,* pp. 116–33. Cambridge University Press, Cambridge.

Tomak, Curtis H.
1994 The Mount Vernon Site: A Remarkable Mound in Posey County, Indiana. *Archaeology of Eastern North America* 22: 1–46.

Tooker, Elisabeth
1978 League of the Iroquois: Its History, Politics, and Ritual. In *Handbook of North American Indians: Northeast,* edited by Bruce G. Trigger, pp. 418–41. Smithsonian, Washington, D.C.

Toth, Jay
2009 *Panther Effigy Mounds.* Annual Meeting of the Midwest Archaeological Conference, Iowa City, Iowa.

Trigger, Bruce G.
1969 *The Huron: Farmers of the North.* Holt, Rinehart and Winston, New York.
1976 *The Children of Aataensic: A History of the Huron People to 1660.* Vol. 1. McGill-Queen's University Press, Montreal.

Turner, Edith
1993 Behind Inupiaq Reincarnation: Cosmological Recycling. In *Amerindian Rebirth: Reincarnation Belief among North American Indians and Inuit,* edited by Antonia Mills and Richard Slobodin, pp. 67–81. University of Toronto Press, Toronto.

Van Nest, Julieann
2006 Rediscovering This Earth: Some Ethnological Aspects of the Illinois Valley Hopewell Mounds. In *Recreating Hopewell,* edited by Douglas K. Charles and Jane E. Buikstra, pp. 402–26. University Press of Florida, Gainesville.

Van Nest, Julieann, Douglas K. Charles, Jane E. Buikstra, and David L. Asch
2001 Sod Blocks in Illinois Hopewell Mounds. *American Antiquity* 66(4): 633–50.

Vickery, Kent D.
1996 Flint Raw Material Use in Ohio Hopewell. In *A View from the Core: A Synthesis of Ohio Hopewell Archaeology,* edited by Paul J. Pacheco, pp. 108–27. The Ohio Archaeological Council. Columbus.

Vickery, Kent D., and Ted S. Sunderhaus
2004 Intrasite Variability and Flint Raw Material Distribution at Fort Ancient. In *The Fort Ancient Earthworks: Prehistoric Lifeways of the Hopewell Culture in Southwestern Ohio,* edited by Robert P. Connolly and Bradley T. Lepper, pp. 167–93. Ohio Historical Society, Columbus.

Voegelin, C. F., and E. W. Voegelin
1937 Shawnee Name Groups. *American Anthropologist* 37(4): 617–35.

Von Gernet, Alexander
1993 Saving the Souls: Reincarnation Beliefs of the Seventeenth-Century Huron. In *Amerindian Rebirth: Reincarnation Belief among North American Indians and Inuit,* edited by Antonia Mills and Richard Slobodin, pp. 38–54. University of Toronto Press, Toronto.

Wallace, A. F. C.
1966 *Religion: An Anthropological View.* New York: Random.

Whitacre, Debbie, and Bob Whitacre
1986 The Whitacre Site (12D246). *Ohio Archaeologist*: 24–36.

Will, George F., and George E. Hyde
1964 *Corn Among the Indians of the Upper Missouri.* Originally published, 1917, reprinted from William H. Miner Co. University of Nebraska Press, Lincoln.

Willoughby, Charles C., and Earnest A. Hooton
1922 *The Turner Group of Earthworks, Hamilton County, Ohio.* Papers of the Peabody Museum of American Archaeology and Ethnology, vol. 8, no. 3. Cambridge, Mass.

Wisseman, Sarah, Thomas Emerson, Randall Hughes, and Kenneth Farnworth
2008 Provenance Studies of Midwestern Pipestones Using a Portable Spectrometer. International Symposium on Archaeometry, Siena, Italy, http://www.itarp.illinois.edu/atam/research/pima/publications.html.

Wymer, DeeAnne
2010 Where Do (Hopewell) Research Answers Come From? In *Hopewell Settlement Patterns, Subsistence, and Sacred Landscapes*, edited by A. Martin Byers and DeeAnne Wymer, pp. 307–26. University Press of Florida, Gainesville.

Yerkes, Richard W.
1994 A Consideration of Function of the Ohio Hopewell Bladelets. *Lithic Technology* 19: 109–27.
2003 Using Lithic Artifacts to Study Craft Production: The Hopewell Case. In *Written in Stone: The Multiple Dimensions of Lithic Analysis*, edited by Nick Kardulias and Richard W. Yerkes, pp. 17–24. Lexington Books, Lanham, Md.
2006 Middle Woodland Settlements and Social Organization in the Central Ohio Valley. In *Recreating Hopewell*, edited by Douglas K. Charles and Jane E. Buikstra, pp. 50–61. University Press of Florida, Gainesville.

Index

About the Author

A. Martin Byers taught for many years at Vanier College, Montreal. He was instrumental in establishing the anthropology sector of the Department of Social Sciences in 1970, the same year that the college was founded. In 1983 he took a leave of absence to pursue his doctorate at the State University of New York at Albany. He completed this task in 1987. After actively teaching, researching, and publishing at Vanier for almost thirty years, he retired and took up a position as research affiliate in the Department of Anthropology of McGill University. He has published several archaeology books, including *The Ohio Hopewell Episode: Paradigm Lost and Paradigm Gained* (2004, University of Akron Press) and *Cahokia: A World Renewal Cult Heterarchy* (2006, University Press of Florida). He and DeeAnne Wymer have recently coedited *Hopewell Settlement Patterns, Subsistence, and Symbolic Landscapes* (2010, University Press of Florida). Although now retired from the research affiliate position, he is still actively pursuing his research while writing on Native North American prehistoric social systems. He hopes to have another book out shortly that follows up the themes of this and preceding books. In particular, his next book draws strong parallels between the nature of the Ohio Hopewell social system that is the theme of this book and the nature of the Mississippian social system.